The Rise of the
American Circus,
1716–1899

The Rise of the American Circus, 1716–1899

S. L. Kotar and J. E. Gessler

McFarland & Company, Inc., Publishers
Jefferson, North Carolina, and London

LIBRARY OF CONGRESS CATALOGUING-IN-PUBLICATION DATA

Kotar, S. L.
The rise of the American circus, 1716–1899 /
S. L. Kotar and J. E. Gessler.
p.   cm.
Includes bibliographical references and index.

ISBN 978-0-7864-6159-2
softcover : 50# alkaline paper ∞

1. Circus — United States — History —18th century.
2. Circus — United States — History —19th century.
I. Gessler, J. E.   II. Title.
GV1803.K67 2011   791.30973 — dc23   2011031235

BRITISH LIBRARY CATALOGUING DATA ARE AVAILABLE

On the cover: Barnum & Bailey chromolithograph, (Library of Congress)
Front cover by TG Design

Manufactured in the United States of America

*McFarland & Company, Inc., Publishers
Box 611, Jefferson, North Carolina 28640
www.mcfarlandpub.com*

This book is lovingly dedicated to
the best sisters in the world:
Betsy Bennett, Amy Zimmerman, Marylou Gillman
and Little Sis, Connie Carpenter

Table of Contents

Preface

The Fort Worth Mail *says:*
A "prominent and well known" citizen remarked yesterday he liked to attend circuses, but preferred the genuine sawdust and spangles. The name of circus is now applied to so many things that it is impossible to tell what the Mail *alludes to. Every very demonstrative exhibition, from a political row to a religious revival, is now called a circus. It is no new thing to say all the world's a stage and all the men and women actors.*[1]

The opening sentence of Chapter 1 is actually an interrogative: When did the circus become a circus? A more perplexing question would be, "What is a circus?" On the face of it, both would seen to be uncomplicated and easy to answer. The circus began in Ancient Rome, with lions pitted against Christians (if not the earliest attraction, then certainly the most infamous). And a circus is performers under the Big Top, with white-faced, red-nosed clowns; acrobats on the high-wire, and brightly attired men and scantily-clad women balancing on the backs of magnificent steeds. Into the mix are thrown bearded ladies and strong men, alongside "freaks" of nature; lion tamers directing ferocious beasts through hoops; and exotic animals prancing, dancing and snarling, all under the direction of a top-hatted ringmaster.

Conjuring up an image of the early days, one might describe a circus as having three rings, and smelling of sawdust, cotton candy and popcorn, where spectators sat on benches running around the near-continual entertainment. Children pulled up canvas flaps to watch for free; women fainted from the sight of seeing the snap of pointed teeth narrowly miss a trainer's arm, and men applauded the marksmanship of a sharpshooter or the prowess of a knife thrower.

What these descriptions really are is part myth, part reality. The truth is wider, more complex and even more controversial. But what would you expect from the world's most majestic form of live entertainment?

There are no easy answers to the first question — even historians do not agree. Some authorities incorporate or discount the Bread and Circuses era; others divide "ancient" (in this case, 18th century Europe) from "modern" (mid–19th century America). Several touch on Philip Astley, the Father of the Circus — unless they are a stickler for terms, in which case Charles Hughes and Charles Dibdin get credit for popularizing the word and thus the circus — but concentrate on the development in the United States.

As for what precisely constitutes a circus, authorities become more specific yet find less common ground. There are those who do not include traveling menageries, arguing that a display of animals without equestrian acts and gymnastics cannot rightly fit the bill. Purists discount from their definition circus-like performances enacted in theaters, hippodromes and music halls, as they do not have the proper buildings or structure. Most disqualify the truly American Wild West Shows and single-artist acts.

Our purpose in writing this book is not to argue the definition or present a monograph of the circus, which, by itself, borders on the impossible. Scant first-hand material exists for the early American pioneers; what is left to the historian are brief newspaper notices, scraps of letters and vague personal accounts. Later, in the era of the newspaper, reports from exchanges (newspapers copying stories from other newspapers) provided more detail but often confused or omitted dates. Worse, copy was occasionally "made up" by the pen of enterprising advertising men ("Baby eaten by Lion!!"), or by editors accepting on face value the worth of a show in exchange for advertising dollars ("A Superb Entertainment Never Equaled in the Annals of the Circus!"). Reminiscences by old-timers faded with the years, and autobiographies tended to be self-serving. Rather, we are interested in the shape and substance of an entertainment form: how the circus, by any name (amphitheatre, hippodrome, grove, company, menagerie, wild animal park) or association of concepts, evolved. We sought to introduce the men and women who were an integral part of the beginning and development through the 19th century. We are interested in the human stories, the innovations, creations, successes, failures, profits and losses of what is loosely called the Circus.

Instead of confining ourselves to any strict interpretation, we sought answers that bring together the whole: Who was Astley, so often mentioned when referencing immigrant performers in the United States? What was a "master" taught and how did he learn the tricks of the trade? How — and why — were pantomimes used; why were dramatic scenes played and what topics did they cover? Why did dramatics disappear and what replaced them? Where did the wild animals come from, how were they transported to the States and who trained them? Why did the well-established art form alter when it came across the Atlantic Ocean? And what did it metamorphose into?

Those questions beg others. Where did the exotic beasts snarling from behind iron bars originate and how were they treated? What happened to circus animals too old to perform? Who cared for child performers, and what about stories of boys running away to join the circus and young women eloping with circus performers? What games did the sideshow gamblers use, and how did they manage to cheat the unwary?

With that end in mind, we begin this book with the earliest Englishmen who assembled minstrels, contortionists, ropewalkers, actors and equestrians on the stage. Providing a background of who they were, we trace their actions, detailing their unique problems and working through their trials and errors. Along the way we introduce the acts, performers, sights, smells, language and feel of the evolving British art form that would eventually become the backbone of the American circus.

With that background, it is easier to comprehend why riding schools grew into equestrian shows, elaborate buildings gave way to tents, and how American tastes dictated the abandonment of dramatic acts and encouraged the merger of full-scale menageries into the circus bill.

Amid the facts, figures, cast lists and traveling schedules is an amazing human story: men and women who sought to earn their living entertaining the public. Some were highly talented horsemen, ever seeking to amaze by "tricks" of bareback riding, swooping, juggling, precision formations, balancing and speed. Others utilized their skills by making audiences laugh; still others walked on ropes, performed feats of strength, displayed magic, imitated the calls of birds, or twisted themselves into knots. Theirs was an ever-changing, day-to-day struggle. Often they were criticized for their itinerant lifestyle, taxed by eager municipalities, lauded as marvels and critiqued as frauds. Some were even drawn to the circus as contract players or independent associates, using the free publicity to draw crowds who might pay an extra quarter to watch them ascend in their hot air or rarefied air balloons.

When life was good, it was very good, and proprietors took in unprecedented sums and lived high lives. The clever reinvested their profits in more elaborate structures, better acts, gaudier costumes. Later in the century, as audiences became more familiar and thus less inspired by the tried and true, operators joined forces, presenting two and sometimes half a dozen established circuses for the price of one. Menageries, once a mainstay of more puritan patrons, eventually were incorporated into the equestrian and clown acts, bringing the whole into line with what is now considered the circus.

When life was bad, it was very bad. The small "horse and pony" shows were relegated to small towns and finally driven into extinction. Laws were passed prohibiting "immoral" performances; taxes grew by leaps and bounds. Moving the entire apparatus from city to city after a night or a week, first by road and water and then by train, was expensive and dangerous. More than one tragedy occurred when elephants refused to cross rivers, or bridges collapsed under their weight. Downturns in the economy and war limited money for entertainment. Inspired managers died and the mantle turned over to less capable hands.

Yet the circus persisted. Men, women and children — for "infants" were an integral part of the 1700 and 1800s circus — refused to give up their way of life. And audiences, who needed a chance to witness the awe and wonder of the unimaginable, and to steal an hour or two from their daily grind to laugh at the antics of clowns, remained faithful. This unique affinity has lasted through the centuries, amid all the modern electronic devices, from film and television to the Internet and ipods.

We hope we have succeeded in meshing the significant with the trivial, the exciting with the mundane, while along the route fleshing out and giving life to this enduring art form. And along the way perhaps we have discovered the answer to the question of what really constitutes a circus. It is that which is in the eye of the beholder: the orb of an eight-year-old with the grin of an eighty-eight-year-old.

1

When the Circus Became a Circus

When you have seen all by bill exprest,
My wife, to conclude, performs the rest.

(Conclusion to a poem written by Philip Astley
for a June 11, 1768, performance)[1]

"When did the circus become a circus?" sounds like a conundrum posed by a brightly-attired clown facing an 18th century audience seated on wooden benches arranged around an outdoor circular ring. And a puzzle it is, for the concept of "circus" and its transformation into what we know today actually evolved across two centuries. More properly, it could be said to be the offspring of traveling minstrels, jugglers, leapers, horsemen and animal parks, dating back to the Middle Ages.

Prior to the five-year period between 1768 and 1773, acknowledged as the "birth" of the circus (although the actual word did not come into common usage until 1782), Europeans sought entertainment at mainstream theaters and opera houses. Those seeking less legitimate sport attended performances of a variety of individuals and small companies offering specific, limited programs. In 1708, German royalty in Berlin attended "Publick Diversions" concluding with the "Combat of the Wild Beasts" in the amphitheatre.[2] The ever-popular "Tryals of Skill," better known as boxing matches, were presented by James Figg at his new Amphitheatre at Hockley in the Hole. During one entertainment, a participant received a violent wound to the head that carried away half his skull, leaving what was feared a mortal wound. A week later, however, having recovered from the "Point of Death," he challenged the fighter who wounded him.[3] Thomas Elmore and Andrew Mac-Colley, Irish masters of the Noble Science of Defense, crossed swords with Englishmen at Stokes' Amphitheatre.[4]

In 1736, a new Amphitheatre was created in Vienna, modeled on Ancient Rome, to exhibit a Combat of Wild Beasts. Oval rows of seating were fixed one above another, with animals released into the arena through porticos and dens beneath.[5] Four years later, at Dresden, the royalty and nobility were amused by combat between a "Lyon and Lyoness, a Panther, a Leopard, a Tyger, a Lynx, three Bears, a Wolf, a Bull, two Buffaloes, a Cow and Calf, a Mule, a Mare, two wild horses, and twelve very furious and large wild Boars."[6]

At the "Desire of several Gentlemen of Distinction," a tyger was baited at Broughton's Amphitheatre in Oxford-Road, the diversion to be followed by several Bye-Battles.[7] In

1748, for lovers of Rural Diversions, cudgeling was offered, the prize being a half crown for every man breaking a head fairly. The program also included "stag" fighting and brusing chickens.[8] Plans were also underway for the construction of a circular amphitheatre, prepared after the manner of the Ancients, partly covered and capable of containing forty thousand persons.[9]

Blood sports were not the only venues for entertainment, of course. In 1712, Punch's Theatre in the Little Piazza, Covent-Garden, offered an Opera called *Orpheus and Erudice*, illustrated with a variety of Scenes and Machines after the Italian manner. On the same day, Her Majesty's Company of Comedians performed at the Theatre Royal in Drury-Lane, offering a popular comedy called *She Wou'd, If She Cou'd*.[10]

By 1742, the celebrated Luminous Amphitheatre in Charing-Cross advertised their building, "constructed of Silver, polished Steel, and cut Glass, exhibiting at one View upwards of two hundred Fountains," several of which represented a star, a fan, a globe and a cross. The whole presented such a pleasing spectacle that his Royal Highness the Duke of Cumberland, expressed himself exceedingly pleased. The same year, new Tennis Courts were established in Holborn, Lincoln's Inn Fields, while gamblers could take their chances on the Lottery, standing at 500 pounds.[11]

The menagerie, or collection of exotic animals, had been a tradition throughout Europe nearly as long as minstrels and acrobats. Sizeable collections were usually the privilege of the wealthy, who kept them in their parks for private viewing. Small side shows exhibited rare or uncommon beasts to attentive audiences, and the possessor of such a creature usually earned a substantial reward. As early as 1742, the "Great Rhinoceros, or real Unicorn" was displayed in Charing-Cross. This beast, taken in the "Great Mogulia Dominions," was reputed to have been transported on a journey of a thousand leagues by land to Patna, then shipped to England aboard the *Lyell* by Captain Acton in 1740.

The rhinoceros was described as being four years old, its body covered with folds like a coat of mail and sealed all over to defend itself from attack by other animals. The horn on its nose, used to strike its sworn enemy the elephant, was whetted on a stone prior to combat. Next in growth to the elephant,

"Two Stallions That Spar" was the evolution of "Combat of the Wild Beasts" and the "Tryals of Skill." The horses, named "John L. Sullivan" (after the famous boxer, who incidentally also tried his hand at circus proprietorship) and "James F. Corbett," came from Arabia and were trained for the circus in the manly art of self-defense at Bridgeport, Connecticut. After a five-month course, John L. and Jim reared on their hind legs, struck a regulation sparring posture, and pawed away at each other straight from the shoulder. They were provided with large well-padded gloves and were securely muzzled to prevent any surreptitious biting. (*Weekly News* [OH], April 28, 1892)

the advertisers swore there had never been such a creature in England "since the Memory of Man."[12]

At this period, these varied public attractions were distinct from one another. Over the next twenty years, circumstances would change. The quest for money and the challenge of competition would draw them together under the banner of several unique individuals. The history and professional relationships of these early pioneers is significant, not only in how they influenced the English circus but in their legacies carried over the water to America.

"Upon the whole, it was not so bad as I suspected."

One of the most interesting characters involved in the evolution of the circus was Charles Dibdin, son of a respectable silversmith of Southampton. A boy in 1757, he served as a chorister in the Cathedral of Winchester, where Mr. Fussel, church organist, taught the gamut of religious and popular music. Much of Dibdin's early knowledge came from scoring the concertos of Corelli and a study of the publications of Rameau. After being refused the situation of organist of Bishop's Waltham in Hampshire on account of his youth, the sixteen-year-old traveled to London. By 1761, he was performing in the chorus at Covent-Garden. He quickly graduated to more prominent roles, partly because of his success in playing the character of Ralph in *Maid of the Mill*, a role refused by more famous performers. Under the management of Mr. Beard, he composed a pastoral piece called *Shepherds of Artificer,* which proved so popular it remained on the play list for the 1762 and 1763 seasons.[13]

Not all his notices were positive, however. On September 5, 1765, when under the manager Mr. Love, Dibdin performed the character of Hawthorn in *Love in a Village* at the new theater in Richmond Green. A critic noted, "Mr. Dibdin is no more like Hawthorne [*sic*] than I am like Hercules: his lank belly, lanthorn jaws, lounging figure, and unmanly gait, but ill bespeak the robust country Farmer.... He superadded a competent degree of want of abilities: Some of the songs he sung tolerably well, and some of them very indifferently." Critiquing *The Busy-Body*, the same reviewer noted that while the Prompter read, "Dibdin gesticulated; but whether or not his gesticulations corresponded with what the Prompter did read, is a question infinitely too difficult for me to determine." Addressing Love, he added, "If you mean Mr. Dibdin any favor, you certainly overshoot the mark; by putting him so much out of his latitude, you make him lose that reputation he gained in Ralph." Surmising Dibdin had been offered the role because of his favored status, he begrudgingly added the production was not as bad as he expected.[14]

The following year Dibdin was still at Covent Garden and thought well enough of to be granted a benefit performance during the production of *Every Man in His Humor*.[15] Benefit performances were a common way of according artists the opportunity of supplementing their income. Commonly, they were allowed to keep full value of any tickets they sold to the benefit. Notices of benefits were displayed at the top of newspaper and handbill advertisements, alerting fans to buy tickets directly from the beneficiaries. Dibdin received a second benefit in May 1767, for a performance of *Cato* and a third at the Theatre Royal on Richmond-Green, where *The Merry Wives of Windsor*, starring Mr. Love, was offered.[16] That same season Dibdin starred in *The Clandestine Marriage*, playing Lord Ogleby, and *Midas*, portraying the title character.[17]

By 1770, Dibdin seemed to have found his niche. Leaving Covent-Garden at the behest of Mr. Bickerstaff, he was introduced to Mr. Garrick, who hired him to compose music for productions at the Royal Theatre, Drury-Lane. While still acting, he wrote music for a pageant, garnering himself another benefit.[18] Two years later he appeared at Sadler's Wells, writing music for *The Monster of the Woods*. At this illustrious theater, newly renovated and with an enlarged orchestra and augmented band, three shillings bought a patron a box seat and a pint of Port, Lisbon, Mountain or Punch.[19]

As his fame grew, Dibdin found his name mentioned as a feature attraction. As the author of a new musical Dialogue, one review remarked, he "adapted the comic tunes to many of the scenes with great propriety."[20] The following year his authorship of *The Opera Ring*, playing at the Royal Theatre, was questioned in the newspapers, charging it to have been written by "a person particularly obnoxious" (Mr. Bickerstaff). After one performance, the manager, Mr. King, promised his audience to "discard Mr. Dibdin forever" if he proved to be a liar. Dibdin made an appearance and declared he had written the words as well as composed the music. This satisfied the house and saved the author's career.[21]

In 1773, the proprietor at Sadler's Wells offered a series of tumbling by Monsieur Ferci and his agile companions, followed by a dance where the principals were humorously habited as Nobody and Somebody. A musical entertainment by Dibdin followed.[22] Finding the "posturing" agreeable, the performing Sigels made an appearance in 1774. Putting "the power of human muscles to the severest test," they excited perfect astonishment[23] and likely left an impression on composer Dibdin — one that he would later put to good use.

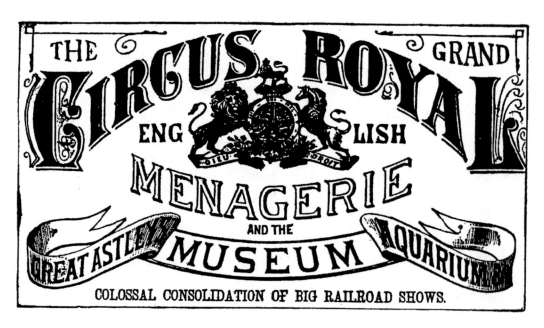

This stylish announcement for the Circus Royal harkens back to the earliest beginnings of the circus by being joined with Astley's Museum and Aquarium. Philip Astley and Charles Hughes might be considered the co-fathers of the circus, both operating exhibitions in London in the late 1700s. It was from their foundations, and with many performers who got their starts at the Amphitheatre and Royal Circus, that the modern circus developed. (*Monticello Express* [IA], September 21, 1882)

Astley and Hughes Get Into the Act

On April 6, 1768, Philip Astley's name appeared in the London newspapers under the small heading, "Activity on Horseback." Four lines of text advertised that Astley would perform "upwards of twenty attitudes on one, two, and three horses" at the New Spring Gardens, Five Fields, Chelsea. Admittance to the performance cost 1 shilling.[24] Thus began the professional career of one of the most influential men in the development and presentation of the multi-faceted entertainment that became known as "the circus."

Astley, a former cavalry sergeant major, opened his Riding School the same year, located next to the White House (or Halfpenny Hatch). Astley and his wife, with his partner, Lambeth Marsh, quickly expanded their operation from teaching horsemanship to ladies and gentlemen of quality, to presenting equestrian performances. By May 30, the pair advertised a number of feats every evening at 6:00 P.M. Included in the demonstrations were fence and defense, sword in hand as in real action; picking up a half crown, a large weight, handkerchiefs and swords from horseback at full speed; sweeping the ground with a hand, "never attempted by anyone," and leaping the bar several different ways.

The pair also rode two horses together, with one foot in each saddle, firing pistols, leaping into the air and demonstrating the manner of Elliot's charge against the French troops in Germany in the year 1761, "when it was said that regiment were all tailors, notwithstanding they gained a complete victory." By June 11, the Astleys added a trick horse that "lies down, imitating death." The words spoken by Astley over the animal began:

> My horse lies dead, apparent to your sight,
> But I'm the man can set this thing to right;
> Speak when you please, I'm ready to obey,
> My faithful horse knows what I want to say:
> But first pray give me leave to move his foot;
> That he is dead is quite beyond dispute.[25]

In July, a comedic act entitled "The Taylor Riding to Brentford" was added to the program. Billy Button (or Buttons), the "taylor" (tailor) tries to mount his horse and cannot. When he finally manages the feat, the horse will not move, and eventually the steed chases his master around the ring. Significantly, this was the first clowning performance in the history of the evolving circus.[26] "Taylor" became an instant hit, eventually crossing the Atlantic, and in various incarnations played to laughing audiences for decades.

The Astleys included a monkey riding on horseback and a tumbling act for a special Christmas week performance. Success followed success, and by 1770, Astley's riding school, located at the foot of Westminster-Bridge, Surry, was advertising "Feats of Activity, with Alterations, and Additions" to the program. Now billed as "The Original Hussar," Astley sprang from his horse to the ground and, "like a tennis-ball," rebounded back to his mount, sprang over its head, then regained his position in time to take a flying leap over a bar. "The Taylor Riding to Brentford" continued to play well, with Astley, "in dress and character," thrilling audiences. Admittance remained one shilling.[27]

With two of the primary ingredients of a circus already in place—horsemanship and comedy—the Astleys next added a race requiring performers, "tied fast all over head in sacks," to run 300 yards, then leap or tumble over a bar two feet from the ground so that they could not get up without assistance. Astley continued his display with the Broad Sword, Mrs. Astley performed horseback feats, and the humorous Little Learned Horse, three feet high, from the Deserts of Arabia, performed conjuring tricks. Doors opened at 5:00 P.M., with a commodious room for the nobility apart.[28]

Master Griffith ("master" indicating an apprentice), a boy of 14 years, joined the troop* in July 1770, under the tutelage of Astley, riding one and two horses in many pleasing attitudes. On July 9, for the benefit of Mrs. Astley, Philip Astley, now billed as "the young English warrior," performed feats with a pack of cards and added Palatine tricks, with lofty tumbling. A side-note to the evening's advertisement observed that Astley was soon to be engaged to perform in Paris. According to notices of the day, their last scheduled show before leaving was July 23, 1770.[29]

With their venue still called the Riding School, the Astleys opened the 1771 season with Astley performing on one, two, three and four horses, "in a Manner far superior than ever exhibited." By the desire of the nobility, he also rode two horses at a gallop while carrying a young lady on his head; enacted the Grand Deception with the Cards, and, while on horseback, picked up a shilling from the ground at full speed while blindfolded. In what may be considered an evolving circus act, "The Drunken Sailor on his Road to Portsmouth" was added to a production of the "Taylor."[30]

Charles Hughes, another horseman destined to play a role in the development of the circus, joined the Astleys in 1771. Born in 1747, the 24-year-old Hughes was already giving equestrian performances at Cromwell's Gardens, and his name would have been recognizable to audiences — enough so that an August 14 advertisement began, "Mr. Astley and Mr. Hughes beg leave to inform the Nobility, Gentry and others..." that despite the wet weather they would continue to perform until Saturday, when they were obliged to leave.[31] After exhibiting in France, the company returned to England for a Christmas week reprisal, conspicuously without Hughes.

Easter Monday being the habitual opening of the

Circuses opened up a new venue for women. They performed alongside men and in solo acts, soon becoming an integral — and accepted — part of the entertainment. The "Wonderful Charest Family," Idalletta and Wallace, were one of many groups performing aerial bicycle tricks in the 1880–1890s. Along with them, at S. H. Barrett & Co. were Miss Jennie Ewers, the Equestrian Bouquet; Charles Ewers, 4- and 6-horse rider; Viola Rivers, the greatest living horsewoman; Orrin Hollis, the great pirouette and double-somersault leaper; the war elephant "Xerxes"; "Little Dot," the smallest full-grown elephant in America; and "Bruno," the low comedy bear. (*Indiana Progress* [PA], June 8, 1882)

---

*"Troop" was the British equivalent of "troupe," from the French word of the same spelling, used throughout the 18th and into the 19th centuries.

not-yet-christened "circus" season, Astley's Riding School offered the little learned Military horse, a new Comic Piece of Activity called "Horsemanship Burlesqued," and different Characters by Mr. Griffiths (the name now spelled with an "s" at the end), and by an unnamed "Native of France."

Literally setting the stage for other women performers (most notable in the rising sport of aerostation, or balloon ascensions), Mrs. Astley was to perform Feats of Activity. "Being the only one of her Sex that has ever had the Honour," she had previously performed before their Majesties in Richmond Gardens, the whole Court of France and at the Grand Camp at Fontainebleau.[32]

Not to be left out, Charles Hughes opened his own riding school, Black Friars Bridge, on April 23, 1772. Boasting a commodious room for the nobility (80 feet long), he and his wife advertised the celebrated Sobieska Clementina (Hughes' sister), with the famous Miss Huntly (later spelled "Huntley") from Sadler's Wells, and a young gentleman who lately had the honor of performing before their Majesties. The ladies rode standing upright on their saddles at full speed, while an eight-year-old girl rode two horses standing upright on the saddles at full gallop. "The Taylor" (original to Astley) was preformed "as usual," along with the Sailor in Dress and Character. Unlike his former associate, Hughes charged 2 shillings for admittance into the Rooms. Those outside the unsubstantial shelter were admitted for one shilling.[33]

Dueling Artistes

While Astley added a performer called Cosmethopila, and his "young gentleman" exhibited "several pleasing heavy balances, never performed before," a public feud broke out between him and Hughes. Unsigned handbills were distributed blasting Astley's reputation, causing him to write a defense in verse, part of which read:

> To stab in secret is a Way
>   The Brave will always shun;
> And Cowards, like the Moon, grow pale,
>   Nor dare they face the Sun...
> As real Worth shall always find
>   A liberal Friend in me,
> So secret Malice from this Hour
>   Shall disregarded be.

Breslaw, a noted conjurer of Dexterity and Deceptions (who was then exhibiting the "Egg riding," a trick whereby a fresh egg balanced on a stick was made to dance around the room by itself, accompanied by violin and mandolina), quickly defended Hughes by noting that, as there were already several Actions against Astley for quarrelling with and abusing different persons, he would not fight a "Paper War." This did not prevent him from questioning Astley's character for turning out his own father, a man "near 80 Years of Age, into the Streets to starve, which very Father is now employed by Hughes, the Horse-Rider, thro' Charity to deliver Bills at 10s. 6d weekly at the Foot of Black-friars Bridge."[34]

To make matters worse, Hughes offered a benefit for "Mr. Astley, sen. and a distressed Family" on June 25. Among the exhibitions promised was a display by Hughes leaping over three horses, leaping over two as they leapt the Bar and leaping over one horse 40 times without stepping between the Springs. An advertisement for the same day noted that at Astley's, their five-year-old son would ride two horses "with such Elegance, Safety, and Ease, as gives general Satisfaction to every one."[35]

Whether to excite business or in plans gone awry, Astley advertised in July that he and his wife intended to depart for Normandy the following Tuesday. After his own announcement promoting his "Horse of Knowledge," which fired a cannon, a pistol and "being the only Horse at present in this Kingdom that will fetch and carry," Hughes begged leave to remind the nobility that he did not intend "setting out for France every Day in the Week for three Seasons," but would remain in England, sparing no expense to make his "unparallelled Exhibition agreeable."

In the same newspaper, he advertised a benefit for Mrs. Hughes, who returned her most grateful acknowledgment to the public for Favors received and expressed her hope the performance would be honored by a Splendid Company of Ladies, for whom the couple would spare no expense while providing for their polite Accommodation. Perhaps tongue-in-cheek, Breslaw, Hughes' friend, announced that he, too, was offering the last night of his exhibition before leaving England.[36] Keeping the sparring alive, Astley published an advertisement entirely in French, announcing his Westminster playbill for July 27.[37]

In the middle of this transitional period, artists with varied talents began drifting to the riding schools. Daniel Wildman, a horseman lately performing at the Jubilee Gardens, Islington, became attached to Astley's. Adding intrigue to his repertoire, Wildman rode with a "curious Mask of Bees on his Head and Face." Several of his trained bees also marched over a table while others swarmed in the air, the whole then returning to their hive.[38]

By August 1772, Astley advertised his Military Horse and Wildman riding "with a curious swarm of bees on his naked Arm, then on his Head, in Imitation of a Bob-wig." He also begged leave to inform the nobility and lesser souls that he had become proprietor of a most elegant "Piece of Machinery with four Fronts, made by the ingenious Artist Mr. Martinet, of Clerkenwell," which had been shown at small theaters to universal applause. This intricate moving machine was enriched with various "Devices of Jewellery Work; the Movement of the Elephant is far superior to any in Europe; the Nabob and the Elephant's Conductors, with the Sun, Tulip, and Saffron Flowers" were elegantly finished. The automata performed various pieces of music, "so that the Eye and Ear are delighted at the same Time."[39] Mechanical automatons were the rage of Europe, and obtaining the device for his School clearly displayed Astley's keen sense of showmanship.

Competing for precious shillings, the two major operators stacked up against one another, offering the following programs in August 1772:

Hughes' Horse Academy

1. The celebrated Sobieska Clementina riding one, two and three horses
2. The eight-year-old girl riding two horses
3. The Young Warrior horse fetching, carrying, walking lame and discharging a cannon and pistol
4. Hughes performing 50 different feats of horsemanship
5. The entertainment, "The English Warrior on his Road to France"
6. "Ben, the Sailor," without saddle, bridle or any other Rigging
7. The Maccarony Taylor in Dress and Character

Astley's Riding School

1. Horsemanship, or Activity
2. Exhibitions of Bees by Mrs. Astley and Mr. Wildman
3. The Broad Sword and Heavy Ballances
4. Comus, Jonas and Breslaw's Tricks with Cards
5. The little Horse
6. The Magical Tables, or the little Military Horse in his Study with four grand Changes
7. A Variety of other Amusements[40]

The circus was coming together. Amphitheatres offered feats of strength and skill; riding schools drew together venues of horsemanship and trick riding. Trained animals provided unusual performances; comedic entertainment included the "Taylor"; gymnasts, contortionists and rope walkers were gaining notoriety; and conjuring and automation provided added incentives for curious patrons. Operating under one open-air arena, the Big Show was less than a decade away from getting its name and establishing a timeless legacy that would reach around the world.

2

The Circus Comes to Town

The public curiosity has been so much excited by the preparations for this new place of entertainment, that there were more people attended last night ... than would three times have filled the audience part of the academy.[1]

Philip Astley, now billed as "late of his Majesty's Royal Light Dragoons," opened the 1775 season on Easter Monday "with a great variety of new Men, and feats of Horsemanship and Activity, in a manner beyond all conception." Breslaw exhibited in Cockspur-Street, Haymarket, with his "Italians Surprising Performances," and Sieur Gaeteno's "Imitation of all Kind of Birds," all for the stiff price of 5 shillings. Those in possession of three guineas could procure Breslaw and his Italians for a private showing.

Astley continued to charge 2 shillings for admittance into the Gallery and 1 shilling for the Riding-ground. As an indication of how tight finances were, in the same notice he took pains to remind patrons he continued to instruct in the polite art of horsemanship, broke little horses properly and taught safe, easy cantering to the ladies. He also published a text entitled *Astley's Method of Riding, a Preventive of Accidents on Horseback* printed for and sold by the author at his Riding School, Westminster Bridge.[2]

With Hughes and his troop out of the country on tour, Astley's Riding School became the predominant attraction in London. Mrs. Astley took over performing tricks with the bees, and three automata figures played pieces of music on different instruments. Also added were "lofty tumbling" acts and Astley's performance with "the little Family, called the Force of Hercules." For the benefit of Master Astley in September, his father appears to have gone into the sleight of hand business, for he advertised catching a bullet fired at him, after which he would immediately show it to the audience.[3]

Productions became larger and more varied. The following season, Astley added a company of Spaniards performing manly entertainment; the *Egyptian Pyramids* (men balanced on one another's shoulders); rope vaulting on full swing; lofty tumbling and still vaulting (typically over a stationary, inanimate "horse" of the type used in gymnasiums today); serious and comic displays of horsemanship; the *Magical Tables,* including four grand changes with birds, lemons, cards and watches; the brilliant *Temple of Minerva,* consisting of various pieces of automata; and a performance on the slack rope called the *Roasted Pig* (in which, apparently, a performer lay on a twisted rope and was spun as if on a spit).[4] Mrs. Astley marched her bees across a table, Mr. Astley demonstrated techniques with the broad sword and *La Force D'Hercule* ("Hercule" being a common name for the strong man in 18th century England). Madam Rossi and her Serpents were added to the program in September before the season ended.

If that were not enough, Astley crowded into his show a variety of amusements taken from the *Boulevards of Paris*, "particularly many deceptions [sleight of hand], experiments, and operations after the manner of Sieur Comus. Perhaps the most interesting inclusion of all, however, resided in the feats of activity on horseback, which included "Mr. Astley, Mr. Griffin, Mr. Phillips, Mrs. Griffin and the Clown." At the conclusion of the program, in what must have been an inspiring spectacle, the *Grand Saloon* was illuminated with several hundred lights, "in imitation of the Colessa at Paris."[5]

It is almost impossible to grasp the scope and awe occasioned by these performances, ending with the arena sparked by artificial light; the touch was pure genius. At this time, before grand structures were built to house entertainments, Astley's Riding School was merely an open-air, circular arena, 95 feet in diameter, hosting a 60-foot ring where activities took place. A main building, 51 feet high, held three rows of seating and was flanked by two smaller ones, beneath which were stables for the animals.[6] After the stimulation of perhaps two hours of nearly non-stop entertainment, beholding the scene engulfed in blazing light (far surpassing what even the most elevated theater could offer) must have left the audience speechless. Who, indeed, would not have wanted to pay his two shillings for such a thrill? Philip Astley was the master, and his talent for showmanship on a grand scale earned him the respectful title "Father of the Circus."

Monday, March 31, 1777, marked the beginning of a new year at the Riding School, with the Automaton Figures receiving top billing. They were followed by Horsemanship, the Slack Wire, the Venetian Performances, tumbling, the little Horse, the vaulting rope, the Egyptian Pyramids and La Force de Hercule.[7] In April, Astley rented the Great Room, Panton Street, Hay-market, where he directed Mr. Brunn, "the celebrated and much admired Saxon," who performed on the Slack Wire. Astley appeared with the little Horse, noted for its "sagacity," and offered a new mechanical invention representing different elegant Fire Works (indicating the device provided different colors). Also added to the program was an exhibit called the Ombres Chinoises (a shadow puppet show, the performers being

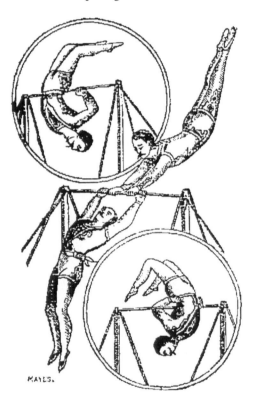

What would the circus be without performing acrobats? This illustration from **Kleckner & Company, 1872,** offers a coming attraction of what spectators would see under the Big Top. Early circus performers worked on the slack- and tight-rope, and only later did aerial performances become common. Nor was it uncommon to see trapeze artists perform their tricks high above the earth suspended by thin ropes from smoke balloons. (***Indiana Democrat*** [PA], August 1, 1872)

small figures of curious workmanship with all the natural attitudes of acting and dancing), featuring the "Diversions of the Spanish Amphitheatre and Bull fighting with Men, Dogs &c.," performed in the French language.[8]

Comedy played a more prominent role, as "The macarony's escape from the shower of rain" (a whimsical scene between a beggar and his wife), "The Disappointed Traveller," and a humorous scene between a cobbler's wife and child, "The cat's escape with the dinner out of the pot," were offered.[9] A display of the "Symphatheyical Clock" came in June. At this time, the advertised company consisted of Philip Astley and his son, Master John (no further mention is made of Mrs. Astley), Sieur Podalo, Mr. Phillips, Mr. Porter, Mr. Dawson, Sieur Carlino, Sieur Colpi and the young Turks, Mr. and Mrs. Griffin, and Miss Huntley. Of note, the second edition of Astley's riding book was offered for sale for 1 shilling.[10]

The schedule of events, calculated to entertain from the minute the doors opened at 5:00 P.M., began with masterly Pieces of Art, the Automaton Figures and Water-works until 6:00 P.M. Thereafter, performances on foot and horseback began. Astley also took pains to note that his buildings formed a most formidable appearance, adding they could not fail to give general satisfaction.[11]

In 1778, while construction was underway at the Riding School (to greatly increase its capacity), Astley rented space at the Exhibition Room, No. 22, Piccadilly. The billing for these performances came under the heading "Rossignol, Sonata, and Astley," and featured Rossignol and his uncommon skill "Warbling, Julking, Calling and Singing" the different notes of birds, as well as attempting to imitate the forte and piano. As a prelude, the Conjuring Horse and learned dog performed their tricks, along with the mechanical mechanisms.[12]

In 1779 Astley opened what he called "Astley's Amphitheatre Riding House." The covered building permitted him to offer entertainment in the evenings, doors opening at 5:30 P.M., with performances at 6:30 P.M. Over the next year, various acts included the "Lilliputian World, or Chinese Shadows," tumbling by Nevit, a clown on horseback played by Mr. Burt, and "Polander's Tricks," meaning feats of equilibrium and balancing on chairs, tables, pedestals and ladders.

With his new Amphitheatre, Astley was able to extend his season, offering winter evening amusements. Although closed between November 4 and 26 for "alterations and additional improvements," he re-opened on the 27th, boasting no additional price for admission to the newly decorated site. Among his winter company were included European horsemen Mr. and Mrs. Taylor, equilibrist Mr. Richer, Master and Miss Richer, Miss Hudson, Miss Vengabley (clown to the Little Family), Sieur Baptista and Sieur Paulo. The expression "clown to" indicated that Miss Vengabley performed in between acts by the Little Family. Most acts, especially equestrian feats in this and into the next century, were typically long and arduous, lasting thirty minutes or longer before the performers were relieved. In order to allow the Little Family some breathing room, an interval of clowning was worked into the program.

A beautiful zebra, previously on exhibition at the Haymarket, was also introduced, being led at a walk around the Riding School. In a separate line, the advertisement noted that the zebra was to be sold for 400 Guineas.

Young Master John Astley, now 13 years old, was also coming into his own as a performer. An "amazing Equilibrium, while riding at full gallop, he danced, vaulted, played an air on the violin and displayed a flag in many comic attitudes; clown to his tricks was performed by Mr. Miller." Less skilled than his father, perhaps, but of a more even temperament, John was called "a prodigy of nature," having exhibited since he was four-and-a-half years old,[13] earning the sobriquet "The English Rose" by Marie Antoinette when he rode at Versailles.[14]

To defray escalating costs of his ever-increasing troop, prices for the new amphitheatre soon rose to 2 shillings, 6 pence (2s 6d) for a box, 1s 6d for an upper box, 1s for the pit and 6d for the gallery.[15]

Starting the new year of 1781 with performances on Monday, Tuesday, Wednesday and Fridays, Astley expanded on his shadow performances, offering a representation of the French landing from their flat-bottomed boats and invading Jersey, together with the British troops attacking, defeating and taking prisoners. Apparently the zebra did not sell, for in his last week of Winter Amusements in April, Astley was still exhibiting the animal.[16]

Importantly, for his Summer Amusements, Astley commented that his performers and horses had been kept in constant practice over the winter, enabling them to present foot and horseback acts at the peak of their skill.[17] This was a significant development, for the upkeep of animals during the winter when they could not be shown outside presented a considerable cost to the proprietor of a riding school or amphitheatre. Smaller companies were often forced to put their performers on hiatus and sell their valuable stock, rather than absorb the price of food and lodging. With covered buildings and his own stables, Astley could now work through the cold months, providing him a considerable edge over his competition. In later years, the upkeep and use of horses would become a serious bone of contention between partners and horsemen.

In October 1781, Astley offered three new Chinese Shadow scenes, including an engagement between the English and Dutch fleets under the commands of Admirals Parker and Zoutman. Also making his appearance was the Great Devil (Mr. Nevit), a master of lofty tumbling and trampoline.[18] (Using the word "devil" in a stage name was a common penchant of rope dancers.) Paulo Redige, a Dutchman whose real name was Pol Roediger, performed as *le petit Diable*. Along with his partner, Alexandre Placide, the pair gained much fame in Paris in the 1770s, and at this time were performing in London. Likely Nevit wished to augment his status by advertising himself as "great," rather than "small." Redige and Placide would later travel to Boston in 1792, where their astonishing feats inspired children to copy their techniques, often resulting in falls from fence rails.[19]

Continuing his winter performances four days a week, Astley reserved Thursdays and Saturdays as practice for his horses. Wealthy patrons were permitted to buy what amounted to season tickets for various places of amusement. Advertisements offering "a renter's share" in the Drury-Lane Theatre or the Opera House were not uncommon, such guaranteeing the purchaser a sight of every theatrical performance for the season. Unlike single-season tickets, however, these offered the owner a literal share of the company. More expensive packages covered a span of twenty years or more, some providing a clear annuity of 20l per annum.[20]

Through the Comic Mirror

The year 1782 would prove historically significant to the evolution of the circus. Already well on its way to encapsulating many of the features that set it apart from fairs and traveling minstrel shows, Philip Astley offered an impressive array of talent for his

Winter Season. Of note, he not only continued to display the zebra, but also added other exotic animals to his growing menagerie.

Part I: Horsemanship

Extraordinary displays of agility on horseback, converting the common saddle into a theatrical stage, on which was exhibited comic and serious dancing in the highest perfection.

Part II: Tumbling

Lofty vaulting over men's heads, tables, horses and hoops, together with feats of strength, including the little family offering different exercises in posturing.

III:

Woman in miniature (24 years of age, 31 inches high, weighing a mere 18 pounds; the beautiful zebra, the little Conjuring Horse and Signor Tabasco's exhibition of Bells.

IV:

Equilibriums on the moving ladder, Polander's performances, imitation of birds and rope vaulting, performed by Mrs. Taylor, Mr. Richer, Mr. Nevits, Mr. Baptist, Mr. Adams and the celebrated Master Astley. Also, the curious Dromedary from Grand Cairo and the Elk from Bombay, ridden around the Riding School by Mr. Miller, "Clown to the Horsemanship."

Conclusion:

The comic amusement of the Ombres Chinoise (or Lilliputian World), offering a rendition of the moon setting and sun rising over Gibraltar, and a singular representation of Mount Vesuvius discharging torrents of flame and sulphur.[21]

By April 13, Griffin performed the "Pantomimical, Farcical and Tragical and Oper-atical" scenes, while Adams was credited with the bird warbling, Richer the ladder-jumping and Baptiste the clowning. Griffin, Jones and Miss Hudson rode three horses and formed a pyramid, and Lonsdale rode full speed with his head on the saddle.[22] It is important to note here that the word "pantomime" in reference to performances outside mainstream theater typically referred to dialogue being delivered in song (like a burletta), rather than a performance enacted without words. The Licensing Act of England, designed to protect actors, prohibited anyone in small companies from delivering the spoken word in acts or "scenes." In order to circumvent this, the "pantomime" and burletta were offered, accompanied by music. If the boundaries were blurred, it was not atypical for the proprietors and the artists to be brought before the Court and charged fines.

Charles Dibdin was a leading song and lyric writer for just this type of small company and had a considerable reputation by the early 1770s. Finding himself favorably compared with Purcell,[23] he continued to reap praise and a considerable fortune. By 1778, he was working at Sadler's Wells, where entertainment of the sort offered by Astley had added rope-dancing and "Several uncommon Feats of Strength and Agility" to the program of tumbling and musical entertainment. As was typical of the time, performers competed in both categories, with one of their headliners, Mr. Rayner, billed not only as a tumbler, but as Dancing on the Tight Rope.[24]

Dibdin, apparently known as much for his temper as his talent (described in his 1814 obituary as having conduct manifesting "the too frequent improvidence of genius ... which chiefly appeared in too hospitable a style of living"[25]) quarreled with the proprietors of

Sadler's and struck out on his own, where he quickly struck gold. Two years before Astley added the Ombres Chinoises to his repertoire, Dibdin and his partners created what was called *The Comic Mirror, or The World as It Wags.* Premiering on Saturday, June 24, 1775, at the Grand Saloon, Exeter 'Change, the "puppet-shew" had London's brightest up in arms before it even opened. A week before the premiere, a review noted, "It is hard to distinguish which anxiety is most predominant, respecting the *Comic Mirror, or The World as It Wags;* the curiosity for seeing it, or the fear of being one of its principal characters, to be held forth for the amusement of the public. Saturday evening next will determine the point."[26]

Both points were carried, as the opening night review observed that the show drew a huge, overflowing audience, and the "various detached pieces and sketches of humour, composed of well-known characters ... seems to be happily tempered with candour and pleasantry." The salon, described as an elegant theater, was painted pink and white and adorned with "lustres prettily disposed," while the music "was principally new, and what could be heard of it, was exceedingly admired." Unfortunately, confusion arose among the scene-shifters and the wire-workers, destroying the effect of one piece. Upon the whole, the audience overlooked the disorder, and great things were expected in the coming days.[27]

In a display of how interconnected small houses were, the September 7 performance was cancelled in lieu of the fact a benefit performance for Mr. Bannister was being offered that Thursday at the Royal Theatre, Haymarket, and the proprietors did not wish to siphon off the paying public.[28]

With success came money, and the Grand Saloon, scenes, frontispieces, figures, dresses and decorations were greatly beautified for the winter season. New titles, such as "Shylock's Plot," "The Milk Maid," and a superb representation of a Masquerade were offered, as well as bird and beast imitations. It did not take long before the satire turned biting, and a picture of "Mock Monarchs" was considered much too severe. "The Ghost of Shakespeare, a Parody," was better received, and new anecdotes were added as soon as "properly authenticated."[29]

Perhaps the character of the Devil, spoken at the Comic Mirror, best sums up the purpose of the playhouse satires:

> ... Take heed then, 'twill shew all your tricks — alas,
> Our Mirror, Ladies, is no flattering glass;
> The truth we bring to view, and strive to give
> A Picture of the Times in which we live;
> Hunt down all Calumny, detect all Lies,
> And boldly shoot at Folly as it flies.[30]

In August, after the Comic Mirror moved to Marybone Gardens, Mr. Breslaw made a special appearance performing his much-admired Deceptions,[31] but by April of the following year Dibdin's temperament and poisoned pen (he exposed some of his greatest admirers and best friends to ridicule) had run its course. The building erected by Sig Torre at Marybone Gardens, including the orchestra, stage, scenes, lamps and dressed figures from the Comic Mirror, were put up for auction.[32]

Dibdin fled to France, where he translated operas into English. This caught the attention of Mr. Harris at Covent-Garden, and Dibdin returned to his native land as house dramatist and composer. Some of the French operas he translated were used at the theater and for several years earned him a considerable sum of money.

Charles Hughes, back in England after touring his Riding School Company through

France, Italy, Spain and Portugal, crossed paths with Charles Dibdin shortly after the latter left his place at Covent-Garden. Deeply in debt, Dibdin proposed a partnership, whereby the two would create a form of entertainment in a more "classical and elegant" style. Bringing in four others to supply the capital, and Colonel West, who owned land near Hughes Riding School, Dibdin later wrote that he determined to call the venture "The Royal Circus," thus bestowing the name which has withstood the test of time.

George Speaight, in his book *A History of the Circus*, postulates that Dibdin took the word "circus" from the time of Charles I, when a circular ride for horsemen in Hyde Park was known as the "Ring" or the "Circus." He also noted that in 1754, John Wood built a circular ring for horses in Bath and called it "The Circus." The more common theory of an association with ancient Roman circuses is also plausible, and as Dibdin himself, clearly unaware of the significance, left no record of why he chose the word "circus," there can be no definitive answer.

Interestingly, Astley's Amphitheatre, which had been in existence much longer and possessed a greater reputation, did not inspire the use of "amphitheatre." Over time, the word was used both in England and America, but eventually fell out of favor entirely, leaving "circus" as the universal name. "Amphitheatre," perhaps, had a closer association with gladiators and blood combat, while "circus" may have represented to the 18th and 19th century mind the idea of sport and exotic animals. From a purely uncomplicated standpoint, "circus" was easier to pronounce and recognize in print for the average semi-literate or illiterate citizen. It also came off better in the title of a handbill or newspaper advertisement, allowing the use of larger print size.

Dibdin had big ideas. With his partners' finances he constructed a "handsome, commodious and neat" building, disposed "in an oval form, at one end of which stands the stage, and round the other end are thrown the pit [boxes and gallery behind, as in the theaters; well constructed and commanding an uninterrupted view of the stage], the center forming a kind of circle for the equestrian performances."[33] The early review continued:

> The stile in which it is arranged, with the light manner of its decorations (the colours being principally a straw-coloured ground with silver balustrades and silver ornaments) gives the whole an air of simple grandeur, and forms a very striking and pleasing *coup d' oeil*. The scenes are extremely pretty, and dresses of the children chosen with taste and propriety, and in the orchestra is placed a very good band.[34]

After only nine performances, the circus was shut down for lack of a license. On October 9, Dibdin and Hughes appeared before the General Quarter Sessions, held at Kingston upon Thames, Surry, to apply for their license. After the Magistrates quickly renewed the customary license for Vauxhall Gardens, council for Hughes and Dibdin, "proprietors of that magnificent building in St. George's Fields," addressed the company. In the course of the debate, it was stated:

> Near fifty children of both sexes, from six years old to fourteen, were to be under the tuition of Mr. Grimaldi,* Dancing Master, late Clown at Sadler's Wells, and were to act Speaking Pantomimes, Opera, Medleys, Drolls, and Interludes, under the

*Nicolini Grimaldi was an actor and "leaper," or gymnast, well known to 18th century audiences. In the 1750s, he performed at the King's Theatre in the Haymarket where one writer noted he was "a man of great strength and agility; he indeed treads the air. If he has any fault, he is rather too comical; and from some feats which I have been a witness to ... it is my opinion that those spectators will see him with most pleasure, who are least solicitous whether he breaks his neck or not." On September 14, 1758, he made his first appearance upon the English stage in a new pantomime dance, The Millers, at Drury-Lane Theatre.[35]

direction of Mr. Dibdin as a Chef d'Ouvre of the place. The Horsemanship, by Mr. Hughes, intended only to be served up as desert.

During the proceedings, the Court received two letters from the Secretary of State, purporting that it would be very improper at this time, "when the police of the country wanted a total reform, to license any new place of public diversion." The Bench divided, 8 for the license and 26 against. It was noted that it was most extraordinary "that any man or men should erect such a beautiful building without a certainty of lawful leave to carry on the purposes intended therein to be performed."[36]

Both Dibdin (from his experience at the Comic Mirror) and Hughes (having operated a riding school for many years) should have known better. Perhaps more interesting was the observation that Hughes' equestrians were primarily consigned as "desert," rather than headliners. That, clearly, was Dibdin's influence, and it did not bode well for their relationship, as neither man was likely to take what amounted to second billing from the other. They eventually succeeded in procuring a license and opened for business at the end of October 1782.

The entertainment for opening night at the Royal Circus began with a prelude, followed by horses making a grand entrance, a grand ballet under the title "Admetus and Alceste" (danced by children), a variety of feats of horsemanship by Hughes and his pupils, and a burlesque pantomimic parody called "Mandarina, or the Refusal of Harlequin."

A review noted the ballet was "admirably well executed and in a stile far superior to the dances generally seen in our theatres. It was decorated with a variety of well painted scenery, and other stage assistance. The horsemanship was excellent of its kind, and not the least wonderful part of it were some feats performed by a boy and a girl, the one eight, the other nine years of age. The pantomimic parody was, as the bill phrased it, a pantomimic *ad libitum*. Lacking structure, the act consisted of a variety of parodies, including the tent scene from *Richard the Third*, and musical parodies on popular songs, ending with a Chinese wedding in which two boys entertained the audience with trumpets. Before the curtain dropped, fireworks were set off, the roof of the stage being open in order to let the smoke ascend without disagreeable smoke or smell, as is generally the case with fireworks exhibited on the stage."[37]

Other reviews were of like praise, adding, "The music was in general pleasing, and in many places, plainly discovered the animated touches and fire of Mr. Dibdin." In conclusion, it was determined the Royal Circus "promises fair to be one of the most frequented public places in this kingdom."[38]

Possibly, the word "circus" did not immediately catch on with the public, for by November 13, advertisements billed the production as "the Royal Circus, Equestrian, and Philharmonic Academy," and throughout the text the company was referred to as "the Academy." Seeking to take advantage of the crowds and make a quick profit, prices were set at: Boxes 4s; Pit 2s. 6d; Gallery 1s. Doors opened at six, and performances began exactly at seven. Perhaps to accommodate the wishes of the Secretary of State, in addition to the present Watch, a horse patrol was provided "from the Academy-Door to ALL bridges."[39]

3

Competition in the Riding School/ Amphitheatre/Circus

Brushing up seems to be the word of the day— the summer places of amusement put us in mind of a lot put up by auction to the best bidder; but which as the most sterling merit, Astley's Royal Grove; the Royal Circus; or Saddler's Wells, time only can discover.[1]

Names being a curious thing, in October 1782, when it became apparent he was to have serious competition from the Royal Circus, Astley began billing his production as "Astley's Amphitheatre Riding School," possibly to add a bit of familiarity to the title as well as to emphasize the equestrian aspects of his show.

That same month he underscored his success in France by introducing the *Inspice et Judica*, a singular method of his own invention that rendered the most vicious horse tractable and obedient, "so much so, that the animal seems to command equal applause with the uncommon Dexterity of his Rider." For the general utility of his system, "his Majesty has been pleased to grant Mr. Astley, his Royal Letters Patent, as a reward for the unwearied pains and expense he has been at; whereby the excellent Horseman still becomes more so, and less skilled ride without danger."

His doors opened at 5:30 P.M., and performances began at half past six. Undercutting Dibdin, Astley charged Front Boxes at 2s. 6d; Upper Boxes 1s. 6d; Pit and Gallery 1s. Among his company were Dawson and Porter (pupils of Astley), Griffin, Baptiste (the clown), Garman, Nevit (the Great Devil), the English Rossignol (bird imitations) and Master Astley ("considered alone in his art").[2] Later in the month, Richer and the Little Family, Mr. Adams doing bird imitations, Masters Langsdale and Jenkins, and a young lady performing horsemanship were promoted.[3]

Acknowledging John Astley's growing fame, his father noted that as the youth, not yet fifteen years old, had been contracted to return to Paris in the spring, it was "indispensably necessary to discontinue his performance on Fridays and Saturdays" in order to give him some necessary relief. The nobility, gentry and others were thereby encouraged to attend performances Monday through Thursday so as not to miss the opportunity of witnessing his extraordinary abilities.[4]

None of this prohibited "Astley, Son and Assistants" from offering riding lessons in the mornings. For the cost of 1 guinea, 1 shilling, plus 1 shilling for the groom, six lessons, taken when convenient, could be obtained at the Amphitheatre Riding School. Interestingly, it appears that some question arose as to the propriety of Astley's techniques, for he was forced to defend Master Astley's saddle of being the common size, and that all horsemanship conformed to his Patent and the law, "any deviation from which never has been, or is the intention of Mr. Astley."[5]

By December, the work Astley commissioned from an eminent artist to decorate his Amphitheatre Riding School was completed. He exhibited trained animals, including the little learned Horse, the Horse that fetched and carried like a Dog, and the most extraordinary Taylor's Horse that appeared between performances of agility on Foot and Horseback. The Ombres Chinoise, automata, Hornpipe (an energetic solo dance, typically performed to music) and Minuet Dancer were included.[6]

January 1783 did not start out well for "Mr. Hughes's Riding Academy, called the Royal Circus." Around January 10, eight hundred neighbors signed a petition claiming the establishment to be a "nuisance, or a disorderly house," delivering it to the Hon. Mr. T. Townshend, a Principal Secretary of State.[7] Hughes was arrested and brought to trial on January 13, charged under the 17th George II ("An Act to amend and make more effectual the Laws relating to Rogues, Vagabonds, and other idle and disorderly persons"), otherwise known as the vagrant act. The Act was divided into three sections, part two describing rogues and vagabonds. In essence, the law, as it applied to Hughes, dictated that anyone performing or hiring to perform for the stage and not being properly licensed was to be considered a rogue or vagabond.

Punishment under the vagrant act was not inconsequential. The convicted could either be publicly whipped or sent to the house of corrections until the next quarter session, at which time he could be ordered to stand six months of hard labor.[8]

The trial itself seems to have been somewhat of a farce. A man named Hyde offered several men a shilling to attend the Royal Circus and note Hughes' activities. One of the witnesses failed to identify Hughes, pointing instead to John Astley. The second identified Hughes from having seen him at the King's Arms after he was taken into custody but could not say he recognized him from the Circus. The third already knew Hughes and could thus identify him. Hyde denied bringing forth the prosecution, but admitted hiring the men, possibly because a conviction would have earned the accuser a ten-shilling reward under the vagrancy act.

The Clerk of the Peace testified that Hughes had applied for a license on October 9 for exhibitions at the Royal Circus, and Mr. Mingay, Hughes' council, had formally moved for a license on behalf of the proprietors of the Royal Circus, but that it was to stand in Hughes' name. The highlight of the case came when Mingay stated that the commitment was drawn on the parish of St. George in Surry County, when, in fact, there was no such parish, the proper name being St. George the Martyr.

Mingay also noted that Hughes was not indictable for "dumb oratory," and "ought to have acted, and performed, to have warranted a commitment." Eleven magistrates voted for "admission" and seven for "dismission." The charges were dropped and Hughes released from custody, "as was also Mr. Astley, upon promising never to exhibit any thing more upon the stage," presumably referring to the type of exhibit in which he participated.[9]

With the lawsuit behind them, both the Royal Circus and Astley's Amphitheatre went back to business. A comparison of their entertainments in April 1783, revealed:

Royal Circus and Equestrian Academy

A Variety of Evolutions de Manege on Horseback

Unparallelled Horsemanship by Mr. Hughes, accompanied by a Lady from Spain and twelve others of the most capital Performers in Europe
A Lecture on The Living Manners with pictures, particularly two Allegorical Paintings of Innocence and Remorse, provoking innocent laughs
Concluding with a most capital Fire-Work[10]

Astley's Amphitheatre Riding School

Unparalleled Display of Manly Agility
The celebrated Master Astley leading the Advanced Guard
The Cabinet of Fancy
Les Ombres Anglois, or The English Shadows
The Little Conjuring Horse and a new Horse Dance by two Redoubtable Horses, rode by Mr. Astley and Son
Concluding with La Fete Chinoise, or the Empress of China on Horseback and Fire-Works representing a Fight between Two Flying Dragons

In June 1783, Astley and son notified the public that in consequence of exhibiting the whole of their new Entertainments in Paris and building a Riding School there, they were closing their Riding School, Westminster, for the summer.[11] Astley thanked the public for their support over the past seventeen years, noting that he would be happy to welcome his patrons at his Amphitheatre Anglois, *Rue et fauxbourg du Temple a Paris*.[12] After numerous "last weeks," Astley's final performance of the year in London came on September 6.

On Saturday, September 27, Hughes also wrapped up his summer season, but the Royal Circus, Equestrian, and Philharmonic Academy opened again for the holidays, offering "The Fairy World," splendid Equestrian Exercises and entirely new music, composed and conducted by Mr. Dibdin.[13]

The Christmas-New Year's week was extremely well received, earning praise for Mr. Grimaldi's pantomime, "The Lancashire Witches," one reviewer noting he "has given a fresh instance of his indefatigable industry, and a proof how well he knows how to make the galleries laugh." The scenery, by Mr. Lupino, Sen., "has a masterly and striking effect as anything ever seen." Miss Romanzini, the favorite of the audience, garnered heavy applause for her performance in "The Milk Maid"; Sestini played the Clown admirably; Dibdin's music was highly spoken of; and Hughes Horsemanship could not be too highly praised.[14]

A review for the upcoming season of 1784 noted that Astley had built a large addendum to his theater, adding a number of French entertainments; the Royal Circus also boasted improvements, but the proprietors earned disapprobation for their "incessant trifling of children." In a poignant observation that would haunt circuses on both sides of the Atlantic for one hundred years, the review continued, "The substitution of grown performers, without encroaching on the system of the Theatres, will certainly meet with the encouragement of the Public."[15]

Astley Flies High

If anything proved the genius of Philip Astley's showmanship, it was his ability to spot a new trend and capitalize on it. On September 19, 1783, the Montgolfier brothers, Joseph and Etienne, oversaw the first public exhibition of a hot air balloon from the courtyard of Versailles. With King Louis XVI and Marie Antoinette in attendance, a sheep, a duck and a rooster were sent skyward. The vessel remained aloft 8 to 10 minutes before safely descending in the forest at Carefore-Mareclia, two miles distant. The Montgolfier brothers became instant celebrities, and news of their momentous achievement quickly traveled around the world.[16]

It is more than likely that Astley, who was in France at the time, was one of the thousands in the crowd standing slack-jawed with awe as the balloon rose from *terra firma*. What he witnessed was an 18th century miracle of flight, undoubtedly leaving him with a head spinning with possibilities. As the concept of raising an aerostat with hot air was not difficult, he purchased, at considerable expense, three small balloons and the apparatus to fill them.

The peculiar airship in this illustration, a century removed from the Montgolfiers, was called the "Great Chicago Air Ship." It exhibited with Wallace & Co.'s 50-Cage Menagerie in 1891. These novelties, still dependent on gas for elevation, rarely got off the ground and, if they did, performed well under expectations. (*Cambridge Jeffersonian* [OH], April 30, 1891)

On March 8, 1784, he began advertising the "New curious Aerostatic Experiments," whereby he proposed to set off his balloons, one of which was 25 feet in circumference, at Hercules Hall, St. George's Fields. Attached to it would be a triumphal car. One balloon was to set off an explosion (probably using a slow match) every 200 feet in the air, and at the height of 4,000 feet, to let off three small explosions in order to ascertain its location when out of sight. A silver tankard was to be awarded to the person who found the large globe and returned it to its owner. Admittance for this novel display was set at 2s, 6d each.[17]

While Lunardi, Blanchard, Charles and Roberts were ascending in Paris, and Monsieur Chevalier arrived in England to demonstrate the techniques of aerostation (with his balloon filled with two thousand gallons of inflammable air), Philip Astley launched his three unmanned balloons from St. George's Fields on March 12. The first caught in the trees and burst, a common fate of globes, big and small. The second was small, of a light brown color, rapidly taking a course toward Essex. The third and grandest, of an oblated spherical form of silk or canvas, had painted on it 24 Divisions, alternately red or maroon and white. Although no "explosions" were heard, the balloon sailed into the heavens to great applause and was soon out of sight. Witnesses speculated that it would remain aloft for many days, making one speculate "the Reward of a Silver Tankard for bringing this wandering Child Home to its Parent, will scarcely be worth the fetching."

With amusing insight, one observer enumerated the large crowd gathered to witness the ascensions:

> Dukes in their Carriages.
> Lords in ditto.
> Ladies of Quality in ditto.
> Ladies of a certain Quality on Foot.

Ladies of all Qualities.
Merchants gasping.
Tradesmen staring.
Boys sinking in the Mud.
Footmen in the Shape of Gentlemen.
Maid Servants in all Shapes.
Tag, rag, and bog Tail, in Parties.[18]

Astley likely recovered his expenses and then some, but with legitimate aeronauts crossing the Channel to England, he could not hope to maintain large audiences. Although not performed within the confines of his amphitheatre, it is important to mark that on this day, Astley became the first "circus man" to experiment with balloons as a means of entertainment. Decades later, American aeronauts, including the famous John Wise, would attach themselves to traveling circuses, and for a time, themselves become circus people.

Astley was not through with his fascination for balloons, and when he returned to his more familiar role as proprietor of what he now styled the "Amphitheatre, and Ambigu-Comic," he immediately worked them into the program. Despite apprehensions that his St. George's balloon would sail for many days, the aerostat probably caught in a tree or descended into the water. Although no description of the balloon Astley used in the amphitheatre is given, it was probably one of his remaining two. And hopefully, some lucky soul earned a silver tankard.

Delaying the opening of the amphitheatre until April 19, he promised that "The performers, performances, machinery, decorations, dresses, music & c." would be entirely new and collected at a very great expense.[19] The theater itself was enlarged and improved by the addition of a new stage for dramatic performances, better adapted to the ease and convenience of the audience by the circular form of the building.

Opening night, April 21, displayed some jitters and a near tragedy, earning Astley mixed reviews. An Equestrian Parade opened the activities, followed by an "indifferent" prologue. The principal novelty was billed as a *Tragic-Heroic-Comic Pantomime*, the subject of which was the rape of Europa. Unfortunately, the audience was unfamiliar with the celebrated ancient fable, and the staff was not quite expert in the machinery. Juno's peacocks were not as manageable as the horses, and Astley, "notwithstanding his skill in raising an air balloon, could not contrive to make the cloud ascend, in which Jupiter and Juno proposed taking their departure." The bull that carried off Europa looked more like an elephant or a rhinoceros and did not keep step. Additionally (whether for good or ill is unclear), the artist appearing in "Peasant of the Alps" was "not squeamishly afraid to display her *white breeches.*

To make matters worse, the performer on the slack rope, in adjusting himself to swing by one leg, owing to the newness of the rope and the polish of his stocking, lost hold and was catapulted over the orchestra, where he lay for some time without moving. Had he fallen three feet nearer the stage he would have been dashed to pieces. After being taken out, he returned and, against public outcry, went on to perform a series of feats on the slack rope "in a stile of the greatest excellence."

The good news was one reviewer's conclusion that Astley showed "great taste, ability, and liberality ... and will meet with universal support." The bad news came in a second review that observed, "Upon the whole, we must declare, that it will be necessary for Mr. Astley to make some great alterations and improvements in his exhibition, unless he will allow his Amphitheatre to be totally eclipsed by the Royal Circus."[20]

While Astley cannot be faulted by his perhaps over-ambitious production, and excused a lack of perfection in the opening night exhibition, the choice of a "tragic-heroic-comic" pantomime on the rape of Europa seems peculiar, given that most of the audience comprised semi-literate or illiterate individuals. Clearly, Astley was hoping to impress the oft-sought "nobility and gentry," who, like the second reviewer, were completely familiar with the story. While it was normal for entertainers to appeal to the learned and the moneyed, as it gave them respectability (and, indeed, many members of the nobility attended Astley's balloon ascensions), it was equally dangerous to reach too far over the heads of the commoners. That said, Astley gave "Jupiter in Disguise, or the Rape of Europa" a typical two-month run before replacing it with the more temporal "Air Balloon, or All the World in the Clouds."

In August, the Riding School was simply called "Astley's, Westminster-Bridge," but by October, it had gone back to "Astley's, Amphitheatre, Westminster Bridge."

Not to be left out, Hughes introduced "the favourite Balloon Song" to accompany a new pantomime called "The Vicissitudes of Harlequin." Dibdin's creditors at this time may have prevented him from applying significant time to the Circus, as Messrs. De Castro and Brooks were credited for new musical works.[21] Dibdin's association with the Circus was not over, however, for in December 1784, he came out with a pamphlet advertised as "Royal Circus, New Songs, composed by C. Dibdin" (or "Dibdin's 12 Circus Songs"), that sold for one shilling.[22] By January 1785, he was back at the Theatre-Royal, Drury-Lane, where a new musical piece of his was in rehearsal.[23]

Two months later, Hughes published a note stating that while he appreciated the offer of unlimited Credit "from different Tradesmen of Opulence," he and Dibdin, "conceiving it to be an injustice (the Royal Circus as a Public Place receiving only ready Money) to require Credit upon any Account whatever."[24]

Opening March 28, 1785, the Royal Circus again advertised that all Musical Entertainments were composed and conducted by Dibdin. One of their new features offered the Automaton Figure of a monkey posturing on the tight Rope. Astley, too, opened on Easter Monday, providing his patrons with Signor and Signora Messica from St. Germaine, with their original Troop of Dancing Dogs and also a Monkey (General Jackoo) performing on the Tight Rope, observing, "This amazing little Animal has been the Admiration of Paris for two Years Past." Astley had also redecorated the Amphitheatre over the winter, adding a large chandelier invented by himself and placed in the Center, illuming the whole and rendering the illumination "less incommodious to the audience."[25]

Over the course of the summer, the two production companies continued to compete with each other as well as with traditional theaters. In April, Astley advertised "The Marriage of Figaro," concurrently playing in Paris and at the Theatre Royal, Covent Garden. Upon being informed the Ballet and Airs were omitted from the production at the Theatre Royal, he purchased the music from the Ballet-Master of the French Comedy, "that it might be a means of adding to the many new Amusements of his Amphitheatre."[26]

Dibdin, always in trouble with creditors, was named in a case brought before the Court of Exchequer whereby he was charged with authorizing the sale of his musical compositions after previously selling the copyright. Astley enjoyed better fortunes, offering for sale a new work entitled *Natural Magic Revealed*, containing twenty experiments exhibited by the most celebrated performers of the present age. In June, attempting to find anything and everything that might cause comment or make money, Astley opened a "Floating Bath for the reception of Bathers."[27]

4

The Evolving Circus

The Royal Grove may with propriety be stiled a hodge-podge; for here you have rope-dancing, singing, pantomime, wire-dancing, the warbling of birds, horsemanship, women vaulting on the slack rope, imitations of hounds, organs, and wild boars, stage dancing, buffoonery, mimicry, and agility of all kinds; in short, the eye and the ear are amused by an incessant variety, and we wonder how in the name of fortune Astley contrives to procure such an assemblage of strange things.[1]

At this point in its evolution, "hodge-podge" seems as good an expression as any to describe the circus. While Astley experimented with various names for his riding school, (including "Amphitheatre" and "Grove," and later "Hippodrome"), the word "circus" prevailed. By mid–1785, a patron could pick and chose between such exhibitions as feats of activity on foot and horseback, burlettas, operettas, burlesques, conjuring, magic, bird calls, pantomimes, automata, puppet and shadow shows, tumbling, leaping, displays on the slack and tightrope, and fireworks. Trained horses, both standard and miniature, were a mainstay, while performing dogs, monkeys and the occasional exotic animal came and went. High and lowbrow dramas set to music ran back-to-back with comedic interludes, while the clown evolved as an important component (see Chapter 25).

The selection of acts depended primarily on the taste of individuals running the operation. In the early years, the word "proprietor" generally referred to the owner. If he were a horseman like Charles Hughes, he featured equestrian exhibitions. Given his background, Dibdin leaned more toward musical productions, while Astley, a far more astute businessman with his ear always toward the "roar of the crowd," tended to be more flexible. He eagerly experimented with the "curious" and innovative, soliciting foreign talent, introducing hits from Paris and offering a wide variety of trained animals, changing his program at least bimonthly.

Toward the end of the 1780s, circumstances began to alter. "Proprietor" remained a word for owner, but "manager" came into vogue, representing the man who directed the day-to-day operations. This was particularly true for shows owned by several parties. Men backing ventures who were not performers hired a manager, typically an artist with a proven track record. How much latitude they granted him dictated whether he used his own judgment in the selection and billing of acts, or conformed to their desires and financial restraints. This was especially obvious with the operation of the Royal Circus.

Philip Astley, who owned the "Royal Grove," or "Amphitheatre," began promoting

"Surprising exercises of the strong man"; and at Sadler's Wells, Patrick Obrien, the Amazing Irish Giant, standing 8' 4", created a sensation with his "juvenility of countenance, and the affability of his manners." In a sense, this could be looked upon as the beginning of the "freak" sideshows that would become so popular in the United States. Prices remained relatively stable and affordable, particularly for the lower classes — admittance to the galleries still cost one shilling, with side galleries even cheaper at six pence.

Competition between the major circuses remained sharp, each attempting to gain the upper hand by exhibiting new and ever-changing acts. In August, upon hearing that Messrs. Placido, the Little Devil, Dupuis, Mannie and the extraordinary La Belle Espagnole were leaving Sadler's Wells for the fair in St. Lawrence, Paris, Astley immediately went out and signed them for a short stay at the Amphitheatre.[2] Stealing performers was not new to any professional troop, and in September, the Little Devil was making appearances at the Royal Theatre.

Perhaps the most interesting "duel" between the two major circuses was fought over an inflammable air balloon. In April 1785, an aeronaut named Stuart-Amos Arnold (an Englishman and former seaman who had lost a limb in the service of his country) advertised in the London papers that he would make an ascension from St. George's Fields on May 10, traveling by air to the Continent. As the site of ascension was in close proximity to the Royal Circus, Charles Hughes became involved, offering to take subscriptions and sell tickets to the event from the Circus Coffee-house.[3]

The timetable did not work out, however, and Arnold was not ready until August 31. Charging five shillings for admittance into the inner circle, Arnold and his associate, Mr. Appleby (who was scheduled to descend in a parachute), had no trouble filling the aerostat with inflammable air. As was so often the case, events did not go as planned. First, an assistant climbed a pole to release the ropes at the apex of the balloon. Blown by a gust of wind, he fell atop the inflated silk, requiring half an hour to get him down. As Arnold and his son mounted their car, and Appleby got into a smaller one suspended below, the balloon broke free. The cords and netting snapped, and the would-be parachutist was flung into the nearby trees. Arnold lost his balance and tumbled to the ground, leaving only the inexperienced child to man the globe. It ascended and was blown out of sight, later exploding in the air. Fortunately, young Arnold survived by being dropped into the Thames near Blackwell. Perhaps worst of all, the crowd of carriages surrounding St. George's Fields proved so great that the paying public was unable to break through what amounted to a barrier to the toll gate, and only 37 pounds were paid into the coffers. In all probability, the accident preserved the life of the hapless Appleby, as the description of his parachute, likened to that of an umbrella, would surely have failed, plummeting him to his death.

Hughes lost no time, quickly offering a benefit on the next two Saturdays "as a small assistance toward enabling him [Mr. Arnold] to repair the damages he sustained in his Balloon." For his effort, Hughes and his managers earned approbation for promoting scientific knowledge as well as gratifying the curiosity of the public. For his part, Astley quickly added a performance called "Harlequin's Escape from the Wreaking in Shropshire with a Parachute." He also translated a new musical piece from the French called "The Lottery Ticket, or Poor Cobler" [*sic*],[4] and introduced a new equestrian exercise called "Still Vaulting," invented by young Astley, which demonstrated "what ought to be practiced by every Horseman, in order to familiarize more effectually the Body to the various Actions of the Horse." They closed for the season on November 10.[5]

In 1786, Astley changed the name of his Amphitheatre to the "Royal Grove" (or "Royal

Grove, and Astley's Amphitheatre"), leaving people to wonder whether he had planted trees in the Riding School or turned it into a foreign Vauxhall.[6] Young Astley (now a star in his own right) and his Troop arrived from Versailles in May and once again performed with his father. Aside from equestrian performances, Mr. Lawrence "threw fourteen somersets, Master Beli eighteen slipslaps and a somerset, and Mr. Lonsdale a round-all, eight feet high, nineteen flipflaps, and a somerset afterwards."

Master Ricketts Makes an Appearance

Jones' Equestrian Amphitheatre, Union Street, Whitechapel, offered the Egyptian Pyramids by Twelve Strong Men, supported and balanced by the English Hercules; horsemanship; "and various other feats of manly activity" too numerous to be inserted.[7] More significantly, the first mention of Ricketts (in this case, listed as "master," indicating he was an apprentice) appeared in a May 6, 1786, advert for Jones' Amphitheatre:

> Horsemanship by Masters King, Rickets, and Sutton; Messrs. Franklin, Miller, and Jones. And a very humourous Piece of Horsemanship by Mons. Baptiste Dubois.

The surname "Ricketts" was misspelled in the notice. John Bill Rickets and his brother Francis would later appear in Philadelphia in 1792, the former going on to become the "Father of the American Circus." Jones' performance that day was to conclude with "The Taylor riding to Brentford."[8] A week later, on May 15, Jones advertised "Rope Vaulting, by Signor and Signora Richer, and a child only three years old. Clown by Master Ricketts." To go along with it was "Horsemanship on one, two, three and four Horses, by nine of the most capital Performers who ever exhibited in this Kingdom."[9] Here the surname was correctly spelled; again, "Master Ricketts" is mentioned by name, an indication that he was highly esteemed. It is also curious to observe that while Ricketts undoubtedly performed equestrian feats, the talent singled out for special mention was that of a clown.

Marking the importance of young Master Ricketts, he and Mr. Franklin were given a joint benefit performance on July 6, 1786. For this performance, "astonishing Exertions of Strength by the English Hercules, in supporting from twenty to thirty men on his Feet and Hands," as well as "the French metamorphoses, or Post Boy tied in a Bag," were offered.[10] This was an early routine of the comedic gender-changing, later introduced by John Bill Ricketts in his 1793 circus as "The Metamorphosis." Ricketts would also offer versions of "The Taylor" in his performances.

In another metamorphosis of a sort, around this time equestrians began substituting the common street saddle with a form of "padded saddle," which gave their skill a different look and added to the mystique. The new saddles were easier to work with and in the beginning constituted less bulk, although as they evolved, pads turned to boards in an effort to facilitate intricate tricks, occasionally becoming large platforms.

Hughes maintained the name Royal Circus, and reviews for the start of the 1786 season concentrated on his equestrian exhibits. Considering him unrivalled in the field of horsemanship, one observer adroitly noted of the remainder, "Music and pantomime very much assist; but in an exhibition of this nature, they must and ought to be considered as subordinate."[11]

The Royal Circus suffered without Dibdin's talent, but it did present wire, tight rope and trampoline acts, as well as featuring Masters Robinson, Davis and Giles leaping from a single horse over a garter (ribbon) and through a tub to alight on the saddle. Mons. Balmatt also threw a back somerset twenty-two feet high and flip-flopped with his legs tied together. The celebrated Monkey, General Jackoo, also appeared.[12] Perhaps the greatest notices came in August when Bucephalus, a horse 16 hands high, was presented alongside the "wild horse," Chilby.

Chilby's history was an interesting one. Hughes obtained him from a man named Dowson, the animal being so savage it required fifteen men to convey it to the circus, leading it "like a mad bull." Apparently unable to handle the horse, Hughes sent it out to Jones at his Whitechapel riding school, where it behaved so savagely Dowson placed Chilby in a pit, declaring it fit only to be baited by dogs. The Magistrates intervened, forcing Chilby's keepers to lower water down to it in a pail affixed to a rope, as no one dared venture near. After the story made the newspapers, Hughes retrieved the horse and put it on exhibition. He seems to have made progress taming the beast, as it appeared on stage "mounted by two equestrian performers, with ornamental fire works on their heads."[13]

In a bit of one-upsmanship, Jones' Equestrian Amphitheatre also advertised "the Wild Horse, Chilliby [*sic*], lately reduced to obedience," prompting a furious rebuttal by Hughes, claiming he had the one and only true wild horse. In a similar ploy, the proprietors at Sadler's Wells advertised that Louis Porter, the Hercules from Paris, would carry on his table 20 to 25 men, upstaging Jones' strongman; while at the Pantheon, Mr. Uncles outdid them all with a bizarre display of his "Grand Fish Balloon and Four Live Eagles."[14]

Astley's season of 1787 was delayed, as his troop remained wind-bound (stranded) for a considerable time at Boulogne. When they finally arrived, he opened on April 28, offering the Royal Troop of female rope-dancers from Paris performing on the slack wire, slack- and tightrope. (The first mention of what became known as a "tight-wire" came in 1850, when Mahommed Caratha returned from Turkey, offering "new equilibres on a small wire." Thereafter, several artists performed on wire, but it was often unreliable, and rope continued in general use. Stranded wire for performances did not appear until the 1830s.[15]) The program was "to conclude with Young Astley's exercises, never exhibited in London."[16] Interestingly, in a notice two days later, the wording was changed to, "The whole to conclude with young Astley's Exercises, never attempted in London." By May 8, the production included dancing dogs and the Learned Pig, and concluded with a pantomime.[17]

John Astley's performance likely was "speaking music" (*musique parlante*), a common offering in France where comedy and tragedy were performed without dialogue. The youth continued at the Royal Grove until the remainder of the season before touring Birmingham, Chester, Liverpool and Manchester with his father, finally returning to his Riding School in Paris.

Early in the 1787 season, a Mr. Becket, Trunk-Maker, Hay-Market, offered an exhibition of "Monstrous Craws, Wild Human Beings" during the week from 10:00 in the morning until 9:00 at night. The price for witnessing these "Wonderful Phoenomena" was 1 shilling. By August, the Royal Grove introduced the "Three Monstrous Craws, *wild born human beings*" in pantomime and then exhibited the originals on an illuminated platform. Although having gone to "great Expense" to procure them for one week before they left England, the price for admission remained "as usual."

The "Craws," consisting of two females and one male, whose "country, language, and native customs ... were yet unknown to all mankind," were supposed to have been blown out to sea in a violent storm, picked up by a Spanish vessel and carried to *Trieste*, and from there to Holland and then London. Perhaps drawn by the exhibition, His Royal Highness, the Duke of York, accompanied by General Grenville and Colonel Lake, made an incognito appearance at "the Grove." After being subjected to the general inconvenience of a crowded house, their presence was made known to Astley, who ordered the performances repeated.

Astley subsequently retained the "Craws" through October, and eventually the "Wild Born Female Monster" become so "tame" that she rode two horses at a full gallop while standing upright, acted together with the Male Monster in the pantomime, and conversed with any person who spoke "Patois," the language used in the "neighborhood of Mount S. Bernards, and in the Alps, within 50 leagues of the City of Coire."[18]

If that were not enough, Astley secured an "Infant Prodigy," lately having performed before their Majesties. This two-year-old, brother to another musical prodigy who played the piano forte at the Royal Grove, amazed with his sensibility and accuracy, while his older sibling was appointed to play Draugts [*sic*] against a celebrated practitioner.[19]

That August, the Royalty Theatre presented Mr. Palmer providing the original "Lecture on Heads," while a new Tragi-comic Pantomimic Entertainment, starring, and under the direction of, Carlo Delpini, called "Don Juan; or The Libertine Destroyed," came afterwards.[20]

The Law Courts Come Calling

Although receiving good press, all was not well with Charles Hughes. Contained within his advertisement for the opening of the season on Easter Monday, 1787, ran the comment, "*The monies received nightly to discharge the growing expenses from the 1st of Jan. 1787, and opening the Theatre this present season, the residue, after paying the Performers, is to be at the disposal of* THE HON. COURT OF CHANCERY" (italics and capitals in original).

Hughes found himself as plaintiff against Davis, Grant, Harborne, Sir John Lade and others, and at the same time defendant against Davis, Grant and others. The cases were convoluted, with both sides professing not to be able to locate the other, and played out better than a drama with comedic overtones.[21]

The case eventually went against Hughes, as it was stated that the defendants owned three-fourths of the interest in the Circus, and the plaintiff, Hughes, only one fourth, thereby requiring Hughes to follow the dictates of those who owned the majority.[22] By 1788, Charles Hughes was wholly dispossessed of all control in the Royal Circus, and the establishment was placed in the hands of Sir John Lade, Bullock and other proprietors. Their first act was to shut up the rooms for which Hughes had obtained a license for the sale of liquor, and add a "proper *Coffee-House*" within the building. At the same time, Nicolini Grimaldi, the circus leaper and comic, who was to have undertaken the management of the stage performances at the Royal Circus, died on March 14 at his house in Strandgate.

Fortunately for the Circus, Philip Astley, who had taken his company to Ireland, encountered so great a success that he prolonged his stay, leaving the Royal Circus for an extended period without any contiguous rival with which to contend.[23]

Hughes remained at odds with the proprietors, although he continued to perform with his equestrian pupils. Mr. Delpini, a familiar name among the public for his talent as a performing clown, assumed control as acting manager of the Royal Circus. By May 1788, instead of lauding Hughes' horsemanship, a review in the *Times* of London concentrated on the Music and Dance, singling out Simonet's new ballet for particular note. Since the *Times* had previously ignored riding school and circus performances (although heavily covering aerostatic ascensions), it was clear they appreciated the change of emphasis ushered in by Delpini.[24]

Although Delpini's time on stage was limited due to his new duties, he wrote new entertainments, including "A New Catch Club" and "The President" (with a Song), and occasionally went back to his roots "at the particular Desire of his Friends," playing the Clown in "What You Please," which concluded the August 4 performance. Only one sentence in an advertisement run in the *Times* (with the headline "Mr. Delpini, Acting Manager, Royal Circus") mentioned Hughes "and his most extraordinary Young Pupils" by name.[25]

Clearly Hughes did not appreciate being relegated to second billing. In what appears to be dueling notices, a September 2 advertisement in the less erudite *Morning Post, and Daily Advertiser* begins with his name in bold capitals and lists his equestrian pupils first. Interestingly, a burletta called "Beau Outwitted, or, Vulcan Triumphant" was written by Dibdin. After another bold, capitalized caption listing "Horsemanship By Hughes," the terse notation stated that a new pantomime by "Sig. Delpini" was to be followed by the concluding "Fireworks on the Famous Bucephalus."

Law courts being a form of entertainment for the 18th century citizen, the three Royal Theatres brought suit against the Royalty-Theatre, the Royal Grove (Astley's Amphitheatre) and the Royal Circus over the Bill for regulating the performance of Interludes.[26]

Philip Astley immediately offered a Consideration to the "Public in general, and more especially, and with the utmost Deference, Respect, and Duty," to the members of both houses of Parliament, defending his character and arguing the case against the proprietors of Sadler's Wells, one of the plaintiffs in the above suit. Charging that the proprietors took advantage of his being out of the Kingdom, he derided their effort "to enable them to go on with their stage performances, and to exclude all other stages performing in a similar way."

Astley prefaced his defense by offering a history of his accomplishments, incidentally offering a unique insight into the rhyme and reason of his life. After being discharged from the 15th Regiment of Light Dragoons in June 1776, he invented new Equestrian Amusements for the public eye, spending more than five thousand pounds in three years to improve his riding school. This activity brought on a severe illness, and in order to preserve his health and give a respite to his horses, he engaged some tumblers and rope-dancers. He continued in this manner until informed that no kind of stage entertainment could be carried on for gain or reward without a license. He consequently obtained that license under 25th George II, the same one used by Sadler's Wells. Believing this to be legal, he continued for eight years, expending 15,000 pounds in improving his Riding School. During that time his stage amusements were unconnected with those of regular theaters, and no complaint of any kind was ever exhibited against him.

His main defense, however, seemed to be his service to his country, for which he submitted a copy of his "Certificate of Service," stating that he enlisted at age 17 and served during the late war with Germany. And that, "at the disembarkation of the troops at Bremerlee, at the mouth of the Weser, by his spirited activity, was the principal means of saving several men and horses, in imminent danger, from the accidental oversetting of the boat." During the battle of Friedburg, when on advance guard, Astley also, under very heavy fire, brought off "his Serene Highness, the hereditary Prince of Brunswick, when his Highness was wounded, within the enemy lines."

The three defendants did not prevail and the bill passed after receiving the approbation of the Duke of Richmond.[27] That meant actors at the Royalty-Theatre, the Royal Grove and the Royal Circus could not have actors speaking lines; all dialogue had to be sung to accompanying music in the form of a burletta.

The proprietors of Sadler's Wells immediately let it be known they had accumulated a fund of "pleasing and elegant Amusement, which no former season, nor any other theatre, ever equalled in one night's representation." Astley's featured new pantomimes and dances, along with young Astley's horsemanship and a Real Gigantic Spanish Pig, measuring from head to tail 12 feet, and 12 hands high, weighing 12 Cwt., ridden by a monkey.[28] The Circus offered similar fare.

With theatrical concerns attracting great attention, another unpleasantness occurred scarcely a month later when Mr. King, manager of the Drury-Lane Theatre, resigned not only his post, but his acting job, under a charge of avarice.[29]

Despite losing in court, Astley's was reported to have had a good summer and fall, for the "frequenters" at the Royal Grove were as numerous as ever.[30] Part of the attraction, no doubt, came from the display of "Philosophical Fireworks." Invented by Mons. Henry, a professor of Natural Philosophy from Paris, the effect of beautiful colors without smoke, scent or detonation were created by inflammable air,[31] a combination of vitriol and metal shavings, of the type used to inflate balloons. Combined with several new, extraordinary pieces of Fireworks, the display clearly made an astonishing conclusion. Astley's season ended November 26.

Now billed as "Mr. Ricketts," John Bill received a benefit performance at Jones' Equestrian Amphitheatre on February 26, 1788. In Part II of the performance he appeared on a single horse with Mr. Sutton (who had also finished his apprenticeship), Master King and Mr. Jones; clown by Mr. Dubois. Part V offered "For the first time this Season, a Trip to Newmarket, or the Jockeys Hornpipe, by Mr. Ricketts, Mr. Sutton, Master King, and Mr. Dubois," and Part IX concluded with "Horsemanship Burlesqued, called the Taylor going to Brentford, upon the Hunter, Manage and Road Horse, by Mr. Humphreys, After which Mr. Ricketts will throw a Somerset from a Board of Fire Works fourteen Feet high, with two Flambeaus in his Hands."[32]

5

Getting Away from the "Circus"

Balloons will soon become useless if the art of flying makes such rapid progress, as it *does at Astley's, and in the manner as practiced there by the troop of* female rope dancers.[1]

The season of 1789 promised to be a tumultuous one. Political events were rapidly unraveling in France, while the health of King George III of England caused great concern. On the entertainment scene, the situation between Hughes and the proprietors at the Royal Circus continued fraying, setting up an ever-escalating conflict with Astley's as the two venues battled over advertisement boasts and competing attractions.

The year started out well enough for Astley, who received 200 pounds for supervising the display of fireworks set off in Stephen's Green in consequence of the King's recovery.[2] Unfortunately, one of the firework displays fell on him, burning his leg. After neglecting the wound for some time, it festered, leaving him lame and weak for several months. Adding more misery, the uncommonly severe winter decreased profits for his Dublin exhibition and John Astley's Paris Riding School.[3]

Events looked brighter for the Royal Circus, as considerable money had been committed to beautifying the house and expanding the stage toward the audience. Such expense had to be recouped, and reductions in other areas were contemplated. Unwisely, proprietors Sir John Lade and William Davis waited until the evening of April 14 to inform Hughes that the horsemanship part of the program was to be reduced to the exercise of horses only, stating that the salary of 7s. 6d paid for the maintenance and performance of each apprentice was too high. An altercation ensued, resulting in the equestrian performance being exhibited, but without the accustomed riders.

The *Times* of April 15 quickly picked up the scandal, noting that the story took flight "on eagle's wings," and was immediately brought to Astley, "who no doubt will hasten to his Amphitheatre with all speed." With the matter to be settled in the Court of Chancery, the advert for April 17 began, "This and every Evening *till further Notice*, Hughes and His Pupils, Robinson, Sutton, Perrira, the General, Stent, Miss Huntley and Miss Crofts, will perform their much-admired Feats of Horsemanship" (italics added). Hurt feelings must have been quickly assuaged, as the same day, the *World* informed the public that the "little disturbance ... in consequence of there being no Horsemanship, is done away, as *Hughes* and his Pupils positively perform this evening."

In a further effort to ensure "Peace and Harmony," the Stage Manager, Thomas Read, subsequently made a public apology to the audience, assuring them that "the cause of the omission of your favourite Horsemanship no longer exists."[4]

That proved true only so far as it went. John Palmer, a principal actor at the Theatre Royal, Drury-Lane, famous for his "Whimsical, Satyrical, Serious, and Comic Olio,"[5] was wrapping up his exclusive contract. The proprietors of the Circus immediately signed him as principal headliner. After his debut on July 20, a review in the significantly important *Times* of July 28 announced, "The popularity and fashion of Palmer's 'As you like it,' has done more for the Royal Circus, than any matter yet exhibited on that stage ... crowded houses every night since Palmer's engagement prove this."

Clearly, the Circus was getting away from the "circus" by depending more on "legitimate acting" than Hughes, if not Dibdin, ever imagined. Indeed, as the French Revolution brought down the Bastille, both Astley's and the Royal Circus went in for extravagant recreations. With John Astley acting as manager during his father's illness, the Royal Grove quickly put together a miniature representation using intricate details of Paris as a backdrop. Premiering on August 6, they beat all competition by nearly two weeks. The Circus, going in for a full-scale enactment, used forty actors to portray the "treacherous Governor's invitation" and the dropping of the drawbridge. For the next several weeks, reviews concentrated on these productions to the exclusion of virtually everything else. Business was good, however, with the pit, boxes and galleries at the Royal Grove (amounting to upwards of 6,000 people) generally filled, bringing in 150l nightly.[6]

As a former soldier, Astley was given credit for bringing stark realism to his "military business," while the Circus advertised their superior effects, causing one writer (signing himself "Impartial") to pen an open letter to the Managers of the Royal Circus, beginning with the quotation, "I hate the Man who builds his Name/ On Ruin of another's Fame."[7] Fortunately, there was some humor to be found, if not within the Royal Circus, than outside, where some wag altered the coronets on several patrons' carriages, changing Earls into Viscounts and Barons into Earls.[8]

By October, Palmer, still headlining the Royal Circus, was credited with performing "As You Like It," playing Olio; starring in "The Catch Club" and "The Triumph of the Liberty, or, The Destruction of the Bastile"*; and headlining the concluding piece, "Don Juan." Hughes' name was sandwiched between, in only two lines of print.[9] The Circus "abruptly" closed the second week in November before a benefit could be offered for one of their actors, Mr. Follett, Senior, who broke his leg and was forced to have it amputated.[10]

Astley's season came to a close on October 29, with a rather telling observation in the press that he offered the best entertainments in point of performers, scenery and machinery, "since he has no proprietors to share with him."[11]

Whether or not the Royal Circus had several owners, it was a lucrative business. On January 7, 1790, the famous Christie's Auction House offered for sale a one-tenth part of the Royal Circus, originally purchased for 15,000l. This share averaged a return ("rent") of 1,360l per year, together with four "Silver Tickets" which admitted the bearer into any part of the House.[12]

The Circus opened on April 5, 1790, featuring:

"Bastille" was spelled with one "l" in the British press during the 1700s.

Feats like this had their origins at Hughes' Royal Circus and Astley's Amphitheatre. As circuses grew, large staff required a great bill of fare. In 1890, Gustin & Smith supplied breakfast for Barnum's circus that included 300 pounds of round steak, 250 pounds of veal chops, 25 pounds of bacon, 50 pounds of ham and 75 pounds of sausages. For dinner, 200 pounds of roast beef, 200 pounds mutton, 125 pounds veal, 75 pounds pickled pork, 200 pounds of corned beef, 200 pounds of neck meat and four livers were delivered. Added to that were 275 pounds of granulated sugar, 75 pounds of butter, 22 bushels of potatoes, a sack of flour, 2 gallons of coal oil, 6 gallons of vinegar, 30 dozen eggs, 4 pounds of pepper, 16 sacks of salt, 10 heads of cabbages, 72 pounds of lettuce, 28 cans of tomatoes, 12 pounds of parsley, 800 pounds of bread, 1,000 buns and 75 pies. The supplier also provided all the wood and milk necessary. (*Piqua Daily Leader* [OH], July 11, 1890; illustration from *Yates County Chronicle* [NY], July 18, 1885)

> Various and new Feats of Horsemanship by Mr. Hughes' Pupils, the Horse Department under the Direction of Hughes
> A new musical piece, "Cymon and Iphigene, music compiled from the works of the late Dr. Arne
> A Grand Spectacle, "Medea and Jason," original music composed by Gluck, starring Mr. Palmer
> A new entertainment, "The Village Fairy"
> Concluding with "Masquerade," under the direction of Mr. Palmer[13]

The events of 1789 clearly had an effect on the new season. Successful presentations of the fall of the Bastille taught the proprietors where the greatest draw lay, and over the winter they made no effort to go back to the roots of the "circus." Hughes' pupils (as opposed to Hughes himself) provided the only equestrian acts, while no gymnastic feats, if presented at all, were featured. This contrasted with Astley, who, by late September, 1789, still maintained a wide variety of acts, including horsemanship, tumbling, rope-dancing and singing, along with the "Representation of the Bastile," and Model of Paris, a representation of the Grand National Naval Review and pantomimes.[14]

Back to Court

It was inevitable that Charles Hughes went back to court, first in April, where he declared bankruptcy, and then in the case "Hughes Against Sir John Lade and Others, Proprietors of the Royal Circus." While the proceedings could not have been pleasant for either plaintiff or defendants, the press it received offered a unique insight into the operation, finances and relationships of the Royal Circus.

The actual suit dealt with the question over whether Hughes should be paid for the keep of horses during the time the Circus was not open for public amusement. Witness Joseph Mead testified that only ten of Hughes' horses were used for Circus performances, and these he used at Sturbridge Fair and to teach riding, the profits of which he kept for himself. Council for the defense painted a sad picture of the proprietors, stating their "adventure" in operating the Circus had been "extremely disadvantageous," and that they had expended many thousands of pounds on its behalf. He further stated Hughes had "misconducted himself most grossly and shamefully, and that there was no prospect of gain while he managed the horse department."

Council also stated that accounts between his clients and Hughes had been settled up on the third of December 1787, and a deed drawn up by a Master Chancery establishing a Committee to determine all future action. The present demand, therefore, went for the seasons of 1788 and 1789. He contended that the relation of servant and master ceased the moment the season ended, and as such, Hughes had no claim on his clients, adding that as Hughes was a one-fourth partner in the Circus (the other three being Lade, Thomas Millington and William Davis), he had no right to bring suit. Hughes' council rebuffed the argument by stating that his client stood "a double character, and that, with regard to the present demand, he was to be considered exactly as a stable keeper."

Somewhat nonplussed, Justice Lord Kenyon observed that it was a "sad thing" to see the parties traveling through the Court of Chancery for six years with different suits, and referred settlement to a third party.[15]

Instead of easing the situation, the ruling only served to exacerbate existing tensions, with letters to the *Times* airing myriad grievances. Hughes claimed that since January 1788, he had received no accounting from the proprietors, nor had they paid him one shilling profit for running the horse department. He claimed the right to be compensated for maintaining the horses, which he should have the use of for his own benefit, just as the stage manager received profits from the sale of Burlettas & c. Hughes added that while the Circus hired a gentleman to "puff" Mr. Palmer at three guineas per week, paid Palmer upwards of 1200l, paid Thomas Read (stage

M'LLE MARIE ELIZE

THE PEERLESS QUEEN OF THE ARENA.

From the beginning, most circus performers were a "here today, gone tomorrow" group. When exhibitions folded, they were put out of work; better offers might come from another circus; injury could shorten a career; or a new star might assume their position. Accolades created by circus writers were easily changed by substituting a different name. In 1867, Mademoiselle Marie Elize was promoted as "The Peerless Queen of the Arena," who stood alone "unapproached and unapproachable" as an equestrian. The removal of one line of type easily introduced another "embodiment of Grace, Elegance and Skill" to the public. (*Sparta Eagle* [WI], May 8, 1867) manager) 500l and the proprietors 500l each for their share of the profits, he had received "£0. 0s. 0d."

Quoting an agreement of April 16, 1789, Hughes stated terms that his apprentices were to be engaged for the season, each receiving 12 guineas per week, and for their clothing and washing, while Hughes (as teacher) would receive 36 guineas in weekly payments of 3 guineas. Furthermore, he was to receive two benefits during the first four months of the season, being given 15 days notice before each, and to hold them before Thursday in the week. By contract, his rights, dating from June 27, 1789, were:

	£.	s.	d.
To keep 10 horses from 27th June, 1789, to the 5th April, 1790 being 40 weeks & 1 day, at 10s. 6d. each, per week	210	15	0
To keep 2 horses from the 27th June, 1789, to the 5th of April, 1790, at 10s. 6d. per week, being 40 weeks and 1 day	42	3	0
Duty for 10 horses in the year 1789	5	0	0
Apprentices from the 20th of April, 1789, to the 8th of August, being 16 weeks, at 12 guineas per week	201	12	0
Apprentices from the 8th of August to the 10th of November, at 6 guineas per week, being 16 weeks and 2 days	84	0	0
	£543	10	0

What he received from the proprietors left a balance of £288, 1 shilling. The names of his apprentices were Giles Sutton, Thomas Stent, John Jefferies, Emanuel Perrirs and Ann Crofts. The proprietors countered by giving a lengthy account of their payments to Hughes, ending with a balance owed of £154, 4 shillings.

Hughes, at the time of bringing suit, was a prisoner under the Rules of the King's Bench, for the sum of £304, "after being arrested on the Circus business [grounds], upwards of forty times. He also owed his attorneys for handling the numerous suits.[16]

John Palmer, himself in jail on a charge of acting without a license, immediately contradicted Hughes' public assertion of his salary, stating he received only £301 in salary and £296 as profit from three benefit performances. In his card or letter, he accused Hughes of wishing to keep him incarcerated and destroying the deal he was attempting to strike with his creditors. In compliance with a request from the actor, Read published a statement avowing that Palmer had only three benefits (as opposed to Hughes' claim of four), and that he paid Palmer 25 guineas for "The Deserter" and a burletta, and nothing for "The Bastile."[17]

Determined not to let the matter stand, two days later Hughes published another rebuttal, claiming Palmer had had two official benefits and two others he shared with another Gentleman, but from which he took half the profits, amounting to £300 for "The Bastile." The profit from "The Bastile" amounting to £1305; Hughes, as a one-fourth partner, received nothing.[18]

It was not over yet. On July 15, Palmer and Barrat were hauled from confinement and taken before the Court of Justice on a charge brought by the associates of the Drury Lane and Covent Garden Theaters of *acting* at the Royal Circus, contrary to the Act made against unlicensed Theatres. (Barrat, from the Norwich Theatre, made his first appearance at the Circus on April 16, 1790, playing the part of Henry in "The Bastile.") After having their request for dismissal denied on the grounds the Circus had a license, it was revealed that the Justices of the Quarter Sessions were not authorized to grant licenses "to such performances as were now exhibiting at the Royal Circus, at Astley's, and Sadler's Wells." Lord Onslow, presiding, declared the entire case a "cruelty" and promised his support to a Bill relieving such "aggrieved persons," and discharged both actors.[19]

Mrs. Hughes had a benefit on June 23, while Mr. Hughes had his own benefit on July 13, 1790. In a rewarding show of camaraderie, John Astley and his troop performed with Hughes, being the first "and positively their last appearance at the Royal Circus."[20] Hughes continued to manage the Horse Department through August, but by September only two of his pupils, the "General" and the "Little Devil," were listed on the bill, and both were advertised for one evening only.[21] Sometime after this, Hughes left for Russia, where he established a new troop of horsemen.

The "Circus" Gains Traction

In 1792, the Astleys changed the name of their establishment to the "Royal Saloon," and Young Astley, who continued to act as manager, adopted a policy of changing the principal entertainments every three weeks. The following year, his production of "The Siege of Valenciennes" became the talk of the town and dominated all other attractions.

Hughes and his Russian "troop" came to England in early 1793, where he quickly joined forces with Handy and his horsemen from the Newcastle and Bristol riding schools. By late March, the equestrians were rehearsing for the opening of the season at the Royal Circus on April 2. Twenty in number, they quickly earned accolades as one of the strongest companies of Horsemanship that ever existed.[22] Early performances included a grand parade, two 30-inch high ponies that jumped through a covered balloon (hoop), Polander's Tricks, and Egyptian and Venetian Pyramids. On May 18, Hughes himself performed at the Circus, welcomed back by repeated warm applause.[23]

By mid–1783, three principal establishments offering "circus acts" presented:

Royal Circus

Horseback by Hughes' Pupils, Handy, Smith, Robinson and Twelve others (formerly Hughes' pupils)

Horsemen Handy and Smith leaping over a Garter ten feet high, and Handy demonstrating Still Vaulting, showing the different methods of mounting a horse without stirrups

Wire, Rope Dancing and Polander's Tricks by the Child of Promise

Slack Rope Vaulting by Mr. Carr and Vaulting over horses by the Whole Troop

The Force of Hercules with nine comical Performers

A Real Fox Chase with Two Foxes and Eight Couple of Mr. Coke's Norfolk's Hounds arranged by Hughes

Concluding with Grand Fire Work; ending by 9:00 P.M. or just in time for the fashionable to attend the Opera.

Boxes 3 shillings, Pit 2 shillings, Gallery 1 shilling.[24]

Royal Saloon (Astley's Amphitheatre)

A Comic Pantomime "Harlequin Medley"

A new piece called "The Disembarkation of the Light Horse"

A new entertainment from the *Arabian Nights* called "Abon Hassan, or, The Sleeper Awake"

Horsemanship with 12 riders, including Master Moulder, only four years of age and the Equestrian Mercury, only 9 years old

Astley's Sagacious Horses and a Pantomime with Mr. Astley, Jun.*

Boxes 3 shillings, Pit 2 shillings, Gallery 1 shilling.[25]

Sadler's Wells

An Allegorical Sketch, "The Hall of Augusta, or The Land We Live In," with a grand Commercial Procession

A Comic Dance called "The Broken Pitcher, or The Village Doctress"

Curious Equilibres and Posture Work

A Series of Scenes drawn from Occurrences on the Continent

Agility on the Tight Rope by Mr. Richer,† from Petersburgh

The Pleasing Extertions of La Belle Espagnole

A Favourite Entertainment called "The Witch of the Lakes"

Boxes four shillings, Pit two shillings, Gallery one shilling.[26]

The Royal Circus worked until June 1, 1793, before closing. The reasons stated were the prior engagement of Handy's horsemen to perform in Manchester, Stockholm and Bath, and Hughes' obligations in Russia. Handy and his troop did leave, but Hughes did not go abroad. Instead, he gathered together another group of former pupils and added a performer named Peter Ducrow, who had just arrived from Holland. Ducrow's specialty was leaping over eight horses and the five men riding them, "with his hand in his breeches pocket."[27]

Back at the grounds of the Royal Circus, a crowded house saw Young Crossman's "Peasant Hornpipe, and Flag Dance, not to be equaled by any Horseman in the Kingdom"; "Le Grand Saut de Trampoline," by Mr. Porter (Clown); "The Humours of the Sack, or the Clown Decried by a Woman"; and the African performing astonishing Stage and Equestrian Performances. There was also the "Fox Chace and Stag Hunt" (with actual animals), Mr. Smith's equestrians and the Musical Child.[28] Later in the season, Porter and Ducrow leaped through the Hoop on Fire, 14' high. The second half of the season ended on October 14.

The Circle of Exquisite Contrivance

Just when it seemed the Astleys had everything going for them, with good crowds in summer and a dual income in winter (John returned to his Riding School in Paris, and "Old" Astley took the "Saloon" troop from Westminster to Dublin), disaster struck. In July 1794, a fire broke out on the Surrey-side of Westminster Bridge, totally destroying the "Amphitheatre," together with several houses in front of the Westminster-road, a public house, and some small dwellings down Stangate. Astley Junior quickly engaged the Lyceum, in the Strand, on a one-month lease. Opening August 28, "Astley's New Circus" offered

---

*It was common in the 18th century to use the title "Junior" to denote a son, even if he did not bear the first name of his father.

†Richer was, in fact, an Englishman. Billed as "Young Richer, the new Phenomenon of agility," who learned the rudiments of his dexterity "from that excellent and long established school of amusement," he went on to perform in the Continent and apparently Russia, newly returned in 1793. His skill was such that his performance was "never equalled in this or any other country," and was "positively the ultimatum of the art."[29]

"A pleasing and capital Variety of Entertainments."[30] Interestingly, this was the only time Astley used the word "circus," and it is compelling to speculate on his motives.

On a fascinating note, part of the entertainment included an "Exhibition of the Telegraphe." Astley, making contact with some of the first Philosophers of the Age, flattered himself "that he is perfectly acquainted with the Nature and Construction of the Telegraphe, so much the conversation, astonishment, and admiration of the day." It is almost beyond belief, and at the same time perfectly logical, that one of the most significant inventions of the era was introduced to the public at a circus! The telegraphe [sic], as Astley explained, was an instrument used in France for the conveyance of certain intelligence at the rate of 250 miles per hour, and "which is effected without the knowledge of any person, except those at the two extreme distances."

Although the curiosity of the English had been excited by the adoption of this machine in France, Astley's demonstration, along with the use of the "key," was the first successful attempt to describe both concept and technique. Perhaps it took a showman's art; certainly it required a master to recognize the import and bring this world-altering discovery to the British. Nearly 100 years later, the American public would be introduced to the electric light in the same manner.

The English, "as ready to relieve the unfortunate, as to reward the deserving," filled the seats in the temporary location, finding the entertainment, "considering all things," surpassed expectations. Using funds from this generous patronage, by September 8, Astley, Sr., was able to oversee the setting of the first stone of his New Amphitheatre, to be erected on the site of the old. The "New Circus" at the Lyceum continued renewing its lease until October 10, when it closed for the season. On October 24, in a display of camaraderie between actors, Astley, Sr., was given a benefit at the Royalty Theatre, Wellclose Square, with the whole of his company united to perform for his sake.[31]

After extensive construction during the winter, the "New Amphitheatre of Arts, Astley's, Westminster-Bridge," opened the season on April 6, 1795, under the patronage of His Royal Highness the Duke of York. This honor was highly significant to the British, and the announcement remained the lead of all subsequent advertisements. Those wishing to become "renters" (meaning to purchase a subscription ticket for the season) were allowed to buy a non-transferable package allowing the bearer free admission to any part of the House before the curtain rose for £2. 12s. 6d.[32]

With $50,000 worth of electric light blazing in the background, the Great Inter-Ocean Railway Show offered 12 traveling museums, 12 grand menageries, 12 first-class circuses and 20 posed war elephants. The promoters promised to give $100,000 to any city they might be in if it was proven they did not give the best entertainment in the world. Such challenges were common, although so carefully worded that no record of any being paid was ever found. (*Oshkosh Daily Northwestern*, June 25, 1880)

The new Amphitheatre was a sight to behold, corresponding, in some degree, with the places for public entertainment designed by the French architect Mons. Louis of Paris, with alterations by Astley, Sr. The ground plan was laid out in the form of a horseshoe, at the head of which lay the "circle of exquisite convenience" for night equestrian performances. In the day, the arena was used for private riding instruction under the name *L'Ecale d' Equitation* (horseback riding ring). By this time, the diameter of the Circle had been set at 42', the distance required for horses to run conveniently at full gallop.

The pit was divided into two parts, one resembling a gibbous, the second an elliptic circle. That part within the columns and next to the circle had seven rows of seats; the other, outside the circle (called the Pit-box), had five rows of staggered seats. Both places terminated in points, providing a good line of sight for scenic exhibitions given on stage.

Passage into the box seats held two shops, one for the sale of musical instruments and sheet music played at the theater, the other for the sale of fruits and confectionary. At the end of the shops was a spacious room for the accommodation of riding students. Adjoining that was the Box Saloon, 52 feet long by 15 high, containing four staircases leading to the lower, side, middle and upper box seats. These seats commanded a full view of the entire performing area.

The gallery contained a spacious seating arrangement, with ease of passage to and from the seats and a good view of all amusements. The mechanism of the stage was entirely new and different from other theaters. Stables (unfinished at the time of the premiere) were for the use of performing animals, built along lines of a common stable. Not unlike the present time, veterans returning from abroad were offered free admission tickets beginning May 12; a temporary building was erected especially to seat them.

Perhaps the most breathtaking and remarked-upon feature of the new Amphitheatre was the decorations, featuring the triumphal entry of Julius Caesar into Rome, copied from a painting in the Louvre. As a tribute to what he had been through in the past year, Astley's prelude to the evening's entertainment was called "The Manager in Affliction."[33]

Among the innovations offered at Astley's for the 1795 season was an entertainment called "The Carousel," consisting of "Tilts and Tournaments, Dance, Exercises d'Equitation, le jeu de la Bague, da Bouquet & c. by the Infant Riders, mounted on 1, 2, 3, 4, 5, 6, and 7 Horses." The "Le jeu de la Bague" (thrust at the flying ring) segment of the Carousel was actually a cavalry drill whereby the cavalier rode at full speed toward a ring suspended in the air, representing his adversary. The exercise was intended to teach the rider the skill of maneuvering his horse with his left hand while defending himself and his mount with the right hand.[34] The season closed October 21, with a benefit for the Little Horse Jockies, who provided great sport in the Poney Races.

Onward to the End of the Century

The year 1794 was not a good one for the Royal Circus. Handy and his troop of horsemen left to play at the Lyceum, Strand. The Circus buildings were allowed to deteriorate, and the property molded into ruin from lack of upkeep. At some point, James Jones and George Jones (late of Jones' Equestrian Amphitheatre, which they lost in April 1788, when the property was let out for conversion into a Chapel)[35] purchased the property and spent considerable money refurbishing it. The Royal Circus re-opened April 3 for the 1795 season, with new paint and gilding creating a neat, rich and elegant appearance. Promising that the horsemanship would keep pace in point of excellence with the business on stage, the proprietors announced the change in ownership, retaining the name and calling their venture the "Royal Circus, St. George's Fields."

The premiere month offered Messrs. Smith and Crossman performing equestrian exercises with eight other celebrated Performers; Smith also appeared on the bill, performing slack rope vaulting and leaping on the Grand Tramplin. No others were mentioned by name. At the same time, Mr. Handy and company (including some familiar names from Hughes' troop as well as his own: the Little Devil, Robinson, Shaw, Carr, Taplin, Saxony, Rollins, Chadwick, Hutchinson, Miss Huntley, Masters Stent, Ackerville, Frost, the Original Child of Promise and Little Mercury) continued at the Lyceum, offering equestrian performances for several more weeks before leaving for an engagement in the country.[36]

The "Little Devil" mentioned was likely Andrew Ducrow, son of Peter Ducrow,

Andrew Ducrow was the great "Napoleon of the arena," renowned throughout the world for his stunning equestrian skills. He appeared at Astley's in *The Gladiator*, in what was called a pantomime, meaning that dialogue was sung as opposed to spoken, in deference to English law that permitted only actors of the legitimate theater (as opposed to circuses) to speak dialogue. The star was described as having an impetuous temper, but being exceedingly generous and unaffected. Later in his career he became co-operator of Astley's. (*Cleave's Penny Gazette* [London], September 15, 1838)

the leaper and strong man. Andrew appeared with his father as an "Infant Wonder" from the age of three or four, and by the age of thirteen was billed as the "Little Devil." (The term "infant" in both Europe and America was used to denote a child of tender years, as opposed to a newborn.) While an excellent equestrian, his acclaim came from performing mime on horseback. He performed through 1818, when he traveled through Europe, most notably France, achieving wide fame. Acclaimed as "the Colossus of Equestrians," Ducrow returned to England in 1823, building amphitheatres all over Britain and eventually assuming co-ownership of Astley's with James West. When Astley's burned to the ground in 1841, Ducrow became distraught, forcing his wife to commit him to a lunatic asylum, where he died the same year.[37]

By September 1785, the establishment was billed as "Jones' Royal Circus," with Williamson Lassells acting as Manager and Author of the Principal Amusements. The bill had increased in variety, with burlettas and ballads to go with Poney Races and equestrian exercises by Smith. For a change of pace, Sadler's Wells offered "a new grand Performance and Dancing, called Chevy Chace; or Douglas and Percy, drawn from the popular ballad of that name ... given in Representation in thirteen Scenes, including the memorable Battle."[38]

Jones' Royal Circus garnered favorable reviews over the next several years, particularly Smith's horsemanship and the writing of C. J. Cross, James Jones' son-in-law, including "The Capture of the Cape of Good Hope," "The Spring Meeting, or Ploughboy's Stake" and "Olympian Revels, or Harlequin Momus." During the winter of 1796–97, they traveled to Edinburgh, offering tumbling, musical burlettas, and "Stage Performances relieved by Equestrian Exercises" under acting manager Cross.[39]

In 1789, back to being billed as the "Royal Circus," wonderful "Trampolin Tricks over a Garter 9 feet high, and a Balloon on Fire," were offered, as well as "The Taylor Riding to Brentford, by Mr. Porter, the first Equestrian Clown and Trampolin Performer in Europe."[40]

Hughes appeared in public only once more — for a London benefit performance for Mr. Quick at Covent Garden on March 21, 1795. On December 17, 1797, a two-line report in *The Observer* (London) noted that "Mr. C. Hughes, of the Royal Circus, the projector, and many years one of the proprietors of that building" had passed away. A minute, sad mention of a man who had spent nearly all his adult life in the business of entertainment. His partner in the Royal Circus, Charles Dibdin, outlived him by seventeen years, dying on July 25, 1814. Although bitter and feeling ill-used during his long career, Dibdin received far more accolades, his obituary stating that as a songwriter he had never been equaled. He left behind 1,200 compositions, most of a light and sprightly nature, along with his conjoined legacies of the Comic Mirror and the *Sans Souci* (meaning "no worries," or "carefree"). In 1745, Sanssouci Palace was made for Frederic the Great, who wished to live there without worry. The term later came into vogue when applied to a short comedy in which public characters and manners of the day were ridiculed.[41]

Closing the loop on the waning century, the Messrs. Jones lured Handy's troop away from Astley's, Madame de la Croix from Covent Garden theater, and Mrs. Wybrow from Sadler's Wells and the Royalty. Cross, under his new title as deputy manager, continued to write for the Circus, gaining more fame for his popular ballet "The Spectacle of Blackbeard." Later in the year, George Jones left the Circus to open a Riding School in St. George's Field. Mr. Cabanel, Junior, became manager of the New Royal Circus for the 1799 season.

And so the 1700s came to a close. At this point the circus had established its foundation. While scenes and pantomimes of prominent current events easily took precedence for a time, equestrian performances never lost their attraction. Wire and rope dancing (not high-wire acts of the future, but gymnastics performed within three or four feet of the ground), agilities on the slack rope, vaulting, contortionists and fireworks were intermixed with entertainments as varied as fox chases, pony races and an adaptation of the *Arabian Nights*. Comedy in the pantomimes and burlettas remained a constant, while clowns, typically on horseback, played an integral role in keeping scenes moving. Acts with bird imitators, card tricks, automata, waxworks, sculptures of famous heads and lectures were worked in and out between singing and dancing. Prodigies, "infants" displaying musical talents, equestrian pupils and innumerable acts involving children of all ages made up a great number of individual entertainments.

Dwarfs, giants, human "monsters" and occasional "freaks" played alongside trick horses, performing dogs, and even birds taught how to discharge toy cannons. Rarely, but significantly, exotic animals, such as zebras, camels, rhinoceros (billed as the original unicorn) and Bombay elk, attracted the curious. All these were the bedrock of what was to be imported to America—along with the name, of course, for despite its on-again-off-again usage in Great Britain, "circus" had come to stay.

Of the three major houses, Astley's was the most written about and most durable. Established before the Royal Circus, it owned seniority over its next-door rival. Clearly, "Old" Astley (as Philip came to be called when John took on more and more prominence) had an astute eye for public taste. His equestrian productions were the marvel of the age, and it was written of "Young" Astley that "were there nothing else to be seen but his equestrian performances, there is not any visitor to the Royal Grove, who would not think himself amply paid back by that alone."[42]

Traveling frequently, Philip was quick to spot trends and transmitted those details to England, where they were immediately turned into sketches or pantomimes. Attuned to the pulse of the times, he also wrote many letters to acquaintances, soliciting eyewitness accounts of significant events. Astley was first with a display of the fall of the Bastille and first to present a representation of the Grand National Naval Review, both of which were highly praised. More importantly, the Amphitheatre/Royal Grove/Saloon drew the crowds, and while it had a smaller establishment than the Royal Circus, its seats were more often filled.

Second in importance, Astley was highly regarded as a person, being a distinguished English war hero. In the hundreds of newspaper accounts from the times, there was never found one single article impugning his character. His son John, trained to the business from the age of four-and-a-half years, followed in his father's footsteps, becoming, if possible, even more popular. With a pleasing personality, boyish charm and gentlemanly manners, Young Astley enthralled the public with his horsemanship, sense of the dramatic and touches of humanity, offering charity events and even appearing with Charles Hughes at the latter's benefit.

Critically, a third advantage was private ownership. Without managers and proprietors with which to contend, the father-son combination was free to follow the dictates of the proven and the impulsive. This served to advantage when they decided to entirely change their program every three weeks. The work involved in preparing the actors for the transition must have been overwhelming, but it was an astute move. Limited engagements prompted people to fill the seats before a new production took the place of an old; no burletta or pantomime became stale, and it always kept the

The One-Horned Rhinoceros was often billed as "The Unicorn," considered by *Theological Commentators* to be the "Unicorn of the Holy Writ," as mentioned and described in the book of Job. The rhino exhibited at the Zoological Institute, Philadelphia, was captured in the interior of Africa, on the Burrampooter River. He was first shipped to London and, as was often the case, purchased by American interests and sent to the United States "at enormous expense." He arrived in December 1831. (*Huron Reflector*, May 26, 1835)

"Saloon" in the newspapers. An eye for what attracted the paying crowds, name recognition, a standard of excellence and a penchant for keeping people guessing established an enduring tradition that lasted until 1893.

The Royal Circus, child of Charles Hughes and Charley Dibdin, had the more elegant building and an excellent ménage, thanks to Hughes' great talent. His pupils were always the talk of the town, and many went on to long, successful professional careers. The Circus also used and promoted the talents of children, often employing scores of them in their pantomimes and scenes. Unfortunately, the Circus was plagued by numerous lawsuits that much injured its finances and almost ruined Hughes. Changing hands several times, it endured an up-and-down history before being renamed the Surrey, achieving enduring success well into the 1800s.

Much had been accomplished: minstrels, jugglers, balladeers, contortionists, magicians, actors, singers, dancers, clowns and horsemen had all been brought into the ring under one roof. The concept, if not the structure, was ready to be imported to America, where the wilds of a new country and an enterprising people would forever put their own unique stamp of performers and menageries "under the tent."

6

The Circus Comes to America

CIRCUS: Mr. Ricketts respectfully acquaints the public that his unparalleled Equestrian Performance, will commence on Wednesday the 3rd of April, weather permitting — For the First Time in America.[1]

The American Colonies in the middle part of the 18th century were young, raw and bursting at the seams with life and vitality. They were eager to establish cities, carve roads out of wilderness, and create a unique sense of identity far different and separate than that of their Mother Country. Men and women worked hard for their livelihoods, and money was scarce. What they spent on entertainment depended on the cultural tastes of their community.

Unlike the countries of Europe, with their long-established traditions of traveling minstrel shows, equestrian exercises and itinerant acting troupes, America literally had to start from scratch. That meant trial and error, combining what they saw as the best of the old with the tastes of the new. Legitimate theaters sprang up in the more populated cities; operas and symphonies from French, German and Italian masters played to the moneyed; but for many, the fascination of the common made wondrous held the greatest appeal. It is not surprising, then, that first menageries and then horsemanship were to become a mainstay of American entertainment. How this transpired, intermixed and ultimately altered the performances left an indelible mark on the entertainment known as the "circus."

The Royal Menagerie, Exeter-Change, was one of the greatest attractions of its day. It not only drew Englishmen to its exhibit of exotic animals, but foreigners from around the world. Among the attractions were the Rhinoceros ("undoubtedly the greatest curiosity in Europe"), the "scientific Elephant, majestic Lion, Royal Tyger, noble Panther, Quagga [a now extinct South American zebra with a yellowish-brown coat and darker stripes], Black Swans, &c. &c."[2] With a growing population in the Colonies eager to share the excitement, exhibitors brought their living curiosities to the New World.

First came the "Lyon of Barbary" in 1716, followed by a camel in 1721 and a polar bear in 1733.[3] In 1724, a troupe of dancers performed in Philadelphia with an act copied from those in Europe, featuring a woman dancing on the rope with baskets, and iron fetters on her feet, "wheeling a wheelbarrow, and spinning with swords, accompanied by the clowning of a Pickle Herring." In New York City in 1753, Anthony Dugee performed juggling and balancing on the slack wire and tight rope. Dugee's wife also appeared as the Female Sampson. Assisting them was a "Negro boy and an Indian."[4]

48

Another Englishmen, Mr. Faulks, rode standing on two and three horses, and vaulted over a single horse at full speed in Philadelphia and New York in 1771; while Jacob Sharpe appeared in Essex, Boston and Salem, Massachusetts, the same year, offering similar equestrian performances. Jacob Bates, displaying his horsemanship in Philadelphia in 1772 and in New York City in 1773, introduced, for the first time in the United States, "the burlesque on horsemanship, or The Taylor riding to Brentford," Astley's famous routine.[5]

The First Continental Congress put an end to any hope of establishing an English-type circus with its large troupe and expansive, carefully structured buildings. On October 20, 1774, an act called the Continental Association listed fourteen articles outlining what they hoped would protect George III's subjects from numerous grievances against the King that threatened their lives, liberty and property. It read, in part:

The Quagga was a South American zebra with a yellowish brown coat and darker stripes, which is now extinct. (*Huron Reflector*, May 26, 1835)

> We will, in our several stations, encourage frugality, economy, and industry, and promote agriculture, arts and the manufactures of this country ... and will discountenance and discourage every species of extravagance and dissipation, especially all horse-racing, and all kinds of gaming, cock-fighting, exhibitions of shews, plays, and other expensive diversions and entertainments.[6]

It would not be until 1785 that Thomas Pool (also spelled "Poole") constructed a menage in Philadelphia, on Market Street, near the Centre House. Here he earned considerable success with equestrian showmanship and the antics of a clown. His particular claim to fame was the various dexterous feats he performed while riding two horses at full speed. He also exhibited two well-trained trick horses. He kept his entertainment open for a little over a year before taking it on the road to Baltimore and Boston.[7] Pool performed in New York in 1786, and by the following year he established himself in Georgia, where his bill included a modernized version of the burlesque, now called "The Taylor Humorously Riding to New York."

Pool advertised himself as "the first American that ever exhibited the following feats of horsemanship on the Continent," stretching the implication, for he was billed in the Windward Islands and Jamaica, where he performed from 1774 to 1784 as "le Sieur Pool, Anglais."[8] Jacob Bates returned to Philadelphia in 1787 and rented Pool's old building, where he established a riding school.[9]

John Bill Ricketts Conquers America

In 1792, John Bill Ricketts respectfully informed the Philadelphia public "that he has erected at considerable expense a circus, situated at the corner of Market and Twelfth

Streets where he proposes instructing Ladies and Gentlemen in the elegant accomplishments of riding. The Circus will be opened on Thursday Next, the 25th October."[10]

Recently arrived from London, Ricketts has been historically credited with being a pupil of Charles Hughes, but in actuality he began his career at Jones' Equestrian Amphitheatre (see Chapter 4). The Amphitheatre closed in April 1788, and by 1790–1 Ricketts had formed a troupe in Edinburgh in partnership with John Parker, a dancer turned equestrian manager, and performed with the Circus Royal there. After touring through Scotland and Ireland, the appeal of a new country drew Ricketts, his brother Francis and some of his artists across the Atlantic.[11]

In his Philadelphia announcement, Ricketts retraced the beginnings of Hughes by opening a Riding School; his use of the word "circus" was in reference to the Royal Circus *building*, not in the manner of performance. He clearly intended to establish himself as a riding master; an article in the Philadelphia *General Advertiser* (November 10, 1792) stated of his school: "Already we find it resorted to by numbers of ladies and gentlemen every morning, who are desirous to perfect themselves in the elegant accomplishments of horsemanship."

Whether it was his intention to expand the riding academy at a later date is not known, but if such was his desire, he was encouraged in it by the same newspaper article, which observed, "Perhaps we may expect to see him make a public exhibition early in the spring," but at present, he is "employed in the business of instruction."

Once he had solidified his livelihood, always a primary concern, Ricketts was free to follow in Hughes' footsteps and offer just such public exhibition as suggested by the *General Advertiser*. On April 1, 1793, *Dunlap's Daily Advertiser* ran an advertisement for the new entertainment, Ricketts noting that he "has erected, at a very considerable expense, a CIRCUS," to open April 3rd. Doors were to be opened at 3:30 P.M. and performances to begin at 4:00 P.M. ("The History of Philadelphia" gives the date of the opening night performance as April 12, 1793.) The building he used was a new one, constructed on the same ground as the old and designed for daylight performances. It held 700 persons, with the price of admission 7s, 6d for boxes and 3s, 9d for pit seating.

On the 15th of May, Ricketts' Circus, "in Market, the Corner of Twelfth Streets," advertised:

A Great Variety of Equestrian Exercises

By Mr. & Master *Ricketts*, Master *Strobach*, and Mr. *McDonald*, who is just arrived from Europe.

In the Course of the Entertainment, Mr. Ricketts will introduce several *New Feats*, particularly he will Ride with his Knees on the Saddle, the Horse in full speed; and from this Position *Leap over a Ribband* extended 12 feet high.

Mr. Ricketts, on a single Horse, will throw up 4 Oranges, playing with them in the Air, the Horse in full speed.

Mr. *McDonald* will perform several COMIC FEATS (Being his First Appearance in America).

Seignior *Spiracuta* will exhibit many Surprizing Feats on the Tight Rope.

The whole to conclude with Mr. Ricketts and his Pupil in the Attitudes of two Flying Mercuries; the Boy pois'd on one Foot on Mr. Ricketts' Shoulder, whilst Mr. Ricketts stands in the same Manner with one Foot on the Saddle, the Horse being in full speed.[12]

For this performance, the doors opened at 4:00, "with the Performance beginning at half past Five o'clock, precisely." The advertisement also noted that Ricketts intended to close the Season within three weeks, "as he is about to take a Tour to some other Parts of the Continent."

Presumably the "Master Ricketts" referred to was Francis, John Bell's brother, who performed leaping and vaulting. Signor Spinacuta was an experienced rope-dancer and animal trainer, having previously worked in France and England. Not listed in this advert was his wife, an equestrian. McDonald was a comedic tumbler. Strobach was the boy who stood on Ricketts' shoulders during the "Flying Mercury" act.

Using trained Philadelphia horses, Ricketts added a flag dance and the "Manual Exercises," or military manual of arms made famous by John Astley. With clear influence from the English masters, Francis threw somersets from an inclined plank and later added the feat of running up the inclined plane with burning torches in his hands. McDonald later included the performance of flipflaps across the ring with his feet tied together.[13]

George Washington attended Ricketts' performance on April 22, 1793. The program for that day revealed:

The earliest rendition of a "pyramid" in the 18th century had performers standing on one another's shoulders in a display of strength and balance. In the 19th century, when performed on horseback, the trick was called the "Flying Mercury," where a boy stood on the shoulders of a featured rider. Along with equestrian feats, the entire family was encouraged to attend the "Mirthful Miniature Circus for the Little Folks," presented in 1879 by Anderson & Co.'s Monster European, Asiatic, African, American, Arctic and Antarctic World's Menagerie. (*Belleville Telescope* [KS], May 22, 1879)

> Mr. Ricketts leaps over a riband suspended twelve feet high and at the same time through a cane held in both hands and alights on the other side with his feet on the saddle, the horse being at full speed.... He will ride a single horse, standing erect, and throw up a bottle and marble, playing with the same in the air, then receive the marble into the mouth of the bottle; he throws up an orange and receives it on the point of a sword, at the same time standing on the saddle without the assistance of the bridle reins, turns about and throws a somerset.... He will put a glass of wine in a hoop, turning it round rapidly, the glass remaining at the same time in its place, takes the same and drinks to the company, the horse being in full gallop.... The whole to conclude with Mr. Ricketts carrying his young pupil on his shoulders in the attitude of Mercury, standing on two horses in full gallop.[14]

Not only did the performance earn high praise, Washington sold Ricketts one of his horses. (Durang notes Washington's white horse was purchased from Robert Morris, of Philadelphia.[15]) A further connection between the two lay in the fact both Ricketts and Washington were Free Masons, Washington himself being head of the Philadelphia Lodge.[16]

After the Philadelphia season ended on July 22, 1793, Ricketts and company went to New York City, where they built an arena on Greenwich Street. Already the beneficiary of positive publicity, the life's blood of the business, they opened on August 7, presenting daily performances at 4:00 P.M. until November 4. In September, Ricketts added "the Metamorphosis," an act requiring him to change costumes and gender on a galloping horse while encased in a sack. The idea of performers working while covered in a sack had been introduced at Astley's in 1770, and "Humours of the Sack" gained much traction at the Royal Circus earlier in 1793.

The indefatigable Ricketts then gathered his company and traveled to Charleston in December 1793, where a building on Tradd Street was erected for their use. Accompanying him were Francis, McDonald and Master Long, who replaced Strobach. This is likely where Ricketts met the "three Mr. Sullys"—Matthew, Lawrence and Thomas. The brothers, along with Mr. and Mrs. Edgar, Mr. Clifford (the celebrated singer from Vauxhall), Mr. and Mrs. Henderson (late of the Liverpool Theatre) and Mr. T. West (from the Bath Theatre), had arrived in Virginia in November 1793, aboard the ships *Union* and *Eliza* from England.

These performers quickly joined the Broad Street Theatre, Charleston, which had been constructed in 1792. Overseen by Thomas Wade West and John Bignall, managers of the "Virginia Company of Comedians," the Broad Street was designed by James Hoban, also the architect for the Executive Mansion (White House) in Washington, D.C. Ground was broken on August 14, 1792, with the structure to be 125 feet in length, 56 feet wide and 37 feet high, "with a handsome pediment, stone ornaments, a large flight of stone steps, and a courtyard palisaded."[17]

The 1,200-seat theater opened in February 1793, presenting dramas with dancing, augmented by a 13-piece orchestra and featuring actors drawn from Northern cities. Opening the winter season on January 15, 1794, the company, which included the Sullys, presented the double bill "The Tragedy of the Earl of Essex" and a comic opera, "The Farmer, or The World's Ups and Downs." Competition, however, was right around the corner. On April 21, 1794, a French-language theater, operated by a Santo Domingan refugee named John Sollee, opened on Church Street. The inaugural performance featured a comedy, "Harlequin Robbed," that included singing and tightrope dancing by Alexandre Placide "and his so-called wife," Suzanne Theodore Vaillande.

Placide, already famous in France and London, had immigrated to Boston in 1792, where he performed before coming to Charleston. There, he not only achieved additional renown, but became equally infamous for his involvement in several affairs. The Sully family also "cut a wide swath through Charleston society: Matthew's sister married Thomas Wade West, manager of the Charleston Theatre, and his daughter Julia married Belzon, the French miniaturist under whom his son, Thomas, studied. Another daughter, Elizabeth, eloped with Middleton Smith.[18]

With France at war with Great Britain, wealthy Charlestonians of an English heritage tended to congregate at the Broad Street Theatre for its productions of Shakespeare, while those who supported the Jacobin side patronized the comedies, vaulting, leaping and light operas of the French Theatre.[19]

The year 1794 found Ricketts' company at Norfolk, Virginia, where they opened on

May 1. McDonald performed the sack metamorphosis, while John Bill and Long offered the "Flying Mercury" on two bareback horses, a considerably more difficult trick than the one performed on saddled steeds.[20] Their exhibitions garnered high praise. One letter to the editor of a Richmond newspaper claimed, "The activity [of Ricketts] is the equal of any I have ever seen in Europe, and his various feats and art of balancing on a horse are far superior to young Astley, or any of his contemporaries."[21] High praise, indeed. Thereafter, Ricketts performed in Richmond and Baltimore, where they worked until September 10.

Having set the standard and proven the success of the "circus," other troupes quickly followed. Thomas Swann, a riding master and farrier from Philadelphia, opened a performing company near the Battery in New York City on September 10, 1794. It featured equestrian feats, with Miss Johnson (described as the "First American Lady") as a principal performer. "General Jacco," a monkey performing on a rope, also appeared, probably the first non-equine performer to appear in an American circus.[22] The monkey's name (an alternate spelling of "Jackoo") was taken from Astley's performing monkey.

Back in Philadelphia, Ricketts used the word "circus" in a letter citing the lack of covered buildings in America as a deterrent to other European performers seeking work in the United States. Performing from September 20 until November 12, he was very generous in returning the favors of patronage by giving benefits for a fuel fund for the distressed poor of the city, and also for the French exiles driven out of Hispaniola.[23]

Ricketts returned to New York, moving into an amphitheatre at Broadway and Exchange Alley. Opening November 24, 1794, he began with an English-style "grand procession of horses" around the ring. Pony races and Polander's Tricks were part of the New York production, with McDonald doing burlesque riding stunts, and Ricketts and Long their Flying Mercury.[24]

During this period, Ricketts offered stage performer John Durang $25 a week through the season and a benefit in each town (minus the expense of lights, music and advertisements) to join his company. Durang accepted, spending his time in New York practicing his equestrian skills. In his autobiography, which would become a mainstay for data on the early circus, he noted that "Mat Sully" was the clown in the ring.[25]

Blazing the trail for the traveling American show, Ricketts opened in Massachusetts on May 12, 1795, at the Boston Amphitheatre, advertising himself as "Ricketts's Equestrian Pantheon." Premiering the "Egyptian Pyramids," he offered the display of two men on three horses, as well as himself turning a somerset over five mounted horses. The program consisted of:

> 1st. A grand entrance with a Roman column
> 2nd. Four triumphal arches
> 3rd. A Roman spire
> 4th. Lion's den down
> 5th. Four arches forming a spire
> 6th. The form of an iron gate, with charges
> 7th. The world renowned upside down
> 8th. Egyptian Pyramid
> 9th. Roman monuments
> 10th. A moving spire
> 11th. Lion's den up
> 12th. A March[26]

They performed at Providence, Rhode Island, and Hartford, Connecticut, where their bill advertised:

> Mr. Sully, the Clown will go through his laughable feats and leaps on a single horse.... Still vaulting by J. Ricketts and Mr. Sully.... Mr. Sully the Clown will perform a string of flipflaps across the circus. The Clown's frolics between two horses. The two Flying Mercuries by Master Long, a child only five years of age, on J. B. Ricketts's shoulders, on two horses at full speed.... The performance will conclude with "Taylor Riding to Brentwood, on Hunter and Road Horse."[27]

The Sully mentioned here is one of the brothers who arrived in Charleston late in 1793, and went to work at the Broad Street Theatre during the time Ricketts performed in the city. Stuart Thayer, in *Annals of the American Circus, 1793–1860*, gives the performer's first name as Matthew, referencing the *Rhode Island Gazette* (Providence), August 1 and 8, 1795. Matthew also appeared with William Sully, both playing clowns, when Ricketts opened in Philadelphia on October 20, 1795. William was cited as being father of the three brothers mentioned as arriving from England in 1793.[28] In his memoirs, Durang never mentioned William Sully.

It is not surprising the Sullys left Charleston. With competition from the local French Theatre proving disastrous, they surely saw the end coming and wished to move on to steadier employment. The Broad Street Theatre did soon fail, and by the end of the 1795-96 season it was out of business. The French and English theaters then merged, using the building of the former but changing its name to the Church Street Theatre.

From Hartford, Ricketts' troupe returned to New York. However long they intended to perform, all amusements were curtailed for the remainder of the season by an outbreak of disease. George C. D. Odell, in *Annals of the New York Stage* (p. 337), noted the cause to be yellow fever, but this is unlikely to be correct. Yellow fever, an infectious disease transmitted by mosquitoes (a fact unknown in the 1700s), was limited to geographical areas with sustained high temperatures, and a prevalence of small ponds and still waters offering abundant breeding grounds. Yellow fever plagued the lower Southern States during the summer, but seldom went higher up the coast than Wilmington. While often cited as a common villain (along with typhus fever, small pox and dysentery), it was more likely an outbreak of cholera from sewer-contaminated drinking water; such an epidemic in 1849 killed one out of every hundred New Yorkers.[29] Ricketts was fortunate he and his traveling company were not singled out as bringing the epidemic to the city, as it was common practice for health inspectors and newspapers to blame itinerants and the poor for sudden, unexplained plagues.

Ricketts opened his "Pantheon" amphitheatre at the corner of Sixth and Chestnut Streets, Philadelphia, on October 19, 1795. The building was of circular form, 97 feet in diameter. A conical roof rose from 18-foot-high white outer walls, reaching 50 feet from the ground. On top was the figure of a flying Mercury. The interior center of the dome was decorated with a blazing star, from which was suspended a chandelier. A handsome portico on the Chestnut Street front marked the principal entrance; from there a lobby ran around to what was called the music or proscenium boxes. The stage was at the south end of the building, large enough for dramatic performances. The center was appropriated to the ring, with boxes running around this circle in the shape of a horseshoe, from which rose 8 or 9 rows of benches, divided into boxes and pit. Stoves provided heating for a capacity crowd estimated between 1,200 and 1,400 persons. A coffee room communicated with these portions of the house, and "Patent" lights were placed on pillars. At the time of its construction, Ricketts' amphitheatre was considered the finest in America.[30] Admission was $1 to the boxes and 50 cents to the pit.

Including Ricketts as a rider, others in the Philadelphia company were Francis Ricketts (rider and leaper), John Durang (vaulter), Spinacuta (rope walker), and Matthew and William Sully (clowns). Mrs. Spinacuta also appeared as a rider, along with Masters Hutchins and Long (riders), Mr. Reano (rope walker) and a band conducted by Mr. Collet. Durang also mentioned Mr. and Mrs. Chambers, Mr. and Mrs. Rowson, Miss Curry, Mr. Bird, two carpenters and a full orchestra led by Mr. Lulier.[31]

Ricketts' specialty at the time was to perform the dangerous feat of riding two horses, each foot placed upon a quart mug set loosely upon the saddle. Francis Ricketts rode on his head, balancing himself on a pint-pot and, while blindfolded, dismounted from a galloping horse, picked up a watch and re-mounted.[32]

January 29, 1796, saw Ricketts proudly display the feats of his trained horse Cornplanter, capable of leaping over a fourteen-hands-high horse; and on February 2, he offered a well-received pantomime, "The Triumph of Virtue." Among the troupe were Indian performers, reportedly from Upper and Lower Canada. Besides Durant, William Langley joined as a clown. Both these performers would go on to have successful careers in the circus. Durang also listed Franklin and son as riders.

As usual, Ricketts went on to New York, where his Amphitheatre opened on May 7. Mrs. Spinacuta joined them on May 26, offering a two-horse performance where she stood with one foot on each of the two galloping animals. Ricketts also offered new dramatics, bringing his show closer to those presented in England. For his benefit, Durang earned "about five hundred dollars," a very considerable sum. Mr. Tomlinson kept the coffee house attached to the circus and took care of it in Ricketts' absence.

The Advent of the Circus Parade

Philip Lailson, a Swede, departed France with his company of performers in the summer of 1796, arriving first in New York and then taking a ship up the coast to Boston. He immediately made preparations for his show, augmenting the talents of his artists with brilliant trappings for the ring and stage. Opening August 11, 1796, perhaps too hastily, one of his equestriennes, Miss Venice (also spelled "Venace" and "Vanice") was thrown from her mount, the horses, still suffering from the close confinement of two sea voyages, being restive and hard to control. This accident was duly noted in a newspaper review, but her grace and spirit "commanded the most animated applause." Others in the company included Mr. McDonald, clown (presumably the same man who had worked for Ricketts until Sully joined); Lailson, equestrian and tight-rope walker; the "Young Swede" and the "Young German," both riders; Miss Lailson, rider; a five-year-old child; and seven others.

Lailson established his company in the arena near the Haymarket Theatre, forcing Ricketts, who also happened to be in Boston, to hastily construct a building on Beacon Hill he styled "Ricketts's New Amphitheatre." Lailson offered more competitive pricing, charging 75 cents for boxes and 35 cents for the pit. After twenty-two days facing stiff competition, Ricketts returned to New York. His winter season ended in Philadelphia, where his company was billed as "The Pantheon and Ricketts's Amphitheatre."[33]

The laws of England forbad performers outside the legitimate theater from speaking dialogue, but that distinction did not exist in the United States. This freedom allowed Ricketts to introduce historic pantomimes into his show. One in particular would surely have appealed to a Pennsylvania audience, the subject being the Whisky Rebellion.

In another significant development of 1796, a young India elephant was brought to New York by a sea captain named Jacob Crowninshield. It was shown there and then sold to Mr. Owen, who toured it through the mid–Atlantic cities of Philadelphia and Baltimore until the early 1820s.[34] Ricketts and Lailson would have been aware of the elephant, and it is interesting to speculate on whether either considered making a deal with Owen to exhibit the animal with their own companies.

After working through the holidays, when Ricketts offered the ever-popular Pony Races, a grand entrance of fourteen horses and riders, and Francis' trained horse American Eagle, he opened the 1797 season in New York at the third of his amphitheatres, this one situated near Greenwich Street. To this establishment was added a Coffee House, where patrons were encouraged to visit during intermissions, supplying an additional source of income.

Among those performing with Ricketts were Master Hutchins, rider; Thomas Franklin, promoted as the famous clown from the Royal Circus; Francis Ricketts, vaulter and leaper; Thomas Franklin, Jr., rider; Mr. and Mrs. Chambers, actors; and Miss Sully, actress.

A broadside for August 4, 1797, advertised "Ricketts's Circus, Lower end of Greene-Street," promising a great variety of Equestrian Exercises, including Ricketts' grand performance with the Broad Sword on the Celebrated Horse Cornplanter. John Durang was Clown to the Horsemanship; Still Vaulting, or a Trial of Skill and A Flying Mercury was performed by Ricketts and Master Hutchins; and the whole concluded with Durang's "The Taylor's Disaster, or Johnny Gilpen's Journey to Brentford." Days of performance were Monday, Wednesday and Friday, with Boxes costing 8 shillings and the "Pitt" 4 shillings.[35]

Lailson opened his season on April 8, 1797, at his own amphitheatre in Philadelphia, corner of Fifth and Prune Streets, extending as far west as the jail wall. The premiere performance included the pantomime "Les Quatre Fils Aynon; or, The Four Valient Brothers," from an old French legend. Members of the troupe included Langley, Sully, Herman (rider), McDonald, C. Vandervelde (also spelled "Vandervelt," a rider who was also responsible for directing the pantomimes), Reano and Miss Vanice. The pantomimists were Pouble, Jaymon (also spelled "Jaymond," a rider), Douvilliers, Poignard, Viellard, St. March, Leger, Savoil, Madame Douvillers, Mrs. Rowson, Mrs. Devan and Mademoiselle Lailson. The company performed French comedies and operas in which Miss Sophie and Miss Tesseire appeared.[36] Joining them was a horse called Bucephalus (after Alexander the Great's wonder horse), a name later bestowed on many circus steeds.

Lailson also developed the advertising ploy whereby he and his magnificently dressed performers, mounted on elegant horses, paraded daily through the streets on performance days. It was a touch of marketing genius, representing the first time an American show dazzled the prospective audience by offering a tease or a preview of star players. Later, managers would use the parade to advantage as they incorporated it into a gaudy entrance into towns and cities, creating a much-anticipated staple of the circus.

In what would become a pattern plaguing circuses, the Friends of Philadelphia were shocked by what they saw as a frivolous tendency of citizens to patronize such amusements and addressed a memorial to the mayor and council, protesting against circuses. In this case, the council was unable to act against the circuses or theaters on the grounds they were "not disorderly," an important distinction that would be interpreted differently in the decades to come.

In September, Lailson moved on to Alexandria, Virginia, before returning to New York. Using Ricketts' Greenwich Street arena, his show concentrated heavily on Jaymond's dramatic productions. Working until late November, he also offered his own equestrian tricks and McDonald's clown presentations.

One of the most important features of the 19th century circus was the parade into town. First introduced by Philip Lailson in 1797, the parade rapidly developed into a gaudy affair whereby the proprietor "teased" audiences by giving them a glimpse of the wonders inside the tent. Star equestrians rode horses elegantly decked in silver-studded saddles; animal tamers rode inside cages with lions and tigers; acrobats performed their stunts down the long road to the circus grounds; and, perhaps most exciting of all, elephants marched to the tunes of calliopes and marching bands. (*Janesville Gazette* [WI], July 17, 1876)

In June 1798 (Odell, Vol. II, p. 32, states the date was February 1, 1798), shortly after opening his second season in Philadelphia, Lailson fell heavily into debt, partially, if not wholly, from the extravagant cost of his over-large company and the "unusual magnificence of the dress and paraphernalia." He declared bankruptcy, and his company disbanded. On July 18, the greater portion of his horses and stage-property were purchased by Wignell & Reinagle for their Chestnut Street Theatre Company, and Lailson's building was offered for sale.[37]

It is probable that the failure of Lailson's company had a profound influence on the development of the American circus. John Bill Ricketts could not have been insensitive to the former's dependence on dramatic scenes, prompting him to take a long look at the differences between American and European audiences. While the United States had its fair share of educated men and women, they did not have what was commonly referred to as "the nobility and gentry." What played well in Europe — the erudite reworking of classic historic and mythological tales — was likely over the head of many hard-working clerks, merchants and farmers. They simply did not "get" the references, or perhaps had little interest in ancient tales. Their tastes lay in more temporal, uncomplicated stories with an amusing theme: *Harlequin in Philadelphia* easily transformed into *Harlequin in New York.*

Americans appreciated horsemanship, clowning, light pantomime and gymnastics. If a more sophisticated audience desired dramatic fare, they went to the theater. This distinction was not lost on Ricketts, who made a profound observation to John Durang by stating, "An equestrian performance blended with dramatic performance would never agree or turn out to advantage, but must eventually fall to ruin"; whereas "a circus within its own sphere ... in America, must succeed and please, and meet the admiration of the public and give general satisfaction."[38]

Ricketts' philosophy was a radical departure from that practiced at the Royal Grove and the Royal Circus. Just eight years earlier, in 1789, managers at the Circus were downplaying Hughes' equestrian performances to concentrate on representations of the French Revolution, first begun by the Astleys. Ricketts' insight in pointing the circus away from its English roots was not only bold but inspired. While it would take decades for the circus to wean itself away from drama and "representations," this was one beginning of the American imprint.

Performer, Machinist, Painter, Designer, Music Compiler, Bill Maker and Treasurer

Acting on this tenet, and well aware of the expense of paying talented artists, Ricketts abandoned his dramatic performers and divided his reduced troupe into two parts. Taking with him Durang, Master Hutchins, the musician Leulier (alternate spelling of "Lulier"?), L. Bird, an assistant groom and six horses — Silver Heels (for "The Taylor," later changed to "Tailor"), Cornplanter (an elegant charger), Governor (for still vaulting), Little Boner (for pony races), Lady Washington and Merry Jacko (two black colored horses), he departed by boat for Albany, New York, on July 19, 1797. After a slow voyage, the ship being compelled to put in every night out of consideration for the horses, they arrived in Albany on July 24.

Ricketts easily obtained the proper permission to perform, and a temporary structure was erected (divided in half — one part for the boxes, covered by a roof, and the second open air for the pits). In one week, the final structure included a place for the orchestra, a moveable stage on which to dance, dressing room and a stable area. A low fence was placed around the ring, supplemented with a chain. The first performance on July 31 garnered $160, with people "boreing holes thro' the board to get a peep."[39]

Albany proved "dull," and the circus might not have stayed long, but a fire that swept through the city on August 5 effectively put an end to a contemplated stay. Durang suggested a benefit performance for those devastated by the conflagration, adding that it would also be a good time to take benefits. On August 7, 1797, Ricketts advertised in the Albany *Chronicle*: "Mr. R. is induced to expect, that from motives of philanthropy, the performance will be honoured by a crowded assemblage of Spectators." The admittance fee was 8 shillings for Boxes, 4 shillings for "pitt." His expectation was met, and for a week or more they played to full houses, Durang clearing $100 on his night and Ricketts taking his benefit on the last evening. Depositing the money from the benefit for the distressed with the "Corporation," or town authorities, they departed August 14.

Traveling by land for Canada, Durang noted several adventures along the way, but his most interesting comment avowed that those in the company never revealed their occupations except when necessary. Since itinerant performers had low reputations, it is not surprising, for they might have received considerably less hospitality from the locals had they known them to be circus people. This perception would become more apparent as time progressed.

Arriving in Montreal on August 25, Ricketts obtained permission to set up the circus three days later. Following Durang's guidelines, the open-air structure was finished in two weeks, complete with ring, stage, dressing room and stables. Box seats were elevated, with the pit underneath that included a coffee room. They opened September 5, with the aid of the 60th Regiment, Royal American Grenadiers, who earned half a crown a day.

Ricketts performed as head and principal rider, while Durang played the clown on foot and horseback ("being obliged to furnish all the jokes for the ring"), and to ride the "Tailor" (compelled to speak in French, German and English). He also played the "sack" (standing on two horses while changing into women's clothes), participated in the Pyramid, still vaulted, danced, played Harlequin in pantomimes, tumbled and performed on the slack rope, introduced the machinery and transparencies, and produced the fireworks exhibition. To these he added music compiler, bill maker and treasurer, providing an excellent idea of what was required of a circus trooper.

The Canadians, never having witnessed such equestrian tricks, thought the riders "conjurers," and were amazed at how the horses were able to dance and keep time to the music. In reality, the opposite was true, but it made for great stagecraft, and Ricketts was prevailed upon to stay the winter. This he agreed to do, building a new circus of stone, including a roof with skylights and a coffee room. Using the pattern of their Philadelphia establishment, box seats were elevated, with the pit in front on the ground floor, and dressing rooms underneath. The orchestra was placed over the door where the horses entered.

Durang's description of his paint job bears repeating, for it is seldom possible to resurrect so vivid an image from the past:

> The dome was a light blue sky colour, cupids bearing garlands of roses round the circle, the boxes rose pink, panels white, with a festooned blue curtain, the ring in panels intersperset with posts and gold chain leading round. The stage department was decorated with scenery, a curtain, a frontispiece, stagedoors, a niche on each with busts of armory.[40]

The new circus was finished September 31 [*sic*], and the company had good business through the end of the year, at which time they offered benefits for local charities to promote attendance. Every afternoon at 4:00 o'clock two regiments of soldiers started the performance by offering a parade, while the band played on an elevated orchestra opposite the soldiers. During off times, riding lessons were offered to ladies and gentlemen. For his benefit, Durang played "The Ghost," and performed Indian dances, bringing $800 into the house.

The last performance was May 3, 1798, and the company left Montreal on May 9, again travelling by land. Reaching Quebec, they constructed their circus buildings within the city walls. Remaining two months "to good business," Durang made $300 for his benefit. Afterwards, the company returned to Montreal for two more weeks of shows. On the last night, Hutchins, the groom, fired a load of dried peas at a group of people gathered on the roof to witness the spectacle without benefit of tickets. Unfortunately, he put out the eye of a young man who subsequently sued Ricketts for $800. Hutchins had to flee for his life and was later retrieved across the border.

After several unsuccessful performances around Troy, New York, the circus went on to New York City, working two weeks before returning to Philadelphia later in 1798.[41]

The second part of Ricketts' divided company, led by Francis, experienced considerably less good fortune. He took with him the two Franklins and Mr. Tomlinson, Junior (caretaker of the New York Pantheon, who agreed to work as clown), and seven good performing horses, including the white horse once owned by George Washington. They traveled through Philadelphia and Lancaster, Pennsylvania, arriving in Baltimore on October 19, 1797. At Annapolis, Maryland, they were unable to make enough to pay their bills, and the sheriff sold their horses. Using $500 sent by the elder Ricketts, they rejoined the primary troupe in Montreal.

The End of an Era

Lailson recovered from his losses in New York and opened the 1798 season on March 8 in Philadelphia with a smaller company. The production featured a new act called "The Death of Bucephalus." Lailson, Langley, Herman and Miss Venice served as riders, with Sully as clown. For the summer session, beginning May 1, the company adopted the name "Summer Circus," replacing the absent Langley with seven-year-old Miss Lailson and Mr. Tompkins. Less than two weeks later, a more nationalistic feel was added by the addition of the word "Federal" to their title.

Apparently the name change did not bring additional fortune. Now called the "Equestrian Circus," they opened in Baltimore on June 4, minus Tompkins and Miss Lailson. After a brief stay, they moved on to Charleston, where their program began with a grand parade. The former Charleston resident Langley was billed as "an American" and Lailson as "a Swede." They garnered favorable press with "The Death of Bucephalus," the horse being praised as equaling in tragic capacity any actor ever seen treading the boards in that city.[42] The circus also offered a variation of the "Taylor" (known variously as "Billy Buttons"), calling the skit "Mr. Rognollet's Journey to London."[43]

Closing on March 2, 1799, Lailson went to the West Indies and later, billed as "Don Felipe Lailson," introduced the "Royal Circus of Equestrian" to Mexico City in 1809.[44] In his autobiography, Durang observed that Lailson's failure in Philadelphia resulted from a too numerous company and the expense of keeping up his building.[45] Faced with similar problems two years earlier, Ricketts had dismissed his theatrical performers and divided his equestrian company, but the effort did not save him for long. It was not yet time for expansive companies to survive the crippling costs of large staff, elaborate costumes or upkeep on circus buildings.

Others soon appeared to take Lailson's place. A new company opened in New York on February 8, 1799, renting Lailson's old building on Greenwich Street. Operated by Thomas Franklin and Johnston (or Johnson), the Franklin Company offered singing, dancing and equestrian acts by Franklin, later adding pantomimes and boxing. After a week off in February, they re-opened and worked until March 19.[46]

The company then moved to Hartford, Connecticut, for the week of April 15–22, advertising Franklin as a clown, and he and Johnston as horsemen. Afterwards, they went on to Baltimore, where they operated through May.

The "Summer Circus," operated by John Walker and his wife, opened in Philadelphia in June 1799. The program consisted of equestrian acts and martial music. The company was short lived; by October the husband-wife team had joined Ricketts.

After closing the Pantheon's winter season on March 23, 1799, Ricketts brought the company to Baltimore, where the circus (the word continuing to refer to the building rather than the company) had been built by subscription for Mr. Franklin, "who did not succeed in performing long." They did very good business, Durang making $300 for his benefit. On May 17, the end of the spring season, Ricketts discharged those in the company not directly involved in horsemanship and moved to Annapolis, Maryland. Business was poor, and they sold the circus (building) for half price and removed to Easton, Maryland, offering ground and lofty tumbling similar to that performed at Sadler's Wells.

One of the few areas where a woman could achieve near-equality with her male counterparts during the 19th century was on the stage. Stage could mean the legitimate theater, ballet, opera or the less formal setting of a circus ring. Women excelled in equestrian feats, particularly the Fox Hunt (that entertainment being especially adapted for the side saddle). In 1876, Cooper, Bailey & Co. promoted the only lady somersault rider in the country. (*Jackson Sentinel* [IA], May 18, 1876)

The Ricketts company traveled extensively during the summer of 1799, including Georgetown and Alexandria, where they advertised for three days "and no one came near the place." Retracing their steps to Annapolis proved no better, and they hurried off to Baltimore "with all possible speed."[47] A building 120 feet by 50 feet was constructed for their use. Typically, these structures were hastily built and torn down immediately after the performers left, the lumber being sold for whatever money could be obtained. The company at this time included the Ricketts brothers, Master Hutchins, Durang and John Walker, with Mrs. Walker performing the featured performance of broad sword exercises and hunt riding (likely copying Hughes' Fox Hunt scenes), and Mrs. Rowson the pantomimes. Women often performed in hunt riding, as the performance was adaptable for sidesaddle. By November they added Mr. Rosainville to provide fireworks, another well-accepted European entertainment.[48]

Back home in Philadelphia, now called "Ricketts' Circus" (as opposed to the "Pantheon"), the company included John Bill, rider; Francis, vaulter and leaper; Durang, rider and tight-rope walker; Mrs. Rowson, actress; Miss Corey, Hutchins and Mrs. Decker, artists. Three ponies, named Boxer, High Flier and Gin Crack, provided the ever-popular races across the stage, down either side of the orchestra and around the two-level ring.

On December 17, 1799, at about 9 o'clock in the evening while the actors were dressing for their roles in "Don Juan," the cry "Fire!" was heard as flames emerged from over the base of the dome at the actors' entrance. Fortunately, none of the 300 to 500 people in attendance were injured. The flames made so rapid a progress that efforts to check it proved ineffectual, and the Circus burned to the ground, along with an adjacent building originally erected for the Episcopal Academy but at the time occupied by James Oeller (also spelled O'Eller) as a hotel. Considerable damage was also done to five new houses in Sixth Street, extending to Sansom Street.[49] At the time, this was the biggest fire ever to strike Philadelphia.

Ricketts' loss was estimated at $20,000; his immediate reaction was to attribute the cause to arson, prompting him to offer $1,000 reward for the apprehension of the incendiary. Subsequent investigation revealed a drunken carpenter in Ricketts' employ named Miller had left a lighted candle in the scenery room. In his absence the flame set the room ablaze, and the fire quickly spread.

Not surprisingly, many citizens viewed the destruction as the judgment of Providence. They were quick to point out the circus handbill describing the fateful pantomime:

> The last scene presents the infernal regions, with a view of the mouth of hell; Don Juan being reduced by his wickedness to the dreadful necessity of leaping headlong into the gaping gulf, in a shower of fire, among the furies, who receive him on the points of their burning spears, and hurl him at once into the bottomless pit.[50]

The fact the pantomime had not yet started, and the fire arose from the roof rather than the pit, likely had little effect on their moral indignation.

In order to keep the company employed, Durang borrowed scenery and costumes from Ricketts and took the performers to Lancaster, where they opened at the end of December 1799. The program included:

> Pantomime, Singing, Hornpipe, *Dancing*, Tumbling, SPEAKING, &c. &c. And in particular an Indian WAR and SCALP Dance by Mr. Durang and Mr. F. Ricketts.[51]

Durang left after two nights to spend the winter at home. Despite being patronized by Governor McKeon on January 2, 1800, the effort failed, and two weeks later Ricketts had to send money to Rowson so they could return to Philadelphia.

Reworking Lailson's Philadelphia building that had collapsed in 1798, John Bill Ricketts began an open air season on April 3, 1800, with Hutchins, Sr., and Master Hutchins, William Sully, Mr. and Mrs. Rowson, Durang and the horse Cornplanter. Lacking a roof over the ring, and with a "gloomy" atmosphere under the partially covered seats, they worked for several weeks, but Ricketts remained despondent and the show abruptly closed April 23, 1800. With John Bill's "mind wandering unrecinciled [*sic*]" he stepped away from his company; some of the performers joined a new show under the direction of Langley, who took them to Charleston.

On June 24, 1799, Alexandre Placide opened the Vaux Hall Garden (also spelled Vauxhall and Vaux-hall) in Charleston. With his wife, the English actress Charlotte Wrighten, he managed the pleasure garden, offering meals and entertainment. By summer he added concert programs with theatrical vocalists who remained in the city throughout the summer months. In 1802, evening musicales with a small orchestra, culminating in fireworks, became part of the entertainment, and in 1804, he added bathing facilities.[52]

Whether the performances had grown stale with repetition or it was the allure of better profits elsewhere, John Bill Ricketts determined to seek greener pastures. While unfortunate for the development of the circus in the United States, his decision cannot be altogether surprising. He achieved great success, but it was tempered and somewhat mitigated by failures. Plagued and financially burdened by devastating fires, he also experienced firsthand how fickle the business could be. Traveling from city to city was exhausting and presented obstacles, not the least of which was the safe passage of his horses. Injury or loss of a trained animal could easily force an entire act or series of acts to be reworked or abandoned. There was also no guarantee of filled seats, as his journeys after returning from Canada proved.

Paying his performers an above-average wage did not preclude turnovers in staff, but it did add to his monetary burden. Even at this stage, when the concept of a circus or equestrian performance was new, he could ill afford to let his stage trappings and costumes become worn or shabby. Illusion, perception and the aura of magic were necessary ingredients for a successful season. With added competition from like entertainers, as well as theaters, play halls and pleasure gardens in the major cities of New York, Philadelphia, Charleston and Baltimore, pressure mounted for bigger and grander buildings, increasingly complex acts and novel entertainments.

The West Indies was already a proven ground for British companies, success bringing rich rewards. After more than a year of inaction, Ricketts determined to try his luck and perhaps improve his spirits among the islands. The brothers Ricketts, along with Master Hutchins and Miller, left Philadelphia late in 1801,* waiting for Matthew Sully to join them in Newcastle before departing. Sully never came, and a ship was chartered, specially outfitted with slings to secure the horses and enough lumber to construct a new circus. Tragically, their vessel was commandeered by a French privateer and taken as a prize to Guadeloupe in the Leeward Isles, where the pirates sold their possessions as prize money.

Facing destitution again, Ricketts sold his prized silver-mounted broadsword and pistols, saved under a pile of manure. With a merchant backer in Guadalupe, he managed to regain his stock and lumber, and constructed a new circus. Several successful performances put him in the black, but ultimate triumph was denied him. Disaster struck when two of the company, including the nine-or ten-year-old Hutchins, died of yellow fever, and Francis was jailed for deserting his native-born wife. Yearning, perhaps, for home, John Bill, without his brother Francis, sold the horses and booked passage for England. The ship floundered at sea and all passengers were lost.

The tragic demise of John Bill Ricketts effectively put a close to the 1700s. The next century would take the circus through its glory days, transforming it along the way — in a fashion that might have surprised the most significant and successful of the United States pioneers.

Historically, the year is cited as 1800, as that was the last time John Bill Ricketts performed in the United States. But as Francis accompanied him on the voyage, the date is in dispute. After the demise of Ricketts' Philadelphia endeavor, Francis accompanied Langley's troupe on its southern tour, remaining with them throughout 1800. By February 1801, he departed for work in Charleston. By August, Langley's company returned to that city and listed Ricketts as one of their riders. If he did actually appear, then he could not have set off with his brother before the fall of 1801.

7

The Century of the Circus

I might as well attempt to describe a piece of music or painting by language, as to express a full representation of the exhibition of the circus.[1]

Chapter 1 opened with the question "When did the circus become a circus?" The next question might be "What is a circus?" As discussed in the Preface, both interrogatives elicit myriad answers. Clearly, common usage of the term originated with Hughes and Dibdin. But did the inclusion of the word make a company into an actual circus?

For purposes of discussing the evolution of the circus in this text, the answer is yes. The rationale is a simple one. Only the wealthy and well-traveled 18th- and early 19th-century American knew of Astley's and Hughes' entertainments. For the remainder of the population, the concept was a new and developing one. While French and English aeronauts routinely had their exploits reprinted in local newspapers across the country, making ballooning a common and familiar topic of conversation, reports of less exhilarating and dangerous forms of theatrics were nearly non-existent. Therefore, when a troupe advertised itself as a "circus," the idea was completely novel. The average American knew only what he or she saw, and therefore "circus" became whatever exhibition appeared in their municipality under that title.

In point of fact, the word "circus" was irregularly employed in the 1700s and early 1800s, with troupes trying it on for size and discarding it as rapidly. Typically, companies preferred the early European designation of "Riding School" or "Equestrian Performances," and only later did they settle on the all-inclusive word "circus."

In the early development of the United States, Philadelphia was always at the heart of fresh ideas and innovation. It is not surprising, then, that it also stood at the forefront of entertainment. Both the American circus and many of the most significant balloon ascensions took place in the environs of the city. With Ricketts and Lailson both departed from the scene, John Durang, well familiar with Philadelphia and its prospects, joined forces with Lewis DeGraff[2] (Durang does not mention DeGraff's name) and put together a company that opened in Philadelphia on July 28, 1800.

Durang rented the old theater on South Street for $20 a night and opened "The Thespian Panorrama" [*sic*]. He offered tumbling, dancing, speaking, pantomime and farce, as well as his own act of flying from the gallery to the back part of the stage through a burst of fireworks. Business was "very poor," but he did manage to salvage $300 at his own benefit.[3]

Occupying the arena once used by both Lailson and Ricketts, Durang wore many hats, performing as equestrian, clown and vaulter, while DeGraff displayed his horsemanship. With them was Mrs. Rowson, also from Ricketts' old company, doing the hornpipe. For their performances they advertised Eagle, the horse. Perhaps finding the show too similar to Ricketts,' audiences did not respond as anticipated, and the company stayed no more than a few days.[4]

Others of Ricketts' old company re-formed under William Langley and traveled to Charleston. On September 9, 1800, he presented a group consisting of himself as rider, Francis Ricketts as rider, vaulter and clown, and Miss Celestine appearing in the pantomime "Death of Bucephalus." Later in the season performances were put on hold so the arena could be covered; it reopened December 27, with the addition of artificial fireworks, and ended in January 1801.[5]

Langley, Francis Ricketts and Johnson went on to Savannah, Georgia, opening February 10, 1801. Ricketts left shortly thereafter, returning to Charleston; the rest went on to Augusta, where they stayed until the latter part of May. By August 3, the company was reunited, Langley advertising the historical note that he had performed in London and Paris.[6] During this period it was customary for performers to flaunt their European ties as a way of giving themselves distinction. If true (for he was a native of Charleston), he likely appeared with smaller groups, learning tradecraft from the many circulating equestrian troupes.

Although Langley announced his retirement to operate a menage, he reappeared in Charleston in April 1802, with a company consisting of Johnson, Robertson, Thomas Franklin, Sr., and Mr. Oldfield, another Charleston native. Robertson soon left to form his own troupe in New York. Thomas Franklin, Jr., and his partner, a man named Lattin, returned to Philadelphia, where they briefly performed at Lailson's old building for a week each in May and June before abandoning the effort. Soon after, they reappeared with Robertson and Company in New York. Langley, McDonald, Lewis, Sully and Johnson eventually joined.

Robertson's Company played at Vauxhall Gardens, New York, where an arena suitable for their use had been constructed in 1802. Their choice of performance ground was an apt one, for the Gardens was situated near the Bowery, already known for its taverns, oyster saloons and minstrel shows. Patrons from the lower wards (as opposed to the upper class elite who patronized Broadway) flocked there in huge numbers, providing both laborers and paying customers. Not yet reaching the nadir of its reputation, Vauxhall Gardens was not far away from its later description as a "cheap rendezvous for infamy... with its many-colored lamps — its bad music and worce [*sic*] ice-cream — its clowns, sawdust, serenauts [presumably a type of cantata], ballet-dancers, and other attractions too numerous to mention."[7]

Sometime between 1800 and 1805, Durang bought an elegant bay racehorse for $100 and named it Cornplanter after Ricketts' charger. He trained it in circus tricks and in 1805, rented Lailson's old circus. In company with DeGraff (spelled "Degraft" in the text), they "went on in some tolerable good order," until Durang had an accident on Cornplanter. Riding in a suit of armor with a visor covering his face, a shower of fireworks startled the horse, who flung its rider over the orchestra and onto the stage. Finding the whole did not pay for his trouble, Durang went back to work for Mr. Wignell, whom he had known from the Old American Company. Together with Mr. Reinagle (the pair who had purchased

Lailson's circus horses and stage props), they operated the "New Theatre" in both Philadel-phia and Baltimore. Interestingly, Durang's salary in regional theater was considerably less than what he earned with Ricketts and the Circus.

During his time with the New Theatre, Durang also entered into partnership with Mr. Francis, a mainstay at the Chestnut Street Theatre, Philadelphia. The pair taught dancing "to the leaders of fashion" for many years before Durang, his son Ferdinand and Mr. Harris, also of the New Theatre, established their own Dancing School.[8] They also traveled around the state, and by 1810 were offering "compositions of theatrical and dramatic performances, historical, comedies, operas, pantomimes and ballet-dances, accompanied with scenery, machinery, painting in transparencies, music and brilliant dresses."[9]

In 1802, Thomas Swann opened a riding school in Southwark, adjoining the South Street Theatre, where he taught riding and gave public exhibitions of horsemanship. That same year he opened an amphitheatre at the corner of Thirteenth and Market Street. Exhi-bitions included a lecture by the manager, equestrian performances, vocal and instrumental music, maneuvers of "the new exercise of the broadsword for cavalry movements, together with readings and recitations by a young gentleman lately from Europe."

Mrs. Scott presented broadsword exercises. Taking a benefit on October 13, she expressed thanks for her patronage and exemplified "the six divisions of the broadsword exercise for cavalry movements in which is exhibited ninety-three motions."

In January 1803, at Lialson's old circus building, Swann, former farrier and animal anatomist, proposed to "cause to be destroyed and dissected" a lame horse, and lectured on the disease known as "hipshot," from which the animal suffered. In 1804, Swann's riding school, opposite Lombardy Gardens, exhibited an African lion. The Jungle Beast was let out of its cage "in a part of the school perfectly secure from the spectators." In this he was preceded by the similar attraction of an African Lion at the Red Lion, Market Street. A Dancing Horse was another attraction at Swann's.[10]

In 1810, Swann moved to the amphitheatre erected by Monsieur Victorien in 1808 at the Centre-House-Gardens. Victorien had given performances on the tight- and slack-rope, and wire and lofty tumbling. That same year, Monsieur Poutingam opened a riding school at the corner of Tenth and Arch Streets. When his enterprise failed, Swann rented out his amphitheatre and kept it until his death in July 1812.[11]

Robertson and Franklin worked together in 1803, performing in Newport, Rhode Island, from February 12 to 21, but no other circus performances were given through the year 1804. In 1805, Durang and DeGraff presented a show at Leaman's Columbia Garden, Baltimore, both men offering equestrian acts, with Durang also giving a wire-walking per-formance. On September 12, Louis Mestayer was introduced as a clown. They played until October 8, when the company moved into the Pantheon, working until January 20, 1806.[12]

The only other circus-type performance of note occurred in Charleston at Placide's Vaux-Hall, where Mr. Berry, a pupil of William Sully, advertised a "Panorama," including ground and lofty tumbling, vaulting, a pantomime and a playlet, accompanied by music. The following year the "Pitoresque & Mechanique Theatre" at Vaux-Hall Garden advertised "an amusement of the Theatre Picturesque and Mechanique," to play Monday and Thurs-day evenings for an admission price of 50 cents (half-price for children).[13] Placide remained in overall charge of Vaux-Hall until his death in New York City in the summer of 1812, but he also managed the Richmond Theatre, where he was involved with the disastrous fire of 1811.

The first introduction of the elephant occurred in 1796 with the importation of a young Indian elephant by Jacob Crowninshield. By 1808, a second elephant, "Old Bet," was brought to America by Captain Bailey, who sold her to his brother, Hackaliah Bailey (alternately spelled "Hachaliah" and "Baily"), an innkeeper in Somers, Westchester County, New York. Realizing he had struck gold, Bailey entered into an arrangement for showing the animal:

> Articles of agreement between Hachaliah Baily of the first part and Andrew Brown & Benjamin Lent of the second part. The S. Brown & Lent agree to pay the S. Baily twelve hundred dollars each for the equal two-thirds of the use of the Elephant for one year from the first day of this month. Baily on his part furnishes one-third of the expenses and Brown and Lent the other two-thirds. August 13th, 1808.[14]

After "Old Bet," came innumerable elephants. The performing elephant Sultan, here being measured to "prove" its tremendous height, was "endowed with almost human intelligence," and "whose startling performances astonish and bewilder all who witness them." (*Defiance Democrat* [OH], July 5, 1873)

For the next eight years Bailey made a considerable fortune from the exhibition. The traveling show operated by Bailey and Edward Finch consisted of Old Bet and a lion. In 1811, while East India jugglers performed at the Masonic Temple, a "great natural curiosity, a living elephant," was exhibited in Arch Street, Philadelphia.[15] Benjamin F. Brown (born in Somers, Westchester County, New York, on January 11, 1799), while working on his father's farm in New York, was hired by Bailey and Finch to care for the elephant. She was, Benjamin observed, "a big one." They showed in barns, displaying the two attractions separately, charging one shilling for the elephant and another to see the lion. He added:

> My brother Christopher was the first man to put up a canvas. He had it in stripes ten feet wide and fifty feet long, and he used to stretch it from the barn doors. In one season we cleared about $8,000 with the elephant alone. You see the expenses were next to nothing. They didn't average twenty shillings a day. We used to have pretty rough times. We traveled in the night, so that folks wouldn't see the animals, and persons collected in the road sometimes, and tried to stop us. Once in Pennsylvania, they collected in this way, and one fellow threw a stone and hit me on the head and knocked me off my horse.

Benjamin traveled with Bailey & Finch for about a year before a disagreement about money caused him to resign his position and return home to help with spring planting.[16] Tragically, on July 26, 1816, a Maine farmer shot poor "Old Bet" on the supposition the exhibitors were taking money out of the state that might better have been spent locally.[17]

The "Importation" of Victor Pepin and Jean Breschard

The first decade of the 1800s was fraught with political disruptions around the world, leading inevitably to the War of 1812. Before President James Madison signed the declaration on June 18, 1812, France and England were already at war. After the defeat of the French at the Battle of Trafalgar in 1805, Napoleon issued the Berlin Decree, forbidding French and neutral ships from maritime trade with Britain. The United Kingdom reacted by expanding the Orders in Council of 1806 (that placed nearly 800 miles of coastline, from Elbe in Germany to Brest in France under blockade) and enacting the Orders in Council of 1807, forbidding trade with the French by the United Kingdom, her allies and neutrals, while blockading French and allied ports.

This led to Napoleon issuing the Milan Decree of 1807, declaring that all neutral shipping using British ports or paying British tariffs be considered as British and seized. These acts prompted both countries to prey on neutral American ships: between 1803 and 1807, the British seized 528 American vessels, and between 1803 and 1806, the French confiscated 206 American ships.[18]

With manpower at a premium, Britain expanded its impressments of American sailors, causing an increase in tension between that country and the United States. By late 1807, when the brig *Eliza Haley* docked at Plymouth, Massachusetts, maritime trade along the northern Atlantic seaboard was depressed. It was neither the time nor the place for a troupe of circus performers to begin their career in a new country, but that is precisely what happened. Victor Pepin and Jean Breschard, traveling from Paris to Madrid and then to the States, quickly moved to Boston, where they hoped to establish themselves.

Erecting tents for rehearsals — the first cited use of tents for circus activity — the team eventually anticipated the construction of a permanent building along the lines of what Ricketts had done in 1795. Toward that end, they were defeated by the Boston Town Council, which declared the trouper's intent to be "too frivolous for these sober times." This compelled them to move to Charlestown, Massachusetts, where they constructed an open-air arena at the end of the toll bridge.[19] The company opened on December 19, 1807, with a handbill of December 29 announcing:

CIRCUS

Messrs. Pepin & Breschard
    First Riding Masters from the Academies of Paris and Various parts of Europe, have erected their *CIRCUS in CHARLESTOWN.*
    New and various exercises of Horsemanship.
    To commence with the entry of the full company well mounted in Military Uniform, who will execute at great Gallop, various Military Evolutions. The Pupils will perform in various Positions on Horseback, Vaulting, and Feats of agility.
    The noble Horse will leap over several Bars, and likewise over two Horses with the younger pupils on his back, which was never done in the United States, but by this Gallant Horse.
    Mr. Breschard will pick up several handkerchiefs and likewise a watch, from the ground, when the Horse is in full speed.
To which will be added, The Nevw and Comical Scene of the CLOWN,
The whole to conclude with the HORSE in FIRE.
    Admittance, Boxes 1 Dollar, Pit 50 cents, Children half price.

In an addendum at the bottom of the handbill ran the following acknowledgment, less an apology than a begrudged acceptance:

> Understanding that the frequency of their performances have operated unfavorable for their Drama to Brethren, they have determined to confine them, for the future, to twice a week, viz, Tuesday & Thursday Evening, which arrangements they trust will give general satisfaction. They would also observe that not being accustomed to announce their performances in public, Bills will be delivered at the Box Office for the succeeding evening.

This clearly indicated that weekend performances ran afoul of the mores of the religious population. This example of how public entertainment in general, and circuses in particular, were viewed is indicative of the times. From the earliest refusal to permit Ricketts to construct a building, to the levy of taxes and permits, magistrates, religious leaders and often editorialists would continue to present obstacles for traveling shows throughout the century.

Pepin performed as the clown and also did the "Fisher Women," an adaptation of Ricketts' "Metamorphosis," whereby he changed costumes and genders while encased in a sack, all while on the back of a galloping horse. The "Horse in Fire" was exactly as it sounded: a horse stood unflinchingly while fireworks were set off around it. Mrs. Breschard was their featured female equestrians and earned laurels for her "astonishing feats of female activity."[20]

Two notices ran in *The Repertory*, both with Breschard's name misspelled:

THIS EVENING, Feb. 2.
A Great display of Exercise, Vaulting and
Dancing on horses, executed by
Messrs. PEPIN & BRECHARD and their Pupils.

The full article in the *Repertory* of February 2, 1808, gave the following information:

CIRCUS
A Great display of Exercise, Vaulting and
Dancing on horses, executed by
Messrs. PEPIN & BRECHARD and their PUPILS.
This will prove one of the most brilliant representations, and will be varied by many interesting changes, and will be closed by the Don Quixote Pantomime with a number of improvements. Among other comical scenes, the attack on the Windmill will excite general mirth, as well as his laughable encounter with the millers. There will also be exhibited a spirited combat between a horse and an ass.
Nothing will be omitted which may contribute to the publick amusement, variety and novelty will concur to attain this desirable end.
Messrs. Pepin & Brechard, alive to every sentiment of gratitude towards a generous publick, will unite all their efforts and skill to merit a continuance of patronage.
Should it rain the exhibition will be postponed until Thursday Evening.
Admittance—Boxes 1 Dollar, Pit 50 cents, Children half price.
Doors to be opened at 5 o'clock, Performance to commence at half past 6 o'clock, precisely.

The circus closed May 7, 1808, and moved to New York City on June 2. The troupe consisted of riders Mrs. Breschard, Pepin, and Mr. Codet; the Young African; Jean Breschard as clown; the Young Chinese as vaulter; and Master Diego, an eleven-year-old youth, performing hoop tricks. Interestingly, the proprietors issued a notice requesting that patrons refrain from whistling during the performance, as that was the signal by which the horses had been trained to stop.[21]

After a successful season, the company moved to Philadelphia, where they had previously purchased land at Walnut and Ninth Streets. Here they constructed an elliptical ring to augment a brick building with an 81-foot dome, atop which sat a flagpole, creating a combined height of 96 feet. Opening night, February 2, 1809, featured Mrs. Breschard leaping her horse through two barrels; Mr. Victorani, rope-walker and vaulter; Mr. Menial, rope-walker; Master Diego, rider; Pepin, hurdle-rider; Cayetano Mariotini; Mr. Codet; and the horses Noble and Monarch.

Following the path of Ricketts, who established short "seasons" in order to travel from city to city to reach fresh audiences (as opposed to Astley and Hughes, who kept far longer seasons, only moving to France, Ireland or Scotland in the winter), Pepin and Breschard next performed in Lancaster, Pennsylvania. Besides the namesakes, the company here consisted of Diego, Codet, Cayetano (clown) and two named horses, Nobel and Conqueror. C. Mercier led the band. Cayetano performed a burlesque "riding lesson" called "Madame Angold," where he dressed as a woman.[22]

They next opened in New York City on July 1, 1809, at a circus (building) constructed at Broadway and Worth. A handbill described the performance:

CIRCUS

This Evening, Aug. 2, 1809, Messrs. Pepin & Breschard, will have the honor to give a brilliant representation of Horsemanship, Vaulting and Dancing.

To which will be added for the first time, the New Pantomime of BILLY, or the Reward of a Good Action, performed with combats, &c. by Mr. P. Grain. — Scene in the adjacent part of a small Village.

Annette, a country girl, Miss Cibert — John Roger, her father, Mr. Simon — Billy, Annette's lover, a simple fellow, Mr. Grain — Francis, do.*

Mr. Menial — Mourtache, 1st chief of robbers,

Mr. Breschard — Rinfort, 2d chief of robbers,

Mr. Caytano — Flamant, captain of the military,

Mr. Grain — Two Travellers, Messrs. Codet and

Allien — An Old Woman, Mr. Fulgence — Soldiers, Robbers, &c.

Doors to be opened at half past seven o'clock, and the performance to commence precisely at a quarter past eight. Box one dollar — Pit half a dollar — Children half price.

It is curious to note that they chose to promote their pantomime, going to the trouble of providing an entire cast list. Possibly the equestrian exercises were too well known to enumerate. The show closed August 26, 1809, and moved on to Boston.

Old Friends Resurface

Competition for Pepin and Breschard came in the form of Thomas Stewart. Opening September 10, 1808, at Providence, Rhode Island, the troupe featured Stewart and "Peter, the Young African" as equestrians. Stewart also performed as clown and provided tumbling exhibitions. A brief stay in Salem, Massachusetts, included Thomas Franklin, Jr., the youthful rider from Ricketts' old company. October 10–20 saw them in Charlestown, where Mr. Bell, the rope-dancer, made his first circus appearance.

---

*"Do" was an abbreviation for "ditto." Cayetano's name was misspelled.

Stewart opened the year 1809 in Salem; by May 31, he had moved into a Boston Amphitheatre constructed for Anthony Roulestone, a local bookbinder and amateur rider. He was added to the bill, as was Francis Ricketts, said to be making his first appearance in twelve years.[23] This was a peculiar exaggeration, for Francis last appeared in Charleston in 1801, although perhaps "years" referred to a particular type of performance rather than a time frame.

The following year, in a review in the *Repertory*, it was mentioned that Ricketts had spent five years in foreign service, been captured and suffered greatly before returning to the United States. The inference being that after his brother set out for England on his fateful voyage, Francis needed employment. Unable to secure a living as a solo performer or with another troupe, he was compelled to enlist in the military. It may also have been that he sought the safety of the armed forces in escaping the charge leveled against him for deserting his native wife.

At some period during Francis Ricketts' stay in Boston, John Durang contacted him in that city, urging him to return to Philadelphia and administer his brother's estate, comprising three lots on Chestnut Street. He reported that Francis came in company with a "Yankey," who urged him to sell the property, which he did for $1,800. The pair then returned to Boston, but within the span of several weeks Francis returned, having lost his fortune to the "Yankey." According to Durang, Ricketts then joined the circus party of Mr. Laudenslager's in Baltimore.[24] Presuming the name to be incorrect, it is possible he joined Pepin and Breschard when they went to Baltimore, but he was back in Boston with the newly formed Boston Circus by January 11, 1810.

On September 19, 1809, Master Samuel Tatnall and his horse Black Jack joined Stewart's company. They worked at Roulestone's Amphitheatre until the latter part of December. A month earlier, Pepin and Breschard had moved on to Philadelphia, performing "Grand Austrian Maneuvers," as well as the favorite "Taylor." As "The Professors of Horsemanship," they opened in Baltimore on December 14 with a company that included Cayetano, Codet, Diego, Menial, Mrs. Breschard and Francoise Seigne as rider.

The Boston Circus opened for business January 11, 1810, renaming Roulestone's building, lately used by Pepin and Breschard. Under the direction of Robert Davis and an actor named Bates, they performed Tuesdays and Thursdays, with a company including Sam Tatnall, Francis Ricketts as clown and Mr. Bell on the slack-rope. In well-established tradition, Roulestone operated a riding school in the mornings and occasionally worked as a circus performer. With them was the horse Nobel. Closing on February 22, they moved to Salem, where the company was billed as "Davis and Leeds." The performers included Sam Tatnall, Peter the African, Francis Ricketts, Mrs. Stewart and Ira Dunn, riders; Mr. Victorani, rope-walker; Mr. Stewart, clown; Mr. Bell, rope-walker; and Robert Davis, vaulter. After a stay lasting until April 3, the troupe resumed its name of "Davis and Company" and returned to Boston for a three-day stand.

On May 3, 1810, "Messrs. Cayetano & Co." were in Newburyport, Massachusetts. Here they erected a board pavilion on an unoccupied lot, furnished with seats in the pit that surrounded the ring; above stood a gallery, with boxes comprising the dress-circle. There was also a stand for musicians. Performances were given Monday, Wednesday and Friday afternoons.

In *Reminiscences of a Nonagenarian*, Sarah Ann Emery described the "Italian troupe" as being "a most respectable and fine looking company, their horses were splendid animals, all the appurtenances in the best style." Because their Grand Military Maneuvers required eight riders and the company brought only six, Cayetano hired two local men, Samuel Shaw and David Emery, to complete the set. The orchestra instruments included a bugle, clarinet, bass-viol and violin.

In a remarkably vivid manner, Sarah Emery described the night's activities, beginning with a bugle call summoning the eight horsemen in single file. After the equestrian military tactics, Master Tatnal performed several gymnastic feats, followed by Master Duffee, "a Negro lad, [who] drew down the house by feats of agility, leaping over a whip and hoop." Codet next performed horsemanship, followed by Mr. Menial, the clown. Other acts included Cayetano's "Fish Woman, or the Metamorphosis" on two horses. She wrote:

> With a foot on each horse, he rode forward habited as an immensely fat fish-woman, in a huge bonnet and uncouth garments. Riding rapidly round the ring, he divested himself of this and several other suits, ending in making his final bow as an elegant cavalier. The Young African next performed feats of horsemanship and vaulting, danced a hornpipe, and other figures, ending by dashing round the ring, standing on the tips of his toes. The horse Ocelot, posted himself in various attitudes, danced and took a collation with the clown. Mr. Cayetano performed "The Candian [Canadian] Peasant," and feats of horsemanship with hoops, hat and glove, terminating by the leap of the four ribbons separated and together. Mr. Cayetano performed the pyramid, young Duffee on his shoulders as "Flying Mercury." Then came the Trampoleon exercises by Messrs. Menial, Codet and the Young African; somersets over men's heads and a leap over six horses. The next scene was the Pedestal, the horse of knowledge posted in different attitudes. The performances concluded with the Taylor riding to Waterford upon the unequalled horse Zebra, by Mr. Menial, the clown. This was a most laughable farce, Zebra being a Jack trained to the part. This elicited a storm of applause, and the play ended with cheer after cheer.[25]

Proving the liquidity of these traveling shows, Ricketts, Bell and Stewart joined Pepin and Breschard when they moved to New York.[26]

The shuffle of performers continued for the next two years. In April 1810, Cayetano took Tatnall, Codet, Menial, the Young African and added Master Dufee to Newburyport, Massachusetts. With an orchestra composed of a bugle, clarinet, violin and bass viol, Menial played the clown and did the "Tailor," Cayetano performed the "Fisher Woman" and the "Canadian Peasant" (both involving a change of costume on horseback), and everyone participated in the "trampolean." Meanwhile, Pepin and Breschard went to Richmond, where they worked from May 5 to May 25. They met together back in New York, playing from June 21 to September 29, and then returned to Philadelphia, performances beginning October 8. Three days later, Thomas Franklin, Jr., joined as rider and clown.

The 1811 season began in Baltimore, where Pepin and Breschard's company consisted of Thomas Stewart, Mr. Bell, Master Felix, Francoise Seigne, Diego, Francis Ricketts, Mr. LaConta, Louis Mestayer and his wife. This season ran from January 10 through April 19.

This proved to be the last time Francis Ricketts appeared with a circus company. After leaving Baltimore he went to Kentucky, where he toured with a Mr. Cross in 1811 and 1812, doing equestrian tricks in the afternoon, and both singing and reciting Shakespearean soliloquies in the evening.[27] John Durang stated, "The last I heard of him, he had been enlisted in the service of the United States laying in camp at Yorktown when I was there, and marched off for the Lakes."[28]

Pepin and Breschard's company traveled to Lancaster, Pennsylvania, in May, with Seigne enacting the "Madame Angold" act. They then moved to New York, where they stayed from June 18 to September 28, finishing the year in Baltimore from November 6 to December 26.[29]

Cayetano, with his own troupe, opened in Boston on January 31, 1811. A handsome handbill depicted three galloping horses with riders in Pyramid formation: three mounted and two hanging from the horses' sides, three men standing behind them on the horses' backs, three boys sandwiched between, two boys with their legs wrapped around the men's shoulders, and a final boy standing on the middle adult's shoulders. The advertisement read:

> BOSTON CIRCUS, on *THURSDAY EVENING*,
> March 28, 1811.
> Grand and Brilliant Representation, composed of Feats Of *Horsemanship, Vaulting, & Agility*, in which the Riders will signalize themselves.
> THE MUCH ADMIRED AND LAUGHABLE SCENE OF THE OFFICER and his RECRUIT, or the two METAMORPHOSES, by Messrs. Cayetano & Codet.
> *Act Second will commence, for the Second Time in Boston, the* GRAND MASQUERADE OF VENICE, as it was performed by the Romans in their Festival Days, in which will be seen a Humourous Combat, between ten persons — After the Combat, will be executed eight different Groups and Pyramids, by twelve persons, as they were to be seen in the Palace Garden of Rome — the whole of the Pyramids to conclude, by an extraordinary Group of fourteen persons, on three Horses in full speed, never attempted by any other Company.... *The conclusion of the evening's performance, will be the famous* Horse Ocelot, surrounded by FIRE-WORKS, who has been taught to it *since in Boston.*
> Doors opened at 6, to begin at 7 o'clock; Tickets to be had at the Box Office of the Circus; Box Tickets 1 dol. Pit 50 cents, Children half price. *Gentlemen that wish for seats or boxes, in season, are requested to call at the Circus, where a Book will be kept, for the purpose of entering their names, agreeable to the Ticket, attendance from 9 till 1, and from 3 to 5.*

Others in the circus included Sam Tatnall, Menial, Duffee, the Young African, Anthony Roulestone and Mrs. Redon, a two-horse rider. "Messrs. Cayetano and Company" next went to Newburyport, Portsmouth, New Hampshire, Salem and Boston. The remainder of the year the company spent in Montreal, constructing a new circus that did not open until November 1811.

Fire and Warfare

Two catastrophic events that effected public entertainment for years to come occurred very close together. The day after Christmas, 1811, was to see a benefit performance for Alexandre Placide, manager of the Richmond (Virginia) Theatre. Ironically, he had intended to hold his benefit two days earlier, but had been ill. On the night of December 11, 1811, a new pantomime, "The Bleeding Nun, or Agnes and Raymond," premiered as the afterpiece to the play "The Father, or Family Feuds." With a full, darkened house there to honor the popular actor, a chandelier was drawn up, with one of the lamps still burning. The stage manager attempted to have the light lowered in order to extinguish the flame, but the pulley did not work well and the chandelier tipped. Quickly flames spread from the lamp to the thirty-five scenes hanging from the roof. Fire quickly consumed the highly flammable panels, jumping to the roof and spreading across the boxes, the dome of the pit and the canvas ceilings of the lower boxes.

Panic spread to the 598 patrons, 80 of which were children. There being only one exit, the door was soon blocked in the melee. Here, many were trampled to death; others died in the flames or perished attempting to jump from upper windows. In all, the estimate of loss of life ranged from 68 to 72 people, of which 54 were women and children. While principal blame was laid at the poor and hasty construction of the theater, larger issues loomed as people questioned how God could have let the tragedy happen. Slavery and politics were two issues said to evoke the Lord's ire, but there were many who pointed the finger at the performers and their "immoral" way of life.

Although Placide wrote many letters around the country, pleading with theater managers to take precautions to prevent similar tragedies in their theaters and playhouses, little regard was given his effort when it came to exonerating the players. Fear, anger and distrust of actors, including circus performers, gripped the nation, and it played a role in diminishing patronage.

Among the rumors circulated after the fact was that Edgar Poe's mother, the actress Eliza Poe, had been one of the victims of the Richmond fire. Actually, she had died two weeks earlier, her last performance occurring October 11, 1811, when she played Countess Wintersen in *The Stranger*. In 1829, Poe used the confusion to his benefit when he claimed to be an orphan, "whose unfortunate parents were the victims of the conflagration of the Richmond theatre," when applying for an appointment at West Point. Considering the governor of Virginia, George W. Smith, Abraham B. Venable, president of the Bank of Virginia, and many Richmond elite lost their lives in the fire, the distinction, such as it was, gave added status to his petition, transforming his mother's status of "actress" (typically viewed with a negative connotation) into that of "unfortunate."[30]

Six months later, on June 1, 1812, President James Madison presented the case against Great Britain; the House voted 79 to 49 to declare war, and the Senate concurred, voting 19 to 13. The War of 1812 officially began on June 18, 1812. For the next three years the major east coast cities, as well as Baltimore and Washington, were threatened (and in some cases outright attacked) by enemy soldiers. Although not the sole cause of depression in the entertainment business, the nation had less time for amusement and fewer dollars to spend.

Cayetano's "Montreal Circus" opened the 1812 season in Canada, where Thomas Stewart and his wife also presented a company of their own. There was some trouble between the two, but as the following handbill reveals, they also worked together, as Stewart appeared in Codet's benefit. The handbill for Codet's benefit proclaimed:

MONTREAL
CIRCUS

Mr. Codet's Benefit;

Mr. CODET respectfully informs the Citizens of Montreal, and its vicinity, that he feels grateful for the frequent applause bestowed on him for his exercises, to gratify and please them at the Circus; he also informs them that his benefit is fixed for MONDAY EVENING next, when his Friends and the Public are respectfully invited to attend, he assures them that his exertions shall not be relaxed, and hopes at that time to give general satisfaction.

Mr. Codet's Benefit;

Grand and Brilliant Representation, Composed of Feats of Horsemanship, & a Grand display of FIRE WORKS.

On Monday Evening, March 9, 1812.

To commence with the Military Manoeuvers; by Eight Riders.

Masters Duffee and Tatnal will execute several feats of Horsemanship, &c.

MR. MENIAL in the character of a Clown will perform Feats of Horsemanship, Buffoonery, &c.

Mr. Steward will distinguish himself with many Feats of Horsemanship, Vaulting, & Agility

The Celebrated African will perform Feats of Horsemanship and Dance a Hornpipe — his horse in full speed.

Madam REDON will on one Horse, execute a great number of Feats of Horsemanship, &c. &c.

Mr. CODET anxious to give general satisfaction to those who will honor him with their presence, will exert all in his power to please, after many feats of Horsemanship, he will leap over four Horses separated and together and will terminate by throwing a back somerset from his Horse, and firing a pair of pistols his Horse in full speed — which was never attempted by any other person but himself.

Master Duffee will introduce the Horse Colin who will sit and lay in different attitudes and will also partake a collation with his master

Mr. Codet will execute the elegant exercises on the SLACK ROPE:

He will perform several different Feats, too numerous to be mentioned. TIGHT ROPE PERFORMANCE;

Mr. Manfredy will do his utmost to give entire satisfaction to the audience by performing a variety of his most tasty Feats.

The Ground and Lofty Tumbling; Will be executed by Messrs. Menial, Codet, Duffee, and Tatnall

Grand and Brilliant Display of FIRE WORKS;

Composed and arranged by Mr. CODET

1st — The Wheel of St. Catherine, which will appear and disappear and change to different forms and colours.

2d — The Lady's Caprice, which will astonish the Spectators by throwing a quantity of fire in the air.

3d — A large Sun, which will change in form and be metamorphosed into a Star.

4th — The Grand Calipers, that will open and shut, and will represent the figure EIGHT.

5th — And last, the Grand Combat between the SUN and MOON, this beautiful piece of Fire Work will surprise the audience by imitating several Forms and many different colours.

The Stewarts were not known to appear in public after their Canadian performance, and Cayetano moved his troupe to Albany, offering their first exhibition on May 13. After a brief stay, the company moved to New York City in June, where they played in less than auspicious quarters, ominously lit by "about 150 candles upon wooden chandeliers, suspended from the roof by a cord."[31] Performers included Mrs. Redon as rider, LaConta as clown and Menial doing the "Taylor." On June 25, 1812, the elephant "Old Bet" became the first animal of its kind to perform with an American circus. The company crafted a platform for her back, with Menial, Codet, Duffee and Tatnall performing the pyramid. By August, the Manfredi family of tight-rope artists joined.[32]

Pepin and Breschard opened the 1812 season in Philadelphia, adding a stage to their newly baptized "Olympick" building at Ninth and Walnut Streets. While continuing their equestrian activities, the pair laid a heavy emphasis on drama in an apparent attempt to draw a wider audience and freshen the look of the bill. Besides the principals, the artists included Bell as rope-walker; Diego (now 15 years old and no longer an apprentice) as performer; Mrs. Breschard, Masters Charles and Felix as riders; and Mr. LaConta as vaulter. On May 9, 1812, the company divided, Breschard going to New York and Pepin to York, Pennsylvania. Neither company could brag of success, Breschard "supplying the equestrian after-piece to dramas being performed by two actors, Dwyer and McKenzie, at the Olympic in New York," which would seem to be a fall from grace. Pepin spent an unprofitable week in Philadelphia, June 29–July 4, and closed without paying his company. After failing to sell his Olympic circus, Pepin lost it to creditors in February 1813.[33]

Yankee Robinson's wonderful performing elephant, "Elfin," holds the pole while two performers display their acrobatics. (*Iowa South West*, September 7, 1867)

Both companies went to Charleston in November 1812. At this point, the venture must have seemed a risky undertaking, as the seacoast city was in jeopardy from the British blockade. The only theater in operation was Alexandre Placide's Vaux-Hall Garden, but since his death that summer, the property had been left to the management of his wife. She began a season in early December 1812, but it ended within the month because of poor attendance, due both to the effects of the war and the presence of the circuses.

Clearly feeling he was in a better position to achieve success, Cayetano built an arena at the upper end of Broad Street, beginning performances on the 16th. The "Circus" bill, considerably expanded from that offered in Montreal, included:

> Grand Military Maneuvers by eight Horsemen
> Horsemanship by Mr. Codet
> Comic Riding by Mr. Menial
> Trained Horse "Syrian" leaping through hoops and hogsheads
> Horsemanship by Master Duffee
> Comic Scene
> "Canadian Peasant," by Mr. Cayetano
> "Flying Mercury" by Cayetano and Duffee
> Trained Horse "Collin" presented by Master Duffee
> The Comic Riding Act "Drunken Soldier" by Mr. Cayetano
> The "Tailor's Journey to Brentford," by Mr. Menial

Mr. Langley, "from the late company of Mr. Lailson," joined the company on November 20; later additions included Codet's slack-wire act, Mrs. Redon and Asa Berry, who performed lofty tumbling.[34] The "Drunken Soldier" was an import, first performed by Andrew Ducrow in England.

Pepin and Breschard opened their season at Vaux-Hall Garden, referring to it as the "Amphitheatre," December 9, 1812, offering:

> Eight-horse entrée
> Minuet on Horseback by Pepin and Breschard
> Still Vaulting by Master Spencer
> Horsemanship by Master Charles
> Vaulting by Mr. Diego
> Trained Horse "Monarch"
> Comic Riding by Mr. Bell
> Mounted Vaulting by Pepin
> Two-horse Riding by Breschard
> Trained Horse "Conqueror"
> Ground Vaulting by Pepin
> "Incombustible Horse" "Tyger"[35]

The fact Charleston had no dramatic theater until 1815, when the Broad Street Theatre reopened under the management of the English thespian Joseph Holman, did not marginally increase circus attendance. Adverse effects from the war made imports difficult to obtain, and even the local newspapers had to reduce the size of their publications for lack of paper on which to print. With money tight, the two circuses merged on December 22, changing locales on alternate weeks.

The combined company, advertised as "Pepin, Breschard and Cayetano," departed Charleston in May 1813 and moved to New York City, with a bill that included Masters Charles, Spencer and Duffee, Diego, Menial, Mrs. Redon and Codet. By late August, they were back in Philadelphia, renting the Olympic for their performances. In November, Francoise Seigne, the rope-walker, joined them. They played until December 3, then moved on to Baltimore. The same month, Mr. Langley began performances with his own troupe in Charleston. The artists included LaConta as rider, ground and lofty tumbling; Don Cayetano Perez, rope-walker; Mr. Bell, rider; Asa Berry, clown; and the horse Conqueror.

For the actor in these early years there was little distinction between "entertainment halls," circuses and "gardens," as they went gracefully from one venue to the other. John Durang was one of the best known to go from theater to circus performances and back to theater, but other memorable names also appeared on handbill lists and in newspaper reports. In 1813, for example, a confectioner and distiller named Lawrence Astolfi opened a summer theater at the Columbian Garden, Philadelphia. Situated on Market Street between Thirteenth Street and Centre Square, the premiere season included Manfredi and Company. They offered the pantomime, *The Imaginary Sick Man*, starring Manfredi as the clown and Louis Mestayer as Harlequin. Mestayer appeared with Pepin in a short Philadelphia season in 1817, and apparently remained in that city. In 1819, Mestayer, his wife and two sons, John and Henry, along with Mons. Dedus, a sword-swallower, offered performances at the Columbian Garden.[36]

8

Equestrian Drama Finds a Home

Whether on foot or on horseback, he showed the port of a King. No Pepin of France that ever rode into Paris with his doughty Austrasians could have claimed greater homage than our martial equestrian as he brought up the rear of his glittering troops — he himself in the costume of a Gallic field-martial. Pepin differed, however, from his royal precursors in one great respect — he had rather more brains.[1]

After opening the 1814 season in Baltimore, "Messrs. Breschard and Co., Equestrians," moved to Alexandria, Virginia. Advertising in the Alexandria *Gazette*, April 19, 1814, the company proclaimed they:

"Have the honor to inform the Ladies and Gentlemen of Alexandria and its vicinity, they have fitted up a CIRCUS at the upper end of Washington street, where they intend to give a few Representations of Exercise of HORSEMANSHIP executed in a superior stile and by the first talents in that line.

The second performance will be this evening, Tuesday 19th.

To commence by a variety of difficult exercises on one horse, by Mr. Seigne.

Mr. Codet will dance a Hornpipe followed by several astonishing Feats to terminate by the great Vaulting.

Mr. Menial, in character of Clown, will endeavor to please the audience, and will execute the still Vaulting; terminating by a variety of Comic Feats.

The laughable scene of the Peasant will be executed by Mr. Breschard, followed by a variety of difficult and astonishing exercises.

The Elegant Horse Conqueror will perform the part of a Domestic Dog, he will bring, at the command of his master, a Handkerchief, Whip, Hat, Basket, &c. and will walk on his knees round the Circus.

Master Spencer will perform several astonishing feats, forward and backward on one Horse, and will leap over 4 Ribbons.

Mr. Breschard will perform on two Horses a variety of feats of dexterity, with apples, forks, cup and ball, bottle, &c.

The elegant scene of the Horse of knowledge who will lie down at command; and put himself in a variety of attitudes.

The whole to conclude with the laughable scene of the Brother Millers, by the whole company.[2]

There was some question of the troupe then moving to Pittsburg (the "h" at the end of the word did not come into common usage until later in the century). What is known, however, is that they advertised a June 13 opening in Cincinnati. This was the farthest west any circus had traveled, and it marked the opening of the American West to this type of entertainment.

Steamboats were just making their appearance on western waterways: the *New Orleans*, under Captain Nicholas Roosevelt, left Pittsburg on October 20, 1811, and reached Cincinnati two days later. The boat arrived in Louisville 64 hours after leaving Pittsburg. After surviving the New Madrid earthquake, encounters with Chickasaw Indians and a nearly disastrous fire, it steamed into its namesake city on January 10, 1812; total time actually traversing the rivers: ten days and nineteen hours.[3] This promised a prodigious growth of cities along the inward waterways, but with the War of 1812 in full progress and New Orleans under siege from the British (the Battle of New Orleans was fought on January 8, 1815), going downriver was not a viable option for Pepin and Breschard. Leaving Cayetano behind, they consequently returned to Charleston, where they opened for business in November 1814.

Still without any theater, the circus was the only professional entertainment open for Charlestonians. Along with Pepin and Breschard, the company included Mrs. Breschard; Masters Spencer, Diego and Boulen; Menial, the clown; LaConta; Codet; Françoise Seigne; and two named horses, Conqueror and Romeo. Mr. Langley also joined on November 19, but thereafter did not appear with any other circus.

Considering the state of the blockade, business may have been slow, or it may have been their desire to double the chances for success, for later that month Breschard, LaConta, Diego, Spencer and Asa Berry moved to Savannah, opening on November 28. Interestingly, people of color were admitted for fifty cents, the same price charged children.[4] Negroes would have been separated from the white audience, but the fact they were allowed in at all, going hand-in-hand with African Americans performing in circuses of the Deep South in the antebellum period, is worthy of note.

Breschard's company rejoined Pepin in Charleston after closing December 22, and the combined circus played until January 3, 1815. At this point, Pepin and Breschard parted ways, the former leaving the country to work in Europe, presumably taking with him Seigne, Peter Coty, Master Boulen and Menial. Codet also dropped out of the record, possibly dying early in 1815.[5]

With Pepin gone, Cayetano added Don Cayetano Perez and his wife, and Mr. LaConta, to his company for their April 17, 1815, performance in Lexington, Kentucky. A "Mrs. Cayetano" was also advertised, possibly being the former Mrs. Redon. They next appeared in Chillicothe, Ohio, in July. By September, the troupe appeared in Cincinnati and later in Louisville, Kentucky, marking the first appearance of a circus in that city, where they remained until October.

By 1815, improvements in the steamboat had opened up the Ohio and Mississippi rivers, providing speedy and inexpensive transportation for produce and travelers. This was a huge boon to cities along these water routes. At this time, the main obstruction to travel was the Falls of Ohio at Louisville. Here the river fell twenty-two feet over a succession of rock ledges, covering a two-mile stretch. Navigation across this stretch proved extremely difficult and dangerous, often requiring an experienced pilot to guide the cumbersome boats through. Attempts could not be made during the seasons of low water, and likely Cayetano waited for a period of high water to take the risk.

By this time, the War of 1812 had ended, although a war of a different sort — this one waged over proprietary rights to the Mississippi, claimed by Robert Fulton — was in high gear. It would not be settled until 1816, when Henry Shreve, a daring river captain, was sued for violating the Fulton-Livingston monopoly. Shreve, a hero of General Andrew Jackson's victory at New Orleans, won his case when the court decided the Territorial Legislature had exceeded its authority by granting exclusive rights to Fulton. This effectively ended the monopoly and opened the floodgates to the Steamboat Era.[6]

Closing in Louisville on October 19, 1815, Cayetano's next destination was Natchez. At this time, Natchez was a thriving river town, effectively divided into two parts: Natchez "Over the Hill" and Natchez "Under the Hill"—the former home to the wealthy and educated, the latter a gathering place for the so-called "River Rats" (keelboaters of a hardened and, at times, lawless disposition, steamboaters, grafters and robbers). Known for hard drinking and wild living, this latter group would have provided a ready-made audience for the circus. Opening on December 29 after a surprisingly long delay of two months, Cayetano planned on staying two weeks, but remained through the year and into the early part of 1816.

Cayetano had his eye on the metropolis of New Orleans, but citing the danger of fire, the city council refused permission to construct a wooden building for the circus. It relented after a second appeal promised the structure would be taken down at the request of the mayor. The required fee of ten dollars was to be paid to the Charity Hospital for each performance.

The circus opened April 6, 1816, with the proprietor undoubtedly hoping for an immediate success. The two-month period between October and December, when the troupe did not perform, the time required to move down river to New Orleans, and the lease of land and expense of the building would have all contributed to a heavy debt. Expectations were apparently met (although subscriptions for a new building failed), for Cayetano remained in the city for the unprecedented span of nearly two years.

At the opposite end of the country, Robert Davis began a new circus endeavor in Boston on October 25, 1815. With Davis performing as rider were Louis Mestayer, clown; Mr. Spriggs, gymnastics; Mr. Diego, clown; James Belmont, gymnast; Sam Tatnall, rider; and Mrs. Mestayer, rope-walker. Performances continued through the winter and ended March 4, 1816. After a two-month hiatus, the Boston Circus re-opened on May 21 with Davis as rider; a Canadian rope-walker, Mr. Chesebrough; Mr. and Mrs. Mestayer; Master James Belmont; and Mr. Spriggs. They only lasted until June 17 and went on to Portland, Maine, performing there from August 8 through October 11. Their year ended at Portsmouth, New Hampshire, where they worked from October 23 until November 1.

The "Hippodrama" by Any Other Name Takes a Bow

The year 1816 reflected the post-war boom: the United States had won "The Second War of Independence" and was now in a position to assert itself around the world. Robert Fulton's monopoly was broken, and itinerant steamboat captains were eager to ferry cargo and passengers up and down the inland waterways. Demand for foreign and domestic manufactured luxuries grew at a prodigious rate, and people spent money, even if that meant borrowing it. Cheap land was an allure few could resist, and Westward expansion began in full force.

It is not surprising, then, that Victor Pepin chose this time to return from Europe and reinvent himself as the king of the American circus. He opened August 12 in Philadelphia, the scene of so many past successes, by refurbishing the Olympic at Ninth and Walnut Streets. Times had changed, however, and finding it difficult to keep the circus operating, Pepin supplemented his income by offering riding lessons, training and stabling horses. His company included Menial, Master Peter Coty, a new addition, Mr. Garcia, and the horses Mentor and Palafox.[7] The double income did not prove adequate and might have marked the end of Pepin's career when luck fell his way.

Horseman James West appeared at Astley's between April (with Ducrow)[8] and July 1801, where "Equestrian Exercises, by the first Troop in England, particularly Mr. West will perform his unequalled Horsemanship."[9] He later formed his own troupe; in 1814, West supplied the equestrian company when the Royal Circus briefly reintroduced circus-type performances. Seeking a wider venue for his talents, he and his performers reached America in November 1816.

Perhaps having met in Europe and anticipated his arrival, Pepin promptly engaged West and his troupe for twelve nights at the Olympic in Philadelphia. Opening November 28, the combined company included riders James West, William Lawson, John Rogers and Mrs. William Williams; Mr. Campbell, clown; Walter Williams; Master George Yeaman; William Williams, clown; J. Blackmore, slack-rope; and Mrs. James West.

During this time, two significant developments occurred: Campbell introduced still vaulting from a springboard (as opposed to a trampoline), and on December 19, the company presented *Timour the Tartar*,[10] a melodrama involving high horsemanship that became a hit with audiences.

Hippodrama

The word "hippodrama" is a combination of "hippodrome" and "drama." In 1796, even the word "Hippodrome" had to be explained to English readers as signifying a place where horse races and feats of the dexterous management of the horse were performed. To that account, the Hippodrome in Constantinople was cited, along with a description of the Turks, their "surprisingly fleet" horses and the practice of throwing the "jirid."[11]

"Hippodrama" has been retrospectively applied to such equestrian productions as *Timour the Tartar*, although the word was

Roman chariot racing, as envisioned by P. T. Barnum in 1886. Barnum's "Farewell Tour" before leaving for Europe consisted of three circus companies, performing in three big rings, each 45 feet in diameter, and upon an elevated stage 60 by 80 feet. In addition to the Roman Hippodrome, there was his Museum of Living Curiosities, the International Congress of Giants and two double-intense menageries. (*Eau Claire News* [WI], August 28, 1886)

not used in the early 1700s. "Melo-drama," or "Spectacle," was used exclusively, referencing high horsemanship or plays where horses were considered as actors.

Clearly, plays involving intricate equestrian involvement were an integral part of theater. As early as 1683, a live "Pegasus" was used in Pierre Corneille's *Andromede*, and the idea of blending mythology, history and horsemanship was interwoven throughout the performances of Astley's Amphitheatre, and later at the Royal Circus and the Cirque Olympique, Paris.[12]

Astley's Amphitheatre in London featured such pieces as "Fair Rosamond," where, "The entry of *Henry the Second* into London, after his victories in France, preceded by a band of horsemen in complete armour, forms a striking object, and very particular ingenuity has been shewn in the manner of discovering the retreat of the fair heroine in Woodstock bower."[13] Astley, Jr., described, "that being desirous of bringing forward Spectacles and Pantomimes at the Theatre, wherein Combats, Processions, &c. are performed on a great number of real Horses, he has, at a very considerable expense (and which has been several weeks in preparation), completed a Moveable Stage, enabling him to produce the following amusements," including "The Death of Abercromby," a Grand Military and Naval Spectacle.[14]

The actual origins of "hippodrama" in its current sense probably began on April 26, 1810, when "An entirely New Grand Equestrian and Pedestrian Spectacle, called *The Blood-Red Knight*, or the *Fatal Bridge*," featuring Messrs. Crossman, Davis, Collet, Makeen, R. Jones, Rose, Mrs. Brooks and Mrs. Astley, premiered at the Royal Amphitheatre. The Spectacle terminated "with a grand attack by land and water on the Usurper's Castle, and Defeat of the Blood-Red Knight, by Warriors on real Horses."[15] It was an instant success, and a contemporary review praised the last scene "as not only the most perfect picture of a battle ever yet exhibited on a stage, but of an *equestrian* battle, two troops of *horse* being seen to skirmish over a bridge and on the stage, during the whole scene, and some of both the horses and their riders being seen driven into the river, or expiring on the land."[16]

It is significant to note that part of the success of Astley's was attributed to an "overflow of noble and fashionable spectators. The singular merits of *The Blood-Red Knight*, and the total exclusion of all improper characters from the lower boxes, may account for the marked distinction and preference bestowed on this theatre."[17]

Astley's season closed October 15, 1810, *The Blood-Red Knight* contributing to "the most lucrative season ever known at any theatre of this description."[18] This prompted larger and grander stage presentations: among the most famous of these crafted in the *Red Knight's* wake were *Blue Beard* and Matthew Gregory's ("Monk" Lewis') *Timour the Tartar*.

The New Theatre Royal, Covent Garden, obtained rights to the Spectacle in 1811. *Timour* was billed in the legitimate theater as a "Romantic Melo-Drama," and repeated "every evening till further notice."[19]

By August, the equestrian play had become so popular a satire of it appeared at the Haymarket Theatre, concluding "with an exhibition of battles, blue lights, and cavalry (half men and half basket-work), in which the last scene of *Timour the Tartar* is closely imitated and burlesqued, in the first style of extravagance."[20] The Christmas Pantomime of 1811 even included a live elephant, "which the Managers with a very laudable liberality have purchased for the entertainment of the town at this season of the year." Thus, Mr. Kemble, as the High Priest, brought forward the Mother of the Gods, "no longer flying on a Goose, or animating the carcase of an Ape (Perouse), but riding on an elephant,— her Car drawn by Lions, Tigers, and winged Horses, the CORYBANTES sounding their brass, and *Timour the Tartar* in the rear." (Charles Kemble is mentioned by Durang [p. 123] as performing with him in the play *Point of Honor* later in the century.)

Interestingly, "malicious critics ... would rather see Lions and Tigers in pasteboard, and a menagerie of stuffed monsters, nay, even respectable actors degraded to the performance of the characters of these beasts, than the noble animals themselves." Insightfully, however, the author ventured to speculate that the elephant would become a fixed favorite,[21] and indeed, elephants (and even lions and tigers) would become staples in the coming decades.

Timour the Tartar continued playing in 1812, with Mr. Farley and then M. G. Lewis as Timour at Covent Garden.[22] Still playing in 1814, it was presented "in all its original splendour, and with the assistance of the Grand Equestrian Troop," along with *The Miller and His Men*.[23] On June 4, 1815, a benefit for Mr. Farley was given,

The bold fact was, if advertising were to be believed, that W. C. Coup's New United Monster Show was "actually worth going 1,000 miles to see." Along with his performing elephants, Coup offered a school of baby sea lions, sea elephants, sea leopards and the baby sea lion, only 14 days old, the first born in captivity. While aquariums are not associated with circuses, they became a rage in the latter part of the 19th century, and no self-respecting menagerie was without its "sea monsters." (*Indiana Progress* [PA], July 1, 1880)

the advertisement noting "a variety of Entertainments, with, (by permission of Messrs. Astley, Davis & Parker) TIMOUR THE TARTAR, in which the Equestrian Troop, and the unrivalled Stud of Horses will appear."[24] The "Grand Equestrian spectacle," as it was called, continued as a British mainstay into the 1830s.

Blue Beard was another spectacle of the genre, popularized in the British theater by April 1791, when a version of the well-known story titled *Barbe bleu* played in Wargrave. The prominent cast included Delpini as the lead character, Lord Barrymore as Pierrot, Anthony Pasquin as the Devil, with Wathen and Miss Richards in supporting roles.[25] Covent Garden offered *Blue Beard, or, The Flight of Harlequin* in December 1791, with a review stating:

> We have lately had occasion to observe that Pantomime is coming into competition with Comedy; and that in general, its story is better imagined, and its incidents adjusted and connected with more skill and effect.
> The present Pantomime is founded on the old and well-known tale of Blue-Beard, and consists of alarming or pleasing events — as poor Columbine is subjected to the power of Blue-Beard, or finds opportunities of escaping with Harlequin.
> The Scenes and Decorations are admirable; particularly the Cottage on Fire; the Flying Chariot; Blue-beard on the Serpent; and his Fiery Palace.[26]

By Christmas season 1797, "the dramatic *mélange* of *Bluebeard*" appeared at the Drury-Lane Theatre, penned by Mr. Colman.[27] Another version, this time an equestrian spectacle reworked as *Black Beard*, appeared at Astley's in early 1800, along with a New Comic

Pantomime, *Quixote and Sancho* or *Harlequin Warrior*, "adapted for Stage Representation, and got up under the immediate superintendence of Mr. Astley, jun.—In the course of the Pantomime will be introduced on the Stage, two Squadrons of Horse, mounted by Warriors clad in Gold and Silver Armour, who will go through various Evolutions of Ancient Warfare." Both garnered rave reviews from "not only crowded but overflowing" patrons, who appreciated the "*four Black Giants*" seen in "terrific array, wielding their large and enormous bodies across the stage."[28] By June 29, the production had earned £4,000 for Astley's Amphitheatre.[29]

Neither *Timour the Tartar* nor *Bluebeard* could be considered highbrow theater, and five years after "the noble and fashionable spectators" filled the boxes at Astley's, both productions were held out as prime examples of "costly nonsense and dumb shews" demanded by "the people who prescribe the taste" of what proprietors must present.[30] The people, in this case, being those of the lower orders, who filled up the seats night after night. And so it proved in the United States, where *Timour* and similar productions, produced as lavish equestrian spectacles, took off like a shot, filling the coffers of stage managers while infusing new blood into the theater and the circus.

"Improper characters" kept from the seats in England included those of rowdy conduct and most certainly prostitutes. James West would learn from Astley's 1810 success. During the appearance of his company in Boston in 1817, he ran the following notice: "No females of a *certain description* admitted in the boxes."[31] While high-sounding in tone, Cyprians comprised large numbers of theatergoers, and it was tacitly acknowledged by wiser men that their money was as good as anyone else's, especially in a more cosmopolitan city like New York.

John Durang noted, "James West made a great sensation here, and their business was tremendous. The Olympic was crowded nightly, to its very extent, and the Old Chestnut street theatre felt the sudden opposition seriously." Although *Timour the Tartar* had previously been staged at the Chestnut and the Olympic, "James West was the first to explore the dramatic possibilities of horsemanship."[32] During its run, *Timour* added as much as $1,000 a performance to the circus treasury.[33]

More specifically, Durang described the production:

The manner with which they did their pantomime business, their combats, and c., took our audience by surprise.

> Ramparts were scaled by the horses, breaches were dashed into, and a great variety of new business was introduced. The horses were taught to imitate the agonies of death, and they did so in a manner which was astonishing. In the last scene, where *Zorilda*, mounted on her splendid white charger, ran up the stupendous cataract to the very height of the stage, the feat really astonished the audience. Perhaps no event in our theatrical annals ever produced so intense an excitement as that last scene. The people in the pit and boxes arose with a simultaneous impulse to their feet, and with canes, hands and wild screams, kept the house in one uproar of shouts for at least five minutes. The next day the success of the piece was the general topic of conversation."[34]

Pepin and West Create Circus History

James West left Philadelphia in January 1817, taking *Timour* to New York, where it played from January 22 to February 28. Next followed stops at Boston (from March 15 to

26) and then at the Providence, Rhode Island Theatre, where *Blue Beard* was added to the program. Concluding toward the middle of April, West returned to Boston, where the cast included J. Blackmore, rider and slack-wire; Master George Yeaman, rider; Mr. Campbell, clown to Blackmore; Mrs. William Williams, rider; with Mr. Stamp, Walter Williams, William West (James' brother), Mr. Parker, William Lawson, Mr. Clark, William Williams, John Rogers, Mr. Dunbar and Mr. Laidley as actor. President John Adams attended a performance on July 3 at Charlestown.

Advertised as the New Circus, and taking full advantage of President Adams' patronage by advertising same, West made a brief appearance at Worcester, Massachusetts, from July 24 through July 30, 1817. One of the features was a "poney" only thirty-five inches high. Again as the "New Circus," West traveled to New York City, offering two versions of "Billy Buttons" before returning to Philadelphia.

Pepin and his company, comprised of Menial and Robert Bradbury, clowns; Welsh, trampoline; Masters Thomas and Peter Coty, and Messrs Phillips, Garcia and Victor Pepin, riders; and two horses, Othello and Mentor, left Philadelphia before West for a January 1817 opening in Baltimore at a circus building refitted by Mr. Grain. Pepin later played in Pennsylvania, rejoining West for the winter season.[35] Also playing in Philadelphia at the time was Le Sieur Blanchard, "known by the celebrated appellation, *multum in pareo* and the astonishers of the world." He exhibited jugglery at Masonic Hall, competing for audiences not only against Pepin but Sieur Breslan and Potter at Washington Hall. It is possible that around this time Blanchard met Day Francis, "the great juggler and magician," who first appeared in the city in 1817.[36] Billed as a "necromancer," Blanchard and Francis would later tour together.

Cayetano continued his venture in New Orleans, adding a pantomime of General Jackson's battle of New Orleans, first presented in January 1817. Over the summer, William West, Menial and Mr. Champeiaux joined his troupe of French tumblers. Tragically, an outbreak of yellow fever took the lives of both Cayetano Mariotini and Champeiaux by November 1817. The company re-formed, with Mr. Bogardus, "first pupil to Mr. Cayetano," Henrietta and Hortense (daughters of Champeiaux), Mrs. Champeiaux, the Young Creole, Mr. Barnett and the horses Antelope and Pluto.

After closing April 5, 1818, Mrs. Champeiaux sold the Olympic Circus building to Messrs. Douvilliers and Barnette (Barnett), who opened *their* show on April 19. Composed primarily of young performers and a "strong-woman" named Madame Jansen, the show closed after less than three months, and the abandoned building was ordered torn down.[37]

By July 1, 1818, a new company, managed by Mr. Vilalliave (also spelled Vilallave and Villalave; "Vilalliave" was the spelling used on a poster for a performance in Worcester), opened in Boston at Roulestone's amphitheatre (Boston Circus). Vilalliave, a well-known tight-rope walker making his first appearance as a proprietor, next went to Salem, and from there to Hathaway's Hall, Worcester, where his handbill advertised:

The Performance Will Commence By The
TIGHT ROPE,
With Balance Pole.

1st *Performer*	The *Little Chinese.*
2d.	The *Young Spaniolet.*
3d.	The *Young Roman.*
4th.	Mrs. *Vilalliave.*

5th.   Mr. *Vilalliave*.

6th.   Mr. *Bedoges*, in the character of a *CLOWN*.

Among the great variety of Feats which they will perform, Mr. VILALLIAVE will dance
on the Rope

A GROTESQUE DANCE,

With a BASKET tied to his Feet, and his Hands and Feet Chained.

There Will Likewise Be Exhibited,

The Dance of the Double Rope,

BY THREE PERSONS

They will afterwards perform a great variety without the Balance Pole, too numerous to
be inserted.

BENDING FEATS,

By the Chinese and Young Spaniolet.

TUMBLING,

By The Company.

Strength of Hercules,

Or

The Egyptian Pyramid;

Performed by Vilalliave.

The Publick are respectfully informed that there will be no pains or exertion spared, to
give a brilliant Exhibition.

Doors open at half past 7, and the Performance to commence at 8 o'clock precisely.[38]

Billed as "Menial and Vilalliave," the company next went to Albany, New York, after
which they dissolved, the latter joining Pepin in Philadelphia.

James West spent the year 1818 in Virginia, constructing a building in Richmond
called the "New Circus." By April 17, the troupe, then in Norfolk, consisted of John Rogers,
riding master; Miss Jones, Master George Yeaman, Master Carnes, riders; Miss C. Dupree,
slack-wire; William Williams, clown; and Mr. Laidley, William Lawson, W. Clark, Mr.
Parsons and Mr. Stitchbury, vaulters. Moving to the theater, they offered *Timour the Tartar*,
May 25–28.

The melodramatic performances proved so popular that West sent the circus people
to Fredericksburg to perform July 25 through August 5. Here, George Yeaman received
billing as "The Flying Horseman," a sobriquet he would use throughout his career. The
troupe then reunited with West in Richmond, where they remained until the end of the
year.

Pepin also performed in Virginia in 1818, opening in Alexandria on February 23. He
and his troupe then moved to Washington, where they, too, presented *Timour the Tartar*.
Next followed a performance at the theater in King George Street, Baltimore, playing *Timour*.

An Uneasy Alliance—The Circus and the Theater

It is easy to see that the concept of "circus people" at this point was neither a set idea
nor a stigma as far as the general public were concerned. West seamlessly glided from athletic performances to "legitimate" theater, sending his gymnasts away not because they were
unwelcome in the playhouse but rather to afford them work. Pepin was also asked to perform *Timour* at the King George and later *Forty Thieves*, another horse-based melodrama.

While *Timour* and *Thieves* were closer to Harlequin than Shakespeare, the productions began their "lives" appealing to the noble and fashionable, only later being lamented as "nonsense" and "dumb"— and that based on upper-class prejudice against the lower orders who filled the seats.

In the future, itinerant American circuses would become associated with rowdy and/or drunken hands, violence and general lawlessness, in part from the swarms of "foot pads" or pickpockets who followed in their wake. Comedies would harbor licentious dialogue, clowns would perform lewd gesticulations and storylines would present suggestive acts. This "immorality," already witnessed to some degree, would later downgrade the reputation of the circus and its performers, making the transition to and from the various acting genres far more difficult. This general bias would eventually compel circus proprietors to promise they would offer nothing offensive to the general audience; and reviews graded them by "moral" standards. The addition of menageries as a separate entity at some circuses (one ticket generally providing admission to both animal displays and tents) afforded a means to escape negative publicity.

Performers took a different view of crossing genres, as evidenced by two theatrical producers, James H. Caldwell and James Entwisle (who managed theaters in Alexandria, Virginia, and Washington, D.C.), who wished to offer spectacles on the order of James West. In the spring of 1818, they offered Pepin the opportunity to present his horse-dramas on alternate days from traditional drama, with equestrians to appear after the plays. They advertised:

> During the season it is the intention to produce, in a style of splendor and magnificence never equalled in this, and which, they presume has not been surpassed in any other theatre several spectacle melodramas, in which all the horses will be actively employed.

The concept may have proved successful, but, as John Durang reported, Caldwell and Entwisle did not get along even before their arrangement with Pepin. The combined company was split into factions, salaries were not paid regularly, and within the troupe, "lines of demarcation were drawn between stage and equestrian" performers. On June 6, 1818, Caldwell withdrew from the partnership, and the theatrical department dissolved. (Caldwell went on to establish theaters in New Orleans, and later operated the first theatrical circuit along the Mississippi and Ohio rivers.)

Taking Campbell, Russell and J. Blackmore from West's company, Pepin made a new partnership arrangement with Entwisle to open the Olympic in the fall. Entwisle went to England with funds to engage performers and procure new material, while Pepin put together a corporation of stockholders to purchase and improve the Olympic Theatre. On October 21, 1818, Pepin bought the Olympic from Charles Bird for $34,000 and then handed it over to William Meredith (an attorney), Dr. Rodman Coxe and Frederick Ravesies (merchants). They, in turn, established a declaration of trust, the property being held on behalf of 115 cultural leaders known as the "Proprietors of the Walnut Street Theatre."

Entwisle did not return when expected, but by prior agreement, Pepin opened the Olympic on November 4, 1818, with a show relying primarily on circus acts. Entwisle finally arrived in Philadelphia in late November, but his project had been a failure. The dramatic troupe closed February 19, 1819, but Pepin continued with his circus until March

22, concluding with a benefit performance for himself.[39] During one performance, "Betty," an elephant owned by Hackaliah Bailey and already being exhibited in Philadelphia, made an appearance on stage.

Pepin next took his company to New York, opening June 22, 1818. They presented:

Grand Mounted Entry
Master Thomas, Horsemanship
Two Horse *Allemande* by Miss Wheland and Sam Tatnall
Mr. Mayhier, Slack-rope
Trained Horse Othello
Mr. Caussin, Feats with a Stick
Master Peter Coty, Horsemanship
Master McCarn, Horsemanship
Madame Caussin, Tight-rope
Sam Tatnall, Whirlwind Rider
Still Vaulting by the Whole Troupe
Mr. Campbell, Clown

Mrs. Williams was added July 6, performing on the slack-rope. The show closed October 5.[40]

Returning to Philadelphia in November, Pepin was joined by the Vilalliaves, whose company had disbanded. Entwisle's dramas took over the major portion of the entertainment until February 20, 1819, when he concluded his efforts; from then until March 20, the circus performed alone.

During the winter run, prices were reduced to encourage business. Competitors in 1819 included Sena Sam, the famous East India magician playing the halls,[41] and an exhibition of the "Mammoth Child," a five-year-old recently arrived from Europe. The child stood 3'7" high, was 3'5" around the body, 25" around the thigh, 15" around the calf and weighed 130 pounds.[42]

The real cause of falling ticket sales, however, came from the panic and depression of 1819, an economic disaster reaching the farthest corners of the nation. After the War of 1812 ended, prosperity reigned. Fulton's monopoly of the Mississippi ended, and huge numbers of Americans traveled west for cheap land, creating a new business of land speculation. Profits soared on the selling and re-selling of western lands, but instead of paying down their debts, speculators bought more land. Banks printed their own money to keep up with demand, eventually leading to inflation. At the same time, demand for manufactured goods sharply declined, causing wages to be slashed and jobs cut. Borrowing increased and personal debt mounted.

Banks curtailed the money they printed, but it was too late. The Bank of the United States, along with state banks, called in their loans; without gold or silver to re-pay, land speculators went bankrupt. Their failure caused local banks to fail, and panic gripped the nation. A cry to return to the gold standard and get away from paper money went hand-in-hand with accusations against imported foreign goods. Cries notwithstanding, the United States went into a depression from which it did not fully recover for six years.

Hoping to inspire business, Pepin enlarged his circus in New York for the 1819 season, beginning May 17. The company featured Miss Wheland, Sam Tatnall, Mr. Bogardus, Mr. Boulen, Masters Thomas, Peter Coty, and McCarn, riders; Mayhier on the slack-rope; Caussin, strong-man; Mrs. Caussin, tight-rope; Campbell and Joseph Welch, clowns; and the horse Othello. On August 11, they offered the pantomime *The Battle of New Orleans*. Business must have been successful, as a benefit for Campbell at "the Circus in New York" netted $1,200.[43]

Pepin next took the company to Boston, where they played at Washington Gardens adjoining Roulestone's amphitheatre, followed by a stand at Newburyport, Massachusetts. On October 28, 1819, Pepin departed for the West Indies, taking with him his wife and two children, Miss Wheland, Mr. and Mrs. Sam Tatnall, Miss Brown, Campbell, Menial, Bogardus, Mayhier, Boulen, Moran, Garcia, Desolane, Thomas, McCarn, Peter Coty and Mr. Beal.[44]

James West built an arena in Washington on C Street between Sixth and Fourth. Performances began January 13, 1819, and ran until February 24, with a company that included riders John Rogers, Master Carnes, George Yeaman, and William Lawson; Miss C. Dupree, slack-wire; William Williams, clown; and Mr. Stitchbury, James Johnson and Mr. Thayer, vaulters. The back of the pit was partitioned off for people of color.

In 1806, President Jefferson appointed a board of commissioners to plot the route for a National Road uniting East and West. The Cumberland Road, as it came to be called, ran from Cumberland, Maryland, through southwest Pennsylvania to Wheeling, Virginia. It opened in 1818,[45] providing passage not only for immigrants and goods, but for traveling circuses. James West's company used this road to move to Pittsburg, where they were greeted by the *Gazette*, which wrote, "Indeed, we must hail this corps with infinite pleasure when we look back and reflect how Pittsburg has been gulled with performances of every kind since the visit of Mr. Pepin"—a somewhat guarded statement, considering the word "gulled" was a 19th century term for "cheated."

West then traveled to Chillicothe, Ohio, and on to Cincinnati, where their general deportment was lauded in the newspapers. In September, "West's Equestrian and Melodramatic Company" performed *Timour the Tartar* at Lexington, Kentucky, with Mrs. West in the starring role of Zorilda. She repeated the act the same month in Louisville. They opened February 3 at Charleston at the Charleston Theatre with *Timour* and later *Bluebeard*. With the company were riders Miss and Master Carnes, and George Yeaman; Miss C. Dupree, slack-wire; C. Breslaw; John Rogers; T. Welch and William Welch, clowns; William Williams, vaulter; and William Lawson.[46]

By September, West's troupe occupied the old circus building on Broadway in New York; after a two-month stand they finished the year in Baltimore. From January 1, 1821, until March 20 they worked in Washington and then returned to Baltimore, opening March 26. During the course of their stay, *Timour the Tartar* and another horse melodrama, *The Secret Mine*, were performed.

Emulating earlier circuses, West next traveled to upstate New York, where they played Poughkeepsie, Troy and Albany before going northward into Canada. The month of June saw them in Montreal, then July in Quebec and back to Montreal for another four weeks, stretching from August 7 until September 4. William West left the company, and his brother took the show back into the United States, where they remained in the Boston area until January 1822.

Victor Pepin remained in the Caribbean until the summer of 1821, when he sailed to Florida from Havana. After a brief season in Pensacola, his troupe next appeared in New Orleans, where they set up at the St. Philip Street Theatre, offering equestrian performances. At this point, the company consisted of Pepin, a nine-year-old boy named Master Emile, Mr. Angot, Masters Peter Coty and McCarn, Menial, the Young American, Bogardus and the horses Conqueror and Romeo. Those not returning were Campbell, Boulen, Thomas, Mayhier and Miss Wheland, who may have stayed in the Caribbean or returned to Europe.[47]

During the winter of 1822-23, Pepin partnered with Mr. Barnet (also spelled "Barnett" and "Barnette"), who, with Mr. Douvilliers, had purchased the New Orleans Circus from Mrs. Champeiaux after the deaths of her husband and Cayetano in 1818. Billed as "Pepin and Barnet," they traveled up the Mississippi by steamboat, appearing at Natchez, St. Louis and Louisville before wintering in Lexington, Kentucky.

The year 1822 was also to witness the last American circus performances by James West. His final season began February 11 in New York, primarily featuring horse dramas. To give them added zest, a camel and an elephant were added June 16 for the production of *Bluebeard*, with Walter Williams also using them in his leaping act. Closing August 5, West announced the sale of his assets to Stephen Price and Edmund Simpson of the New Theatre, New York, and returned to Europe, later partnering with Andrew Ducrow in 1824.

Victor Pepin distanced himself from the eastern seaboard, and James West's departure put a literal and perhaps figurative end to another chapter of circus history. From 1816 onward, Pepin was a major force in the development of the genre John Bill Ricketts had established in the United States; joining with West in 1816, the pair not only carried on the tradition, but traveled to many distant cities. Along the way, they added the horse melodrama, where trained animals were truly the featured performers, earning a considerable fortune from their endeavors.

Men, women and apprentices from Europe received training, experience and exposure to the American way of life. A number would carry on their careers under new managers, surviving in what would become a cutthroat but always exciting business. More often than not, like Pepin, they would stay in their adopted country and, when their time came, be buried beneath its soil. Some, like West, would return to their roots, no doubt inspiring the Old World with the life's blood of the New.

The times, they were a-changing. In 1875, P. T. Barnum announced that "in consequence of injury that would result to the magnificent wardrobe of Barnum's Hippodrome, if exposed on the street, and on account of the fact that the lady riders and charioteers cannot endure the fatigue of the street parade, the procession will consist only of the superb band of music, on foot, followed by the blooded race horses, ridden by jockeys." (*Freeport Journal* [IL], July 28, 1875)

This was as it should be, for the Circus was the living stage for human endeavor: challenge, creativity, perseverance, success and failure on both small and grand scales. Ahead lay the explosion of new faces, the development of complex gymnastics, the daring of equestrian feats, the laughter of clowns and the addition of menageries. Behind sat the foundation, once constructed of wooden buildings, which harbored the hallowed halls and ethereal memories. These would give way to canvas tents that in turn would create layers of new commemorations, pushing ever onward.

9

"In the Rude State of Nature"

The feats performed by Mr. Hunter on the tight-rope and his horsemanship without saddle
or bridle requires no comment; no person can have an idea of them unless he sees for himself—
they are said to be the most astonishing ever attempted by any man.[1]

With James West gone, the New York team of Edmund Simpson and Stephen Price had effectively eliminated competition for their New Theatre. The playhouse, located at 21, 23 and 25 Park Row, about 200 feet east of Ann Street, backed Theatre Alley. Designed by the French architect Marc Isambard Brunel (who fled his native country to avoid the Reign of Terror, and was then the city's engineer), construction costs ran out of control, forcing changes in the design and resulting in a rather plain exterior. Eventually costing $130,000, the three-story structure measured 80 feet wide by 165 feet deep. It followed the European design of placing a gallery over three tiers of boxes overlooking the horse-shoe-shaped pit.

Neighboring Bridewell Prison, the local poorhouse, and a field of squatters, the first performance at the New Theatre on January 29, 1798, grossed $1,232, paid by an overflow crowd of about 2,000 patrons. In 1805, the New Theatre was sold to John Jacob Astor and John Beekman, who maintained ownership until it was demolished in 1848. In 1807, the English architect, J. J. Holland, remodeled the interior, adding gas lighting, coffee rooms, more spacious boxes and repainting the ceiling. Stephen Price became manager in 1808. An English actor, who spent much of his time in England, Price established the British "star system," presenting English drama, Italian opera and "upper-class bills."[2]

In 1810, Edmund Simpson, another imported English comedic actor, became stage manager for Price, the lessee. Simpson, known for his studious and painstaking performances, also displayed "a hardness of manner that interfered with his popularity." Permanently crippled when his leg was broken in an accident with the stage machinery, he and Price introduced the noted British players of the day to American audiences. In 1821, he became working manager under Price.[3]

The theater burned down in May 1820, but was rebuilt the following year. As New York City's only theater, showbills dubbed it "The Theatre," and during the early 1820s, it enjoyed its most profitable period.

Now in control of West's circus, the pair sent the company, under Sam Tatnall, to Philadelphia, where they leased the Walnut Street Theatre and refitted it for equestrian performances. Adopting the old name of "The Olympic," they played twelve weeks, beginning September 21, 1822. William Lawson served as master of the circle and John Parker as ballet-master. The equestrian/circus troupe included Tatnall; George Yeaman; William Williams, slack-rope and clown; Mrs. Williams, slack-wire and pantomimist; Champlin, balance and wire-dancer; James Belmont, clown; Miss C. Dupree, slack-wire; John Rogers, rider; and Messrs. Carnes, Roper and James Johnson.

It was during this engagement that Price and Simpson brought the equestrian James Hunter from England, where he had played at Astley's. Hunter's specialty was riding "in the rude state of nature," or without saddle or bridle, an entirely new concept to American audiences. The appellation "wonderful" was quickly bestowed on him for his style of riding, and spectators crowded the Olympic to watch and applaud his skill.[4] Stuart Thayer, in *Annals of the American Theatre*, stated that after Hunter introduced what was later to be called "bareback riding" (the term did not come into common usage for decades), equestrians were divided into two categories: those who could copy James Hunter's style and those who could not. Bareback riders commanded twice the salary of "pad riders," and no pad rider ever achieved a great reputation after Hunter.

Riding "without dress" also meant that a horseman had little control over his animal. This led to the position of riding master, whose duty it was to keep the horse at a steady and appropriate pace. Eventually, this would lead to the title of "ringmaster."[5]

It did not take Sam Tatnall long to realize this new style of riding would soon dominate horsemanship. He and his pupil Charles LaForrest ("LaForest") secretly practiced to learn the technique and achieved so much success that they proposed to perform it in the ring.

Realizing his uniqueness was in jeopardy, Hunter immediately appealed to Price and Simpson in New York, and they prohibited the pair from performing their feats "without saddle and bridle" in the circus. Rebuffed, Tatnall appealed to the public and succeeded in bringing them over to his side. With or without permission, for his benefit night Tatnall made up his own program and displayed his horsemanship with great success.

Along more theatrical lines, James Roberts made his first appearance with the company in a piece he had written, giving imitation of popular actors.[6]

The company next moved to Baltimore in December. Sam Tatnall was replaced by George Blythe, another transplant from Astley's, where he had been billed

Riding "in a rude state," or bareback riding as it came to be called, was introduced in America by James Hunter in 1822. Once witnessed by astonished patrons, the art of performing without a saddle became a mainstay of circus performers. Clowns were frequently used to assist riders during their performance. The paper-covered hoop the clown holds was referred to as a "balloon." (*Herald and Torch Light* [MD], April 19, 1871) as an equestrian and also served as the "director-general for the London Amphitheatre." Also added were Mr. and Mrs. Parker, Mr. Maxy (Maxcey), a Kent bugler and Mr. Honey, a clown. During this season, James Hunter also performed on the tight-rope, as well as displaying his equestrian talent. They remained there until January 15, 1823. (Thayer reported that Hunter made his first appearance with the Price and Simpson company beginning December 9 in Baltimore, and around the same time Tatnall formed his own troupe and set out on his own. This timeline would indicate Tatnall left to perform his own version of bareback riding at the Lancaster, Pennsylvania Circus, as indicated above, beginning January 7. Despite his success, he returned in March.)

The Price and Simpson company performed in Washington from January 18 until February 28, with George Blythe, Parker, William Lawson, George Yeaman, Carnes, William Williams, Laidley, Lee, James Johnson, Mrs. Parker, James Hunter and the horse General Jackson. Some of the company then returned to Baltimore, but the horsemen, particularly Blythe and Tatnall, were summoned to New York, where their expertise was put to good use performing *Timour the Tartar* at the New Theatre.[7]

With Price and Simpson the absentee owners, George Blythe became director of the ring, with Daniel Reed acting as manager for the Philadelphia season beginning on May 1, 1823. Mr. Asten replaced William Lawson as riding master. William Dioneford, a young actor from London, and Master Turner made their first appearance with the company. Two novelties of the season were *Ali Pacha*, or *The Greek Struggle for Liberty*, premiering for Hunter's benefit, and a patriotic drama, *The Two Sisters*, or *Heroines of Switzerland*, written by W. Barrymore.[8]

After one month the company went to New York and opened June 2 at the Broadway Circus, judiciously avoiding competition with the New Theatre (re-named the Park Theatre around 1826). This was especially important, as the Chatham Garden Theatre was built in 1823, and, for the first time since West's departure, offered a real challenge to Price's dominance.[9] Opening day at the Circus offered:

> Grand entree, twelve horses
> Scotch ballet by Parker, Roper, Yeaman and Mrs. Carnes
> The trained Horse, General Jackson
> Horsemanship by the Entire Company
> Horsemanship by Master Napoleon and B. Turner
> Comic Song by Mr. Roberts
> Horsemanship by Mr. Blythe
> Still-vaulting by Yeaman, Tatnall, Parker, Turner, Lee, Lawson,
>   Johnson, Asten, Roper, Rogers and Sessford
> Horsemanship by George Yeaman
> The "Hunter Tailor" by Yeaman and Parker

James Hunter and William Williams joined the troupe on June 10, with Williams billing himself as "Chatterbox Gabblejoke," a *nom de plume* he would use often. An English character actor named Joseph Cowell, who had worked for Price and Simpson since 1821, took over the management of the company in July. They returned to Philadelphia for the winter season.[10]

Joseph Cowell divided the company after the season ended in December, sending one part to Boston and the other to Savannah, Georgia. They reunited in New York in May and returned to Philadelphia in August. With Cowell as the chief manager, his staff included Mr. Gale as melodramatic manager, George Blythe as equestrian manager, Lawson and

Rogers as ring-masters, T. Honey as prompter and John Parker as ballet-master. Scene-painters were Henry Wilkins and Henry Isherwood, an artist who garnered much praise for his painted scenery.[11]

Artists at the Olympic included George Yeaman, and Masters George Sweet and Sylvanus Spencer, riders; William Lawson; William Williams, clown; Mr. Roberts, comic song (who achieved success with the character of "Bob Logic," which became his signature specialty); and Mr. Parker, hornpipe. In a new and "horrifying" act, James Stoket, a slack-rope artist, performed the new trick of seemingly hanging himself by the neck as though he were on the gallows. Although renounced by the moral authorities, it became a success with the paying public.

As Price-Simpson productions were always heavily stocked with dramas, *Lafayette*, or *The Castle of Olmutz*, written by Samuel Woodworth of New York, was performed October 1. *The Cataract of the Ganges* (a new horse-drama already playing at the New Theatre, New York, starring George Blythe) was introduced in Philadelphia, the company using real water on the stage for added effect. A third play, *Tom and Jerry*, was presented for Cowell's benefit night.[12]

A Riot in Pittsburg

Constructing a circus in Lexington, where they spent the winter months, Pepin and Barnet offered *Timour the Tartar* as one of their main attractions. For the performance of February 25, 1824, Pepin made a plea in the *Kentucky Reporter*, soliciting "sympathy and love for all oppressed Patriots," and in particular "the gallant Greeks, who are now struggling to regain their long-lost liberty." Such an act was more common in Europe than in the United States, where performers shied away from expressing political sentiments. On September 1, 1824, for example, a Mr. Smithers offered a balloon ascension at the Mermaid Tavern, Hackney, England, to aid the Greek nation "in their desperate struggles against the Infidel." Pepin, better known and in a far more advantageous position to raise money, risked his reputation and that of the circus by taking such a stand, and the attempt was admirable.

Perhaps more significant was his comment "...even our own Congress refusing to utter one cheering word in their behalf!" Deriding the government was a dangerous petition, but, interestingly, Pepin, the English-born man, used the words "our own," signifying his personal ties to the country. In fact, Pepin never returned to the land of his birth. After his death in 1845, he was buried in an unmarked grave in New Albany, Indiana, across the Ohio River from Louisville, where he made his home in his declining years.

After tours in Louisville and Cincinnati, the company arrived at Pittsburg in September. Here, to augment his income from circus performances, Pepin apparently opened a riding school "to teach young ladies, &c. to ride gracefully." The newspaper article continued (with asterisks in the original):

> One evening when riding out with other young ladies, accompanied by Mr. Pepin, she [one of his pupils] pretended that her horse was frightened, and caught Mr. Pepin by the hand for protection, but in such a way that he understood her at once. He afterwards received several letters from her, one of which being first intercepted went to disclose **** between them, which he positively denies.

The affair became public knowledge, and she was sent to the country, a letter-writer at the time musing, "'Tis strange that a young girl, worth from 10 to 15,000 dollars, and perhaps not more than 16 years of age, should fall in love with an *old man*, with a wife and a family, but so appears this fact."

On the evening of September 20, when the circus was crowded, a mob surrounded the building and began throwing stones. Things rapidly got out of hand, and they endeavored to tear down the circus. The company had to stop the performance and call for assistance. A lull ensued while women and children were cleared out, then hostilities recommenced between the mob and the circus men, "the latter of whom were all well armed." One of them fired into the crowd, killing a man. This caused the townsmen to think twice, and they disbanded. The circus man "was admitted to bail. But the whole circus company had to seek protection in the common jail, for two or three days."[13]

The dead man was subsequently identified as Hartzell, a laborer not engaged in the fray,[14] and the shooter as a man named Murray, an actor who had been with the circus in Cincinnati. Interestingly, in June 1825, John McFarland, editor of the Pittsburg *Democrat*, was brought up on two indictments for riot, the first involving the death of a man at the Circus and the second for participating in a meeting where Mr. Clay was burned in effigy. The jury could not agree, and the charges were dropped.[15]

At this point, Barnet parted company with Pepin and moved his troupe to Washington, Pennsylvania, thereafter disbanding. Pepin returned to Louisville, where he offered riding lessons.

Pepin toured the summer months of 1825, finding business bad. On November 14, 1825, he ran the following notice:

> This is the first time in my life that I have appealed to the generosity of the
> public, but when my consort, with four children, pierce my heart with their cries
> of want, it cannot be deemed derogatory in letting the world know it, when it is my
> only wish to do all in my power to render assistance to them as a husband and
> father ... V. Pepin.[16]

Pepin engaged in a little melodramatic hyperbole, for his wife and children had remained in Philadelphia during his long absence from that city. Whether or not his plea was answered, he was able to take the company back to Louisville in December. In 1826 he attempted another tour, but in June 1826, Mrs. Pepin filed for divorce. Her petition stated that her husband did not supply her with enough money on which to live and had been involved in an adulterous affair with a circus rider. She was granted a divorce in February 1827.[17]

Victor Pepin gave his last circus performance on February 17, 1827. It was a benefit for the victims of a recent fire in Alexandria, Virginia. He retired to Louisville, making one last appearance in Philadelphia, the scene of so many past triumphs. According to John Durang, Pepin was poor and friendless, seeking an opportunity to give riding lessons as a means of earning a few dollars. The effort does not appear to have been successful, and on February 18, 1831, the managers of the Arch Street Theatre gave him a benefit night. Among those appearing in his honor was the great thespian, Junuis Brutus Booth, forerunner of the Booth acting family.

Perhaps finding the city too full of memories, both good and bad, Pepin traveled to Baltimore the same year, working as a riding instructor. In 1837, he received another benefit night by Fogg & Stickney. He eventually returned to Louisville, where he died in 1845.[18]

James W. Bancker of Albany, New York—
American-Born Proprietor

A descendant of the early Knickerbockers, a name that today still rings recognition to upstate New Yorkers (and which for many years graced the masthead of the evening *Knickerbocker News*), James W. Bancker entered the circus business on February 27, 1824. His building sat at Division and Green Streets in the Capital City, and his performers included the Young American, Mr. Byrnes, William Gates, Master Jacob Burton and the horse, White Surrey.

Already in Albany was "The Grand Caravan" menagerie, managed by John Martin. It featured Tippo Sahib,* a great male Asian elephant imported by Mr. Foster of Philadelphia in 1819. The two establishments bordered one another, and a single ticket could get a patron into both shows; this represented the first time a circus and a menagerie worked in tandem.

When Martin's menagerie left on April 22 to tour, Bancker enlarged his troupe with some familiar names: William West arrived from Montreal, where he had been working with William Blanchard; Bordoleaux, Gonzalo and Westervelt came from New York City, where they had been performing with John Rogers; and Charles Sibery and Miss. C. Dupree also joined. By the end of June, the cast included William West, William Gates, Mrs. Stickney, John Stickney, Master Jacob Burton, Mr. Ostron, Mrs. Thompson and Bancker. They performed in an arena on State Street owned by Samuel B. Parsons of Charleston.

The company played their last performance on June 23, and moved across the state to Syracuse and Rochester, where Bancker offered the *Miller's Frolick*, based on the story of *The Miller and the Coalman*. Destined to become a circus favorite, the concept was a simple one: a miller, dressed in white, meets a coalman, dressed in black. They mark each other in an escalating farce that ends when both are covered with the other's dust and become indistinguishable.[19] At one point, the circus may have crossed into Ohio, for an advert noted, "Exhibition! A Large and learned elephant at Cole's Tavern. Admittance 12½ censts [*sic*]. Children half price."

By November 1824, Bancker was back in Albany, where his company performed until January 26. The circus was subsequently taken over by Samuel McCracken in 1825, and moved into Samuel Parson's new amphitheatre in 1826. Even with the Erie Canal opening up the city, earning a living in entertainment was difficult. In 1824–25 a theater was built on South Pearl Street by a stock company. Opening May 13, 1825, under the management of Charles Gilfert, the first season starred Edwin Booth. The following year Edwin Forrest became a member of the company, playing under Edmund Kean. Despite the fact these were three of the greatest names in legitimate theater, competition from the circus proved too much, aided by the fact they charged a mere 75 and 50 cents for admission. After two seasons, Gilfert departed, taking his theatrical company to the Bowery.[20]

Joseph Cowell remained in charge of Price and Simpson's circus, taking it to Baltimore

---

The name "Tippo," alternately spelled "Tippoo," or "Tipu," and with the word "Sultan" substituted for "Sahib," was derived from the name of an Indian ruler, the sultan of Mysore from 1782–1799. As a name for an elephant, it was meant to convey strength and power, and an association with India. Americans were well familiar with events in India, as the British were involved in a protracted war with the sultan, and news of Lord Cornwallis and Lord Wellesley's success quickly reached across the Atlantic.

in December 1824. Isherwood, who had done such fine work in Philadelphia for the owners, did the same here with the arena. Performers at this time were James Hunter (equestrian and tight-rope), Mr. Parker, George Yeaman, Mr. Lee, Mrs. Thompson, John Rogers, Ben Stoker (slack-rope), T. H. Blakely, Mr. Jamie, Alexander Downie, Masters Spencer and Sweet, and William Lawton as ring-master. The attraction was *Tom Thumb the Great*, a successful burletta imported from England. Washington was the next venue, where the troupe divided, some going to Alexandria, Virginia.

After touring through Augusta and Charleston, they reunited in Philadelphia on May 6, 1825. A foray to the New York Broadway Circus followed, Hunter going on to Montreal and Yeaman joining the Lafayette Circus, newly formed under proprietor C. W. Sandford. They returned to Philadelphia in August, where the company then included James Hunter, Ben Stoker, John Rogers, Sam Stickney, Davis, Parker, Lee, Isaac Asten, T. H. Blakely, Mr. and Mrs. William Williams, George Blythe, and Masters Hunt, George Sweet and John Whittaker.[21] During this time, with Philadelphia lacking any theatrical companies, the circus faced no large-scale competition.

By fall, additions to the company included Collingbourne, a London dancer and pantomimist, and James Kirby, a famous clown and scene painter from the Drury Lane Theatre and Astley's. Astley's had, by this time, undergone a change of ownership and several name changes, possibly prompting Kirby's defection. Similar to many American companies, Astley's Amphitheatre had expanded its dramatic presentations to the point where it was half dramatic, half circus, or, as a contemporary Kentuckian would express it, "half horse, half alligator." A letter from London, dated August 15, 1825, observed, "The feats in horsemanship are nothing extraordinary. Hunter surpasses them."[22] Others in the troupe included John Hallam, comic actor, who first appeared as Joe Steadfast in *The Turnpike Gate*; Palmer

Circus dancing evolved rapidly. In 1869, Yankee Robinson's Consolidated Shows offered the "Ballet of Beautiful Ladies Amazon March" as one of his featured attractions. The elaborate costumes would have added a great deal to the proprietor's expenses — far more than the nondescript performers, many of whom might earn no more than $10 a week. A far cry from a star, who could command ten times that amount. (*Elyria Independent Democrat* [OH], June 2, 1869)

Fisher and his wife (who later became Mrs. E. N. Thayer); Miss Aspinall, dancer; and Harry Moreland, vocalist, who afterwards married Miss Aspinall.

The event of the Philadelphia season was a production of *The Talking Bird*, first performed on October 14, with scenery painted by Kirby and Williams. Kirby also acted two parts and played the clown. The story conveyed the supernatural idea of Paradise, with John Durang noting, "The machinery of this piece was never surpassed in this country, if indeed equaled."[23]

Curiously, the sole item meriting mention in exchange newspapers was that a young man from Tennessee, making his first visit to Philadelphia, had his pocket book, containing $1,500 in U.S. bank notes, cut from his pocket while attending the Circus.[24] Such news items, clearly more important to editors of the day than a description of acts, had a cumulative effect in creating what would be a negative connotation of the circus in general and circus people in particular.

Samuel McCracken took over James W. Bancker's circus in 1825, billing it, appropriately enough, "McCracken's Circus." It left Albany for Hartford, appearing there in early May. Offering members of the Connecticut General Assembly free tickets to the show, McCracken brought his company to the attention of authorities, who then charged him with violating section 88 of a 1773 law, prohibiting "on any public stage or place whatsoever any games, tricks, plays, shows, tumbling, rope-dancing, puppet shows or feats of uncommon dexterity or agility of body," at the risk of incurring a fine of $60–$200.[25] An attempt to suppress the circus passed the House but was finally tabled in the Senate. The ramifications, however, would resurface the following year.

McCracken's Circus went on to Poughkeepsie, Syracuse, Canandaigua and Rochester that season.

Connecticut Blue Laws

The Lafayette Circus of C. W. Sandford, constructed on the island of Manhattan, opened for business July 4, 1825, and ran its premiere season through March 26, 1826. During this period the company consisted of Sam Tatnall, J. W. Bancker, John Stickney, William Lawson, William Harrington, Chris Hughes, Alexander Downie, A. Herbert, Mr. Stimpson, Archibald Madden and Master Charles LaForrest, who had served as Tatnall's pupil in 1822–23. (LaForrest subsequently married Sophie Eberle, sister of performers Harry and David. Apprenticeships, as in any other profession, were a way in which a youth could train for his specialty. Apprentices were frequently bought and sold between masters.) Also included were Bogardus; Rhigas (strongman); Eberle and his trained horses Romeo and Napoleon; Master Charles Brown, an eight-year-old; Masters John S. Whittaker and Benjamin Stickney (younger brother of John and Sam); and George Yeaman soon joined. W. Burroughs served as theater manager, and James Hunter equestrian manager.

Sandford offered horsemanship and equestrian melodrama, including *Timour the Tartar* and *Bluebeard*. One of his principal attractions was an automaton trumpeter, "or a machine in the shape of a man, that performs all sorts of tunes on a trumpet." The process "whereby wood and wire can be made to perform the functions of the human lungs and throat" proved fascinating to spectators, and the *New York American* urged the curious to "see for themselves."[26]

The invitation to witness the marvels of the circus did not apply in Connecticut. In March 1826, James Hunter took his troupe to Hartford, where they established themselves in a building on property owned by a private citizen. It must have been a rude structure, with seats but no stage (at least not one traditionally defined by theatrical usage). The magistrates, having already argued against public displays of entertainment when Sam McCracken passed through town the year before, were quick to act.

On March 13, the performer was arrested for violating Connecticut Blue Laws and brought to trial before the County Court in the case *Sunday Inhabitants v James Hunter*. Witnesses testified as to the type of feats performed by the defendant and observed that four or five hundred persons were present at the circus. Hunter countered by stating his circus was erected on private land and no one was admitted without a ticket. After two failed attempts to reach a verdict, Hunter was "convicted and fined $60 for the crime of 'uncommon dexterity and agility of body,' in riding a horse without saddle or bridle in the Circus lately erected at that place, and leaping through a hoop, walking a slack wire, turning a somerset from a horse, still-vaulting and dancing a hornpipe dexterously to music."[27]

For his own part, Hunter published a card expressing the better part of valor:

> Mr. Hunter, being about to leave Hartford, takes this public method of expressing his acknowledgment to its citizens generally, for the very kind reception given him during his short stay among them.... He leaves Hartford with no other feeling than those of good will toward its citizens — he leaves it in the hope of one day revisiting it under happier circumstances.

The actual statute under which he was convicted was not repealed until 1852.[28]

An early pioneer of the "star system," Hunter spent the rest of the year going from troupe to troupe, making brief appearances. This enabled proprietors to advertise his name and thus draw crowds without being obligated to pay his high salary for any length of time.

Several significant events involving individuals destined to play a huge role in the development of the circus occurred in 1826. A partnership between Nathan Howes, Aron Turner and Sylvester Reynolds formed a company, which appeared in Portsmouth, New Hampshire, in July. Members featured were Nathan Howes, riding-master and performing "Billy Buttons"; Masters Wilson and Seth B. Howes (younger brother of Nathan), riders; Mr. Regan, clown; Reynolds; and Mr. Pennoyer. Sam Stickney joined later in the season. By December, they moved into the Washington Garden, Boston, joined by James Hunter and Richard Hians, with Wilson Howes mentioned in their advertisements. Reynolds died in Maine later that year.[29]

Also bowing in 1826 was the Washington Circus, a partnership between Jeremiah P. Fogg, Isaac Quick and Abraham H. Mead, all from Westchester County, New York. Members of the troupe were Sam Stickney, William Lawson, Walter Raymond and Master J. Raymond, Major DeGroot, Chris Hughes and Master Levi J. North, here an apprentice to Isaac Quick (North would earn fame in the circus business as one of its greatest riders). Samuel P. Stickney, the equestrian, was born in Boston in 1808. While only 19 years of age, he had accompanied Fogg west with the second circus that ever crossed the Allegheny Mountains.[30]

In December 1826, "a very amusing and somewhat dangerous occurrence took place at a small circus in the Bowery, in which there is an exhibition of wild beasts, such as elephants, tigers, lions, &c." A tiger and tigress broke out of their decrepit cage, quickly catching and eating a llama, "as cordially as the cobbler and his wife hung over a cider barrel in New-Jersey." The keeper attempted to catch them by throwing nooses over their heads, but finding that impossible, retreated behind the elephant. As the tigress charged, the pachyderm caught the animal in his trunk and flung her aside. After a second attempt, where she was wounded, the tigress retreated to her cage. The male tiger then attacked a lion, but became caught in the bars of the cage and was rescued by the keeper. Not surprisingly, the affair became the "table-talk of the Bowery" for a week.[31]

Elephants, lions and tigers constituted a large menagerie for a small circus in the Bowery and were expensive to keep. By comparison, the Royal Menagerie, England, displayed numerous representations of beasts, birds and reptiles from the American continent. The collection also included "pig-tailed babboons" and "ring-tailed monkeys," as well as serpents, such as the boa constrictor and other snakes of monstrous size: "They lie coiled up in boxes, with blankets thrown over them, and the temperature of the room artificially raised, to form a suitable climate."[32]

The same month, after a devastating fire on Suffolk Street, New York, destroyed $10,000 worth of property, driving 100 poor people from their homes, a benefit was given by the Mount Pitt Circus for their relief.[33] While it could hardly be compared to the 5,000 francs donated by the King of France, the Dauphin and Dauphiness to the Messrs. Franconi after their French circus burned,[34] it was a gesture of great generosity for a small company (Mount Pitt was several miles outside New York City) and certainly in keeping with the American circus tradition.

Tradition is, of course, what the circus was all about, as one generation passed along its memories to the next. It is equally true that the memories of childhood never quite matched the realities of adulthood. Writing in 1867 about his first experience at a circus in November 1826, an unnamed writer described:

> At last, just before dark, the show came in. They did not have large tents in those days. They usually got under a shed, and hung a canvas in front. It seemed to us that they would never get the thing ready. But finally, just at dark, the *fiddle* and *triangle* struck up, the show was ready, and the ground was getting white [with snow].
> We handed our shilling to the doorkeeper and passed in. There was a lion, a buffalo, a pony, and three or four monkeys.

Equally stimulating for the writer was the discovery of "tracks of a strange animal," soon rumored to be that of a lion or an elephant, escaped from the circus. "Hunters who had never quailed before the panther, the bear or wolf entered the forest with a suspicious look for a long time after the discovery." And sadly, he concluded,

> It is a positive fact, however, that circuses, unlike everything else in our country, do not make any progress; in fact, they are not as good as they were thirty years ago, though we have to admit the influence of age upon our tastes.[35]

A different tradition associated with the menagerie/circus that would develop over the next several decades was the close rapport between wild animals and their keepers. One early account came from Brighton, England, where a young man approached the cage of a vicious hyena. "In an instant the hyena exhibited symptoms of the greatest delight, bounded about the cage in an ecstacy [*sic*] of joy, and rubbed himself against the young man's hands, appearing overjoyed with his caresses." It was later discovered the animal had been taken, when a cub, by the youth to England and sold to a menagerie. Although seven years had passed since parting, the animal remembered "the gentle treatment he had received," reversing the idea that hyenas were a supposedly "*untameable animal*."[36]

10

The Circus Tent

Just as the theatre had the greatest difficulty in ridding itself of circus adjuncts, so now the circus blundered on, unable to divest itself of theatre incumbrances.[1]

As the economy stabilized and a mobile population created cities from obscure towns, new opportunities arose for those involved in the entertainment business. The main drawback for circuses to venture forth into areas with small populations had been the difficulty of travel and the expense of constructing a building in which to perform. As with their European counterparts, American proprietors generally required at least a covered, semi-permanent structure with indoor lighting and stoves in winter to heat the enclosure. If a standing theater existed, it might be adapted for the circus; but more often, managers built their own establishments, setting out the rings, stage and seating at considerable expense. After playing for a week or a month, these temporary buildings were offered for sale and usually sold for the cost of the lumber. Buildings of a more permanent nature were often rented out in the absence of the company, but this added to the bookwork and placed additional demands on the owner.

To reach out-of-the-way towns where business might be conducted for a day or two before moving on to a neighboring village, new arrangements, less costly and easier to manipulate, had to be devised. Necessity being the Mother of Invention, the concept of the "Pavilion Circus," and thus the one-night stand, came into being.

Various individuals have been given credit for developing and implementing the idea of the pavilion, later known as the tent circus. If a company did not advertise in the newspapers, thus leaving a public record of their activities, cast members and acts, its structures and routes become difficult to trace. In lieu of autobiographies (which are typically inaccurate as to dates and names), contemporary diaries or letters, it may be impossible to precisely offer a date when the first *circus* use of a non-permanent structure took place.

Prior to the mid–1820s, John Bill Ricketts had briefly experimented with a four-sided walled structure with a canvas roof, but he did not persist in its use, as the idea of a circus was to remain fixed for an extended time. As noted above, early proprietors chose to build wooden structures, at times so elaborately constructed that they were able to return to them season after season. This gave a sense of permanency to the circus and enabled owners to elaborately decorate and paint buildings in glittering colors. In the eye of the beholder, this added legitimacy to the acts and put the circus on a level with the theater. Such sentiments were particularly true in Europe, where Astley's Amphitheatre, the Royal Circus and Sadler's Wells offered magnificent rings, seating, well-lighted and heated interiors, and amenities such as coffee houses and "souvenir" shops where programs and sheet music could be purchased.

Statues were placed atop roofs, gilt and glitter indicated affluence, and box seating provided a level of comfort for the more well-to-do. But Astley, Hughes and the proprietors who followed were, in a sense, members of the community. They lived in the area where their riding schools and circuses were constructed, and were well known men. They had a nearly limitless population from which to draw patrons, added by the influx of people from the country and an ever-changing tourist contingent. When British companies toured during the off-season, it was usually to Ireland, Scotland or Wales, where they could expect to entertain large crowds unfamiliar with their acts and skill sets. Returning to their home base after these absences, anticipation was high for the introduction of new spectacles and performers, as well as a reunion with old favorites.

In the United States, cities were smaller than London or Paris, and thus the opportunity for large, sustained remunerations was limited. A stand of months or even weeks was usually enough to see revenue drop significantly. Moving great distances to the next large city was cumbersome and expensive, and, when operating on a limited budget, potentially disastrous. With no income being garnered, horses still had to be fed and stabled at

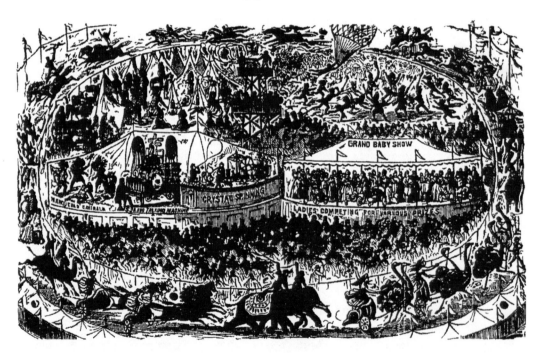

A world unto itself: Within the confines of Yankee Robinson's circus, anything and everything could be witnessed. This fascinating illustration reveals Hippodrome races with elephants, ostrich herding, Roman chariots, English jockey and camel races. Spectators packed inside to view the Grand Baby Show, Ladies Competing for Various Prizes, Crystal Spinning and the $30,000 Talking Machine. While a balloon sailed overhead, an English stag hunt was performed, performers danced, and the elevated platform housed a full brass band and orchestra. (*Daily Chronicle* [MI], September 25, 1880)

night, lodgings procured and sustenance provided. A trip by boat, although faster, was equally expensive and more dangerous, as rough water was often the cause of horses being injured or washed overboard, along with equipment and occasionally the unwary employee.

Westward expansion created new cities but did not solve the problem of venue. If short stays, followed by brief forays to the next town were to be contemplated, then temporary shelters were needed. Unlike the phenomenon of aerostation, requiring little more than rope fences and seating, where the most expensive ticket brought the spectator closest to the balloon and ascensions were cancelled during poor weather, circuses required a more structured arrangement to provide hours of nearly non-stop entertainment.

The advent of the pavilion or tent, constructed with a duck roof, provided the answer. These could be erected in a short time, were easy to transport, and provided a buffer from the weather. This structure was actually the end result of the interim arrangement whereby four walls were constructed and covered on top with canvas, used by a number of circuses at the time. It would take years of trial and error for the tent to take permanent shape, and for canvas to become lighter and more pliable (thus permitting more expansive arenas), but once the idea took hold, it made possible what was to become known as the Traveling Circus.

On November 22, 1825, the following notice was published:

PAVILION CIRCUS

The proprietors of this concern respectfully inform the citizens of Wilmington that they will give Equestrian Exhibitions this evening in the Circus at the Cross Keys Tavern kept by Mr. Vandever on the Kennett Road. If the weather should prove favorable there will be a performance tomorrow evening; otherwise this evening will be the last.[2]

Joshua Purdy Brown, of Somers, Westchester County, New York, operated this circus, partnering with Lewis Bailey. The company next moved to Alexandria, Virginia, where they performed until the end of December. The year 1826 was spent traveling through Virginia; on May 29, the company spent one day and moved on, marking the first documented time a circus deliberately played a one-day stand. Calling themselves the "Virginia Pavilion Circus," they reached Winchester by June before crossing the state line into Maryland. At Hagerstown, the following newspaper note heralded their arrival:

Mr. Brown, the proprietor of an Equestrian Corps, has erected a Pavilion Circus in this place. The papers received at this office from the section of country in which this Corps has been performing, represent the horses attached to it as being the best taught, and the performers the most active and accomplished, of any that have preceded them.[3]

From there it was a brief foray into Pennsylvania, but their extensive travel underscored a significant new consideration. When a circus stayed in a city for any considerable time, the performers were obliged to pay their own room and board. But with a tent circus, although the owners no longer suffered the cost of constructing a building, they were faced with a more cumulative drain on their budget: that of sustaining their performers on the road for the duration of the season. That, plus the necessity of keeping wagons, horses and teamsters on the payroll, demanded a near-constant source of income. Therefore, if a town provided good crowds, they might stay several days; if not, they were forced to press onward, seeking new business. What tenting brought to the circus by way of mobility, it lost as far as stability was concerned.

Brown's company, as it appeared in Alexandria, Virginia, in October 1826, listed: Benjamin Brown (cousin of J. Purdy Brown) and Daniel Champlin, riding-masters; James W. Bancker, rider; Masters Prosser, Andrew Levi (apprenticed to Benjamin Brown), Birdsall and George Sergeant, riders; Messrs. Campbell and Lewis, clowns; William Myers; and Master Lipman and the horse Conqueror.[4]

Benjamin F. Brown had originally been hired to care for the horses; Charles Siberry was a horse-breaker, and Brown soon became his assistant. After picking up the knack of breaking horses, he devoted much time to teaching boys to ride. His efforts earned him the respect of Bailey & Brown, and they divided their establishment, sending part of it south under the charge of Benjamin. The company traveled through Tennessee, Kentucky and Ohio, "the scene of many bloody frays."

"Tonight's the night for fun and jokes, so patronize the clown, good folks"

Although Brown had success with the pavilion tent, the idea did not catch on immediately, and things went on as normal with other traveling circuses. In May 1827, Joseph Cowell bought a half interest in the Broadway Circus from Edmund Simpson, and on May 14, the pair advertised their intention to construct a circus in Baltimore. The company itself toured Philadelphia and Wilmington before returning to a leased theater in Baltimore. In November, they played Providence, the cast including George Blythe, Mrs. Williams, Stickney, Ben Stoker (the Yorkshire Phenomenon) and Master George Sweet (Young Flying American). They ended the year in Boston at Washington Gardens, where Matthew Buckley and Master Collet were added.

The Lafayette Circus (building) was auctioned in March 1826, and subsequently turned into a theater; C. W. Sandford's troupe spent the summer in Boston, returning to New York in November, where they joined the Mount Pitt Circus. Their program began with a grand twenty-four-horse parade. Moving back and forth between the Mount Pitt and Lafayette Circus (the latter having failed as a theater), performers during this time included Benjamin Stickney, Archibald Madden, Davis Richards, Sam Tatnall and Masters John Whittaker and Charles LaForrest. Those joining later in the season were Master Conlon, a London rider; Mr. Pullis, slack-rope; Isaac Asten, trampoline; Napoleon B. Turner, with his two-horse act; Mrs. William Blanchard, with Master William, Elizabeth and Cecelia Blanchard; Harry Eberle; and John Richer.

By July 25, in Boston, the company, credited as being the "Mount Pitt Circus," rented a live sloth for display.[5] Returning again to Mount Pitt, they performed from September 1827 until April 1828, offering *Timour the Tartar*, where they garnered the review seen at the head of this chapter. Clearly, the combination of circus-theater and theater-circus had not yet been firmly delineated, leaving both to borrow acts and performers from the other.

In one of a long series of incidents that would reappear in newspapers throughout the century, the *Adams Sentinel* (PA) of March 28, 1827, reported on a fatal accident that took place at Danbury, Connecticut, two weeks prior. A youth named Hart Crosby, desiring to become a Circus Rider, attempted to throw a somerset. In doing so, he fell and struck his head, dislocating the neck joints. Noting this was the second time such an accident had occurred, the newspaper added, "From this we may hope a caution may be derived, that will deter young men from engaging in a pursuit not only so dangerous to life, but demoralizing to community." Unfortunately, the allure of the circus was such that boys would continue to pursue their dreams, often with dire consequences.

In 1828, the American circus had seemingly come full circle when the editors of the *New York Post* began an article by stating, "At Astley's Theatre in London, which is a kind of circus, where equestrian feats are displayed, animals exhibited, and pantomimes, and melo dramas performed...." The story concerned an elephant "saying more than was set down for him" by extemporizing his part during a performance of *Blue Beard*. After conveying the hero over the mountains with great propriety, the animal lunged toward the audience, threw his forelegs over the railing and planted them in the pit.[6] More interesting than the "buffooneries" was the editor's lead-in. Although the circus had its beginnings in England, it had already become so firmly established in the United States that writers were able to step back and call one of the founding companies "a kind of circus."

In some respects they were correct, for the idea of the American circus had taken deep root. Thirty-five years after John Bill Ricketts opened in Philadelphia, there were approximately seventeen circuses operating in the United States. Five would not last the year (all but one were tied to older metropolitan cities, including the Price and Simpson company in New York), but the rest were willing and able to take on the changes of the expanding country. Throughout 1828, circuses would play in such diverse cities as Natchez, New Orleans, Mobile, Cleveland, Raleigh, Lynchburg and Norfolk, Virginia, and Savannah, Georgia.

Old favorites continued to perform, often going from one circus to another as schedule and terms dictated; others began their own companies. One of these was Matthew Buckley, late of Price and Simpson's. After a short stay in Philadelphia, where the company "no doubt" gave general satisfaction, indicated by the "profitable run during the short stay of the company there," people in Wilmington, Delaware, anticipated seeing "the best selected corps of Equestrians which has ever visited this place." Situated near Mr. Vandevet's on the Kennet road, where J. Purdy Brown had played in 1825, "The Circus," as it was billed, advertised "grand Performances at the Circus" through October 11, while advising, "All persons having any demands against the Circus, will present their accounts on Saturday morning to Mr. Buckley."[7]

"The Circus" went on to Philadelphia, where it played *Timour the Tartar* at the Arch Street Theatre in mid-November. William B. Wood opened the theater, constructed on Arch Street, west of Sixth, on October 1. It was built by Haviland, the architect, and presented a handsome front and an interior well suited for plays, with seating for 1,500.[8] Wood relinquished management duties December 24 on account of "the disorderly and ill assorted company, whom he could not undertake to govern." The season ran until December 29, the final days under the management of Mr. Roberts.[9]

"Some circus riders," "Some circus company..."

In January 1827, the Washington Circus (Fogg, Stickney, Quick and Mead) moved from Columbia, South Carolina, to Augusta, Georgia. Among the group were John Rogers and his 9-year-old son Charles J. (from Price and Simpson); Mr. Welch; and Chris Hughes, clown. The whole were under the direction of William Lawson. Among the "players" were a group of monkeys riding Shetland ponies under the name "Dandy Jack," most likely a take-off on the popular 18th and 19th century colloquialism "Jack Dandy," meaning a fop or a little insignificant fellow.

In February, the Washington Circus joined forces with the Lafayette Circus of Asa Smith and John Miller at Savannah, advertising thirty performers, among whom were Chris Hughes, John Rogers, and Dan Minnich, clowns; Dan Ricardo and W. H. Creighton; Dan Champlin and Masters C. J. Rogers; J. Raymond and Levi J. North, from Fogg's company; with Asa Smith, Master Smith (his son), Master Burroughs and George Yeaman. Twenty-five horses were also listed, including Arab and General Marion (presumably from Francis Marion, the "Swamp Fox"). Levi J. North took his first benefit in Savannah, Christmas Day, 1827, performing the sack metamorphosis act, before the company broke up.

The Washington Circus worked the early months of 1827 in Charleston before Fogg, Quick and Mead dissolved their partnership. Jeremiah P. Fogg and Samuel P. Stickney entered into a new partnership that began September 1 at the new Washington Circus and Theatre, situated on Old York Road between Tammany and Green Streets, Northern Liberties, Philadelphia. Performers included Mr. Eggleston,* strong-man; Dan Minnich, tight-rope; Isaac Asten; Gil Gullen, slack-wire; John Richer and Sam Stickney, riders; Chris Hughes and Dan Ricardo, clowns; and Masters J. Raymond, Levi J. North, and C. J. Rogers, riders. James Hunter appeared by September 16, performing on the tight-rope.[10] After performing a week in Cincinnati in 1827, they eventually moved to New Orleans aboard a flatboat, stopping at each town along the route. They took the old American Theatre there and ran it successfully for a season.[11]

On June 10, 1829, the Washington changed to a theater; a large stage was erected, the ring changed to a pit and seating arranged to accommodate 1,200. Fogg and Stickney were still listed as managers, although no circus performances were offered. Doors opened at 7:00 P.M., with the curtain rising at 7:30 P.M. Boxes cost 50 cents and the pit 25 cents. Among the performers frequently cited were Mrs. Stickney, with Mr. Stickney occasionally giving readings. The theater played from June 10 to August 4, 1829.[12]

Fogg and Stickney also toured during 1829. Among their company were listed Dan Ricardo, J. Raymond, John S. Whittaker, C. J. Rogers and John Richer.

On March 3, 1830, the *Lycoming Gazette* (PA) reported a tragic story. A young woman born without arms named Pauline Snyder was taken to Albany, New York, where she hoped to earn enough money to support herself by exhibiting her ingenuity in cutting and sewing with her feet. At Albany, she was entrusted to two men belonging to *some circus company*, named Shay and Jackson. They took her to Newark, joining a clarinet player named Dickeson. After exhibiting Pauline throughout Pennsylvania and making a great deal of money, they abandoned the penniless woman among strangers at Harrisburg.

If a preponderance of pickpockets (being legally charged with the performance of "uncommon dexterity and agility of body"), manslaughter and stealing from the afflicted were not enough bad press, the circus suffered one of the most bizarre incidents in the

---

On July 22, 1829, a "melancholy occurrence" happened at Hagerstown, Maryland. During the performance of some circus riders, one of the company, named John Eagleston, attempted to disperse a number of boys who were throwing stones and other "missles" at the riders. He threw a billet of wood into the crowd, unfortunately striking a shoemaker by the name of John Hart. The man died the following morning, while the "perpetrator of the deed left this place early yesterday morning."[13] The spelling of the surnames are different but the pronunciation likely similar, and it is possible they were the same individual.

history of any entertainment genre. William Harrington took his troupe through Washington and Virginia in the early part of 1829, arriving in Sunbury, Pennsylvania, in August. There, the Deputy Attorney General of Northumberland County "drew up an indictment against the Circus Company then performing in that place, in which the riders, tumblers, &c. are charged with witchcraft" The following is given as part of the indictment:

> ... Mr. Herrington [*sic*], Mr. Downie, Master Downs, Clown Stokes, Mr. Beacon and Sergeant Andrews, possessing the power of *Witchcraft, Conjuration, Enchantment and Sorcery*, and being moreover persons of evil and depraved dispositions, and as magical characters having private conference with the *spirit of darkness*, did, at the borough of Sunbury, in the county aforesaid, on the nineteenth day of August, in the year aforesaid, in the Circus aforesaid, expose to the view of divers and very many people of this commonwealth, various feats, acts, deeds, exhibitions and performances of magic, and witchcraft such as Grand parade, &c.[14] [italics in original].

The jury refused to indict and ordered costs be paid by the county.

Attitudes changed slowly, but prospects for entertainment venue profits rose considerably when the Pennsylvania legislature passed an act in April 1830, permitting "the owner or manager of any theatre or circus within this commonwealth, to make application for the privilege of selling vinous and spiritous [*sic*] liquors." The fee was $75 for one bar, or $50 for two or more bars.[15]

Apparently there were no witches in Baltimore, or at least none charged with such, for the new Theatre on Front and Low Streets opened September 10. William Blanchard's company christened the building with a company including Mrs. Blanchard, tight-rope; Elizabeth Blanchard, slack-rope; George Blanchard, "Peasant's Frolic"; Master William Blanchard, riding without saddle or bridle; a "Billy Buttons" sketch with George Blanchard, Messrs. Peters and Marshall; Master Eaton Stone, horsemanship; and Harry Eberle, comic song. Receipts for opening night were $1,041,[16] a "magic" take by anyone's standards. Business prospered, with 2,800 patrons filling the seats of the "New Theatre and Circus" for the first exhibition of *Timour the Tartar*.[17]

Occasionally, reviews of a circus were more entertaining than their subject matter. In 1873, the editor of the *Defiance Democrat* (Ohio) began, "If the circus is an evil which cannot be exorcised except by the introduction of seven devils for the one you turn out, would it not be well for the best society to give its influence, and thereby elevate it to its original intent and purity?" Apparently, J. E. Warner's "Great Pacific" Circus was an exception, for the editor concluded that Warner "is a gentleman worthy of patronage." (*Defiance Democrat* [OH], July 5, 1873)

Mr. Page, an Albany resident who had previously worked with Blanchard in 1828, formed his own circus the following year, working upstate New York. On December 30, 1829, he advertised an Equestrian Performance in Syracuse at "the Circus House in this place." Box tickets were 50 cents, Pit 25 cents, and children, accompanied by their parents, half price. The notice further advised, "No smoking allowed in the circus, and proper officers are engaged, who will be vigilant in their duty, to see that order is observed."[18] The latter warning was typical, attempting to reassure patrons while warding off potential thieves and troublemakers. That it did not work is part of circus lore.

As the decade wound down, several prominent names disappeared from circus annals, either by death or leaving the field. George Yeaman died November 27, 1827, in North Carolina; Joseph Cowell returned to his roots as an actor, where he performed until 1856; George Blythe left to operate a riding school in New York City and died on Staten Island in 1836. William Lawson stopped performing in December 1829, and died of cholera in New York in 1832. James Hunter left the country in early 1829, and returned to England; after being convicted of a petty crime, he was transported to Tasmania, where he continued his career.[19]

For those remaining, there were big shoes to fill, both literally and figuratively. Much had been accomplished; for most in the field, the circus had provided a profitable livelihood. Apprentices such as Levi North had made their debuts and would go on to achieve stardom. The circus tent, if not yet universally accepted, had become more popular and would soon dominate arenas, allowing people in smaller communities the privilege of seeing the circus in their hometowns. Mixed programs of equestrian and agility acts still shared billing with melodramas, but that was changing. Traveling menageries were on the rise. Perhaps more importantly for the American circus, homegrown talent was replacing European stars, and the decade of the 1830s would see this promise come to fruition. And while sharpers, riots and questions of morality were on the horizon, there would be no more witchcraft trials.

11

"Horrible: A Man Devoured by Tigers"

The honely ginevine speciment in the huniversal globe of the East Ingy rhinosycross, wot was cotched on the top of the North Pole, by Capt. Ross: and of the wonderful hoorang hootang as volloped three ottentois in Van Demon's land, and vos only cotched arter it had drink't three gallons of rum toddy.

The above description was offered by an itinerant showman at the Camberwell fair, England.[1] Roughly translated, it states:

> The only genuine specimen in the universal globe of the East India rhinoceros, that was captured on the top of the North Pole, by Capt. Ross: and of the wonderful orangutan as walloped three devils in Van Dieman's Land and was only caught after it had drunk three gallons of rum toddy.

The spiel itself was a take-off on Charles Matthews, a famous cicerone of a London menagerie. The humor, as easily understandable to Americans as the British, played on many subjects, including poking fun at the pronunciation of a foreigner, and the obsession of reaching the North Pole that was prevalent from the early 1800s. (Arctic explorer John Ross garnered great fame in the 1820s and 1830s for his voyages and discovery of the magnetic north pole.) Animals as exotic as the rhino and orangutan (one slang for orangutan was "ourang outang," often used in political humor, particularly against Abraham Lincoln) were thought to live in Van Dieman's Land, a reference to Tasmania. Rum toddy, a popular alcoholic drink, stands for itself.

Menageries were coming into their own in the 1830s, and newspaper leads were "wild" about them, not necessarily from the fact they exhibited exotic animals but from the stories such traveling caravans provided. And there was never far to search before one titillating report after another found its way into public consciousness — either of the tragic and graphic, or of the heartrending and tender. How many were published with strict adherence to truth is hard to judge. Unless written tongue-in-cheek, such adventures were sincerely penned, albeit with an eye to sating the public's taste for vicarious blood and gore.

In 1833, the *Hampton Whig* described the "temerity and concequent [*sic*] destruction of the keeper of a menagerie," the story being all the better as the Menagerie had exhibited in that town a few months prior. It seems the keeper of the tigers "was torn to pieces and literally eaten up by them" near New Haven, Connecticut. Having been in the habit of entering the cage, "at the evident hazard of his life," this time the tigers prevented his getting out for several hours. The keeper was only saved when rescue came and offered the big cats their accustomed food. The following day, the keeper repeated his folly, "when they fell upon him and instantly tore him to pieces."[2]

Keepers were not the only ones in danger from caged wild beasts. In July 1835, the *Boston Transcript* reported that while the cage of a leopard was being cleaned, the sweeper turned his back, allowing a curious thirteen-year-old boy to get too close to the open bars. The leopard instantly seized his arm, lacerated it severely, and drew him inside. After hearing his cries, three circus men extricated him from the perilous situation, happily saving his life and incidentally their jobs. The boy was taken home, reportedly out of danger but with both arms dreadfully torn and bitten.[3]

The same year, the *United States Gazette* ran a story about a tiger from a menagerie in Philadelphia that "contrived to escape from his cage, and having a good appetite, he beset the little Shetland pony that belonged to the same concern. In another minute he would have torn one of the circus men to pieces but for the prompt interposition of some attendants."[4]

Tigers and leopards were not the only animals to be feared. During the exhibition of a circus at Hornellsville in 1837, the elephant was in the outer yard being fed by spectators when a drunken man named Mason snatched a wisp of hay from its mouth. The "offended animal encircled him around the body with his proboscis, drew him forcibly against his tusks, and raised him about ten feet and let him fall. He struck his chest and survived about three hours.... The keeper made a present of $40 to his widow."[5]

Escaped animals were another danger involved with the confinement of wild creatures within close proximity of human beings. Unfortunately, in many menageries and circuses, negligence was a common occurrence; drunkenness and/or extreme carelessness led to unwanted danger. Sometimes, as in the following story, events were resolved peaceably; most, however, had tragic results for the poor animal.

In 1833, the *New York Commercial Advocate* ran an article concerning the escape of a "Puma, or Panther" from the Menagerie in the Bowery. When it bounded from its cage, screaming people scattered in all directions, no one having the temerity to stop the animal. After strolling down the sidewalk, it eventually entered a ,shop, cleared the room of occupants and went to sleep upon a bundle of flannel, where it was eventually found and recaptured by its keeper.[6]

Two years later, a leopard

In 1876 P. T. Barnum promised "A Noah-like Menagerie, three times the largest ever moved, and including Barnum's $25,000 Behemoth, the only LIVING HIPPOPOTAMUS in America; all others advertised being base frauds." Barnum himself was not unknown to frauds, but never minded accusing another exhibition of false advertising. (*Belleville Telescope*)

made its escape from the New York Menagerie, walked down Broadway and was finally discovered near Harlem by "sportsmen" tracking him with hunting dogs. It required thirty shots by the intrepid hunters to bring him down.[7]

Nor were elephants immune from seeking a taste of freedom. In 1833, the *Providence Gazette* reported that two elephants belonging to the National Menagerie escaped at Taunton. They eventually responded to the command of their keeper, but not before taking the liberty to "destroy some half dozen carriages that were in the yard, and to which they had manifested strong disapprobation."[8] Another elephant, lately exhibited in Baltimore in 1837, managed to get free from the Menagerie and swim the Delaware near the Brandywine, only being secured by the attendants when they built a fence around him.[9]

Similar to the event of 1833, an elephant belonging to a menagerie at Cincinnati broke loose one night and killed a zebra and a horse, besides injuring several others with its trunk. The writer observed:

> What is very remarkable, the Camel and several horses which were equally exposed, escaped his wrath entirely, being not injured in the slightest degree. This fact goes strongly to show the sagacity of the elephant, and their sense of injury, for it is not likely that he would have made such bloody work without some cause — it being by no means characteristic of the animal. There is no doubt, but that the animals which have thus been roughly handled, had some time or other offended his elephantship, and that he has now punished them in proportion to the extent of their several offences.[10]

Not all stories ended in bloodshed, even if that were the intended outcome, as dumb beasts proved more sentient than their two-legged counterparts. During a lion-baiting in New Orleans in 1832, a bear was placed in the cage of a 24-year-old African lion, with the intent that the lion would tear it to pieces. Contrary to expectation, after the bear made several unrequited lunges at the lion, the King of the Jungle "after some time elapsed, placed his paw on the Bear's head as if to express his pity for its helpless situation, and evinced every disposition to cultivate friendship." A reporter, dubious of the tale, went to inspect the situation for himself and discovered both animals together, the lion remaining constantly awake "to guard his weaker companion from danger." The manager relayed that "the Lion suffers the beast to eat of whatever is thrown into the cage, until he has enough, but will scarcely touch food himself." The reporter concluded, "This seems to us astonishing indeed, and will no doubt attract the notice of naturalists."[11]

After all was said and done, however, the menagerie was first and foremost an adventure. A boy's first exposure to the wonders of natural history, written many years later, perhaps best sums up the experience:

> Strange and wildly tropical was the commixed odor of the saw-dust, ammonia, and orange-peel. An undefined sensation of terror seized us on the trap-stair, while descending into the interior of the caravan; for a hideous growling, snarling, baying, barking and chattering, warned us that the inmates were upon the alert, and between the entrance and the quadrangle there seemed danger of a protruded paw....
> There was "Nero," the indulgent old lion, who would stand any amount of liberties.... What a nice beast the elephant was, and what an appetite he possessed! From nine in the morning till six in the dewy eve, his trunk was a mere vehicle for cakes.... Then there was "Wallace," a rampant, reddish-maned animal ... [who] was characteristically tenacious of his dignity, elevated his tail in defiance, and would not tolerate the affront of being roused by the application of the long pole.... [Next] lay the

Trained animals became a mainstay of circuses and menageries. Among the performing animals were an elephant that rode a bicycle, a pony that waited on him, and a monkey valet. Many animals were dressed as clowns; while oxen seesawed, zebras did tricks, pelicans raced, and even boa constrictors took part. (*Monticello Express* [IA], September 21, 1882)

> awful form of the Royal Bengal tiger, for whose innate ferocity we needed not the vouchment of the keeper.... Need we be ashamed to confess that we recoiled from the dangerous proximity with a scream of abject terror; and in so doing, came within the sweep of the trunk of our former friend, the elephant, who, possibly conceiving that our cap contained inexhaustible stores of gingerbread, picked it from our head, and instantaneously added it to the miscellaneous contents of his stomach...?
> We shall not speak of the serpents ... nor of the zebra whom we greatly coveted for a pony.[12]

The Menagerie Comes to Town

Animal importation became a primary concern for the establishment, maintenance and continuance of the menagerie. Many creatures were either purchased in England or imported through British agents because of their ties with Asia and Africa. More ambitious American concerns occasionally hired their own hunters and sponsored expeditions to obtain animals for exhibition. In July 1833, a shipload of animals arrived from the Cape of Good Hope and were incorporated into the concern called the "Boston Company," comprised of Eisenhart Purdy, Rufus Welch, Zebedee Macomber and Eman Handy, an expansion of the small menagerie "Purdy, Welch & Co.," Boston.

The animals were exhibited in Boston on August 26, 1833, in what was later billed as the "New Menagerie, Purdy, Macomber & Co. props." By July, Macomber was dispatched to the Cape of Good Hope in quest of more animals, while "Purdy, Welch,

Macomber & Co.," with Mr. Putnam as keeper, exhibited a tapir (a large hoofed animal from Southeast Asia, related to the horse), promoted as "the hippopotamus of the New World." The menagerie spent the winter at Maelzel's Hall, Philadelphia, using the name "Zoological Institute."[13]

This scene depicts the capture of a "Mysterious Malay Mountain Mammoth" by the Reiche brothers. "Quedah" was believed to be a descendent of prehistoric creatures that roamed the earth in ancient times. Menageries with entire herds had come a long way from the first elephant brought to America in 1796. (*Yates County Chronicle* [NY], July 18, 1885)

In late June or early July 1834, after a four-month hunting excursion and a six-month round-trip by sea, Macomber returned on the ship *Susan* with a "singular cargo" of birds and beasts. Brought ashore, the caged animals were stowed in a shed where reporters were permitted to view them prior to their being moved to larger quarters. During a walk-through of the tightly packed area, Macomber described a young eland as "a modest and very quiet animal, we believe of the Antelope order, about ten months old, and with straight horns of great strength and symmetry." Supposing the animals would soon go extinct, the hunter explained that the creature had been feeding at a stream with its mother; the dam "was off like a shot," while the young was secured without difficulty.

Next were five gnus, captured by driving a herd between two high rocks; eighteen were taken, some of which refused food "and worried themselves to death." There were also quaggas (a South African zebra with a yellowish-brown coat and darker stripes that has since become extinct) and zebras, captured by lasso. Included in the collection was a gazelle; an African or Bengal tiger; monkeys; jackals; hyenas; a porcupine; a lioness; and a "Morgay," used here in reference to a member of the cat tribe, possibly because it was spotted. (By definition, a "morgay" is a small spotted dogfish or small shark.) There was also a creature referred to as an "Ant Bear," and a collection of "very valuable and curious" birds, including "Secretary birds," fifteen pelicans, four ostriches, Ibis birds and a gigantic crane.[14]

After several months fitting up the exhibition, the company went on tour with upwards of one hundred animals in about 30 carriages, the whole requiring the care of fifty men. Included in the caravan was a splendid music band. They passed through Bristol county and several towns in Rhode Island on what would seem to be a series of one-day stands, attracting huge crowds everywhere they went.

The menagerie carried with it 12,000 feet of canvas for three large pavilions; but even so, these did not provide enough space. Arriving at New Bedford in September, the crowd was so great that many were compelled to wait for admittance; while at Newport, "all classes and ages" of people demanded to see the most valuable zoological collection ever put together in the United States, forcing the proprietors to stage a second exhibition.[15]

One of the most important aspects of this menagerie was the inclusion of a keeper, or animal trainer. This person would care for and establish a rapport with the animals, eventually teaching them tricks and becoming part of the show. The concept caught on, and by 1835, they were to be found in nearly every menagerie. Keepers (albeit by title rather than name) often found themselves the subject of newspaper articles. In March 1835, for example, the keeper of Messrs. Welch, Macomber and Co's Menagerie was prominently featured in a story of the hungry elephant. The pachyderm had already become somewhat famous for directing visitors with his trunk to a recess under the stairs leading to the picture gallery, one of several non-animal exhibitions. Patrons soon discovered that was where the animal's grain and fruit was stored and where it was fed.

One evening, after a short absence, the keeper went to bed, supposing his assistant had taken proper care of his charge. He was soon aroused by the elephant, which had stepped over a three-and-a-half-foot bar to "growl" at his bedside. The animal twisted its trunk around one of his arms and directed him beneath the stairs; there it overturned a barrel, intimating that he had had no supper. Nor would the elephant allow the keeper to sleep before he had procured the usual quantity of oats and potatoes.[16]

Many of the animals Macomber captured (he made a final trip late in 1834) were eventually divided among several menageries when they incorporated under the title of the Zoological Institute in 1835.

The Zoological Institute

In what may be considered astonishing cooperation among proprietors and managers, nine menageries already in operation in 1835 came together to form one large group. Called "The Zoological Institute," concerns included June, Titus, Angevine & Co.; Raymond & Ogden; Lewis Bailey & Co.; Purdy, Welch & Co.; J. R. & W. Howe, Jr. & Co.; Mead, Miller & Co.; Kelly, Berry & Waring; and Ganung, Strang & Co. The initial capitalization amounted to $329,325. For every $1,000 investment, one share was issued, with additional shares for sale at $100 each. Directors of the concern were James Raymond, Hiram Waring, Caleb S. Angevine, Lewis Titus and William Howe, Jr.[17]

One purpose of the Institute was to create and direct routes that would not bring shows into competition with one another. This was the same philosophy adopted by steamboat operators along the Lower Mississippi. There, lines were created along a single trade route, each leg of the journey being controlled by a member of the association. As with circuses and menageries, the object was to drive business away from rogue or non-member boats. Each partner kept his own receipts, and at its best, departure and arrival times were greatly improved. The steamboat concerns did not have the financial power or authority of the Zoological Institute, however, and lines seldom lasted more than two or three seasons.

Purdy, Welch & Co. became the Zoological Institute, Philadelphia. For their exhibition at Norwalk on June 6, 1835, they advertised as "The Association's Celebrated Menagerie and Aviary, From Their Zoological Institute, Philadelphia." At 3:00 P.M., midpoint between the hours of operation (1–5 P.M.), they announced the Keeper would enter

An early woodcut from 1834, featuring a menagerie lion belonging to J. P. & J. T. Bailey & Co.'s Splendid Menagerie and Circus. In the early days of circus advertising, bold print and italics were used to generate excitement. It did not take long before posters, hand-bills and newspaper advertising included illustrations of exotic animals to identify the beasts no one in America had ever seen. This show boasted three lions and a keeper, who would enter the cage at 3 o'clock to "caress" them. The zebra was brought from the Cape of Good Hope. (*Huron Reflector*, July 8, 1834)

the cage containing the Lion, Lioness and Leopard, followed by the cage of the Cape Lion and Lioness, and finally enter the cage of the "black-maned African Lion and Leopards." The advertisement continued:

> This group of the most formidable and unconquerable of all the natives of the forest, furnishes to the mind of the spectator an insuperable barrier to the belief, that the art of man could subjugate to his will and control these wild and ferocious animals. Yet, his credulity must at once be dissipated when he beholds the Keeper in their Cage, playing and frolicking with them, and all enjoying their wild pranks with as much seeming delight and innocence as children do their holyday gambols.

A One-Horned Rhinoceros, billed by custom as "The Unicorn," was described as 12' long, with the circumference of the body almost equal to the length, and in height 8'. The animal on display was four years old, captured in the interior of Asia on the Burrampooter River and shipped to London, where he was imported to Philadelphia "at an enormous expense, in December 1831." While undoubtedly true, the phrase, "at an enormous expense," was to become a standard in menagerie handbills and newspaper prints in an attempt to impress prospective customers.

The elephant Siam, claimed to be superior to any exhibited in Europe, was 9' high and weighed 9,000 pounds, with tusks nearly 3' long. As an added attraction, the elephant was adorned with a saddle, "trimmed and decorated after the European style," of sufficient capacity to contain six persons, "who may ride upon his back with perfect safety and pleasure to themselves."

The Menagerie and Aviary occupied 29 spacious carriages and wagons, drawn by 75 splendid gray horses, and required 50 men, including 14 Musicians, to complete its operation. Tickets were 25 cents, with children under 10 years half-price.[18]

Raymond and Ogden's Menagerie began in 1830 or early 1831, after they secured a rhinoceros belonging to the Flatfoots Association, so called because they claimed exclusive rights to entertain wealthy upstate New Yorkers by declaring, "We will put our foot down flat and shall play New York, so watch out."[19] The expression, "put your foot down" (meaning "to take a stand") originated from the Flatfoots' campaign.

The rhino was a three-year-old male brought to the United States from Calcutta aboard the *Georgian* in 1830. Weighing 1,590 pounds, it was imported for Dr. Burrow (Burrough) from Philadelphia. The animal was exhibited from December 9, 1830, through January 3, 1831, at 48 South 5th Street, Philadelphia, and was sold at auction after the show ended, being purchased by James Raymond and Darius Ogden.[20] Under the title of "New and Rare Collection of Living Animals," the rhinoceros was advertised with a religious theme as being "considered by Theological Commentators the Unicorn of the Holy Writ, as described in the book of Job; the character strictly corresponds with the description." In 1833, the animal was still listed as being 3 years old, but weighing 3,700 pounds.

In December 1832, Raymond and Ogden added an elephant calf, Ahder-Ali, then 2 years old. The following year, they hired Mr. Gray as Keeper for their growing collection that included an Asian Burthen Camel; a full-grown African lion, "who will suffer his keeper to enter his den," requiring a feat of unparalleled courage; a Royal Bengal Tiger; the Anaconda Serpent from the Island of "Bornea;" a Condor of South America; an African Leopard; a Puma, or South American Lion; a Cougar from South America; a pair of Panthers; a bear; a species of baboon; and a "Rompo," or Man-Eater. (a "Rompo" typically referred to a mythical creature found in Africa or India, combining the features of a hare, badger and a bear with human ears, that was said to feed on dead people.) In this case, "Rompo" referred to a hyena. The menagerie also offered "the interesting performance of the Semi-Equestrians on their *Shetland Ponies*." The expression "semi-equestrians" was commonly used in advertisements, referencing trained monkeys. A Band of Music, "far superior to any with similar collections," accompanied the menagerie.[21]

By the end of the season, Hiram Waring joined James Raymond and Darius Ogden, and the concern became known as Raymond, Ogden, Waring & Co's Menagerie. In 1834, they traveled through Ohio, stopping at Sandyville, Canton and Paris, making one-day stands on the 27th, 28th and 29th of October, respectively. Promising an ample treat for all who called upon them, the company noted that "every attention will be paid to render the exhibition orderly and instructive." The latter was added to differentiate them from a circus, about which numerous critics throughout the country continued to write editorials on the lack of educational value in watching pure entertainment.

THE ELEPHANT.

"The Elephant," Siam, exhibiting with the Menagerie and Aviary from the Zoological Institute, Philadelphia, stood 9 feet high, weighed 9,000 pounds and possessed tusks nearly three feet long. He was provided with a splendid saddle, trimmed and decorated after the Eastern style, of sufficient capacity to carry six persons with "perfect safety and pleasure." (*Huron Reflector*, May 26, 1835)

Elaborating on their previous advertising, the text noted that the Lion Keeper would enter the den of the Lion and Lioness "and commence fondling these terrors of the desert, by opening their mouths, and putting his hand in their tremendous jaws, & c.— He will also chastise them fearlessly and safely." Again, the assurance was offered to alleviate family fears about the inadvertent shedding of blood by overzealous keepers. While there may have been those drawn to the performance for just that reason, 19th century women and children were carefully protected from violence, and any suspicion of such would have kept them away.

In addition to the same animals listed for 1833, the menagerie boasted an African Ostrich, a Wolf, an Ichneumon (mongoose), Parrots, Monkey and Baboon species. Interestingly, they dropped the word "Rompo" in favor of "hyena." The exhibition was accompanied by Music from an Extensive Band "expressly engaged for the purpose," offering National Airs, Marches and Overtures, with "a taste and science surpassing any now travelling." For their accommodation, a barouche drawn by four elegant horses was provided.

Seats were constructed on a safe and approved plan for the reception of 600 to 800 persons, to which ladies and juveniles were first entitled. Hours of exhibition were from noon to 3:00 P.M.[22]

In 1836, the "Mammoth Exhibition, Under the Management of Noell E. Waring, From the Zoological Institute, New York City," played Hancock, Clear Spring, Hagers-Town and Green Castle, Maryland, in the month of October. The menagerie advertised a crane, emeu, eland, a pair of African ostriches, a pair of kangaroos, a lioness, a royal tiger and tigress, an elephant, rhinoceros (weighing 6,628 pounds), a pair of Arabian camels, a zebu, a white bear, zebra, quagga, jackell [*sic*], hyena, leopard, a pair of panthers, jaguar, gnu, buffalo, Hindostan bear, white pelicans, a vulture and a pair of cockatoos.

Waring's Exhibition of "Natural History" was accompanied by the celebrated National Band of Music, which announced the arrival of the Grand Cavalcade, the whole arranged in a splendid Pavilion, "adequate to contain ten thousand persons at one time." Seats were provided for Ladies and Children.[23]

Perhaps the most well-known menagerie (primarily because of their advertising, which was extensive) was the concern of the brothers John L. and James M. June. Together with Lewis B. Titus and Caleb S. Angevine, they began exhibiting in 1830 at Washington Gardens, Boston, with a rhinoceros, a pair of monkeys and a mongoose. Adding more animals the following year, they traveled under the name "American National Caravan Menagerie." In 1832, they supplemented the exhibition with two elephants, "Romeo," a ten-year-old, and "Juliet," alternately using the titles "American National Menagerie" and "Titus & Angevine."

By 1833, calling themselves the "National Menagerie," they added Mr. Roberts to the company. Formerly keeper at the Tower of London Menagerie for ten years, Roberts entertained the crowds by entering the tiger's den. Shortly thereafter, he was severely mauled, and his death opened the door for the man who would become known as the "Great Lion Tamer" (see Chapter 12).

Another tragedy was reported on November 4, 1834, stating that a keeper from the Menagerie of June, Titus, Angevine, and Co. was destroyed "a short time since" by an elephant. According to the story, the elephant balked at a bridge over the Susquehanna at Columbia, Pennsylvania. The keeper tantalized it by offering apples, then gave the fruit to its companion, a smaller elephant, "at which the larger one became so enraged, that he seized the man with his trunk, and dashed him against the side of the bridge — killing him instantly."[24]

In the same newspaper, an article reprinted from the Wabash *Courier* (probably Indiana) reported a "shocking accident" at Covington, whereby an individual named Black offered several pieces of tobacco to an elephant. Noting, "To that noble animal, nothing can be more repulsive," it seized the man, wound its trunk around him and dashed him to earth, killing him almost instantly. The report added that the tragedy should be a lesson to all who visit such exhibits not to place too much confidence in the docility of animals, as "the nature and disposition of such are not readily understood."

In a less deadly affair, two elephants belonging to a menagerie at Middletown, Connecticut, "prostrated" a fence surrounding an apple orchard and regaled themselves on fruit to their perfect satisfaction.[25]

Not above his own adventures, Romeo, upon entering the Menagerie with his companion Juliet, spied a former master against whom it held a grudge. The elephant promptly crossed a street and gave chase, sweeping away a fence and partly tearing down a shed in his eagerness to get at the object of his ire. The man escaped, and Romeo was "arrested by the hook & speak of his master" and conducted quietly back to the Exhibition.[26]

In 1830, Benjamin F. Brown operated his own show. In describing his experiences, he noted:

> It was a circus and a menagerie. The menagerie consisted of a few worn out, old animals. We were down to the West Indies and South America. The biggest card in my show was a boy named Levi, a Jew. He was a wonderful rider. We had a piece of canvas twelve feet wide, then a hoop eighteen inches in diameter covered with paper, a balloon, it was called, and Levi held in his hand a hoop nine and a half inches in diameter. He'd jump over that banner, through the balloon and through the little hoop all at the same time. That was called a big feat in those days.

Cruising the Windward Islands and the Caribbean Sea, the circus experienced many close escapes, as pirates were an ever-present threat. Once, when leaving one of the islands, Brown was warned that the *Rover*, a well-known piratical craft, was lying in wait. The circus was aboard a new brig with a captain who knew the waters well, so they took the risk. Unfortunately, after reaching open water the wind died to a dead calm. By night, they heard the splash of oars, indicating the pirates were approaching. The captain issued the eight muskets and five pistols he kept aboard, remarking, "We might as well defend ourselves as to let them take us. They'll make us walk the plank, anyway." Just as the attackers came into view, the breeze came up, the sails catching the wind. A chase followed, lasting into the following night, when they succeeded in escaping.[27]

"J. P. & J. T. Baily & Co.'s Splendid Menagerie And Circus," possibly under the ownership of Hackaliah and/or Lewis Bailey ("Baily" interchangeably spelled "Bailey") was created out of "Bailey, Brown & Company," a small menagerie operating late in 1832. The initials may refer to Hackaliah's other two sons, James and Joseph; Solomon Bailey served as the animal keeper. Hackaliah was the promoter who toured with "Old Bet," the elephant, from 1808 until 1816. Lewis Bailey had an extensive circus background, having previously partnered with J. Purdy Brown. Oscar Brown, Purdy's brother, had taken over the circus when Purdy unexpectedly died on June 6, 1824.

In 1833, the company billed itself as a circus and menagerie; it continued this tradition into 1834, promoting a rare assemblage of animals besides "the best trained and most skillful performers in the union." Typically, menageries would form a circle of their wagons and place the ring inside. This menagerie and circus advertised 13 spacious wagons, specifically mentioning that the exhibits would be arranged under one extensive pavilion adequate to contain twelve hundred persons, with seats expressly for ladies and children. Gentlemen were expected to watch the performances while standing.

The keeper would enter a cage containing three lions each day at 3 o'clock, and there caress them. They also displayed a Royal Tiger from Bengal; a "Bear, from the frozen ocean"; a Hyena and Black Bear in one cage; a Panther and Leopard grouped together; a Cheta [*sic*] from Bengal; a Jackall [*sic*]; a Crested Porcupine from Africa; a Zebra from the Cape of Good Hope; a Puma; Lama from Peru; a pair of Leopards; and a great variety of "minor animals of the monkey tribe." Their tour through Ohio included Sandusky City, Norwalk, on July 11, Urbana, Dayton and Cincinnati.

Putting animals of different species together in the same cage may have been done for the sake of economy, or merely, as the *Examiner* mused, because "the nature and disposition of such are not readily understood." In any case, the practice resulted in dire consequences to the menagerie at Norwalk in 1835. A leopard and a lion, two "playmates" that appeared extremely fond of one another, got into a fight. Before the keeper could enter the cage and separate them, the lion was killed. The beautiful young animal was valued at $1,000, a very heavy loss to incur.[28]

In 1830, "Macomber and Howe's Menagerie of Living Animals" was formed, soon dividing into two companies, the second of which was called "Howe & Birchard's Menagerie." In October 1832, the Howe brothers, James R. and William Jr., formed a caravan that opened in New York City in December. The performance featured the elephant "Columbus" and included a thirteen-piece band.[29] In 1834, they hired Mr. Whiting as their keeper and were billed alternately as "J. R. and W. Howe, Jr. & Co.," and simply "Howe & Co."

With the assistance of investor Lewis B. Lent, they expanded their menagerie, purchasing a half-interest in June, Titus and Angevine's rhinoceros, polar bear and leopard. Unfortunately, in August of that year at Hartford, they met with a severe loss in the death of the rhinoceros, valued at $800. The first notice they had of the demise was the altered notes of the laughing hyena, which changed to a low, hollow moan.[30]

The rhinoceros mentioned here is credited with being the first of its species to reach American soil. In 1829, a male rhino was captured in Assam when about 3 months old. From August 1829, it was kept by a Rajah in Calcutta, who sold it in 1830. It was shipped to Boston for the Flatfoots Association, with permanent quarters at 37 Bowery, New York City. Assigned to the caravan of June, Titus & Angevine, the animal was exhibited at Washington Gardens, Tremont Street, from May 14 and was then moved to 350 Broadway, where it remained on display for June and July. Showing the animal under the "American National Caravan," June, Titus & Angevine then toured with it at Philadelphia in September and October, and at Washington, D.C., in December. In 1831, it remained with the American National Caravan; in 1832–33, it toured with the same company, also billed as the Grand National Menagerie, owned by James M., John J., Stebbins B. and Lewis B. June.[31]

Not uncommonly, bad luck plagued traveling caravans. On May 30, 1838, as Raymond & Co.'s Menagerie was crossing the river at Franklin, Ohio, the bridge fell. Five men and eight horses were drowned.[32]

For the proprietor of a menagerie, other things besides the death of a prized attraction could lose them money. Upkeep for the animals was a huge overhead, particularly the meat-eaters, and that may have been one reason the "*Morocco Lyon*" was sold at Mr. Dyer's Auction Rooms in April 1835. The sale drew a large crowd, hoping to get a gratuitous look at the Lion, but "he appeared only by proxy." The highest bidder proved to be an agent for the Menagerie in Boston, who paid the very high price of $3,330.[33]

In 1836, the "Great Attraction: Frost, Husted & Co.'s Great Gymnastic Arena, and Circus Company" appeared on the scene. I. P. Frost, with his partner N. R. Husted, advertised an "immense establishment" that required the services of upwards of 70 men and horses to complete its operations. Touring Huron county, Ohio, with their combination circus/menagerie, they appeared at Norwalk on the 16th and 17th of August, again using the reassurance that "nothing will be introduced that can offend the most delicate or fastidious."

With them was Mr. Rockwell, the great American rider (as opposed to a European performer—appealing to nationalistic tastes was becoming more important); Mr. Conklin, the Herculean horseman, acknowledged to be the greatest vaulter in the United States (having thrown 61 summersets at two trials); Langley, the celebrated Dramatic Equestrian; Walker, the horseman of all works; Gilkison, the Modern Hercules; Burgess, the Comic Singer; Calender, the Posturist; Messrs. Teets, Johnson and Williams; the two Master Dales; the Clown, Stone; and the undaunted equestrienne, Mrs. Bensel.

Their Band of Music, consisting of 12 members, announced the arrival of the Company in towns by playing several popular airs. They were conveyed in a splendid barouche carriage made expressly for the purpose and drawn by four horses. Lest there be any doubt, "the whole at an enormous price." Admittance to the Boxes was 50 cents, and the Pit was 25 cents.[34]

In 1837, Frost toured Ohio, Virginia and North Carolina before appearing at Charleston in December. After a stop at Savannah in January 1838, he shut down his company without public explanation, giving evidence that while the majority of men entering the menagerie and circus business were successful to a greater or lesser degree, there was no guarantee of profit or continuance of their enterprise.

12

The Era of P. T. Barnum and the "Great Lion Tamer"

The people are repeatedly wrought to excitement and take sides most enthusiastically in trials of skill, when, if the truth were known, the whole affair is a piece of management between the prominent parties.[1]

By 1835, half-way through the decade, menageries and circuses had already established themselves in the mid–America states, throughout the South and as far away as New Orleans. Roads had improved considerably, permitting rapid overland travel by wagon, and many companies owned their own caravans to facilitate moves from one town to the next.

For those companies working the Atlantic seaboard, the opportunity to travel by sea presented a cheaper and more rapid method of covering large distances. At this period, steamboats were the preferred vessels. Rapid inroads had been made in convenience, and steamboat lines offered frequent departures, providing passengers with a fairly reliable timetable for arrivals. This allowed caravan operators to advertise at their destinations with a good degree of certainty of meeting deadlines. Steamboats were also able to carry heavy cargoes, which was particularly important when large animals, such as elephants and rhinoceroses, and iron cages were involved.

That said, steamboats brought with them their own risks, and the list of casualties resulting from accident was harrowing. The Edinburgh steamer *Royal Tar*, listed at 400 tons, which made it a mid-sized boat, carried 12 guns and spent 1835 transporting British troops to St. Sebastian and then cruising off the coast.[2] The following year, under Captain Thomas Reed, it was in Canada, working the passenger trade. On October 21, 1836, the *Royal Tar* left St. John's, New Brunswick, bound for Portland, Maine. Along with 90 to 100 passengers, the caravan of Macomber, Welch & Company was taken aboard. In order to accommodate the large menagerie, two of the lifeboats were left behind. This would prove a fatal mistake, and the events that transpired represent a classic example of a steamboat disaster.

Prior to leaving port, the regular engineer had been dismissed by the owners from motives of economy, one of the firemen being promoted to that office (but with a smaller salary). In turn, another fireman was advanced to second engineer, although neither man was qualified for the position.

While crossing Penobscot Bay, within about two miles of Fox Island, it was discovered that the boilers had run dry. This was a matter of critical negligence, and the captain immediately ordered the boat anchored to remedy the situation, despite the fact a heavy gale was blowing. A second act of negligence was committed by improperly filling the boilers; an hour later, fire broke out in the boiler room. A third instance of negligence occurred when the engineer abandoned his post (one of the greatest taboos committed at sea) and, without giving alarm, took 15 persons in the largest lifeboat and set off for land. When the fire was discovered, the captain committed a fourth error by ordering his crew to fight it without alerting the passengers, any number of whom could have been summoned to assist. In Captain Reed's defense, it should be noted that boiler room fires spread rapidly, and once started, were nearly impossible to contain.

In yet another deviation from protocol, for the captain was traditionally the last man off the vessel, Reed took the last remaining lifeboat and set to leeward, picking up the then-panicked passengers who were leaping into the water.

Distress signals were sent, and a Revenue Cutter came to their assistance. Tragically, it had no boat of sufficient size to render aid, and, having gunpowder on board, Lieutenant Dyer, in command, found it prudent to keep a safe distance. Reed remained in the water attempting to rescue the drowning, but it was only with some difficulty that he could convince the crew to get near the burning wreck, as the men feared the elephant would go overboard and the resulting waves sink their boat. Eventually, six horses were backed overboard, three instinctively swimming for land, the others swimming around the boat; all eventually perished. Mogul, the elephant, moved to a portion of the boat not yet burning and mounted his forefeet upon the rail, where he remained until the fire was nearly upon him, when he leapt into the water. It, too, began swimming for land, but as the *Royal Tar* had by this time drifted four or five miles out to sea, it eventually drowned, along with two camels. Those creatures confined in cages were left to burn to death.

In 1852, Raymond & Co. and Van Amburgh & Co.'s Menageries United offered two lion tamers, Van Amburgh and Mons. Crawford, performing simultaneously in separate dens. Their animals included lions, tigers, leopards, cougars and panthers. For one price of admission, the public could view over 150 living wild animals, exhibited under a spacious pavilion 300 feet in length by 100 feet in breadth. (*Kenosha Democrat* [WI], May 29, 1852)

Between 27 and 33 passengers, including six children and four crewmembers, also drowned, and an elderly Irish woman was burned to death. The loss in money and other property, independent of the boat, was placed at $150,000; that of Macomber, Welch & Co., exclusive of the value of the elephant, was placed at $16,000, besides the private funds of the hands, four of whom perished in the disaster.[3] The tragedy put an end to the menagerie of Macomber, Welch & Co.

H. H. Fuller, formerly an independent circus operator with his brother, A. R. Fuller, operated the Olympic Circus in 1835. The "principal manager" was described as being "entirely destitute of common decency, morality and common sense."[4] H. H. Fuller later became the manager of Macomber, Welch & Co., and survived the sinking of the *Royal Tar*. In September 1837, he operated another concern, this one called the "Boston Amphitheatre, or Circus," which appeared in Bangor, Maine, "under their Pavilion, at the Merchant's Exchange" on the afternoons of 25 and 26 September. Immediately after the circus, the side exhibition presented "Sculptural and Historical Paintings," together with the learned monkey Don Pedro. Entrance to the exhibition was from inside the large Pavilion.[5]

The quality of an early circus woodcut varied greatly, depending on how much money the proprietor had to spend on advertising. This illustration of a trick horse from 1837 was offered by H. H. Fuller, who managed the Boston Amphitheatre, or Circus. Among his other attractions were Scriptural and Historical Paintings and the learned monkey, Don Pedro. Interestingly, later in the century some managers went back to using old images like this to play on the nostalgia of adults and recreate their childhood memories of the "old circus." (*Bangor Daily Whig and Courier*, September 21, 1837)

On the economic front, by 1836, inflation had gotten out of control, currency had depreciated, and the enormous extension of bank credit had reached a saturation point. President Andrew Jackson issued the Specie Circular in an attempt to control banks from privately printing money by returning to the gold and silver standard. This prompted a run on the banks, and during 1837 alone, nearly 800 banks failed because they did not have enough specie to make good on the paper dollar. Widespread devastation followed: businesses failed, people were thrown out of work, credit became impossible to obtain and prices plummeted. These dire circumstances likely led to the collapse of the Zoological Society, once again creating independent operators out of circus and menagerie owners. No longer having the benefit of planned routes and intra-trade of exotic animals, they were on their own, and survival became a matter of personal concern.

Tricks of the Trade

Aron Turner ("Aaron") was an American original who, like others to follow, became known as a circus manager, rather than a performer, although he did serve as riding master.

He was a partner with Nathan A. Howes and Sylvester Reynolds in 1826, mortgaging his farm to raise his share of the expenses. His older son, Napoleon, who became a renowned circus rider performing without saddle or bridle, made his debut March 30, 1823, at age seven with Price and Simpson's Company, followed by a tour through Canada with the Blanchard family in 1824.[6] Aron's younger son, Timothy, was also a circus rider as well as an owner.

Turner's Columbian Circus joined the Zoological Institute in 1835, taking on considerably more status with an influx of new attractions. In April 1836, he made an arrangement with Phineas T. Barnum, then little more than a small-time operator, to hire Signor Vivalla, one of Barnum's contract performers, for the summer. The situation leading up to their association gives a fascinating insight into the somewhat seamy side of American entertainment — one, however, that would not change drastically for decades, possibly a century or more.

The year previous, Barnum had witnessed the performance of an Italian, billed as "Signor Antonio," who displayed remarkable feats of balancing, plate spinning and stilt walking. As this skill was new to him (as it was to most Americans), the promoter engaged Antonio's services for a year at $12 a week plus board and traveling expenses. Deciding the name did not sound sufficiently foreign, Barnum re-christened him "Signor Vivalla." As he did not think it "policy" for Vivalla to speak English, although he was fluent in the language (having spent several years in England), Barnum also acted as his spokesman.

Leaving New York after a successful venture at the Franklin Theatre, where Barnum earned $150, they spent a successful week in Boston and from there traveled to Washington. Unfortunately, heavy snow made for an unprofitable stay, compelling Barnum to borrow enough money to take them to Philadelphia, where they opened at the Walnut Street Theatre. During one performance, Vivalla was hissed by the crowd; Barnum ascertained the disapprobation came from a balancer and juggler named Roberts, who declared he could do all that Vivalla could. After exchanging some harsh words, Barnum ran a card in the newspapers headed "*One Thousand Dollars Reward!*" followed by a statement promising that sum to any man who could publicly accomplish Vivalla's feats.

Certain Roberts could not meet the challenge, but savvy that the contest was sure to attract attention, Barnum then contrived a scheme whereby for a fee of $30 for one month's service, Roberts would agree to do anything asked of him. Using the press to stir up considerable anticipation for the match, the house was "crowded to suffocation." Vivalla won, as pre-arranged between the participants, and the contest netted $593.25, of which Barnum received $197.75.

During the month of Roberts' contract, they repeated the "contest" once more in Philadelphia, before taking it to Dinneford's Franklin Theatre, New York, and various other places. Afterwards, Barnum took Vivalla through Connecticut and New Jersey, where he met with poor success, owing to "expenses, licenses, etc., frequently exceeding the receipts."

In April 1836, Barnum's path crossed that of Aron Turner, whom the former described as "an old showman." They agreed to connect Vivalla with Turner's circus, Barnum writing that the artist was paid "the nominal salary of $50 per month and two half-clear benefits, and $30 per month for myself; and also in consideration of Vivalla's and my own services [including acting as ticket-seller, secretary and treasurer], I was to receive one fifth of the entire profits of the circus company." At the time, Barnum was paying his performer $80 a month, so that with the two salaries collected from Turner, he was left with the chance of 20 percent of the net receipts for his profit.

The "paraphernalia" of the company included wagons, carriages, tents, horses, ponies, band of music, with about 35 men and boys. It did not take Barnum long to realize that the stories of the "old showman's" frugality were well deserved. Their first day on the road, instead of stopping to dine, Turner bought three loves of rye bread and a pound of butter, distributing portions to each man. For this he paid 50 cents and watered the horses, having tarried less than fifteen minutes.

Together with the two Turner boys and Joe Pentland, the clown, whom Barnum described as "one of the most witty, original, and chaste men in his line in the country," they traversed, at what must have been a grueling pace, New England, New York, New Jersey, Pennsylvania, Delaware, Maryland, Washington, D.C., Virginia and North Carolina, the "house" growing better as the season advanced.

Clearly, Barnum looked back on his experiences of this season with fondness. He wrote in his autobiography:

> Aron Turner, the proprietor of the circus, was an original genius; a good judge of human nature, a man from whom much information might be derived. He was withal a *practical joker*. By his untiring industry he amassed a large fortune, and was not a little proud to inform the world that he commenced life without a shilling. Frequently have I heard him say, "Every man who has good health and common sense is capable of making a fortune, if he only *resolves* to do so.... There is not such a word as '*cannot*' in the English language. Never say you *can't* do a thing — and never cry 'broke' till you are dead."

"My dear Barnum," Turner commented after playing a practical joke on the young entrepreneur, "it was all for our good. You will see that this will be noised all about town as a trick played by one of the circus managers upon the other, and our pavilion will be crammed tomorrow night." And so it was.[7]

In 1838, Aron Turner operated the "American Arena or Circus Company." July 3–7 he was at Bangor, on a lot near the Penobscot Exchange, with his "extensive and beautiful Stud of Horses, and Company of first rate Equestrian Performers." The scenes in the Circus promised "an assemblage of talent and manly activity, unsurpassed by any other establishment." The arena was fitted up with every comfort and convenience, with admittance remaining at 25 cents for adults and half price for children 10 years and younger. A day performance was offered on the National Holiday of July 4; otherwise, doors opened at 7:00 P.M.[8]

The same year, Samuel H. Nichols opened his "Victory Arena, or Nichols' Extensive Circus." Nichols began his career as a clown for J. Purdy Brown in 1829, but his history from that period until 1838 is unknown. Based in Albany, New York, his company performed in that state, New Jersey and Pennsylvania. On August 25, at Gettysburg, the entertainments commenced with a "Superb Cavalcade and Allegorical Representations of the Four Quarters of the Globe, America, Europe, Asia and Africa, showing a succession of intricate Maneuvers; with Eight Beautiful and highly trained Horses, and actually performing the difficult mazes of the Waltz and Star Dance." With an eye toward those shows that had come before, his advertisement indicated, "The Public may rest assured that every thing here announced will actually be performed."

Mr. S. Miller, the Celebrated Equilibrist, was introduced, while Miss Caroline Devine

(Nichols' niece) and Master William Nichols (his brother) appeared in the circle at one time, mounted on the *Unparallelled Twin Ponies!* (Kanko and Osceola), going through "their celebrated and much admired Allemand" (an instrumental dance with close embraces and turns, in this case probably resembling a square dance on horseback, traditionally spelled "allemande"). William also rode on his head, and enacted the scene of his "Flat Head Warrior, or armed Horseman of the Missouri," as well as portraying the "Manners and Customs of the Aborigines."

Nichols also introduced another niece, Miss Elizabeth Devine (sister of Caroline), who rode a single horse representing many beautiful, daring and Classical Attitudes, "never before attempted by one of her age, being only 12 years old." Clown to the whole performance was Mr. G. Knapp.

Positional and Proccan* Artists went through many Transformations and Contortions; Master John Aymar, the young scenic rider, performed as young Nimrod on his beautiful horse *Mazeppa;* Mr. Howes introduced the Wonderful and Learned Water Poodle "Dog Monk"; and a number of Comic Songs were added. The whole concluded with a Laughable Afterpiece entitled the "Black and White Marketmen." Despite the poor economy, Nichols charged 50 cents for Boxes, 25 cents for Pit, and children under ten half price. They gave two daily performances, one at 2:00 P.M. and the other at 7:00 P.M.[9]

In July 1841, Nichols had his "Albany Amphitheatre, or Great Western Circus" in Ohio with an Equestrian Troupe under riding master Henry Needham. Mons. Le Tort was a featured horseman, as were a number of "accomplished Ladies." Accompanying the troupe was a "superior Band of ten members."[10]

Under the management of Messrs. S. H. Nichols & Co., the "Victory Arena and Grand Western Circus" performed in Michigan in 1843, which was, for mid-century American, the "west." On this tour, his company featured Mons. Guillott, who waltzed "with a cannon on his shoulders, weighing 400 pounds, with the grace of an *Ellsler,*† bend an iron bar across his arm as if it were a reed, and perform other Sampsonian feats equally astonishing."[11]

Gilbert R. Spalding, a druggist by trade, had financed Nichols' Albany Amphitheatre, but foreclosed on it early in 1844. Changing the name to "North American Circus," he took over the reins, touring New York and the Midwest that season. Advising the citizens of Southport and Racine, Wisconsin, on July 9, 1844, that he "has not disregarded the taste of the public, which imperiously demands the exclusion of everything immoral or objectionable," he promised every comfort and amusement.

In his company were William Stout, herculean equestrian, and his "interesting" pupil master Nevilles; John Smith, the celebrated Negro dancer and Singer, with Piccaninny Coleman, the inspiring Banjo player and their "Jaw Bone Minstrel Band"; H. Gardiner, the Melo-Dramatic Equestrian and Gyminst [*sic*]; Thomas McFarland, the Champion Vaulter (having thrown 60 successive somersets; by 1845, he would be known as the "Duke of *Somerset*"[12]); B. Carrole, Equestrian and Acrobatic Wonder (who threw a Double Somerset, turning twice in the air); James McFarland, tight rope performer; Mr. Baldwin, the Equilibrist, Juggler and Contortionist; Young Hare, the little equestrian Hero; and Mr. McKnight, the Yankee Samson (who fired a cannon weighing 1,000 pounds from his breast).

The use of the word "proccan" is obscure; it may possibly refer to some sort of dance derived from a church festival.
†*Fanny Ellsler (1810–1884) was a European stage performer known for her grace, agility and beauty. She toured the United States from 1840 to 1842, earning immense success in a number of ballets.*[13]

Also featured were Miss Heilen Rallio, the female equestrian; Miss Delsenore, the beautiful and accomplished Rider; and Knapp, the Buffo Clown. G. Griswold was the Advertiser.[14]

Spalding opened in Albany for the 1845 season, ending in New Orleans. In 1846, he reversed his travels, returning to Albany. Charles J. Rogers joined Spalding in 1847 as a rider and became his partner. By 1848, the North American Circus was advertising itself as "The Largest and Grandest in the World." Appearing in Wisconsin for the summer, they had a Double Water Proof Pavilion seating 4,000. Edward Kendall served as bandmaster, and H. M. Whitbeck as agent. Along with C. J. Rogers was W. W. Nichols, J. W. Smith, J. McFarland, John Shundle, Victor Piquet, J. Blackwood, S. D. Baldwin, R. Rossiter, E. M. Dickenson, Bandana Brown, Sam Johnson, G. O. Knapp, Alex Rockwell ("King of Grotesques," an English performer who earned accolades at the London Opera House as the *clown of clowns*), Joe Wiley, T. Sparks, W. Russel, J. Adams, and Mademoiselles Thompson, Rockwell, Wayne, Wright and Delsenore.[15]

Perhaps one of the most astonishing instruments to appear in the circus was the Apollonicon, introduced by Spalding & Rogers in 1849. They described it as "by far the most stupendous musical project of the age, composed of over 1000 distinct musical instruments, more powerful than a band of 50 musicians, and *driven by 10 horses* in procession."[16]

Benjamin Flight and Joseph Robson, two of London's most celebrated organ-makers, developed the Apollonicon, premiering it in July 1817. A description from the *Harmonicon*, 1831, described it as:

> A very large chamber organ, furnished both with barrels and keys, and whose sounds may be produced either by action of machinery, or by the hands of a performer. The stops are between 40 and 50, and by their combination give very perfect imitation of every wind instrument used in a modern orchestra.[17]

The Apollonicon was popular in British theaters and coffee houses in the mid–nineteenth century, and Spalding's introduction of this self-acting barrel organ must have seemed a modern marvel. If the instrument were not enough, they also offered a Dramatic Company under the direction of H. F. Nichols, proprietor of the Adelphi Theatre, Washington, D.C. Others performing were the Carlo Troupe, under Signor Felix Carlo (known throughout Europe as "The Man of 1,000 Tricks"), C. J. Rogers, W. W. Nichols, E. Perry and J. McFarland, among others, with C. F. Conner, Agent.[18]

The "French, Hobby & Co.'s Baltimore Menagerie and Circus" opened in 1834, marking

Although a snake, traditionally a symbol of evil, was used by Joseph E. M. Hobby to promote his exhibition, he also noted that "there shall be nothing introduced in the performance that can offend the ear of the most fastidious, but the whole will be conducted with the utmost order and decorum." His reptile collection of Asiatic serpents included an "immense Anaconda, or Terror of Ceylon, the Boa Constrictor or Strangling Serpent of Java, the Pompoo or Python from Madras, also, that extraordinary Reptile, the Amphis Beana, from Calcutta, the connecting link between the Serpent and Worm." (*Adams Sentinel* [PA], August 13, 1839)

J. E. W. Hobby's first foray into the business. Their best-known performers were Henry Madigan and William B. Carroll, who presented scenic acts. W. H. Creighton was the clown, and Nicholas Johnson, in his first year, offered a "flying wardrobe act." After performing at Norfolk in August 1838, the Menagerie made headlines under the banner "Novel Sight." Their elephant, refusing to board the ferry to cross between Norfolk and Portsmouth, resisted the threats and coaxing of its master until it was finally determined to lead him to the water's edge near Town Point and let him swim over. This he did, "his long snout protruding out of water, his motions resembling those of a porpoise. Refreshed by his bath, and in good spirits, he landed safe on the Portsmouth side."[19]

On August 13, 1839, the *Republican Compiler* ran an ad for the "Menagerie and Circus United," J. E. W. Hobby (Manager), using an illustration of a camel. On the same day, the *Adams Sentinel* ran an ad with similar text, calling the concern the "Circus & Menagerie Exhibition United," Joseph E. M. Hobby (Manager), and printing a picture of a coiled serpent. (The initial "M" was frequently interchanged with "W.") The caravan was to play Gettysburg on August 22. The wording underplayed both the circus and menagerie aspects, commenting briefly on "a variety of new and interesting feats of horsemanship, and other varied scenes of amusement, and Equestrian Exercises," with Scenes in the Circle featuring a fine collection of Living Animals.

After reassuring the public nothing introduced in the performance would "offend the ear of the most fastidious" (tacitly acknowledging that clowns and circus people in general were often known for their lewd dialogue), and that commodious seats were erected for visitors, the main thrust of the notice described an exhibition of the "most extensive collection of PAINTINGS" ever offered. These represented everything from Conflagrations to Shipwrecks. In addition, a collection of Asiatic Serpents, consisting of an Anaconda, or Terror of Ceylon; Boa Constrictor, or Strangling Serpent of Java; the Pomboo, or Python from Madras; and the Amphis Beana from Calcutta, "the connecting link between the Serpent and the Worm," appeared.

Unlike other combination circus/menageries, where one ticket bought admission to all attractions, Hobby charged 50 cents for the equestrian and animal performances, and 25 cents to get into the "Specimens of the Fine Arts" and serpent collection.[20]

Van Amburgh, the "Brute Tamer"

Contemporaries described Isaac Van Amburgh as a man of personal strength with a peculiar cast to his eyes, being "singularly made. His body is perfectly round, but rather thicker than broad. His bones large and firmly set, and his flesh almost muscle. Yet from the peculiar conformation of his body, he seems to have all the grace and lightness of a Mercury."[21] Measured at 5 feet 10½ inches, he had "hard, straight hip bones; shows no particular calves bulging out of the legs; and is, altogether, much the same size up and down."[22]

Born in Fishkill, New York, in 1808 (Ephraim Watts stated he was born July, 1811), Van Amburgh descended from the "Knockatokkers" (Knickerbockers), the original Dutch settlers. At age 15, he went to New York City and worked as a clerk for a relative. By age 20, he left his warehouse position and by 1833, was connected with the Bowery Theatre.

At some point, when the lion tamer did not appear for a performance of "The Lord Lion," he volunteered to go into the cage in his stead. Cane in hand, Van Amburgh talked to the lion, and in a few seconds "they became quite intimate." The lion died soon afterward and the company broke up, Van Amburgh joining the New York Zoological Institute (June, Titus & Angevine), as an assistant. When Roberts, the Institute's keeper, was severely mauled, possibly "eaten up," Isaac Van Amburgh replaced him.[23]

Van Amburgh quickly became a star, billed as the "Great Lion Tamer." One act in particular drew rave reviews. Together with Masters Hayman (a 9-year-old boy) and a lamb, he entered the Cage of Animals, "a novelty never attempted by any person but himself. The success which has attended to the exertions of this gentleman to obtain the perfect obedience and command of the various animals is without a parallel." When the beast did not show aggression for the child or the lamb, questions arose over how the trick was performed. Since Van Amburgh entered the cage at 3:30 P.M., and the animals were fed between 3 and 4 o'clock, speculation centered on the idea that if they were especially wild before a performance they were fed beforehand to calm them down, and if they appeared manageable they were fed afterwards.

"Van Amburgh, the Brute Tamer": Isaac Van Amburgh took London by storm with his trained lions, earning accolades for his "power of man over the instincts and propensities of the brute creation." Dramas were written around the lion tamer's prowess, involving a character's interaction with the animals. At Astley's, Van Amburgh starred in *The Brute Tamer of Pompeii; or The Living Lions of the Jungle.* One of "Van's" feats of showmanship was to have a ferocious lion gently lick the head of a lamb. (*Cleave's Penny Gazette of Variety* [London], September 8, 1838)

Van Amburgh toured with the menagerie through 1837, at which time he was sent to England because (as Watts, his biographer, put it) Lewis Titus' elder daughter fell in love with him. An 1838 London review summed up the biography by critiquing that Watts "gives a marvelous account of the boyhood, growth, education, and deeds of the 'Great Tamer;' of whose extraordinary *pupils* also, divers strange anecdotes are related. They may all be true — but, however —"

In any case, Van Amburgh left June, Titus & Angevine July 7, 1838, headed for Astley's in London. Lewis B. Titus' name was linked to Van Amburgh's, and he supplied animals for the exhibition, although there were early mentions in the British press that the lions and tigers used in Van Amburgh's European performances were originally purchased from Mr. Copps, of the Tower.[24]

Van Amburgh actually did take lions and tigers to England. They were shipped to London while he arrived at Liverpool, the usual place of demarcation for American travelers.

His subsequent reunion with the animals was described as one of the strangest ever presented, as the beasts immediately recognized their trainer and crouched, crawled and lashed their tails with every demonstration of delight.[25]

A private-day exhibition was quickly arranged on August 23 at Astley's. Among the ten animals displayed with the star performer were three lions, a lioness (another report states there were two male and two females), tigers and leopards, all shown in two large cages occupying the entire front of the illuminated stage. The "Brute Tamer," it was said, rendered the animals subservient by "some mysterious influence," adding that the animals' "docility and obedience to the commands of their keeper (more through fear than love)" was truly wonderful.

In what would become the standard by which all lion tamers on either side of the Atlantic were to be judged, Van Amburgh entered the cages with no other weapon or defense than a whip, occasionally dashing the creatures to earth with considerable violence. During his performance, he rode one lion, put his head into the mouth of another and provoked them by the art of "teasing made easy," without the least symptom of mutiny among his subjects. He also reprised his American act of introducing a lamb into the cages, allowing it to frolic about the enclosed space; when it was placed by the mouth of a lion, the beast licked it* and suffered it to be rested on its head.

Van Amburgh next selected a leopard, guiding it through a variety of graceful evolutions. When Van Amburgh put his finger in the air, the big cat, "as if frantic with delight, sprang first on the back of the lion, then on the shoulders of the man, who evidently had to succumb to the enormous weight of the creature." At the conclusion, the great Ducrow (who, at this juncture, was co-manager with Astley Jr.), with his usual courtesy, ordered the pony stables to be opened for inspection.

The exhibition was pronounced "most extraordinary," the only objectionable portion coming when Van Amburgh placed his head in the lion's mouth.[26] If "Zoological Anecdotes" were to be believed, Van Amburgh was not the first to gain fame by putting his head in a lion's mouth. At the beginning of the 17th century, at a menagerie in Cassel (Kassel, Germany), it was reputed that a woman who had care of the lions frequently performed such tricks. Unfortunately, during one such attempt the animal made a sudden snap and killed her on the spot. It was speculated that a strand of hair had irritated the beast's throat, causing him to cough or sneeze, thus closing his jaws around the keeper's neck. Having some sense of the misdeed, it exhibited signs of deepest melancholy, lay down beside the body and soon pined to death.[27]

Van Amburgh's official premiere came four days later on August 27. The advertisement indicated that, for the first time in England, there would be a display of the "extraordinary Living Lions, Tigers, Leopards, and other trained Animals, from the Zoological Institution, New York, introducing the performance of Mr. Van Amburgh, the Conqueror of the Brute Creation.... Mr. Van Amburgh and his Living Animals, will perform in a new entertainment called the Brute Tamer of Pompeii; or, the Living Lions of the Jungle."[28]

Rave reviews followed "The Brute Tamer of Pompeii." The plot of the piece ("forgotten in the interest excited by the extraordinary character of the exhibition") had Van

---

*Later reviews often noted the propensity of beasts to lick Van Amburgh's head or hands as proof of affection; this actually resulted from another trick of the trade whereby the keeper smeared his head and hands with an unguent of which the animals were particularly fond.[29]

Amburgh playing Malerius, condemned to death for plotting the assassination of the Emperor of Pompeii, enacted by Mr. Campbell. As punishment, he was thrown in with wild beasts. The stage contained two dens, the first containing a lion, lioness, a tigress and a leopard; the other holding a leopard and a full-grown lion. Van Amburgh fondled the lion, put its paws upon his shoulder, and leapt over its head; he had the lion and lamb lie down together, pulled back the lips of the lion to prove it had not been rendered toothless, then put his head in its mouth. Gone was the squeamishness of the earlier reviewer; opening night provided very great applause at this daring, with the reviewer noting, "Mr. Van Amburgh has such perfect command over the animals, there is nothing at all unpleasing about it."[30] Interestingly, the act with the lamb and the lion drew particular attention, it being astutely observed that in olden times such wonders would have been called "miracles," and the performer ascribed with superhuman powers.[31]

Van Amburgh became an instant celebrity, and as the season wore down, proprietors clamored for his services, adding that "in conjunction with his partners, Mr. Titus and Mr. June," he had already realized many

Isaac Van Amburgh was one of the first and greatest of the "Brute Tamers" in the 1800s. Under the auspices of Lewis Titus, he went to England in 1837, astonishing Londoners with his power over the beasts. After performing at Astley's, Van Amburgh went on to the Drury Lane, earning the ire of the patriotic "Actors by Gas-Light" via their caustic observation, "For Alfred Bunn to plaster the walls of Drury Lane with pictures of Mr. Van Amburgh, and still dare to call the place a 'National' theatre" is an absurdity. (***Bell's New Weekly Messenger*** [London], November 25, 1838; illustration from ***Postville Review*** [IA], May 17, 1876)

thousands of pounds, "and their trip to England will put many more into their pockets." After fulfilling the engagement at Astley's, it was rumored he would go on to Paris, perhaps taking with him the lions and tigers originally purchased from Mr. Copps, of the Tower.[32] In fact, Van Amburgh began dual performances, appearing at Astley's in the evening and at the Royal Gardens, Vauxhall, in the afternoon.

The "Tamer" apparently also had an interest in ascending in the *Royal Nassau* balloon with a Bengal tiger, under the auspices of Charles Green, the renowned aeronaut. Aerostation in the 1830s was a huge phenomenon, and thousands of tickets were sold. Unfortunately, the Union Hall magistrates, proprietors of Vauxhall Gardens, decided not to permit the ascension at the last minute, fearing the panic that would ensue if something went wrong and a tiger were let loose on London. The loss of revenue amounted to thousands of shillings.[33]

Being famous, of course, had its downside as well as its rewards, and rumors began circulating in the *John Bull* that "the gentleman with the Dutch name" had a tiger, "subjected to his wonder-working control," turn on him, with the beast only being subdued after a severe conflict. Reporters from the *Chronicle* and *Courier* promptly came to Van Amburgh's defense.[34] The performer himself was finally compelled to write a letter to the

Morning Post, hoping to "remove the doubts of the skeptical." He stated the perceived difficulties were no more than part of the performance in which the tigress "springs upon and throws him on the ground, and stands upon his body."[35]

A more revealing quotation described his technique:

> To get a lion down and allow the tamer to stand on him is most difficult. It is done by flicking the beast on the back with a small tickling whip, and at the same time pressing him down with one hand. By raising his head and taking hold of the nostril with the right hand, and the upper lip and lower jaw with the left, the lion, by this pressure on the nostril and lip, loses greatly the power of his jaw, so that a man can pull them open and put his head inside of the beast's mouth. The only danger is lest the animal should raise one of his forepaws and stick his talons in; and if he does the tamer must stand fast for his life till he has shifted his paw.[36]

Describing his novel and practical theory to account for his success, Van Amburgh confessed that from the first moments with the beasts he talked to them as though they were human beings. "They believe that I have the power to tear every one of them in pieces if they do not act as I say. I tell them so, and have frequently enforced it with a crow bar."

The "Lion Tamer" continued to be received with *roars*, and Ducrow extended his season much longer than was customary. Van Amburgh proved to be Ducrow's greatest hit since the *Battle of Waterloo*, and it was reported that the pair made six hundred pounds each week.[37] Other accounts stated Mr. Titus earned fifty pounds a week for the services of his lions and tigers, and that Van Amburgh earned fifty shillings a night.[38] When Astley's finally closed October 20, both Ducrow and Van Amburgh opened at the Theatre Royal, Drury Lane, on October 22.

It was reported that at Drury Lane, the wild animals were not fed the entire day and kept behind the scenes in the dark until needed on stage. They were allowed food only after a successful performance.[39] Similar to the United States, the feeding process became something of a show in itself. Young Queen Victoria made three trips to Drury Lane Theatre in January 1839, to watch the pantomime with Van Amburgh and his beasts, then she and her suite were taken on stage after the audience left to witness the lions in their dens devouring raw meat with violent rapacity.[40] Her keen interest created such a curiosity that the manager determined to make the feeding a part of the exhibition.[41]

On February 27, 1839, the American packet-ship *Mediator* arrived at St. Katharine's Dock, bringing a large collection of wild animals for Van Amburgh, said to have formed part of his concern in America. Among them were a pair of lions, a tiger, a leopard, and a spotted hyena, the first of its kind ever brought to England. On the voyage over, the hyena gave birth to one infant. The lions were immediately taken to Drury Lane for the proprietor's, Mr. Bunn's, benefit.[42]

Van Amburgh closed at the Drury March 23, thanking the audience for himself and his companions, "his majesty the lion, and her majesty the lioness," who "beg to assure you that they have no desire to return to their *deserts* in Africa, since your kindness has bestowed upon them *desserts* so far beyond their expectations here."[43] He returned to Astley's and then toured Manchester, Lancashire and Dublin, where his stay was extended six nights. Next followed performances in Liverpool; at the Clifton Zoological Gardens he was badly bitten by a lion. The wound became infected, requiring Van Amburgh to rest for several days before returning to the stage.

He arrived in Paris August 4, where an interlude, *The Emir and the Sultana*, was composed for him. During this whirlwind tour he was received to great acclaim before returning to England. There he received a consignment off the *President* on August 11, consisting of a "stupendous elephant and two hyenas."[44]

Once more at Astley's, Van Amburgh put the newly arrived elephant "through some extraordinary feats, which astonished the spectators."[45] He did not stay long, but transferred back to the Drury Lane, where he was once again blessed with a visit from Queen Victoria, on February 12, 1839.[46]

As a reward for pleasing the Queen, she commissioned a painting by Edwin Landseer, R. A., entitled "Van Amburgh and His Animals" (also known as "Van Amburgh Between a Lion and a Tiger"; a second painting was titled "Van Amburgh in His Den"). Copies of it were exhibited at Drury Lane, and it became quite the talk of theatrical circles.[47]

Success bred imitators, and the winter season of 1839 opened at St. James' Theatre on February 4, with M. Taudevin being advertised as having equal mastery over lions, tigers and leopards. The announcement was not well received by the press, who preferred more legitimate performances.[48] Nor did Astley wait long to replace Van Amburgh after his departure in September. On October 10, at a private showing, he introduced John Carter, "the celebrated American Lion-driver," who "surpassed Van Amburgh" and reportedly "instructed him in taming of animals."[49] One of Carter's most noted tricks was harnessing a majestic lion to a triumphal car and then driving it "with all the dignity of the conqueror of this heretofore untamable king of the forest."[50] Carter had been in America in 1838, associated with the "A. Hunt & Co." Menagerie and Circus, where he worked with a lion, lioness, two leopards and a lamb in an act similar to Van Amburgh's. He went to England after the season ended.[51]

Billed as "The Lion King, the ninth wonder of the world," Carter opened October 14 to rave reviews in a drama entitled "The Miracle, or Afghar the Lion King." It was printed that while "Van Amburgh was considered a wonder," Mr. Carter was still more wonderful.[52]

If it could be said any one event solidified Van Amburgh's reputation, it came in 1839, when a new African lion was added to his menagerie. With Van Amburgh never having seen the beast, it was supposed he would not dare enter its cage. He did, however, lying down by the animal's side and allowing it to lick his face and hands. He then took the lion by the jaws and made it roar and bark in the same fashion as those he nightly exhibited. His "extraordinary power over animals" was thus confirmed in the eyes of the public, the news even traveling across the Atlantic to America, where the oft-told story became part of his lasting reputation.[53]

The history of this lion was an interesting one. The animal was sent to the president of the United States as a gift from the Emperor of Morocco. Complying with the law that prohibited a republican functionary from receiving royal presents, Martin Van Buren's staff sold the animal to Lewis Titus for £620, the money given to the authorities in New York for the benefit of the poor. The animal was then shipped to Paris, where Van Amburgh was performing at the Porte St. Martin Theatre. The above scene took place at the request of French authorities, who demanded a display before they would allow so dangerous a beast to appear on stage. Van Amburgh succeeded in convincing them of the safety of the act and was permitted a license.[54]

Van Amburgh's charm diminished somewhat when he was bitten by one of his lions during a performance. He finished the performance but took little care of the wound. It became infected, and by November, his life was thought to be in danger.[55] He recovered and received a commission to perform at Rouen in February 1840, but, unfortunately, was again bitten by a lion, this time in the arm. The attack was so severe he was compelled to beat the lion on the nose in order to make it release him.[56]

Fate seemed destined to catch up with Van Amburgh's "arch rival," for in April 1840, John Carter, while at Cahors, was himself bitten. He was lying on the stage in a feigned sleep when a young tiger was sent in. The animal closed with a spring and "in two minutes the stage was flowing with blood." The tiger was beaten off, but came back a second time, gouging Carter in the throat. The "tamer" struck it on top the head with a hammer and rendered it senseless at his feet. Carter's wounds, particularly those in the throat, were considered serious but not fatal; it was hoped the tiger would survive.[57]

Van Amburgh returned to Astley's Amphitheatre in June, but apparently worked solely with his "Living Elephant," earning mixed kudos whereby it was difficult to say which received the most applause — the animal or its instructor.[58] The wry nature of the review could come as no surprise to any performer who has ever worked with a "scene stealer" (applied equally to children as to animals) and likely hurried him back to the stage in his accustomed role. By this time, Carter had been hired to perform at Astley's (now under the management of Messrs. Ducrow and West), with his animals in cages and on the open stage, compelling Van Amburgh to move to the Royal Surrey Theatre (the reincarnation of the Royal Circus). On June 28, he first appeared as a Dramatic Character in an entirely New Historical Spectacle, entitled *Mungo Parke; or The Arab of the Niger Karfa*, in which he was "attacked by a Leopard and a Tiger, in the Wild Beast's Lair," finally encountering the whole Herd in their Dens.[59] The new piece was well received, despite the fact the adventures of Mungo Parke, the celebrated African traveler, had no plot and was merely conceived to display Van Amburgh's prowess in controlling the fierceness of the animals.[60]

Van Amburgh and Carter attempted to outperform one another during the next two years, culminating in the former's development of a grand procession leading into the cities he visited, much like American circuses were doing. In Exeter, in June 1842, the parade was led by a splendid carriage, rich in gilding and blazonry, in which sat a dozen members of the band of musicians. The carriage, driven by Van Amburgh, was accompanied by outriders and drawn by eight cream-colored horses. Following the band with their wind instruments came elegant blue vans carrying the beasts in their cages, drawn by four horses. Bringing up the rear was the trotting elephant, arrayed in Eastern fashion with a "Houda" on his back in which were seated a number of young gentlemen.[61]

Underscoring the danger of the profession, while performing at Falmouth that August, Van Amburgh had one of his fingers bitten off by a lion, preventing his appearance the following day.[62] A month later, at the English Opera House, Carter suffered two accidents, being twice bitten in the hand by the same lion in the course of seven days.[63] Van Amburgh followed Carter to the Opera House, making a public entry into London with his grand procession. With the sanction of the Lord Chamberlain, he intended to convert the Opera House into a circus and menagerie. The grandstanding of Van Amburgh to convert the Opera House may have been an attempt to recreate his glory days in the Kingdom, but he was highly criticized for the effort, his procession being described as "a specimen of the grossest vulgarity, unbecoming any establishment, but that of a booth at a fair, and in every respect derogatory to the fair fame Van Amburgh once enjoyed."[64]

Cognizant of the fact "lion taming" had started to wear out its welcome, Van Amburgh

Older's Grand Museum, Circus & Menagerie not only featured the Cardiff Giant but Madame Sanyeah, pronounced by the press to be the handsomest woman in America. This Cretan lady appeared "in her original, indescribable terrific Mid-Air Flight of 100 Feet. Nothing like it was ever accomplished before, by any gymnast, male or female." This illustration is an excellent example of an indoor aerial exhibition in a stately building, such as the Opera House. (*Monticello Express* [IA], October 13, 1870)

(listed as Mr. J. A. Van Amburgh) and Carter joined forces in January 1843, at the Theatre Royal, Lyceum and English Opera House, renaming it "The Grand American Amphitheatre of Dramatic and Equestrian Spectacle," and widening the scope of their presentations. Levi J. North and the "Matchless American Equestrian Company" were added to their playbill, as well as Madameselle Camille Leroux from Franconi's in Paris.

Spending considerable money to create an equestrian arena for "the elite of the Wonderful Equestrian Artistes of America," they opened January 16, with Carter, "The Lion King," appearing with Van Amburgh in a New Historical Burletta Spectacle, combining their collections of Lions, Tigers, Leopards, and other Wild Animals. They also boasted New Scenery, Gorgeous Costumes and Properties, and an Increased Band, all under the Dramatic Director, Mr. J. T. Haines.[65] The circus was well contrived for the stage, which was hollowed for the purpose, with every movement visible from all parts of the house.[66]

The dramatic performance was *Aslar and Ozines, or the Lion Hunter of the Burning Zaura* (Van Amburgh playing Aslar, with Carter playing Ozines), followed by feats of equestrianism "very cleverly constructed on the stage." A little accident prevented Carter from coming up to his "call," later explained, to great laughter, that he had "broken his tights." The horsemanship was judged extremely good, as was the Virginian banjo player, Mr. Sweeney ("Sweeny").[67]

As an example of how difficult it actually was to incorporate wild animals, no matter how well trained, into acts, the January 17 performance featured a "diffident panther" pushed by visible hands from his den, while a lion completely refused to play his part. Worse for "Ozines," a lion began chasing him, resulting in the actor making "an unpremeditated leap from the anxious eyes of his pursuers." Fortunately, the American equestrian scenes starring Levi North proved surprising, fully redeeming the evening's entertainment.[68] Other members of the troupe included Mrs. W. West, Master Rine and Mr. Ayman throwing back somersets on horseback.[69]

By February 6, the Performances in the Circle expanded to include Richard Sands, another American who had come to England the year previous, while introducing the tent to British circus goers. Sands performed on two horses, and Master Buckley (one of the American performing Buckley family) also appeared on horseback. With them were Lipman and Dale, who, together with Sands, offered, "vaulting extraordinary, and great trial of skill."[70] The following week, Sands played "Courier of St. Petersburgh," Mr. Buckley (presumably another member of the family) played the "French Reaper," and North performed in a Star Act, the whole concluding with the elephant Bolivar.[71] Lipman garnered much praise for turning upwards of forty somersets.[72]

John Carter departed the Lyceum in March 1843, possibly at the behest of his new wife, who did not approve of his perilous occupation. His timing may have also been influenced by Van Amburgh's financial troubles, due, in part, to flagging enthusiasm for his "emasculated lion, and the fat o'er-burthened tiger, and the sleek obedient panther." On March 26, it was announced the English Opera House would close, with Van Amburgh losing money on his speculations from enormous expenses; North, Buckley and Sands stayed until the last.[73]

Although not featured in the newspaper advertisements, Mr. Aymar (spelled "Aymer" in the British papers), "the celebrated American Somerset thrower," excited much admiration in his peculiar department at the English Opera, "under the management of Van Amburgh and Titus." After the house closed, he joined the circus company of Mr. Batty, then the proprietor of the Royal Amphitheatre. While attempting a double somerset, a feat considered nearly impossible, he failed to land on his feet, instead falling on his head, resulting in instant death. This was the second tragedy of its kind, Mr. Smith, the great trampoline performer and vaulter, having died in precisely the same manner several seasons prior while working for Messrs. Ducrow and West at Astley's.[74]

For his own part, Van Amburgh went back on tour, performing during Passion Week at St. Neots, Huntingdonshire. Back to his familiar tricks, he offered a grand procession of 46 horses, including his eight cream-colored steeds, then provided an exhibition of his lions and other wild animals.[75] The American Company continued its tour throughout 1843. In February 1844, Titus purchased a male and female lion from Havre at a cost of £240 for Van Amburgh. The three-year-old male was nearly four feet high; both were transported from Africa by the concern of James Watt.[76]

Reclaiming some of his past glory, Van Amburgh and his American Company were booked for a brief stay at the Royal Amphitheatre in March 1844. With them were Brown and Sweeney, the banjo players.[77] From there it was on to Gloucester, where receipts were £140 a day, and Bristol, where Bolivar, the elephant, had to be placed in front of the caravans in order to preserve sufficient space while Van Amburgh performed.[78]

At Windsor, in July, where crowds were estimated at 1,500 persons, Van Amburgh received a royal command to appear at the Castle. Unable to attend because of a performing commitment, he sent Mr. Wallett with two lion cubs (whelped on the 26th), a lion and lioness, where they entertained the Queen, Prince Albert and the Court in her Majesty's drawing room. She appeared much pleased with the playfulness and gambols of the animals.[79]

Making short, one-and two-day stands, Van Amburgh's company traveled throughout Kent, stopping at Canterbury and Rochester, while his rival, John Carter, the Lion King (now apparently with the blessing of his wife), performed at the Royal Amphitheatre, being praised for his bold daring that "far exceeds that of Van Amburgh." The review also noted that Carter's "system of treatment appears different," and his acting was far superior.[80]

Although his tour appears to have been successful, in March 1845, Van Amburgh determined to return to the United States. On March 17, at the arena of the Roman Amphitheatre, Cooper-Street, Manchester, Messrs. Lucas of Liverpool auctioned his property, including an elephant, giraffe, several lions, harnesses mounted with silver, and vans. While the harnesses brought high prices, there was little bidding on the beasts: a black-maned lion sold for £350; Cobbold, of the Edinburgh Zoological Gardens, purchased a male lion cub, about 8 months old, for £12, 10s; a female cub of the same age sold for £35. A six-year-old lion sold for £310. Bolivar went for £750 and the giraffe for £400.[81]

Some of the animals were retained, and on October 1, an old male elephant was moved through Newington toward the St. Katherine's Docks. Leaving at 3:00 A.M., it was hoped the beast could be removed to the ship without attracting a crowd, but such was not the case. The elephant refused to go quietly, tearing up roadside gardens, destroying fences and inflicting damage on a "Tom and Jerry shop." Van Amburgh was finally called, and the animal's two forefeet were chained together and ropes fastened around its body. Fifty-six men pulled, prodded and threatened, finally being compelled to strike it with pikes and pitchforks.

Crossing London Bridge proved extremely difficult, and by the time the elephant was induced to cross, it was bleeding from the right ear and left foreleg. Once at the dock, it boarded the *Toronto* without further difficulty and was placed in a small wooden house on deck. The

Before Barnum's "Jumbo" elephant came on the scene, the Great Forepaugh Show advertised "Bolivar" as the largest and heaviest elephant in the world. Most adult circus-goers understood that the art used to promote circus performers, human or animal, was more exaggeration than truth. If the man standing beside Bolivar were a mere 5 feet tall, that would make the elephant over 17 feet. (*Defiance Democrat* [OH], July 6, 1882)

entire process required nearly 24 hours.[82] The ship, 700 tons burden, under Captain Tinker, with 60 steerage passengers as well as Van Amburgh's collection, left port on Saturday, October 4.[83]

Thus ended the sojourn of Isaac Van Amburgh through the British Isles and France. In summarizing his accomplishments, it is clear that during the early years he was an uncontested star, earning accolades from the lowest wage earner to the Queen of England herself. He set the standard by which Carter and other big cat trainers would be judged. At the height of his career, he earned huge sums of money and, by bringing his menagerie across England, Ireland and France, introduced thousands of people to his peculiar talents.

Clearly, Lewis Titus spent a great deal of money to see that Van Amburgh had the best of everything, from an influx of dangerous animals to silver and gilt-covered trappings. The cavalcades were written of with awe, and for a time, at least, his productions at the English Opera House were the talk of the town. That he over-extended himself is obvious from the result, but it is equally true that by the mid–1840s, the public had become somewhat jaded regarding lion tamers and stage dramas featuring wild animals.

On a less positive note, from newspaper articles and reviews, Van Amburgh seems to have been less than personable. While possessing charm enough to please the Queen and have his portrait painted by royal order, others found him difficult, stubborn and perhaps suffering from an over-inflated ego. How much this influenced his eventual return to America is hard to gauge, but there seems little doubt it was time for him to go home. While he could not have seen into the future, the move proved advantageous, as he had a long and prosperous career ahead of him as one of the "lions" of the American circus.

13

Variety, Novelty and Splendor

The elephant belonging to a large menagerie now in Mobile, has been confined in jail,
whether for debt, suspicion of debt, bigamy, burglary, or what not, we are unable to state.[1]

The first giraffes introduced into the United States came in June 1838. Transported from Cairo aboard the *Prudence*, two individuals landed in New York under the auspices of the Boston Zoological Association (Welch, Macomber and Weeks). Another pair was imported from England aboard the *Carroll* that fall. One giraffe meant for exhibition died while being loaded at Cape Town and was consigned to a taxidermist; it was subsequently leased to James Raymond.[2]

Considering Americans had never before seen a giraffe, it was described as being covered with a spotted coat like a leopard, and possessing a tail like a lion, a neck like a camel, legs like a horse and divided hoofs like an ox. Living on vegetable food, it chewed its cud similar to the camel and demonstrated the slender tongue of an ant-eater. The largest were described as being 20 feet high and possessing the prominent eyes of a rabbit.

It is difficult to imagine how that confusing picture conveyed an accurate idea of the animal, but it likely stirred a desire to see one in the flesh. In 1847, hunter John Clayton, under the auspices of Macomber & Company, went to the great Kalahari Desert in South Africa. Discovering a herd, Clayton described the technique of capturing one alive: After selecting the smallest giraffe, he threw a lasso over its head, sprang from his horse, and, holding the rope loosely, brought it to ground by gently exerting force around the neck, thus cutting off oxygen. Keeping the cord at moderate tension, he approached the convulsed victim, leapt astride its head and used the long neck as a lever to keep it on the ground. Forced to maintain this position until help arrived, coils of rope were used to bind the legs, the hunters being ever wary that if allowed to throw aloft its head, the giraffe, although a foal but a few months old, would break free from the restraints and become "furious in defense of its freedom. It will not only strike at its assailants with its fore and hind feet, but actually pursue them, until brought to the ground by the suffocating noose. In these struggles, many Giraffes expire; and even after they are secured and placed in the waggons, they become so mutilated by struggling as to die within a few days."[3]

It is important to note that many of the techniques for capturing and exhibiting exotic animals were harsh to the point of being brutal, and seldom in the literature is any remorse exhibited when describing such incidents. Life was often violent in the 19th century, and people accepted it almost as a matter of course. From the death of giraffes being captured and transported, to a lion tamer's bloody battles with his charges, it is more likely to find acceptance and approval than the contrary. While voices surely cried out, and Societies for the Prevention of Cruelty to Animals were established in Europe and the United States, for the most part, the ends justified the means; and if exhibitions, reaching almost to the point of blood sports, were offered, people eagerly paid to see them.

From his hunting excursion (the oft-used expression for such ventures, in itself denoting violence and death), John Clayton brought two giraffes to New York. One of them became attached to the New York Circus and Arena Company, also known as Hall, Nathans, Tuffs & Co. In July 1839, this concern was purchased by Rufus Welch, John Clayton and Jonas Bartlett. Under the title of "Giraffe and New York Circus Arena Company" (a combination of the Giraffe Company and New York Circus and Arena Company), they toured Pennsylvania in August 1839, appearing in Gettysburg on the 17th. Advertising a pavilion large enough to hold 3,000 spectators, the managers promised scenes in the circle comprising interesting feats of horsemanship and equestrian exercise, as well as a display of the giraffe, or Camelopard, "the greatest wonder of the animal kingdom." Hours of exhibition were from 1:00 to 5:00 P.M., with admittance 50 cents (children half price).[4]

In mid–1840, another ship arrived in New York, this one from Alexandria, Egypt. Aboard were four giraffes and three gazelles intended for a menagerie in the city.[5]

Giraffes were not the only peculiar animals on display in 1840. In January, a stray ostrich was witnessed on the road between Belchertown and Ware, New Hampshire, "running free at top speed." It seemed that while Macomber's caravan was headed east, it encountered a stage going west. The coach paused to let the menagerie pass, and as it was making its way through, a gust of wind struck the cage sitting high atop the wagon and upset it, breaking the teamster's leg. The cage hit the ground, and the bird escaped. Since it was described as "outstripping the velocity of the fleetest horse," it may very well have enjoyed its freedom for some time.[6]

One of the greatest wonders of the menagerie was the rare giraffe, described as spotted like a leopard, tail like a lion, neck like a camel, legs like a horse and divided hoofs like an ox. Although they were a great draw, giraffes were never common in menageries because of the difficulty in transporting them from their native Africa. It was not uncommon for traveling shows to advertise exotic animals and then not produce them. Such deceptive practices gave proprietors a bad name, and cities were always threatening to pass ordinances prohibiting such false advertising. (*Indiana Progress* [PA], August 8, 1872)

The Western division of the "Circus & Caravan" of June, Titus, Angevine & Co., Proprietors of the Bowery Amphitheatre, New York, under the direction of Ira Olmstead, toured Michigan in the summer of 1841, offering "Splendid and Combined Attractions of Equestrian and Gymnastic Performances, With a beautiful collection of Living Wild Animals, Comprising the Stupendous Giraffe, the Elephant, and every variety of Wild Beasts, Birds, and Reptiles." Performing one-night stands at Concord on July 27, followed by stops at Homer on the 28th, Marshall on July 29 and Battle Creek on the 30th, they had, by this time, perfected the business of rapidly setting up, carrying out the acts and dismantling the pavilion within a span of hours.

With Richard Sands as Equestrian Manager, the company offered horsemanship by American and European riders, the Rivers Family (late from Astley's) and others "in every department of the Olympic Exercises." Accompanying them was a Band of Musicians performing popular tunes. The menagerie, it was noted, had "intelligent and obliging keepers" who took great pains in responding to the wishes of the audience. G. R. Brunson was their advertiser.[7] Sadly, their giraffe died at Richmond, Iowa, in November; it was valued at $20,000.[8]

CIRCUS AND CARAVAN.   Splen-
id and Combined

The giraffe was one of the most amazing animals displayed to astounded circus and menagerie patrons in the 19th century. (*Independent Treasury*, Ohio, August 31, 1842)

The Eastern division of the company, under the direction of Wilson Howes, traveled through New England in the summer of 1841. By September 14, the company appeared at Bangor, Maine, on the vacant lot at the rear of the Penobscot Exchange for one day only. For those inclined to more historic tastes, playing opposite them was the Lewis, Bartholomew & Co.'s "Celebrated Dioramas," depicting the Battle of Bunker Hill, as well as the Romantic Spectacle *The Fairy Land.* Admittance was half that charged by the circus, being a mere 25 cents, without distinction of age. And if neither satisfied, in the wake of the "Aroostook War" ending, "War! Trainings! Game" was commencing for those who wanted to play soldier.[9]

A third circus belonging to June, Titus & Angevine, called the "Bowery Circus" or "Bowery Amphitheatre," performed under the management of Henry Rockwell. They toured primarily through the state of New York and the northeast. In March 1842, a zebra and an elephant died within an hour of one another. The body of the elephant, valued at $2,000, was to be divided between two medical schools in New York; staff immediately began quarreling about respective portions. Early indications were that the animals had been poisoned by something placed in their food, but as other animals ate the same fare without sickening, it was assumed they died from some unknown epidemic.[10]

The Circus and Caravan of June, Titus, Angevine & Co., R. Sands, Equestrian manager, offered "every variety of Wild Beasts, Birds, and reptiles, that easily sets itself up for the old joke: 'Mr. Showman,' said a greenhorn at a menagerie, 'can the leopard change his spots?' 'Yes, sir,' was the reply, 'when he gets tired of one spot, he can easily go to another.'" (*Tioga Eagle* [PA], January 4, 1855; illustration from *Democratic Expounder and Calhoun County Patriot* [MI], July 23, 1841)

The Western division of June, Titus & Angevine, still billed as the "Circus & Caravan," toured the Midwest in 1842, advertising at a one-day stop at Marshall, Michigan, on August 9: "The only living Giraffe, or Cameleopard in America, it being 17 feet in height, and weighs 1780 pounds." John R. Shay served as the Equestrian Manager. Among their attractions were the four Hungarian Cousins; the "Vaulting Phenomenon, Mr. Lipman, who has actually thrown 71 somersets at one trial, the greatest feat on record"; Paolo Conovo, the India Rubber Man, who exhibited "every limb out of joint, twisting his body with the ease of India Rubber. Physicians and Anatomists declare that unless the man is formed without bones, his postures are not to be accounted for; besides others in every department of the Olympic Exercises."[11] Following were appearances at Milan, Michigan, on September 2; Norwalk, Ohio, on the 3rd (a considerable distance away); Florence on the 5th; and Elyria on the 6th.[12]

In December, the combined circuses of June, Titus & Angevine appeared at the Bowery Amphitheatre. During this time, the elephant Siam attacked Charles Howe, knocking him with his trunk and throwing him against a wall. His condition was considered fatal and brought to a close the partnership of the above-named proprietors. They had acted together for twelve seasons, and while they went on to separate careers, theirs was one of the outstanding partnerships of the time.[13]

Injury and death from wild animals continued to mount. In Troy, New York, a boy crawling under the canvas came out directly beneath the cage of a leopard; the animal seized his arm, severely lacerating it.[14] A leopard was also the culprit at the Menagerie in New York. Considered "tame," it was not confined in a cage but merely secured by a chain. For some reason it lashed out at a four-year-old girl, caught her with its mouth and so dreadfully lacerated her as to endanger her life, one of her eyes "being nearly torn from its socket."[15]

Escaped animals also proved a problem. In Louisville, a tiger, newly obtained at the cost of $4,000, got free from its cage. Finding capture impossible, the only alternative was to shoot it before harm came to local stock or citizens.[16] Animal fights, as well, continued to make news. In a menagerie at Philadelphia, two strange elephants were introduced to three others. The old residents resented the intrusion and attacked the newcomers, nearly demolishing the interior of the menagerie. A ten-ton portion of the flooring fell on one of the combatants, ending his participation and finally allowing the keeper to restore order.[17]

Because of, or perhaps in spite of, such melees, exotic animals continued to be imported into the United States to sate the tastes of the paying public. In May 1843, the brig *Sea Flower* arrived in New York from Trinidad, Cuba. During a six-month voyage, it sailed 6,000 miles, visiting fifteen harbors. Among the captured were a Royal and black tiger, an African leopard, a "Poona bear" (19th century term for a bear from Pune, India), an African gazelle, a lioness, a Rocky Mountain bear and four serpents. They were said to be for the menagerie of June, Titus & Angevine, and likely were distributed between the partners.[18]

America, of course, was not the only nation obsessed with wild creatures. In 1841, it was estimated that in Europe there existed 225 lions, 289 tigers, 302 leopards, 270 panthers, 67 elephants, 10 rhinoceroses, 2,700 wolves, 78 rattlesnakes, 216 boa constrictors, 1,040 hyenas and 96 crocodiles.[19]

No Females Need Apply

The Philadelphia Circus of Noell E. Waring, under the working title "Raymond, Waring & Co.," left its namesake city after a five-month season, where "over 170,000 persons" composed of the "beauty, fashion and moral portion" of society had attended their entertainments. At Hagerstown, the proprietors continued their purported piety and social snobbery by producing "every thing with the strictest observance to perfection." They further stated, "In the chasteness, daring, and intrepid performances that will be offered, the gentlemen composing the company" are particularly celebrated. To this end, they boldly proclaimed:

> In order to give a character to their exhibition equal to its standing for Talent, the Proprietors have determined that NO FEMALES shall in the smallest degree be connected with the performances or travelling of the Exhibition, but that the reputation of their Amphitheatre shall be advanced beyond the slightest possible shadow of obloquy, by the propriety and upright conduct of the Performers in private, and chaste, talented and astonishing performances in public. This they regard as a very essential and highly important part of the exhibition, as the introduction of Females into an Equestrian Establishment is not calculated to advance its interests, while they not unfrequently mar the harmony of the entertainments and bring the whole exhibition into disrepute. It was never ordained by Nature that woman should degrade the reputation of her sex by a display of Gymnastic Feats, which are not calculated for any other than the stalwart man.[20]

After that tirade of chauvinism intended to play to the "moral, religious, intelligent, and refined" societies of the day, the proprietors went on to describe the Spacious Pavilion, with seats "so arranged as to make a few hours spent in witnessing the performances a pleasure instead of pain, as has heretofore too frequently been the case."

Scenes in the Circle included "Acrobat Evolutions of Manly Agility," still-vaulting, gymnastics, Pyramidical Devices and Chinese Pagodas, chivalric Pageants interspersed with a choice variety of Comic and Dramatic Entertainment, and horsemanship with new Scenic Acts. They also introduced a Group of Burmese Ponies in the Epsom Pony Races, including a Grand Entrée with Elfin Steeds and Fairy Riders conducted by children connected with the exhibition. Presumably the children were all male; no apology was offered for child exploitation. A card printed after the above, lauding the praises the company received in Philadelphia, ironically erred in misspelling Waring's given name as "Noel."[21]

No females need apply: the Philadelphia Circus of Raymond Waring broke from successful tradition by stating in no uncertain terms, "NO FEMALES shall in the smallest degree be connected with the performances or travelling of the Exhibition.... This they regard as a very essential and highly important part of the exhibition, as the introduction of Females into an Equestrian Establishment is not calculated to advance its interests, while they not unfrequently mar the harmony of the entertainments, and bring the whole exhibition into disrepute." This illustration of a male balancing on his head high above the ground accompanied the above pronouncement. (*Hagerstown Mail* [MD], August 21, 1840)

Elephant "Pranks" and the "Animal Subduer"

The "Grand Zoological Exhibition" that played Philadelphia in the winter of 1842–1843 represented three combined shows of James Raymond and his partners: Hubbell & Co.'s Menagerie; Raymond, Ogden & Co.'s Menagerie; and the Philadelphia Circus (also billed as Waring & Raymond). They wintered in the city and set out in the spring. Early that season, huge numbers attended the parade down Broadway, where four elephants drew the music wagon. The elephants were covered with white cotton cloth to the knees, "making great display of their legs and ivory.... Ropes were fastened to their tusks and they were urged by simple pounding on the rear.... They glided along with the ease of scows ... their trunks playing about close to the pavement."[22]

Later that summer, the "Unparalleled Zoological Exhibition" appeared at Bangor with what was to become a signature attraction of Raymond exhibitions: a parade into the city featuring the Music Car drawn by four mammoth Elephants.[23]

This came about by a series of events bringing together six of the seven elephants then in the United States. In 1842, Raymond already possessed "Columbus" (Lynes Menagerie), "Pizarro" and "Ann" (Hubbell & Co.), and "Hannibal" (Waring, Raymond & Co.). When June, Titus & Angevine folded in the winter of 1842, they sold "Siam" and "Virginius," two of their three elephants, to the Raymond concern. Drawing "four-up" with elephants had never been accomplished before, but Albert "Put" Townsend, a former keeper of Siam, then with June, Titus & Angevine, had the expertise to make it work.[24]

Of these, perhaps the most infamous elephant was formerly connected with the combined menageries of Humphrey & Lynes in New Orleans. In 1841, while transporting the elephants along the riverbank, Mr. Crumb, keeper of Humphrey's elephant, spoke some words to it. Its companion, "Pizarro," took exception and struck Crumb with his trunk, knocked him from his horse, then carried him away in his mouth. The body was later thrown over a fence near Algiers, after which the elephant became unmanageable and caused great alarm in that city.[25]

Elephants certainly appealed to American awe and wonder, and proved as great an attraction as the stories spread about them. Most common were articles on their sagacity. A typical newspaper article of the 1840s described how a four-year-old boy was watching the progression of a menagerie into the Bowery when a company of troopers came galloping down the street in the opposite direction. The child, becoming confused, could not get out of the way and would have been trampled but for the intervention of an elephant that seized the little fellow with his trunk and pulled him to safety.[26]

"Pranks" followed a close second, typically detailing some misguided spectator giving the elephant tobacco, followed by its ire and subsequent destruction of property — or of the miscreant who taunted it.[27] Much of the reporting relied on humor, or what passed for humor in the mid–19th century. One example went as follows:

> The keeper of a menagerie was lately seen beating one of the elephants with a large club. A bystander asked him the cause. "Why," said the keeper, "he's been flinging dust about the tent, *and he's big enough to know better.*"[28]

Another detailed the escape of an elephant after a violent storm. Charging into town, it entered a bread store and began devouring all the bread, crackers and cake. When a wagon delivering supplies came up, the animal "poked out a long nose and tumbled the cart over the horse's head — proving that there are more ways than one of putting 'the cart before the horse.'"[29]

Transporting elephants also proved trying. In late July 1843, four elephants attached to Raymond & Company's Menagerie left Fall River for Bristol, Rhode Island, the management offering benefit performances for sufferers of a late calamity. When the company attempted to board the ferry, three elephants refused. One animal was successfully transported, but the others plunged into the water and swam the mile distance.[30]

In late April 1844, another incident took place, this one involving the elephant Columbus, which was being driven from Philadelphia to Camden, New Jersey. The keeper, urging the animal along, pierced its ear with a long, hooked rod. After crossing the Delaware and moving into the Cricket Ground, Columbus seized the weapon with its trunk, broke off the hook and attacked his keeper, throwing him to the ground from a considerable height. A second keeper intervened and was also tossed into the air. A large dog (dogs were typically companions of elephants) soon quieted it. Both keepers were seriously injured, one possibly fatally.[31]

Attached to the Zoological Exhibition was Jacob Driesbach, an American from upstate New York. Leaving Schoharie about 1830, he went to New York City. Being possessed of a social and familiar disposition, with a "knowledge of human as well as *animal* behavior," he gained notice by his power over animals, eventually earning a job in a menagerie.[32] By 1842, he was working as a lion tamer at the Bowery Theatre. That May, he joined D. R. Lines' menagerie, one of James Raymond's shows. With Van Amburgh in England, "Herr" Driesbach rapidly became the most famous lion tamer in the States, billed as "the unrivalled animal Subduer."[33]

Like those who came before and who would follow, he was not immune from accident. At Philadelphia on December 21, 1842, while the tigers were being changed from one cage to another, one slipped away and attacked Driesbach, pinning him to the floor. Despite the keeper's desperate struggles, the outcome might have had dire consequences, but for some reason his "tigership" offered a majestic growl and retreated to his den.[34]

Perhaps with this accident in mind, advertisements for the Zoological Exhibition in 1843 noted that animals were "secured in strong iron cages." After performing in Haverhill and Portland in August, a two-day performance at Bangor offered a splendid, spacious pavilion, prepared especially for the occasion, capable of containing 10,000 persons. With his Leopards, Panthers, Tigers, and majestic Lion, Driesbach played a character described as an outcast banished to the forest. After a staged fight with a Brazilian Tiger, he secured the animal's den, harnessed his noble Lion to an ancient Car and drove over a road erected across the Pavilion. The act concluded with a "whole caravan of wild animals let loose upon him at the same time, who will then playfully exhibit his skill in subduing and controlling this matchless exhibition."[35]

Iron bars were only useful when used. On March 8, 1844, while at Baltimore, Driesbach took a favorite leopard to a coffee house. Companions of a 12-year-old boy pushed the child against the big cat, which reacted in rage by taking the boy's head in his mouth and severely wounding his face. Driesbach rescued him by thrusting his hand down the leopard's throat. In consequence of his negligence, he was arrested and sent to prison, afterwards being released on $1,000 bail.[36]

A splendid, spacious pavilion, capable of containing 10,000 persons, lured ticket-buyers to Raymond & Co.'s Zoological Exhibition. In it, Herr Driesbach played an outcast banished to the forest. After defeating a fierce Brazilian tiger and securing him in his den, the hero harnessed his noble lion to an ancient car and drove it over a road erected across the pavilion. The story concluded with a bold, grand and daring display of courage when the whole caravan of wild animals was set upon him. Driesbach's character triumphs by "playfully" subduing and controlling the beasts. (*Bangor Daily Whig and Courier*, September 2, 1843)

Incidents such as this gave the circus/menagerie a bad name, and, unfortunately, violence associated with traveling caravans was not unique. At Canaan, Maine, a fight broke out between members of Raymond & Co.'s Menagerie and a gang of disorderly citizens. After an inno-

Raymond & Waring promised their menagerie was composed of nearly EVERY EXISTING MEMBER of the brute creation, from the continents not only of AMERICA, but of Europe, Africa, Asia, New Holland, and the Isles of the Pacific. Herr Driesbach, the LION TAMER, also had in possession the "most terrible Lion ever caught," that saved his life when tigers, leopards and other beasts attacked him in the exercise cage. (*Marshall Statesman* [MI], August 18, 1846)

cent man named Spaulding was killed in the fracas, a vigilante committee brought in several members of the menagerie, while two others fled.[37]

"It was a sight worth walking ten miles to see."

"Grand Cavalcade! One Elephant In Harness!" read the advertisement for Raymond & Waring's Great Zoological Exhibition from the City of New York for a performance at Platteville, Wisconsin, in August 1846.[38] For their "Zoological Caravan" appearing in Marshall, Michigan, that same August, they advertised "Two Tremendous Elephants in Harness!" Accompanying the Michigan company was Herr Driesbach, tamer of the largest lion ever caught. "This lion is at present in his possession, and has repeatedly saved his life when exercising tigers, leopards and other beasts in the Performing Cage!"

Circuses and menageries changed names almost as frequently as they did proprietors. Mr. H. Hopkins first appeared in 1834 with a menagerie. In the winter of 1837, he joined forces with Matthew Buckley and Henry Rockwell as "Buckley, Rockwell, Hopkins & Co." The following season, they toured as the "Mammoth Arena and Circus Company" through upstate New York until Rockwell left to assume the duties of riding master for June, Titus & Angevine. By November, the concern took on Thomas Tuffs and became "Buckley, Hopkins, Tuffs & Co." In 1839, the show was sold to Hall, Nathans, Tuffs & Company.[39]

In 1843, the Philadelphia Zoological Garden united with the New York Institute (one of Raymond's concerns) under the direction of H. Hopkins and Co., and exhibited at Gettysburg. They offered "New and Splendid Scenery, done in oil painting by one of the best artists of Philadelphia," adorning the sides of 25 wagons, each depicting "animals of different descriptions." John Schaeffer, the "subduer of the savage denizens of the forest," appeared in scenes entitled "*The dreadful doom of the Sultan's slave.*" The "thrilling" situations included:

> The outcast slave banished to the forest of Falhut, expiring from hunger and fatigue; when a fierce Brazilian Tiger darts like lightning upon him from an upper cavern.
> The eastern despot's most awful sentence!!! Forfeited life spared on condition of training a wild lion to harness, which is accomplished, and the slave rides across the road in an ancient car.

The piece concluded with a whole caravan of animals let loose at the same time upon the Indian Slave, "who will gradually subdue, and playfully exhibit his remarkable skill in elegantly grouping the matchless zoological exhibition."[40]

Hopkins & Co. may not have been all that it was cracked up to be. In October 1843, the Ohio *Repository* got into an argument with a rival newspaper over a favorable review the former gave the menagerie. Prior to that, however, the *Repository* had published a very *un*favorable review and was then accused of recanting, owing to Hopkins' threat to prosecute. The editor denied the charge, insisting that on Hopkins' invitation they had visited the menagerie, realized their error and repaired the misconception.[41] Either scenario was equally plausible.

It is as well for the editor of the *Repository* that he did not get too close to the elephant, for in 1844 at Mount Pleasant, Ohio, it killed a man who had given it tobacco.[42] On March 10, 1845, the *New Orleans Bee* reported a tragedy involving Hopkins & Co. occurring outside the city and centering on *the same elephant* that killed its keeper at Algiers in the spring of 1841. According to the report, two elephants and a camel belonging to the menagerie of Hopkins & Co. were being driven in advance on the route to Clinton, the female elephant and the camel being chained together. Four miles from Baton Rouge, the male elephant, Pizarro, refused to cross a bridge. The keeper procured a horse for the purpose of driving it over, but as he mounted, the horse shied, throwing the keeper to the ground. This incited the elephant to gore the man with his tusks, toss him into the air and eventually deposit the body in the woods. It then returned to the other two animals, gored the camel, broke the chain that attached it to the female elephant and carried the dead body into the woods. When the caravan caught up, they fired at Pizarro without effect. Word was sent to the U.S. garrison, and 30 or 40 soldiers shot it 50 or 60 times. When the balls merely flattened against the tough hide, a field piece was sent for. In the interim, another keeper used a spear to inflict so much pain that the elephant screamed and yielded.[43] More elephant trouble plagued the company when it lost "Siam" in December 1845, at Zanesville.

Raymond & Waring's Menagerie was the object of a midnight visit by a reporter from a Cincinnati newspaper in April 1847. Proclaiming the trip worth a ten-mile walk, the writer arranged an interview with Herr Driesbach, who promised to show him the animals during their hours of repose. In what must have made fascinating reading for subscribers, the article first dispelled the assertion of natural historians by revealing that elephants actually slept lying down. He further described how lions, tigers, leopards and panthers slept together, "paws affectionately twined about each other, without regard to species or nativity." In cages where there was more than one animal, explained Driesbach and Thomas Cart (night watch of the menagerie, known as "Uncle Tom," and at this time the oldest showman in the United States), it was the custom for one cat to keep watch while the others slept. The sentinel paced back and forth, occasionally lying down but always with his head toward the front of the cage and never sleeping until relieved.

It required 500 pounds of hay per day to feed two elephants, while the carnivorous animals consumed from 100 to 120 pounds of meat every day. Added to that were large quantities of apples, potatoes and turnips purchased for the monkeys, birds and small animals.[44]

If the midnight interview was a warmhearted story, what followed less than two weeks later was not. After leaving Camden, Virginius and Pizarro, two elephants belonging to Raymond & Waring's Menagerie (the latter obtained from Hopkins & Co.) refused to get on the ferry for transportation across the Delaware River. Their keeper, Mr. Nutter, led the yoked pair to the Marine Railway in Southwark, where they were to swim across. Swept by the strong current, they actually swam two miles before Virginius tired. The pair gradually sank beneath the waves, their pitiful trunks extended above water for as long as possible before their strength gave out. Nutter described their final minutes by saying they seemed conscious of their fate, and their last looks toward him "were of regret and agony," as if sorrowing to leave him. Despite the animal's a history of violence, Pizarro was described by Nutter as a "docile animal," and he grieved his loss.

The elephants were valued at nearly $30,000, and their friends in Philadelphia mourned their tragic loss.[45] "Columbus" was brought up from another of Raymond & Waring's menageries at Pittsburg to take their place.[46] "Siam," another elephant belonging to the company, had died in December 1845, at Zanesville.

Things did not go well. At the end of December 1847, immediately before a performance in Philadelphia, the chain by which Columbus was held came loose and the elephant walked into the ring. William Kelly struck the animal with his goad, so irritating him that he twice swiped the keeper with his trunk, dashing him to the ground, breaking his right leg and thigh. The animal subsequently went on a rampage, smashing cages containing two hyenas, a wolf, jackal and twenty monkeys, killing some of the smaller ones.

Two elephant-dogs of the type used in India to hunt the creatures were set on Columbus; being unable to withstand his wrath, they were severely injured. Mayor Swift, having been summoned to the scene, called for muskets from the armory of the Washington Grays; before they arrived, Herr Driesbach tried to subdue the animal by his well-known voice, but failed to calm it. J. J. Nathans, of Welch's National Circus, suggested placing a noose on the ground where the animal might tread. When the foot landed in the middle of the rope circle, it was pulled tight. The crew tried to hold him, but even this failed, and Columbus eventually attempted to mount the box seats that descended from the front gallery to the arena. Finding they would not sustain his weight, he retreated to the arena, where a number of hooks fastened to ropes were lampooned into his ears, finally bringing him to submission.

Various reports indicated that Kelly, who had been unacquainted with the elephant, had his leg amputated; the *Cleveland Herald* reported that he died a few days later.[47]

By 1848, Raymond & Waring's Grand Menagerie was using ten Grey Horses to pull their New York Brass Band in a chariot measuring 20 feet high, 30 feet in length and weighing 8,000 pounds, to the summit of the canopy. The new artist featured for the May 16, 1848, perform-

Raymond & Co.'s Mammoth Menagerie featured Herr Driesbach, one of the most successful and popular lion tamers of the day. His pupil, the "Lion Queen," practiced "almost Superhuman Exhibitions of *fearless address* and *admirable courage*" by having the lions crouch at her feet in abject fear, proving the "superiority of the human mind over brute force and ferocity." Unfortunately, this "superiority" was achieved by brute force and did not often succeed. In 1850, an unnamed "Lion Queen" fell victim to one of her subjects. (*Rock River Pilot* [WI], June 7, 1848)

ance at Marshall, Michigan, was "M'lle Cybelle" (also "Madame"), the "Lion Queen." Taught to practice *self–possession, fearless address and indomitable courage* while performing her "almost SUPERHUMAN EXHIBITION" by Herr Driesbach, pupil and master demonstrated the most untamable animals crouching at her feet.

In addition to 60 Men and 100 Horses, the Menagerie boasted:

Cage No.

1	contains a Canadian Elk;
2	an African Zebra;
3	an Emu, or New Holland Ostrich & Kangaroo;
4	a pair of Peruvian Llamas;
5	Powees, Macaws, Parrots, Armadillo and Egyptian Weazel [*sic*];
6	Zebu, or Sacred Bull of Burmah [*sic*];
7	full grown Lion, Lioness and Leopard;
8	Asiatic Lioness, Tiger, Puma and African Leopard;
9	Royal Bengal Tiger, the only one in the United States;
10	Four North American Panthers;
11	Pair of Brazilian Tigers & Prairie Wolves;
12	Pair of spotted or grave robbing Hyenas;
13	Senegal Leopard, & beach or strand Hyena;
14	Russian and North American Brown and Black Bears;
15	Monkey Family, Ichneumons, Badgers;
16	Collection of prepared Beasts, Birds and Reptiles;
17	Boa Constrictors & Anaconda Serpents.[48]

One animal that did not make the list was reputed to be a cross between a Bengal tigress and a lion. Born around November 1847, at Raymond & Waring's Menagerie, the story went that a woman who had recently lost a child took it to "raise at her breast," the opposite of the Romulus and Remus tale of ancient Rome. Stepmother and infant (a male with the head and forepart being completely lion, but with a striped body and resemblance to a tiger) were said to be thriving.[49]

14

A *Small* Field of Competition

Here's the monstrous elephant;
I'm all a tremble at the sight!
See his monstrous tooth-pick, boys!
Wonder if he's fastened tight?[1]

The newspapers billed it as "Rival Attractions"—Raymond & Co.'s Mammoth Menagerie and General Tom Thumb, both exhibiting in Chicago in June 1848. The Chariot of the Menagerie, drawn by ten horses, attracted general attention, while Gen. Tom Thumb's miniature carriage, ponies and footmen had "irresistible charm."

"General Tom Thumb," born Charles Sherwood Stratton in Bridgeport, Connecticut, on January 4, 1838, was destined to become one of the most common faces and talked-about individuals of the 19th century. An unusually large baby, he reportedly weighed 9 pounds, 8 ounces at birth and grew normally for the first six months. At this point he stopped growing, and by late 1842, had not grown nor gained weight, not reaching two feet in height and weighing less than 16 pounds.

P. T. Barnum had the four-year-old brought to New York and quickly realized the possibilities of exhibiting him. He engaged the boy at $3 a week for four weeks, putting out the announcement in his Museum bills that "Gen. TOM THUMB, a dwarf of eleven years of age, [has] just arrived from England!" Barnum lied, of course, but justified it by stating that a small American child would hardly excite the public's interest.

After careful tutoring from the master, Tom Thumb, by his "native talent and an intense love of the ludicrous," became a fresh "novelty," touring the country with Fordyce Hitchcock, Barnum's friend.

An astonishing trip through Europe began in 1844, where the "General" met with unqualified success, charming Queen Victoria on several occasions and meeting other heads of state. By January 1, 1845, Barnum entered into an equal partnership with Mr. Stratton, Charles' father, each taking half the considerable profits. A favorite "levee" of his became the play *Hop o' My Thumb*, written by Barnum's friend Albert Smith.

After returning home, Barnum and Tom Thumb toured the eastern states, meeting President Polk and his wife in Washington in April 1847. Receipts from a 12-day stand in Philadelphia garnered $5,594.91; a one-day performance at Providence drew $976.97. With expenses given as $25 to $30 a day, the pair earned a tremendous stake. In November 1847, they traveled to Havana and from there took a boat to New Orleans. Traveling up the Mississippi, they reached Pittsburg in May 1848. From there, Barnum gave up his role of showman and returned home to Bridgeport while his agents continued with Tom.[2]

It is easy to understand why the General's arrival in Chicago incited "an immense crowd of urchins, and some of mature growth." He was advertised as a "distinguished MAN IN MINIATURE, weighing only 15 pounds, 16 years of age, 28 inches high," being "perfectly symmetrical in all his proportions, intelligent and graceful beyond all belief, and smaller than any infant that ever walked alone." Announcing that he had performed before 6,000,000 persons during the last 4 years, morning, afternoon and evening performances of two hours each were offered. In these, he sang, danced, imitated Grecian statues and gave representations of Napoleon Bonaparte and Frederick the Great.

Besides displaying Presents and Jewels received from the crowned heads of Europe, a daily parade of Miniature Equipage presented by Queen Victoria, consisting of the smallest horses in the world and a Chariot attended by footmen in livery, passed through town. Admission was 25 cents, children under 10 years half-price.[3]

While Tom Thumb thrilled audiences, Raymond & Waring's Menagerie continued to experience myriad problems. At Renselearville (Rennselaer), New York, high winds blew down the huge tent. Some 1,800 persons were underneath when the canvas collapsed, eliciting shrieks, groans, curses and supplications during the melee. Luckily, none of the animals escaped, and the performance was continued out of doors. Ironically, Waring was a native of that city, and this was his first visit home in 25 years.[4]

General Tom Thumb, the "Distinguished Man in Miniature," was one of the most recognizable and famous performers of the age. In 1848, he was listed as weighing only 15 pounds, being 16 years of age and 28 inches high. Typically, he was billed as being "perfectly symmetrical in all his proportions, intelligent and graceful beyond belief. The Little General's performance included songs, dances, imitating Grecian statues and resentments of Napoleon and Frederick the Great. Also showing with him was the Miniature Equipage presented him by Queen Victoria. (***Daily Sentinel and Gazette*** [WI], June 9, 1848)

P. T. Barnum's American Museum, New York, proved so successful that the great showman decided to take it on the road. Newspaper articles of the time (often lifted directly from advertising copy or dictated by a circus press man) noted that every feature of the mammoth establishment was of a peculiar and interesting nature. General Tom Thumb was attached to the establishment, and three of his more famous "personations" are depicted in this illustration. The "normal sized chair" is used to accentuate the General's diminutive height. (***Democratic Expounder*** [MI], July 22, 1852)

Raymond and Waring were not finished with "Acts of God." In November 1848, a "Thrilling Incident at the Menagerie" appeared as a lead story in the newspaper. This might have been construed as good news for the Menagerie, especially as it referenced a feature "not previously announced in the bills." Rather than depict a surprise animal act, however, the story recounted another violent gust of wind that blew down the canvas forming the large pavilion, just as Miss Adelina, the "Lion Queen" was performing. Spectators and cages were completely engulfed "in one common mass of confusion."

The roars of terrified beasts, screams of patrons and the pelting of the pitiless storm rendered the scene truly appalling, but, fortunately, panic was merely momentary as the managers cleared the wreck. Fears for Miss Adelina's safety were allayed when she emerged unscathed, albeit with a dead leopard at her feet. Apparently, the moment the canvas fell, two leopards and a tiger made a leap for her, but the noble lion bounded between them and protected her. Alviza Pierce, the keeper, reduced the snarling beasts to subjection, and the Lion Queen was happily relieved from further participation.[5]

Marking an eventful year, Raymond & Waring's animal problems persisted. On July 16, 1848, at Galway, Illinois, the elephant Columbus again got loose and tore away the bars on the cage housing the rhinoceros. The two engaged in a life-and-death struggle, the "unicorn" eventually thrusting his horn into the underbelly of the elephant. It then made its way to a swamp, where his keepers despaired of capturing him. A large reward was offered for his safe return, which remained in doubt. Columbus was not expected to recover; the loss to the menagerie amounting to $20,000, and "what was worse, they cannot be replaced."[6]

Some good news came when the rhinoceros ("the only one in America since 1836") made it out of the swamp and spent five months of the winter season with the company in Zanesville, Ohio. Interestingly, the entire company "won friends and good opinions" during this period, and their return for another winter stay was contemplated with satisfaction.[7] The "Driesbach Menagerie," as it was familiarly styled, did, in fact, return to Zanesville for the winter of 1849-1850, using Mr. Hundley's unoccupied Foundry building at the intersection of Market and Third streets.[8]

Another of Raymond & Waring's caravans featured Alviza Pierce, the Lion and Tiger Tamer, said to be the rival of Van Amburgh.[9] It was likely that with this menagerie the "Lion Queen" met her fate. On January 20, 1850 (the actual event probably occurring a month pervious), it was reported that during a performance a lion scratched her leg, and in moving back, she tripped. This inspired the animal to attack, with fatal results. The given name of the performer was not included, but as Miss Adelina was the last listed "Lion Queen," it may have been she to whom the article referred. Not surprisingly, another "Lion Queen," this individual a young girl attached to Wombwell's Menagerie, London, was killed by a tiger in 1850.[10]

The Original Returns — Almost from the Grave

Isaac Van Amburgh, to whom Pierce was likened, had returned to the United States from England in 1845, and played the Bowery Amphitheatre from December 18 until April 4, 1846. On April 20, a combined parade of Van Amburgh's caravan and Sands, Lent & Co.'s Circus opened the new season. Each company sported heavily carved bandwagons for the event (Van Amburgh's being a copy of one used by the English circus man Charles Hughes). James Raymond quickly copied their style, and through the turn of the century this type of bandwagon became synonymous with circus parades.[11]

Sands, Lent & Co., in their second season since returning from a tour of Europe (1843–1845), offered a diminutive theme featuring twin ponies "Lamon" and "Pythina" performing Waltzes, Tricks and Exercises; the scientific and wonderfully trained Fighting Ponies "Deaf Burke" and "Tom Spring"; the fairy steed "Cinderella," purchased at Franconi's in Paris; and a Lilliputian Troupe of 12 Ponies. Along with Richard Sands were juvenile riders Masters Juan Hernandez* and Walter Aymar; scenic rider and Equestrian Master Thomas Mosley; Mr. Huggles on the slack rope; the India Rubber Man, Henry Conover; Joe Pentland, Clown to the Ring; and 2nd Clown and Buffo Singer Sam Lathrop.[12]

Notoriety, for Van Amburgh at least, had its price. On June 16, 1846, the *Woonsocket Republican*, Rhode Island, published a report that he had been killed by a Tigress after foolishly approaching her at feeding time.[13] An enterprising lithographer quickly began circulating his depiction of the scene, and the report spread like wildfire, appearing in numerous British newspapers, including *Bell's New Weekly Messenger*, *The Nonconformist* and *Church and State Gazette*, as early as August 9. The story was eventually revealed to be a hoax, "got up by the N.Y. Penny press to make a *sell*," while foreign papers were alerted to the truth by the English clown, Mr. Wallett, who was with the performer in Boston.[14]

Truth proved equal to fiction the following year when, after a lengthy illness, Van Amburgh went back to work at Baltimore on March 31. After entering the cage of a lion and two leopards, he petted the lion before turning to the leopards. At this point the lion, without any show of anger, bit him in the breast. After a shriek of pain, the tamer left the cage and was attended by Dr. Gibson, who discovered teeth marks fully indented on the breast and back but no flesh opened. It was concluded that after his long absence away from the animals, he had lost some power over them.[15]

Acting for an agent of Lewis Titus, Van Amburgh left for England in December 1847, with the object of purchasing trained horses and to scout for talent in the equestrian, vaulting and tumbling line. After purchasing albinos, piedbalds [*sic*] and "spotted chargers," two or three elephants for £100 each, as well as the whole of his camels from William Batty, then proprietor and manager of Astley's Royal Amphitheatre,[16] Van Amburgh went back to performing.

Opening Easter Monday, April 24, 1848, Van Amburgh starred in *Morok, the Beast Tamer*, written by Bayle Bernard, founded on a passage in Eugene Sue's novel *Wandering Jew*.[17] He took a benefit performance on May 15, afterwards moving to Vauxhall Gardens.

Van Amburgh's sojourn to England ended, and he returned to the United States. On November 11, 1848, his caravan (Van Amburgh & Co.) sustained a serious loss from the ever-present danger of fire, although in this case arson was suspected. A barn in Lambertville, New Jersey, burned, killing twelve of Van Amburgh's finest horses; the loss was estimated at $3,000.[18]

One of the more enduring circuses established in the 1840s was that of Henry Rockwell

---

*Juan Hernandez (1832–1861) was a contemporary of Levi J. North and enjoyed an almost equal reputation. Alternately billed as James Hernandez, he was described by Richard Hemmings, a famous somersaultist, as having a fair complexion and hair, being 5'3" high. Hernandez, whose real name, according to Hemmings, was Mickey Kelley, visited England in 1852, and was pronounced the greatest equestrian that had ever appeared at Astley's.[19]

& Oscar R. Stone. In July 1844, under the title "Rockwell & Stone's New York Circus, or American Olympiad," Stone's half of the company featured a splendid Bugle Band under the direction of Mr. Vose, drawn in a Magnificent Chariot by six Arabian Horses.[20] Rockwell toured with the other half, hiring the Rivers brothers and also featuring a splendid carriage. In November, they reunited in the Bowery for a winter production.[21]

The 1845 version of Stone's New York Circus featured Monsieur Cassimer, styled "the Greatest Drummer in the World" by Louis Phillippe, who had made him chief drum major of the French Army. Cassimer's talent for Stone was to beat upon twelve drums at once in a rapid and elegant manner. Stone himself, called the "far famed equestrian of the west," performed, along with G. W. Sargent, the "famed Shakespearian rider." W. W. Hobbs, the youthful equestrian and vaulter (advertised as having thrown a backwards somerset while the horse was at full speed, the only successful rider to achieve this difficult task), appeared with John Gossin, the Clown surnamed "Grimaldi of America." Mrs. Gossin, female equestrian; D. Minnich, vaulter and slack rope dancer; C. Champion, youthful double leaper and double somerset thrower; Victor Piquet, posturer; Master B. Stephens, equestrian prodigy; Alonzo Hubbell, the American Samson; and the Nubian Melodists, a band of African Singers, completed the star attractions. Their featured exhibition was the "Andalusian Entry!" a sublime Spanish spectacle with splendid steeds gorgeously caparisoned.

Rockwell's half of the "Mammoth Circus" for 1845 comprised 120 Men and Horses, covering New England and Pennsylvania. He featured "Holiday Sports of Old Spain! Or the Bull Fight" (that had played at Boston for more than fifty nights), with the horse Black Vulture being disguised as a Bull. Charles, Frederick and Richard Rivea, the "human phenomenons," offered "Gymnical Trials," feats on the Cord Aerial, and classic *Union of Statuary*; and Master R. Rivea performed the Polander's Ladder, standing on his head for five full minutes.[22] For a single performance at Harrisburg, Pennsylvania, the circus drew 2,700 people.[23]

Rockwell & Stone's New York Circus, or American Olympian, was "Instituted for the advancement of refined Equestrian and Gymnastic Exercises," with their stud of beautifully marked and highly trained Arabian horses, "unmatched for Fleetness, Sagacity and Docility." (*Bangor Daily Whig and Courier*, July 8, 1844)

Tragedy struck on May 23, 1846, at Raynham, Massachusetts. While helping take down the equipment during a heavy storm, Oscar Stone sickened, dying three months later at the age of thirty-one. Hearing of his death, the troupe of Welch & Mann's Circus draped their canvas with crepe and wore mourning bands for a week.[24] C. R. Banks, who had been with the New York Circus as treasurer, assumed management of the company and maintained that position in 1847, when the New York Circus (H. Rockwell & Co., Proprietors) played New England.

Along with their Equestrian and Olympic Games, and the sagacious pony "Fanny Ellsler," the New York Circus featured Mrs. D. Johnson, pastoral horsemanship; Mrs. Camilla Gardiner, equestrian; Miss M. J. Johnson, juvenile aspirant; W. C. Johnson, whose ring performance included the reining and managing of nine horses simultaneously; George Sweet, rider and tight-rope walker; L. J. Lipman, principal act rider; Signor Felix Carlo, the Italian Clown who assisted D. Gardner; A. Lierpine; A. McFarland; H. Smith; Maller; and Masters M. McFarland and Jackson. Henry Steinman conducted and arranged the Bugle Band of twelve musicians.[25]

Tragedy of a different sort struck the circus family on December 15, 1847, at St. Louis, where Rockwell's Circus was in winter quarters. A former actor in the company named Harrington booked passage on a steamer for New Orleans, designing to take with him a boy named William, 8 or 10 years of age. The child had been committed to Harrington's care by his mother when only a year old. Typical of the period, Harrington adopted and trained him, and he became a valuable member of the company. Hiram Franklin, a partner in Rockwell & Co.'s Circus, did not wish to lose William. After carrying him off the boat, Franklin had himself appointed guardian. On discovering the deception, Harrington found Franklin at the Mansion House and shot him with a six-barreled revolver. The ball entered the side of his face, knocking out two teeth; the wound was serious but not considered mortal. Harrington next went to the Frederick House and attempted to shoot William Lake, another member of the circus. Failing that, he turned the pistol on himself and committed suicide.[26]

Ironically, William Lake (real name William Lake Thatcher) ran out of luck in August 1869, at Granby, Missouri. A loafer named Jake Killian tried to slip into the circus without paying. Lake confronted the "dead-head" and had him arrested. Killian later returned, paid his way in and shot Lake dead. Lake's wife, Agnes Lake Thatcher (*née* Agnes Mersman, born 1826), a tight-rope walker, lion tamer and financial manager, became proprietor of the "Hyppo-Olympiad and Mammoth Circus," and operated it for three years. In 1876, she married "Wild Bill" Hickok.[27]

William Hubbell, who had managed the second of Rockwell's New York Circuses, managed the European Circus in 1849. The company featured the Antonio Family (Antonio, Lorenzo, Augustus and Alphonso); Mons. Orlel and Lovett, clowns; Signor Shobiski, slack wire; Signor and Signoretta Altonio; Mr. and Mrs. Sherwood; and M'dlle Antonietta Duvat. Exhibitions included Equestrian feats, Slack Rope, Slack Wire, Ground and Lofty Tumbling, a Grand Entrée and Comic Afterpiece, Negro Concerts and Breakdowns (dancing). Reviews for this show were generally flattering.[28] The circus lasted but a single year.

James M. June and Aron Turner joined forces again in 1844, under the banner "June & Turner's Circus! From the Bowery Amphitheatre, New York." Traveling through the Midwest, by 1845 their troupe consisted of Napoleon B. Turner; Timothy V. Turner; William H. Stout, clown and rider; James W. Myers, scenic rider and Riding Master; Mr. L. Freeman, contortionist; and Messrs. O. Bell, Liming, Keenan, Vanbonhurst and Her, with Masters Nevilles and Tom. Reducing the cost of tickets to 20 cents, they hoped "to receive a share of patronage from a liberal public."[29]

"Combined, Enlarged, and Improved" for 1847, "June & Turner's Menagerie and Circus" featured James M. June as manager and William June as agent. Adding animals provided the excuse to raise prices (admission to both attractions cost 40 cents, with children half price). Performers listed were Timothy V. Turner, Equestrian Director; H. W. Nichols as Clown; James W. Myers as Riding Master; and S. B. W. Post as Leader of the Band. Their Grand Pavilion was new, covering an area 160 × 76 feet, constructed of weatherproof material and large enough to accommodate 3,000 persons. Mr. Post's New York Military Band was carried by a Chariot drawn by Eight Cream colored Horses wearing harnesses richly silver-mounted in pattern work, manufactured by Francis of New York City.[30]

Interestingly, in an August advert, they gave the dimensions of the Pavilion as 150 × 75 feet and omitted the word "silver" when describing the harnesses.[31] No description of the animals was given, but in a review in September, it was remarked, "The Menagerie embraces a large and very fine collection of animals."[32]

A different combination appeared in 1848, as June and Titus joined forces to present the Equestrian and Zoological Circus and Menagerie, boasting 150 Men and Horses. The ticket price for this exhibition was 25 cents (no half-price offered). Feature performers included William Carroll; Mrs. Carroll, the equestrian; Messrs. Swift, Bacon and Conover; Masters Johnson, Aymer and Williams; Sam Lathrop as Clown; and Mr. Huntington as Ring Master. The menagerie contained Romeo, the elephant, with Miss M. A. Randolph, another "Lion Queen," appearing with lion tamer Mr. Shimer. J. G. Sloat acted as agent.[33]

Welch (misspelled as "Welsh"), Mann and Delevan's Great National Circus, with James W. Bancker, agent, traveled throughout New England and the mid–Atlantic states in 1846, featuring the by-now standard Cavalcade, with a "costly Chariot" drawn by ten cream-colored horses. Their great water-pavilion tent measured 20,000 square feet and was capable of containing 3,000 persons. Among their performers were J. J. Nathans, a 2-, 4-, and 6-horse rider (with occasional balancing of the infant Frank Pastor on his head while the steeds galloped at full speed); Riding Master Horace F. Nichols; two Clowns, John May and John Whitaker; Signor Germani, the Italian Juggler; C. G. Rogers, scene rider; W. Nichols, a "chaste principal Act Rider of the French and American Schools"; W. Kinkade, young equestrian hero, on his jet-black filly "Lucy Neal"; E. Wood, the great personificator [sic] of the Red Man of the Forest; Mrs. Woods, chaste Female Equestrian; the youthful George Dunbar, Equilibrium and personal Posture; Neal Jameison, banjo; and Frank Brower, dancer. Admittance was 25 cents.[34]

Welsh, Mann and Delevan's Great
NATIONAL CIRCUS,

The attractions for Welch (misspelled in the ad), Mann and Delevan's Great National Circus, 1846, read like a Who's Who of the Circus World: James W. Bancker, agent; J. J. Nathans, the unsurpassed 2, 4, and 6-horse rider, with the "infant" Frank Pastor, who rode on Nathans' head while the steeds were at lightning speed; riding master Horace F. Nichols; clowns John May and John Whitaker; Signor Germani, the Italian Juggler; C. G. Rogers, scenic rider; W. Nichols, principal rider; W. Kinkade, young equestrian hero; E. Wood, the great personificator of the Red Man of the Forest; Mrs. Woods, female rider; George Dunbar, Chinese Equilibrium and personal Posture; Neal Jameison, banjo player; and Frank Brower, dancer. (*Star & Republican Banner* [PA], May 22, 1846)

With the departure of Alvah Mann in 1847, Welch & Delevan's Great National Circus toured Wisconsin, Michigan and Ohio. Rider Levi J. North joined the company with his trick horse "Tammany"; J. J. Nathans performed and served as Equestrian Director; and N. Johnson was Riding Master. Also returning were John May, Mrs. Woods and Mr. E. Wood, with Frank Pastor offering "touching infantile" acts on a single horse. With C. Griswold serving as agent, James Bancker returned to performing, along with G. Dunbar, F. Brower, N. Jameson and J. Stickney (playing an Ethiopian character).

Colonel Alvah Mann died in 1855, aged 46 years. A well-known and popular figure, he was the builder and first manager of the Broadway Theatre in 1849. According to his obituary, after losing the property and nearly all his savings, he entered circus management, "likewise considered unsuccessful." W. E. Delevan and General Welch were among those attending the funeral.[35]

Welch & Delavan's Great National Circus, 1847, featured the brilliant equestrians Levi J. North (with his dancing and trick horse Tammany), J. J. Nathans and John Glenroy (pupil of Mr. Cadwallader), the barebacked horse rider, whose somerset, or throwing himself head over heels while his courser galloped at great speed and alighting firmly on the horse's back, was proof of the eminence that might be obtained by unceasing practice and undaunted resolution. (**Huron Reflector**, October 19, 1847)

One of the "noblest features of the Company" was John Glenroy, the great bare–backed horse rider, leaping through balloons and over silken raised barriers. A pupil of George Cadwallader, Glenroy was said to be the first to perform a somerset on a bare–backed horse, accomplishing the feat in 1846. Among the equestrian attractions were two "eccentric ponies, Black Moggy and Jenny Lind."[36]

One of the more interesting stories surrounding this circus involved an Anaconda that swallowed a rabbit whole. A doctor was called, and he dosed it with calomel. The snake subsequently died, and Welch sent the body, coiled in a full whiskey barrel, to the physician as part payment for his trouble. The doctor being away, the barrel was placed in the back room of his hotel, where several patrons discovered it. Unaware of what the barrel actually contained, they tapped it and drank the liquor. When the doctor returned, he found the anaconda in a state of decomposition and buried it. Returning home, he mentioned to the stage driver the "suckemstance" of the snake, causing the driver to fall into a fit of convulsions. When finally recovered, he articulated, "D — n your infernal snake! I thought the liquor had a thundering strange flavor!"[37]

The story was decidedly more amusing to the doctor than the proprietor, for the loss of the anaconda was substantial. In 1848, a boa constrictor measuring 30 feet was brought from the African coast to Salem, Massachusetts, by Captain Williams of the

Allen. Lewis Titus' agent offered $7,000, and P. T. Barnum's manager, Fordyce Hitchcock, offered $7,500, but the owner held out for $11,000. No mention was made of who eventually won, but as the snake laid 57 eggs, weighing 70 pounds, there was enough to go around.[38]

Not uncommonly, an erroneous report on the death of Levi J. North emerged after a hurricane struck Welch & Delevan's Circus while performing at Kingstown, Indiana, that September.[39] In another unsurprising notation, that fall John Glenroy's apprenticeship ended and he was released from Cadwallader's contract. The youth remarked that during the entire time he never received fifty dollars from his earnings, Cadwallader appropriating it all for himself. Frank Pastor, an apprentice of J. J. Nathan, observed that as learning to be an equestrian and acrobat "were not legally recognized," his apprentice papers said "farrier and veterinary man."[40]

In 1848, Welch's National Circus, from the Chestnut Street Amphitheatre, Philadelphia, introduced the Sylvic Gas for lighting the immense Establishment, which was introduced into the center of the beautiful Pavilion, in a large Coronet of Silva brilliancy. The orchestra was under the direction of Richard Willis, surnamed the "King Bugle Player." His noble stud of horses and ponies were culled from the "pride of Arabia, the choice of England and France, and the selections of Scotland." (*Republican Compiler* [PA], July 24, 1848)

Gas Illumination and the "Armamaxa"

One of the more intriguing additions to Welch's National Circus when it played Gettysburg on July 27, 1848, was Sylvic Gas used to illuminate the pavilion. Noted to be "one of the most extraordinary and wonderful improvements in travelling exhibitions," a large fixture was placed in the center of the tent, casting a large "Coronet of Silva brilliancy" across the arena.[41] As with aerostation, when balloons were inflated with gas, temporary pipes were run from a gasometer belonging to the local gas company and filled. In this case, the pipes would have been attached to a large lamp or chandelier.

The introduction of this particular gas was extremely new, the apparatus for the generation of sylvic gas having only been invented in 1848, by Benjamin Franklin Coston. A scientist of repute, he left the Navy Department in 1847 over a contract dispute and went to work at the Boston Gas Light Company. Sylvic gas was derived from rosin and provided an extremely bright illumination. It quickly became popular and was supplied by gas companies for city lighting, and use in factories, churches and even the Astor House. Tragically, Coston died on November 24, 1848, from exposure to toxic processing chemicals. Significantly, his wife Martha later developed a pyrotechnic night signal flare and code system used by the United States Navy during the Civil War.[42]

This proved the only time piped gas was advertised this season, most likely stemming from the fact that smaller cities could not provide the article.

In September, at Marshall, Michigan, Welch, Delevan & Nathan's National Circus, J. W. Bancker, agent, introduced another wonder, this in the form of the "Armamaxa," or Imperial Persian Chariot, drawn by 30 horses. The chariot was manufactured by J. Stephenson and Co., 27th Street, New York, and was fashioned after the Imperial Chariots of Persia during the reign of Cyrus the Great.

The sides of the Chariot were divided into six panels, separated by richly gilded scrollwork in the style of Louis XIV. The scrollwork was bordered by frill molding and ran along the top and bottom of the Chariot.

Equestrian J. J. Nathans' style was described as "manly, energetic and masterly." In his scenes of *Centaur and Infant Achelles* he was assisted by the Infant Artist ("Infant" referring to a child rather than a babe in arms) Frank Pastor, who, for his grace, beauty and courage, was considered "the most wonderful child in the world." Also appearing was Frank's younger brother, William, in a series of personal gymnastics. It was not uncommon for children of tender years to perform arduous and often dangerous circus tricks. Later in the century, circus proprietors would run afoul of the newly formed Society for the Prevention of Cruelty to Children, which protested their work under evolving child labor laws. (***Marshall Statesman*** [MI], September 5, 1848)

The seat was covered with a rich hammercloth (a cloth that covered the coach-box in which hammer, nails and bolts were carried in case of accident) of purple velvet, trimmed with deep silver fringe, pendant from a border of blue and yellow velvet, the whole decorated with eagles, equestrian figures, stars and flowers, and wrought in gold and silver. The Charioteer appeared borne along between the expanded wings of two mighty dragons, "apparently of massive gold," which crouched above the fore wheels of the Chariot.[43]

A contemporary in Philadelphia, describing the events of New Year's Eve, 1846, wrote that a circus, holding 3,000 people, was crowded to excess every night; the menagerie, he added, was also well patronized, centrally located and admirably filled with a very large collection of beasts and birds. A splendid attraction of this exhibition was the chariot, 20 feet in length and 17 feet high, manufactured by John Stephenson, New York, where workers spent nine months on its elaborate carvings:

The driver's seat is at one side, supported on the shoulders of an Atlas, while the figure of a Triton, blowing his conch shell, ornaments the other side. The sides of the chariot are embellished with paintings of an East India tiger hunt, surrounded with animals carved in a manner true to nature. A splendid canopy surmounts the whole, on the top of which is perched an eagle. The supports of the canopy are exceedingly appropriate — coils of serpents sustain it in front, while the figures of giraffes do the same service in the rear. At the back of the car is a full sized lion's head and front, and the swing — [illegible] are ornamented with the heads of crocadiles [sic]. The ornaments are all carved out of solid blocks of wood and richly gilded, while the groundwork of the chariot is painted in rich scarlet. Its cost was about $5000, and is only used upon the entrance of the company into the cities and towns they visit during their travel about the country, when it contains the band attached to the menagerie, and is drawn by two or four elephants. Its weight is so great that ten or twelve horses are required to draw it.[44]

If any image brings to mind "circus," this is surely it: extravagant use of images and color, shiny gold and silver decoration, reference to ancient cultures, brilliant emblazonry, graceful portions. At the midpoint of the century, Americans responded to Big, Bold, Impressive and Expensive. Circus advertisements extolled harnesses trimmed with silver and "chariots" covered with decorated panels — the Armamaxa literally threw out all the stops, proprietors hoping to impress and draw massive crowds. The enormous expense was a gamble, but one based on sound business principals.

The effort accurately mirrored what was happening along the rivers, where steamboat owners painted their vessels bright blue or yellow, crafted images of bursting suns or mythological goddesses, gilded palings, and provided plush couches and gourmet meals to first cabin passengers. It was all "smoke and mirrors," of course, meant to last no more than several years before the superficial gilding wore off, the paint faded, the panels buckled and the thin hulls gave way.

It was the illusion of the moment that counted; that which inspired the farm family, the clerk and the small businessman to "pony up" his hard-earned money for two hours of exposure to the grand and sublime. Steamboats and circuses provided the ultimate escape, offering make-believe worlds and exotic adventures. The circus and menagerie business was, first and foremost, just that: a business. Owners, managers and artists wanted to make money, and toward that end they understood the effect of glamour. Entertainment of the 1800s was not meant for children, as the circus might be construed today; it provided escapism for the men who toiled in the fields or who were locked in offices and factories twelve hours a day, six days a week. The humor was adult, the clown's gesticulations frequently lewd and bawdy. Circus proprietors took great pains to advertise educational or non–offensive acts, but paper promises were often more lure than fact.

In reality, traveling entertainers, whether they were actors, mesmerists, patent medicine pitchmen, lightning rod salesmen or circus performers, lived hard lives, and many had bad reputations. Numerous newspaper articles detailed how members of these lower orders committed robberies, perpetrated frauds, instigated brawls or lured children away from their parents. Many circulated in fast company; greater still were the chronic drunks. Gold and glitter was the ticket to counter, or at least thinly cover, reality with fantasy. And, to a large extent, it succeeded.

New on the Bills

J. J. Nathans, listed by the National Circus in 1845 as a *two and four horse rider* (italics in original), graduated to a 2, 4 and 6 horse rider in 1846. He was assisted by Frank Pastor; while Pastor's brother William was apprenticed to Nathans in 1848 and performed personal gymnastics. Richard Rivers, Signor Germani (presenting the "Hindoo Miracles," as well as appearing with two Learned Dogs), Edward Wood, Frank Brower and Ring Master N. Johnson continued with the circus for the 1848 season. New on the bill were scenic riders Washington Chambers and James Hawkins.[45]

The following year, the National Circus again toured the Midwest. Besides their Armamaxa, the proprietors offered an expansive entertainment harkening back to the earliest roots of the circus, consisting of Scenic Acts, Gymnastic Feats, Globe and Barrel Exercise, Vaulting (both single and double), Leaping, Equilibriums, Tumbling, Pyramidical Devices, Posturing, Comic Singing and Dancing, Comic Burlettas, Interludes, Promenades, Cavalcades, Masquerades & c.

The New York Knickerbocker Brass Band, under Thomas C. Casram, performed the fashionable airs of the day, while four European Stars (Lavater Lee, C. Lee, and Eugene and Theodore Lee), termed the *Necromancers, or the Bottle Magicians,* offered magic. Nathans offered 1, 2, 3, 4 and 6 horse riding. The rest of the troupe included J. Gossin, the "clown of all Clowns"; Niel Jameson (Neal Jameison); Robert White, gentlemanly Riding Master; E. M. Dickinson, Gospel singer; Madam and Mr. Woods; Washington Chambers; J. Hawkins; B. Mallory, Comic Posturer and Dancer; Antonio Pastor, ground and lofty tumbling; Frank Pastor, the "Pet of the Circle"; and Master William Pastor, Exercises.

Dan Rice, the true character of the age, earned his own circus in May 1848, partnering with Gilbert R. Spalding in an exhibition called "Dan Rice & Co.'s Metropolitan and Hippodramatic Circus." It began in St. Louis, with Van Orden as manager and John Glenroy (and later Henry P. Madigan) as principal rider. Rice's wife, Margaret Ann Curran, made her debut as a rider the same year. By August, Rice made enough money to buy out Spalding, Van Orden leaving with him. After performing on steamboats at the beginning of 1849, the circus began land travel with wagons. Around this time, Spalding and Van Orden reappeared, investing $2,300 for a half share of the concern. Things did not go well, and by season's end, Spalding foreclosed on Rice, taking everything but one horse, while Van Orden foreclosed on Rice's farm.

In 1850, Rice borrowed money to operate a small circus, beginning his tour in Buffalo. William B. Carroll, principal rider, used his own horses. The sting of losing his former circus did not sit well with Rice, and in order to publicly vilify Van Orden, he penned less-than-flattering songs that he performed in the ring. The object of his ire sued for libel and had Rice arrested. Rice made bail, but Carroll deserted to Spalding's circus, taking his horses with him. With two friends, Jean Johnson and James O'Connell (the tattooed man), Rice advertised the concern as a "One Horse Show," eventually reaching New Orleans. Success followed, enabling Rice to purchase the steamboat *Zachary Taylor,* said to be worth $9,000.[46] Despite his inability to handle money, bouts with alcoholism, and what might be considered a zany personal life, Dan Rice became a stalwart of the Circus Era, eventually earning legend status.

Not So Trifling Annoyances

If two constants in life are death and taxes, even circuses were not immune. Cholera, one of the most dreaded plagues of the 19th century, struck with frightening regularity. The disease was spread by drinking water contaminated by excrement of infected persons, but that was not known in the first half of 1500s. When an outbreak occurred, accusations generally fell on immigrants along the waterways and traveling people who were thought to spread contagion. In 1832, at Jacksonville, a circus performing there was blamed for the deaths of patrons who attended their performances. Several principal artists also died, and the company was broken up.[47]

This instance was well remembered, and when cholera struck in Iowa in 1849, the Burlington City Council refused a license to the menagerie. The manager did succeed in obtaining permission from the county but eventually declined to fulfill the engagements. A circus in town at the same time, also refused a permit, removed to the bank of the river on the Illinois side, offering free ferry rides to anyone wishing to attend their performances. Tensions ran high, however, and several fights broke out during the evening.

In a different twist, instead of being blamed during the Jamaican cholera epidemic of 1850–1851, the large van of Wortley's Circus was used to carry off the dead.[48]

Measles was another scourge of the 19th century, and when monkeys in Forepaugh's Circus contracted the disease, newspaper accounts reported it had spread to farm children in Chataraugus County, New York. To prevent the spread of disease, in 1886, at Brownsville, Texas, a Mexican circus was placed in quarantine by being "dumped into an old warehouse on a barren sand island ... and told they would be kept there twenty days." They appealed to their Consul, complaining of suffering inflicted on their women and children.[49]

License fees were another drain on circus and menagerie coffers, and were not to be discounted lightly, as they brought substantial revenue to municipalities. In 1842, for example, Milwaukie [sic] passed an ordinance charging any persons wishing to exhibit "animals, wax figures, sleight of hand, rope or wire dancers, circus riding or theatrical entertainments for gain" a fee of not less than $5 or more than $50 per week.[50] By 1845, the legislature of Pennsylvania charged theaters and circuses $200, and menageries $40, a year to perform in Philadelphia. This fee did not exempt them from municipal taxation.[51] Costs mounted quickly: for the period of December 1, 1845, to November 30, 1846, the state collected $1,180.50.[52] Business must have slacked off somewhat in 1847, as Pennsylvania only received $930, but estimates indicated that 1848 would bring $1,000 into state coffers.[53] If 1848 did see such a take, 1849 surpassed it, garnering $2,210 in license fees. The year 1850 was expected to surpass that, bringing $3,000 into the treasury.

To put fees into perspective, in 1849, alone, Philadelphia garnered $3,000 from "Pedlar's Licenses"; while Broker's Licenses brought in $12,000; Patent Medicine Licenses $3,000; and the combination of Billiard Rooms, Bowling Salons and Ten-pin Alley Licenses $5,000. Canal and Railroad Tolls (another incidental fee circuses paid) amounted to a stunning $1,825,000 in 1849.[54] By April 12, 1850, the Philadelphia legislature proposed an increase, raising license fees to $500 per circus.[55] Not to be left out, in July 1849, the Common Council of Detroit levied a fee of $100 *per day* for those "showing the elephant."[56]

Besides taxes and death, prejudice could be added to the list of not so trifling annoyances. An article entitled "Demoralizing Amusements" summed up the matter. Singling out circuses, the author opined:

We do not care what the show bills may say, as to the morality, or decency, or dignity of these establishments. We know that every one that drags its filthy tail over the country is heralded by boasts of a peculiar freedom from anything objectionable. We know that ladies and children are confidently invited to attend their pure and refined exhibitions, in which "nothing is allowed which would offend the most delicate modesty," and they do attend them. We are unmoved by these pretensions, first because they are always false....

Vulgar antics, "disgusting and degrading frivolity," and obscene jokes by the painted clown were enumerated, along with an observation that "these travelling pestilences" drag after them a vast train of "almost indispensable depravity... half a hundred of profane, licentious and reckless men, who poison the very air, with the exhalations of city pollution." In conclusion, the author called for a complete ban on such exhibitions in Ohio, similar to what had been tried in Vermont.[57]

Another newspaper article from Ohio concluded, "Such amusements we believe to be wholly inconsistent with Christian character, destructive to piety, ruinous to the early religious impressions of the rising generation, and a hindrance to the conversion of irreligious neighbors."[58]

Despite disease, taxes and printed attacks, circuses and menageries were well established in the American consciousness and set to parade into the decade of the 1850s.

15

"A Regular Out-and-Outer"

What is the difference between the trunk of a tree and the trunk of an Elephant?— One leaves *in the spring, and the other* leaves *whenever the menagerie does!*[1]

Circus humor even provided a chance for businesses to get into the act:

HURRAH FOR BARNUM.

Barnum is some Pumpkins they say, but he charges a Quarter for a Show—While I charge nothing for a sight of the Tallest Yankee, and the Cheapest, Neatest and Best SHOES in TOWN.[2]

Joseph Andrew Rowe opened his "Olympic Circus" in San Francisco in late October 1849, finding fertile ground among the gold miners and immigrants flooding the city. On opening night the "circus company of very fair materials" took in "the very snug little sum of $3000—a pretty good beginning."[3] Dave Long, the clown, a recipient of this prosperity, earned $12,000 a year for his efforts,[4] and in December that year, he was bought into the circus as a partner. Other performers included Senor and Senora Levero, tight-rope; and Master Raphael and Mrs. Rowe, riders. The show moved to Sacramento in May 1850, before returning to San Francisco. In November, it traveled to Hawaii.[5]

Another "Great Olympic Circus" (late of Astor Place, New York), with many performers from Sands, Lent & Co., chartered the steamboat *Cinderella* to carry them to Newport, where they set out tents on July 8, 1850. Among those performing were Messrs. Richard Rivers (proprietor), Hiram W. Franklin (the man shot in the head in 1847), Burnell Runnals, John Glenroy, N. Johnson, George Honey and H. Conover. John Tryon served as manager.[6]

Another familiar name, Aron Turner, operated simply the "Circus" under the heading, "A. Turner & Co., Proprietors. Under the direction of Dr. E. Ganung." Promising, "on no occasion will ribaldry be used by the clowns or singers," the troupe included Napoleon B. and Timothy V. Turner, J. Estley, James W. Myers, S. Maller, R. Hoe, Mons. Henry Haslett, J. Maine, Moses Lipman, with Masters Ward and Wyath. The leader of the Band was S. Neave, and Director H. Neave. Working throughout Pennsylvania and New Jersey, Timothy Turner's four-horse act and James Myers' clown performance as a "comic genius" were singled out for attention in reviews.[7]

A year later, adding Van Amburgh's animals, "A. Turner & Company's Combined Menagerie & Circus" featured the elephant "Abdallah" as it traveled through Pennsylvania.

Among the human performers were the 6-horse rider Napoleon Turner and the "Clown of All Clowns," John Meyers.[8] With all under the same pavilion, the price was 25 cents, or "cheap enough," as the newspaper noted.[9]

Gerald C. Quick & Company's "Mammoth Menagerie" purchased animals from Van Amburgh, being formed from his company and that of June, Titus & Co. (James June having gone to Ceylon for P. T. Barnum in 1850). Also exhibited were Langworthy's trained Ponies, which waltzed and danced.[10]

"Sands, Lent & Co. American Arena" (also called "R. Sands and Co.'s Hippoferean Arena" in the same advertisement) performed throughout New York and the eastern states in 1848, with a cast that included Richard, Jesse and Maurice Sands, Joe Pentland, Sam Lathrop, Albert Aymar, Master Walter Aymar, Henry Ruggles and Signor Perez. Master of the Arena was J. A. DeCamp, with H. P. Madigan serving as equestrian director. Their elephants were Romeo and Jenny Lind. The year 1849 was similar; but in 1850, the company advertised two eye-catching features: a grand procession with the East India Car, drawn by three huge elephants, and the "Chariot of Queen Mab," drawn by Twenty Lilliputian Ponies. Master of the Arena was Frank Whittaker; Equestrian Director William H. Stout; clowns Sam Lathrop and William Aymar; James W. Foshay was Treasurer; and Gerald C. Quick was Manager and Director.[11]

For the citizens of Fort Wayne, Indiana, one summer week in 1850 must have seemed like heaven. While Sands played there August 28, Crane & Co.'s Great Oriental Circus appeared August 23 and 24. With their 240 Men and Horses, Children and Ponies, John P. Crane offered the "Monster Dragon Chariot, Drawn by 10 Camels," followed by a "Fairy Chariot, Drawn by 12 Diminutive Ponies" not more than 36 inches in height, driven by Master A. Ward. Their pavilion accommodated 5,000 spectators. Mr. P. Fous directed the New York Sax Horn Band. With them were M'lle Rosa; Joe Pentland, clown; H. P. Madigan, equestrian; Henry Gardner, Dramatic Horseman; John Shay, Equestrian Juggler; Mr. Liming, Trick Clown; Signor Bliss, contortionist; Messrs. Murray and Reed, Acrobatic Artists; and Twin ponies, Damon and Pyfillas. The pet Pony Don Juan danced, waltzed and starred in "The Charioteer's Dilemma," while the camels performed in the Oriental Pageant "The Sultan's Hall in the Desert."[12]

Arriving at Wellsboro, Pennsylvania, on October 10, Cranes' Oriental Circus was heralded by one review as the best troupe of gymnastic and equestrian performers. The reviewer singled out the Dragon Chariot, with its 10 Syrian camels, the superb Oriental costumes and the celebrated clown Joe Pentland.[13]

Sands and Quick combined their circus and menagerie for 1852, offering "Wild Beasts and Equestrian Exercises, with a pageant of 'St. George and the Dragon.'" In August 1852, a "hoax" was perpetrated by their agent in putting out a story that Richard Sands had died while attempting to perform his antipodean feat of walking on the ceiling. A great deal of sympathy for Sands' fiancée was "wasted" by the agent's "adroit movement" to obtain free publicity.[14] J. J. Nathans, Frank and William Pastor, John Lovett & H. W. Day (clowns) were featured. An added bonus was having the Pavilion illuminated by Portable Gas Chandeliers.[15]

In 1855, Sands and Nathan combined in an exhibition called the "American Circus," with Sam Lathrop as clown and four elephants (Pizarro, Timour, Selim and Saib, from Astley's). Lewis June served as agent. The show was described as being "a real old-fashioned, simon-pure sort, only a great deal more so."[16] The following year, Sands & Nathans' advertised only two elephants, "Victoria" and "Albert," which marched with military precision,

Cooper, Bailey & Co., Proprietors, promised "A World of Amusement" with their "Great International 10 Allied Shows," where one ticket admitted the bearer to everything. "Everything" included a combined double circus and double menagerie, camel races and every child's favorite, "The only Den of Living Performing Flesh Eating Hyenas!" (*Jackson Sentinel* [IA], May 18, 1876)

balanced on their hind legs and stood on their heads. Richard Sands performed his Antipodean feats, or "a man walking like a fly"; J. J. Nathans served as Equestrian Director; C. Bassit was Master of the Circle; and five clowns, Sam Welser, Ben Huntington, Toney Bliss, Bob Connor and Fred Denver, filled out the bill.[17]

Just as Noell Waring had gone home to upstate New York in 1848, so, too, did "Herr Driesbach, the Lion Tamer," return to his roots in Schoharie during the hiatus in January 1850. The locals hoped his visit might be to cure his state of "single blessedness."[18] Whether or not he had his eye on a lucky lady, he returned to Zanesville, Ohio, by March, where Raymond & Co.'s Menagerie was wintering. Unlike Van Amburgh, whose personality was occasionally standoffish and imperial, by all accounts, Driesbach was a pleasant man who enjoyed performing for an audience of reporters. Armed with a book containing extracts of newspaper articles praising his extraordinary powers, he gladly conducted tours of the animals and offered private shows,[19] displaying a love of his "pets."[20]

Putting on a display before leaving Zanesville in April, the concern had the opportunity to show off its newly acquired Polar or White Bear. The menagerie also included a rhinoceros and the usual collection of big cats.[21] From Ohio, the company traveled through Michigan and Wisconsin, offering pony races with monkey riders.[22] On June 31 [*sic*], an all-too-frequent accident occurred, where a youth was thrown from the elephant, dying the next morning.[23]

For Students of Natural History

A story of a different sort, and with a happier ending, revolved around Herr Dries-bach's "rival," Isaac Van Amburgh. Enjoying a successful tour through Toronto, where 3,000 persons nightly came to witness the lion tamer's performances,[24] another Tamer named Signor Hydralgo was in the cage with a panther, a Bengal tiger, an African lioness, a spotted leopard, a cougar and a hyena. Toward the end of the performance, after a tiger was struck with the whip to make him leap, the animal turned on Hydralgo and brought him to the floor. Van Amburgh, who had been on the other side of the arena, rushed to his aid and quickly had the enraged beast "under his feet in perfect subjection." For his bravery in saving his friend, Van Amburgh received three hearty cheers.[25]

On February 13, 1851, while the menagerie wintered at Zanesville, a lioness gave birth to three whelps, the first born west of the Allegheny Mountains. Within the past three years, this same lioness had given birth to twenty cubs but had raised only two pair. Sadly, these cubs died two days later.[26]

For 1851, Raymond & Co.'s and Van Amburgh's Combined Menageries toured Ohio and Pennsylvania, offering over 150 specimens of wild animals, including the Rhinoceros, White Polar Bear, Van Amburgh's ten Lions and the beasts of another tamer, Mons. Craw-ford (presenting an altogether different performance from Van Amburgh's), comprising an African Lion and Lioness, Senegal Leopard, Asiatic Tiger and two cougars.[27]

November 1, 1851, marked another sad day for animal lovers, as the elephant Colum-bus, of Raymond & Co., died at Lenox, Pennsylvania, while crossing a bridge. The timbers gave way under the five-ton weight, and the poor creature dropped 15 feet into the water. He was valued at $15,000; and his age was put at 150 years, being traced back to the year 1701, when he was brought from Bengal to England.[28] In September 1854, a suit for the recovery of $20,000 was brought against the town of Adams for the death of Columbus. It was the first-known case of its kind in the United States.[29]

Raymond & Van Amburgh's Combined Menageries traveled through Michigan, Wis-consin and Pennsylvania in 1852, adding two elephants, Hannibal and Kaaloo-Ali (also spelled "Kaloo Alia; this was temporarily re-named "Romeo"), to their collection. Mons. Crawford and his own trained big cats continued with them. Admission remained 25 cents for adults and 15 cents for children. By October, a new concern called "Welch's National Circus, Raymond & Co.'s and Driesbach's & Co.'s Menageries United," under G. Berry, Manager, played throughout Pennsylvania. The "Cortege" through town included Carriages and Cages containing the animals, drawn by 120 horses. Heading the procession came Neuper's Philadelphia Brass Band.

The lion tamers for this circus were Herr Driesbach and Signor Hideralgo, presenting "A Double Performance in 3 Immense Performing Dens," or a three-ring circus. From Welch's (late of Niblo's, New York, and National Amphitheatre, Philadelphia), came James G. Cadwallader, 4- & 6-horse rider and Equestrian Director; S. Langworth, Master of the Circle; R. Williams, 1st Buffo Clown; and E. Davis, 2nd Shakespeare Clown. With them were L. J. Lipman (Scenic Rider); Davis Richards, bare-back rider, with his Wild Prairie Steed; E. M. Dickinson, Comedian and Comic Singer; J. Sweet, impersonating the Red Man; Master Williams, juvenile Gymnast and Antipodean; and Williams and Davis, with "Puns, Jokes, Bon Mots & Witticisms."[30]

In December 1853, while performing at the Broadway Menagerie, Jacob Driesbach had a close call. On entering the den containing a lion, lioness, three leopards and a Brazilian tiger, the animals became intractable due to the glare of the lights. The tiger attacked, knocking him down. The lioness attempted to intervene, but missed her aim, striking her master. Mr. Moffet, the principal attendant, dragged Driesbach away, with the tiger's teeth still holding fast. It eventually let go, and a physician was called. The injuries were considered only flesh wounds.[31]

Injuries of a more tragic type occurred on March 21, 1854, when "Gunjer," the rhinoceros on display at the Broadway Menagerie, died from internal injuries sustained the past summer when he fell through a bridge a distance of 30 feet. He was brought from Calcutta four years previous, and was estimated to be 10 years of age. Gunjer was valued at $10,000. Barnum took possession of the remains.[32]

The Broadway Menagerie traveled to Pawtucket, where it played June 3, 1854. Early on June 5, the company packed up for a trip to Fall River. After traveling seven miles, the elephant Hannibal became furious, broke free and went on a rampage, overturning four wagons encountered on the road, injuring a number of passengers and killing three horses. Mason Barney and another man chased him for several miles but had no success in preventing further damage. It was not until Hannibal exhausted himself and lay down about ten miles from Shade's Ferry that he was captured, secured in chains and carried over the ferry to Fall River. At one point, the elephant was clocked at running one mile in three minutes.[33]

Hannibal exhibited more violent tendencies on June 6, when the menagerie played at New Bedford. It nearly escaped again by breaking two of the three chains holding it,

Raymond & Co. and Van Amburgh & Co's
MENAGERIES UNITED.

The public was "particularly informed" that the union of these two menageries, to last only for the year 1852, created the largest collection ever concentrated in one exhibition, consisting of over 150 living wild animals to be exhibited under a spacious pavilion. The Grand Procession was headed by two monster elephants, Hannibal and Kaaloo-Alia, each beautifully caparisoned with a "Magnificent East Indian Hoodah." (*Milwaukee Daily Sentinel*, June 2, 1852) causing considerable anxiety. The company paid $700 in damages for the prior week's rampage.[34]

Late in December 1854, "the Herr" announced his intention to retire to his farm in Potosi. The menagerie continued touring under the Driesbach name, in 1856, advertising Eaton Stone, bare–back rider; William Worrell, star clown; with Madame Zamesou from the Cirque Nationale, Paris, making occasional appearances with the company.[35]

While coming into Newark, Ohio, in May 1856, a story of a different type, concerning one of Driesbach's elephants, made headlines. His keeper fell from his horse in a fit, bringing the caravan to a stop. An attempt was made to aid him, but the elephant would not allow anyone near the prostrate man. After picking him up in his trunk, the elephant tried to place him back on the horse. Failing that, he settled him gently on the ground and continued to guard the body, letting no one close. At length, the keeper awoke and commanded the elephant to let a physician attend him. The animal obeyed, all the while expressing extreme anxiety for his keeper's well being.[36]

The menagerie ventured through Iowa, where, disturbingly, the scarcity of food became so acute the animals nearly starved to death. They became so reduced in strength that Mr. Wheeler, the agent, sent around notices stating it would be impossible to exhibit any but the giraffe between Iowa City and Dubuque.[37] The effects of near starvation may have taken its toll, for in December the giraffe died at Cincinnati. The only one of its kind in America, it was valued at $5,000.[38] Less than a year later, in the summer of 1858, Hannibal the elephant died in Canfield, presumably from old age.[39]

After several years away from his animals, a reunion with Driesbach occurred in Dubuque, Iowa. When a lioness that had been a particular favorite of Driesbach saw him, she wagged her tail and appeared frantic with joy. When he spoke to her, she kissed him and placed a paw in his hand. A witness observed that he could not make up his mind about who was the most delighted: Driesbach to know he had not been forgotten, or the animals to be once more in his presence.[40]

Spalding & Rogers' North American Circus, C. C. Willits, Agent, rode into Newport, Rhode Island, on June 5, 1851, on their "Apollonicon," the masterpiece of Musical Science and Mechanical Skill built by Henry Erben of New York at a cost of $10,000. Drawn by 40 horses, four abreast, it carried Karl Furhman and his band of 50 Musicians. Their draw was a complete Dramatic Corps presenting such features as *The Spirit of '76.*[41] The following month, the name changed to Spalding & Rogers & Van Orden's "People's Circus," with Equestrian, Dramatic, and Zoological exhibitions. This Triple Combination was based upon the North American Circus, under the joint supervision of Den Stone, Senior Proprietor of Stone & McCollum's Circus, including most of the original company of Dan Rice's Circus. W. T. B. Van Orden served as Manager, with Hunt & Wilder as Agents.

The main attraction was "The Lion Queen Marie," only 8 years old, with her faithful dog Fiddo, who entered the Leopard's Den. A one-day performance took in $1,000, a heavy contribution from a county where wheat was selling at less than 60 cents. After the last performance, some persons connected with the circus were involved in the death of William Wallace Axiel, whom they "dispatched" after his drunken disruptions. As was often the case when circus perpetrators quickly quitted town to avoid prosecution, no immediate steps were taken to arrest them.[42]

The "galaxy of stars" advertised by Agent J. W. Wilder for August 1852, included C. J. Rogers; W. B. Carroll, two-horse rider; Walter Aymar, bare–back rider; J. McFarland, tight-rope walker; Madam Gulime Carolie, equestrian; Mrs. H. Ormond, Broadway actress; Miss Mary Carrol, equestrian danseuse and lion tamer; Master Clarence, trick rider; A. P. Durand, aerobatic performer; Mons. Thorn, French Hercules; G. O. Knapp, the People's Clown; Cool White, Dramatic Jester; H. Magilton, Trick Clown; and the Motley Brothers, George and Henry. Along with their Apollonicon, they featured Lilliputian Trick Ponies. Prices were 50 cents for Boxes and 25 cents for Pit.[43]

Perhaps the most interesting event involving a circus in the 1850s was Spalding & Roger's second exhibition, called "The Floating Palace Circus," a steamboat superbly fitted up with armchairs and cushions for 2,000 persons, from which spectators viewed the performances. Affectionately styling it a "horse boat," local papers assured potential customers it was "no humbug."[44] Unfortunately, the authorities at Baton Rouge seized the boat for evasion of the License Law and taxes. Forced to abandon the vessel to authorities, the owners commenced a suit against them for illegal seizure and detention, contending that their customary license exempted them from taxation for State and Municipal licenses.[45]

Advertised as "Twice as Large as any other Circus in the Union," the galaxy of stars for 1853 included J. C. Rogers; W. W. Nichols, Bare–Back Rider; R. White, Maitre duc Cirque; Master Clarence, Trick Rider; Mons. Le Thorn, French Hercules and cannon ball Juggler; Mons. Henri, the Man Monkey; J. McFarland, tight-rope walker; Mrs. H. Ormond, Broadway actress; Charles Brown, Gymnast; Mrs. W. Lake, Creole Gymnast; J. W. Paul, Yankee Sampson; with C. J. Rogers, Manager, and J. M. McCreary, Treasurer. Forty horses drew their "World Renowned Apollonicon."[46]

The following year, Spalding & Rogers combined their Floating Palace Circus with

SPALDING AND ROGERS' NORTH AMERICAN
COLOSSAL DRAMATIC EQUESTRIAN CIRCUS!
Twice as Large as any other Circus in the Union.

This illustration depicts the "World Renowned Apollonicon, Drawn in Procession by 40 Horses, four abreast, [driven] by J. W. Paul, one of the strongest men in the world." (*Marshall Statesman* [MI], June 15, 1853)

their North American Circus, the companies comprising the elite of the profession, "North and South," not an inconsequential statement, given the growing unrest in the country.[47]

Not all circuses earned the left-handed compliment of being "no humbug." In 1851, while traveling through Wisconsin, Mabie's Circus, notwithstanding the "puffs" of the newspapers, received a less than favorable review. Calling it "shabby," one reporter for the *Janesville Gazette* advised all citizens to "save their shillings and keep away.— The Supervisors charged them double the amount [of a license] any similar concern was ever charged before, on the ground that they were a nuisance."[48]

Being a "humbug" did seem to pay off, for the Chicago *Advertiser* observed:

> We learn that our citizens have been gulled out of about $3,000 during the stay of that traveling humbug, which was here on Friday and Saturday. We hope there are not as many fools in Milwaukee.[49]

Apparently there were, for a blurb in a Wisconsin paper noted:

> Another One-Horse Circus is in town. How many more are on their way here, we know not. They are generally successful in scraping coppers, and pleasing the lowest tastes, if in nothing more. They are getting to be great nuisances.[50]

Next to a failure to distribute free tickets to city editors, the quickest way to get on the bad side of a newspaper was by refusing to advertise. When a show came to Platteville, the *Independent American* gave it a gratuitous notice by reprinting a review from its sister newspaper, the *Monroe Sentinel*, on May 19, 1853: "Butler's Circus exhibited its novelties in this town on Friday last. The performances are spoken of as being perfectly stale." A slightly kinder notice in August observed that Butler's actors were to be pitied, as performing in the sweltering Wisconsin summer was not to be envied. The next mention of L. G. Butler's Circus came two weeks later. After pitching their tent at Platteville, the sheriff arrived with an attachment on the establishment, shutting down operations.[51] The circus survived, eventually upgrading the show in 1854 with the addition of the Antonio Brothers, Dan Gardner, two of the Lipmans and James DeMott. In November, Butler erected an amphitheatre in Chicago, the first indoor arena in that city.[52] The circus played through 1855 and then dropped out of sight.

Mabie seems to have learned the lesson Butler ignored. On August 3, 1854, he took out a large advertisement in the *Fort Wayne Times*. Whatever price he paid proved worth every cent, as the show earned editorial praise by being "celebrated" and "wonderful," with the added bonus, "Boys! lay up your quarters for the show." By this time, E. F. Mabie's circus had teamed with E. Ganung's menagerie. Artists included John J. Nathans, Equestrian Manager; A. Pastor, Master of the Ring; S. B. DeLand, Manager; Solomon J. Lipman, Clown; Hideralgo Beasley as Lion Tamer ("Hideralgo" was Beasley's stage name, assumed when working for Raymond in 1850–1853; here he is billed as a combination of both); Miss Emma Nathans, equestrian; and the Brothers Seagrass on the 30-foot equilibrium pole called the "Perche Equipoise."[53] As a side venture, E. F. & Jeremiah Mabie owned a flouring mill (a water mill grinding wheat into flour) in Delavan, Wisconsin, valued at $16,000. It was said to perform excellent work.[54]

Mabie's newly organized menagerie and circus for 1857 featured S. B. Deland, manager; W. H. Stout, Equestrian Director; J. Essler, Ring Master; Tony Pastor, Clown; Garry Demott, Grotesque Merryman (another name for clown) and Professor Beasley as Keeper of the Menagerie. (The gratuitous use of the word "professor" was common throughout the 19th century, particularly among aeronauts, to convey the impression of wisdom and skill. After the Civil War, "Colonel" briefly assumed predominance.) The show boasted a

Grand Procession drawn by 4 Elephants, feats of posturing by the Conklin Brothers, "Dislocating and Muscular Experiments" by Barkley and equestrian by Mad'lle Leaman.[55] Things went well enough that Mabie was able to purchase new cages for the menagerie animals, leaving the old ones behind at Delevan to the delight of the children, who used them to catch those citizens "tight," or otherwise found in a "place of suspicion," and lock them up.[56] Mabie did suffer a bump on the road, however, when the sheriff place a levy on his elephant for $125.[57]

Where Do Elephants Come From?

If more evidence of circus profitability were needed, in 1849, P. T. Barnum "projected a great traveling museum and menagerie." Partnering with showman Seth B. Howes, to take full charge of the operation, and Sherwood E. Stratton (Tom Thumb's father and by now a wealthy man), the trio selected Stebbins B. June and George Nutter to procure them twelve or more elephants and other wild animals. Leaving New York in May 1850, aboard the *Regatta*, under Captain Pratt, the pair made for Ceylon.[58]

After arriving at Point de Galle, a seaport on the southwestern extremity of Ceylon in early October, they attempted to purchase elephants from the governor, or the temples, which owned large numbers, but the newly installed governor "seemed to be in a confused and unsatisfactory state," and was unable to help. Additionally, many roads had been

destroyed by rain, and what elephants there were had been put to work repairing them. Consequently, they went on to Colombo, the maritime capital, sixty miles distant. In a letter written December 30, 1850, June noted that he advertised for elephants, "but the results did not give me a very favorable idea of 'the benefits of advertising.'" The price for elephants rose to such an extraordinary pitch that they determined to start for the interior and hunt their own.

With a party of natives, June traveled northwest of Kandy, while Nutter explored the southern part of the island. Although battling the discomfort of the rainy season, it favored their expedition, for elephants preferred it, ranging in the thick jungle covering the tableland and hills around the base of the mountain chains. At Anara-

Phineas T. Barnum was a giant in the 19th century, alternately called a genius and a humbug. That he was a keen businessman with an eye for what would appeal to the public there can be no doubt. In his own words, he was "early impressed with the value of money, and the necessity of getting it." Over the course of his career, he brought Jenny Lind to America, created the American Museum, introduced such schemes as the Woolly Horse and the Mermaid, and presented General Tom Thumb to the world. His traveling exhibitions and the Greatest Show on Earth set the standard (whether real or imagined) by which every other concern was judged. A shameless self-promoter and a man who knew and manipulated the press to his advantage, his name still stands today as being synonymous with the circus.

jahpoora, June discovered a herd and made a *kraal*, or pen. After ditches were dug, heavy posts were set upright in the ground, closely bound together with withes, and made firm by other posts resting against them on the outside, as stays. There were three sides, leaving an aperture on the fourth for an entrance slanting outward like the mouth of a funnel.

When the *kraal* was finished, natives ran at the herd, shouting and firing muskets, forcing the elephants inside. To catch and secure them, two trained elephants were sent inside. After selecting one individual, the trained elephants calmed it, then wound their trunks around that of the wild elephant, holding it in a vice-like grip. Natives then fastened ropes around the captive's hind legs. He was made fast to a tree and kept without food or water for three or four days until "tame." At that point, the animal was taken to a stream and watered. In the course of ten days to two weeks, the animal became docile enough to be driven at large with the tame beasts.

An alternate way of catching an elephant was to wait until it had fallen asleep under a tree, and then lightly touch its foot. Thinking a fly had landed, the animal would raise its foot, and the hunter would slip a noose around it. The process was repeated with the other foot, and when it woke up, the elephant found itself completely bound. Ceylon elephants were divided into two classes: the *tuskar*, or tusked elephant, and the *oliar*, or tuskless elephant. Of the two, the former were more valuable and were principally sought by native priests for service in the temples.

The most dangerous of the elephants was the *rogue*, an animal of unsocial disposition. June succeeded in capturing one, as well as another male he described as being larger than either Columbus or Bolivar. Before the largest was shipped to Point de Galle, he demolished a banana plantation. He also attempted to escape on the road to Colombo, but was caught in a newly irrigated paddy field after sinking to his knees. Recapturing it proved difficult, and, tragically, it died from wounds received in battle.

While on the road, several *mahouts* (natives) departed, taking one elephant with them, so June had thirteen left by the time he reached Port de Galle. In an interview given upon his return, June stated nine elephants were placed on a large lighter (barge) and carried over to the *Regatta*, where they were stowed in the hold. Prior to transfer, the rogue broke free and scattered the onlookers. Once on board "he behaved remarkably well during the passage." One of the younger elephants died after leaving the Cape of Good Hope and was thrown overboard. The others arrived safely after a voyage of 12,000 miles. A letter to the editor, dated September 19, published in the *New York Express* stated that one of the three ships Barnum sent to Ceylon and Borneo was lost at sea.[59]

A native Cingalese accompanied the animals. He went on tour, watching as the elephants peacefully devoured the gingerbread contributions of admiring thousands.[60] That sentiment accurately represented the feeling of the "admiring thousands" but was hardly accurate. Not only were the captives deprived of their natural right to freedom, behind the scenes the elephants were trained with goads, often having their delicate ears injured by the sharp points when a keeper lost patience. As already documented, traveling was another potential nightmare. In October 1852, the Menagerie of Sands, Quick & Co. was in St. Johnsville, New York, when tragedy struck. Two elephants refused to cross a bridge; they might have been driven around it by going through a cornfield, but the owner demanded an exorbitant fee the agent refused to pay. Through carelessness on the part of the keepers, "Romeo" and "Juliet" were forced onto the bridge at the same time; their combined weight caused it to break, precipitating them fifteen feet to the bottom. Juliet was too injured to move, and Romeo refused to leave her. Force was used without effect, compelling the menagerie men to bring out a large mastiff, obtained several years before from the farm of Henry Clay in Lexington. The dog, habitually used to drive the elephants, set upon Romeo for the purpose of separating him from his mate. Although in dire fear of it, Juliet made a desperate effort to protect Romeo. During the struggle, the handlers were able to drag both elephants to the beach.

Juliet being too injured to go on, the company built a protective shed for the pair, with the intent of collecting them later. Romeo, much bruised and stiffened, was not dangerously hurt, but Juliet was past all help, having broken her shoulder and otherwise being badly crippled. After three weeks, water in the creek rose, threatening to drown Juliet. The keeper desired her to move to higher ground, and when she refused, he attempted coercion with a pitchfork. Romeo wrenched it from his hand, broke it and flung away the pieces. Juliet lay there until she died, and only then did Romeo consent to move away with the keeper.[61]

These elephants, along with a third, were captured together around 1842, and brought to England, where they were purchased by Jeremiah Wombwell ("Old Jerry Wombwell"), the famous London proprietor of three menageries, who, ironically, had recently died in December 1850. At the time of his death, he owned five elephants that he had taught to perform in dramatic pieces in the principal theaters of Europe. Romeo and Juliet were sold by him to Sands & Quick and brought to America, where they became known far and wide.[62]

The more animals that perished or became injured, the greater the need to procure more. In 1851, Lewis Titus left for Europe to purchase rare specimens. In January 1852, he sent back a Cassowary, a bird native to the Indian Archipelago. It was described as a type of ostrich with remarkable "plumage" ("neither *feather* nor *hair*"), standing five feet high and possessing the strength of a horse. Also in the shipment were pelicans, two emus, and white and black swans.[63]

On the other hand, humans handling wild animals also ran great risk, occasionally from unusual sources. At Frankfort in 1850, Mr. Kreulzburg, the keeper of a young Hyena, was bitten in the hand. The wound brought on an attack of hydrophobia, from which he did not recover.[64]

P. T. Barnum, the Great American Humbug

In April 1851, word got around that P. T. Barnum was collecting a "monster exhibition, to be called 'Barnum's American Museum and Menagerie.'" It was promised to travel through rural districts of the country, with wagons built by Thomas B. Pierson. Among the attractions were to be Tom Thumb; the Wisconsin Giant; Mr. Nellis, the man without arms; and Mr. Pierce, the lion tamer.[65]

The opening months did not go well. In June, a "demonstration manifested itself against Barnum" at Princeton, New Jersey. The citizens pronounced his show a "humbug" and, after following the exhibition, dragged one of the wagons into the canal.[66] A month later a severe storm in Narragansett Bay blew down the tent just as Mr. Nellis exhibited his infirmity.[67]

Under the titles "Asiatic Caravan, Museum and Menagerie of P. T. Barnum" and "P. T. Barnum's Grand Colossal Museum and Menagerie," the 1852 Traveling Exhibition featured ten elephants drawing the Great Car of Juggernaut, and a baby elephant one year old and only 3½ feet high carrying General Tom Thumb, then described as being 20 years old, weighing 15 pounds and standing 28 inches high. The baby elephant, it was noted, had been weaned on its passage from India. Also included was an "infantile Camel, only six months of age, the first ever born in America."

The Pavilion of Exhibition, large enough to hold 15,000 spectators, featured Mr. Nellis, the man without arms, who loaded and fired a pistol with his toes and played the Accordion. In pure 19th century style, Barnum noted, "Mr. Nellis in these performances exhibits a wonderful example of what indomitable energy and industry can accomplish, even when laboring under disadvantages apparently the most insurmountable." Another 19th century fascination was wax statues. Barnum's collection included life-sized figures of presidents and foreign dignitaries.[68]

Twenty-five cents bought admission to see Tom Thumb, the entire Collection of Wild Animals, the Wax Statuary, the baby elephant, Mr. Pierce's performance in the dens, and Mr. Nellis & co. Two performances were offered daily, from 1 to 4 and 7 to 9 P.M.[69] Playing opposite Barnum in Zanesville was "Johnson & Co.'s Great Consolidated Equestrian, Dramatic, Olympic and Histrionic Establishment," with W. H. Stout, W. Aymar, G. Dunbar (Master of the Arena) and two star clowns, Jennings and Brower. G. B. Johnson was the manager.[70]

Twenty-five cents a ticket may not seem like much, but the profit for Barnum's menagerie reached $60,000 in 1851, even with "incidental expenses" (such as Tom Thumb's salary of $200 a week, or $10,400 per year—an income equal to the combined salaries of Daniel Webster and John J. Crittenden).[71] In four years, receipts for the menagerie reached nearly one million dollars.[72] That meant a great number of tickets were sold, and to the average New Yorker, it meant traffic jams. When Barnum's Menagerie played the city, it was not uncommon for Broadway, from the Museum as far as the eye could see, to be effectually blockaded by innumerable conveyances, all working their way toward the show. Those on other business lamented the situation and called for "the relief of Broadway," but there was no denying the irresistible urge of locals and tourists to "see the elephant!"[73]

At the same time traveling exhibitions offered the wild and the bizarre, aeronautics in the United States had become a virtual institution. While it is almost impossible to conceive, as balloons and circuses are not typically thought of as co-existing, at this period aeronauts and circus men competed for audiences. In many Midwest newspapers, appearances by Barnum's exhibition ran opposite the typical "clip art" balloon illustration featuring such celebrated "professors" as John Wise. And just as circuses and menageries combined, it would not be long before balloonists were brought into the fold, working in tandem with midgets and lions — in the same vein as Barnum scheduled his circus to play opposite smaller "side shows," drawing away their audiences.[74]

Equally interesting was that in the passage of time between Ricketts and Barnum, the circus had gotten "old," or at least more commonplace. A humorous article from 1852 enumerated the spectators, past and present, as a fair assortment of ladies, white, brown and colored, with the usual quota of gentlemen, loafers *en masse*, considerable grumbling and a few fights. Rain perforated the "*water tight* canvass," the "elephant looked about as he did twenty years ago, only twice as natural, and the rhinoceros' hide was as thick as ever, and the leopard had not as yet changed his spots." All in all, however, the "show" was a regular "out and outer," and quite satisfactory.[75]

Whether from the notoriety of Barnum's name or from actual fact, more articles associated the activity of counterfeiters and thieves with his exhibitions over any other. "Look

Out for Counterfeiters!" was a common theme, describing how $10 bills were passed "by some fellows who were following in the train of the Circus and Menagerie." The men passing the bad money went in advance of the show, got off their bills and hastened for parts unknown.[76] More specifically, reports out of Milwaukee warned of "something rascality" closely connected with Barnum:

> It is not to be wondered at! We can hardly understand how any man could travel or in the least stand connected with such an outrageous swindle and not feel an itching to get his hands into somebody's pocket or till, or steal clothes from a line or chickens from a roost.[77]

Even confectioners were not exempt from suspicion. A gang of Barnum's adjuncts, working outside the menagerie, passed bad money by giving change from the purchase of huge candy sticks. Nine total, including a soap vender, were apprehended.[78]

If there was no such thing as bad publicity, then Barnum must have been elated by the free press his Menagerie received. The *Waukesha Press* called it "one of the grossest swindles ever practiced on the amusement loving public."[79] The *Independent American* went further, stating the Menagerie "has made thousands of dollars out of one of the most meagre [*sic*], half-starved, dilapidated collections of curiosities and animals we ever took the trouble to see."

Warning that the exhibition richly deserved the description of "humbug," the writer added, "Tom Thumb and the armless individual ... are well worth seeing.... The car of Juggernaut, which was to enter the town with such Oriental pomp, would not compare in magnificence with the establishments of most traveling tobacconists, and was drawn by six dwarfish elephants, instead of ten, according to the bills.... The Menagerie consisted of a few consumptive looking animals.... The most curious feature of this company was their determination that no reports should get out side of the canvass until all had invested their dimes." Notwithstanding, between 5,000 and 7,000 tickets were sold.[80]

Worse was yet to come. On August 16, while at Belvidere, Illinois, a drunken man named Dibble created a nuisance at a small side show following Barnum's Menagerie. Baird, who was performing with an alligator, took offense and shot him dead. He was arrested and made bail of $2,500. Reports concluded, "So another murderer escapes the penalty of the law for this paltry sum."[81]

In November 1854, Barnum put an end to his Menagerie by selling off his animals at East New York through the firm of Hammond and Tattersalls. Messrs. Sands, Titus, Quick, Cushing, Nathans, Robinson of Cincinnati and 100 spectators attended the auction. The lot of seven elephants sold to S. B. Howes for $2,300, who also purchased two lions, one lioness, two Asiatic lions (male and female), a Bengal tiger, leopard, zebra, black bear, two hyenas, an alpaca, prairie wolf, monkeys & c., along with cages, wagons and canvass, for $2,500. Barnum bought back two giraffes (that he subsequently displayed in a production called "Hot Corn" at his Museum), and purchased an elephant to work his farm at Bridgeport. The rhinoceros went unsold; Barnum would have bought it, but found it "would not draw" at his Museum. One hundred and twenty horses were also sold "low." It was felt that the "winter of discontent" for all showmen had forced Barnum and his partners, Seth B. Howes and Sherwood Stratton, to this act, money being tight, the cost of feed high and menageries unprofitable.[82]

After "humbugging the world for two or three years" with his menagerie, Barnum earned an almost funereal tribute:

The Greeks, upon viewing the expenditure around the shrines of Diana, the Ephesian goddess cried out, "Great is Diana of Ephesus." The American people, in view of the manner in which Mr. Barnum has grown rich, might cry, Great is Barnum of America.[83]

But he was far from through. There was "Barnum's Baby Show," in which he "got up an exhibition of specimens of the human race," and the World's Fair in New York to keep him occupied.

General Tom Thumb, Barnum's most celebrated celebrity, went on to tour with S. B. Howes' Menagerie & Circus. Among other performers for the 1855 season was Parker, the "Tamer of Wild Beasts"; Samuel P. Stickney (who pioneered the four-horse act); Madam R., juvenile horsemanship; Miss Sallie ("Sally") Stickney, bareback rider; Signor Felix Carlo and son, the Italian Trick Clowns; Bobby Williams, clown; and W. Armstrong, somerset and scenic rider.[84] The following year, Tom Thumb toured alone, performing his songs, dances and Grecian statue imitations.[85]

In 1855, Howes joined forces with Myers & Madigan, with J. M. Nixon serving as director of the combined exhibitions. Along with a giraffe and a rhinoceros, the troupe included Jim Myers, clown; Miss Rose Madigan, equestrian; and Messrs. T. King, LeRue, W. Armstrong, H. P. and Master Madigan, Thompson and Nixon. A new pantomime, *The Master of Bagdad*, closed the exhibition.[86]

While in Toronto on July 16, 1855, a brawl broke out in a house of ill fame involving several circus men and locals from the Hook and Ladder Company. The circus men getting the better of it, the firemen vowed revenge. After the evening performance, they instigated a fight, succeeding in tearing the canvass with knives, tumbled a wagon into the bay, burned the ticket wagon, attempted to burn a cameleopard and eventually succeeded in burning the entire wardrobe and tent.[87]

General Tom Thumb (real name Charles S. Stratton), the "man in miniature" who captured the hearts of 19th century people across the globe, started out his career at age 5. Brought to P. T. Barnum from his home in Bridgeport, Connecticut, he was not above two feet in height and weighed less than 16 pounds. Granting himself some poetic license, Barnum immediately signed the boy to a contract, whereby he was to earn $3 per week for four weeks. Charles' name was changed; Barnum instructed him in stagecraft and introduced him to the world as being a dwarf of 11 years, just arrived from England. In a sense, the latter became true, for Tom Thumb would make a staggeringly successful tour of Europe, becoming a favorite of Queen Victoria. (Photo in authors' collection)

This was not the first time a peculiar riot occurred in Canada. In 1830, at Montreal, some journeymen tailors took offense at a circus performance of *The Tailor's Journey to Brentford*. Two days of fighting ended with a great deal of destruction and numerous injuries.[88]

16

"Gulling" the "Dear People"

We incline to a tolerable strong belief that the great World's Fair in New York will turn out the mammoth humbug of the coming year.... One thing is certain; it will afford a rich harvest to pickpockets, swindlers, circus owners, showmen, gamblers — or, in polite language, "sportsmen."[1]

The Crystal Palace, constructed for the World's Fair, opened in July 1853. As suggested, it "gull[ed] certain amiable dupes known as the 'dear people'" in transactions too numerous to mention; but it also brought to New York City an influx of foreign performers, including an Alligator that passed through Philadelphia on his way to New York. All 14 feet of it arrived in a box weighing 750 pounds. "He resisted manfully — or rather alligatorfully — his removal to the Express wagon, and his only notice of numerous requests to 'hold his jaw,' not to 'unfold his tail' and other characteristic remarks was a most violent splashing and a determined demonstration of hostility." He was eventually deposited on the wagon and dispatched on a "sea-teamer" to serve as a "specimen of 'American industry.'"[2]

One foreign exhibition constructed independent of the Fair was Franconi's Hippodrome. The building was 400 feet in length by 200 wide, with accommodations for 10,000 spectators. It was to be covered with a canvass roof, capable of being removed for balloon ascensions.[3] Henri Franconi subsequently toured in 1854 with his Parisian Chariot Riders, with J. G. Cadwallader as Director and W. H. Stout as President of the Games.[4]

James M. June & Co. toured in 1852 with The Great French Circus and their "Magnificent Car of Neptune," but in 1856, June and Turner gave way to G. F. Bailey & Co., which traveled under that name with the explanation, "Successors to June and Turner's Combined Circus and Menagerie." For this exhibition, W. B. Carroll served as Equestrian Director, Dr. Woolston was Master of the Ring, and H. Hough and J. W. Ward performed as clowns. Their featured performer was La Petite Marie, a ten-year-old child who entered the Den of Wild Animals, displaying "her indominable [*sic*] courage, equal to the celebrated Van Amburgh." In October, Mr. Sands performed equestrian tricks and the dramatic scene "The Jolly Jack Tar."[5]

The Railroad Circus and Crystal Amphitheatre operated in 1853, with W. T. B. Van Orden, proprietor, under the ownership of Spalding & Rogers. The performances featured Dennison Stone, the celebrated New Orleans Clown and brother of Eaton Stone; H. P. Madigan; and H. F. Nichols.[6]

Van Amburgh spent parts of 1853 through 1855 aboard the "Floating Palace," John J. Drake, Chauncey R. Weeks and Gilbert R. Spalding, proprietors. The boat lay at the foot of Canal Street, New Orleans, where the lion tamer was to be seen entering the cages of various "varmints."[7] On December 30, 1854, one of the varmints, a monster giraffe, fell overboard while being transported off the steamboat *Philadelphia* and drowned. It cost Van Amburgh $15,000.[8]

Van Amburgh's Menagerie and Den Stone's "Circus of the People, and Tyler's Indian Exhibition United" joined forces later in 1855, and toured Michigan, Wisconsin and Iowa. Den Stone was billed as "the original inventor of Bon Mots" and "The Clown of the Era,"[9] an attempt to differentiate him from his brother Eaton. The following year, Van Amburgh combined with two European and one American Circus Companies, offering the equestrian Cook Family (Henry, Sr., John Henry Cook and young Harry Cook); the Francisco Brothers (Frank Carpenter and Louis Francisco), gymnasts; Den Stone, Clown; and Professor Langworthy, Lion Tamer.[10]

G. F. BAILEY & CO., SUCCESSORL TO JUNE & TURNER'S.

This eye-catching illustration helped announce the change of ownership from June & Turner to G. F. Bailey & Co. in 1856. It was not uncommon for new owners to promote the name of readily recognizable proprietors, capitalizing on their reputation for putting on a good show. Among Bailey's performers were W. B. Carroll, equestrian and Equestrian Director; Madame Carroll in her celebrated *Floating Vail*; the famous *La Perche*, performed by the Lee Brothers; and La Petite Marie, who entered the Den of Wild Animals, displaying courage equal to the renowned Van Amburgh. (*Weekly Argus and Democrat* [WI], August 5, 1856)

Richard Rivers (Equestrian Director) and Edwin Derious (Manager) teamed in 1851 to present a circus, by 1854 called the "Grecian Arena Circus." That year, they offered a brilliantly lighted pavilion by means of portable gas, manufactured on the grounds. For the comfort of their patrons they also provided seated elevations around the entire space.[11] "Comfort" was a relative term. In 1863, it was lamented that "some genius has not [yet] invented a cushion or seat to be used at the circus. The amount of torture and agony we experienced the other evening during a three hours sitting on a hard board was beyond expression.... The next time a circus comes, we'll bring a pillow or stand up."[12]

By 1855, the pair introduced Russian performers. This did not help their bottom line, for in September, the Grecian exhibitions in Delaware were "very thinly attended," and likely they did not clear expenses. Joe Pentland's Circus, playing after them, offered different "appendages" and was better attended, "though this was scarcely to be compared with the attendance formerly at these shows."[13] In hopes of improving the gate, Rivers & Derious renamed themselves the "Grand Oriental Circus" in 1857, offering a full company of Chinese Artistes."[14]

For his circus, Pentland, the famous clown, offered Davis Richards, the Wild Eccentric Horseman; balancing by Nicolo and Sons; Frank and William Pastor; and the Oriental

Dragon Chariot.[15] By 1857, Pentland advertised, "Old Friends with New Faces," featuring Richard Hemmings (tight rope), T. King (the California Leaper), and Madame and Mons. De Bach, French equestrians.[16]

Two incidents of note involving animals occurred in 1856. The first happened at Hagerstown, Indiana, on April 25, when a lion attacked a cougar. Langworthy, the trainer, rushed into the cage and attempted to intervene, but the lion succeeded in tearing the cougar to pieces. The Professor managed to save his own life by grabbing an iron instrument used for cleaning cages and beating back the lion. Van Amburgh immediately returned to his zoological building in Cincinnati to replace the animal so fearfully destroyed.[17] The second incident was at Newport, where a lioness, enraged that her cub was taken from her, tore through the iron fastenings of her cage, killing a dog and a tiger cub, and demolishing several cages containing rare and valuable birds before the keeper succeeded in chaining her.[18]

Under the heading "A Great Menagerie Keeper Dead," the *Philadelphia Bulletin* announced the passing of the greatly loved and respected Gen. Rufus Welch, lessee of the National Circus and Theatre, in that city in December 1856. Welch was born in New Berlin, Chenango Valley, New York, in September 1800. His obituary stated that he went west when 11 years old and soon thereafter became connected with the circus business, then in its infancy in the United States. One of his many journeys extended over 2,000 miles into the interior of Africa, from which he delivered many animals, including giraffes, claimed to be the first ever imported to America.[19]

Hyatt Frost was one of the most durable managers of the 1800s, marking his 39th year with Van Amburgh's Menageries in 1885. (*Elyria Republican* [OH], August 6, 1885)

The year 1857 saw the merging of three exhibitions under the auspices of Spalding & Rogers: the North American Circus (New England circuit), the Floating Palace Circus (Mississippi and Ohio Rivers; steamers *Floating Palace, James Raymond* and *Banjo*) and the New Railroad Circus (Middle States). Hyatt Frost served as manager; Den Stone was the Clown; Langworthy the Lion Tamer; and Nicolo's Performing Dogs and Tippo Sahib, the Performing Elephant were the star attractions. In 1858, the Great Broadway Menagerie and Van Amburgh's Menagerie toured together. Interestingly, a note in the *Davenport Daily Gazette*, September 23, 1858, noted that although attendance was "pretty good," it was down from previous years, showing that the people "have got surfeited with such pastimes, or else that they feel the scarcity of small change." The same two companies exhibited together in 1859 (still advertising Hannibal the elephant, one of their less famous beasts renamed), calling themselves, "The Only Moral and Instructive Exhibition in America."[20]

Circus Stories

While the newspapers were filled with such stories as "Elephant Escaping," "Lion Attacks Keeper," and "Spectators Trapped Under Canvass," five in particular stand out as expressing the feel and the temper of the American Circus and Menagerie in the 1850s. The first occurred when the *Lady Elgin* was making her way up the lake, carrying a large collection of animals. When the wheelsman suddenly found it impossible to change course, everyone looked overboard for some obstruction. What they discovered was that the elephant, Siam, had gotten into the water and wound his trunk around the chain, preventing navigation of the boat. With some difficulty, his keepers persuaded him that "such liberties could not be allowed" and finally managed to get him back aboard.[21]

In 1857, a Canadian official, in his zeal to hunt contraband goods, stuck his hand inside a wooden box, only to discover the slimy folds of a huge anaconda belonging to Van Amburgh's Circus. Quickly withdrawing it, he ordered his clerks to "pass the snake" without delay.[22]

In Cincinnati the following year, a city official saw a large group of children gathered outside the menagerie, longing to get inside. The gentleman bantered with Van Amburgh to set a price, guessing there were 80 in number. The showman agreed to admit them all for $3. As they filed past, it was revealed there were actually 140, and the appearance of so many youngsters added quite a feature to the show.[23]

In 1859, at Philadelphia, a little girl named Sarah B. Noble, in spite of precautions taken to inhibit approach to the animals, sneaked into the area of the dens. After petting the lion, she attempted to caress a tiger, but the animal quickly sank its teeth into her arm. Her screams created intense excitement among the child actors rehearsing a performance of *Cinderella*. One of the circus men thrust a pitchfork into the tiger's mouth, and a crowbar was used to make it release the captive. Miss Noble was rushed to Pennsylvania Hospital, where it was found necessary to amputate her arm.[24]

Finally, a story begun by the *Cleveland Plaindealer* made the newspaper rounds. It stated that some new keepers belonging to Van Amburgh's Menagerie spit tobacco juice into the eyes of a lion to make it roar. The lion broke free and leapt at the men, but being temporarily blinded, it missed his mark and struck his head against a pole, splitting himself from head to toe. Van Amburgh rushed in, seized the cleaved parts of the lion and clapped them together. "But imagine Van's agony when he saw that he had put the lion together in the wrong way; that two of the animal's legs were up and two down!" But the lion got well, and when he got tired of walking on two legs, he flopped over and walked on the other two. "He is said to be a curious looking lion."[25] The tale, of course, was a complete fabrication, but it found good play and likely a few smiles when people discovered they had been duped.

"The Great Calliope Coming"

"The Great Calliope Coming! Wait for the Steam Music." Boasted to be "The only Instrument of the Kind in Existence!" the musical instrument most closely associated with the genre had its circus beginnings in 1857, when James M. Nixon and William H. Kemp's "Great Eastern Circus" introduced it to the public. So enormous that it had to be drawn by 40 horses (4 abreast in two chariots), it heralded the arrival of the circus. Nixon & Kemp described it:

The Calliope

A stupendous and harmonious instrument, played with steam pipes, the only one now on exhibition, and equal in power to a brass band composed of more than a thousand musicians. It can be heard for miles around, while its notes are as clear and harmonious as those of a full and perfect orchestra.[26]

The word "calliope" stemmed from the Greek, meaning "beautiful voiced." In Greek mythology, Calliope was the daughter of Zeus. The 1850s were what might be called the Golden Age of Steam, with steamboats the most readily identifiable steam engine of the times. Because these boats had an abundance of steam, calliopes were often used on these vessels, sometimes replacing the steam whistle in announcing arrivals and departures. Its use in circuses (which had to carry the instrument in one carriage, and an independent apparatus for steam generation, including a boiler and an engineer, in a second) was the

The Parisian Steam Calliope was advertised to emit the most ravishing music that could be heard for miles: "Nothing like it ever seen before; worth fifty miles to see." Early versions of the calliope required two wagons, one to draw the steam-making apparatus and a second for the instrument. This later version was combined in one, but undoubtedly played the same off-key music that has become synonymous with circuses ever since. (*Burlington Weekly Hawk-Eye* [IA], May 7, 1874)

next obvious step, as the music served to alert people for miles around. While an expensive adjunct to posters and newspaper advertisements, the calliope's bold tones reached a wider audience and stirred immediate recognition from an illiterate populace.

The whistles of a calliope were tuned to a chromatic scale through a difficult process that required frequent repetition to maintain quality sound. Since the pitch was affected by steam temperature, notes were often off-pitch, and as the calliope became more common, the less-than-perfect sound became more a feature than a detraction.[27]

By 1867, the calliope had reached the West, where "that steam thing, whatever you call it, is heard in the land," and where it was humorously written:

> For him there bears no ray of hope,
> Who does not call it calliope;
> While he is blind who cannot see,
> It should be called cal-li-o-pe.[28]

Expressing what more than a few believed, it was also observed that the "steam piano" furnished "the most delightful music we ever listened to — for suicidal purposes."[29]

Along with their new musical device, Nixon & Kemp featured Kemp, the English Clown; Tom Linton, Trick and Stilt Clown; R. W. Smith, Buffo Singer; Walter Aymar, Wild Hurdle Jumping Rider; and James Ellsler and J. Haslet, Tumbling and Vaulting. Horace Nicolls served as Equestrian Master. A gratuitous exhibition by M'lle Louise on the single wire, extending from the ground 350 feet to the head of the circus flagstaff (an elevation of 80 to 90 feet), was offered before the Calliope was placed inside the Great Pavilion and the doors opened to the paying public.[30] Nixon & Kemp did not advertise the calliope in 1858, replacing it with Ned Kendall in his Grand Musical Carriage.[31]

Free exhibitions before a performance were becoming more frequent toward the end of the 1850s. Levi J. North's "Colossal Circus" featured a pre–performance exhibition of aerial high wire, performed by "Professor" McFarland, who traveled 80 feet from the ground to the flagstaff. North himself performed Principal and Scenic Riding; Horace Smith was the Two Horse Rider and 100 Somerset Thrower; and the bill also featured Anthony Pastor and Ben Jennings as Clown.[32]

The Calliope reappeared in Sands, Nathans & Co.'s American Circus and Great Elephant Exhibition in 1858. The "most Powerful and Melodic of all Musical Instruments," it was said to cost $86,000 and be capable of playing any musical composition, either operatic or otherwise. It was supplied with steam by an Engine, while an Accomplished Artist played the keys, "which are like those of a piano." The entire instrument required two Chariots to contain it, and the music, creating an "intense sensation," was said to be heard 12 miles distant. Victoria, Albert and four other elephants gave performances, and Sam Lathrop, the "Gentleman Clown," offered his Stump Speech.[33]

A typical example of a humorous political dialogue was offered during a performance of Whitby's Circus, Philadelphia, in December 1860:

> Ring Master: Well, sir, have you read the President's Message?
> Clown: Of course I have. Every intelligent and influential gentleman like myself,
> always reads the Message of the President of the United States.
> Ring Master: Well, sir, what did you think of it?
> Clown: Sir, it is a great message; a powerful message; an unanswerable message.
> Ring Master: About that, sir, there is some difference of opinion.
> Clown: No, sir, there is no difference of opinion; there can be no difference of

THE CALLIOPE!

The Calliope was billed as the most powerful and melodious of all musical instruments, costing Sands, Nathans & Co.'s American Circus $86,000. It was capable of playing any musical composition, either operatic or otherwise. (*Hornellsville Tribune* [NY], July 8, 1858)

opinion upon that subject. The president is perfectly right sir. He is in favor of all sides of the question![34]

Victoria and Albert were subsequently sold to Dr. Charles Bassett, who brought them to California, where they were purchased by William Hendrickson, partner of John Wilson. They toured with them in 1859 as part of the Great Elephant Show and Circus, making a great deal of money on the venture. Sadly, when crossing the river from Columbia to Murphy's Camp, the elephants opted to swim the river. Victoria made it to the other side, but Albert had trouble, causing great distress before their keeper, John Peoples, calmed them down. By June 14, Victoria began to fail, and she died June 28, at Iowa City. An autopsy revealed heart trouble, stemming from the day she thought she had lost her mate in the river. She was buried in the first circus ring ever made in town.[35] The elephant was so famous, the lead in the *New York Times* simply stated, "*Victoria* Died on the 28th of June." She was valued at $20,000. According to Mr. Moyce (the gentleman who kept her and took charge of her in the ring), the cause of death was lung fever.[36]

Dan Rice, the celebrated clown, continued to bear a grudge against Gilbert Spalding, and in 1852, was sued again for libel, this time for "causing to be printed a series of doggrel [*sic*] verses." He was fined $1,558.[37] By December, he was back in New Orleans, where he had previous success in a show called "Dan Rice's Museum and Menagerie."[38] The popular Rice, who would "positively appear at each exhibition," operated his fleet of menagerie canal boats through Indiana, Ohio and New York in 1853. With him was "The Performing Lalla Rookh — a splendid collection of wild animals, including a white Syrian Camel, the wild Boy of Ceylon, Chinese Family & c."[39] Reviews for the "Hippodrome and Menagerie" noted, "Every body has heard of Dan, the great jester, and very prince of clowns; and every body, of course, will go to see him. His company and performances are spoken of as being far ahead of the ordinary run of travelling circuses." Featured were the trained elephant and grizzly bear.[40] A good name and good reviews brought in the crowds; the *Cincinnati Commercial* reported that during the last 116 days, while traveling through Ohio and Western New York, Rice's receipts amounted to $80,400, or an average of $700 per day.[41]

The year 1854 proved equally rewarding. In June, Rice cleared $13,000 with his show. Not much of a seer, however, he left $1,000 in Jackson as a bet Fillmore would be the next president.[42] "Dan Rice's Great Circus Show" of 1855 featured the elephant Lala Rookh walking the Tight Rope; Mrs. Dan Rice; M'lle Frank Vic; Frank H. Rosston, 6 and 8 horse rider and Maitre du Cirque; Young Jean Johnson, Tight Rope Dancer and Scenic Rider; Charles Noyes, the Little Giant; and Master Charles Read, the Infant Prodigy, and his counterpart, Little Mike Lipman.[43] As an indication of how hard it was for child performers to adjust to a man's world, "Little Mike" filed for bankruptcy in 1868, citing $32,600 in debt.[44]

A history of Dan Rice, given in the *Reading Gazette,* stated that some 14 years ago (which would make it 1841) Dan left Reading with an exhibition that turned out poorly. Judge Heidenrich of Berks County found him in a bad condition, bought him a suit of clothes, and lent him a horse and wagon. Destitution soon overcame him, and he sold the horse and wagon in order to raise the means to take his ill wife home to Pittsburg. He obtained work in a theater, where the Judge found him "still poor and seedy." Instead of reproaches for selling his horse and wagon, the Judge offered to outfit him a second time, which Rice refused.

In 1855, while performing at Reading, the now-successful Rice met the Judge for a third time, took him for a ride in a brand new carriage drawn by a cream-colored Arabian pony, then presented both to his friend in exchange for what he had sold so many years before. "An honest man, and a man of honor, is Dan Rice, the circus clown!"[45]

Fame, in a manner of speaking, caught up with Rice and Barnum in 1859. L. B. Lent's Mammoth National Circus combined with Gen. Rufus Welch's National Circus from Philadelphia, L. B. Lent's New York Circus from Niblo's Garden, New York, and Col. Charles May's Great Southern Circus from Mobile and New Orleans. The company included Dan Gardner, Sam Welsor and William Kincade, clowns, along with Young Dan, the smallest Grimaldi ever known (the term "Grimaldi," meaning clown, being a tribute to the brilliant English clown of that name); Frank H. Rosston, Equestrian; Henry Bartine, Slack Rope Walker; William Kincade, the 100 Sommersets Man; and the "Educated Mules" — named *Dan Rice* and *P. T. Barnum.*[46] William Kincade would die in Baltimore in December 1868, age 38 years.[47]

Dan Rice may have gotten one-up on the educated mules by an advertisement for his "Great Show." In speaking of the rhinoceros, he noted, "This animal will be turned loose into the arena, and perform incredible feats; proving, by its submission, that what could not be done in the past, has, *in the future*, been accomplished" [italics in original].[48]

17

Circuses and Menageries
in the Civil War Era

Brig. Gen. Phelps, in command at Ship Island, is a very plain man in his dress and in speech very slow and precise. It is said when Col. French's regiment arrived, he walked up to a squad of Capt. Kelly's Zouaves, whose particular dress attracted his attention, and asked, "What-part-of-the-show-do-you-belong-to?" "Capt. Kelly's Zouaves, sir," replied one. "Oh, soldiers!" said the General. "I thought you were circus riders."[1]

Tensions between North and South came to a head on October 16, 1859, with John Brown's attack at Harper's Ferry, Virginia. This armed conflict pushed both sides to the point of no return, and preparations for war assumed an ominous tempo. Circuses were not immune from sectional differences, and an interesting story surfaced about "Yankee" Robinson (real name Fayette Ludovic Robinson). He was in Raleigh at the time of Brown's attack, and business fell off sharply. He went on to Charleston and played three weeks before going to Savannah, where it seems the locals objected to his name. Sensing trouble, "Yankee" and his performers escaped into the woods, losing all their belongings.[2]

The word "Yankee" had long been associated with Northerners, but its origins dated to Colonial times, when early settlers faced serious conflict from a tribe of Native Americans called *Yankoos*, meaning "invincible." The word was eventually corrupted to "Yankee" and became attached to the hard-fighting immigrants.[3] Robinson returned to the "free states" and toured under the title "Circus & Theatre: Yankee Robinson's Double Show," with H. Shepard, manager; Yankee Miller, Stage Manager; and Frank Phelps, Manager of the Arena Performances.[4] The entertainment was not actually a circus "but a dramatic troupe interspersed with circus performance."[5]

Dan Rice had a different experience at the beginning of the war, which found him down South on a steamboat in the Mississippi. Finding business "hard skinning" in Southern waters, at one point he was arrested and escaped with some difficulty. Taking the precaution to arm his boat with 50 muskets and two cannon, he saw a steamer off the Cumberland River and, as a "joke," launched a shot across her bow. The clerk waved a secession flag, to which Rice responded by firing another. A second man quickly ran up the Stars and Stripes, and the vessel was allowed to go in peace. Rice noted that he declined returning South "just yet."[6]

In April 1861, circus men played a role in transmitting war information to Washington.

After being wrecked off Cape Hatteras, several men from Nixon's Royal Circus made their way to Norfolk, where they observed the Rebel Army, "to be in force about 11,000 strong," encamped behind strong entrenchments.... They say the troops are well armed, clad and fed and unmistakably anxious for an attack from the U.S. Army and Navy."[7]

While it would seem the nation was too preoccupied for entertainment, such was not the case, at least in the northern states. Even President-Elect Abraham Lincoln, on his way to the Executive Mansion in 1861, hurried away from the mayor's reception and "visited Barnum's Museum." A devotee of circuses and menageries in Springfield, it was said he could repeat what the clown had "got off" long after the performers had left.[8]

Mr. Lincoln carried his love of circuses into the Presidential Mansion, inviting his old friend Dan Rice to visit whenever he was in Washington, going so far as to provide his presidential carriage for the trip. Once, he even used the clown's lowly social status to scare away a prominent Republican who had arrived to present some unwanted resolutions.[9]

While not interested in fashion, Mr. Lincoln might have been interested to see a young performer by the name of Jules Leotard display his revolutionary gymnastic feats. Debuting in Paris on November 12, 1859, he exhibited his talent by springing up and seizing two iron rings suspended from the roof, raising himself up by strength of arm until his entire weight was borne by his wrists, then lifting his legs in the air until his head was down and his body perpendicular above. By degrees, he let his body bend back until his feet were below the wrists and remained in that position several seconds. The act required employing different sets of muscles, one to raise his body and the other to counteract the tendency of the rings to fly asunder.

Leotard also exhibited other skills on a ladder, moving upward by use of his hands.[10] He would become an expert on the trapeze, moving to the Alhambra Theatre, Leicester Square, London, in May 1861, being paid £180 per week. In 1867, George Leybourne wrote the lyrics to the song "The Daring Young Man on the Flying Trapeze" about him. Leotard thrilled audiences until 1870, when he died in Spain from smallpox or cholera. His name is used today in reference to the skin-tight, one-piece

In typical circus fashion, Kleckner & Co. advertised a world-renowned combination of artists who had traveled through all the principal cities in Europe and America, where they were received with unbounded enthusiasm. The performers in this illustration wear body-fitting tights, first introduced by Jules Leotard in 1859. (*Indiana Progress* [PA], August 8, 1872)

garment he designed, created to be flexible, permit unrestricted movement and, not incidentally, show off his physique. The *maillot*, as he called it, quickly went from the circus to French ballet; by 1886, the English had re–named it the "leotard."

Leotards quickly developed into tights, drawn on as tightly as two or four arms could get them and fastened by a leather bolt around the waist. The bolt had to be drawn at such tension that performers considered it torture, and the famous Louise Montague once remarked that she would accept $25 less salary if she were not compelled to wear them.[11]

The Anatomical "Rule of Orange"

A new sensation brought great interest to an American performer using the stage name "Zoyara." Niblo's Garden, New York, under the management of James M. Nixon, opened on January 16, 1860. Among the attractions were equestrians from Cooke's Royal Amphitheatre, London. One performer was singled out for special notice: "Mlle. Ella Zoyara, the principal lady of the company, is a very remarkable performer, and the graceful daring of her 'acts' brought down the heartiest applause of the house."[12] It did not take long, however, for her gender to be called into question, and the newspapers were filled with stories about the artist.

When Zoyara traveled with Nixon's company to Boston (March 5–April 6, 1860), the question seemed settled, for it was reported that Signor Amodio, of the Italian Opera, was to marry her.[13] When that happy event did not come off, several young gentlemen waged a bet that they could determine the true nature of things by employing the "Orange Test." This was based on the contention that if that fruit were thrown to a lady, she would "involuntarily extend the folds of her dress to afford the largest lap for it to fall in, while if you throw an orange to a gentleman the result is the reverse, for he immediately closes his knees to prevent it falling to the ground, should he not catch it."

After securing an interview, the test was tried: Zoyara reacted according to the feminine theory. In order to be sure, a second orange was thrown, when, "wonderful to relate, the masculine order of closed knees took place." The youths were "dumbfounded," and left "convinced that there are exceptions even to their anatomical rules of orange receiving."[14] On July 30, the company returned to Niblo's, "bringing with it that charming mystery whose charms, at least, are no mystery at all, the androgynous Zoyara."[15] Later that year, despite the pending sectional conflicts, Nixon's Royal Circus traveled through Virginia and North Carolina, where one review observed, "The celebrated M'lle Ella Zoyara certainly proved by her equestrianship that she is entitled to her European as well as American reputation as the best female performer on horseback."[16]

"Zoyara's" abilities as an equestrian, as well as the mystery surrounding her/him, proved exceedingly lucrative for Nixon, and imitators followed. Several used the name "Zoyara," while others opted for other exotic names. In Cleveland, "Mlle. Jennies Leon" became a sensation as another she/he personality. Leon had "the symmetry of limb — the plumpness of arm — the fullness of shoulder and bosom, so characteristic of the well-formed girl," and could, "if we may be allowed the expression ... wiggle enchantingly." The neat deception was very successful in Cleveland, Washington and Pittsburg, as "she" received numerous presents from those smitten by her stage charms. Leon, apparently, was a 17-year-old youth who began his career with a band of Ethiopian minstrels as a "wench dancer." Leaving that business, he was unable to get work in the theater, "as male dancing [was] not attractive," and so retained his skirts and drapery. The exposure of his gender, observed the *Plaindealer*, was not intended to injure him in business, but was made because the secret must come out, "particularly if he should decide to marry any one of his numerous lovers."[17]

Nixon's Royal Circus returned to Niblo's Garden March 28, 1861, where the original "Mlle. Zoyara made her appearance in a brilliant equestrian act and was warmly received by the audience."[18] The plot thickened in November, when the King of Sardinia presented Ella Zoyara his celebrated stallion Favorita, "as a tribute to her great equestrian skill and to her virtue as a lady." The gift was eventually brought to trial in *James R. McDonald vs. Spencer Q. Stokes et al*, questioning ownership of the horse. Q. L. Stokes (probably S. Q. Stokes) testified that he was a circus manager, and that Ella Zoyara was a boy whom he had picked up in Europe and dressed in girl's clothing; he added that "Miss Ella" had since eloped with another Miss, to whom he had since been married.[19]

Americans were not the only ones inundated by fantastic reports in the newspapers. In 1838, one London newspaper listed the absurdities of theatrical life: "To publish the *beer inspired concoctions of numerous dirty gentlemen,* and call them the '*opinions of the press....*' To think that the public can be gulled by seeing a piece that they *know* has been *damned* the previous night designated as the '*greatest hit ever known....*' For ladies, when about to be treated in a 'ROUGH WAY,' pausing to adjust a ribbon, or put aside a curl. For an actress to appear as a chambermaid of a tavern dressed in jewellery, the price of which would purchase the lease of the house and fixtures ten times over." (*Bell's New Weekly Messenger* [London], November 25, 1838; illustration from the *Herald and Torch Light* [MD], April 19, 1871)

Brien's (O'Brien) National Circus and Model Show for 1863 advertised "Charles Reed, the Retro-Equestrian, formerly principal Artiste in 'Dan Rice's Great Show,' and known as the 'Sensational Rider,' and impersonator of the mysterious female, ELLA ZOYARA, [who] will execute his 'Daring Somersault Act.'" Even more fascinating, O'Brien also "borrowed" Margaret Ann Curren, the present Mrs. Charles Warner (formerly Mrs. Dan Rice; Warner had served as Dan Rice's treasurer for several years), who assumed the position of Directress of the Performances, the first time a woman had been so honored. Miss Libbie Rice, her daughter, appeared in a "propemonde capacity."[20] Not to be left out, in 1866, De Haven's United Circus offered M'lle Jenny Day, "the fairy like creature whose smile entranced," who also "*turned out to be a boy*" [italics in original].[21]

The same John Wilson who had operated the Great Elephant Show and Circus in San Francisco joined forces with "Zoyara" to form Wilson and Zoyara's Great Circus. Zoyara proved a great attraction, being reviewed as "the most renowned equestrian that has ever been in California."[22] Wilson's Circus closed in October, planning to depart soon after for Australia. The local newspaper expressed a wish that in view of all the excitement Zoyara created in the Atlantic cities, the manager induce Miss Ella to appear in male attire before leaving, noting, "We think it would prove a winning card."[23] Wilson actually toured the United States in 1865, departing for Australia in 1866. The *New York Times* of March 18, 1866, reported that the bark *Alice*, bound for Australia with the circus of Wilson & Zoyara, was wrecked soon after leaving Tahiti, with all hands lost. This was false, as Wilson safely reached Australia and toured there between 1866 and 1868.

The case of *Chris. Lorrey and Others vs. Omar Kingsley* came before the California Supreme Court in February 1865. The suit against Kingsley (identified as the former equestrienne Ella Zoyara, who had by this time assumed male attire) was brought in order to recover salaries of members of the Stokes Circus Company. The defense lay on the fact that Stokes was sole proprietor and hirer of the troupe, and that Kingsley was not liable "as a partner or otherwise." Notwithstanding, the jury awarded the plaintiffs $1,550.[24]

The story of the she-he published in the *Californian* revealed that James M. Nixon had traveled to Europe seeking an extraordinary female rider to save his circus from financial ruin. Failing that, he discovered a youth performing in Paris and convinced him to play the part of a female equestrian. After testing the disguise with success, the pair came to the United States, where "Ella Zoyara" became a celebrity, in part because of questions concerning her gender. The story went that Nixon's wife became jealous of the time her husband spent with another woman, forcing him to confess the truth. Her retort "Don't you think I know a man from a woman when I see one?" certainly complicated matters.[25]

Omar Kingsley died in 1879, after which a variation of his history appeared. It stated he was born in St. Louis about 1840. At the age of six, he ran away and became apprenticed to Spencer Stokes, a circus proprietor of Philadelphia. Using his "beautiful boyish face, a profusion of rich, black curly hair, and slender form," he assumed the name Ella Zoyara, attracting no particular attention. Kingsley/Zoyara later accompanied Stokes to Europe, where he rode as a female. The story goes that in Italy, King Victor Emmanuel became attracted to him and presented "Ella" with a black stallion that Stokes took possession of and sold in Madrid. Returning to the United States, Kingsley earned fame as a great female equestrian, secretly marrying the equestrienne Sallie Stickney, daughter of performer Robert Stickney, of Cincinnati. Zoyara traveled to California in 1863, debuting with John Wilson's circus, once being observed in male attire "swearing like a gulf pirate." Kingsley toured in Australia with Wilson in 1875, arriving in India in 1877. There he appeared at Bombay until the time of his death from smallpox on April 3, 1879.[26]

In 1884, old-time circus manager and performer Richard Hemmings added a fuller account. He stated that the artist was born of French parents in New Orleans and became apprenticed to S. Q. Stokes at the age of seven years. His true surname was known only to Stokes, but the boy was called "Little Sammie" and taught to ride. When he was eleven, Stokes changed his name to Ella Zoyara, and the youth assumed female attire in professional and private life, no one in the company suspecting he was not a girl. Hemmings stated he was playing at Astley's in London when Zoyara first appeared there, accompanied by a little girl about the same age, who could have been taken for his twin. Grown to womanhood, she became Stoke's wife.

After eight years of successful deception, the ruse was discovered, but "Sammie" never seemed to recover, having assumed the role and personality of a woman too long. He afterwards rode under the stage name "Omar Kingsley," but he could never break himself of the effeminate manners and habits acquired during the long masquerade. After a troubled marriage to Sallie Stickney, he remarried again and had one child by his second wife.[27]

As far as authentic women were concerned, a significant feat was achieved in G. G. Grady's Unprecedented Old-Fashioned American Circus in 1869, when Mrs. Lily Lane appeared as "The ONLY FEMALE CLOWN that has ever been introduced before the American public." On the same bill was M'dlle Adah Inez Montlcain, the only female Hurdle Rider in the world, who performed with her trained steed "Minnehaha."[28]

A Variety of People, a Variety of Incidents

In one sense, the War years of 1860–1865 were different than any other time in circus history, and in another sense they represented the axiom "life goes on." Reviewing newspaper articles, some mere snippets and others four-page editorials, perhaps gives the best idea of how American entertainment survived, how it affected and was affected by the conflict, and where it stood at its bloody termination.

The story begins in the House of Representatives, where elected officials debated, during this time of trouble, whether to "tax the luxuries and recreations of life." Toward that end, tea and coffee were offered up as such, as were circuses. The question then arose, "What is a circus?" Among the more obvious items were added "prestidigitations, ringmaster and clown performances."[29] Once that was clarified, there had to be a circus. February being the month when plans were made for the coming season, in Janesville, Wisconsin, operators commenced breaking in and training ring horses, &c. For this purpose proprietors built a closely boarded-up amphitheatre ring, 40' wide and 12 to 20' high, covered with canvas. Men, horses and equipments were gathered and placed in readiness for April 1, when they planned to set out.[30]

In March, exotic acts were readied. Eaton Stone, the celebrated circus rider, went out west to train a herd of buffalo. After training the beasts for the ring, he proposed hitching several to a wagon and driving them around as common cattle. He also had a calf, which he attached to a cart "and indulge[d] in a pleasure ride once in a while."[31] In Washington, Captain Berens of the Milwaukee Turner Rifles trained his soldiers. Himself a former strong man in the North American Circus, he gave exhibitions of strength to reporters "that would have done honor to the best circus performer in the country," and offered one of his privates to turn somersaults for their benefit.[32]

At the National Capitol, six theaters and two circuses "were in full blast," with the circus tents being used for religious services on Sunday.[33] It was not all fun and games, however, and "pioneers" (soldiers performing such tasks as road work) who the night before attended a circus, were called away by "marching orders." The circus performers in this case were members of the regiment, earning from $100 to $200 for their performances.[34]

Attending a circus could also be a dangerous petition, as one soldier discovered. Accosted by a female who wished him to escort her to the performance, the pair were arrested afterwards and taken to Police Court, where the soldier was told if he paid $15 he would "save himself from trouble." That he did, without ever knowing the charge.[35]

Once the season began, advertising men were sent to spread the word. Every eligible place about the streets was placarded a week or two in advance with "bills of all imaginable colors, and about as big as the side of a barn."[36] Competition being fierce, soon after they were put up, agents of a rival circus arrived. "With remarkable sharpness and not to say honesty," they pasted their equally flaming bills directly over those of the former. When the proprietors of the aggrieved exhibition returned and discovered the shrewd trick, they coolly guessed "they would take their bills down," industriously tearing them off, removing at the same time those of their rivals.[37]

A name re–familiarized to Americans via the television series *The Life and Times of Grizzly Adams* (1974–1982, starring Dan Haggerty) was James Capen "Grizzly" Adams, a hunter and trapper famous in his own day for capturing and training grizzly bears. Born in Maine, he passed a rough life in the woods before leaving for California in 1848, at the age of 48 years. The next decade was spent in the coastal mountains, where he cultivated the friendship of the savage beasts, not altogether successfully, for he lost the upper part of his skull while fighting a fierce Rocky Mountain grizzly.[38] In the spring of 1859, Adams came to New York, exhibiting his animals on Thirteenth Street under the name "California Menagerie," where they danced, laughed, grieved, climbed, turned somersaults and did "everything but speak."

Adams became a familiar figure in New York, taking his morning stroll accompanied by one of his bears and a small band playing bass drum and piccolo flute. In May 1860, while exhibiting an immense grizzly named "Colonel Fremont," he received a severe wound to his arm. Two months later "Old Adams" had recovered sufficiently for Barnum and Nixon to hire him to perform with the latter's circus on its Connecticut tour. In October 1860, while on the horse cars of the Dorchester road, the jolting caused his old head wound to reopen, and blood spurted forth with great violence. Taken to the home of friends, he died there on October 25. His autobiography, revised and finished by Theodore H. Hittell, came out the same year. Adams' menagerie lived after him, later incorporated into Cooke's Royal Circus.[39]

Where there were crowds there must be politicians. In July 1860, the "Douglasites" held a mass meeting in Washington on the day of the circus. The purpose, "of course," was to claim the crowd going to the show was actually there "on account of their mass meeting. Smart trick, that, to get up a crowd."[40] Governor Sam Kirkwood, on a stumping tour through Iowa, also took advantage of the circus to get an audience. It did not work out very well for him, however, as the clown announced, "He had never seen the Governor ride a horse, nor tumble in the ring, and he believed the only somersault he ever turned in his life was a political one. As for a speech, he could make as good a one himself."[41]

With the war in full swing, transportation, or, more precisely, location, became a thorny issue. Early in 1861, Ben De Bar's troupe contracted for an engagement in New Orleans, but in October, when it came time to fulfill his contract, the question arose, how could he get there? And if he could succeed in transporting a company there, how would the speculation succeed? Old Jack Huntley, late manager of the Arkansas Circus, solved his problem by joining a company performing in Cleveland; Robinson & North's Equestrian Company went to Canada.

If transportation for people was a problem, moving heavy animals continued to prove vexing. In 1863 the Metropolitan and Quadruple Combination consisted of George F. Bailey & Co.'s Grand Circus; Herr Driesbach's Menagerie (including lions captured by his hunters and brought to America in April 1862); Sands, Nathan's & Co.'s Performing Elephants; and Gerald Quick's Hippopotamus. (Richard Sands' name continued to be used, although he died "fearfully suddenly" in 1861 in Havana of brain fever. Unmarried,

"The Great Show is Coming!" The Metropolitan and Quadruple Combination (consisting of George F. Bailey & Co.'s Grand Circus; Herr Driesbach's Extensive Menagerie; Sand's, Nathan's & Co. Performing Elephants; and the Gigantic Hippopotamus or Behemoth of Holy Writ) featured Sam Burt, the hurdle and bareback rider; Philo Nathans, classic equestrian; the Denzer Brothers, acrobats; Charles Rivers, 2- and 4-horse rider; and James Ward, American Humorist and Extempore Clown. This 1863 Civil War–era combination performed opposite W. A. Reynolds' display of fireworks from two large balloons, celebrating the opening of the Mississippi river by the capture of Port Hudson. The same illustration was used by the Quadruple Combination the following year, where it was promoted as the largest traveling Establishment in the Country. (*Janesville Daily Gazette* [WI], July 17, 1863; *Cedar Valley Times* [IA], May 26, 1864)

he left an estate of $250,000, divided between friends, relatives and a number of old employees.[42] As proof of how lucrative proprietorship could be, another famous circus man, Gerald C. Quick, died at Philadelphia in 1869, leaving $200,000 in cash to his brother, nieces and nephews.[43])

While traveling from Buffalo to Detroit, the elephants and hippo, along with their keeper, Ali the Egyptian, were sent on the propeller, *S.D. Caldwell*. The cages were too heavy, so the animals were kept loose at the bow. Within several miles of their destination, the hippo, valued at $40,000 (lately shown at Barnum's Museum and the only one in the country), "vamoosed" by jumping overboard. After leading Ali on a merry chase, a large black mastiff that slept in the hippo's cage was sent into the St. Claire River after it. The dog directed it to shore by barking, and both creatures were quickly re-captured.[44] The hippo continued to make headlines, sharing press with its human performers, "the men and women in underclothes."[45]

Bad roads were blamed on an accident that might have had far more dire consequences. On the way from Watertown to Oconomowoc, Wisconsin, a driver lost control of his wagon, and a cage containing a lioness and her whelps slipped off. In attempting to right it, the leg of a cub became pinned, driving the mother into an uproar. Her fury proved contagious, creating a horrific row among the other lions. The noise so frightened the camels and elephants drawing the bandwagon that they panicked, threatening to break free and escape. At a point when the roaring and confusion threatened a general melee, the lion tamer arrived. Deducing the root of the problem, he freed the cub, thus quieting the lioness and ultimately permitting the other keepers to control their animals.[46]

With staggering losses only a bad road away, it was no wonder proprietors sought other ways of assuring themselves a steady income. After closing a profitable year in 1861, Dan Rice laid in a crop of clover at his farm[47] and dabbled in oil speculation, making a strike in 1865.[48]

Hedging Bets and Lesser Crimes

Rice was not the only one to hedge his bet. Matthew and Lorenz Van Vleck (who operated the Mammoth Circus with Dan Castello in 1862–1863) were owners of one of the heaviest mineral lodes worked in Wisconsin.[49] Two proprietors of Lake & Robinson's Circus bought shares in the *Cincinnati Enquirer*. Unfortunately for them, the newspaper burned to the ground on February 26, 1865, their part in the venture being totally uninsured. The loss was estimated at $300,000.[50] While the *Enquirer* conflagration was considered an accident, another fire in Philadelphia was blamed on William R. Donaldson, a circus clown whose name appeared on the roster of the Great Western or Victory Arena, 1845, and John Tryon's Winter Show, 1847.[51]

Gambling of a different sort than that practiced by Lake & Robinson was far more closely associated with the circus, not always with the intended reward. In 1863, a Pittsfield gambler "came up to increase his pile on circus day and got whipped" for his trouble.[52] Closer to home, Alexander Prentice, traveling with Bailey & Co's. Circus, was arrested and fined $50 and costs for gambling. He had "a showcase full of jewelry, from a $100 gold watch down to a two cent brass ring, and a few dice, by a few throws of which greenhorns were induced to throw away their money in vain expectation of drawing a big prize." Three others were involved, but they "skedaddled" in time to save their $50 each.[53]

Lesser crimes were incurred by Dan Castello's Circus in 1866, when they rented the North Public Square in Burlington, Iowa. An outcry was raised over the low fee of $10 charged the company when damage incurred from the construction of the ring included the destruction of embankments and grass crushed by horses, wagons and spectators.[54] And then there was the "impudent pea-nut venders and side shows" with attaches, who persisted in "selling candy, peanuts, tickets for a bogus concert, song books &c. &c." while insulting people via the blackguards rude and violent language.[55]

The law case *J. C. Julius Langbeen by his Guardian vs. James E. Kelly & Van Amburgh*, 1864, brought forth another interesting topic: a man was forcibly ejected against his will by the ushers of Van Amburgh's Circus, New York, for sitting in an area reserved for women and children. Despite his violent and profane language in resisting, the jury found he was entitled to damages of $150.[56] As one way to compensate for such miscellaneous expenses and possibly receive a gratuitous supply, Hyatt Frost of Van Amburgh's wrote a testimonial promoting "Dr. Tobias' Venetian Horse Liniment," remarking he found it "the best article ever tried by the Circus Company."[57]

None of this helped the reputation of circus people. A recurring theme was summarized by one editorial complaining, "We hear of this company of vagabonds throughout their entire route, and we hear no good of them in any place. Their exhibitions are obscene — as all circus acting is — and the accompaniments, drinking, gambling, pilfering, quarreling, &c. finish out the picture."[58]

Despite such pious grousing, the simple enjoyment of wild animals, equestrian and gymnastic showmanship became even more important during the bleak years of retreats, advances and death tolls. A typical description of a combined circus/menagerie gives substance to what these traveling entertainers meant to people desperate for relief.

> About noon, the town was literally crowded, and about that time the circus band heralded the approach of the caravan. The usual procession, headed by the three elephants drawing the individual with the unpronounceable name (Hippopotamus), the train of cages, and the usual escort of horses and paraphernalia is familiar to all. The crowd was as mixed as such gatherings usually are. The grave farmer with his wife and little ones; the simple, unostentatious rustic with his modest, healthy looking "gal," and the more dashing young dandy, trimmed out with all the tailor's latest art (not forgetting the jewelry store), and the belles, admiring and admired, their beauty — when they possessed it — smothered under a super-abundance of dress, generally climaxed with that nondescript article worn where a bonnet used to sit, formed a picture.[59]

Fleshing out the variety of people and the variety of incidents at the circus:

> There were those who knew about natural history, and volunteered information whenever you asked a question concerning the animals; there were those who came only to see the menagerie department, and who would not have staid [*sic*] except to see the hippopotamus and performing elephants — they belonged to the "first families," and seemed a little ashamed of a curiosity which ought to belong only to the vulgar people; there were those who laughed whenever the clown spoke, believing it to be their duty to do so, and thinking that if they did not, everybody would imagine they had never been to a circus before; there were those who had never attended such a place of amusement before, and who strained eyes and ears to their utmost tension, lest they should lose a gesture or a word; there were those who had been in the afternoon, who had actually stood face to face and conversed with the ring-master and the manager of the "What Is It?" and who therefore knew all about it — knew when the clown was expected to beat all the others turning summersaults, when he was expected to be witty, and what his next joke was going to be — knew that Ali was a real Egyptian, and not a highly colored Irishman, as was suspected by an ignorant fellow near at hand — knew whether the horse stumbled on purpose or not — knew all about the hippopotamus and the elephants, and had been made acquainted with everything worth knowing connected with the whole institution; — it was pleasant to have them sit directly behind you, because they spoke with loud voices, and you at once became enlightened upon a great many important particulars with reference to which you might otherwise have remained in ignorance.... There were lovers there, clinging to each other's hands for fear of losing each other. There were a thousand other kinds of people there ... each one of whom filled a place which would have been a void else. You will always find them at the circus.[60]

All this was summed up by the *Iowa City Republican*: "A circus with a bear, dog, mule and monkey show, draws thousands at fifty cents a piece. The commencement exercises of the State University, free to all are hardly noticed."[61]

The War Years had their great combination circuses and their "one horse circuses," which could hardly fail to meet expectations:

> The elephant was like all other elephants, and flapped his ears as usual — the horses look like all other tired and jaded horses. Men with Frenchified name and

tawdry accoutrements jumped and kicked up their heels, to the great astonishment of the little boys, while the clown sung coarse songs in a very bass voice, and cracked stale jokes to the evident delight of a few appreciating minds."[62]

The "most interesting performance of all," however, was that "of taking in the quarters."[63] With money being the "soul" of the business, a considerable amount was at stake in the law case *Marie Macarte vs. Richard H. Platt*, whereby the plaintiff alleged she was employed by the defendant under a contract by which she was to perform at his circus as long as he remained proprietor, for the weekly salary of $180. She had performed several weeks but Platt discharged her; she was ready to continue her performances. The defense justified discharging Macarte on the grounds she had conducted herself in such a manner as to injure his business. The case settled in favor of the defendant.[64] Macarte had been a big star, debuting in America in November 1846, as the leading performer with Nathan Howes' New York Bowery Circus. Born in Paris in 1824, she specialized in the "change act," where she rode at top speed altering costumes into characters as varied as a nun and Gypsy fortune teller.[65] She later worked for Haight & Chambers' New Orleans Circus, Menagerie & Museum. In 1867, while on tour at Lansing, she was thrown from her horse, receiving serious injuries.[66]

Haight & Chambers promoted a den of Asiatic lions, worked by Herr Lingal, and the smallest baby elephant ever imported, measuring three feet high and weighing less than 500 pounds. Interestingly, a Galveston newspaper observed that while the regular price of admission was $1 in currency (paper), if paying in specie (coin), the cost was *forty cents more*. Two months later, the same newspaper noted the circus was slightly attended, due in part to the fact they charged $1 in coin but only 50 cents in currency. The policy did not pay off, as in January 1868, the sheriff seized their assets. Mystery surrounded the circus failure, although it maintained a good reputation in Houston for offering three benefits for the purpose of building fences to keep cattle from roaming over graves. The proprietors had one more grave to protect the following week when James Day, one of their own, committed suicide because he was owed $600 at the time of Haight's disorganization and despaired of receiving what was owed.[67]

Municipalities continued to levy fees: the Equescurriculum paid $70 for the privilege of exhibiting in Adams[68]; another circus company was fined $50 for exhibiting without a license (later reduced to $5 and costs)[69]; and a comment with relevance today lamented that all the money collected from circus licenses were to be reserved as a special fund, but instead went into the general treasury.[70] If anyone needed a reminder the war still raged, property of a different type was sacrificed when the Union Army at Nashville confiscated circus horses and forced the men to work on fortifications.[71]

Life and death, birth and regeneration remained daily reminders of the earth's cycle. On April 29, 1864, some good news was delivered to war-torn Americans with the announcement that a double-humped camel in the Manchester, England, collection of Messrs. Sanger, gave birth to a fine young calf, only the second in England. The mother took kindly to her young and suckled it with an abundance of milk. The calf weighed 58 pounds and measured 3'6". It was brown in color, with black humps. The humps were uniform in size, parts where they would grow indicated by small patches of thin, loose skin, resembling oil-skin.[72]

The curtain dropped in April 1865, with the Obsequies of President Lincoln. Acknowledging the national tragedy, the bands of De Haven & Co.'s Circus and that of Lake & Co.'s tendered their services to the sad procession in Washington.[73]

18

Everything's Hunkidori: Moral Exhibitions, Aggregations and the "Ku-Klux-Kan"

Lovers of the marvelous are informed, in this morning's paper, that a man will eat rocks and then swallow a sword, and also exhibit a dwarf negro woman thirty inches high and 57 years old.[1]

The decade of the 1860s continued and expanded upon the concept of "bigger is better" by combining smaller concerns into one mammoth exhibition, changing names almost as often as performers and animal attractions. Nixon's Royal Circus added Grizzly Adams' California Menagerie in 1860; the R. Sands' Grand Combination Circus of 1860 became "Sands and Nathans with George F. Bailey & Co.'s Grand Circus" in 1863. Later the same year, the "Grand Union Triplicate Combination Circus" included R. Sands' Complete Circus Co., with Melville's Great Australian Circus and Henry Cooke's ("Cook") Mammoth Troupe of Performing Dogs and Monkeys, before transforming into the "Metropolitan and Quadruple Combination" of Bailey's Grand Circus, Herr Driesbach's Extensive Menagerie, Sands' and Nathan's & Co.'s Performing Elephants and The Gigantic Hippopotamus.

L. B. Lent's Great National Circus Company, also known as the "Equescurriculum," included Tom King's Olympic Circus, Joe Pentland's Circus, Wallace's Troupe of Acting Bears, Deer's Educated Sacred Bull, the Wonderful Leaping Buffalo, and Prof. Langworthy's Corps of Performing Dogs and Monkeys. The names changed in 1865, when the concern advertised Lent's Broadway Circus, Mons. François Tourniare's Great French Circus, William Ducrow's Circus Royal (London), Old Grizzly Adams' Troupe of Acting Bears, Forrest's Trained Buffalo, Evans' Educated Sacred Bull, and Prof. Wallace's Corps of Performing Dogs, Monkeys and Ponies. That year, Lent sold his share in the Equescurriculum and purchased the New York Circus, as he no longer desired to travel.

In 1866, Lent added Senor G. Chiarini's Royal Circus. Jose Chiarini was born in Rome around 1826, and apprenticed under his father at Cayetano Chiarini's circus, until age 16 when he began a tour through Europe. Honing his skills at Astley's, he came to New York in 1852 as one of Franconi's managers. He took his own circus to Havana, featuring equestrian acts that included his daughter Josephine. With his agent, Lorenzo Cuppia, they played in Mexico and the southwestern United States before joining Lent.[2]

The Antonio Brothers' (Guiliamo, Lorenzo, Augustus and Alphonso) Great World Circus (1860–1863) included the clowns Albert Aymar, Tom Osborn and Tom Tipton, and Mr. Stowles' "Fire Act," whereby he went through the Volcano of Fire. Van Amburgh's Zoological and Equestrian Company (1860) featured wagons made by Messrs. Field & Butler, New York, and offered the War Elephant Hannibal and Tippoo Saib; Herr Lengle ("Lingal" and "Lengel"); lion tamer Nat Austin; the English Performing Clown; and James L. Thayer with his Educated Mules. Along with a mid–season name change to "The Great Van Amburgh Show," James Melville, the Great Australian, was added. By 1863, it was styled "Van Amburgh & Co.'s Mammoth Menagerie and Great Moral Exhibition," and by 1864, it had metamorphosed into "Van Amburgh & Co.'s Menagerie in Connection with Gardner & Hemming's American Circus."

De Haven's Great Union Circus (1860) became George W. De Haven & Co.'s United Circus in 1865, with Levi J. North as Equestrian Director; A. Haight as Treasurer; Signor Charles Bliss, the great antipodean; Albert Aymar; and balloon ascensions. The winter company, under the title "The Great United Circus," added "Old Sam Lathrop," the famous clown, and Master Castello on the high wire. Under the proprietorship of William Shephard, "George W. De Haven's Grand Imperial Circus" of 1868, George De Haven, manager, featured principal performers Joseph Tinkman and Gus Lee, clowns. For one of the first times, the "Boss Canvasman" was credited to Hank McGuffin. Proprietors Alderman & Ladd presented "De Haven Combination of Circus and Animals" in 1869, again with George De Haven as manager. With them appeared Sam Lathrop and Billie Andrews, clowns; Joe Tinkman, Double Somersaultist; the Lazelle Brothers; and Amelia Bridges and Mad'lle Marie, equestriennes.

The 1863 version of Thayer & Noyes' United States Circus and Hippozoonomadom featured champion rider James Robinson, Albert Aymar, George Derious, Thayer as jester, and Noyes with his trained horse and monkey. The 1865 edition, called Thayer & Noyes' Great United States Circus and Van Amburgh's & Co.'s Menagerie, included the famous lion tamer; Hannibal the War Elephant; and James Cooke as jester. In 1867, having separated from Van Amburgh, Elias White became lion tamer. On July 4, upon entering the cage, one of the males attacked him, fastening his jaws in White's shoulder. The circus men were required to use iron bars to rescue him, but the injuries

Miss Ella Zuilla (also spelled "Zuila") was billed by the 4-Paw Show as the "only female Blondin," a reference to the famous 19th century tightrope walker. She crossed the high wire 60 feet above the heads of the audience, with the added attraction of being blindfolded, with her feet encased in sacks. Another part of her act was to carry a man upon her back as she crossed the wire. (*Daily Chronicle* [MI], September 25, 1880)

were not considered severe. "The affair caused great excitement in the audience."[3] White recovered and was with the circus the following year; attractions included Glenroy's Elephant and a performing monkey called "Hun–ki-Dori," likely the origin of the common expression, "Everything's hunkidori," referring to an event that was "just fine."

In 1869, Thayer severed his connection with his partners (C. W. Noyes went on to produce the Mammoth Crescent City Circus in Texas), calling his concern The Zoolo-hippozomadon with Prof. White's Den of Performing Lions. With them was the Elephant Lala Rookh and performer Albert Aymar. Proving anything was worthy of jest, one of their "sensations" was the Grand Cavalcade of the Ku-Klux-Kan [*sic*], or, The Clown's Cavalry, forming "one of the funniest and most laughable sights ever witnessed." While it is hard to envision bicycle performances as early as 1869, the company also featured artists on the Bicycle Velocipede.[4]

Everything was not "hunkidori" with Thayer, for in October 1869, the sheriff of Hamilton County served a writ of attachment on the property. Clarry & Reilly of New York issued the original suit, claiming $2,926 for printing. Eight others immediately joined:

> Franklin J. Howes, $750 for 5 weeks service as equestrian manager, use of his trained horses and the performance of his wife, an equestrienne who was to receive $150/week
> Charles Abbott, clown, sued for $363, the balance of his $70/week salary
> Frederick A. Dabois, sued for $565, balance due on $1,000 due for advertising services from April–October
> Joseph H. Neal, gymnast, sued for $428 from his salary of $35/week
> Joseph Burdeaux, gymnast at the same pay, sued for $320
> Charles H. Lowry, equestrian, same pay, sued for $238
> James Blakely sued for $900 on a judgment recovered elsewhere

A receiver was set to sell the entire property.[5] In March 1870, four of his lions were sold at a sheriff's sale in Cincinnati for $5,200.[6] A month later, Thayer organized another circus at Erie, prompting an editor to note, "Those circus people don't stay failed any more than newspaper men."[7]

James L. Thayer, considered one of the great humorists of the age, began his career as a physician. His father, Captain James L. Thayer, was one of the first settlers of Milwaukee, being a pioneer in navigating the waters of the Rock River. Humor was always topical, and when an American prizefighter beat an English champion, Thayer's song found rousing enthusiasm:

> Pray give me your attention,
> And I'll not detain you long;
> It's the topic of the day,
> So I'll rhyme it in my song—
> About the brave "Benecia Boy,"
> Who proudly took the field,
> And fought old England's Champion,
> And made the Lion yield.
> CHORUS-Horra, three cheers, for Heenan is the Boy,
>   We'll give him a reception when we get him back to Troy.[8]

Also coming to grief was the Great Australian Circus Company, "so called because no member thereof has ever been in Australia." At Riverhead, Long Island, the treasurer decamped with $4,000. Along with the Long Island Railroad Company, residents presented bills for hay, corn, oats, cider and pork. Lacking money to pay, the managers and several actors were arrested and lodged in jail. As the performers had not been paid for some time, George Rebbel and Hendrick F. Gafgen "fell back on their old business and resorted to highway robbery." Several other actors were charged with having acted in a like indecorous manner toward the burghers. Among the animals seized were the lions owned by Miss Minnie Wells, who threatened to take the issue to court.[9]

George De Haven had better luck in 1870, while performing in Meridian, Mississippi. He just happened to be at the telegraph office when a message came in over the Western Union wire for lawyers to hold his circus for debt. Casually asking whether the message had to do with circus matters, he offered to deliver it and fulfilled his promise four days later, after arranging his affairs so that his circus was not "holdable." Finding his plans thwarted, Joseph Cone, to whom the money was owed, sued the telegraph company for a substantial consideration.[10]

Similar names were another sticking point. Robinson & Lake's Great Menagerie and Circus (John Robinson and Bill Lake, proprietors, Col. Thomas Usher Tidmarsch ["Tibmarsh" and "Tidmarsh"], manager, and H. Ruggles, Advertising Agent) offered Archy Campbell as the Rural Joker and "Farmer's Almanac of Fun"; James Robinson, the famous equestrian, and Master John Robinson (sons of John Robinson); John Alexander Robinson (John's nephew); Bill Lake (the "Southern Clown") and Sam Long (the "Universal Jester"); along with the great Russian Elk, captured by John Robinson. To avoid confusion and distinguish themselves from others in the field, their agent, Fred H. Bailey, published a disclaimer stating that "the so-called 'Yankee' Robinson is not at all interested nor at any time connected, in any shape whatever, with the establishment of Robinson & Lake."[11]

Tragedy struck on April 25, 1866, when ruffians demanded entrance to Robinson's circus, then playing at Crittenden, Kentucky. Being denied, they abused the national flag, flying overhead, and instigated a brawl. Initial reports indicated James Robinson had been killed, while his brother John and "Big Jim" Robinson (boss canvasman, no relation) were severely wounded. John, the father and proprietor, then at home in Cincinnati, rushed to his circus in company with Dr. Mursey. When it was all sorted through, it was revealed that John Alexander Robinson had been mortally wounded, dying on April 30, "Jack" Robinson had been shot in the leg, and Big Jim probably mortally injured.[12]

In a less than sentimental aside, it was noted James Robinson earned $24,000 a year.[13] He went to Paris the following year, performing at the Theatre du Prince Imperial with his little son.[14] Two years later, he returned, headlining James Robinson's Champion Circus Combined with Kenyon's Menagerie.[15]

"For the Era We Live In"

Yankee Robinson himself offered the Colossal Moral Exhibition "For the Era we live in" in 1866, promoting the only Yankee-born elephant, a huge selling point to recently reunited Americans, and Tom Thumb's Cortege. His "Bran [a common substitute for "brand"] New Show" of 1868 featured the Abyssinian elephant "Roscius," the Egyptian Wallapus, and the Sea Cow.

One of the largest exhibitions of the immediate post–war era was Forepaugh's Gigantic Circus and Menagerie, Adam Forepaugh, sole proprietor; Frank M. Kelsh, Manager; and

Dr. Richard P. Jones, Director of Publications. Jones, a respected agent for over 20 years, committed suicide in 1869, after receiving a telegram stating his wife had deserted him.[16] Desertion and unfaithfulness from both partners in a marriage was not uncommon among circus people: in 1864, Mrs. Caroline L. Nixon, wife of James Nixon, the famed proprietor, divorced him on the grounds of "improper communication with a well-known danseuse." At the same time, the danseuse instituted an action for divorce from her husband for "cause."[17] Dan Rice's wife, a deacon's daughter, sued for divorce in 1881.[18]

Forepaugh's menagerie, separate and distinct from the circus, but with one price of admission to both, offered "Babie Annie," the elephant (later spelled "Baby Annie"); Sam Long, the Southern Clown; James DeMott, bareback

The **Silver Mountain Equestrian Bears,** in their astonishing and almost human performances, were only a small part of Yankee Robinson's Colossal Moral Exhibition "for the era we live in," making its rounds in 1867. Other attractions included Tom Thumb's Cortege (as opposed to Tom Thumb himself), George Sears as the Great Lion Tamer, and the "Only Yankee Born Elephant, just weaned from its mother." (*Iowa South West,* September 7, 1867)

rider; Thomas King, Scenic Rider; James Ward, Clown; Theodore Tourniaire, Hurdle Rider; and Prof. Langworthy, Lion Tamer. They boasted 22 massive dens, "finished in the most gorgeous and recherché styles of fine art, and decorated with emerald and gold,"[19] beside beautiful depictions of animals on the sides. The Second Annual Tour in 1868 added "Romeo" to the menagerie, advertising "the largest and smallest elephants in the world." That year, George Forepaugh was credited as the elephant trainer and Prof. A. J. Forepaugh as the Lion King.

In November 1868, while at winter quarters in Philadelphia, Forepaugh's building burned down, resulting in the destruction of the wagons and circus equipment valued at $17,000, none of which was insured. A Bengal tiger escaped but was recaptured without incident, and, fortunately, all the large animals were spared injury.[20] Forepaugh recovered from the devastation, and the 1869 season was billed as "Adam Forepaugh's Great Zoological and Equestrian Aggregation," with the "Advent of the Great 4 Paw Mastodon." Old Romeo, as well as two infant elephants, were listed beside 25 dens of animals and a herd of Camels and Dromedaries. In one of his skits, Sam Lathrop, the clown, described the "Bond question" in all too familiar language:

> The people have to get up at 5:20 and work until 10:40 in order that the bond-holders may lie in bed until 10:40 and retire at 7:30. The meaning of the 5:20s is, that it takes the labor of 20 men to support 5 bondholders in idleness, while the laboring man gets $5 of his earnings and pays $20 to the bondholder."[21]

With the war over, circuses made their way back south, although conditions were hardly favorable. As a member of Orton and Older's Great Southern Circus, the famous clown "Yankee Sullivan" (real name Billy Andrews) wrote a letter home to Dubuque, Iowa, in 1867, remarking, "The company has been showing its way through Arkansas with great success, although the war has left the majority of the inhabitants as poor as a church mouse."[22] Although feelings still ran hard, one review for the Great United Circus (Andrew Haight, proprietor) harkened back to Antebellum times. Sounding as though it came out of Disney's *Song of the South*, it noted about a performance in Texas, 'The Concert of the Negro Minstrels brought back to memory, very forcibly, that musical phenomenon, a happy-go-lucky, rolicking, sleek skinned Southern slave."

"Rolicking" of a different sort took place in 1867, when members of the Alabama Convention at Montgomery visited Castello's circus. "The colored delegates desired to seat themselves among the whites, but the ushers inexorably confined them to 'de brack track' subdivision."[23] The following year "two Negro men were brutally and fearfully beaten" in Wilmington by attaches of Dan Castello's circus.[24] Segregation continued to rear its ugly head. In March 1868, a United States soldier in uniform attempted to take a mulatto woman into the circus at Galveston, announcing he "was an advocate of equality and intended to carry it out." When the manager was informed, the couple was removed to the black side. The following year at Sparta, Georgia, "a personal difficulty" broke out between a few whites and blacks attending the circus, in which one Negro was killed and another mortally wounded.[25]

Dan Rice, the "American humorist," thrived during the war years, bringing his "Great Show" east in 1861. Described as neither a circus nor a menagerie, it was "a grand exposition of the *Wonders of Nature and Art, including Highly Trained Animals and remarkable Exploits of Athletic Power and Agility ... Combining Amusement with Instruction!*"[26] The following year, Mr. Stickney engaged him for the National Circus at the Bowery Theatre, in company with his comic mules[27]; and in 1863, Dr. G. R. Spalding (frequently misspelled "Spaulding"), of Albany, paid him $25,000 for the season, or the equivalent of President Lincoln's salary.[28]

A man whose name frequently appeared in the newspapers for his charity, Dan Rice contracted the Chicago sculptor Volk to build a $4,500 monument to the memory of the deceased soldiers of Erie County at Gettysburg.[29] During court proceedings in 1865, word leaked out that Dan

THE GREAT CONSOLIDATION CIRCUS!

The Great Consolidation Circus included Ben Maginley's Celebrated European Circus, W. B. Carroll's New York Circus, J. H. Woods' Great World Circus and Howes' Champion Circus. Bigger was always better, and as the decades passed, people expected more and more for their price of admission. Uniting into a single unit also had the advantage of putting smaller, unattached "mud shows" out of business and brokering better prices along the way. (*Sparta Eagle* [WI], May 8, 1867)

Rice's Circus and Menagerie was backed by John O'Brien and Forepaugh, who hired Rice, supplied the animals and paid $25,000 for 27 weeks, with expenses, for the use of Rice's name.[30]

That same year, Rice appeared with Howe's European Circus at Galveston. Though he earned $1,000 a week, it was his politics rather than his wealth that came into question. There were hard feelings among Southerners concerning the monument he erected in Pennsylvania. His explanation that the inscription, "To the brave Soldiers who fell at Gettysburg," also included Confederates apparently proved satisfactory.[31]

"Colonel" Rice returned to the Gulf States in 1866, reporting that, except at government institutions, the United States flag was rarely seen below the mouth of the Ohio River. Even menageries that habitually flew the flags of all nations failed to raise the Stars and Stripes, his show excepted. In Mobile, rumors started that Rice had led the advance guard of Gierson's raiders during the war, and threats were made on his life. He was encouraged not to perform

DAN RICE'S
GREAT SHOW

Dan Rice, American humorist and circus proprietor, possessed one of the most recognizable names in the circus world of the 1800s. Rice continually reinvented himself over the course of his illustrious career (which included bankruptcy, lawsuits for slander, bouts with alcoholism, friendship with Abraham Lincoln and religious conversion). This 1861 advertisement for his Great Show promised he was "Not Dead, as some of his enemies have reported, but now comes to greet the good friends who sustained him in the hour of adversity, with a combination of startling wonders, such as has never before been witnessed in the West." (*Hudson North Star* [WI], July 31, 1861)

one night, but, placing a revolver between the center pole and the hoisting rope, in full view of the audience, he "gave them a plain talk." Some disturbance followed, but the offenders were arrested and the show went on.[32]

Dan Rice's Mammoth Menagerie and North American Circus, featuring the Asiatic elephant Romeo and his keeper, Stewart Craven (who had captured and trained the animal six years before), performed at Gettysburg in April 1866. The equestrian department included Miss Annetta Aymar, Mr. and Mrs. Sam Stickney (misspelled in the ad), S. D. Baldwin, George Darious and H. King.[33] Later that month, Rice was called upon to testify before the Reconstruction Committee about his recent tour through the South. A transcript, from the Washington correspondent of the *Commercial*, was widely reprinted. The questions concentrated on how Southerners likened their animals to renowned Federal figures.[34] That same year, Rice was nominated as the Johnson candidate for the 19th District, Pennsyl-vania.[35]

Another war-related "sort of a circus, only not so attractive, and not half so respectable," involved a set of Mosby's brigands (John S. Mosby was an infamous Confederate guerrilla, operating in Virginia) coming north to go through "the tomfoolery that they call a 'tournament' in Virginia."[36] It is hard to imagine any Union man paying to see this, as the idea was perceived as extremely tasteless.

"One if by land, two if by sea...."

Transporting circus equipment, personnel and animals over great distances was never an easy task. Choices for the 19th century proprietor consisted of travel by road, water and, as the decade progressed, railroad. Each method had advantages and drawbacks. Gilbert Spalding and Charles Rogers' circus was, both fortunately and unfortunately, attracted to disaster. In July 1860, their show-boat *Raymond* was at Cairo, Illinois. Antonio, one of the cast who had been up late playing chess, heard an explosion originating from the steamboat *Ben Lewis*. He, Tom Watson (clown) and a deck hand immediately put out their yawl and were the first upon the scene of the burning boat. The river was filled with passengers holding onto various bits of debris. They took aboard two ladies, six men and a boy who were clinging to the rudder, thus saving their lives.[37] The circus subsequently spent nearly three years abroad in South America, the West Indies and Cuba before returning home in mid–April 1864. Having voyaged over 16,000 miles (the only mishap being the loss of two men to yellow fever) and given $20,000 in charitable benefits and donations, the company returned to New York on the brig *Hannah*. The steamer wrecked near the harbor, resulting in the loss of two horses, amphitheatre and costumes from the Ocean Circus, as well as the personal belongings of the 28 artists.[38]

Notwithstanding, the Great Ocean Circus, with Charles J. Rogers as Managing Proprietor, went on tour, featuring South American per formers with young Charles Fish, the bareback rider (who would become one of the great equestrians of his time); Billy Pastor, gymnast; Tom Stewart, Maitre de Cirque; and H. W. Ruggles and "The Marvel of the Age, Prof. Austen's celebrated newly invented Family Steam Carriage," a self–propelled vehicle reputed to travel 30 miles per hour, stopping only for a bucket of water or handful of faggots."[39]

At first glance, it might appear the Family Steam Carriage was conducting people around the dawn of the 20th century, but it actually made its circus debut in 1864, during the Civil War, when it was gratuitously displayed in the ring at every performance of Spalding & Rogers' Great Ocean Circus. A wonder of mechanical ingenuity and triumph of inventive skill, the car promised "to supersede the use of horses on ordinary thoroughfares." The vehicle was reputed to steam along at 30 miles per hour, "stopping for a bucket of water or a handful of faggots, only; and more docile than a horse, it halts instantly, turns dexterously, or proceeds at funeral pace at the bid of its driver." (*Daily Milwaukee News*, September 4, 1864)

A disaster of epic proportions occurred on October 3, 1866, when the steamer *Evening Star*, recently departed from New York to New Orleans, was struck by a gale and sank. Among the passengers were thirty members of Spalding & Bidwell's Circus Company, with all their stage appurtenances but no horses. Also aboard was a French opera troupe of 60 singers and ballet dancers under the direction of Paul Alhaiza, who had only arrived from Europe two days earlier. Additionally, a large number of "flash" women hired by mistresses in New Orleans to ply their trade in that city and numerous "respectable" passengers filled the vessel.

Tragically, members of the French troupe did not speak English and thus could not understand instructions. In the ensuing riot, however, it may not have mattered, as there were only four life preservers aboard and limited space in the lifeboats. Of the estimated 300 passengers, only 16 survived, none of them women or children. Captain Knapp also perished in one of the lifeboats.

The value of the *Evening Star* was $500,000; peculiarly, it was completely uninsured, and speculation arose that it was un–seaworthy and so uninsurable.[40] If true, it was a damning circumstance for the company. The cargo, valued at $1,000,000, was privately insured.[41] Unlike railroad owners, who were required by law to insure cargo, no such mandate applied to steamboat operators, and it was fortunate shippers in this case took precautions.

The year 1868 included two accidents involving circuses. The first occurred on January 25, when the steamer *Emerald* struck a snag, creating a hole under the guards. Fortunately, the boat was brought to shore, but cages belonging to John Robinson's circus, holding a learned hog, a bear, tiger, four monkeys, a box of snakes and a dog, were on the hurricane roof and were thrown into the water.[42] On June 11, the side-wheeler *Ocean Wave*, charted by De Haven's Circus to transport it to St. Paul, took fire on the return trip and was destroyed. No lives were lost.[43]

In light of the above, the transition from road or steamboat travel to the Iron Horse was a logical one. With most cities and towns near a depot, it became an easy matter for a proprietor to plot a route for the entire season, send out his advertising men and employ trains for the typical quick one- or two-day stops before moving on to the next place

The transition from wagon or steamboat to railroads enabled exhibitions to travel faster and to stop at more towns, but it was an expensive way to travel. (*Star and Sentinel*, Pennsylvania, August 21, 1879)

along the line. The mode was expensive, however: in October 1871, Robinson's Circus paid $126 a day for transportation from Chicago to their next stop in Illinois, including stoppages.[44]

Larger concerns charted a train, decorating the cars as they once painted their wagons and caravans by splashing brightly colored illustrations of roaring lions, threatening elephants and death-defying acts by gymnasts and equestrians. Flat cars also offered the advantage of strength, being capable of carrying the immense weight of iron cages. Railroads provided townspeople the opportunity of meeting the train at the station and watching as the animals and paraphernalia were unloaded. It then became a matter of personal preference and financial consideration whether to indulge the public in the accustomed parade to the circus grounds. Contrast these two exhibitions, both from 1868:

Bailey's Quadruple Show provided an immense procession, headed by a chariot drawn by eight dromedaries and assisted by two elephants, followed by a dozen horses pulling wild animal cages, "all making one of the best poor men's shows ever exhibited. This is a striking feature. Bailey's show upon the street is for the benefit of those who cannot afford to go and see, and this part should be appreciated by those it benefits."[45]

On the other hand, Stone & Murray's Circus traveled "exclusively by Railroad, on special trains chartered at immense expense. Therefore, no attempt will be made to deceive the public by a Street Parade of empty wagons, drawn by horses hired in the place of exhibition. The attractions of this Circus are in the Pavilion."[46]

Arrangements with the Union Pacific Railroad were negotiated in 1869 to transport a circus and menagerie across the continent. In this first-ever venture of its type, stops at principal towns were to be made along the way from the Missouri River to the Pacific Ocean.[47]

On September 28, 1870, L. B. Lent's Circus was on a chartered train of the Erie Railway at Turner Station when an express train rammed it from behind. Mr. Whitbeck, the circus director, was killed when a pole was driven through his body. No animals escaped, but the loss was placed at several thousand dollars.[48] Proving that no method of transportation was safe, in May 1871, a train struck one of Barnum's wagons near Crawford, New Jersey, killing three men and dangerously injuring two others. The wagon, loaded with provisions, was totally demolished.[49]

By and large, although railroads offered more convenient transportation, circus people preferred to "rough it" by traveling in caravans, despite the fact it entailed greater hardships on animals and personnel. Moving by road was also more remunerative to proprietors, and a full dependence on railroads never became the norm for smaller concerns.

"Roughing it" took on a new meaning in 1870. John Robinson's Circus and Menagerie was at Tallahassee, Florida, and had to get to Quincy for the next performance. Although warned that crossing swampy country was dangerous, the manager replied that the agent had already made arrangements for him to go through, and it was not in his nature to back down. Consequently, Professor Lewis Houston, in charge of the animals, set out, taking with him the elephant Empress, a Bactrian camel, a white Arabian camel, a thoroughbred mare and colt, and two dogs. Beginning at night, they came to a ford, the elephant entering the water first. Before the caravan was two-thirds across, the dogs were attacked and killed by alligators. The Bactrian camel became the next target, and, despite efforts by the elephant to save it, the animal perished, having only its head retrieved by the faithful elephant. The roar of terrified beasts and the smell of blood brought scores more alligators to the scene, and the colt was soon killed. Houston eventually made shore, having sacrificed the Bactrian, valued at $5,000, the colt and both dogs.[50]

Tragedy, certainly, was not contained to transportation issues, and the newspapers were filled with incidents involving individual performers. One such occurred in Moscow in late 1866, with the death of bareback rider Davis Richards while performing at the Cirque-Reuz. In the midst of his Olympian act, Richards' foot slipped when getting down from the shoulders of his comrade. He fell off the rump of one horse and struck the ground with such force as to paralyze his whole body. On being lifted up, he sent love to his wife and died within 24 hours.[51]

Nor were circus owners immune from tragedy. In November 1870, Henry Whitby of the Great American Exposition, who had been on a tour

Under the category "all's fair in business," the Great 4 Paw Mastodon Aggregation warned prospective patrons, "Caution: There is an effort on the part of certain individuals to put upon the roads a small concern, under the title of Forepaugh's Menagerie and Circus. I hereby warn the public to beware of all such impositions. There is only one Forepaugh's Menagerie and Circus on this continent, and the public can easily distinguish that by its superiority over all other Shows." The trademarks of this establishment are: the Mammoth Tents, one for the Menagerie, the other for the Gigantic Circus; 2d: Thirty massive dens of Living Animals; 3d: The War Elephant, Romeo. (***Democratic Expounder and Calhoun County Patriot*** [MI], June 30, 1870)

in the South, was shot at Raysville, Louisiana, and died at Vicksburg, Mississippi, from his wounds.[52]

One circus performer who lived to tell the tale was Thomas Nathans, a clown who began his career with Benjamin Brown in 1828, and later traveled with the New York Circus in 1837. Long retired and gone into the dry goods business by 1866, he told the story of his youth. One day when the lion trainer struck for higher wages, he volunteered to take his place. The lion immediately seized him below the small of the back. The fear of being chewed, and the pain of the laceration and disappointed ambition blanched his hair in a moment, and he emerged, no longer a fair-haired youth, but a white-headed old man.[53]

On a more "uplifting" note, the gymnast of a Chicago circus was caught by a hook on the trapeze and was completely peeled of his tights from the waist downward. He was carried off after falling, not much hurt, amid the shrieks of the crowd.[54] Equally amusing, one performance not on the bills created more humor than the scheduled acts. In order to show the docility of the elephant, the animal was asked to walk over the supine body of a lady volunteer. All went well until a heavy "squall" came up, drenching the woman with water, followed by a terrible flow of manure. The audience comprehended the situation, "and the screams and roars of laughter" filled the tent. "There wasn't a doubt remaining in the docility of that elephant."[55]

Mighty Monarch of the World!

Carloads of Living Wild Animals, Including the Giant Elephant,

"EMPRESS"

And the Blue-Horned Horse.

When circus proprietors took out expensive advertising, they expected small perks in return. Free mentions throughout the newspaper, such as, "Don't fail to witness the grand free street parade of the Circus Royal and English menagerie"; and "Friday, Sept. 22, is show day, and this is the last circus and menagerie that will visit our city this season, so everybody should come in and see it," were the payback. (*The Upper Des Moines* [IA], September 13, 1882)

Striking the Tent

The mid–to–late 1860s saw several changes in the circus world. The first involved an alteration in nomenclature. Words such as "Stereopticon" were added to Nixon's New York Circus; "Zampillearostation" meant flying through the air (Champion Circus); "Horse opera" became synonymous with small exhibitions; clowns were referred to as "modern Grimaldis"; other humorists became specialized as "Court Jesters," "trick clowns," "performing clowns," "Singing Clowns," "Quintessence Clowns," "Quaint and Comical Clowns," "Changeable Acts clowns," "Monarch of Clowns," "People's Clown," and "old and favorite clowns," being regionalized as the "Great Southern Clown" or "Yankee Clown." They offered "Funnygrams," "Rural Jokers" and "Farmer's Almanacs of Fun." On an important note, in 1869, Port Faust became the first Negro clown, working at G. G. Grady's Unprecedented Old-Fashioned American Circus.

Buckley's Hippodrome and Universal Fair offered spectacular Roman chariot races around a track constructed under the tent. In an amazing display of ingenuity, circus hands arrived scant hours before a performance and set up the massive tents in a matter of hours. Hippodrome tracks were quickly dug into the ground, seating was set into place with interlocking pieces, and sawdust scattered around the performing rings. At the end of the last act, the entire concern was taken down, packed and made ready for the road, all within a 24-hour period. (*Logansport Daily Star* [IN], July 17, 1874)

In order to maintain a rigid schedule, "striking the tent" was honed to a fine art. After the last performance, usually around 10:00 P.M., the circus hands, doubling as van drivers, commenced tearing down the canvas, rolling it up and packing it away in the wagon. The seat planking and uprights followed, aided by artificial light created by wrapping alcohol-soaked cotton wrap atop 6-foot iron posts and planting them in the ground. Half a dozen lights provided enough illumination to cover the entire lot.

Once everything was packed, the men either returned to the hotel or slept in the wagons until the entire troupe was called at 2:00 A.M. Breakfast was served, then the animals were hitched to the wagons. Most individuals had an idea where the best sleeping places were to be found and crawled into them. Roads were often indifferent, with poorly marked signposts. If the assistants were called upon to extricate wagons from mud holes, they likely missed out on sleep entirely, indulging "in profanity to an alarming extent." However, such cursing was found "not only to help the wagons along, but to ease the mind greatly."[56]

Reaching the scheduled town, they paraded to their previously rented lot and immediately begin the task of setting up for the afternoon performance. The canvasmen raised the center pole, placed additional uprights and spread the canvas. Once the plank seating was arranged, the rings (arenas) were constructed, and whatever props required put in place. Only then did the workers get a chance to rest. For their effort, these least glamorous of the profession earned $20 a month and board.[57]

The dressing room was a small tent at the rear of the larger ones. To reach it, a passage had to be made through tethered horses and groups of assistants. Twelve or fifteen performers crammed into the small space, many with marks upon their bodies "in every conceivable place," wrapped in bandages. Elastic knee-caps were used to strengthen the knees, usually the first parts of the body to weaken, while artists frequently suffered from bruised kidneys and breast injuries. Trivial matters, such as shoulder and ankle sprains, "were unworthy of notice." Heaps of porous plasters and quantities of glycerin, enough to fill an apothecary's shop, were used in one season.

It was here, too, that performers rehearsed their dialogue. Many of the clowns in this period were old artists who, having matured in the circus business, and being perhaps too elderly or too crippled to continue more strenuous work, adopted this less taxing part of the trade. Others, like "Jim" Melville, the famous equestrian, became too infirm to perform but stayed on, in his case becoming a judge of the hippodrome races.[58]

Contrary to the popular belief that clowns were the epitome of all that was spontaneous and witty, their jokes were carefully prepared by another and committed to memory with "awful labor and unremitting diligence; his political speeches are not voluntary outbursts of patriotism that they simulate and his very antics are but ghastly specters of his past agility."[59]

Superstition was another aspect of behind-the-curtain circus life. Crossing oneself at the approach of a cross-eyed person was thought to stave off bad luck, and the appearance of a hunchbacked man in the morning brought luck for an entire week. Nothing, however, could ward off doom when an umbrella was opened inside a building. Individual superstitions included never sweeping the floor after sundown, as it carried away luck; broken mirrors portended injury or death; and the loss of a garter, breaking a shoestring or losing a button from a shoe indicating the loss of a lover. The breaking of a needle while mending a garment indicated the owner would live to wear it out, while stumbling going upstairs damaged matrimonial prospects for a year. Many performers refused to transact business between 12 and 1 o'clock in the day. Whistling was also taboo in dressing rooms, while black-faced actors were forbidden to wear mustaches, some companies going so far as to prohibit anyone from wearing facial hair on the upper lip. James Bailey refused to hire any man who sported a cane.

Certain actors were considered "mascottes" (or "mascots"), meaning that the prospects of improved play were enhanced by his or her presence. The opposite also held true, and those considered "Jonahs" were shunned at all costs. When told a certain equestrienne had brought bad luck to two previous companies, Barnum paid her full season's salary and dismissed her. In 1889, when Lowande's ten-cent circus exhibited at New Brunswick, the band went on strike, the reserve seating gave way, the center pole broke (injuring a canvasman), the cash box of the lemonade man was stolen, and a horse came down with "Pink Eye." The manager determined there was a "Jonah" among them, and vowed that as soon as he was discovered, he would be fired.

In 1897, despite the lack of rolling stock, Otto Ringling refused to purchase a railroad car on the grounds he had once ridden in it and been "hoodooed," another word for jinx in vogue in the 1890s. One hoodoo in particular thought to bring bad luck was a yellow flageolet (a small fipple flute resembling the treble recorder), and it was avowed that no circus man would have one in the band. In 1897, when several lions died, a giraffe was lost to accident and a chimpanzee died of consumption, the animal tent was considered hoodooed and the boss animal keeper was fired.[60]

The "tenting season" for a "show," as the circus and menagerie was technically termed, generally began in April and lasted six or seven months, depending on the weather. Attractions were seldom, if ever, changed during the season, and only then if the company added a star performer along the way. In an average year, 16 or 17 shows traveled the country.

Costs and profits of the circus business varied from year to year, with the future of the concern dependent on the bottom line. In 1848, Adam Forepaugh's exhibitions opened April 1, near Philadelphia and closed October 24, at Connersville, Indiana, making 177 "show days," with only one day missed on account of weather. During this period, the caravan traveled 2,936 miles. Expenses, exclusive of salaries, were:

Aggregate cost of show lots	$2,424
Licenses	$4,996
Hotel bills (90 people, 207 days)	$22,448.70
Stabling and feeding stock	$27,023.80
Newspaper advertising	$3,829.39
Bulletin board, wall advertising	$3,858.60
Distribution of bills	$3,086.04
Beef for animals, 150 pounds/day	$2,910.93
Total Cost	$70,567.45

Combined salaries averaged $250 to $300 per day; including depreciation, and board, which averaged out to approximately $12 a week per employee, the aggregate being about $800 a day. Receipts for the season were $194,700, leaving a profit of $53,100, out of which had to be deducted the cost of wintering the animals.[61]

Careful proprietors were capable of amassing fortunes. How that trickled down to performers depended on their status. First class riders earned $75 to $350 a week with expenses, with the average for a rider of merit being $100 a week. The lower orders who could stand on their feet three times around the ring made $20 to $30 a week with expenses, and the "pretty good" rider earned $30 to $60 per week. Female equestrians earned $30 to $150 a week according to ability and "shrewdness in making an engagement." Good riders with several children or apprentices commanded a very large salary.

Leapers (at this period meaning men who threw somersaults over horses) earned as much as $75 a week for that act alone; gymnasts usually went in couples, receiving $30 to $125 a week for the pair. Contortionists got $20 to $60 per week for kinking themselves. Clowns earned $20 to $120 a week according to ability and reputation. A popular clown was worth more than an equally skilled one, as his name had value on the advertising bills. His salary might go as high as $1,000 a week, which included the services of several apprentices, the use of various horses and animals, and the use of his name in advertising.[62] Those who carried out two or more branches of the business received a proportionally larger salary; for instance, the dog-man with the French poodles received the pay of two.

In 1869, the principal shows were:

The New York Circus (L. B. Lent)
Stickney's Empire City Circus
The Great European Circus
James Robinson's Champion Circus
Stone & Murray's Circus
Forepaugh's Grand Equestrian and Zoological Aggregation
The Oriental Circus (J. M. French)
The Hippoolympiad and Mammoth Circus ("Boss" Bill Lake)
Dan Castello's Big Show

Dan Rice's Own Circus
John Robinson's Great Combination Circus and Menagerie
Colonel Ames' Mammoth Circus
The Crescent City Circus (W. Noyes)
Chiarini's Circus
Bailey's Circus and Menagerie
Yankee Robinson's Consolidated Shows
James Thayer's Circus
Van Amburgh & Co.'s Great Golden Menagerie[63]

Receipts for New York theaters and circuses for 1866 revealed an aggregate take of $2,188,559, broken down as follows:

Niblo's Garden	$345,987
Winter Garden	$203,740
Wallack's	$195,456
Olympic	$168,277
Barnum's	$133,886
Van Amburgh's	$217,396
Academy of Music (4 months)	$120,151
New York Circus	$219,052

Besides these, seven others had receipts from between $58,000 and $72,000. The lowest return was the Fifth Avenue Opera House, at $10,046.[64] In 1867, receipts of the

Circus humor was part and parcel of the business. One oft-repeated joke concerned a woman's first visit and went like this: "As we entered the tainted enclosure I said to my husband, 'How terrible the wild animals growl, don't they?' I was almost frightened to death till he told me it was only the vendors of peanuts and prize packages plying their rogation." (*Warren Ledger* [PA], May 14, 1880; illustration from *Elyria Independent Democrat* [OH], June 23, 1869)

New York shows exceeded those of London or Paris. Twenty-two establishments in New York and Brooklyn earned over $3,000,000, with Niblo's ranking first, followed by Wallack's and the Olympic.[65]

The number of cages containing wild animals was a huge selling point for menageries, as it offered proof positive that those with greater numbers offered superior attractions. In 1871, various concerns broke down as follows:

	Cages
Van Amburgh	21
Van Amburgh (Western)	16
G. G. Grady	3
G. F. Dailey	12
Wooton & Haight	1
Rosston, Springer & Co.	11
James Robinson	8
Cole & Orton	1
John Robinson	16
Sheldenburger's	9
Handenburgh's	7
O'Brien's	20
R. A. Olden's	8
J. E. Warner's	10
Adam Forepaugh	32

Circuses, such as Lake's and Noyes', that did not have a menagerie attached were listed as "0."[66] Forepaugh was the clear winner and did not hesitate to advertise the fact, bragging that the "Two Tent" concern grew from 16 small, old-fashioned cages in 1867, to 30 massive dens, requiring 120 horses to transport them; while four years before they only needed sixty.[67] Ever growing, Forepaugh's show saw the German ship *Walbeaur* bring in a cargo of "New and Fresh Animals" for the menagerie in 1870.

Advertising and reputation were the name of the game, as evidenced by a notice of Barnum's Circus that astutely observed, "Probably a show by any other name would be as good, but it would not draw half so well."[68]

19

Sawdust and Spangles

Today, Robinson's great circus. Tomorrow, election. Wednesday, drunks on its result. Thursday, the great game of base ball. Friday, the Golden Menagerie. Saturday, head aches caused by the week's dissipation, with clear soda and sherry and egg. Sunday, repentance.[1]

"Come one, come all! Only fifteen cents to view the living curiosities — see for yourself the unique, never-before-witnessed treasures of the Natural Museum." Thus cried a typical door-keeper outside the side show entrance, enticing gullible patrons to part with their coin. Few could resist the allure of loud, constant, superlative-laced chatter, and besides, who would not want to see the "living" stuffed whale? Hawkers of such concerns were the original, most prolific and, in a sense, most innocuous of the more readily acknowledged swindlers and fakers accompanying a circus.

If circuses could be said to be the repositories of the weird and the fantastic, two examples stand out — one, a natural phenomenon and the other, an equally fascinating scheme. In 1871, Lent's New York Circus featured the "Cynocephalus," described as "an animal which rivals the greatest human riders in feats of Equestri-

"The Wonderful Cynocephalus" was reputed to be an animal that rivaled the greatest human equestrians. It was pronounced by the press in Paris, London and New York as the most remarkable novelty and powerful attraction ever seen in the Equestrian Arena. The animal was captured in Zanzibar by its promoter and trainer, Mons. Jean Martell. It performed with Lent's New York Circus in 1871, but, unfortunately, "left the troupe soon after" and was never seen again. (*Wisconsin State Journal*, July 5, 1871) aniam; and has been pronounced by the press of Paris, London and New York to be the most remarkable novelty and powerful attraction ever in the Equestrian Arena."

Captured in Zanzibar by its owner and trainer, Mons. Jean Martell, the creature gave impressive imitations of human riders.[2] Unfortunately for Lent and Mons. Martell, the Cynocephalus "suddenly left the troupe at Bay City, Michigan, and has not since been captured."[3]

The advertising headline read: "Dimensions of the Great Stone Giant! or Petrified Man, Exhumed Oct. 16, 1869, in Cardiff, Onondaga Co., New York, One of the Wonders of Older's Museum Circus & Menagerie."

Length,	10 ft. 4½ in.
Length of Head from chin to top of head,	21 in.
Length of Nose,	6 in.
Across the Nostrils,	3½ in.
Width of Mouth,	5 in.
Circumference of neck,	37 in.
Shoulder, from point to point,	3 ft. 1½
Length of Right Arm,	4 ft. 9½ in.
Across the Wrist,	5 in.
Across the Palm of Hand,	7 in.
Length of Second Finger,	8 in.
Around the Thighs,	6 ft. 3½ in.
Diameter of the Thigh,	13 in.
Through the Calf of Leg,	9½ in.
Across the Ball of the Foot,	8 in.

DIMENSIONS OF THE

Great Stone Giant!

Or PETRIFIED MAN,

Exhumed Oct. 16, 1869, in Cardiff, Onondaga Co., New York,

ONE OF THE WONDERS OF OLDER'S

Museum Circus & Menagerie.

Length,	10 ft. 4½ in.
Length of Head from chin to top of head,	21 in.
Length of Nose,	6 in.
Across the Nostrils,	3½ in.
Width of Mouth,	5 in.
Circumference of Neck,	37 in.
Shoulders, from point to point,	3 ft. 1½ in.
Length of Right Arm,	4 ft. 9½ in.
Across the Wrist,	5 in.
Across the Palm of hand,	7 in.
Length of Second Finger,	8 in.
Around the Thighs,	6 ft. 3½ in.
Diameter of the Thigh,	13 in.
Through the Calf of Leg,	9½ in.
Length of Foot,	21 in.
Across the Ball of the Foot,	8 in.

WEDNESDAY, October, 19th, 1870.

Purported to be "the identical petrification that caused such commotion among the press a few months since,"[4] the Cardiff Giant became the great astonishment of the age. Nineteenth century Americans were led to believe this monster was an actual human being, turned to stone from its long interment in the ground. It became an instant celebrity, and although later investigations revealed it to be an imposter, the truth never seemed to diminish the giant's appeal. Immortalized by Mark Twain in his masterful piece of wit "A Ghost Story," the Giant (or one of its many pasteboard imitations) went on tour, attracting the curious by the thousands. Despite

The Cardiff Giant was one of the best "humbugs" in an age of the duped. First discovered in Cardiff (Cooperstown), New York, the Giant was reputed to be the petrified remains of an ancient man. People from all over the country flocked to see him before the "body" (or one of its many duplicates) was taken on tour by Older's Museum, Circus & Menagerie. It did not take long before the truth of its man-made origins came out, but that never lessened the Giant's appeal. The monster was the hero in Mark Twain's witty "A Ghost Story." (*Monticello Express* [IA], October 13, 1870)

the fact reviewers noted, tongue-in-cheek, "The 'Cardiff Giant' was the center of appeal, and a pretty fair specimen of sculpture it is, too," its attraction has lasted until the present

The purpose of advertising was to offer in pictorial form as many different attractions as possible in order to strike the fancy of the public. In 1870, Van Amburgh & Co.'s Mammoth Menagerie offered the "Hartebeast," an animal of the antelope species never before on exhibition. Along with this "newly discovered beast" was Seigrist's Great French Circus combined with Lowanda's Brazilian Circus Troupe, all under the management of H. Frost. The accompanying text, which few bothered to read, merely informed the public that "The Brazilians are a circus by themselves, equally wonderful on the ground as on horseback," and "The Spaniards will appear at each exhibition." (*Wisconsin State Journal*, July 25, 1870)

century, where the original, somewhat worse for wear, lies at the Farmer's Museum in Cooperstown, New York, opposite the National Baseball Hall of Fame.

Pardon A. Older's association with the Giant was curious. While Barnum was making a Cardiff Giant for his museum, Older entered into a scheme with his friend Mr. Wood, Barnum's partner. They made a mold of Barnum's giant, and by spring he had an exact duplicate, 10 feet long and weighing 3,600 pounds. He had an immense wagon made for it, and kept it behind bars and under lock and key. Billing it as the "only Original," it proved the biggest money-maker he ever had, earning him $50,000 the first summer. During the third season, in order to relieve himself of the weight, Older had a duplicate of paper mache [*sic*] constructed, and made the switch at Manchester, Iowa. The "original" duplicate was sent to his home in Independence, where he stored it in his livery stable. By 1899, he was still in possession of the original.[5]

End-of-season reviews for Older's were somewhat less than charitable, one noting it had come and gone "and with it a great many crippled horses, a few animals, considerable circus, and numerous half dollars."[6] Another wished the proprietor would discharge the small army of thieves who followed in its wake.[7]

On the opposite end of the scale, Van Amburgh's "Show" received favorable notices: "The elegant imported and domestic horses were beautifully caparisoned, as also were the riders tastefully and brilliantly costumed. In place of that old and stereotyped edition of nets common to most rings, we found substituted a new and original programme. Instead of the threadbare sailor-boy (we have wished drowned a hundred times), we found a classic act, with backward and backward back somersault, under full speed. There was no stuffed and padded Indian with his manufactured gibberish, but the genuine South American in his native tongue absolutely terrifying in his dangerous and difficult scenes without saddle or bridle."[8] Positive publicity resulted in a $3,000 gate for two performances at Elkhorn two weeks later.[9]

One attraction of many circuses was the balloon ascent. Aeronauts who earlier traveled from town to town soon found competition from circuses siphoning off their livelihood. To survive, many opted to follow the tented shows, either as independent contractors or, more often, as hirelings.

While experience was required for a successful flight, the balloonist's fate depended as much on the age of the vessel, the method of inflation and the weather. Because disappointment in failing to "go up" meant bad press, and bad press meant the possible loss of a job, aeronauts all too frequently ascended under adverse conditions, leading to crash landings, debilitating injury and, not uncommonly, death.

In a tragically typical scenario from 1871, Professor Torres, associated with Grady's American Circus, inflated his balloon via the quick but dangerous method of generating hot air from a furnace set in the ground, funneling it through a chimney into the mouth of the aerostat. Once the restraining ropes were released, the balloon rose, the rider hanging by a trapeze from which he performed airborne tricks. Unknown to Torres, flames from the fire had been communicated to the lower part of the basket and quickly spread up the globe, bursting it in mid-air. While the audience considered this "the most exciting exhibition of this kind ever witnessed," Torres crash-landed and was dragged a considerable distance before being rescued.[10]

Later that same year, Torres was drowned after his balloon fell into the river and help came too late. His position was immediately assigned to a man named Fisher, who made six ascensions a week for a salary of $13. This, too, was a common and often inexcusable "remedy" employed to fulfill promises depicted on the bills. Men with no training in maneuvering the unwieldy aerostat were sent up, causing one observer to note, "The track of the circus company is marked by the broken limbs of these daring young men."[11]

The most notable death of aeronauts occurred on July 15, 1875, when Professor Washington Donaldson, the great balloonist then working for P. T. Barnum, ascended with a young newspaper reporter from the *Chicago Evening Journal* named Newton S. Grimwood. The balloon apparently hit a storm over Lake Michigan and disappeared. Grimwood's body was eventually discovered 33 days later; no account of Donaldson's fate was ever fully substantiated. In a cruel twist on "the show must go on," on July 21, long before word of the men's fate had been received, Barnum hired Professor Samuel King, another aeronaut of repute, to assume Donaldson's "recently vacated" place.[12] By July 24, he was with the circus and performing. While expressing regret over the accident, Barnum assumed no responsibility.

A World Under Canvas

The thrill of attending a circus in the 1870s continued the tradition honed by over fifty years of experience and expectation:

> For weeks the dead walls, high fences and special bill boards have been gaudy with astonishing pictorial representations of impossible feats of strength, skill and brute intelligence. The small boy has been saving his pennies for the approaching show, and the suburban tiller of the soil has had his other boots oiled up and standing ready, with his best clothes to be worn to the city. Tuesday morning the wonderful crowd of knights and knightesses, bejeweled and upon prancing steeds, in procession with the elephant and camels (packed like book-worms), all headed by a glittering chariot filled with discoursers of sweet music, dazzled the eyes of the juvenile, and made his pulse beat mountain-high with anticipation of the crowd and general bewilderment of the afternoon performance. About the mammoth pavilion were gathered side-shows, peanut and pink lemonade stands, gingerbread, bananas, and whole fields of urchins, for whose hardened stomachs these tempting luxuries were designed by the cunning and enterprising hucksters. Flags flew, and great banners, with life-like portraits of enormously fat women, exceedingly thin men, and brilliantly-colored serpents, hid the landscape.[13]

The decade continued to feature old favorites: P. T. Barnum's "Greatest Show on Earth"; the Great Forepaugh Show; Howes & Cushing's United States Circus (including Pearce's Performing Lions and the Great New York Circus, Sanger's English Menagerie and the Iroquois Indian Troupe); L. B. Lent's Leviathan Universal Living Exposition; John H. Murray's Great Railroad Circus; John O'Brien's Six Separate Shows Combined (including Warner & Co., Dan Rice's Circus, Handenburger & Co., Sheldenburger & Co. and O'Brien's); "Old" John Robinson's Great World Exposition; Yankee Robinson; D. W. Stone's Grand Circus and Musical Brigade; and Van Amburgh's Great Golden Menagerie with Hyatt Frost's Roman Circus and Royal Colosseum.

Added into the mix were Baird, Howell & Co.'s Oriental Circus, Caravan, Museum, Menagerie and Balloon Show; W. W. Cole's Great New York and New Orleans Zoological and Equestrian Exposition; Cooper, Bailey & Co.'s Great International Allied Shows; W. C. Coup's New United Monster Shows; the European Zoological Association (Sells' Brothers, proprietors); the Great International Caravan; Maginley & Co.'s Museum, Circus,

Menagerie, and Trained Animals; Montgomery Queen's Great Show; Dan Rice's Great River Show; Robbins & Co.'s Great Moral Museum, Circus, and Menagerie; and A. B. Rothchild & Co.'s Royal Victoria Menagerie.

James Robinson and Charles Fish continued to dominate equestrian performances, while miniature celebrities garnered headlines. Principal among them were Admiral Dot (also called "Commodore Dot"), the "smallest man in the world, being 18 years of age, 25" high and weighing 20 pounds); Commodore Nutt; the 4-year-old Franky (Frankie) Flynn, the 1876 sensation (23 inches, weighing 12 pounds); and the Burdette twins (Fanny measured 32 inches and weighed 50 pounds; her marriage to a six-foot man, W. H. Bristol, and the birth of their 8-pound child in 1878 became "big" news around the country).

Captain Martin Van Buren Bates (the title coming from his service in the Confederate Army with the fifth Kentucky Infantry) and his wife, Anna H. Swan, were advertised as the Tallest Man and Woman on Earth, each standing 7'11½"; Charlotte Moxley (real name Angelina Teeples) toured as "The Giantess," standing 6'2½" and weighing 723 pounds; and Captain George Costentenus, the Tattooed Greek, whose body was covered with 388 pictures and figures in blue and red, with indigo and cinnabar inks, was the wonder of all. Barnum advertised him as "the most memorable of Mortal Marvels," being a

Captain Martin Van Buren Bates, reported to stand seven feet, eleven-and-one-half inches tall, was born in Whitesburg, Kentucky, November 9, 1846. Anna H. Swan was born in Colchester County, Nova Scotia, and was said to be the same height as her husband. Raised as a farmer, Bates served in the fifth Kentucky Infantry, Confederate Army, during the Civil War. He is seen wearing a Confederate uniform in this daguerreotype. The pair were married June 17, 1871, at St. Martin's Church, Trafalgar Square, London, after which they were introduced to Queen Victoria. The couple made a fortune touring as the largest man and woman in the world, eventually buying a farm at Seville, Ohio. (Original daguerreotype in authors' collection; *St. Louis Globe-Democrat*, April 28, 1880)

noble Greek Albanian who was tattooed from head to foot in China, Tartary, as punishment for engaging in rebellion against the King. The Cardiff Giant, or reasonable facsimiles, made the rounds; Millie Turnour became "Queen of the Air"; Dan Rice's Blind Talking Horse, Excelsior, and the Comic Mules, Pete & Barney, thrilled the crowds; Pete Conklin, "America's Clown," made people laugh; while George Melville and William DuCrow offered bareback and hurdle rides, and artists being shot out of cannons became showstoppers.

Every menagerie worth its salt had an elephant. Cooper & Bailey advertised ten: Chieftain, Mandarin, Princess, Empress, Victoria, Titania, Khedive, Juliet, Romeo and Price, the Clown elephant. Along the way, Empress was replaced by Mamma, and Victoria was advertised as "about to become a mother." Among the sideshows, dignity was hard to find. While "Lewis, the only actual African Circus Rider," played inside the tent, a two-headed Negro girl was displayed outside. "Freaks of nature" combined both human and animal exhibitions. Along with tattooed men, fat women, giants and midgets, mid-century oddities included the Giant Devil Fish; $100,000 worth of "Broncho horses"; Mademoiselle DeGranville, "The Lady with the Iron Jaws"; and "Monster Living Sea Lions."

Mr. Loyal was one of the great attractions of the Great Forepaugh Show, 1880. After he crawled into the barrel of the Monster Cannon, it was loaded with powder and ignited, sending the artist whirling through space, to be caught by a lady hanging head downward on the lofty trapeze. (*Titusville Morning Herald* [PA], May 12, 1880)

Such excitements easily slid into the realm of folklore. In 1871, a report surfaced that a child at Pittsfield, Massachusetts, was born with the body of a boy but with a head shaped like an elephant, including floppy ears and nose elongated into a trunk. The defects were explained by the fact his mother had been frightened by a circus elephant a few months before giving birth.[14] In 1876, the report of a "nondescript" human child with the head and habits of a bear was explained away by the superstition that his mother, "at an unlucky time," went to a menagerie showing at Genesee county and was frightened by a huge polar bear.[15]

Life was never easy for the denizens of the Big Top. Topping the list of dangers was occupational hazard. Accidents to lion tamers and elephant keepers were routine; following them were aeronauts and trapeze artists. In 1871, M'lle Ellsher's fall of 25 feet was due to the unsteadiness of the high wire.[16] In 1875, M'lle Victoria fell from her trapeze, breaking through the safety net and severely cutting her thigh. With true professionalism, she limped away to make room for the banjo player. An editorial in the *Richwood Gazette* (Ohio), February 4, 1875, adeptly commented on the incident:

> There is an undeniable
> heartlessness about the
> amusement-seeking people,

or else a constant recurrence of these trapeze accidents would not be possible. *When a man pays a dollar to see a woman hang by her toes, there is a certain portion of the money which is a tacit payment for the chance he has of seeing her fall* [italics added]. The story about the party who followed the circus for years to see the performing lion eat his trainer is not an improbable one.

Humorously, but no less true, the *New Orleans Picayune* noted a general complaint that in 1879, *the circus elephants were exceedingly small and never kill a keeper.*[17]

The omnipresent Grim Reaper had more than one way to catch the unwary performer. Joe Pentland, the famous circus clown, died at the insane asylum on Blackwell's Island in February 1873. In 1879, while working for Cole's Circus, a young tumbler named White misplaced his feet while throwing a double somersault and broke his neck.[18] Old age caught up to the famous equestrian "Uncle Sam" Stickney, who died at the residence of old John Robinson in Cincinnati in 1877.[19] Thomas King, who spent twenty-five years in the sawdust arena as an unparalleled leaper and later as ring master for Barnum, died at Baltimore in October 1877, age about forty-two. Even younger was Ted Almonte, the British clown who later thrilled many Americans and served as vice-president of the Equestrian Benevolent Association. He died in April 1878, apparently suffering a heart attack after concluding a performance.[20]

A year after the burning of the steamer *Oceanus*, upon which members of the Great International Circus perished, members of the troupe then playing at Hickman, Kentucky, disinterred the remains of George Constable, one of the unfortunates, and gave him a decent burial in the city cemetery. With the entire company weeping like children, the clown, Jack Lawton, gave a moving testimonial.[21] Funerals for circus people often differed from those of ordinary citizens. In England, after the passing of the famous clown Billy Watson, the entire troupe in full costume accompanied the body to the grave. With them was Jacko, the Barbary ape, dressed in mourning and riding a Shetland pony. After placing a daisy quilt on the grave, Billy's brother clowns turned somersaults over the spot.[22]

Death was seldom dignified with such honor. More commonly, an actor or hand who died from injury was placed in a rough box, his associates paying $15 to bury him and then quickly departing.[23]

Nor was death reserved for those under the canvas. In 1878, John Strickland, who had charge of Barnum's chariot racing in the Hippodrome from 1874 to 1875, and also served as one of the most trusted drivers for Montgomery Queen, S. B. Lent and others, died while driving one of Barnum's six-horse teams home on a personal errand. On the return trip, the horses took fright, and even his skill could not rein them under control. After the empty wagon struck the tracks of the street railway, the axle snapped. Strickland was propelled forward, falling under the wheels, sustaining a crushed skull.[24]

Animals as well as their human counterparts suffered the pain of losing a friend. In 1876, after the accidental death of her beloved dog companion "Carlo" (a 19-year-old cross between an English setter and spaniel), Betsy, the old elephant of Cooper, Bailey & Co.'s Circus, led the funeral procession into the ring. Betsy lowered the body into the grave while four other elephants, seemingly aware of their loss, knelt beside her. Betsy then filled the hole, later giving utterance to mourning sounds when asked about her friend. That evening during the performance, she stopped by the grave, pulled up the stake that had been placed at the head and threw it away. Charles Warner (known as "Alligator Charlie"), who had charge of the elephants, related many stories of how Carlo would encourage Betsy to cross bridges by standing on the crossway and howling, thus summoning her to his assistance. Once there, she was easily led across.[25]

Death on a large scale occurred on Christmas Eve 1872, when a fire broke out in the boiler room of Barnum's Hippotheatron, New York. Previously condemned by the Fire Marshal on account of its inflammable material, defective flues, gas, and heating apparatus, the building was quickly engulfed in flames. It was believed smoke killed numerous monkeys, two Bengal tigers, two sea lions, two polar bears, an Arctic seal, ten camels, one eland, the "Horned Ox of Tartury [sic]," and a lion and lioness, but torturous fire killed four giraffes and one elephant. Two other elephants, the old Jeanette and the youthful Gypsy, ran into the street and escaped, where they were taken under control by one of their keepers and a favorite dog. They, along with the sole surviving double-humped camel, were led from danger. Altogether, Barnum's losses were detailed as follows:

Loss on building	$80,000
Loss on animals	$125,000
Loss on curiosities & c	$25,000
Loss on fixtures	$20,000
Loss on properties	$5,000[26]

The Equestrian Benevolent Association held a benefit for the attaches on January 7, 1873, arranging to assist them in replacing their wardrobe and effects.

Accident, violence and old age were familiar and understandable foes in the 19th century, but disease struck inexplicable terror. In the age of "every man a physician," where diagnostic tools and antibiotics were unknown, pitchmen hawked remedies promising to cure the most virulent ravages. When these cures (typically containing little more than alcohol and burnt sugar or cocaine) failed to work, people needed someone — or some thing — to blame. James Murphy, Jr., the 8-foot-tall Irish Giant who traveled with Barnum for three years, died in Baltimore at the age of 33 from bronchial disease contracted, it was alleged, from his circus work.[27]

Far more ominously, when an epidemic of yellow fever broke out at Shreveport, Louisiana, in 1873, the cause was attributed to "Mexican vomito," brought to the state by the Transatlantic Circus, a strolling company from Vera Cruz "which had traveled along the line of the Texas Pacific Railway, and had left the seeds of contagion along their route."[28] Interestingly, a later report accused the circus of "distributing small-pox as it goes,"[29] testimony to the fact that disease was not well understood. Such accusations often followed itinerants, especially foreigners, and quarantine or sterner measures were frequently taken against them. Responding to another outbreak in 1878, and perhaps not insensitive to those who might be blamed, old John Robinson donated half the receipts from a Quincy, Illinois, engagement, and his company donated $256 more, making a contribution of $1,006 for yellow jack sufferers.

Small pox reared its ugly head again in 1894, when Washburn's circus was prohibited from unloading at Plainfield, New Jersey. The precaution was taken on account of a report that one of the employees had been stricken with the disease at Orange. The managers petitioned the mayor for a permit to exhibit but were turned down. The following year, an epidemic in Butler county, Maine, closed down all circuses, picnics, shows and revival meetings in the area. In 1898, the Hall circus was accused of bringing small pox to Pueblo, Colorado, creating a great scare in the towns it played at along the route to Hutchinson and Newton, Kansas.

Scares were sometimes just that, but the dread of disease was enough to cause serious financial damage to circus owners. Buffalo Bill's show was booked at Lowell, Massachusetts, on July 1 and 2, 1895, but a report from the Pennsylvania Board of Heath accused the exhibition of carrying small pox. It turned out the report was a fraud, instigated by a rival concern that had played the same scheme successfully against Washburn. In that case, Washburn discovered the perpetrator and sued for $50,000 damages.[30]

The Hippodrome and the "Greatest Discovery of the Present Age"

In England, "hippodrome" was inevitably associated with horse racing. At Bayswater in 1837, a racecourse of that name offered a steeple-chase course of two miles, a race course of equal length and an exercise ground.[31] By 1851, the concept expanded when William Batty opened a Hippodrome in the Kensington Road featuring equestrian acts.[32]

By the 1870s, the word had gained common acceptance in the United States, where it was described as "not a circus in any sense of the word — [it] is a novelty, and possesses many features of interest.... The main features of the hippodrome is competition."[33] Competition, American style, assumed many varied forms. In 1877, W. W. Cole's Great New York and New Orleans Zoological and Equestrian Exposition offered an elliptical racetrack 30 feet wide, where 8 times around equaled 1 mile. Twenty different races on the Hippodrome Track were featured, while two circus rings inside the area provided other entertainment.[34,]

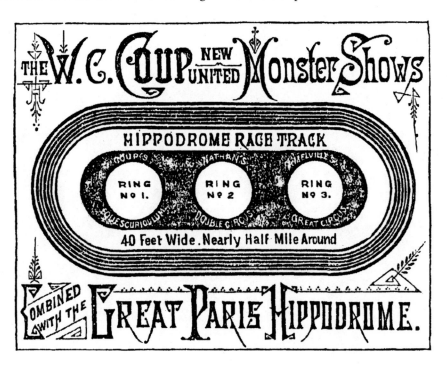

In the 1870s, hippodrome races became fashionable, and major circuses hurried to promote their race tracks. Typically, eight times around the track equaled one mile, with the largest being 40 feet wide and nearly half a mile around. Although all circuses were "proverbial humbugs," W. C. Coup's New United Monster Shows provided horse and chariot racing around the track while also offering nonstop entertainment in the three inner rings. (***Boston Daily Globe***, April 24, 1881)

Buckley & Co.'s World's Race Festival and Twenty Center Pole Menagerie provided patrons with "A game of LaCrosse with 100 Iroquois Indian Chiefs" in 1874.

> While the Prussian band is playing (sometimes in excellent tune and sometimes not), the grand entree occurs. After this 20 lithe and perspiring Indians give the spectator something to warm up on, in an exciting game of LaCrosse. As they go tumbling in and out of the ring, checking and slashing, running, jumping, and yelling, the coolest person in the audience yields to the excitement, rises from his seat with breathless interest, and at the conclusion of the game mops and mops, and wonders how long his system will bear up against such a torrent. Then comes a Roman charriot [*sic*] race, the clumsy vehicles being driven by ladies, and drawn by horses at a dead run. Sometimes Miss Baker's team wins, sometimes Madame Connelly's steeds.[35]

Contests, of course, were staged, particularly when money was involved. In 1873, a $1,000 bet was placed on a foot race in Dubuque. The participants "had run only about 20 yards of the 240 staked off when both accidentally (?) fell, and it was considered a draw" (question mark in original).[36]

Wagers of a different sort also became routine in the 1870s, whereby proprietors offered "Challenges" to other exhibitors in an effort to substantiate their superiority. In 1875, Barnum issued a card to the public, offering $5,000 in each of the following categories if they could be disproved:

1. He had more thoroughbred horses
2. He spent more money on wooden amphitheatres and accommodations
3. He had more travelling musicians

In 1877, P. T. Barnum "cheerfully" offered to pay $50,000 to anyone who could prove they had the equal of his $30,000 stud of "Six Superb Educated 'Trakene' Stallions." Introduced altogether, they simultaneously, and as one company, executed the most astonishing acts and evolutions, with all the activity, precision and intelligence of an army drill, even standing erect as soldiers. (*Cedar Rapids Times*, August 30, 1877)

4. He had more performers
5. His silver armor, purchased from Messrs. Kennedy, Birmingham, England, cost more money than the entire wardrobes of any other company
6. He was the only company who had a Congress of Nations
7. That it was produced better than anyone else's
8. He was the only man who imported English hounds for a stag hunt in his Hippodrome
9. He had the only "Fete at Pekin"
10. He managed and originated more shows than anyone
11. His Hippodrome contained more cloth than any other
12. His dressing rooms are larger than anyone's
13. He employs more railroad cars
14. He spent more money on novelties
15. He provided the greatest balloon ascensions
16. He carried more canvasmen to erect his buildings
17. He has more improvements in travelling exhibitions
18. His is the largest and finest traveling exhibition

Should a showman or individual disprove any one claim, Barnum promised to appropriate the sum to any charitable institution chosen by the mayor of the city in which they were

More astonishing than any exhibit, the Great Forepaugh Show promoted the Edison electric light. Requiring a 50-horsepower, high-pressure engine to illuminate the tent, most people got their first exposure to the "Miracle of the Century" beneath the Big Top. W. W. Cole's Famous New York and New Orleans Circus was not far behind, as this fantastic scene depicts. Decades earlier, Londoners received their first exposure to another miracle of the age, the telegraph, displayed for their edification at Astley's. (*Titusville Morning Herald* [PA], May 12, 1880; illustration from *Star and Banner* [PA], August 21, 1879)

accepted. He concluded by promising his Hippodrome was "not the old, old Circus, but every act entirely new and startling, and is under more expense than three of the largest shows on earth."[37]

Interestingly, not everyone appreciated the new and startling. More than a few lamented the passing of the "legitimate," or old-fashioned, circus, remarking of the present day (1875) that there was "no ring, no sawdust to speak of: no clown; no music, with the band up on the ordinary benches. Instead an endless sea of canvas; a race track a mile long, more or less; the audience on the other side so far off ... the clown clothed in civilians' dress, and distributing some accidental humor to a select few...." Too much horse, too much elephant ... more monkey than is absolutely necessary. "It is all good I grant you, but is there not such a thing as satiety in the way of animal and canvas?"[38]

Performers, too, longed for the old days. A British clown responded to the request to speak of the clowns of the present day (1872) by responding, "That's easy done, in a very few words—there ain't any.... What is wanted in a clown is gag, and a real clown ought to be up to any amount of improvised gag.... I call no man a clown who can't answer the gallery [respond to the crowd].... The Victorian audience may be rough and ready, but I should be sorry to risk my skin by one word of coarseness. As for answering the gallery, you mustn't do it too often, or they look for it."[39]

His comment about crude language hardly held true for America, where newspapers were filled with editorials condemning circus performers. To counter their bad reputation, proprietors responded by running ads promising "moral" exhibitions or acts designed for the "whole family." That they failed to sway the public is underscored by continued lambasting in the press throughout the age.

Next to the advent of the circus tent, probably the greatest change in the circus came from the introduction of electric lighting. Though it was already in use in London and Paris, by 1879, W. W. Cole's "Famous New York and New Orleans Circus," and Cooper & Bailey's combination "Great London Circus, Sanger's British Menagerie and the Famous International Allied Shows" were at the forefront of this new technology. Since many Americans had never seen an electric light before, their first introduction came by way of the circus.

Cooper & Bailey advertised, "Dense Night Converted into Dazzling Day by the Electric Light. 18 Electric Light Chandeliers, equal to 37,000 Gas Jets. Requiring 30-Horse Power Engine; 40-Horse Power Boiler; 900 Revolutions Per Minute; 28,000 Yards Insulated Telegraph Wire. Cost us $15,000."[40] Cole's advertising put out that "the electric light is 'a beacon blaze, without blur or blot ... that produces a dazzling and bewildering effect.'"[41] Furthermore, it was promised, newspapers of the finest print could be read two miles distant from the light, and blue was blue and green was green, as was not the case with gas light. Offered as "Heaven's own gift to man," electricity was predicted as the light of the future, with the actual daily cost of operation a mere trifle.[42] The only drawback was reported to be a disagreeable flickering.[43]

A Time When Palm-leaf Fans and Cool Lemonade Are Fashionable...

Thus was described the start of the circus season, 1878. Those shows traveling by railroad included Cole's, starting from St. Louis, and three concerns beginning from New

York City — Barnum's (under the proprietorship of Barnum, Nathans, Herd, June and Bailey), the London Circus (owned by Parkes, Davis and Dockrell), and Stone and Brownson's. Van Amburgh's Menagerie continued its tour through the South,[44] although it was recognized that few companies visited the Southern States "on account of the outlawry which has existed for years ... resulting in the deaths of Young Robinson and Managers Ames, Whitby, Spaulding and Lake, who were all victims of the bullet or the knife, being murdered in cold blood."[45] (Lake was shot to death in 1869, at Granby, Missouri; John Alexander Robinson was shot at Crittenden, Kentucky, in 1866; Colonel Charles T. Ames was shot at Dawson, Georgia, in 1870, while trying to pacify a drunken man having an altercation with the doorkeeper of a side show; Harry Whitby was shot at Raysville, Louisiana, in November 1870, and died at Vicksburg; and Henry Spaulding, manager of Dan Rice's circus, was shot at Baxter Springs, Kansas, in 1872.)

Pageants into the city expanded into numbing displays of grandeur, with monster music cars (the steam calliope being "the marvel of the age") drawn by dromedaries; star attractions, such as George Conklin, the Lion Tamer, seated in the midst of his pets; and Hindoo [*sic*] snake charmers inside glass-plate dens.[46] Hundreds of people came from surrounding counties to view the shows, some riding on another wonder of the age — the Pullman sleeper.[47]

For their Grand Procession, the Great European Zoological Show promised "Sedan," the War Elephant, two miles of ornate cages, gorgeously painted and gleaming with all the colors of the rainbow, and the Great Morlacha, lion tamer, representing "the thrilling picture of Daniel in the Lion's Den."[48] Baby elephants rode on tableau cars, a horned Ethiopian Horse pranced, and "ludicrously educated dogs, goats and monkeys" followed.

There was no greater attraction than elephants, and in 1878, Sells Brothers' 7 Elephant Great European Railroad Exposition promised five performing baby elephants to go with their two adults. Among them were a pair of nursing twin baby elephants, the "first and only" ever exhibited anywhere, to be seen nursing in the arena. This pair was but 30 inches high and less than a year old. The elephant trainer, who appeared in the circle (ring), was often dressed in native garb to add to the authenticity of the production. (*Warren Ledger* [PA], October 11, 1878)

Barnum's Grand Street Pageant included:

Grenadier Cornet Band, 20 pieces
Massive Car containing Representatives of the British Government
Chariots drawn by Ponies driven by Youths in Costume
20 Principal Lady Hurdle Riders
Droves of Racehorses carrying their Jockeys
Car containing the Sultan of Turkey and his Beauties

Emperor Wilhelm and Staff, Bodyguard on horse
Four-horse Chariots with Lady Drivers
Elephants and Camels
Car containing Egyptian Ladies
Indians, Hunters and Trappers in the Costumes of the Plains
Hunting Horses and Hounds used for the Stag Hunt
Car and Chariots representing other Nations of the Globe
Leorichi's tribe of Indians upon Native Ponies

Among the most talked of attractions of the 1870s were the nursing baby elephants of Sells Brothers' "7 Elephant 7 Great European Railroad Exposition," which were introduced into the ring along with bottles, "their piercing squeals for more pap exciting much merriment."[49] Automatical curiosities moved by steam engines and Robert Houdin's life-sized automatons were displayed alongside likenesses of the Presidents of the United States. In 1875, for controversy, W. W. Cole of the New York and New Orleans Circus ordered the creation of wax figures representing Henry Ward Beecher and Beecher's wife, and Theodore Tilton and his wife.

In this grouping are two adult and five baby elephants attached to Sells Brothers' 7 Elephant Grand European Railroad Exposition of 1878. Elephants were paraded down the street from the train depot to the circus grounds, offering those who could not afford a ticket a sight of the magnificent beasts. (*Warren Ledger*, October 11, 1878)

The proposed exhibition garnered immediate notoriety, as the four individuals were embroiled in what was considered the 19th century's most famous scandal. Although the two men had once been close allies in the abolitionist movement and worked together on the *Independent*, a Congregationalist New York newspaper, Tilton's advocacy of "free love" assumed what might be considered a hypocritical stage when he sued Beecher for "criminal intimacy" with his wife. The subsequent trial in 1874 ended in a hung jury; two upholsterers, Joseph Loader and his assistant Price, supplied affidavits against Beecher and were sent to prison for perjury.[50] The trial remained a topic of conversation for years.

Beecher did not take kindly to Cole's exhibition that included the wax figures wearing genuine cast-off clothing of the originals, and hired a private detective to investigate. Immediately before the doors opened at the premiere showing in Burlington, Iowa, a temporary injunction was issued, forcing Cole to place sheets over the quartet. The lawsuit hinged on whether Beecher could establish his right of property in maintaining exclusive ownership of his face, his name and his words, a question with wide implications to the present day.[51] The *Daily Republican*, May 24, 1875, noted, "It is an excellent advertisement for both parties, but the circus man is going to get the best of it."

Behind the "Day of Wonders"

It was no surprise that Artemus Ward, the American humorist, once wondered why it took three grown-up persons to take one child to the circus, and even less wonder that W. W. Cole offered a reward of $100 to the newspaper paragrapher who could write a four-line announcement without reference to the "small boy" who was always accused of being the only person interested in the circus, when nine-tenths of patrons were adults.[52] People of all ages were in agreement that the greatest accolades given a circus, truly making it "something new under the sun" (written about Burr Robbin's circus), were that it exhibited all it advertised, prohibited gambling about its premises, had courteous ushers and polite, square-dealing refreshment venders, all under the control of a manager who paid his bills without grumbling or quibbling.[53]

To achieve this, traveling entertainment had, of necessity, metamorphosed into a complicated business with a scope and magnitude exceeding anything early proprietors could have dreamed. Literally thousands of displays bewildered patrons, requiring nothing less than an army of field agents to keep it running.

Adam Forepaugh boasted that $450,000 was spent in presenting his massive exhibition to the public, that included the parade, "a moving panorama, one mile and a quarter in length. See the procession, and then if you think the Show is not all that it claimed to be, don't patronize it." The point being, obviously, that Forepaugh gambled no adult viewing the parade could resist paying 50 cents for a ticket. (*Herald and Torch Light* [MD], April 19, 1871)

In the early part of the century, proprietors were also performers, usually headliners who drew the crowds and hired talent, plotted routes, and negotiated contracts with locals, including rental of property and paying municipal fees. As the decades passed, more and more proprietors devoted themselves to business matters, sometimes having no more physical connection to the show than lending their name to the title. Within the sub-specialties that developed to handle responsibilities was the general manager, or superintendent. He was the brain behind the circus, keeping all modalities working together and on time. Typically a current or former showman, he judged what audiences required, conceiving and executing plans toward that end.

Next in order of rank came the supervisor, whose task it was to oversee the whole concern. The position required an eye for business and a talent for cultivating personal relationships with the performers and the public. Summer heat drove circuses as far north as practicable; if the concern operated during winter months, they gravitated toward warmer climates or permanent structures. An agent traveled along the prospective route before the season started, making advance arrangements with town authorities. For those exhibitions still traveling by wagon, he also inspected the roads, calculating travel times from point to point.

In larger or united circuses, this agent had any number of assistants, including advance agents who arranged accommodations for the staff and animals. Often called "the genius of the show," the best agent knew every town, hamlet and crossroads, and were on familiar terms with each editor and his peculiarities. "He knows when to spring the 'Behemoth of Holy Writ' on the natives, and when to advertise the sacred crocodile." Reputed to actually forecast weather, the brightest spent the winter studying statistics relevant to the coming year.[54] A few had dubious reputations among hotel operators, working contracts with the verbiage "forty men, more or less" (the "more" habitually occurring a greater percentage of time than the "less").[55] On occasion, if no appropriate hotels were available, the agent would direct the circus to bypass the city entirely.[56] A first class agent received $100 to $200 a week in salary.

Equestrian managers looked after the training of the horses and determined the feats to be performed; the boss canvasser had charge of the tents, superintending the arrangements for erecting and removing them; while the boss hostler oversaw the care of the animals. Quartermaster agents arranged the purchase and preparation of food. With over 500 people to feed, huge cooking rooms were arranged where roasts of veal and beef, bushels of potatoes, and gallons of milk and coffee were prepared for consumption in the dining rooms. Other agents set up and operated the dressing rooms, taking charge of a small army of seamstresses who worked the sewing machines, making and repairing costumes. The treasurer was not only responsible for finances but had under his control the master ticket agent and his subordinates, whose responsibility it was to actually sell tickets.[57] Ticket sellers were rarely praised for their work, the exception being George W. Zebold, credited with being the "champion ticket seller of the world." To earn this title, he displayed a rapidity of distributing tickets and making change for the Great Eastern Circus and Menagerie. For his services, he actually had a medal presented to him, valued at $500.[58]

Advertising agents had charge of advance publicity, and under them were the newspaper (press) agents, whose business it was to cater to local dignitaries and editors in expectation of favorable reviews (discussed in Chapter 23). A press agent earned from $50 to $100 a week. With a wry tip of the hat to the glamour of this profession, one reporter wrote, "When a circus agent loses his $800 diamond pin he doesn't squander a dollar by advertising it. He simply encloses 40 cents in a letter and sends it to a New York establishment with instructions to send him another just like the last."[59] Fake diamonds were not to be confused with the 40-carat ring worn by Adam Forepaugh, said to be worth $40,000, or the 15-carat diamond collar-button, for which he paid $3,000.

Diamonds played the dual role of personal adornment and being the most convenient form of portable property. If a circusman ran out of money on the road, a diamond held better pawn value than a watch worth twice as much, and many considered the jewel a "silent partner." Circus people frequently saved their money by investing in diamonds, and occasionally merchants traveled with exhibitions, first selling the gems and then buying them back or loaning money on them when the possessor was hard up.[60]

Primary among the tools employed by an agent was the dispensation of free passes, a dual bone of contention and humor among those not included. It was noted an average Philadelphia Alderman could get away with 16 complimentary tickets,[61] while the city clerk of Cincinnati once demanded 47 tickets from Dan Rice, prompting him to quip about whether he wouldn't take the elephant and ticket-wagon instead.[62] Occasionally, tricks would be played on the good will of circus men, as the case of three Portage men proved. They pretended to be reporters from the *St. Laurent Courier*, the *High Bluff Advertiser* and the *Poplar Point Gazette*, none of which actually existed, but the ruse got them inside for free.[63]

Often, goodwill free passes were handed out to businessmen, who, in turn, offered them to their customers as an incentive to purchase their products. Such was the mania of "dead-heads" to obtain them that men "who count their wealth in tens of thousands" would visit a shop dozens of times merely to obtain gratuitous tickets, spending more in street-car fare than it would have cost to buy the tickets.[64]

"The Knights of the Silken Fleshings, Saw Dust and Spangles"

On May 15, 1872, one of the most disgraceful scenes ever occurring in Chicago involved the Great Eastern Menagerie, Museum, Aviary, Circus and Balloon Show. The afternoon performance attracted a large audience, and in expectation of earning an even greater sum, managers continued selling tickets for the evening show long after the house was packed to overflowing. An attempt was made to offer a performance while "cheap-looking clowns made frantic appeals to the crowd to sit down." Finding no place to sit, the ever increasing numbers swelled into the ring; men began shouting, the band could not be heard over the roar; and "the stale jokes of a man who in the afternoon brutally abused a little boy to make laughter for a vulgar crowd, were drowned in the uproar." Amid shoving and pushing and not a little violence, the masses took possession of the ring, "and the show came to an abrupt termination."[65]

This would not be the last time the Great Eastern ran into trouble. The following year, reviews noted, "There were but few specimens on exhibition, and they were borne down sadly by the weight of years, many of the animals looking as though they had recently recovered from an attack of Asiatic cholera."[66] They were not the only ones to suffer from bad publicity. In 1877, one reporter wrote of a mercifully unnamed circus, "The half dozen wagons or cages that contained the *animals*, looked as if they had been built before the flood, and been in constant use ever since without having been repaired or painted, while the horses used for drawing them were ring-boned, spavined, splint and blind, and so near starved to death that they could scarcely travel." Three of the drivers struck for back pay; in order to prevent his best horses from being sold, the proprietor "got down to the bottom of his calf-skin, scraped together a sufficient amount of usufruct to pay the claim, some $67."[67]

Below the fading glitter, managing a circus was a difficult affair, and on average, five or six shows failed every year. The numbers were higher in presidential election years, as periods of intense political excitement kept people away from more legitimate forms of entertainment.[68] In 1871, Stowe's Circus escaped closure by mortgaging its property; the settlement in this case being primarily due to Joe Tinkham, the leading man in the troupe, whose popularity creditors felt would eventually help turn the concern around.[69] Couch & Co.'s Circus failed in 1873 because of "hard times and bad pay of the managers."[70]

Howe's & Cushing's circus failed in Fall River, Massachusetts, in 1876, when the performers, led by Fredersticks, the champion jockey rider, led a strike after not being paid

Politics and circuses seldom made good bedfellows, as electoral campaigns tended to draw men's attention to the political rather than the sawdust arena. This early political cartoon depicts Secretary Blaine, who attended the circus the evening previous and was seen enjoying the elephants go around. Among the circus characters in his "dream" were those involved with the Pension Bureau Scandal, the "Free For All Presidential Handicap, 1892," the Billion Dollar Congress and the Chinese Mission. (*The World* [NY], May 15, 1892)

for six weeks. The proprietors arrived from Boston, made good the claims on the circus and gave small amounts to the actors, after which an attachment was placed on the property.[71] Howe's London Circus also suffered a levy to be placed on it while in Georgia in 1877, with its property to be sold by the sheriff on the 29th of January.[72]

One of Barnum's circuses collapsed at Atlanta in August 1877, with debts of $210,000 and assets of $120,000. On November 30, 1877, the sheriff of York county, Pennsylvania, sold property belonging to O'Brien's Circus, including one band wagon, one pole wagon, one baggage and nine animal wagons, and one buffalo and a sacred cow "left behind some time since."[73] Occasionally, a bit of humor was injected into the proceedings. In 1873, when John H. Murray's Great Railroad Circus was attached by the sheriff in Bridgeport, Connecticut, for the sum of $350, the proprietor paid up in 25-cent script, sending the creditors home with distended pockets.[74]

Even the mighty were not immune from paying the piper. In February 1878, Montgomery Queen, proprietor of the California Circus and Menagerie, filed voluntary bankruptcy, with liabilities of $166,000 and nominal assets of $31,223. A large number of creditors were performers, with a considerable amount due for printing and money loans. Among the secured creditors were:

E.D. Calvin, assistant manager, owed	$6,525
George S. Cole, Treasurer, owed	$3,538
James Cook, clown, owed	$1,164
John S. Strickland, boss hostler, owed	$700
Woodie Cook, rider, owed	$630
Buffalo *Courier* Company, owed	$18,000
James How, owed	$8,991

Most of the assets consisted of stock valued at $30,000, including a hippopotamus and two elephants.[75] The circus was scheduled for sale by auction at Louisville, Kentucky, on February 21, 1878.[76]

Not all was simple in the way of collecting debt. When the Southern Circus and Menagerie came into Hagerstown, the proprietors could not pay for transportation. The cars were seized and switched off upon a siding. Upon the railroad agent, Mr. Way, fell the duty of feeding the animals, and they soon ate up considerably more than the amount of the claim. Worse, Way was obliged to keep the zoological specimens from devouring the village children, who congregated around the menagerie every evening, thus making his company liable for damages.[77]

Nor were auctions the best way of recovering money. In 1875, after the wardrobe of Barnum's Universal Exposition Company was put on the block, the sale of 162 horses, ponies and mules was offered. With the crowd filled with showmen smelling a bargain, the two primary bidders were Nathans and a representative for Old John Robinson. Altogether, only $20,000 was raised, with thoroughbred horses selling for as low as $15 to $75.[78] A year later, when Cooper & Bailey's Great International Circus was disposed of at auction (the proprietors fitting up an entirely new outfit for the 1876 season), their Cardiff Giant was bid off by Mr. Wolfinger for $35. A reported added, "The original pretend fossil, while it lay in a New York swamp, was certified to as genuine by Boynton, a geological lecturer, who was badly fooled or paid as Silliman* was in the Emma mine." The 30-foot-long stuffed whale went for $42.

By 1889, the Cardiff Giant was reported to be lying in a small garden in El Paso, where it had been obtained to defray a board bill and transportation expenses. Customers were in the habit of chipping off pieces, and one of the legs had broken, revealing an interior filled with a heavy frame of iron rods holding it together.[79]

Circus losses garnered little understanding or sympathy from the average citizen. They viewed the business in small terms:

> You go to a circus, and pay 50 cents to get in. To find a decent seat, you pay 10 more; to see the best thing in the show, you must pay 25 cents more, after the show is over. But the best thing of all is the side show outside, where will be found all the living wonders of the world, which may be seen for 25 cents more. If you are dry, you can drink for ten cents. If your gal wants a stick of candy, or a measure of peanuts, you can get them for ten cents.[80]

*Benjamin Silliman was a geologist hired to assess ore at the Emma Mine in Alta, Utah. His gross overestimation of the value led to financial ruin for many British investors. The reference to his being "paid" referred to broad accusations in the early 1870s that he had been bribed to provide untruthful reports.

Circus owners thought anything but small, however. Although times were hard, a Georgia newspaper growled in 1873 that a circus in Atlanta took in $3,000 at one performance.[81] The same year, John H. Murray (one of the youngest managers in the country, who worked his way from the ring to the possession of an ample fortune) cleared $75,000 at the end of the season.[82] In 1876, some circuses reduced the price of admission from 50 cents to twenty-five in acknowledgment of "hard times," but profits continued to roll in. In August 1877, the *Staunton Vindicator* reported that Robinson's circus earned $7,600 from a week's work in Bland and Craig counties,[83] and Coup's circus made $6,000 during two performances in Bradford.[84] It was not surprising, then, that it was written, "The circus men are opposed to silver, this thing of having half a ton of it to haul around is said to be inconvenient."[85]

To make money, a circus proprietor had to spend it. An aggregate of John Robinson's company for the ten-year period, 1864–1874, revealed that his costs (excluding staff and performers) were:

Hotel and livery	$700,600
Advertising	$490,000
Incidentals	$135,550
Smithing	$25,450
Lots	$25,000
Lights	$24,497
Woodwork	$26,224
Harnesses	$15,957
Licenses	$151,448
Railroad transportation (past 6 years)	$226,000

During the 18 years the company was in operation (to 1874), it traveled over 111,853 miles.[86]

Thoroughbreds such as these used in racing were part of the huge expenditure required to operate a circus. (*Freeport Journal* [IL], July 28, 1875)

During the season of 1876, Burr Robbin's company traveled through seven states: Wisconsin, Iowa, Minnesota, Nebraska, Kansas, Missouri and Illinois. He showed in 137 towns and traveled 3,132 miles, 340 by rail and 2,792 by wagon. The longest drive was 36 miles from Seneca, Kansas, to Marysville, and on two occasions he drove 35 miles each day, with an average distance of 22½ miles, only missing one performance (at Parkersburg, Iowa) when the teams became "mud bound."[87]

In 1879, Burr Robbins' season opened May 3 at Janesville, Wisconsin, and closed at Reedsburgh on October 16. Business was good, not being afflicted by the usual spurts and fallings-off which generally characterized a show. He covered Wisconsin, Illinois, Iowa and Minnesota, making 143 single-day stands, or 286 performances, paying $6,020 in licences. The show traveled 2,960 miles exclusively by wagon. During the season, there was consumed for feed 510 tons of hay, 13,600 bushels of oats, 5,100 bushels of corn, 170 tons of straw, 34,000 pounds of meat and 17,000 pounds of bread.[88]

Carnivorous animals were fed six days a week, eating about 16 pounds of beef or liver at a meal. They were never fed on Sunday, as it was deemed healthful for them to fast one day. An elephant consumed 50 pounds of hay and 3 pecks of oats per day during the summer; the hyena was served 5 pounds of rib bones and scrap beef, while the hippopotamus received only immense quantities of milk. Sea lions ate only fresh fish, eating 8 to 10 pounds daily; while the monkeys were the cheapest, in point of food, of any animal.[89]

Two of the largest concerns in 1877 were Barnum's and Forepaugh's. It was estimated that to start a circus of their magnitude, half a million dollars was required, which included a "sinking fund" to cover expenses during hard times. Salaries in the 1870s reflected changing economic conditions from the previous decade. Experienced equestrians earned about $125 a week: Charles Fish received $150; the top man in that "line," Jimmy Robinson (working in Australia in 1877), earned $500 in gold. Mid-range riders earned $80, while lady riders readily commanded $300. Clowns did not receive large salaries, as was generally supposed, averaging about $35 a week, with the superstar of the era, Dan Rice, receiving $1,000 per week.

Gymnasts, acrobats, leapers and contortionists commanded the smallest wages, as the supply exceeded the demand, taking home from $15 to $30 a week, with contortionists earning at the high end. Most lion tamers received $25 a week. Extremely lucrative salaries were paid to Ben Lusbie, the "lightning ticket seller" of Forepaugh's, who received $3,000 for the season; while Fred Lawrence, the advance advertising agent, earned $4,000 during the season. The lowest-paid members of the company were the "pets"—the sons and daughters of performers who earned for their parents $10 to $30 a week. An entire band of music performers cost $1,000 a month in salaries. The elephant man was paid $10 a week, with attendants (one to every three cages) earning $20 a month.[90]

One of the most common complaints about circuses was that they drained money from a town and left nothing in return. That was hardly the case. Aside from human and animal subsistence purchased from local farmers (hay costing $10 a ton and oats 35 cents a bushel), a large circus used 2,500 feet of lumber per day and 800 large sheets of poster paper. Four thousand programs might be used for the one-day stand; town newspapers gained by extensive advertising; and the average cost of licences was $75 for each municipality.[91] And these numbers did not include the benefit to hotels and diners patronized by those coming in from outlying areas, not to mention any incidentals purchased by the performers themselves.

20

"Fully in Keeping with the Present Age"

Foreign papers get locations in this country sadly mixed up, and occasionally tell some startling tales. Sangalli, the danseuse, is now doing Europe, and is in Paris. She has evidently been putting up a job on some newspaper man. She makes herself the heroine of the following thrilling tale:

Once, when a manageress of a traveling circus in the wilds of Ohio, she was suddenly attacked by a band of savage Sioux Indians, led by Sitting Bull. Everybody fled, and all was consternation and despair, many persons being drowned in the tempestuous waves of the Amazon. Suddenly, this heroine sprang upon an unsaddled horse, rallied around her P. T. Barnum and a few other of her employees, and with a revolver in hand attacked and dispersed the murderous red devils. Kansas City rewarded her with a commemorative medal, and Col. Buffalo Bill, of Lieut. Gen. Sheridan's staff, knelt at her feet and offered his hand and fortune.[1]

The first half of the 1880s were characterized by huge syndicates, or the mammoth bringing together of circus concerns. Miles Orton's Anglo-American Circus included the Royal German Menagerie, Le Gran Circo-Zoologico and the Mystic Circus of Japan; P. T. Barnum united his Greatest Show on Earth with James A. Bailey and James. L. Hutchinson's Great London Circus, Sanger's Royal British Menagerie and the Great International Allied Shows. S. H. Barrett & Co.'s New United Monster Railroad Shows included the Oriental Circus, Egyptian Caravan and Universal Exposition of Living wonders. In 1882, W. W. Cole advertised the 12th consecutive year of Nine Shows Consolidated. W. C. Coup's New United Monster Shows included the Great Indian Show, Ricthel's Flying Machine (1880), Melville's Australian Circus, Wood's Famous Museum, Colvin's Superb Menagerie and the New York Aquarium.

Adam Forepaugh's New and Colossal All-Feature Show bragged "a score of years under one ownership and management," including a bit of deceptive advertising with the bold pronouncement of "100 Elephants" preceded by a very tiny-print qualification — "Quarter of a ..." — making, in actuality, a mere 25 elephants. The Great Inter-Ocean Circus included Batcheller and Doris' Great Railroad Show, O'Brien's Great Show, the Southern Hippodrome and Prussian Circus, L. B. Lent's New York Circus, Campbell's Zoological Institute and Imperial Circus, Henderson's Egyptian Caravan and Oriental Circus, North American Indians, Prof. Ward's Conservatory of Beasts and Birds, the Traveling Museum of Living Wonders, Mullet's Aquarium of Marine Monsters and Sanger's Great London Circus, later to move to Barnum's.

June & Co., Nathans & Co.'s Railroad Shows had attached Colvin's Zone Exhausting Menagerie, Juke's Automatic Museum and Fryer's Pony, Dog and Goat Circus. Myers & Shorb's Big United States Circus & Hippo-Zoological Aggregation combined with the New Great Eastern Circus, Caravan, Museum and Mammoth Racing Balloon Show. Old John Robinson's 10 Big Shows began 1884 under the management of John Robinson, Old John's grandson, marking its 59th Annual Tour; the Sells Brothers 6 Enormous Railroad Shows offered 6 tents, 100 cages, 10 elephants, 20 camels and 3 rings, expanded to 4 rings in 1884, but reduced itself to 50 cages. The old Van Amburgh name (in 1885, promoting its 65th consecutive year [1820–1885], with Hyatt Frost entering his 39th year as manager) combined with Frost, Stone & Co.'s Roman Circus and Colosseum.

Man's obsession with flying machines that were capable of navigation accelerated toward the latter part of the 1800s. Although many aeronauts had not given up on the idea of steering balloons or of using one to cross the Atlantic, others sought to combine the balloon with engines as a means of achieving both navigation and distance. Ricthell's Flying Machine (1880), displayed as part of W. C. Coup's New United Monster Shows, was one such invention, requiring the operator to manipulate fans and peddle for power. (**Indiana Daily Messenger** [PA], June 30, 1880)

The consolidations were necessitated in part because of a growing trend "that everyone wants more for their money than they ever did before." Burr Robbins' effort typified the unification. During the winter of 1880, he brought together owners of nine different organizations and proposed the idea of merging them into one immense concern, making a stock association of it and having it duly incorporated and chartered under the state of Wisconsin, where he lived. They chose the name "Burr Robbins & Colvin's Great American and German Allied Railway Shows," and appointed a Board of Directors and elected a president. Orders were given for the construction of a monster railroad train, and agents dispatched to Europe to secure talent and novelties. The Governor of Wisconsin granted them a charter,[2] and they went on the road with two monster menageries, a herd of giant elephants, and the Great Triple Circus (featuring the famous rider Charles W. Fish).

"All for fifty cents" was the cry of P. T. Barnum's Great Moral Show, and its bewildering display of the world's wonders were summed up in an article from the *Olean Democrat* (New York), August 12, 1884. Taken almost verbatim from Barnum's advertising, it read: "The word 'great' doesn't do justice to it. It is immense, stupendous, unparalleled, and fully in keeping with the present age of great things — the age of the telegraph, the tele-

This handsome illustration was used in the masthead of Van Amburgh's New Railroad Shows, Charles Reiche & Brothers, proprietors. Hyatt Frost, manager, had been with the exhibition since the beginning and marked his 39th year in 1885. (*Yates County Chronicle* [NY], July 18, 1885)

phone, the railroad, the electric light — the age of big things in literature, art, science and invention."

Reaching the point where the "good old days" referenced the 1860s and 1870s, the reviewer harkened back to circus parades where a single band was drawn by a dozen horses, a courageous man sat in a cage of lions, and one carved chariot in gilt and gold trailed "a couple of elephants and a dozen old wagons." The procession of 1884 included a dozen bands, half a dozen men sitting with lions, tigers, hyenas, thirty elephants and twelve chariots. Inside the great tents, where "one tenth of his animals would have made a great menagerie," were "specimens of uncivilized and strange races [which] is a whole by itself." Continuous performances across two rings and an elevated center stage offered six simultaneous acts.

In a rare deviation from Barnum's "script," the reporter noted that people called the parade only "fair," found the white elephant a disappointment and complained they did not feel they had gotten their money's worth. Was it all too much? Had Barnum, Robbins and the others become so large that no amount of entertainment sated the public? Possibly. The season of 1884 was a disastrous one for traveling troupes of all kinds, and for 1885, Robbins announced he was scaling fares back to 25 cents.

W. C. Coup devised one of the more intriguing exhibitions of the railroad age. Known throughout the south as "Coup's Rolling Palaces," the idea was to have a train of cars specially built so as to be connected at will into one long pavilion. Inside was a museum, a huge aquarium, a "Congress of Freaks" and, lastly, an "auditorium department," where brief vaudeville performances were given. The entire display was brilliantly illuminated by dynamos and cost $100,000. Coup did not have the upfront money and was forced to take on "commercial capital." After one extremely profitable season, his backers took control and ran it into the ground. Finally, the specialty train was brought to Chicago and sold for $7,000 to a variety theater manager. He sold the cars piecemeal, and for years, fragments of the concern were operated by fly-by-night showmen "with all sorts of strange freaks."[3]

The Handsomest Woman in the World

One of the great schemes of the 1880s was Adam Forepaugh's contest to discover the "Handsomest Woman in the World." Perhaps it all started in early 1881, when his agent, Charles H. Day, sent Forepaugh's life-sized portrait to the *Janesville Gazette*, where it attracted the attention of all.[4] Having success with his own face, he decided to offer $10,000 for the loveliest lady, on condition that she "give her services for 20 days as the main participant in a grand daily pageant," talent not required.[5] Those wishing to appear as "Beauty" were to send their portraits to Charles H. Day.

By April, over 3,000 pictures had been received, and newspaper accounts around the country had a field day "announcing" the winner. One report from the *Reno Evening Gazette*, April 1, 1881, named Annie Pauline Scott, of Monongahela, Pennsylvania, described as "tall and shapely, with a bosom full and undulating ... symmetrical waist, filling her

Miss Molly Brown, Champion Female Rider of the World, was described by the Circus Royal in 1882 as being the handsomest female bareback rider the world had ever seen. In 1881, Adam Forepaugh had the bright idea of holding a contest whereby the most beautiful woman in the world was chosen from contestants around the country. Miss Louise Montague was selected to win the $10,000 prize. Unfortunately, the contest was fixed, with the winner being chosen from within the ranks of the Forepaugh Circus. Nor was Miss Montague to actually receive the huge prize. Rather, she was expected to earn her way at a salary of $30 a week. Being intelligent as well as beautiful, she eventually instigated numerous lawsuits for the entire sum, eventually settling for far less than was advertised in the scheme. (*Monticello Express* [IA], September 21, 1882)

bodice nicely and seemingly superlatively huggable." Unfortunately, the young lady declined to travel with the circus, preferring to gamble with "a well-worn deck of Hart's best playing cards," observing, "that old duck Forepaugh couldn't get me to travel with his show for no money. Will you take a hand at $1 limit?"

The *Lebanon Daily News* (Pennsylvania), April 2, 1881, denounced the Reno report and suggested a lady from Milwaukee, who was "between a blonde and brunette [with] large, full dark eyes, light hair, a Grecian nose, small mouth, and full oval cheeks."

On April 4, an official announcement was made in Philadelphia appointing Louise Montague "Queen of Beauty." The 21-year-old hailed from the Ninth Ward, New York City; her selection was made after Forepaugh personally interviewed several of the candidates. Louise was described as a "semi-brunette, her lips suggestive of a cherry, teeth regular and pearly ... a large but not disproportionate mouth; large expressive brown eyes, a symmetrical nose and an intelligent cast of countenance."[6] This heralded appointment was followed in May by the classic circus scheme of appointing for the "Beauty" a male rider to appear as her nobleman, who just happened to "belong to one of the leading houses of the old Hanoverian kingdom."[7]

Things rapidly fell apart. In June, the "wicked" editor of a Peoria paper threatened to publish the names of the losers in Forepaugh's contest, causing serious consternation among relatives of the ladies concerned. Adding insult to injury, word leaked that the entire project was a "humbug," the Queen actually belonging to his circus; and rather than receive the $10,000 prize, she was to be paid $30 a week and expenses.[8]

Miss Montague's "intelligent cast of countenance" quickly asserted itself. Just four months after her appointment, she was discharged and threatened to sue, not for a paltry salary, but for the entire $10,000 prize.[9] Ongoing negotiations finally settled on a $333 a week salary, with Louise also agreeing to portray the pageant character of Lallah Rookh departing from Delhi. The real-life story was not destined for a happy ending. In November 1881, she filed another suit, this time against the Louisville & Nashville Railroad for damages sustained in a train wreck the past September. In consideration for lost wages, pain and suffering, and the inability to perform due to a "scarred and mutilated limb," she demanded $20,000 in compensation,[10] settling in April 1882, for $1,000.[11]

Alas, the story would not die. In December, playing to the public's taste for the sensational, Barnum offered $10,000 for the most handsome man in the world; while in 1882, Batcheller and Doris featured the "$10,000 prize beauty" alongside Millie Christie, the two-headed woman. By September, Laura S. Keyser, known professionally as Louise Montague, filed another suit against Adam Forepaugh to collect her $10,000. During the trial in Philadelphia in February 1883, the beauty's lawyer, James H. Heverin, made a ferocious attack on Forepaugh's character; Forepaugh promptly brought suit for slander.

Beauty prize suits continued: in a separate trial, Louise claimed $10,000 for breach of promise and won $150; another suit against Forepaugh demanded compensation for when the plaintiff fell from the back of an elephant. After that was disposed, another for the $10,000 prize was to begin.[12] In June, two cases for injury and breach of promise resulted in a $650 reward. The final suit for damages was pending in a Fort Wayne court, where it was noted, "As he has lots of money and the grit to stay by all litigants, he is liable to come out on top."[13]

The best incident to come out of the Beauty Contest occurred in June 1881, during a circus parade in Chicago. A practical joker cried, "The 10,000 beauty has gotten loose."

The crowd ran in every direction. Some women fainted, and one was thrown from a window, nearly killing a telegraph operator. Those who have seen 'the most beautiful' think the people were justified in being panic stricken.[14]

The "Selling" of a Presidential Assassination

James A. Garfield was shot in Washington on July 2, 1881, by Charles J. Guiteau, and died on September 19. After a bizarre trial, during which the assassin claimed he was not guilty because Garfield's murder was the will of God, he was convicted on January 25, 1882. "Great diplomatic schemes" were immediately undertaken by rival circuses to obtain the murderer's clothes worn at the time of the assassination. On March 31, three months before his execution, an agent of Coup's circus visited Guiteau in jail and succeeded in purchasing two suits of clothes: that which he wore at the time of the assassination ($250) and another worn at trial ($100). When informed the suits were to be exhibited on plaster casts of himself made by the sculptor, Wilson McDonald, Guiteau was elated at the idea.[15] Reportedly, George Scoville, the murderer's agent who arranged the sale, "found himself outwitted by the alleged lunatic, who promised to pay him a commission and then refused to pay him a cent after getting the money."[16] Counsellor Reed finally forced the prisoner to pay for Scoville's services.

McDonald, aided by Clark Mills, spent three weeks in the cell; he described Guiteau as a "human animal in his appetites and his passions." Claiming the man had made no friends while in captivity, the sculptor studied the prisoner's skull from a phrenological standpoint, concluding he had "absolutely no love, no gratitude, no sense of decency, no courage, while his self-esteem is enlarged abnormally. He is cruel, absolutely having no heart." Guiteau was, he added, patient under the examinations because it glorified his vanity, thinking the American people were anxious to see him, if only in effigy. He was, McDonald said, expecting to be out soon, when he would go on a lecture tour.[17]

Although Scoville proposed to get up petitions for a commutation of sentence to life imprisonment, Charles J. Guiteau was executed by hanging on June 30, 1882, in the District of Columbia. Amid continuing jokes that Guiteau sold a suit of clothes to every circus in the country,[18] Coup went on tour with the Grand Historical Tableaux, representing the assassination, for which there were "no less than five hundred figures, appropriately costumed with correct likenesses of all the persons connected with the trial, such as Judge Cox, Judge Porter, the jury, council, etc."[19]

While exhibiting at Oshkosh in June, a local report indicated that while the chariot and Roman races formed an interesting feature, the wax figures of the late president and the assassin Guiteau "were hardly seen by the crowd, although they were historically correct."[20] Guiteau's second bullet, which missed Garfield, was also sold to a circus exhibition that hoped "to realize a handsome sum."[21]

"Mr. Jumbo, New York"

"Look for me — I am coming!" the baby elephant says in bold advertising print. And coming he was — to Cooper & Bailey's menagerie, where he was born in Philadelphia on March 15, 1880, after a gestation of 20 months and 20 days. Two months prior to giving birth, Hebe, the mother, had stood in the center of a large stable room with both hind legs chained to posts. The birth seems to have been uncomplicated, and her baby was "demonstrated beyond cavil" to be the only elephant born in captivity, shattering scientific belief that no elephant would successfully breed in confinement. The infant weighed 215½ pounds, stood 34 inches high and was measured, from base of trunk to the root of tail, at 37 inches.[22]

Hebe was an Asiatic elephant, 23 years old; the sire was Mandrie, age 25. Their "queer-looking" black baby was described as being not much larger than a Newfoundland dog, with a very diminutive trunk and a disposition to run at things blindly, like a colt. At the moment of birth, six elephant onlookers set up a tremendous bellowing, madly throwing about their trunks, standing on their hind legs and bellowing. This frightened Hebe, and she broke the chains holding her, grasped the baby in her trunk and threw it 20 yards across the room. She followed, destroying a stout wooden fence and a stove. Amid the continuing roar of the other elephants, the keepers reunited mother and baby, but she was too distraught to suckle it, forcing attendants to put a long rubber tube in the infant's mouth, pouring milk through a funnel.[23]

Hebe finally displayed maternal instincts and nursed it on her own. During the baby's first bath, taken in the Blackstone River, his mother caught him between her forelegs, lay down in the water and rolled over. Satisfied with the effort, she directed him to shore and prevented his return, although he showed a strong disposition to do so.[24]

The "little-big baby" was an instant sensation, and hundreds flocked to watch it nurse when the menagerie began its season. The infant had two years to reign supreme before the universal topic of the day turned to the arrival of another elephant, this one by ship from England. In his unique style, P. T. Barnum made the announcement, published in newspapers everywhere:

"Pretty Baby Talk: The Baby Elephant says, 'Look for me — I am coming!'" And so it was, arriving with the Great London Circus, Sanger's Royal British Menagerie and the International Ten Allied Shows, James E. Cooper and James A. Bailey, proprietors. (*Newport Daily News*, May 26, 1880)

The Colossus of elephants is now here — Jumbo. The people of two hemispheres excited over the purchase. Just arrived from the Royal Zoological gardens, costing thirty thousand dollars. The mighty monarch of beasts landed amid the enthusiastic shouts of half a million of people! All England against its departure. All America bound to have him. Brought here against the regrets of Queen Victoria and the Prince of Wales, and despite the injunctions of the law and the voice of united Europe. Ridden upon by the Queen and Royal family and by over a million children; its loss mourned by every child in Great Britain. Now on exhibition every afternoon and evening in connection with the greatest show on earth.

Jumbo, brought into the United States on April 9, 1882, without payment of duty on an affidavit being made that he was imported for breeding purposes, arrived in his cage around midnight, attracting large crowds. Sixteen horses dragged, and two elephants occasionally pushed, the cage to the gardens, but the entrance proved too low for the box, compelling Jumbo to stand in the street until morning, when the cage door was opened. Reluctant to emerge, he was finally coaxed out and introduced to his new surroundings, while men set out oiling and polishing his body. When introduced to two of Barnum's 21 elephants, it became apparent they were mere "pigmies" beside him. At that first meeting, Jumbo trumpeted and wagged his tail. The others breathed hard and elevated their ears before three elephant trunks met and caressed in midair. They "blowed" and grunted, giving every indication of pleasure. When introduced to Queen and her baby elephant, Jumbo began a flirtation but ignored the pony-sized baby. A special railway car was ordered constructed, the bottom of which would just clear the rails, enabling the car to pass under bridges.

Jumbo was an instant hit with the American public; and the English mails brought many packages and letters to their lost pachyderm, simply addressed to "Mr. Jumbo, New York."[25] Jumbo was 25 years old when brought to America. According to the history Barnum

For an all-too-brief time, Jumbo the elephant was the wonder of the animal kingdom. Billed as "Majestic, Powerful, Mastodonic, Wonderful," he was brought to the United States from England, where his sale to P. T. Barnum was considered a national calamity. For months after his arrival, the transatlantic mails were filled with letters from British children addressed to "Mr. Jumbo, New York." (*Logansport Journal* [IN], September 6, 1883)

provided, he was captured in Africa as a young animal by a party of Arabs and transported to France, where he was displayed in the Jardin des Plantes. When still young, he was secured by the Royal Zoological garden, Regent's Park, London, by swapping other animals. He was not considered a wonderful elephant at the time, but by age 7 or 8, he began to grow very fast. With prodigious growth came a change in temperament, and he was put under close confinement for fear he would injure someone. After 17 years, the council of the Garden decided to sell him and accepted Barnum's $10,000 offer, although Jumbo's removal from the country was considered a national calamity.[26]

Barnum did not wait long to take the "world renowned" Jumbo on the road. Huge crowds waited by the train depot as early as 4:00 A.M. for the circus to arrive, eagerly watching as the army of employees began their work. The first act was to release the pack-horses. Work-horses occupied eight cars and were packed in tightly, 16 to 20 animals per car. Ring horses occupied two cars, and were kept blanketed or already saddled to save time. Once the gangplank was set in place, they followed each other out in quick succession. Each team had its own driver and carried the exact load every time.

After the horses were released, chariots, wagons and cages followed. They were unloaded by means of an inclined plane stretching from the platform car to the ground. Once the car was emptied, the next, closely coupled, was pushed into its place, obviating the need to uncouple each car and readjust the plane, or have an incline plane for each. This saved labor and hurried the process of hitching the horses and getting them off to the circus ground.

One car contained giraffes, horned oxen and like animals. Next out were the ponies, mules and zebras, which also had their work to do in transporting parade vehicles. Those animals that were on exhibition but were not confined to cages followed. Four elephants occupied one car, two cars contained six elephants and one had four, plus the baby elephant. Jumbo had a private car he occupied with his English keeper, Scott, who had been with him since he was three years old and stayed with him at all times. Elephants were chained in the cars, but with enough length to lie down. They all descended on the inclined plane except Jumbo, whose car was lower than the rest, allowing him to step out.

Long before the unloading was completed, work began at the circus grounds. In 1882, C. H. McLean supervised 125 men. The ground was laid out according to a survey and properly staked off. The circus tents went up first, followed by dressing rooms, stable and dining tents, the last being the menagerie canvas. To achieve this, long stakes were driven at short distances from

Adam Forepaugh advertised "The Only Trained Giraffes on this Continent" with this illustration of a giraffe drawing a circus chariot. Along with the giraffes were 15 performing elephants, 100 wild beasts, 100 great actors, 50 trained Arabian horses and a human being fired from a monster cannon. (*Marion Daily Star* [OH], August 19, 1880) one another, ropes were placed in position and fastened to the canvas. Outside poles went up first, followed by four peak ones; last up were the red and blue poles that divided the rings from the hippodrome track. The side canvas was placed around the tent; ropes were fastened to it and run through the top of the short poles, finally being pulled up in a peak to enclose the structure. This required an hour and a half. Once completed, boards for seating were positioned, one section fitting into another. In three quarters of an hour, seats for 15,000 were in place.

Nearly all heavy laborers who traveled with circuses wore a small leather band, bound tightly and sewed into place, around their right wrist. Those outside the circus considered the use a superstition, but the men claimed the band was strengthening, as it kept the cords of the wrist well moistened, feeling they could work harder and longer with the device.

The rings, previously marked, were rapidly plowed up and covered with sawdust. Next followed the stringing of lights. The procedure remained constant from stop to stop, allowing for a polished routine in setting up and dismantling. Not everything worked according to plan, however, and during a stop at Newport the smaller elephants broke away and ran up the street, fortunately being caught before inflicting any damage.

Those waiting at the depot got to see Jumbo free of charge, but he was quickly transported and placed under canvas, his feet being too delicate for the street parade. Not incidentally, with Jumbo being the "big card," it did not pay for Barnum to display him long without taking a ticket for the performance.[27] Shortly before 9:00 A.M., the procession began. Gilded chariots, bands, lions, tigers, leopards and snakes were exposed to public gaze; camels were ridden and elephants led, ridden or harnessed to wagons. Horses paraded by the score, along with zebras and ponies, the steam calliope, and fantastic male and female figures "that bore no resemblance to anything on the earth, bowing and scraping and making merry from their aerial positions."

Many paid their money just to see Jumbo, the "monstrous animal and they went away feeling repaid. No one was disappointed in him. He was as large as had been reported [11' 11", weighing 8 tons], but he was not handsome." Lacking grace or beauty, Jumbo was described as the most amicable of beasts, always ready for something to eat, delighting children who fed him cookies, peanuts and whole loaves of bread. "Bridgeport," the baby elephant, "as gentle as a kitten," played near his mother, Queen, and permitted children to ride on his back.[28]

Tragedy struck September 15, 1885. After a performance in Ontario, Jumbo and the trick elephant "Tom Thumb" were taken to their special car positioned on a sidetrack, opposite which lay a steep embankment. As a freight train approached, Jumbo's keeper tried to get him down the embankment, but he would not go. The keeper then attempted to position him between the circus train and the main track. During the process of moving the elephant, the engine struck Jumbo on the right side, carrying him 100 yards as he roared in pain. Jumbo was terribly mangled and died in about three minutes. In the crash, the baby elephant received a compound fracture to one of its legs and died several hours later.[29]

Although Barnum had insured Jumbo for $500,000 on his journey across the ocean, that marine policy expired upon the animal's landing. He was uninsured at the time of his death, there being no company in the country offering policies for accident to livestock. The only type of protection available was fire insurance, which not only required enormous premiums but would not have applied in this case. Although ostensibly brought to the United States for breeding purposes, Jumbo left no offspring. Obituary notices ran all over America and England announcing the passing of the children's favorite.[30]

At the time of his death, Jumbo's measurements were: circumference of forearm, 5' 6"; around the foot, 5' 6"; twice around the foot was his height of 11'; length of trunk 7' 4"; around his tusk, 1' 3½"; length of foreleg, 6'. The animal was skinned and his hide sent to the Smithsonian Institute.[31] The bones were assembled with wire and put on display, a peculiar advertisement from July 22, 1886, reading: "JUMBO — As Large as Life and Quite as Natural."[32]

The General Manager of the Canadian Grand Trunk Railway denied responsibility for the accident, citing reports that the circus men cut down the fences and were driving Jumbo across the track when he was killed. Had they taken the trouble to go by the regular crossing, the signalman would have warned them of the oncoming train and the accident could have been avoided.[33]

The case of Barnum, Hutchinson & Co. against the Grand Trunk Railway of Canada to recover $100,000 was heard in April 1887. The railroad claimed Jumbo had "very slight value," based on testimony that it had been sold by the London Zoological Society "on account of his fierce and unruly character." They rested their defense on the fact a clause in their contract with the circus stated they were not liable for any loss greater than $15,000. The plaintiffs argued that the railroad clause was illegal and presented depositions from George Artinstall, Jumbo's trainer, and Matthew Scott, his keeper, both of whom had returned to England.[34] Mr. Childs, attorney for Barnum, withdrew the suit and settled out of court for a reputed $5,000 cash and an agreement by the Grand Trunk Railway to "haul the circus, eighty cars, over its rails free during the coming season." That made the final disposition about $10,000, Barnum having paid $4,800 to the same railway the previous year.

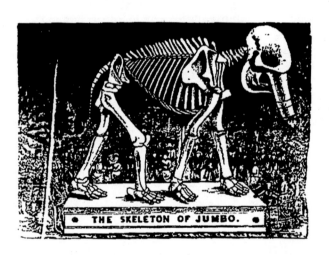

Although having the reputation of a bad disposition, Jumbo, the gigantic elephant transplanted from England "at enormous expense" (a favorite advertising expression), proved to be wildly popular for P. T. Barnum's United Monster Shows. Tragically, while being placed inside his private traveling car, he was struck by an oncoming train and killed. Being uninsured, Barnum, Bailey and Hutchinson, the owners, were forced to sue for damages. Rather than be satisfied with the $10,000 won at court, the industrious Barnum had Jumbo's bones polished and "articulated," and took them on tour, promising them to be "As large as life, and quite as Natural." (*Oshkosh Daily Northwestern*, August 17, 1886)

The Hard Life of Circus Animals

Circuses and menageries fixed the commercial value of animals because they were the largest buyers. In 1894, the relative worth of each stood at:

Elephant	$10,000 each	Antelopes	$185–300
Giraffe	$6,000	Deer	$75–100
Hippopotamus	$4,000	Moose	$500
Rhinoceros (one horn)	$3,000	Ant-eater	$400
Rhinoceros (two horns)	$4,000	Hartbeast (a kind of antelope),	
Lions	$800–1,200	wart hogs and sloths	$350
Lioness	$1,000	Cheetahs, alpacas and guanacos	$300
Tigers	$1,000	Tapirs	$400
Grizzly bears	$500–1,000	Sea lions	$300–400
Polar bears	$800	Seals	$50
Other bears	$50–200	Zebras	$250
Camel (one hump)	$350	Llamas	$200
Camel (two humps)	$400	Emus	$175
Ostriches	$800	Mountain lions	$100
Gnus	$700	Armadillos	$50
American buffalo	$500	Porcupines	$25
Rocky Mountain goat	$500	Wolves	$75
Panthers and leopards	$250	Kangaroos	$150
Hyenas and pumas	$175	Monkeys	$20–75

Ironically, the animal accorded the greatest worth was the trained circus horse, valued at $2,500.[35]

Training circus animals was an "interesting spectacle" to human observers, but likely less so for the brutes. To teach an elephant to lie down on command required a harness and the service of five other elephants. The pupil had a cable attached to each leg and a band around his body, each attached by rope to trained elephants. At the word of command, the elephants pulled the ropes so the pupil's hind legs were pulled out from under him and his forelegs drawn apart. Unable to maintain balance, another elephant at its side pushed; the pupil howled and went over on his side. While this was being done, the trainer spoke a word. After the "flopping process" was repeated several times, the animal associated the command with lying down and learned the trick. Elephants frequently practiced on their own after rehearsal, developing the fine points so that when brought into the ring they appeared perfectly docile and capable of the most intricate performances.

Oxen being taught to walk on their knees were trained in a similar manner, being brought to their knees by ropes and then pulled forward until they learned what was required.

Such training measures were not considered harsh, but no one could ignore the horrific accidents involving circus animals that were all too common during the 19th century. Aside from transportation accidents, fire was a major cause of death and destruction. On May 22, 1879, one of the worst fires involving such animals broke out at the Five-Mile House outside Detroit, occupied by P. M. French's menagerie. His collection consisted of "Sultan," the elephant, seven lions, a tiger, zebra, sacred cow and calf, three leopards, a wolf and a Rocky Mountain deer. Just prior to their being leased out to a zoological garden in Chicago, fire broke out in a hayloft, spreading so quickly that within 15 minutes the barn was one sheet of flame. Tortured cries of the animals filled the air, but as it was impossible to rescue them, the entire group was cremated.[36]

Sunday, November 20, 1887, proved another tragic day when fire broke out at Barnum's winter quarters in Bridgeport, Connecticut. Nearly all the principal animals for the show, including four elephants (Alice, Sampson, a white elephant and another), five lions, seven leopards, six panthers, four kangaroos, six horses and a great number of smaller beasts, were burned to death. One elephant escaped, but was found drowned in the Sound that it had attempted to cross in its terror; a lion also escaped, but could not be recaptured and was shot by circus employees. Otto Mabie, an elephant trainer, heroically saved the other eighteen elephants. Insurance, placed through Staples & Co., covered $7,125 for the building and $35,000 for the animals, including $4,500 on the elephants and $2,250 on the hippopotamus. Barnum placed insurance recovery at $65,000 and actual losses at $500,000. The fire was supposed to be the work of an incendiary. A number of animals from Wombwell's menagerie were purchased to replace those lost.[37]

Accident proved another daily risk for performing animals. In 1885, one of W. W. Cole's rope-walking horses, valued at $5,000, fell from the tightrope and was placed under care of a veterinary surgeon. There was no help for the animal that had spent 26 of its 30 years in active circus service, and it died shortly thereafter.[38] A year later, Adam Forepaugh, Jr., proposed walking his horse, Blondin (named after the famous tightrope walker), across Niagara on a cable. Fortunately, he was prevented by Henry Bergh, secretary of the Society for the Prevention of Cruelty to Animals.[39]

An accident of a different sort happened to one of Dan Castello's circus elephants. A painter left a pot of green paint in the animal's railroad car. The curious beast sampled it, liked the taste and finished it off, including the brush. It immediately became sick, suffering terrible diarrhea before recovering.[40]

VanAmburgh, Chas. Reiche & Bro's NEW RAILROAD SHOWS.

Next to the pavilion or tent, the greatest change to circuses came when traveling companies switched from wagons to the iron horse. Traveling by railroad was more expensive, but offered speed of mobility, allowing exhibitions to stop at every town along the route, perform an afternoon and evening show, pack up and move on. This eased the wear and tear on the larger animals that were forced to walk long distances and cross unstable bridges, but also subjected occupants to ever increasing and often fatal railroad accidents. (*Elyria Republican* [OH], August 6, 1885)

Sometimes miscalculations were involved. A dog belonging to Sands, Nathan & Co., for which they refused $500 a week earlier, died in a fit at Albany.[41]

More common were the innumerable stories about wild beasts escaping, typified by a report from 1882. Two leopards escaped from O'Brien's circus while being conveyed by train from Camden to Mt. Holly, New Jersey. After chase was given, both leopards were crushed by the wheels of the train.[42]

Disease also took its toll on animal performers. In October 1872, a "Canadian horse epidemic" was thought to have been introduced into Rochester by a traveling circus. It was considered a form of influenza, characterized by tears from the eyes, a watery discharge from the nose, general languor and cough. The disease spread rapidly, and within 24 hours, 300 cases in Buffalo proved fatal, while O'Brien's circus company had 200 horses under treatment.[43] By November, Barnum's circus had to postpone its performances because of the disease. During the three-day shutdown, Barnum's animal "Doctor" astutely filled the stable with steam (to induce sweating) that checked and eventually extinguished the disease. Surprisingly, none of the other hoofed animals, such as zebras, bovines and the Shetland pony, became infected; however, the lions and tigers suffered the same symptoms as the horses.

By mid–November the "sneezing disease" had spread to Washington, Philadelphia, Virginia and Chicago. The outcry reached as far as England, where a demand of quarantine was brought against Fish and Rowland, two circus riders who transported sick horses to England.[44]

In 1884, two of O'Brien's horses were found to be suffering from the highly contagious disease, glanders. After being inspected by a veterinary surgeon at the request of the mayor, two animals were ordered killed and others isolated, the observation being made that the entire concern ought to be shut down and the proprietor arrested for traversing the country with such animals.[45] In 1885, six of Burr Robbins' circus horses were destroyed at Tipton by order of the Assistant State Veterinary Surgeon for the same disease.[46]

The war elephant "Romeo" (known among showmen as "Old Canada") was the most famous of his day, being celebrated as vicious, vindictive and dangerous. His "fits of madness" were nearly impossible to control, and his keeper, Mr. Craven, of Forepaugh's menagerie, resorted to what most certainly must be considered inhuman treatment to contain him. In 1866, while on exhibition in Philadelphia, the 10-foot high, 5-ton animal showed signs of ill humor. He was placed in a cage 28 feet square and secured by chains

Elephants were a circus and menagerie standard, and crowds of all ages appreciated watching the animals perform tricks, perhaps more than any other attraction. In the ring, the well-trained animals played comic roles to perfection, but the life of a captive elephant was anything but easy. Many suffered foot and leg injuries from traveling long distances, and numerous accidents were recounted of animals falling from bridges or suffering from extreme discipline. (*Janesville Gazette*, July 17, 1876)

so that he was positioned midway in that space. Food and water were kept from him for seven days. Hardly quieted by starvation, a dozen loads of rifle shot were fired into his head, one destroying his right eye. When even that did not quell his anger, a tackle was brought in and chains made fast around his feet. He was hoisted up and then maneuvered onto his side, during which time he was shot in the trunk and side. This time the punishment worked; after a night of being forced to remain on his side, Romeo was released and performed his usual tricks in the ring.[47]

There is no question that Romeo was a dangerous elephant, killing his keeper, Mr. Williams, at Hatboro, Pennsylvania, and several others during his life. Rather than "retire" him to pasture, his "card" was so great an attraction that George Forepaugh, his keeper, continued to show him. In 1869, during another rampage in which Romeo nearly killed Forepaugh and did destroy a favorite dog, it was felt necessary to "take him." This was accomplished by confining him beyond the power of resistance and then beating him until he trumpeted submission.

If block and tackle were not available, guy stakes were driven into the ground at a distance of 100 feet in front and behind the animal, to which ropes were secured, running through falls and blocks, which, by adroit management, were attached to fetters around the animal's legs. When accomplishing this in 1869, birdshot was fired into the sensitive trunk, causing rage and pain. With everything in readiness, the elephant's legs were brought from under him until he lay recumbent. His legs were then tied together, and a man drove a spear deep into his flank, ordering with "sharp, derisive tones" to "speak." Romeo refused, and an 8-hour-long torture session commenced, the handlers beating him with iron rods and wounding him with the spear innumerable times until he "begged long and loud for mercy." The proud keepers then bragged, "A child can now drive him with a rye straw."[48]

Numerous other examples of Romeo being "brought into submission" with pitchforks could be cited over the years, but in June 1872, the poor animal became a victim of "scientific surgery." At the beginning of the season, he was more than uncommonly "raising thunder," the cause eventually determined to be acute suffering from copious infected leg wounds of long duration. Being an old elephant, his flesh was slow to heal, and a lack of knowledge about how to treat elephant sores, coupled with many misapplied remedies, brought Romeo to death's door. When Forepaugh's menagerie reached Chicago, it was determined he could go no further. Forepaugh summoned Dr. H. W. Boyd, a professor of surgery and anatomy at the Chicago Medical College, who had performed several autopsies on elephants. R. J. Withers, veterinary surgeon connected with the stables of the City Railway, accompanied him.

They found Romeo standing quietly in a bed of hay, with his four festered feet in tubs of water. It was determined the wounds required debridement; George Forepaugh stood guard with a pitchfork as the hour-long operation commenced. Several pounds of flesh were removed from the wounds, Romeo setting out "a low rumbling like distant thunder" that vibrated through the tent, setting every animal in the menagerie into a chorus of noise. After being pitch-forked into submission, a quiver ran through the elephant's frame, and after that, "during three mortal hours of terrible pain, the animal displayed only the noblest qualities of fortitude."

Under the direction of Boyd, Withers cut, gorged, tunneled and chiseled into the legs, digging out a pound or two of flesh at a time. Each time the knife was removed, blood copiously flowed, total loss being estimated at three bucketsful. When bone was finally revealed, huge, white-hot soldering irons were shoved into the openings to cauterize the bleeding. During a two-hour procedure, while Romeo "quivered like an aspen," 30 rods were thrust into the leg openings, despite the fact the bones showed fractures and did not meet properly. The elephant eventually weakened and became groggy from loss of blood. The operation was stopped, and the wounds were washed with lotions and bound. As a reward for his heroics in enduring intractable agony, Romeo was offered a candy stick, "but he refused it with a solemn shake of his head." The article concluded:

> It is perhaps needless to say that Romeo expressed himself disgusted with surgery, and declared that he would rather die than submit to such treatment — and die he did.[49]

It would have been far more humane to submit Romeo to euthanasia, as was done to an elephant belonging to Wombwell's concern. Said to be 120 years old, it suffered from diseased feet, and it was felt that the kindest thing to do was put it down. After administering chloroform, large doses of prussic acid and strychnine were given, but without effect. More chloroform was given in the hope the animal would die under its influence, but it wore off. The drug was given a third time to prevent any pain, then the carotid artery was cut. In a few minutes, the huge animal died without a struggle.

More horrific were animal executions. In 1888, the elephant "Chief," traveling with Adam Forepaugh's circus, was determined too violent for safety. It was first suggested to the Robinson Brothers, his owner, that the 25-year-old, weighing 10,000 pounds, should be put to death by electrocution, but it was later determined to put him to death by strangulation. A rope was secured around his neck, and two elephants, Basil and Bismarck, were ordered to pull the ends. After the two were commanded to use all their power, Chief tottered and fell, and died in 20 seconds.

The year 1893 was a particularly brutal one for elephants. In March, the elephant "Old Tobe," chained by his keeper while undergoing punishment, died; while "Zip," the children's favorite, expired in Baraboo, Wisconsin, of reputed heart failure.[50]

Occasionally, treatment of both an innovative and trial-and-error approach was required to maintain or heal an injured animal. Routine care for elephants included paring their toenails, which was done several times a year. One by one, the animals were ordered forward and commanded to roll onto their side. The keeper would then straddle one leg and begin the operation with a draw-shave. The sharp edge cut through the tough, callous substance with ease, the chips showing a light yellow color with pinkish tints, measuring 3 to 4 inches thick on some parts of the foot. Afterwards, bits of nails and glass that had lodged in the foot were removed to prevent injury. The animals seemed to enjoy the procedure.[51]

In 1851, Mr. Chapart, a French dentist, performed the feat of pulling out a tusk from the mouth of a mammoth elephant belonging to Hughes de Massilia's menagerie. "Alysha" was "chloroformised" and tied with ropes, after which the roots of the tusks that had been broken several years earlier were removed. Weighing more than 18 pounds, it was hoped the removal of ivory would prevent recurrence of toothache similar to that which had excited him to commit much mischief.[52] On the subject of ivory, an 1885 report indicated that 65,000 elephants a year were slaughtered in Africa for their tusks, concluding, "The elephant and the buffalo will soon be numbered among the mastodons of a past age."[53]

Chloroform was also used as a means of subduing irate dangerous animals. During a private performance of the Nickel Plate circus, animal trainer Charles McCurran entered the cage of Prince, the largest African lion in captivity. While he was going in, Prince seized the opportunity of going out and promptly lunged at the spectators. While they scattered, the lion directed his attention toward a trick Shetland pony; and before anyone could stop him, the big cat slit the helpless animal's throat. Unable to beat back Prince with iron bars, it was decided to chloroform him. A hole was broken into the floor above the animals, and two large sponges soaked with the drug were shoved under the lion's nose. In a few moments, the animal fell asleep and was safely removed, but too late to save the pony.[54]

The above cases in which chloroform or any type of anesthetic were used on animals would appear to be rare. Typically, as in Romeo's case, beasts were expected to endure what humans thought best, which is not to suggest circus animals were always maltreated or proper care denied them. John Carney, superintendent of the Zoological Gardens, Cincinnati, succeeded in a novel experiment to heal what might be considered the pride of the king of the jungle. One of the lions at the exhibit had his tail bitten off by a vicious hyena; the creature continually chewed at the wounded tip, and it was feared he would worry himself to death. Carney ordered a very small cage constructed so that when the beast was coaxed inside it could not turn around. Once secured, the end of the tail was medically treated and covered with a black snakeskin. When released, the lion appeared perfectly satisfied with the improvement and gave no further trouble.[55]

A different "tail story" came out of Boston in 1885. A frenzied four-year-old Bengal tigress, weighing 500 pounds and measuring six feet long, bit off her own tail while on exhibition in Connecticut. The wound did not heal, and the sore stump caused intolerable pain. The howling set the other animals wild, leaving the concern in a continual uproar. Dr. Al Watts, an Englishman, was sent for when the circus reached Boston. He ordered the tigress secured by ropes, and, when accomplished, he went into the cage and operated to remove the remaining stump close to the rump. In order to keep the tigress from injuring herself, a log of wood was placed between her teeth. Before the surgery was completed, she had rendered the wood to splinters, and a pine board was substituted. The animal's cries were perfectly fearful and her struggles so powerful she managed to free one paw, swiping it at the doctor. He barely escaped and completed the 30-minute operation outside the cage. After removing the ulcerated portion, the wound was washed with a weak solution of carbolic acid and water. Orders were then given for her hind legs to be released. Taking advantage of this freedom, she rose upon her haunches and made a tremendous effort to free herself. Just as suddenly her strength gave out and she collapsed, almost lifeless. Upon recovery, "she appeared as happy as the skillful surgeon who had imperiled his life for hers."

In 1894, surgery was performed on "Jim Blaine," the Royal Bengal tiger. It was determined he was suffering from appendicitis, and a New York specialist agreed to remove the inflamed organ for $750, the owner stipulating that no ether or chloroform be used. After securing the animal, the surgeon made an incision, cut away the sac, then removed nearly a quart of suppurating matter. After washing the wound, he followed with "an injection of antiseptics" before closing with silver thread.[56]

The question of what to do with circus animals too old to perform was perplexing. Most were passed down the chain from smaller to smaller shows and dragged around the country until death finally claimed them. Even less dignified than that, in May 1851, flaming advertisements of a "Grand Buffalo Hunt" drew a crowd of 15,000 to the racecourse at Cincinnati. The buffalo "turned out to be a dyspeptic old bull, that had been cast off as no longer able to follow in the train of a menagerie." After being shot with bows and arrows, lances and tomahawks, the buffalo, "*perfectly* resigned to his fate, and after receiving six arrow shots from the bows of various red men, the poor fellow got up and walked quietly into a dirty pool of water near by and as quietly gave up the ghost" (italics in original).[57]

When W. W. Cole sold out in 1887, he had three circus horses of which he was particularly fond. Not wanting them sold and "put to work," he decided the kindest thing would be to put them down. Toward that end it was suggested bleeding them to death, but a liveryman suggested the use of chloroform as a less painful method. The three horses were collected in the tent, along with Cole and his performers. The first little mare was called by name and asked to kiss them all good-bye. "The intelligent animal, stretching forward her head, kissed each one. This was more than they could stand, and the sacrifice was put off." It was eventually decided the liveryman, W. B. Leonard, would find someone to take charge and keep them in good order until old age claimed them.[58]

October 19, 1872, marked the death of Dan Rice's horse "Excelsior Jr." After spending 18 of its 20 years as a circus performer, enduring blindness for much of its life, the beloved animal caught cold, rendering it deaf. It was sent to a stable where it soon passed away, Dan announcing the event to his audience with tears in his eyes. Excelsior's sire, Excelsior Sr., Rice's splendid trick horse, had been with the performer since the start of his career when he had nothing more than a "one horse show." That animal died in Baltimore in 1858, and was buried with honors.[59]

The most difficult question to address when discussing animal care and safety during the 19th century was what exactly constituted cruelty. Opinions varied, as illustrated by an incident involving P. T. Barnum, who, unfortunately, made a grandstand display out of the question. In 1880, Mr. Bergh and Mr. Hartfield of the Society for the Prevention of Cruelty to Animals issued a formal mandate forbidding Barnum from allowing the horse Salamander to leap through flaming hoops. Armed with his lawyer, Barnum stepped into the ring, and after giving a long speech on his own dedication to animal welfare, proceeded to order the hoops lit. He then "walked leisurely through the first ring, put his hands into the flames, and then walked toward the next ring, while the audience cheered wildly." Superintendent Hartfield went into the ring, took hold of a hoop and slightly burned his hands, but not enough, apparently, for him to enforce the stay.[60]

21

Privilegers, Flash Folk,
Fakirs and Bunco Men

Beware of the oily-tongued individual, the light-fingered gentleman, and the catch-penny concerns connected with the circus on Monday next.[1]

If a 19th century citizen were to be asked to describe a circus, the answer would undoubtedly focus on the equestrian skills of bareback riders, the astonishment of "living wonders," and the stale jokes of brightly clad clowns, which in itself became an industry for jokes:

> A correspondent, speaking of a circus performance in Arizona, says: "The show went on, regardless of the fact that there were two dead men lying under the seats." It is supposed that the clown got off a new joke. We have always maintained that somebody would get hurt if the thing ever happened.[2]

After taking a deep breath, the speaker would likely elaborate on recurring themes stretching throughout the decades: circuses not offering what they advertised and the proliferation of low life that followed in their wake.

Of the former, a typical "humbug" of 1870 concerned the Parisian Circus of the Macarte sisters that "originated, as its name implies, at Par — Des Moines, about six weeks ago, and consists of a lot of street loafers, &c. who have purchased Orton's old canvas and started out to 'gull' people."[3] On a larger scale, an 1884 report noted of Sells Brothers' Circus:

> The dens of polar bears, the lairs of crocodiles, the herds of elands, the lairs of serpents, the droves of moose, etc. which were so vauntingly boasted of by the management, were all a myth — not having any existence whatever except on paper.... The coal black sacred elephant and the monster three-horned rhinoceros were also among the grand invisible features of the menagerie that failed to materialize for the edification of the curious, but why this was thusly no explanation was given.[4]

The latter is perhaps amply summed up by an editorial from 1872, that began

> The circus which exhibited in this place on Thursday was accompanied, we are informed, by the usual sharpers, gamblers, &c. Three card monte, the usual sweat board and other devices for cheating greenhorns were practiced openly in defiance of the law.... The unwary who risked their money were fleeced as they deserved to be

In 1875, the year of this advertisement, Howe's Great London Circus made its first tour of the United States by railroad. Promising the most gorgeous street procession ever given, the combination included the Grecian Hippodrome, Sanger's English Menagerie and the Iroquois Indian Troupe. (*Burlington Weekly Hawk-Eye* [IA], June 10, 1875)

for being so simple as to risk their money against professional blacklegs. So common has this thing become that the visit of a circus is attended with nothing but evil.[5]

It need hardly be reiterated that thieves, swindlers and gamblers of all sorts followed circuses as independent hangers-on, in well-organized gangs and as "privilegers," or those individuals who purchased rental space in proximity to the show on which any sort of business might be conducted. Licences granted to a circus ordinarily covered all its belongings, including side shows. With limited expenses, it was not infrequent that while circuses lost money during a season, its side shows made handsome profits.[6]

Side show privileges for large and popular circuses sold for as much as $30,000 a season, and occasionally circus men with familiar names who had been ruined by a disastrous year regrouped by buying such permissions and advertising themselves along with the main entertainments. Advance sales allowed them to put together new acts, and, if successful, entirely new shows emerged from these leases or privileges.[7]

Most sellers fell under the category of "fakirs." Loosely applied, the term included petty crooks, whose plan of operation was to rob people so ingeniously that they liked it, but also merchants who bought an article for 10 cents and sold it for $1. The term also applied to "petty performers," such as those who walked around on crutches and made a good living selling cheap lead pencils to sympathetic purchasers.[8]

"Candy privileges" covered the sale of confectionary, nuts, fruits and lemonade in the main tent. The particular specialty of these "candy-butchers," as they were called, was to collect 3-cent pieces, skillfully giving the similarly looking coins out as dimes when providing change. Twenty-cent pieces also went for quarters, and it was once believed that it was circus men who suggested the minting of that particular coin. When a half dollar was given, a deft sleight-of-hand easily substituted a quarter. If called upon for delivering incorrect change, the 25-cent piece was presented as evidence of what the buyer "actually offered."

"Candy butchers" plied the trade of selling erstwhile "taffy," exclusively working the top benches where the "country bumpkins" sat. Their trick was to fill his girl's lap with oranges, candy, popcorn and fans, "making the young man pay thirteen or fourteen prices for the rubbish."[9] These "fly workers" traditionally had colorful names, such as "Canada Jack," "Frisky Coleman," "Kid Barton" or "Bahama Ben." "Insolent young ruffians" who sold peanuts were universally held "in a manner that deserves unlimited censure." When 200,000 quarts of peanuts were sold at a circus during a two-day period[10] (making $18 from an 8-quart bucket), it is easy to see that salesmen earned a substantial living

Drinking water was rarely available, forcing patrons to buy lemonade from a stand operated by a contractor who had purchased the monopoly.[11] The product varied in quality, prompting several oft-repeated jokes:

- A circus lemonade man happening to be in a market the other day, and seeing some of the yellow fruit, pointed to it and said: "What's them things?"[12]
- Why is it that the circus elephant never kills the clown or the lemonade man? [13]
- And under the heading "Why We Laugh": Hooray! A circus lemonade man has been shot in Kansas.[14]

Pink, or Strawberry Lemonade, was made by the barrel, using ten cents worth of tartaric acid and five cents worth of analine [sic], sugar and two lemons.[15] (Aniline was an oily poisonous liquid used in the 19th century for making dyes, medicines and explosives.) Dealers easily made $50 a day selling their "filthy slop" for 10 cents a glass. The expression "circus lemonade" came to mean a spiked, or alcoholic, mixture. If beer were also sold, drunken and disorderly conduct was sure to follow.[16]

"Ticket privileges" involved the right to sell daily tickets to the main show in advance of the opening of the ticket wagon at a slight increase in price. Thousands of people found it more convenient to pay an extra dime than struggle in the crowds. For larger circuses, the fee for a year might be as high as $7,000.[17]

Similar to candy butchers but with larger denominations, the most commonly employed trick was to issue incorrect change, most often done during rush periods. In one instance, a $5 bill might be offered for two tickets, with the seller engaging the purchaser in an argument over price. Unable to compromise, the seller would return the money and the buyer would leave, realizing too late that what he thought to be his original $5 was instead only a $1 bill. If the buyer tried to pay in coin, the seller would complain he had too much silver and request paper money. In the ensuing exchange, the thief would confuse the patron as to what was actually paid, carefully pocketing the excess for himself. If a $10 bill was offered, the scalper drew four $1 bills and a $5 and asked the buyer to place his $10 on the money. With a slick movement, the sharper hid the $10 and the $5 in his pocket and the customer went away with the four $1 bills, not noticing the theft.

Money-takers might also be "forgetful" that a patron had already paid his entrance money and demand a second payment, or sell a 25-cent ticket outside the tent, then demand an additional 25 cents at the entrance, claiming the buyer had purchased a reserve seat pass worth 50 cents. Most never realized the deception until too late; others felt the small loss was not worth arguing over. When a "guy kicked up a rumpas," some fakirs smiled, pretended innocence and made correct change, but most ignored the loud cursing. If the victim complained to authorities, he rarely obtained redress, and when an operator was brought up on charges, the punishment hardly fit the crime. In 1882, a man operating a confidence game was charged $1.00 and costs.[18] Less frequently, the matter was brought to the proprietor, who might refund the difference on the stipulation the matter be kept quiet "so as not to injure the reputation of the circus."[19] Charging for infants and very small children was also against the norm, with the proprietors of Batcheller & Doris' ("Dorris") Show singled out as among the worst in that category.[20]

Nor were peddlers immune from ire, either from the practice of overcharging for the purchase of pop beer, peanuts, gingerbread and lemonade, or from "repossessing" items once sold. If a person carelessly dropped a souvenir, the odds were good that the vendor would quickly snatch it back and deny any knowledge of having sold it.[21]

In 1883, attaches of O'Brien's circus succeeded in giving short change to the tune of between $2,000 and $3,000 during a short sojourn in Emporium.[22] A year later, one industrious ticket seller paid $1,000 for his privilege and made $6,000 by being slick with his fingers.[23] Smaller concerns generally sold ticket privileges for $50 a month, which did not include room and board, so the seller had to make a good many "mistakes" to come out with a profit. The best generally cleared $300 to $360 at the end of each month.[24]

Penalties for ticket-sellers being "pulled" were typically light, and most got away with little or no fine.[25] In anticipation of such circus swindling, a merchant at Dansville strung a sign across his grocery store, perhaps not so humorously stating, "Don't go somewhere else to be swindled: walk in here."[26]

Another bold scheme was for a man to mount a box and begin selling tickets. He was on the up-and-up until someone passed him a large denomination bill. Shoving it in his pocket, the fakir jumped off the stool and disappeared into the crowd, pulling off his false mustache and walking into a dressing room where he changed clothes. He then returned to repeat his "trick" again and again. If, in the course of an evening, no one offered a $20 bill, he offered a free ticket to anyone who would, saying that the show did not want so much silver, as it was inconvenient to carry. Once in his hand, he was off to the races.

The "flim-flam," so artfully portrayed in the film *Paper Moon*, consisted of offering to pay for an item with a $5 bill and taking change. Before leaving, the confidence man would remark that he did not wish to carry around so much change and asked for a $10 bill, giving back the $5. Quickly departing, he earned $5 profit.[27] In another case reminiscent of *Paper Moon*, a sharper following Forepaugh's circus swindled a farmer. Under the pretense of making him an agent for a Bible company, he demanded the farmer pay $1,500 up front to show good faith. The man paid and the swindler disappeared.[28]

"Concert privileges" covered variety shows given after the tent and ring performances ended. These shows had no license or advertising expenses, promoting their acts by having bellowing fellows offer tickets during the main show. However, higher end side shows often had heavy outlays in salary, as specialty performers were often the highest paid. If attached to popular circuses, they provided handsome profits. On the other hand, events did not always turn out well. In 1871, after an exhibition of the Commonwealth Circus ended, the usual sale for the minstrels began. Being unable to sell a large number of tickets, the manager pocketed the receipts and summarily dismissed the assembly. A riot ensued, resulting in many serious injuries and the death of one man. Seventeen circus men were eventually arrested and held over for trial.[29]

Two other privileges of the type agreed to in smoke-filled backrooms crossed the border into illegality. The first conferred the right to pass counterfeit money to the "yokels" along the circus route; the second, known as the "clothes line privilege," allowed crooks to conduct petty thievery along the line of the circus march. In both cases, the thieves would be men personally known to the managers, and they paid liberally for permission to ply their trade and "work" the crowds.[30]

Circus men, of course, had their own language, communicating to one another in slang so as not to be well understood by the public at large. Everyone was called a "guy," the most important being "main guys." Countrymen were "jays" and "hayseeds," "blokes," and "suckers." Money was "bunt," "tin" or "cases." Beer and other drinks were "lush," clothing "togs" or "harness," food called "grub," conversation as "weedings," the verb "to see" rendered "stag," eyes were called "ogles," a hat either a "dicer" or a "cady," while ladies were spoken of as "dames," girls as "molls," an argument as "guff," clowns as "joeys," and bank bills as "flimsies."[31]

Some word origins were more obscure than others. The circus and theatrical term for a ticket was "squidge," supposedly stemming from the 1860s, when a Negro boy attempted to get into a Southern circus without any money. He was told he could not pass into the tent without money or its equivalent. The child went home and told his parents he could not go to the circus unless he got some money or a "squidgulum." When told of the tale, the ticket-taker was very much amused and passed it along, the name "squidge" or "squidgulum" rapidly catching on.[32] "Hey, rube!" was the term used to warn others of danger.

Counterfeiting and 3-Card Monte Men

Selling spurious tickets was one way a thief could make a good living at the circus. Counterfeiting was a better one. By the mid–1880s, photography had reached a high art, and it required little more than a camera to photograph legitimate tickets, and print and sell the forgeries as genuine. Edward Cloustou, of Boston, was considered one of the best in this line, but in 1882, he was caught in the act at Barnum's Circus in Schenectady, New York, and locked up.[33] Counterfeiting paper money was also a well-honed line during the 1880s, and newspapers were filled with stories of circus hangers-on who spent their entire careers following shows and dealing out bad money.

The usual trick was to purchase items of small cost and receive good money for bad, or to give bad money as change to unsuspecting patrons. Less common was bogus silver; in 1886, about $15 in false coin was reputed to be left behind by circus people in Brandon.[34]

False identities went hand-in-hand with passing bogus checks. In 1883, a man calling himself "Manning" presented himself at Bangor, claiming to be an advance agent of Forepaugh's circus. With suave manners and a fine appearance, he cashed checks for $35 and $250 at local banks, and afterwards ran off with a 16-year-old girl, whom he promised to marry. He was known to spend money lavishly in a reckless manner. After swindling the hotel at which he stopped, the adventurer escaped, with the law on his trail.[35]

The most common way confidence men passed bogus checks was to sell them "short" to greedy men hoping for a quick profit. At Fort Worth in 1884, two men traveling in the wake of the circus played the trick by offering a draft for $970 and taking $340 in return.[36] When the "pigeon" attempted to cash it for full value, he soon discovered his costly mistake.

The "sawdust boodle" or "counterfeit money dodge" was a similar game, whereby the operator arranged to sell counterfeit money to a dishonest local willing to "deal in the queer." The fakir showed a sample package, using good money to impress the victim of his forgery, even encouraging him to take it to the bank for inspection. When he was convinced, they agreed on a price, typically $40 good money on $100 counterfeit. If the fakir wanted a quick turnover, his confederate engaged the momentary attention of the greedy buyer while the "sharp" changed packages, substituting one filled with white paper or sawdust, leaving a good note on top so as not to be obvious. A third associate pretended to be a detective; his partner "spotted the law" and warned the buyer they were being watched. Urged to "take the boodle and skip," the mark did so. On a more elaborate scale, the fakir took an advance of $40, providing the buyer with a "note of hand" due some weeks ahead for whatever money was exchanged. The order, of course, was never filled.[37]

One of the most successful swindlers of the age was Ross Raymond, who started his career as a reporter for a San Francisco newspaper in 1872. Realizing his talent for swindling, he traveled eastward. In Cincinnati, he got into an altercation with circus owner John Robinson's son, who cut him badly. Making the best of the scar, Raymond went on to claim it was a war wound, finding that it improved his career.[38]

Candy fakers (or "fakirs") played a scheme whereby they laid packages of candy and some of their own money in the lap of their victim, promising that hidden within were valuable prizes. After the spectator was lured into thinking he might discover something of great worth, he took out his own money to pay for the packages. By changing and re-changing the money, "and giving out the appearance that he himself is rather muddled about making change," and getting the victim into a sort of "mesmeric trance," the "candy fiend" gathered up all the money and quickly disappeared in the crowd.[39] Lotteries where $5 bills were supposedly hidden in small packages (usually containing costume jewelry) lured smalltime gamblers into buying dozens of worthless ones in the hope of striking the prize. This was also called the "soap game," where players paid a dime for a cheap cake of soap in the hope their package contained money, a silver watch or other valuables. To prove the game was legitimate, occasionally a partner "won" a timepiece or the large denomination bill from the "most execrable of all swindlers, the soap vender."[40]

Larger lotteries promised prizes upwards of $1,400 for a mere outlay of $500. Convinced the chances of winning the big prize hidden in a jewelry or trinket packet was in their favor, countless fools were suckered into the game, either finding they had purchased something worth a few cents or being cheated by an incorrect counting of change.[41] Two swindlers often worked these games, the first being the soap seller and the second pretending to be "in the know" as to where the prize packet was hidden. The victim would buy a chance and, in exchange for the inside information, agree to split the winnings. He never won, and the con artist quickly disappeared.

If a man dared summon the authorities to report the fraud, it was likely another of the swindlers, this one dressed as a "collar" ("cop"), would appear and "arrest" the confidence man. That would be the last time the "chump" saw either of them.

Raffles were similar to lotteries, but in one instance, at least, the game was played "fairly." A showman raffled off a lion in every town he visited, opening the cage door and announcing "Take your prize" to the winner. The crowd stampeded away in terror, and the unlucky owner, finding the operator would not sell the cage, generally paid the circus man a second time to keep the brute.[42]

"Shuck" was the name of the sweat board game, played with dice and a green cloth marked 1–6. The game was played by "flipping the bones," or rolling the dice, the gambler betting the number thrown would correspond to that on which he placed his money. The game required little up-front capital, and a skilled fakir knew how to throw the dice (loaded or otherwise) so as to roll a number on which no coins rested, easily winning most hands from the unfortunate "gilly." A sharp fellow could earn $10 a day. If reported to the police, most merely disappeared into the crowd, leaving behind their board and a small pile of silver.

The "ring racket," worked around most big shows, consisted of one "operator" picking out a dishonest-looking man in the crowd and asking if he dropped a valuable ring. Upon receiving a negative reply, the two examine the "diamond," the fakir remarking that it must be worth $15 or $20. Since the finder was a stranger, soon to leave the city, he offers it to the "mark" for $3 or $4, suggesting the townsman turn it in for the reward or, if unable to find the owner, keep it for himself. The deal being made, the "winner" soon discovered the jewelry to be worth no more than 50 cents. Confidence men bought fake rings in bulk from Chicago.[43]

Another swindle was performed by four men: the most respectable was called the "doctor"; the second, possessing a sedate and dignified bearing, played the "judge"; the third was called the "sender"; and the fourth the "dealer." The judge pretended to be in the market for land and asked the land seller who he might borrow money from. Given that information, the judge treated the potential lender to wine and cigars and invited him to the circus. There they discovered the doctor winning heavily at banco. Having earned the loaner's confidence, the judge suggested they put their money together and bet against the game. The townsman goes to the bank and withdraws his money, secretly followed by the sender, who then alerts his cohorts. The townsman loses and is so distraught that the judge, who feels terrible that he let his "friend" down, promises to return in two weeks and make good his losses. In four cases out of five, the townsman does as bidden and does not report the scheme to the authorities, giving the men more than enough time to make their escape.[44]

Pickpockets, who in the early days of the circus, worked with the consent of, and shared profits with, the owner, continued to ply their trade throughout the century, but as independent agents. These "light-fingered gentry" typically "worked" the area around

Bigger was always better, and that philosophy pertained to the circus parade as well as the attractions. Proprietors spent lavishly to offer gilded, brightly colored carriages leading the circus parade into town. This was especially true before the advent of railroad circuses when companies traveled by road. Warned ahead of time by thousands of posters and hand-bills, citizens lined the streets. All business activity ceased until the parade passed — except for the "light-fingered gentry" or pickpockets, who found parades the best time to ply their trade. (*Janesville Gazette*, September 2, 1871)

the ticket wagon, where people clutched money in their hands for quick transfer, paying less attention to watches and pocketbooks. Otherwise, they canvassed the outskirts of the crowd (avoiding close quarters were they might be observed), taking advantage of people's divided attention when eager to move ahead in line.

Another place to pick pockets was during the entrance parade when men gathered along the route, eyes fixed on the attractions. Few were immune from the light-fingered gentry, as this note from 1872 recounts:

> The fellow that thought he was too smart to have his pocket picked came to the circus. He borrowed money to get home with.[45]

A straightforward-looking man standing by a glass case partitioned off like an egg crate operated the game of "dropcase." In some of the numbered compartments were money and dazzling jewelry. The player rolled the dice, hoping to throw a number corresponding to a prize. The odds on him winning a large prize were nil, as the dice were "rounded," always landing one or two above the lucky number. "Wheel games" (roulette) were played the same way, with the victim spinning a numbered wheel and claiming the prize corresponding to the number on which it stopped. The "peg and ball" involved a ball suspended by a string from a frame under which was a board. The object was to swing the ball and knock out the peg. When the board was level, this was achieved with some skill. However, as soon as the victim paid and attempted the task for real, the board was tilted slightly, preventing him from winning.[46]

Three-card Monte was probably the most common of the gambling games swindlers practiced at circus side shows. It consisted of a dealer indicating the target card (usually the Queen of Hearts or the Ace of Spades, viewed as lucky), then placing it face down on a table alongside two other cards. He then rearranged the three cards, and the player attempted to select the money card. If he did, he won; otherwise, he lost his bet. Play was often encouraged by having a confederate "win" to prove the ease with which money might be made.

Sleight of hand and the technique of "throwing" (where the dealer concealed a non-winning card in his hand and deftly substituted it for the money card when setting out the pasteboards) were so calculated that the player had no chance of winning. If a dealer chose to include the money card, he performed the same substitution if the mark picked the money card. Many monte operators worked with a partner whose job it was to convince the mark he could point out the money card for him. Sharpers were so good at playing the switch game they were virtually undetectable, even by other professionals. A sampling of newspaper reports says it all:

> • A country delegate lost forty dollars in an ambitious effort to bust the three-card monte man at the circus on Tuesday.[47]
> • Wesley Pontious, a respectable citizen of Dayton, had a little fun with the three card monte men the day Hilliard's circus stopped there. Wesley is out $240 in cash, and four millions in self-conceit.[48]
> • The festive "monte men" plied their little three card game at Bedford, while the circus exhibited there last week. Verdant citizens indulged in a little exercise with the delusive pasteboard, and several amounts they were out averaged from $50 to $200. Several persons in this county can sympathize with them.[49]

Another form of "gambling" displayed how there might also be an amusing twist to the outcome:

> "No more gamblin' for me," said a countryman on his return home from the circus. "I've had 'nough.'"
> "What kind of game did you tackle?" asked another countryman.
> "I dunno what it's called. A man standin' on a corner had a music-box and a little iron monkey fixed to it with a plate in his hand. As fast as I'd put a dime on that plate, the monkey would fire it under the box. I didn't win a single bet."[50]

If an organ-grinder and his iron monkey were not amusement enough, an 1884 report out of Tonawanda, New York, stated a firm there was making a "merry-go-round," described as "something after the principal of the 'flying circus,' with saddle-horses, carriages, animals, etc. on which about 250 people may sit comfortably. It is operated by a portable engine, and considerable speed can be attained." Interestingly, in 1897, when an old warehouse was cleaned up, hundreds of pieces of a merry-go-round were discovered, placed there by the inventor's widow, who hoped to find a purchaser for them.[51]

The "shell" or "pea game" was played the same as 3-card Monte using shells hiding a pea instead of cards. Another common name for the game in the 19th century was "thimble rigging," where thimbles concealed the trinket or prize. "Lung testers" offered less of a game than a challenge, giving "dudes" and "ruralists" the opportunity to see whether they could blow enough air into the tube to reach the top. Not uncommonly, older men who lost their edge performing higher risk circus schemes went into this line of work, donning the checkered pantaloons, high peaked hat and big mustache associated with the trade.[52]

One fraud involved con men writing to parents of children thought to have joined the circus demanding "burial money" for their "deceased" son or daughter. Another involved less than stellar performers, desperate to attract people to their acts, resorting to a scheme whereby they advertised for 50 or 60 men for a job not specified and having them apply for the position at an advance ticket wagon. Large crowds made it appear such an artist was in high demand and inspired others to buy tickets for their show.[53]

Nor were circus proprietors immune from working the enthusiastic to their benefit.

Like other "competitions" performed in the circus, outcomes were typically prearranged. W. C. Coup's New United Monster Shows appeared at Boston, April 25, 1881. Ticket sales must have been good, if this humorous notation from the *Chester Daily Times* (PA), January 3, 1881, is to be believed: "Adam Forepaugh, whose testimony must be deemed conclusive unless ample rebutting evidence is offered, says that Boston is the best circus city in the country. Boston is yet to be heard in her own defense." (***Boston Daily Globe***, April 24, 1881)

In the mid- and late-1880s, the idea was put forward to organize the best non-professional wheelmen, runners, jumpers, gymnasts and champions of every kind to participate in World Olympic games. Such displays became highly remunerative, providing the owners with a cheap form of entertainment, as it cost them no more than traveling expenses and outfits.[54]

Not to be left out were the patent medicine men who sold liver invigorators and consumption (tuberculin) cures. Both remedies were made of similar ingredients — water, whisky and one or two extracts. In Dayton, Ohio, one fakir sold 130 bottles of liver invigorator and 208 bottles of consumption cure in four hours on the principal that "when you appeal to a man's avarice you hit him hard; when you get him to thinking his liver is out of order, or that he is consumptive, you can take his last cent."

Glass bulbs filled with reddish fluid were purported to test blood, and "although any one of average sense must know they are frauds," even physicians lined up to pay their ten cents. In summary, "About the only thing connected with the outside of a circus which is not a fraud on the public is the electric battery."[55]

Other schemes had far more serious consequences. Numerous reports detailed how circus followers were known to send free tickets to farmers, robbing their homes when they knew the family to be away, or committing breaking and entering along entire streets the night the circus performed. Riots were frequently associated with drunken circus men, leaving townspeople injured and property damaged. Typically, the manager or members of the circus would raise bail, and the offenders slipped away with the circus. Less common, but by no means isolated, were reports of circus men committing outrages on young women. In such cases, local authorities hunted down the perpetrators. If the criminal were a white man, he might serve 18 months in prison; if he were black, threats of lynching followed his capture.

In the 1880s, it became fashionable for managers of large conglomerates to hire and loudly advertise detectives for the protection of their customers. These men usually perched atop wagons, not bothering to watch men's hands, for they could not see them. Instead, they studied faces, identifying those who looked ahead and behind themselves as likely pickpockets. Once they detected a theft, the detective jumped down and easily apprehended the thief because of his unawareness at being spotted.

A less-promoted form of protection involved the circus taking care of itself. Under an advertisement calling for 40 "bill posters" to augment an existing force of 60, the "Jobs Wanted" sought "good war workers, true to their employers, hustlers ready day or night for any emergency. Not afraid to fight for their side." The use of "hustlers" in this instance indicated initiation into a rough and tumble group used to protect circus property and personnel from attacks by circus goers, who seemed "to look upon show people as their natural enemies outside of the canvas."[56]

Constant travel took circuses to many out-of-the-way places, and newspapers were filled with stories of riots taking place. Some were occasioned by the consumption of beer and alcoholic sarsaparilla, the still palpable tension between races, and the persuasive aura lingering around traveling companies that they were filled with schemers, cheats and robbers. While posters and ads proclaimed "Moral Shows" (originally used in reference to menageries, but later expanded to prohibit acts performed by scantily-clad women, swearing, cussing, lewd behavior and ribald jokes), such was not usually the case. Men, stimulated or angered by what they saw, or incensed over crimes attributed to circus followers, were quick to pick fights. If not curtailed by private armies, the loss of valuable property and animals easily stretched into thousands of dollars, while numerous deaths by gunfire piled up horrific statistics.

22

The Original Monster Makers

When Barnum says Forepaugh's sacred elephant is a store elephant manufactured by a wild English shiek [sic] for the American market, we are bound to believe there is some truth in it, for the reason that there never has been any truth in anything else he has said, and even Barnum ought to tell the truth once in awhile.[1]

In 1848, P. T. Barnum bought a strange-looking horse, bereft of mane or any hair on its tail, but covered in a thick wool curling tight to its skin. When Colonel Fremont was lost among the snows of the Rocky Mountains, newspaper accounts expressing apprehensions for his safety made the soldier a household name. News soon came that the officer was safe, and Barnum seized his chance for a quick dollar. Issuing an advertisement that a "Nondescript or Woolly Horse"—part Elephant, Deer, Horse, Buffalo, Camel, and Sheep—discovered by explorer Fremont, was to be exhibited in New York, he created an instant phenomenon.[2] This "woolly horse" was not the first "freak of nature" to be displayed to a gaping American audience, but it set the tone. Colonel Benedict's papier-mâché whale and Major Bunnell's three-headed cow (1866) followed, thus perpetuating the exhibition of what showmen called "living curiosities."

"Wild men" were extremely popular in the late 1870s and early 1880s, one of the earliest being "The Wild Man of Afghanistan," who was, in actuality, a simple mulatto discovered by Tom Courtland in a poorhouse in Ulster County, New York. He was made up to appear exotic and earned a great deal of money for his promoter. Circus men were quick to copy "drawing cards," and as late as 1885, Barnum was advertising "Arada, the Wild Man" in what would be a continuing theme of trickery. "There never was a real, out-and-out, Simon-pure, gilt-edged wild man in any show in this country," stated Hank Stone, who made his living engaging attractions for circuses and side shows.

The key was "making" novelty attractions. Sam Ashbridge displayed a "wild nigger," or man-gorilla, complete with tusks, that drew crowds. The tusks were actually created for the poor fellow after his own upper teeth were pulled. The appliances came out over the lower lip, and for a single season the show was the talk of the town. "Zulus" were another drawing card during the 1880s, although they were more popular in Europe. The reason for the discrepancy stemmed from the fact "there were no natural points about a genuine Zulu that differed from those" of an American black. In 1883, Stone guessed there were a dozen Zulus brought to the country, but there were "enough on exhibition to form a regiment."[3] Stories dithered back and forth as to whether this or that company had "specimens from Zululand," evoking tests known as the Hartford experiment, from an 1880 trial where a Mr. Wilder discovered Barnum's Zulus were fakes by finding them ignorant of the Zulu native language.[4]

The Negress Princess Amazulu was billed as a "real Zulu woman," but after getting drunk in Scranton, Pennsylvania, she was sent back to Rhode Island, where she kept a beer shop. In 1882, the Great Circus advertised a group including "Cannibals, Zulu Kaffres and Modoc Braves." One of the best summaries of the situation came from the *Oshkosh Daily Northwestern*, May 6, 1880, when it stated, "Every circus this season will have its wild Zulu along, thus giving employment to many respectable colored men."

The "recipe" for making Circassian women, "the cheapest kind of curiosity," was even easier. After dying her hair, a brunette braided her tresses over long pins and saturated it with stale beer before retiring at night. In the morning it stood straight up on the head like porcupine's quills. (The beer imparted a wiry consistency without destroying the gloss or leaving it sticky.) Occasionally, a little shellac was added for stiffness. Barnum hired the first such, dressed in costume and purported to be a stranger from a foreign land. Actually, she was of French extraction and had toured France and Germany before being engaged by John Greenwood for Barnum.

When making "albinos," redheads were required. "A human hair is a tube, nearly white and transparent. The coloring matter is inside. When the coloring matter is bleached out of red hair it leaves a shade of white more nearly resembling the hair of a true albino."[5] Real albinos were rare: the white Moors of Madagascar were four true albinos; the husband was an Italian by birth and the wife an Australian. They had a little boy and girl, and were billed as the Lucosie family. On the opposite side, "artificial negroes" were manufactured in Paris by using iodide, "opening a brilliant future for young men as black servants, circus negroes, etc."[6]

For a time, Barnum's Tattooed Greek, Costentenus, the

7 Enormous Metropolitan Menageries! 7

UNITED!

50   Blazoned Cages of Wild Beasts!   50

S. H. Barrett & Co. do not clearly identify the creature headlining their 1882 advertisement (the best guess is that it represents "Bruno, the Low Comedy Bear"), but it looks suspiciously like the Cynocephalus exhibited by Lent's New York Circus in 1871. Perhaps the missing beast was finally captured and Mr. Barrett decided to keep the peculiar-looking little animal for himself. Not unlikely, the printer found the illustration, showed it to Barrett's agents, and they liked the mystery. Considering the same advert promised the company showed everything it advertised, it is probably fortunate few ever challenged such claims. (*Indiana Progress* [PA], June 8, 1882)

Captain Costentenus was the first tattooed man to be exhibited in the United States. His Burmese tattooing was done in blue, red, indigo and cinnabar inks. At the height of his career, the Greek Wonder made a fortune, but fame was fleeting. Eventually, the ink faded, and many other would-be stars copied his style, including Martin Hildebrand, who was tattooed by a jeweler named Decourcey. Hildebrand's tattooing took one year, the operating lasting 6 to 8 hours at a time. His principal pictures were on patriotic subjects, about 50 in number, and covered his entire body except the face. The entire process required more than 3,000,000 sticks. Those unwilling to spend the time, or endure the pain, attempted to find fame by using stencils instead of piercing. (*Boston Daily Globe*, February 7, 1881; illustration from *Cedar Rapids Times*, August 30, 1877)

"Living Work of Art," was a huge novelty with the public, but "he didn't hold his color well," eventually looking like "faded calico." The second tattooed Greek was Harry deCourcey, who was born in Brooklyn. He was tattooed by Martin Hildebrant especially for exhibition and was followed by the Tattooed Australian, whose body was "pricked" in Philadelphia. Women soon joined the fraternity, one of whom was alleged to have been brought to this country at great expense by John Robinson. The newspaper's comment: "Humbug."[7] Another solicited work at $40, but when it was discovered she was merely stamped with indelible ink, she offered to travel for $20. The actual operation of tattooing was extremely painful, and for an individual to be covered over half their body required three months.

A trick of another sort occurred in 1881, when W. C. Coup's New United Monster Show advertised the "Beautiful Flying LuLu, the Cloud Flyer," who hurtled through the air by means of a huge iron catapult, attaining an altitude of 90 feet, then descending in a semi-circle of nearly 200 feet. Seeing a woman shoot through the air had an almost supernatural feel, filling the audience with awe. As with Zoyara in the early 1860s, however, LuLu was actually a man. In show business since he was a boy, nearly his entire career was spent portraying a female gymnast; and although his sex was always a matter of speculation, he was, in essence, another circus "fake."[8]

In 1883, keeping it all in the family, R. R. Moffitt, "a handsome piece of Mosaic work," married Miss Leo Hernandez, the "Spanish Bearded Lady." The husband, past age 40, had previously been married to the "Russian Giantess," a 500-pound Venus who died of dyspepsia in 1880. Before that season ended, he married a "Circassian beauty" of Milesian [*sic*] extraction who died in 1882. John Geary, the bride's stepfather and circus sword-swallower, gave her away. The bride wished to shave her 3-inch beard before the wedding, but the groom feared her "curiosity" would not grow back and refused to allow it.[9] That made the Spanish Bearded Lady an exception, for most women in that line wore false beards.

Hannah Battersby was the biggest woman in show business, advertised at 720 pounds, but actually weighing closer to 500. Jessie Waldron, a 16-year-old, standing 6'6", followed at an advertised weight of 600 pounds, weighing in actuality closer to 450. Emile Hill was the lightest of the fat women, weighing a mere 250 pounds, but her diminutive 4-foot frame made her large circumference a great curiosity. Fat women were the easiest "curiosities" to pick up. By adding an immense amount of padding about the waist and the use of a bustle, they appeared much larger.

Lu Lu was a featured performer for the Sells Brothers' Millionaire Confederation of Stupendous Railroad Shows and Grand Free Roman Hippodrome. She was terrifically hurtled through the air from a huge iron catapult, attained an altitude of 90 feet, and then descended in a semi-circle of nearly 200 feet. This was "a Daring and Blood-Curdling Act, never before accomplished." (*Davenport Weekly Gazette* [IA], June 15, 1881)

The life of a circus Fat Woman, with constant travel and an unhealthy diet, had its consequences. Fannie Conley, a Negro advertised as weighing 624 pounds, died at age 34 from suffocation by turning over on her face during sleep and being unable to extricate herself on account of her weight.[10] Rose Leslie, 5'3", weighed 615 pounds and died at age 25.[11]

Living Skeletons were the result of disease and could not be manufactured. To the scientific mind of the 19th century, several "skeletons" were the result of consumption and dyspepsia, but the rest were inexplicable. Some of the earliest men to perform in this line were Calvin Edson (an accomplished violinist before being struck by disease) and Isaac W. Sprague. Colonel Martin P. Avery, formerly an adjutant of ex–President Hayes' regiment, was brevetted a brigadier general for bravery, sustaining severe wounds that never healed, rendering him a living skeleton. Skeletons were generally ravenous eaters, but Avery lived on ice cream and milk. These individuals were made to look thinner by dressing in black; in contrast, fat women wore light or bright materials to augment their flesh. It was not unusual to exhibit them together for contrast.

To qualify as a "giant," men had to be at least 7 feet high. To augment their natural height, they wore boots with high heels, high hats and long coats, creating the appearance of at least three more inches. Most giants exhibited in uniforms to make them seem imposing, raising their arms slowly to give them a massive air. In contrast, Captain Bates, of W. W. Cole's circus, typically appeared in a dress suit, although he occasionally posed in his Confederate uniform. Promoters generally felt Chinese giants, such as Chang, Barnum's Chinese giant (circa 1881), showed to best advantage because of their long gowns. This permitted a slight adjustment of their height, giving Barnum the leeway to claim his performer's height as nine feet.

The cost of contemplative show life could add 25 pounds a year to their weight. Goshen, the giant exhibiting with Barnum in 1883, had once been a slave in Owens County, Kentucky, and earned $100,000 when exhibiting by himself.[12] Forepaugh's giant, H. C. Alexander, amused people by lighting his cigar from the street gas light. Once on tour in London, he peered into a second story window and saw a man murder his wife. On Alexander's testimony, the criminal was convicted and hanged.[13]

By the 1880s, "Hindoos" became big side show attractions. In 1883, Barnum advertised "Savages — 6 Zulu Warriors, 18 Nubian, Pagans and Mohammedans." Forepaugh promoted "30 Moslem Mamelukes and Moors.... Followers of Mohammed; Believers in the Koran; Sun-burned Sons of Sahara." John Robinson offered a Troup of Hindoo Jugglers in 1881;

"Hindoo" Snake Charmers were always a draw for the circus. Most "Hindoos" were actually African Americans, although "Rajah Hajah," the "celebrated Egyptian snake charmer" was pure Irish. (*Eau Claire News* [WI], August 28, 1886)

while Sells Brothers had a Troup of Hindoo Magicians in 1883. Negroes usually played Hindoo and Egyptian roles. They were also selected to impersonate snake charmers, although Rajah Hajah, the celebrated Egyptian snake charmer, was pure Irish. An example of how tragedy turned to profit occurred at Madison Square Garden, when one of the snakes died of "sore mouth." The manager ordered it cut in half, and by the following day George O. Starr, one of the most experienced showmen, had concocted a story about Rajah's fearful encounter with a boa constrictor, only managing to save his life by a desperate struggle, resulting in the snake being severed.

One young snake charmer, billed as a Hindu, was a "smoked Irishman," the 19th century term for a child born of an Irishman and an East India mother. After traveling the world with his act, he came to America in 1884, and found work at Coney Island, where he received billing as the only snake charmer in the United States. Unfortunately, he was swindled out of his money by Bowery sharks and soon applied to the British consul for passage to England.[14]

Sword-swallowers were as common as paving stones, and only 1 in 10 were what they purported to be. The rest had trick swords or worked the process by sleight of hand. The best was a black man in Chicago who blew flames out of his mouth.

The key to being a popular "curiosity" was to possess a talent for conversation, honed by time and experience. Spectators liked talking to the living exhibits, and this drew the crowds. One of the best conversationalists in the business was Sir Walter Stuart, the man without arms or legs. He was very intelligent, and people seemed to forget they were talking "to a monstrosity."

Wages for such industry standards as fat women, skeletons, dwarfs and Circassian ladies were generally as low as $5 a week, the market being glutted with them. The greatest wage earner of the curiosities was Batcheller & Doris' Two-Headed Lady, Millie Christie, billed in 1883 as having "Two heads, two hearts, four arms and four lower limbs, united in a single body." They noted she had recently been engaged in Europe and brought back to America "at an expense of $25,000." Gliding through a graceful waltz before gaping audiences, Millie earned $500 a week, being the only one of her kind.

Millie Christie's attraction lay in the fact she was not offensive. Being repugnant was a drawback to Moral Circuses, and while the attraction called "The Man with the India-Rubber Skin" had the ability to pull out his lower lip and cover his forehead with it, he offended good taste, diminishing his value.

If one considered the life they led, being a circus "freak" had all the ear-markings of a terrible existence. For the select group billed as headliners, however, there may have been some compensation. Tom Thumb earned a "snug fortune," while Millie Christie made $60,000 to $75,000. Unfortunately, she lost the greater part of it backing the circus of a friend. Hannah Battersby and her skeleton husband were worth $10,000; Captain Bates and his wife accumulated $50,000 and had a fine farm in Ohio. If Lucia Zarete, the Mexican midget, had received all the salary she earned, she would have been worth $25,000. Not atypically, her manager, Frank Uffner, kept the bulk, minus the $4,000 to $5000 he paid her father. Eli Bowen, the legless man, had $6,000 in the bank, and Cooper, the giant, nearly that much.

The oft-expressed fraternal feeling among "curiosities" was typified by Hubert Ferrer, long known as the Toronto giant, and Edward Skimeer, the armless wonder. In 1865, when both were in their 70s, they lived together in a little cottage outside Bridgeport, Connecticut, where a colored man and woman, for many years a stableman and wardrobe keeper, looked after their wants. The four were all dependent on a small monthly assessment collected at every circus, museum and side show in the country.[15]

Dog-Faced Boys, Missing Links, Manufactured Freaks and Sacred White Elephants

In 1885, P. T. Barnum's Greatest Show on Earth advertised another living wonder, this one under the heading "Jo Jo, the Dog-faced Russian boy." Also referred to as the human Skye terrier, the unfortunate was described as having a very dog-like expression. To appease the skeptical and garner himself some free press, Barnum had the youth examined at Madison Square Garden by a number of eminent physicians. Stripping him to the waist, they revealed his back covered with hair, like that upon his face. He possessed only five teeth, two in the upper and three in the lower jaw. His attendant, it was stated, was teaching him to speak, and he was already able to utter a few words. The opinion of the doctors was that Jo Jo was "an extraordinary freak of nature."[16]

JoJo, P. T. Barnum's "Dog Faced Russian Boy," was one of the features in what was variously styled the circus freak show. In order to authenticate the child, Barnum had him brought to Madison Square Garden, stripped to the waist and examined by various authorities. The experts declared him "an extraordinary freak of nature." (***Boston Daily Globe***, June 4, 1885)

The same year, John B. Doris' Great Inter-Ocean premiered Krao as the greatest living wonder. With Charles Darwin's 1859 groundbreaking book, *On the Origin of Species*, required reading for the enlightened mind, this child, reputed to be the "missing link," drew huge crowds, quickly becoming the principal attraction of the circus. Far from a wild animal given to climbing trees and acting like a monkey, the little girl still presented a startling figure. Standing about three and a half feet tall, "with a very dark colored face, heavy black hair growing down on the forehead nearly to the eyes, large dark eyes, a flat nose, minus any cartilege [*sic*] whatever, and full lips," the girl had a slender figure — not graceful but gifted with agility and litheness. She was capable of turning her fingers backward until the ends touched the back of the hand and had two pouches in her mouth where she stored bits of food. She was articulate, spoke fluent German and English, and was capable of autographing her photograph.

She reportedly came from Siam, where she lived with her parents, being regarded by the natives as a mere curiosity. She was purchased for $360 and later sold for $45,000 to Signor Farini, the celebrated discoverer and exhibitor of curiosities. After being exhibited around the world, she ended up in the hands of Dr. George Shelby ("Shelly"), Farini's nephew. She was under contract with the Inter-Ocean for 30 weeks, earning $800 a week, presumably for Dr. Shelby.[17]

When the genuine article would not do, or if exotic animals were unavailable or too expensive, circus men turned to a New Yorker named Patterson, whose job it was to turn out artificial and occasionally living freaks. He made everything from a stuffed mermaid and sections of sea serpents to a five-horned ox and winged mules. One order required him to produce a cow with four horns, two of which grew out the eyes. To accomplish the feat, he glued the horns over the animal's eyes, the horns being taken off at night. Unfortunately for the cow, she became blind after a short time and had to be replaced. Patterson also set glass eyes in the middle of a bull's forehead or in his hips "so naturally that almost any one would be deceived."

Just after the war he received an order from the Lipman show in Cincinnati to make ten zebras out of mules. Patterson stenciled the mules in black and cream colored stripes over the course of six weeks and earned $500. The animals fooled the crowds, but after a week a rain storm washed out the coloring, making the beasts so frightful looking they had to be sent back to Cincinnati.[18]

During the 1880s, there was hardly any curiosity receiving more attention than the "sacred white elephant." P. T. Barnum had a "$200,000 White Elephant purchased from King Thebau"; W. W. Cole's Entirely New Colossal Shows exhibited "The Sacred White Faced Elephant of Burmah"; and the Great Forepaugh Show advertised "The Sacred White Elephant, 'Light of Asia,'" and later "Theodorus," the White Elephant. A typical story, such as that presented by the Inter-Ocean in 1880, ran that for thousands of years, the white elephant was an object of religious veneration in far-flung places like "the Empire of Ava." For 2,500 years, no sacred elephant was allowed to leave the kingdom; not until the conquest of the Ottomans in the east was such an animal known. After the English government forced its way into the interior of the empire, a single specimen was procured "at enormous cost" and brought to America, the sole property of the Inter-Ocean.[19]

Other circuses immediately jumped on the proverbial bandwagon and procured their own white elephant, although rumors were rife that "white" came as the result of paint rather than birth. To prove the authenticity of his own white elephant, P. T. Barnum invited doctors of divinity, scientists and medical men into Madison Square Garden in 1884 to prove his beast's legitimacy. The spectacle included "Tody" Hamilton, prince of Burmese elephant trainers. The first thing Hamilton

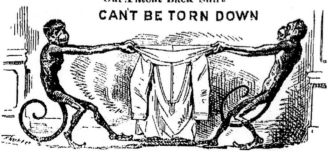

Freaks of nature were not solely the proprietorship of menageries. In this advertisement from 1883, a clothier promised his patent shirts could not be torn down by the proverbial "missing link." (*Alton Daily Telegraph* [IL], June 20, 1883)

The fascination in 1884 was the Sacred White Elephant. Heavily promoted by Barnum and Forepaugh, huge crowds flocked to see the animal worshipped in Siam, only to be disappointed when discovering "white" actually meant a lighter shade of grey. Barnum's constant bickering with Forepaugh as to whether the latter's elephant was truly a Sacred White Elephant or a whitewashed one disillusioned the public, and by 1885, they had all but disappeared. (*Olean Democrat* [NY], August 5, 1884)

did was to dip his fingers in water and rub the animal's hide, triumphantly remarking, "No whitewash there, gentlemen."

Barnum's partner, George F. Bailey, spoke a line of native dialogue, and Barnum gave a speech about Toung Taloung being the "best specimen of the Burmese sacred white elephant in existence." In true Barnum style, the guests then partook of some delicious buffalo sandwiches and expressed delight at their visit.[20]

It did not take long for the matter of "white" elephants to become a good joke, with the press reporting:

- When a western circus gets caught in a shower, the white elephant is locked up in a water-proof safe.
- The western circuses must be using a very inferior article of paint. Any good paint will stick for two years in any number of showers.[21]

Matters turned ugly in 1884, when Barnum charged the Forepaugh circus with having a "store elephant manufactured," and offered to back his judgment with a deposit of $20,000 to some local charity if he were wrong. The counter, of course, was that "white" did not mean "white," and an elephant might be white without actually being white.[22] This prompted more good humor, with the press noting, " If sacred white elephants are really scarce and command a high price in Siam, it would pay to start a sacred elephant factory in this country, and export sacred animals to Siam. It can't cost much for white wash and other chemicals."[23]

Accusations flew back and forth, but the truth of the matter was that white elephants truly were not white, as in "pure white," but rather of a slate color. Over-advertising saturated the market — having the sacred elephants stand on Burmese rugs, fastened by golden chains, attended by high priests and set under Oriental canopies — turning initial affection into indifference. People found they preferred the "commonplace, old-fashioned family elephant." The experiment did leave a lasting impression, however, as the expression "white elephant" (meaning a valuable property that is more expensive than its worth or usefulness) came into general usage. As it turned out, 1884 "was not a good year for sacred white elephants."[24]

Forepaugh's "Light of Asia," reputed to be the daintiest beast with a trunk, was sponged every morning with tepid sweet milk and fed half a dozen oranges. An hour after, it was given bread, milk and two dozen bananas, costing the proprietor $10 a day, as opposed to $2 a day for a regular elephant.[25] By November, after standing outside in the cold, the "Light of Asia" died of lung fever resulting from a cold, costing the circus $32,000.[26] By 1885, there was a near total absence of sacred white elephants, which some attributed to a glut of advertising and the heated exchanges between Barnum and Forepaugh, which killed the elephant as a business venture.[27]

23

Canvassing the Landscape

A bill was introduced in the Missouri legislature to compel circus managers to do as they advertise. This will have the effect of doing away entirely with the circus business.[1]

In 1875, the rural newspapers of North Carolina announced that the failure of a circus was due entirely to a lack of advertising, adding, "Let this be a warning to others."[2] P. T. Barnum would have agreed, observing in the same year:

> We can easily lose half a million of dollars next summer unless we can so awaken and electrify the country in advance, as to induce everybody to join in getting up excursion trains to hit the few centres where we exhibit. That's one reason why we send one of our immense tents ahead and literally "canvas" every town.[3]

Circus advertising was big business, and it was the goal of every manager to have boys "almost dislocate their spinal columns by twisting their heads to look at the circus posters."[4] Indeed, posters were gotten up with great skill and with no small degree of merit. They attracted universal attention, "for it is almost as gratifying to see a picture of a man in impossible positions, or a woman flying through half a dozen balloons, as to see the reality."[5] These advertising marvels, naturally, were exaggerated and augmented with bold colors. Jumbo the elephant was depicted as large enough to let a coach and four, with a driver high atop, roll under his belly; tricks were depicted "as well nigh incredible"; and there were always lions and tigers with their mouths so wide apart that one reporter was inspired to write, "No animal can enjoy life with his mouth stretched seven feet, even in a woodcut."[6]

Bright, eye-popping hues and images of the fantastic and the anatomically impossible abounded: A yellow lion with a blue mane and pea-green tail; a boa constrictor tied up in a double bow knot where the seven primary colors were mingled in heterogeneous confusion; a steed clearing a church steeple; a beautiful lady with shapely limbs hanging between two trapeze bars; a graceful man sitting on his elbows eating oysters with his heels.[7] Circus posters were better than life: they were imagination come true.

Placarding a city meant the circus was coming and nothing would stop the intrepid bill poster from getting out the word. The process of "billing the town" evolved slowly. In 1823, John Robinson sent out his agent on horseback, saddlebags containing all the bills necessary for six week's worth of advertising. The earliest posters had no illustrations, relying on bold print and italics to get their message across. Simple woodcuts, crudely engraved on pine or dogwood and painted in colors, depicting men forming pyramids and equestrians leaping through the air followed. These evolved into elaborate lithographs so detailed that likenesses of proprietors, neatly tucked in beside the circus name, elevated them to the status of performers.

That said, it is interesting to observe the almost circular path taken by circus advertising. By the 1880s, the idea (as opposed to the actuality) of "old-fashioned" circuses became more prevalent. Technology had radically changed the face of the world: electricity lit cities, telephones provided instant communication, bicycles replaced horses, and experiments in engine-propelled vehicles brought navigation across land and air to the brink of reality. Adults, always the mainstay of the circus, harkened back to simpler times. To connect with these childhood memories, simple block woodcuts and line drawings began sneaking into advertising, drawing back audiences who had not given a thought to anything but business for decades.

Well aware of the power of advertising, the entertainment industry set aside funds exclusively for this purpose. Traditionally, this meant "more is better," and scores of boys and men were locally hired to "hang paper," first in store windows (in exchange for complementary tickets, referred to as "window privileges"), then on sides of buildings, until every square inch was covered. Next came temporary billboards, erected by advertisers or enterprising townsmen who anticipated leasing the space. While a good idea in theory, in practice men occasionally got greedy, selling space to two competing circuses, causing rows. More competitively, an advance agent for Batcheller & Doris was caught pasting over the dates of J. H. Murray's circus, earning himself a $45 fine.[8] Things got so bad, the Wabash railway company issued an order forbidding brakemen from hanging circus posters in the cabooses.[9]

The "want of reverence in American advertising" certainly pertained to "handbill slingers." In 1881, a circus-advertising wagon followed the Memorial Day parade, only desisting when an irate participant pressed the point of a sword against the nose of his horse. The driver, incidentally, complained of an infringement of his rights to use a public highway.[10] Lightning bill-posters were renowned for their skill, muscle and agility, but amateurs had their own sense of pride. In 1878, one "poster" bit off the fingertip of a competitor, getting his cheek "chawed" in return. Worse, in 1872, a circus bill board blew down, severely injuring an old lady. Reaching to extremes, one circus agent distributed a lot of his most handsome bills to prisoners in the county jail, which the local newspaper observed "added insult to injury."[11]

It was possible to go overboard, and editorialists struck back

It was a common joke in the 19th century that circus artists always managed to capture the menagerie animals at the exact moment they opened their mouths to roar, one wit noting that it was cruel to depict lions and tigers and hippos with their jaws so extended, even if they were only drawn on paper, as it must be very tiring for them. (*Waterloo Courier*, September 11, 1878)

by complaining that men "without character or standing" so deceived the public by "glowing announcements and flourishing posters" that the public began to look upon traveling exhibitions with suspicion.[12] In 1883, such anger at being deceived led to violence when a mob used breech-loading guns and revolvers to express their dissatisfaction when O'Brien's circus did not perform as advertised. During the altercation, Charles Henderson, one of the proprietors, was fatally struck in the eye and head, and a driver shot from his wagon.[13]

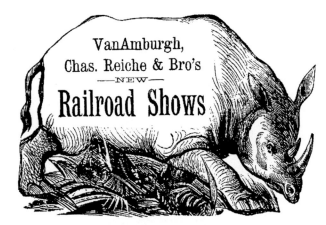

The Circus is First - Class

Circus men and menagerie animals were not the only ones to travel by railroad. Huge exhibitions had their own advertising agents, and these men also went by rail, in lavishly decorated, specially designed cars. Proceeding the circus with an army of "posters," they "billed" every available window, barn and building with colorful advertisements, going so far as to construct their own billboards for greater-than-life depictions of circus art. (*Elyria Republican* [OH], August 6, 1855)

Posters were applied with paste (thus giving rise to the name "paste brigade"); and it required four barrels of flour, the primary component, to cover Pittsburg with circus posters. Unfortunately, glue did not dry during rainy days, and after a storm, hundreds could be found scattered around the city. This worked out to Col. Stambaugh's advantage in 1883, when he demonstrated a sample of his paste on Van Amburgh's bill posters. They were so impressed that 300 barrels were ordered for distribution out west.[14]

Once the circus had gone, towns were left with hundreds of posters, bill boards and fences erected solely for advertising. The *Lebabon Daily News*, Pennsylvania, lamented the fact and demanded the City Commissioners speedily remove the eyesores around the park, which was made so desolate that birds forsook it and the grass turned yellow.[15] When not promptly removed, posters were prone to being defaced, eyes gouged out and plugs of tobacco shoved into noses. (In fairness, political faces were even more likely to be ruined than those of circus men.)[16] For those that survived, there existed both a nostalgic and financial value. Lithograph speculators gathered up the 15-cent posters and sold them back to the circus at half price. Circus companies cut off the old dates and reused them. An enterprising collector could earn $30 to $35 a day for his efforts. This had its amusing side when semi-literate assistants relied on phonetic spelling, in one instance writing "Ft. Wain" instead of Fort Wayne.[17] Going one better was the advertisement promoting "wacks figgers" for W. W. Cole's circus.[18] Which leads into one of the better puns associated with posting. A "paste mixologist," ignoring a sign reading "Post no bills under penalty," was confronted by the irate owner of the fence, who demanded whether he could read. Answering in the affirmative, the bill poster continued, "I'm posting over penalty."[19]

Being a bill poster must have had its attractions. In 1879, Dr. James L. Thayer, the circus proprietor, became manager of the Pittsburgh Bill Posting and Distributing Company.[20]

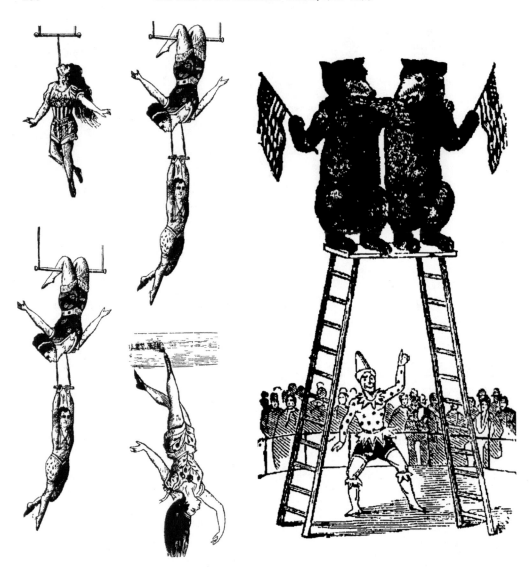

Left: P. T. Barnum's 1875 Great Roman Hippodrome was part of an overall exhibition that "10,000,000 Satisfied Auditors [spectators] the Past Year" witnessed. His Amphitheatre held 15,000 people, which cost from $1,000 to $3,000 to build at every stand. That included a racing track one-fifth mile in length, acres of wide-spread canvas with the largest seating capacity in the world. Attractions included an army of men, women and children, hundreds of thoroughbred imported horses, gilt and gold besprinkled chariots and tableau-cars, solid silver and jeweled armor, glittering paraphernalia and the most elaborate, brilliant and expensive costumes ever beheld. (*Freeport Journal* [IL], July 28, 1875). *Right:* "We stop the press to announce the advert of Yankee Robinson's Consolidated Shows," ran the lead to an 1869 newspaper article. Editors were only too glad to offer positive press to circuses, as they often "wanted to appropriate nearly one whole page of our paper" in order to "convey to the minds of our readers something of an approximate idea of the magnitude of this vast consolidation." Getting out the word was big business, and circus proprietors spent small fortunes "posting" a town with literally thousands of handbills and posters, some the size of a barn. (*Warren Ledger* [PA], July 1, 1869)

With a wink and eye toward the reputation of posters, if not the "poster-ers," Matt Morgan, caricaturist, tired of exaggerating, resolved to confine himself to strict truth and moved to Cincinnati, agreeing to draw pictures for circus bills at a salary of $200 a week.[21] Former clown Richard Burden, another man familiar with exaggeration, left the profession to become a city bill-poster in Winnipeg.[22]

Gimmicks, Ploys and Mystic Advertising

In the middle of the 1880s, circus advertising utilized creative ways to get out the word on the cheap. One of their most important jobs was to develop a rapport with local newspapermen. One scheme involved informing a reporter that the circus boss required a good man to write up star notices at $75 a week, all expenses paid. The agent then showed a letter he had written to the circus manager, strongly recommending him for the job. The letter went into the mail but was always incorrectly addressed. The agent plied the same game across the state, leaving behind reporters filling their paper with circus news favoring his "employer" that cost the concern nothing but a few lies.

Close association with newspapermen garnered positive press. After taking out paid advertising and thus earning good will, it was not uncommon for reviews to be written in the newspaper office under the supervision of the advance agent.[23] These were based on laudatory reports the agent kept in a portfolio and appeared nearly verbatim from city to city. Or reviews were merely reworked advertising copy with complementary statements added by local reporters. This laudatory technique was justified under the philosophy, "There is positively no poor whisky — though some whisky is better than others."[24]

Occasionally, however, the tables would be turned. When the manager of a circus asked the *Denison News* (Texas) to do some advertising and accept tickets instead of money, the editor did not dicker, writing, "Excuse us if you please. Dead-head tickets to the circus are hereditary perquisites of newspaper men."[25]

A "stake-driver" for Barnum used another ploy, slapping bills on tombstones in Presbyterian and Methodist cemeteries. If discovered by a preacher, the excuse would be, "Them's all Bible scenes, anyhow, and represents Noah getting' his menagerie together in the ark." The ploy did no harm, as neither denomination went to the show, Midwestern towns primarily being composed of "'Piscopalians and Unitarians."[26]

Chalk artists were one of the earliest forms of advertising. In describing the "old circus," Peter Sells, one of the famous Sells Brothers, remarked that during the era of Dan Rice's Floating Palaces, his agent, Charles Castle, would float down the rivers from Pittsburg to New Orleans, using only a piece of chalk. Appearing two weeks before the circus arrived, he announced its coming by using chalk to write the dates on warehouses, ferryboats and wherever he could find room.

An offspring of the chalk artist was the soap artist, who covered a shop window with soap film and then ornamented it with elaborate script and images promoting circus attractions. The best could decorate a full-sized plate window in half a minute.[27]

Another creative method was used by a western circus who distributed primers for children, complete with illustrations of all the animals contained in the menagerie. When the show arrived, the value of the advertising became apparent in the eagerness of the young ones to see the exhibitions.

Predating the Burma Shave advertising by nearly a century, "mystic advertising," as it was called in 1871, used "dodgers" to attract attention. For example, the first posters would pose a question: "What is it?" The following day others would appear: "Why is it so precious?" A third might continue, "Why does a baby travel with a trunk?" The answers would be revealed by the last, describing a cute baby elephant, with a trunk for a nose, traveling with the Great London Circus.

An advance agent on his way to Galveston in 1891 perpetrated one of the most outlandish schemes on record. Hoping to obtain some free advertising, he gathered two-dozen empty pop bottles and bought the same number of steaks from the ship steward. Rubbing the meat with arsenic, he wrapped them around the bottles, incidentally carrying circus bill posters, and tossed them overboard, calculating that sharks would devour the food, be poisoned and float ashore. He anticipated that they would be cut open, the bills found and the entire thing written up in the newspapers. The plan worked perfectly, except that upon reaching the city, he was met with notes from every editor in town, offering to write the story "with a snap camera cut of the shark" at the regular rates.[28]

Perhaps the best cheap advertising was to burn an old circus tent and send a note to the newspapers, detailing its (exaggerated) cost, the "rescue" of animals, the heroism of the staff, the name of the show and subsequent tour dates.[29] Circus writers easily constructed stories of escaped lions and the extraordinary measures taken to re-capture them, throwing in a "shower of lead" or a child eaten by the wayside for added measure. Or they might describe a canvas man who turned out to be a British nobleman in disguise; an elephant fight, dripping with gore; or a tragic accident of a trapeze artist who heroically dragged his/her crippled body through the remainder of the performance.

Particularly good articles were printed on soft paper in the general style of a newspaper story. Columns of market reports were printed on the back of this slip, and then the edges were scissored in a careless, zig-zag style, giving the finished product the appearance of a truthful article clipped from a legitimate paper. The advance agent, well supplied with these bogus clippings, passed them out to editors in every town he worked. The consequence was that the article was widely reprinted, and readers flocked to the show to see the lion that escaped, the pugnacious elephant or the injured artist.[30]

Fabricated stories occasionally took on a life of their own. In 1874, an advertising man issued the statement that his "mammoth, golden, Semiramisian band-wagon ran over and killed 'Black Eagle,' the last chief of the once-powerful Iroquois tribe."[31] It was later picked up and reported as fact by various exchanges. Unfortunately for historians, it is impossible to distinguish the legitimate from the spurious unless collaborated or denied by subsequent reports. Typical of such a case was the report of the "Wild Santa Barbara Children." Details of their discovery (in Decatur, Illinois), names (John and William Henry), descriptions (short, deformed, goggle eyed) and exhibitor (Prof. Athous and his Great National Museum) were provided, down to the "red-hot irons" kept by the cage in case they escaped. First described in the *Decatur Republican* on March 20, 1873, the "Santa Barbara Children" became humorous local legends, reappearing in the *Daily Republican* (Illinois) on February 9, 1874, when the children were reputed to be "at large," and again in the *Republican* in 1886, when a local citizen was arrested for "using language offensive to John Henry Evans, one of the wild 'Santa Barbara Children.'"

"Show literature," as it was called, had its own cheering section. Labeled "a standard of modern journalism," circus posters were used to rebuff "Conceited Britishers," who

The Mirimba Band of P. T. Barnum's Greatest Show on Earth, 1886, was described as "Mystics of Intensely Interesting Features," collected at an Enormous Expense. "Mirimbas" were not the only "interesting" people collected by Barnum. In 1893, J. B. Gaylord, long a foreign agent for the showman, "collected" cannibals from Queensland, Australia. He paid £20 a head, knowing the natives would be "perfectly satisfied with their condition as long as they had plenty to eat and drink and all the tobacco they wanted. They were also very fond of rum, and, in consequence of "being treated too well," seven died on the voyage to America. Occasionally, "interesting" meant fabricated, as in the case of the "Wild Santa Barbara Children." (***Galveston Daily News***, June 11, 1893; illustration from ***Logansport Daily Pharos*** [IN], July 22, 1886)

claimed America had no literature. Toward that end, a writer who described a hanging with the words "Fatal sore throat" was urged to give up journalism and go into the circus poster business. Even the weight of a brain belonging to a deceased poster writer was compared favorably to that of Napoleon and Daniel Webster, as it required a "genius" to perform such a task.[32]

Which is not to say writing circus advertisements was easy. In 1891, a specialist in the field who had just prepared 600,000 words for Barnum's show observed:

> People have become so accustomed to the big adjectives that go with the circus
> bill that a moderate statement of all the wonders to be seen within the big tent
> would not attract attention. They are an important part of the show, but it is very
> exhausting work this year finding adjectives big enough.[33]

In the latter part of the 19th century, circus proprietors went out of their way to prove the expression "there is no such thing as bad press" false by liberally attacking their com-

W. W. Cole's 1876 "Declaration" in celebration of the centennial of the American Revolution speaks for itself: "When in the course of human events it becomes necessary for Managers of Show Business to dissolve the Old Fogy Bands which have connected them with Obsolete ideas, and assume among the inhabitants of this great nation an Independence of action. We hold these truths to be Self Evident: that all men are created equal; that they are endowed by their Creator with certain inalienable rights: that among these are life, liberty and the pursuit of HAPPINESS IN SHOW BUSINESS. That to secure these rights, Plans are instigated among Showmen, deriving their just power from the consent of the Show Going Public. That whenever any style of show becomes hackneyed it is the right of any Wide Awake Manager to inaugurate a new Departure." To that end, Cole promised to ignore the old "thumb marks of Show History" and create an entirely new organization with a "Brand New Show on a Stupendous Scale." (*Indiana Progress* [PA], August 24, 1876)

petitors in the newspapers. One incident in 1883 sparked a lively debate between P. T. Barnum and W. W. Cole. After Cole outbid Barnum at auction on a huge elephant, the latter took exception to the former's advertising claim that "Samson" was the largest Asiatic elephant in captivity, protesting in the *Sentinel* and extensively distributing handbills arguing the fact. Responding to Barnum's claims as being "false as Hades," Cole wrote to the *Daily Free Press* (Wisconsin), reiterating his claim with relish by noting the acquisition had been a thorn in Barnum's side since his agent failed to purchase the animal. Paying only $6,000 because of a false rumor "from disinterested parties" regarding the brute's docility, Cole met Barnum's challenge to "put up or shut up" by offering $25,000 for any animal the equal of Samson, giving the Union National Bank, Chicago, the Bank of Metropolis, New York, and the Third National Bank, St. Louis, as holding his money to meet the offer.

Chiding Barnum for his unsuccessful attempts to either loan Cole his animals "for a certain sum of money" or to become partners with him, he asked why Barnum failed to compete with him along his published route and wondered if the proprietor would bring his actual show or substitute two or three concerns that merely used the Barnum name in their advertising. The letter went on to enumerate Cole's acts as being the best in the world, concluding with:

> Advertise your show honestly. Do not cover my bills, do not circulate posters telling people I am not coming, nor tear down my lithographs and bills. Attend to your own business honestly. There is room enough for all.[34]

The following year, Barnum may have derived some satisfaction from an incident involving Samson in Hailey, I. T. (Indian Territory). The elephant severed his chains, attacked his keeper, hurled aside a cage of lions, killed two horses and then attempted "to paint the town red." The circus people begged the townsmen to shoot the monster, and thirty bullets were later found in his hide after he was eventually roped and quieted. Damages amounted to $10,000.[35]

Throwing dispersions on the competition as a whole was another oft-used ploy, forcing proprietors to respond in their own advertising. In 1882, this addendum appeared:

> MIND THIS. There is a concern advertised to come here before the arrival of the Great Forepaugh Show, which claims to be a consolidation of "5 enormous shows," and asserts that it uses more cars, has more men, horses, etc. than the Great Forepaugh Show. It also asserts, in its frantic efforts to keep from starving for want of patronage, that the Great Forepaugh Show has been cut down, reduced, etc. The above statements are ALL INFAMOUS LIES.

The notice was followed by a comparison:

So-Called Enormous Shows	Great Forepaugh Show
17 Flat Cars	27 Flat Cars
3 Stock Cars	6 Box Cars
3 Box Cars	10 Stock Cars
3 Passenger Cars	*6 Passenger Cars*
31 cars in all*	49 CARS in all

(Capitals used in original, and columns printed out of order; *Forepaugh's arithmetic was also slightly askew, giving the "Enormous Shows" too many Cars.)

As hard as it is to believe, before the turn of the century street advertising was done by electricity. The route of the electric line through the business section of a city was adorned by red and white banners suspended from the cross guy wires of the electric system. Two banners were attached to each wire, one on each side of the street, so that as far as the eye could see were gaily illuminated circus banners.[36]

Bill Posters, Advertising Brigades and Mer-men

In 1871, there were about 275 professional bill posters (who employed from 2 to 20 men each), who earned, in whole or part, their living from the trade. To "bill a town" was an expensive undertaking: per thousand, an engraving with one illustration and a sole color cost $15 to $20; multi-colored posters ranged from $22 to $35; larger, more elaborate posters, engraved on blocks (including the cost of engraving), cost $120 to $150. A circus had to spend from $200 to $300 to bill a town, depending on how long the billboards were occupied.[37] A bill-writer received a similar salary to that of a press agent, making the tidy sum of $50 to $100 a week, with top men receiving as mush as $200 a week.[38]

Newspaper advertising also consumed great expense. For the season of 1879, Burr

The concern of Barnum & Co., Den Stone's Colossal Circus and Howe's Great London Circus offered this enticing illustration of two equestriennes competing in a chariot race. Barnum, who appreciated a joke as well as anyone, would have appreciated this story, written in vernacular. "Lions B. C.: Lecturer: This movin' scane, gintelmen and ladies, represints 'Daniel in the Lions' Den.' This is Daniel betwixt the lions. Auditor: Be them wild lions or circus lions? Lecturer: I pity the ignorance of the like of yez, sor. This was B. C., before circuses." (*Newark Daily Advocate* [OH], August 6, 1886; illustration from *Alton Weekly Telegraph* [IL], September 24, 1874)

Robbins paid $7,150. An average of 400 feet of paper was "billed," and 300 feet of boards erected every day. Over six months, 143,000 sheets of colored paper were used and 858,000 programs distributed. Paste, in the form of 14,300 pounds of starch, was utilized to affix the advertising, making the $6,020 spent in licences seem almost paltry by comparison.[39]

Whether true or not, the story of a bear in the newsroom "bears" repeating. It was common knowledge that itinerant circus companies paid poorly, and the advertising editor who did not get paid in advance likely did not get paid at all. Such was the case in 1874, when the Great European Circus and Metropolitan Caravan tried to escape town without paying the printer. The sheriff attached the Rocky Mountain bear for a $12 debt, and it was brought, caged, to the composing room, where it consumed $15 worth of meat in two days. On the third day, the bottom fell out of the cage, and as the bear seemed to want to roam around and inquire into the business, it was thought wise to allow him. He remained there a week, preventing the *Argus* from issuing any newspapers. The bear finally climbed out a window and sat on the roof. During its foray as "editor," it upset the type, soaked itself in ink and then rolled over every square inch of floor. Thereafter, a new policy went into effect whereby advertising in the *Argus* was to be paid in advance.[40]

The 1880s witnessed the proliferation of the "Advertising Brigade," so-called because armies of agents traveled in specially designed railroad cars. O. J. Boyd was in charge of O'Brien's car, a marvel in its own right. Handsomely painted outside, the interior contained large drawers on either side, built in size and shape to contain various kinds of paper. Boyd had a private office with a marble-topped desk, surrounded by easy chairs and a folding berth. Closets, filled with work and street suits, fit in odd corners, while wash rooms, desks for his assistants, a paste room, a flour room and a boiler for furnishing steam to make paste occupied the rest of the space. The car carried fourteen tons of paper, which lasted only ten days; while a barrel and a half of flour was used every 24 hours in making paste. Billboards aggregating 1,000 feet in length by 12 feet in height were covered daily.

For the 1883 season, O'Brien's circus used 200 tons of printed matter, 300 barrels of flour, and pictorials covering 200,000 feet of board. The show advertised in 2,219 papers, and bill posters traveled 28,800 miles around the country, posting bills in 9,000 small towns. This effort resulted in the sale of 592,117 whole (adult) tickets, 319,270 children's tickets, 53,903 complementary tickets and 6,270 clergymen's tickets. The show traveled 11,306 miles, visiting 24 states and Winnipeg, showed 185 days and never missed an advertised stop.[41]

Barnum's shows used three gorgeous advertising cars, one of which burned near Stevensville, Canada, in 1881. This state-of-the-art railroad car, built by Barney & Smith in Dayton, Ohio, measured 63 feet long. James Walker, New York, painted the exterior at a cost of $5,000, one side depicting a pageant scene and the other a grouping of animals. The interior was furnished in black walnut and ash. Its loss was placed at $20,000, exclusive of $5,000 worth of advertising bills.[42]

It was often written that viewing circus art, depicting roaring lions, performing leopards, agile female gymnasts and creatures never seen on this or any other planet, was almost as good as going to the Big Show. Such sentiments would not have pleased circus proprietors, who depended on ticket sales to meet their bottom line. However, they spent heavily on splashy posters and handbills to advertise their coming, and the artwork admirably served the purpose. (*Janesville Gazette*, July 17, 1876)

Not every printing house was capable of reproducing the size or colors required for circus posters. In the 1870s, the *Buffalo Courier* provided such a service on an extensive scale, having 30 cylinder presses turning out multi-hued circus bills. They also maintained a poster show room, providing extensive viewing of their work.[43] In 1883, Strobridge Lithographing Company, Cincinnati, created for Cole's circus the largest lithograph ever printed as a show bill. Seventy feet long by twelve feet high, it depicted ten main scenes, including 45 acts, with Samson the elephant as large as life. Each copy took 105 sheets of paper and used six colors. The cost was $10 each, and Cole ordered 1,000 copies.[44]

A small, old-fashioned studio on Houston Street, New York, was a unique place circus men went to have huge posters created. From this shop, two brothers oversaw the creation of circus illustrations from January until May, did painting work for seaside resorts and traveling shows in the summer, and filled orders for museums and fairs in the fall.

Circus art ranged anywhere from the size of a four-story house to a 22-foot painting. White muslin canvasses were stretched on frames and artists stood on scaffolds, several painting and another sketching charcoal outlines. One order to grace the western door of an aquarium included a life-sized dolphin and sea lion, accompanied by a human female, "entirely innocent of clothing" from the waist up and fish from the waist down. Beside her was a mer-man, smoking a cigar and watching her drink champagne. Another project promoted a "facial artist," first revealing his normal countenance and then, beside it, portraits of the same face in caricature of a parson, Dutchman, schoolboy, Irishman and temperance lecturer. Chang, the giant, was painted 30 feet high, dwarfing normal people, who reached only to the tops of his shoes.

In answer to the popular circus advertising scheme "What Is It?" artists depicted a "dead brown" individual with limbs at highly impracticable angles, balancing a white-spotted Negro boy on his head.

One request to the proprietors from P. T. Barnum read:

> Send us three more twenty-two foot paintings. One of Maori giant, a big Indian
> with spear, shield, helmet, and feathers; another of fat woman — make her very fat;
> third of shadow man — he's a living skeleton; don't give him any substance. Yours, etc.

The largest of the scenes required a mere two-and-a-half days to complete and cost the buyer $140. Ordinary sizes of 10 or 15 square feet ranged from $50 to $75. The brothers kept a library of books on natural history to assist in their depictions. If given an order to paint aborigines, for example, they researched their collection to give the figures correct features and surround them with appropriate foliage[45] (designing, it would seem, a more accurate picture than the "creations" actually playing the characters).

By 1885, there were nine major printing establishments doing circus work, located in New York, Chicago, Boston, Detroit, Cleveland, Buffalo and Cincinnati. With 200 companies, ranging from top-of-the-line circuses to one-horse concerns, as well as theaters and individual stars purchasing their own advertising, the total spent per year on show work reached $500,000. When times were flush, profits soared, but in lean years much printing was done on credit. Not infrequently, printing houses were obliged to furnish money to keep losing concerns afloat, thereby becoming virtual partners in the management. In 1896, Lemen Brothers circus passed into the hands of the United States Printing Co. of Cincinnati, the printing company having a claim of $12,500 for paper used during the season. In a reverse scenario, the bill-posting firm of Broadway & Treyser sold its entire interests to Burr Robbins, W. W. Cole and R. C. Campbell, circus managers, who then conducted business under the name American Advertising and Bill-Posting Company. [46]

Waxing philosophical, the *Boston Journal*, with a touch of poignancy, summed up the circus poster, and perhaps the heyday of the circus, by observing:

> Today it glitters in the sun, resplendent with more colors than all the colors of the spectrum produce ... and the eyes of all men behold and marvel at its magnificence. Tomorrow ... it will be torn down ... by the loud-yelling rag and bottle gatherer, or the melancholy goat ... swallowing with ignorant relish, not only Jumbo and all his associates, the Zulus and the "Behemoth of Holy Writ," but also the genial Mr. Barnum himself.... Verily the circus poster is a type of human life, which today exalteth [*sic*] itself and tomorrow is the victim of swift-pursuing and sharp-toothed fate.[47]

24

The Allurement of
Sawdust and Tights

*Senator Norwood Said: Ladies and Gentlemen and Fellow Citizens: I hope you will not
consider me fickle because the night of the speaking was changed. It was fixed for tomorrow
night, but was changed on account of the circus. I am not able to speak against four elephants,
twenty-four painted horses, and a brass band. I understand John Robinson's circus would
break up a Methodist camp-meeting, and I thought discretion the better part of valor.*[1]

Second only to Gypsies stealing children were the tall tales told of circus men: how
they abducted children, hid runaways, apprenticed and occasionally abused juvenile performers, and eloped with girls and women. In fact, so closely associated with circuses were
these stories that scarcely a month went by without reading reports of such incidents. It
was certainly true that the wandering circus life held a strong appeal and drew people from
every station in life to join the ranks. Some thrived and went on to have successful careers;
some repented their rashness and abandoned the pursuit after a few weeks. Children, literally sold by their parents or apprenticed to the circus, endured grueling, often dangerous
lives. Females who abandoned the comfort of their homes on the promise of marriage by
sweet-talking performers seldom thrived. Heartbroken parents sought out their offspring,
encountering mixed results; enraged spouses employed the long arm of the law for redress.

How many of the incidental stories are true is hard to say; one story begot another,
and reporters were not above creating sensations to sell newspapers and lurid magazines.
On the whole, it is likely most were factual to some degree, and they paint a picture of
the evolution of a country, and the young and old who inhabited it.

The most common circus incidents were those involving runaways. A typical notice
ran:

> BOYS MISSING. — Two boys aged nine and eleven, named Alexander and Thomas
> Barton, left their home in Burlington before breakfast on Friday morning. They were
> last seen at the circus on that day, and are supposed to have followed it west. Alexan-
> der has dark hair and brown eyes, Thomas black eyes and hair. Alexander wore a
> light check roundabout and white hat, Thomas had a palm leaf hat but no coat.
> Both boys wore yellow pants. Any information of their whereabouts will be grate-
> fully received by their parents.[2]

A snippet of news items covering a 25-year period includes: Andy Sullivan was a
typesetter when the urge bit him and he became a jig dancer, traveling with Orton's Circus.

Employing traditional circus superlatives, W. W. Cole's Great New York and New Orleans Museum offered "The Most Gorgeous Street Pageant Ever Seen!" Admission in 1878 was 50 cents for adults and 25 cents for children. Although it was a childhood passion to try and slip in for free, the *Daily Journal* (Indiana), June 4, 1882, noted, "'In the bright lexicon of youth there is no such word as fail,' says Bulwer, but Bulwer never tried to crawl under a circus tent." (*Postville Review* [IA], May 18, 1878)

A young girl ran away to join the circus and leaped from a train going 30 miles an hour to avoid capture; her hoops saved her life. Two young, respectfully connected girls from New Orleans were taken away by a woman calling herself Mrs. Robbins; she took them to Cincinnati, making great promises if they would learn circus riding and minstrelsy. Two young ladies of Tipton, Iowa, ran away with the circus last week, not being able to resist the allurements of sawdust and tights. A widow from Bellefonte is seeking her son, Samuel Hartman, who attached himself to Robinson's Circus, since which time nothing has been heard of him. Miss Naonie Horne, a good looking girl of 17, joined Sell's Circus; her father telegraphed the chief of police in Atlanta, who arrested and returned her. She says she will run away again. Joseph Kesell, aged 16, ran away with Forepaugh's Circus; it is generally believed the boy is concealed by parties connected with the show.

Occasionally, the wayward would be found: A minister recognized his brother at Chillicothe, Missouri, after a separation of 30 years — he was a circus clown. Among the actors in a circus, a lady found her son from whom she had not heard a word for 18 years.

Once in a while runaways had great adventures. In 1871, a 13-year-old named Neil Rogers joined Robinson's circus, making his way to New Orleans, where he shipped as a cabin boy bound for England. He traveled around the world, reaching Barbados, where he was inadvertently left behind. He spent a year and a half working for a French plantation owner before arriving in San Francisco in 1875, where he went prospecting for gold before

This illustration depicts the "Adam Forepaugh Shows," under the sole ownership of James E. Cooper. After Forepaugh's death in 1890, Cooper, a former partner with P. T. Barnum, bought rights to the name and the exhibitions. Cooper died suddenly in 1892, however, paving the way for James A. Bailey to buy the property. Bailey, another partner of Barnum's who had already assumed control of the Greatest Show on Earth after Barnum's death in 1891, became king of the circus business. (*Oshkosh Daily Northwestern*, June 13, 1891)

becoming a bartender in Deadwood City. After a successful venture with a Jewish capitalist named Wolf, he earned $3,800 and returned home, where he intended to remain and support his mother in her old age.[3]

Henry Stark ran away from home, and one of the cooks at Forepaugh's named "Shorty" took him in. He traveled from Jefferson City, Missouri, to Sedalia, Kansas City, then to Texas and finally New Orleans, doing odd jobs to earn his board. In Philadelphia, "Mr. Forepaugh and a Mexican who owned a portion of the circus quarrelled and the circus was broken up." Henry eventually made his way to New York, where he was turned over to the Society for the Prevention of Cruelty to Children.[4]

Stranger still was a report making the newspaper rounds of little Jimmy McGinniss, who ran away with James A. Bailey, the circus man, who adopted him. He took Bailey's name and, at the man's death, succeeded to his business. He later returned home and royally entertained his relatives, the moral of the story being: "Small boys need not imagine that adopting managers grow on trees."[5]

Closer to actual fact for most runaways was the story of a boy inflamed by circus posters who came to believe nothing but the life of sawdust and spangles could ever satisfy him. After doing odd jobs for the boss canvasman, he was assigned to the cook and the drudgery of carrying water to the elephant. After being cuffed by rude hostlers and nearly bounced off wagons, he found he would not be "dressed up in spangled tights" and taught to ride. Finding show business far from his wide-eyed dreams, the homesick lad learned a hard lesson in life.[6]

Returning home taught a different lesson to a boy who had run away with Forepaugh's. Rather than killing the fatted calf, his father "whaled" him with a piece of hickory "until his back looked like the Star-Spangled Banner."[7]

Reminiscent of the methods used to kidnap teenagers away from cults in the 1960s, the Jesuits "took charge" of a young equestrienne in 1861, had her re-baptized a Roman Catholic and placed in a school at Regla. The prognosis for her redemption was not good, however, as it was held that once the scent of tan-bark and saw dust was imbibed, it "is never eradicated from the human breast," and within a few months the girl would be back as "the pet of some circus company."[8]

One of the more bizarre stories came out in 1860, concerning the son of wealthy people residing in Concord, New Hampshire. The lad supposedly ran away to join the circus, eventually becoming a very skillful rider. Years later, his brother found him in Natchez and persuaded him to leave the ring. He returned home, entered Dartmouth and seemed to be making a good life for himself when the circus arrived, its "tinsel and music" working a fatal charm on him. He yielded to it and, "since returning to the breakneck calling of the ring," tragically died after being thrown from his horse while performing a bareback act through streamers and hoops. The tale was picked up by all the exchanges, later to be declared a "sensation story" got up from the "Cincinnati, Cleveland and other Western papers, to create a sensation."[9]

A sensational story of another sort was published in 1867, noting the infatuation of young Robert Lincoln, the president's son, with the circus. "Considered by his mates somewhat wild," he was once lured away by a circus exhibition in Springfield, "and when his friends found him, Bob was almost in the costume of the Texan, *i.e.,* with nothing but hat and boots. A good drubbing soon took the romance out of him."[10]

"Another Abduction"— Carried Off by Circus Employees

The newspaper leads read, "Another abduction," rather than merely "Abduction," giving an idea how frequently such incidents occurred. They almost always started out, "Last week Caldwell's circus visited Waverly..." or "On Monday last as the circus which had been exhibiting at Nicholson left town..." and followed with, "Mrs. Robinson discovered that her two daughters, 12 and 14 years old, had disappeared..." or "The news of the abduction, as it could be called nothing else was sent to her brother...."

Details were also depressingly familiar. "Men attached to a circus which recently exhibited in Tiftin, enticed a young girl to leave her home and go with them," or "Angie is 16 years old, and was detained against her will by the ticket seller." Bereaved parents sought redress by the law; vengeful brothers followed the trail, all too frequently discovering that the men responsible "had been discharged a few days since," and no one knew their whereabouts. In 1881, George Freeman, a former circus performer, was arrested after becoming separated from his companion and four-year-old Charles Bulo during a nutting expedition. The child never returned home, and it was supposed Freeman's partner stole the boy to sell him to the circus.[11] Toney White and Harry Harrison, two circus performers, were charged with the abduction of Minnie Banish, a 15-year-old girl from Chicago.[12] Even familiar figures found their names in the newspapers under unfavorable circumstances. James Robinson, the circus rider, was sued in Cincinnati by a mother seeking to recover possession of her son and daughter, who were being trained for the circus.[13] As late as 1883, slavery reared its ugly head when a young Negress was stolen by Robinson's circus. They made a dancing girl out of her, and she stayed with the company until it visited Havana, where she was sold on the block, human bondage still being legal in that country.[14]

A kidnapping in 1885 reached across the Atlantic when Thomas McCue was stolen from a circus exhibiting in Cleveland and taken to Europe, where he was trained as an acrobat, receiving brutal beatings and starvation when he tried to escape. Fortunately, while in Rotterdam, the cruel treatment came under investigation by the authorities, and he was sent home.[15]

Arguably the first kidnapping for ransom in American history involved little Charlie Ross, a four-year-old abducted from Germantown, a suburb of Philadelphia, on July 1, 1874. The kidnappers believed Christian Ross was wealthy and sent a suspiciously poorly written ransom note, demanding $20,000 for the return of his son, and warning that he not call in detectives or the child's life would be forfeit. Authorities advised Mr. Ross not to pay and to respond to the demands through the personal columns of the newspaper. That tact failing, Pinkerton detectives were summoned, and a nationwide search began. On August 22, the agency issued a three-page circular, on which was the only known likeness of the boy (at age two-and-a-half). Also included were questions to be put to any child thought to be Charlie. (Question: Who is your uncle on Washington Lane? Answer: Uncle Joe. Question: What horse does mamma drive? Answer: Polly.)

Ironically, a $20,000 reward was offered, the same amount originally demanded by the kidnappers. On September 1, Pinkerton issued a single-sheet flyer containing a lithograph of a painting commissioned to update the child's age; later, Charlie became the first missing child to have his face distributed on a product container when his likeness was embossed onto cologne bottles.[16]

Police searched nearly 200 Gypsy caravans within a year and an half of Charlie's disappearance[17] and investigated thousands of leads, many centered on circus men. In September 1874, at Goshen, Pinkerton men thought a young circus performer was Charlie, but reluctantly determined his tumbling skills were too great to have been learned in such a short time.[18]

The most interesting connection with a circus came in 1875, when W. W. Cole's show displayed wax figures of Charlie and his family. In promoting the exhibition, Cole announced that the parents offered $5,000, the ladies of Philadelphia added $3,000 more, and he put up $2,000, making a $10,000 reward for the child's recovery. Performing in Canada at the time, the circular drew hundreds of people from the countryside. Charlie's father traveled north of the border, where he discovered two wax figure displays, one labeled "The Intemperate Family" and the other "The Ross Family." None of the figures looked anything like the Ross members. Without identifying himself, Mr. Ross spoke to the proprietor, who professed that the wax images were taken from life, made under his own supervision and approved by the father, with whom he was very intimate.

When Ross finally identified himself, the unnamed proprietor "was the worst taken-down man I ever saw in my life." He finally confessed to Ross that the figures were originally the "Temperate Family," renamed to play off the missing child. He added that when the boy was found, he would pay $1,000 a week for 30 weeks to exhibit him.[19]

In 1887, a man named S. G. Sellers came from Mitchell, Canada, to Erie, Pennsylvania, for the purpose of meeting Mr. Ross. He stated that 12 years ago, a family came to Mitchell from Erie with a boy identified as Charlie by his resemblance to a wax figure seen at a circus. The husband having recently died, the wife stated the child was the missing boy whom they had kidnapped. She later recanted her statement, fearing recrimination from the law.[20]

A report in 1888 involved a man named L. G. Reno, who told a strange tale with all the earmarkings of a Mark Twain satire. Reno stated that Charlie had been living in Coop-erstown, New York, for many years, telling the story that he had been kidnapped by a circus man and woman, put on a steamer bound for New York, and from there taken to Cuba, where he suffered extreme cruelty by a couple attempting to make a circus performer out of him. An Episcopal minister rescued him, kept him for a year and then sent him to New York under the guardianship of a steamboat captain who eventually placed him in the Cooper orphanage, Cooperstown, the matron of which was a daughter of James Fen-nimore Cooper.

After the child was identified as "Charlie Ross," his parents were sent for, and they positively identified him. Mrs. Ross, however, being rendered insane from grief some time past, suddenly refused the child, and he was left behind when the Rosses returned home. According to the story, Mr. Ross often visited him, wrote frequently and paid for his cloth-ing for several years. Various distractions, including the insanity of his wife, drove the father into despair, and he eventually lost interest. Although this Charlie eventually returned to Philadelphia and identified his boyhood home, none of his relatives except Mr. Ross acknowledged his identity.[21] Peculiarly, this story first broke on January 22, 1875, when reports of a stolen boy taken from a circus company in Havana and brought to an orphanage in Cooperstown, New York, was avowed to be Charlie, but it "proved otherwise."[22]

The case was never officially settled, and Charlie Ross' name became synonymous with missing children. For decades after his disappearance, whenever a child disappeared, newspapers began with the lead "Another Charlie Ross case."

Dastardly Affairs of the Heart

Another sort of running away from home, in a more or less voluntary sense, is illus-trated by the numerous cases of young women losing their hearts to dastardly circus per-formers. While it is likely girls of little means and less hope comprised the majority of those eloping, newspapers concentrated on the daughters of respectable, well-to-do families. A typical story from 1868 described the daughter of a Philadelphia banker and graduate of a first-class boarding school who made the acquaintance of a "roving, rakish young man" working for Yankee Robinson's circus. She soon wore "short dresses, and neat tights, and displays her ancles [*sic*] and accompanying charms as liberally as her more experienced sisters" of the ring.[23] A strikingly similar incident occurred the same year and at the same circus, but this time involving a highly educated clergyman's daughter from Albany, New York. Although her father followed and eventually caught up with his daughter, she refused to return home unless her husband was allowed to accompany her. The father refused, and despite Yankee Robinson's intervention, describing the "vicissitudes of the life she was leading," she chose to stay with her spouse.[24]

Courtships in such cases were done in "leap year fashion." In 1871, three members of a circus troupe performing at Lebanon, Indiana, each succeeded in carrying off wives, leaving the chagrined bachelors of that city to "take private lessons on the balancing pole and in the sawdust ring."[25] More explosively, a young Los Angeles lady eloped with the cannon-ball man of Jackley's Circus.[26] In 1886, it was observed that if a circus clown named Bennett, working for Sells' Circus, expected to keep Dolly Grubbs of Cincinnati, "he would have to do considerable acting" to get away with it.[27]

An oft-repeated scenario involved a 16-year-old girl, one of those "shallow-pated [sic], brainless children, who are carried away by the tinsel show, and pawnshop gilt of a circus." Meeting one of the tumblers on the street, "he enticed her to a house where they drank, and her ruin was accomplished." After promising to send money so she could meet him in the next town, where they would be married, he deserted her. In her despondency, she again resorted to intoxicating liquor and was arrested in the streets. It was supposed the brute would be arrested and the woman would benefit from "a lesson that will no doubt last a life time."[28]

Single women were not the only ones enticed away from lives of comfort. Mrs. Williams, of Delaware, attended the afternoon performance of the circus. There she met "one of those oily-tongued fellows who wear the tinsel and taggery of the ring," who convinced her to leave her husband and baby and run away with him. Her relatives caught her at the railroad depot and returned her, expecting that she would be "wiser if not sadder than before."[29] Mrs. Jennings, wife of Captain Jennings of the schooner *Idaho*, eloped with James Reynolds, "The People's Clown" of O'Brien & King's Circus, who also happened to be married. The pair were caught and jailed. Making bond, Mrs. Jennings exonerated Reynolds from blame, citing her own infatuation, but refused to go home, abandoning her child with her mother and leaving with her paramour.[30]

Elopements resulting either in marriage or fraudulent unions left scars for the victims but occasionally proved financially beneficial for the perpetrators, for it was often noted that fond fathers "bled freely" to get rid of erstwhile husbands, often to the tune of $1,000 "endowments."[31] If not bribed away, wives were left behind, as in the case of a circus tumbler who drew his pay and went back East, leaving his wife a "grass widow."[32] Cast-off wives had a hard time, and not a few stories represented them as being found in houses of ill fame or committing suicide.[33]

Less frequently were stories of happy endings. In 1880, the newspapers ran numerous articles about how Hattie L. Bnrg [sic] ran away with a circus performer named Tom Searles. Tom took exception to the disparaging notices and wrote to the local newspaper, stating that the woman left home with the blessing of her mother, adding that the pair were married the same evening. He defended himself by stating, "My salary is large enough to enable me to keep her a lady as long as I have my strength. — We have a Pulman [sic] Palace Sleeping Coach and she has a section with every home comfort." The editor willingly published the correction.[34]

Child Performers in the Circus

"The fact is admitted by an interviewed showman that the feats of beasts and children in the sawdust arena are, in the main, produced by torture. From the biggest elephant to the smallest girl on an equestrian's shoulders, compulsion under the fear of severe punishment is the incentive."[35] This sentiment was frequently repeated in the 19th century, and there can be no doubt it held more than a grain of truth. Before the advent and enforcement of child labor laws, many young performers suffered greatly while learning their art.

For many, the circus could not be said to be their chosen profession. In 1870, the case of Honora Shananan vs. James Bowen et al, Commissioners of Charities and Corrections, drew considerable attention. Circa 1862, the plaintiff delivered into their care her daughter, whom she alleged they gave to Mrs. Perry of Illinois, keeper of a circus. This mother sued for damages; in defense, the commissioners admitted guilt but claimed there was no official wrongdoing. Their demurrer was sustained.[36]

In 1871, the story of circus rider Frank Morgan came to light. His father, overstocked with "numerous progeny," sold him, as a small child, to the circus for $25.[37]

In the early days of the circus it was not uncommon for performers to "adopt" children for the express purpose of training them to the profession. Annie Carroll, the equestrienne, was one of those. Professor "Pop" Carroll, who operated a school for the training of circus performers, located near Van Nest station on the Harlem River branch of the New York-New Haven-Hartford railroad, found her in an English village and made a star of her, keeping the $200-a-week salary for himself. In 1883, still under contract to Carroll and by that time paying him $40 a week, she married Eddie Snow, an acrobat from Barnum's. Snow had also been a pickup, discovered by John Snow, the rider and contortionist, who found him in Pittsburg.[38]

In 1866, then with Forepaugh's Circus, Dan Rice was near Schenectady, New York, when he made the acquaintance of a six-year-old girl. She became so enamored with him that her parents indentured her to Rice, and he began her training as a rider. He changed her name to Lizzie Marcellus, and her talent eventually earned her $100 a week from Barnum. In the summer of 1873, before Lizzie was of age, she fell in love with an Italian performer named Cardona, and the pair were married (against "Uncle Dan's" wishes). Cardona proved a jealous husband, and he tried to slit her throat. Rice and William H. Stowe (a "blackface clown" working for Rice, and son of the well-known circus man) saved her, and a suit for divorce was brought in Chicago. It was granted in 1875, and shortly thereafter she married the 24-year-old Stowe. Tragically, the Stowes, along with their two young children, a boy of seven by her first husband and their five-year-old daughter, were burned to death aboard the *Golden City*.

The custom of performers marrying was widespread, and in the 1880s, contracts were issued to families rather than individuals. Their children necessarily went into the business, and if successful, the group earned a comfortable living

One of the most skilled apprentices coming from a circus family was Alice Lake, daughter of Bill (a clown) and Agnes Lake (slack-wire performer), of Robinson & Lake's circus. Alice was taught to ride from infancy and would have been a star for many years, but on crossing Lake Pontchartrain, a large diamond cross became detached from her throat and fell overboard. She clutched for it, lost her balance and was never seen again.

Rose Madigan, another rider, was a pupil of her father's. Rose and Sallie Stickney were great female riders, trained under Sam Stickney. (Sallie eventually eloped with the female impersonator Ella Zoyara/Omar Kingsley, by whom she had three children. They eventually divorced, and she died in extreme poverty in January 1886. She had been forgotten for many years and was buried by the Actor's Fund.[39]) Sam Stickney also taught his son Robert.

If children were not stolen, purchased or born into the business, they learned the trade through apprenticeship, a span seldom lasting less than six years. Billy Morgan, the hurdle jumper, was an old-time apprentice boy, as was the great Charles W. Fish, who served under Charles Rogers of Gilbert R. Spalding & Rogers. James Robinson, apprenticed under John Robinson and William Dutton, served his apprenticeship with William Lake.[40]

Levi J. North,* the famous rider, was one of the best old-time trainers, and his circus was comprised primarily of apprentices. Boys commenced their training by learning to ride a pair of ponies and graduated to bareback riding. To teach this, a "mechanic" was used, consisting of a pole set in the middle of a sawdust ring with a high arm on which was attached a rope fastened to the rider's belt, the other end being held by the instructor. As the horse galloped around the ring, the pole and arm revolved. In this way, if the pupil slipped, he was saved from falling. Practice lasted 3 to 4 hours a day. When the company was on the road, a short rope was tied to the pupil's belt and fastened to a ring in the saddle. That prevented him from falling on the ground.[41] Once mastered, the apprentice graduated to the "pony act," where he was dressed as a jockey, riding around the ring on two ponies, waving his cap and urging greater speed. During the performance, the young rider contrived to slip and fall between the miniature steeds, eliciting applause from a sympathetic crowd who feared he might be crushed. This effect was merely a trick of the trade, for the rider wore the same rope fastened around his waist that would not permit him to fall.

The child learning acrobatics began with posturing scenes. In his or her first exposure to the ring, there was little to do but stand in the proper position and receive a toss from a senior member of the group. Next came the "split," consisting of spreading the feet apart until the legs were at extreme right angles with the upright body. "Bending," or throwing the head back as far as possible toward the heels, followed. When perfected, an adult placed his hand under the back of the child and, with a toss, threw the feet over the head, transforming a bend into a somersault. When this was mastered, vaulting, "battoute flaps," spring-board somersaults and cart-wheels were taught, the entire process consuming several months.

To learn the tight-rope business, the novice began on the rope positioned at the same height as a regular performance, the rationale being to accustom the child to heights and give space for the 12-to-20-foot-long balance pole. To protect the young performer from injury, men were stationed on either side of the rope, into whose hands the learner unavoidably fell until perfecting the art.[42] Perhaps to allay fears, an article in *The Boy's World* (March 22, 1884) offered the "Origin of the Safety-Net," attributed to Marcus, the Roman

---

*Levi J. North was described by Richard Hemmings as being "simply an Apollo on horseback. He was about five feet six inches in height, with a ruddy, fair complexion and light hair, which, like most performers of his day, he wore long, while his face was always smoothly shaven. His every movement was the embodiment of grace, and he was as daring as he was graceful. He is said to have been the first rider who ever turned a somer-sault on horseback. He was a very versatile performer, being not only a great rider, but a great acrobat as well." For a period of 40 years, North was one of the most famous and widely known in the circus profession.[43]

magistrate. The story went that while watching the performance of a boy rope-dancer, the child lost his balance and fell to his death. The grieving Marcus thereby decreed that ever after, a safety net should be spread beneath gymnasts as a protection against such fatal accidents.

A letter published in the London *Pall Mall Budget* in 1885 described how boys 8 or 10 years of age went through morning drill. Clad in only a shirt and trousers, the child was required to make a certain number of somersaults without stopping, from one line drawn in the dust to another. "In order to come back to his starting line he had to pass every two or three minutes, giddy and panting, between the cushioned ring and a gentleman, one of the proprietors of the circus, who held in his hands a long, heavy, cutting whip..." If the boy succeeded, "Mr. Merryman" let him pass with a smile and one long, playful cut across the shoulders, "a facetiousness which always elicited a howl from the

Children being taught the high wire act were started on the wire at the same height they would perform in the ring in order to familiarize them with the distance and to allow them to manipulate the balance pole, similar to the one depicted in this illustration. (*Marion Daily Star* [OH], August 19, 1880)

victim and a grin from the grooms." But if he failed, as was often the case, his arms being too weak to support the body in the reverse position, Merryman's cutting whip "traveled, with an indescribably horrible sound, from the nape of that child's neck to the calves of his legs," the flimsy clothing offering no protection.

The letter ended with the reflective comment, "Now I shall never go into a circus again, for whenever the young gentleman in pink tights and spring spangles should appear smiling, his sallow cheeks smeared with rouge, somehow or other a horrible vision of a whaled back would come before my eyes and the swish of that terrible whip would sound in my ears."[44]

The smile was a tradition demanded of circus people. A showman reminisced about how a boy was trained as a hurdle rider of four ponies. The act was typically performed by an adult on full-sized horses, standing on the back of one animal and managing them all by reins, finally leaping, along with his own steed, over the hurdles. One apprentice spent the entire winter learning the trick and finally mastered it, his terror of the teacher being greater than the horseback danger. When performing before an audience, however, he found it impossible to smile. "Instead, a distressful expression of fright came into his face. That would not do and he was literally clubbed until he smiled."[45]

The training of a danseuse was equally torturous for a young child. Sent to lessons with nothing in the stomach but a cup of coffee, without socks or shawl, a seven-year-old's feet were "imprisoned in a groove-box, heel against heel, and knees turned outwards," until the feet accustomed themselves naturally to fall in a paralleled line. This was called *se tourner*. After half an hour in the groove, the girl was obliged to rest her foot on a bar and compelled to hold it in a horizontal line with the hand opposite the foot to be exercised, a technique styled *se casser*. After this, the child was required to study other forms, day in and day out. Even a week off from practice resulted in two months of redoubled, incessant toil. Fanny Bias and Fanny Elssler (who performed with the New York Circus in 1847) were two of the most famous danseuses.

In the ballet *La Peri*, there existed a leap so dangerous that dancer Carlotta Grisi risked her life every time she attempted it. Not surprisingly, the same Englishman who followed Van Amburgh for three years waiting for the beasts to devour him, attended the ballet expecting the leap to prove fatal to Carlotta.[46]

Danger was not always confined to the circus. Youths observing the daring feats of performers wished to emulate them, occasionally with disastrous results. In 1865 a 16-year-old named Charles Dimock from Chicago came home from the circus and tried to copy the trick of an artist he had seen "hang" himself. He did not get it right and was found dead in the barn with a rope around his neck.[47] The same fate befell James Dayton, aged 14, from Washington, whose mother found him dead after he tried copying a trapeze act seen at the circus.[48] And then there were incidental accidents. In 1873, a small boy discovered a hole in the circus tent and applied his eye to the aperture. Unfortunately, it happened to open into the equestriennes' dressing room. One irate star resented the intrusion and stabbed the watchful eye, resulting in the boy being taken to the hospital and the lady bound over by a magistrate.[49]

If that were not enough, it was alleged that reading novels, pretending to be a pirate or attending the circus was enough to warp a youth's personality so that he would grow up to become a murderer, robber, pirate or circus performer.[50]

On a less depressing note, the "Great Western Circus," composed of juveniles holding their own performances in "Gen. Smith's barn, which has been well cleaned," made gross receipts of 55 cents by charging an admission of 5 cents for adults and "one-half price, or 25 pins" for children. This gave the company "a good start on their next exhibition."[51]

Child Labor Laws

At age seven, Leocatia Coles was apprenticed by her widowed mother to a well-known trainer of youthful acrobats and riders. Papers were drawn up, stipulating that the trainer was to have her until she was 18 years old, and that she was to be "instructed in the art and mystery of the circus and acrobatic business." In return for her service, Leocatia was to be fed and clothed and to have eleven quarters schooling during her apprenticeship. She was taken to Frankford, where "infant wonders" and "juvenile phenomenons" were turned out.

Under the guidance of the ringmaster's whip she was taught to leap and ride bareback, to stand on one foot and hold the other out at a sign-board angle with one hand, to pirouette and to jump through paper-covered hoops known as "balloons." After learning all she could, the child was assigned to a woman traveling with O'Brien's circus and billed as "Katie Brown." She was also given a 12-year-old "sister," who had appeared as an infant wonder before outgrowing the appellation. The woman who had charge of Katie traversed the continent with her, saving money by hiding the child under her skirts to avoid paying fares. Katie's mother bought her fancy gauze dresses, tights and slippers, and the child never received an education.

Under the law regulating children's work in circuses, acrobatic or song and dance acts, in 1878, Mrs. Coles applied to have her daughter returned. Leocatia was taken in by the Society for the Prevention of Cruelty to Children and not returned to her parent until proper assurances were given that "Katie" would not again be indentured to the circus.[52]

Laws reflecting protection of children were relatively new to the United States during the latter quarter of the 19th century. In fact, laws governing the protection of animals preceded them. Henry Bergh, a New York philanthropist, founded the American Society for the Prevention of Cruelty to Animals (ASPCA) in 1866. Not until 1875, again with the assistance of Bergh, were efforts made to formalize such laws for children, beginning with the New York Society for the Prevention of Cruelty to Children (SPCC). Under the guidance of Elbridge T. Gerry and that society, a New York campaign to remove child performers from professional stages resulted in passage of An Act to Prevent and Punish Wrongs to Children (1876). Not surprisingly, the intense response of the theater industry resulted in a protracted political struggle.[53]

Reports on enforcement of the New York State law (used as a precedent by other states) were spotty. In 1875, the Pony Circus, scheduled to perform at the Howard Athenaeum, was withdrawn from the program in compliance with the request of the Committee of the City Council (Boston) upon licensing public entertainments, which acted on representations made by the Society for the Prevention of Cruelty.[54] In 1882, Manager Fisher, of Robinson's circus, was fined $100 in Oakland, California, for allowing a child of tender years to ride and perform in the circus. Nathaniel Hunter of the SPCC prosecuted the case.[55]

On November 16, 1883, a warrant was issued for the arrest of Adam Forepaugh, Jr.; the charge was assault and battery. The case stemmed from a 15-year-old boy named Leo Lawrence, who charged that while he was training to become a professional circus rider at the winter quarters of the Forepaugh show, corner of Lehigh avenue and Richmond street, Philadelphia, he fell off his horse. This so incensed Forepaugh that he struck the child over the head and face with a loaded whip and then prodded him in the back with an iron prong commonly used in subduing elephants. The case was to be prosecuted against Forepaugh for employing a boy beneath the minimum age allowed by law, which was sixteen.[56]

Lacking specific laws in Ohio, the ASPCA took charge of a Cincinnati case involving Gertrude Missun, a girl who had been on exhibition at the People's Museum. The girl's mother, a widow from St. George, Delaware, originally gave her to a man named Craig when the circus passed through town. After five years of brutal treatment by Craig, who had become her manager, Gertrude was found wandering aimlessly in Lincoln Park. It was speculated she would be returned to her mother.[57]

One of the more noted cases of child abuse involving circus men had to do with a child named Harry McCabe, alias Harry Sebastian, who was rescued from Montgomery Queen's circus in August 1876. According to the mother, she gave the child away to Sebastian Quaglienti, a rider then belonging to Howe & Cushing's circus, being unable to care for him after a separation from her husband. The parents later reconciled and searched for the boy, finding him in San Francisco, where he was an infant equestrian. After it was discovered he had been badly handled by Quaglienti, he was taken from the circus on the night of a performance at Oakland under the supervision of Charles Sonntag, acting as an agent of the New York SPCC. During the rescue, Sonntag was nearly mobbed by circus people.

According to testimony given before Judge Dwinelle, Harry was given away without the father's permission but with the consent of the mother, obtained by deception and fraud, and was illegally held by Quaglienti, who trained him for the circus. Quaglienti denied the charges, stating he received the child from the Commissioners of Charities and Correction of New York, upon whose care Harry had been thrown because his parents abandoned him. The child was then a year and a half old and was received in delicate health and destitute of clothes. Quaglienti swore that he cared for the child as if he had been his own, was never cruel to him and never trained him as a performer.

This testimony was flatly contradicted by Lawrence Dee, Quaglienti's groom. He stated he had seen Quaglienti strike the child after the boy made a mistake in the ring, or when on the "mechanic," using a whip, a stick and twisting his ears. Sonntag added that when taken into his custody, Harry had eight or ten large bruises on his body.

Harry was remanded into the custody of his father, to whom he would be sent when recovered from illness; the Supreme Court of New York appointed John D. Wright, president of the New York SPCC, general guardian. In conclusion, Judge Dwinelle said that

W. B. Reynolds' Consolidated Shows or Trained Animal Exposition announced they had "The First and Only Show in the World Exhibiting a Wonderfully Trained Moose." According to their advertising, they had an "outlay" of $5,000 to bring their "Original, Costly and Novel" show to the public, especially emphasizing the rare and hitherto considered untamable quadruped moose. Training animals often resulted in harsh treatment. When a report was filed with the Society for the Prevention of Cruelty to Animals, the Society would investigate and intervene when necessary. (*Evening Gazette* [IL], April 30, 1892)

"too much censure could not be indulged in toward those charitable institutions whose officers recklessly placed children under the care of those who make a profession of what is known as 'perfecting children for the ring.'"[58]

A follow-up article from November 1886 noted that the late Ed. D.C. Cittridge, a rich lawyer, became interested in Harry and adopted him, making the boy "worth about $2,000,000," which he would inherit upon obtaining his majority.[59]

At the annual meeting of the American Humane Society in 1887, it was reported that 121,655 cases of alleged cruelty to animals had been investigated; of these, 100,000 animals were relieved and over 10,000 persons arrested. The organization aided 31,000 children in investigating 52,000 alleged cases, prompting the arrest of over 10,000 persons.[60]

Child welfare concerns were also being addressed in Europe. In 1884, the Seine Tribunal of Paris sentenced an Italian named Maguayo to 15 days imprisonment and fined him 2,000f for engaging the services of his eight-year-old daughter as a trapeze artist to the managers of a circus, where performances were of a most perilous nature. For the services of his daughter, Maguayo was to receive 2,500f a month.[61]

Child welfare cases did not always go the way that common sense, if not the law, dictated. Although the New York law of 1876 made it a misdemeanor to employ a child under 16 years of age "for or in any business, exhibition or vocation injurious to the health, or dangerous to the life or limb of such child," interpretations varied widely. In 1885, a case involving a 14-year-old girl employed in a steam laundry came before the court. While feeding collars and cuffs into an ironing machine, her finger caught in a button-hole. The machine drew her hand between the rollers, crushing and burning it. In a suit for damages, the Court of Appeals decided in favor of the employer after taking into account the law about children employed in circuses and acrobatic performances. Their interpretation was based on the idea that while the law forbade the employment of a child in a business or vocation dangerous to life or limb, *it did not mean employment in a respectable business, like work in a laundry. It meant a disreputable employment, such as a circus* (italics added).[62]

25

The State of the Circus

Old men go to the show to renew their youth, young ones to witness what proved a source of delight even during the days of ancient Rome, of Olympus and England, when the old time rural sports were in vogue — athletic skill, feats of strength and tests of speed. You cannot cloy or surfeit this insatiable interest. It is as much a part of humanity as life itself. That is why the circus lives, why innovations are frowned upon and met with rebuff and failure.[1]

The Interstate Commerce Act, passed February 4, 1887, placed railroads under Federal guidelines, making this the first industry so regulated. The intent was to prohibit railroad monopolies from setting prices, excluding competitors and controlling regional markets. Specifically, the law required "just and reasonable" rate charges, prohibited special rates or rebates for individual shippers, prohibited "preference" in rates for particular localities, shippers or products, forbade long-haul/short-haul discrimination, and established a five-member Interstate Commerce Commission.[2]

The law affected circuses by denying railroads the right to offer rebates or lower prices to large concerns in exchange for securing their exclusive patronage. By the end of February, circus managers were reported to be raising a purse of $10,000 in Cincinnati to test the constitutionality of the law.[3]

Doomsayers were swift to predict the demise of traveling shows: New York's *World* announced, "The season has come when the rural population revels in the pleasure of the circus. But it looks very much as though this spring's crop of clowns and trick mules would be very short."[4]

By September, the law was not only blamed for drowning two-thirds of the circuses, it was feared that the Virginia peanut crop, amounting to 1,600,000 bushels, would become "a dead drug in the market."[5] The truth proved not quite so dire. Harry Evarts, press agent for Sells Brothers show, pronounced the present season "good," notwithstanding the drought and the Interstate Commerce Law. Although it cost the proprietors $3,200 to move 360 people, animals and equipment from one town to another (a 30 percent increase over the previous year), he still predicted a winning season.[6]

Circus owners had much to contemplate over the winter of 1887–1888. The larger circus companies had hardly felt the effects of the law the previous year, as their contracts with the railroads had been made before the law went into effect. The old tax rates had been so low they "had hardly been felt." On their expiration, proprietors were forced to pay a standard rate for hauling the cars, as well as a passenger-rate charge on every employee accompanying the show. Barnum anticipated it would cost him $6,000 a day, declaring it "simply prohibitory." He was in good company. Railroad barons bemoaned the potential loss in earnings from the circuses, as well as a revenue drop from excursion trains from outlying points to central places where shows were given.

It was estimated that of the 43 nickel-plate (railroad) circus companies on the road in 1887, no more than half could afford to travel by rail, resulting in a return to the wagon train approach or outright failure. Voicing the opinion of the majority, newspapers declared, "It is evidently good bye to the glories of the sawdust ring."[7] Fortunately, such was not the case. Although the law proved constitutional, most circuses continued making their accustomed tours.

An Acre or Two of Teeth

Throughout the decades of the 1880s and 1890s, the larger circuses continued to show healthy profits. In pictorial form, this popularity of the Big Show was expressed as a "sea of faces," or an ocean of countenances from the "hillside of seats" whereby thousands of eyes, looking white by contrast with darker shades of clothing and soot-stained canvas, sparkled in excitement. By contract, it was commonly held that in cities not more than one spectator in three showed his teeth when he found something amusing, but in rural areas, nine out of ten did so when something humorous was performed.[8]

A summary of receipts from the last decades of the century revealed that in 1880, Burr Robbins' circus took in $2,400 for one performance at Londonville, Ohio,[9] while Cooper & Bailey's circus averaged $7,000 a day touring the New England States.[10] In 1881, Forepaugh's circus took $12,000 out of Milwaukee from 13,000 people, 3000 of whom had no seats.[11] The year 1884 proved poor: Forepaugh lost $140,000 that season, and Barnum reportedly lost $40,000 in one week, supposedly from vendors regarding circus men as "common prey" and charging them four times what food and supplies normally cost.[12] Four years later, the season of 1888 suffered — not from the Interstate Law, which ultimately proved to have minimal effect on profits, but from the fact presidential years were generally associated with lower business.[13] Rebounding quickly, three weeks before the end of the 1889 season, Sells Brothers circus had earned $248,000 in profit, marking this the best year ever for the concern.[14]

Under the heading "When it was good..." a number of circus proprietors were extremely wealthy men. In 1889, it was calculated that Seth Haines, former owner of the London Circus, retired with $1,500,000; John Nathans and Lewis June were said to be worth $150,000 each; John Robinson left an estate of $800,000; Adam Forepaugh possessed $1,500,000, most of which was invested in Philadelphia real estate; while the grand old humbug, P. T. Barnum, had amassed between $4,500,000 and $6,000,000 from his show ventures.[15]

Under the heading "When it was bad..." Melville's employees were forced to live at city expense after the circus was attached on June 24, 1889, at Biddeford, Maine. Two days later, they applied to the overseers of the poor for aid and were provided with passes to Boston.[16] An even sadder tale came out of Fort Dodge, Iowa, in September 1890, when four of Barnum's "Nero" ballet girls were discharged for alleged drunkenness. All four had been hired in London at a stated salary with the promise they be provided transportation home at season's end. As the year drew to a close, they reported that management made it a practice of discharging some of the performers in each town for trivial breaches of discipline not noticed earlier in the year. All discharged women were foreigners and penniless.[17]

Their situation prompted speculation on how they spent their salary. In an 1887 interview, Mrs. Burr Robbins stated that no matter what pay a performer received, little was saved. She professed that few gambled, but after a show all rushed to the nearest restaurant, spending lavishly on evening spreads.[18] Brilliant wardrobes, whether for personal or professional life, cost a great deal, and it is not unlikely the remainder went for liquor.

Equally revealing was the fact that while a circus advertised a star's exorbitant salary to increase his value to the public, such was not actually the case. In 1881, Mme. Dockrill's salary was advertised as $1,000 a week when she actually earned $450 a week. The remainder was calculated on the cost of her traveling and hotel expenses, the carriage placed at her disposal, the transportation of her six horses and the man hired to look after them. Broken down to actual pay, Chang, the Chinese giant, received $200; Tom Thumb $325; and Mme. Cordova, the rider, $300 a week.[19]

The Wild, Wild West

In 1882, Captain A. H. Bogardus appeared with W. W. Cole's circus and menagerie, offering exhibitions of marksmanship. Along with his two pupil-sons, Eugene and 5-year-old Master Henry, they offered fancy trap shooting and rifle work "surpassing belief." Advertisements in May offered a Gallery of Wax Statuary, Aerial Bicycle Riding and Russian Roller Skating, with Bogardus, "The Crack Shot," listed twelfth out of 58 attractions.[20]

Among Bogardus' accomplishments were the America medal, 1871; the Lorillard medal, 1874; the championship medal of the world, won at London, 1875, and the glass ball championship, Long Island, 1877. An achievement of a different type was his patented invention of glass balls and traps, used as a substitute for pigeons, "as in practicing, thousands of them were slain." An objection to glass balls being the broken glass left on the ground, the development of clay pigeons was introduced. These were felt to more accurately simulate flight and would eventually replace live birds.[21]

As his fame grew, Bogardus was billed as "Champion Wing-Shot of the World," capable of "hitting 100 birds with 100 shots." In 1886, his "Wild West Exhibition" joined Adam Forepaugh's New and Colossal All-Feature Show, where he and his four sons received top billing.[22] The act featured a delegation of Indians, cowboys, trappers and scouts, with Indian ponies, wild buffalo, elk and the old Deadwood coach used to illustrate life on the plains, over a half-mile race track.[23]

After Bogardus defected, Cole brought in Dr. William F. Carver's "Wild West" Combination, that presented an imposing historical parade headed by Red River Tom's cowboy brass band, mustang races, and rifle and pistol shooting, and concluding with Indian circle fighting, the method of savage warfare used against "the gallant Custer" when he and his company were annihilated in the Yellowstone Valley in 1876.[24]

If one show had a Wild West attraction, others must follow. In 1887, Chevalier Ira Paine appeared with Frank A. Robbins' circus, billed as the "Master Shot of the World." Advertised with him was Charles W. Fish, the "sole, undisputed champion of bareback riders."[25] Not everything went according to schedule, however. In July 1877, four people were shot during the Wild West performance of Sells Brother's Circus, one fatally; the injured included a woman, an Indian and a spectator. It was supposed loaded cartridges had been substituted for blank ones.[26]

While thrilling to the eye, the genuineness of Wild West performers was often the subject of humor. A generic description included a dozen men never before this side of the Connecticut River; the regular spotted horses; several Pequod [sic] Indians from Massachusetts; a yearling calf; and a spavined steer with a piece of buffalo robe tied over its shoulders.

The men who are supposed to represent cowboys are helped onto their horses, and if the horse is less than twenty years old they are usually tied on, and then they chase the steer over the great, undulating plain of the circus ring, and shoot at him with wooden guns and bother the poor animal till he turns around and shakes his head and scares them away.

> The yearling calf is then led in and after the man takes the halter off, and kicks at it so it won't follow him back, the cowboys proceed to rope it with clothes lines. They go rushing around the range, and run into each other, and two or

Not your father's circus: aerial bicycle riding became the rage by the 1880s, as this illustration of W. W. Cole's Circus, Theatre, Menagerie depicts. One of the "World's Greatest Wonders," the exhibition included a gallery of wax statuary, a bicycle college, Russian roller skaters, a museum, encyclopedia and races. (*Logansport Pharos* [IN], May 23, 1882)

three of them fall off and get stepped on and are pulled out by the clown, who stays in the ring to make it seem natural and just like a western round-up. All this time the calf is standing still and scratching his head on the center-pole. The cowboys continue to ride around and yell feebly and catch one another's horses with the clothes lines, and lose their hats and get off to pick them up, and some of the horses will balk and the riders will climb down and try to lead them. After the audience has grown tired and about half of it has gone, the head cowboy, who is supposed to be Buffalo Bill, falls off and grasps the calf by the tail and Texas Jack walks up and slips

Forepaugh's Grand 3-Ring Circus promised 20 lady bareback riders, but by the 1890s, the major attraction of American circuses were the Wild West shows. Captain A. H. Bogardus and family were heavily promoted as champion pistol shots. Accompanying them were "numbers of Indians, cowboys, scouts, and pathfinders, in all kinds of wild west entertainment. Truthful, historical, romantic and comical scenes." Perhaps the last was the most accurate, as performers who had never been west of the Mississippi were often cast in such roles, typically becoming the butt of popular jokes. (*The Morning Review* [IL], May 3, 1891)

> a bed-cord around its neck and leads it away, while the Buffalo Bill goes along behind and pushes it when it acts balky. It is a wild, wild show, and any body at all nervous shouldn't go near it.[27]

The acts, and subsequently the humor, reached as far as England.

> When one of Buffalo Bill's braves was thrown from his Indian pony and severely injured at the Wild West Show, in London, last week, Mr. Gladstone sent a telegram of condolence to show his sympathy for the down-trodden people of Ireland.[28]

William Cody, the original Buffalo Bill, joined forces with Forepaugh, promoting "the one genuine Wild West show" in 1889, but by 1892, America's historical fantasies had been replaced by the "Fall of Nineveh, featuring 1,000 men, women and children, $150,000 in gorgeous costumes, $50,000 in special scenery, $30,000 in armour, swords, shields and spears, 200 beautiful ladies in the Grand Ballet, all on the best equipped stage in the words, 300 FEET LONG AND 55 FEET WIDE" (capitals in original).[29]

Of Mr. Merryman and Circus Music

Colonel W. C. Crum, press agent of Forepaugh's circus, made the remark in 1887 that

> The day of the clown is nearly over. Formerly they were half the show, but now they attract little attention. The enlargement of the show is chief cause. The big shows now have two or three rings, and the circle of seats is so far off that the people cannot hear the jokes of the clowns. In the old days an average clown received from $100 to $200 a week.... Dan Rice, who was considered the greatest of them all, was paid $1,000 a week.... At the present day the pay of the clowns ranges from $20 to $50 a week.[30]

The inability of "Mr. Merryman" to deliver "wheezes," or funny stories, made him nearly superfluous to the late 19th century circus.

The Evolution of the Circus Clown

In the earliest days of the formal entertainment that would become the circus, it became fashionable to introduce a tight-rope dancer between dramatic performances. Accompanying him was a clown, whose job was to chalk the artist's feet and make bad jokes or puns while the artists rested. This clown developed from Shakespeare's, whose characters traced their roots to the jesters and buffoons kept by royalty.

The first burlesque acts of horsemanship were introduced at Astley's in his first season in 1768. By 1780, a clown on horseback appeared in the bills. In the 1870s, Carlo Delpini succeeded the elder Grimaldi at the Royal Circus, where he initiated the catch phrase "What you please," which became a circus standard. Baptiste Dubois worked at Jones' Amphitheatre in Whitechapel, first performing a comic riding act, the "French Post Boy's Journey from Paris to London," effecting a change of costume and probably gender while inside the post boy's sack, predating the first performances of the "Metamorphosis." His "rustic booby" character of the

Clowns were not the only ones telling jokes when the circus came to town. Little Johnny's father told him he would rather his son study than go to the circus because maybe he would grow up to be president. Little Johnny alertly responded, "Father, there's about one million boys in the United States, isn't there?" "Yes." "And every one stands a chance of being president?" "Yes." "Well, dad, I'll sell out my chance for a circus ticket." (*Warren Ledger* [PA], May 14, 1880)

English yokel played Astley's, the Royal Circus, Drury Lane, Covent Garden, and the Edinburgh Equestrian Circus, and was a favorite at Sadler's Wells, where he was clown to Richer's tight-rope performances. During his act, Dubois danced a reel with a set of hats that he kept spinning like tops before kicking them up and catching them on his head.[31]

Fair booths and hucksters across Europe had their Jack Pudding, who became, after Joey Grimaldi's time, plain "Joey" in England, "Hans Wurst" and later "Staberl" in Germany. In France, the nickname became "Paillasso" or *Le Pitre*, and in Italy, the comic appearing at fetes and farces became "Stentorello." In the mid–1830s, the Shakespearean clown emerged. Charles Marsh claimed credit for the style, but it was a well-educated Bohemian, W. F. Wallett, who, after failing as a stage actor, reemerged in the ring as the "Queen's Jester," the greatest Shakespearean jester of the age. As such, he gave recitations in the dress of a Medieval jester and never descended to tumbling. By the 1850s, Wallett's dialogue incorporated a wordplay quickly adopted by others:

> Whether the weather is cold, or whether the weather is hot, we shall always have weather, whether we want it or not.

In lesser circuses, the humor was a stretch to the Elizabethan playwright, with dialogue no more closely related than the clown pretending to have a toothache and declaring, "To draw, or not to draw."[32]

By the 1840s, the Frenchman Auriol (Auriols Flaschentanz) was the idol of the Parisians. The performer was a very small man but excessively graceful, and the creator of many acts that were borrowed and traveled around the globe by imitators. His specialty was the pyramid of bottles and chairs, tumbling on stilts and turning somersaults on horseback through hoops, all the while speaking no more than his signature, "La-la-la."

About the same time, at Astley's, the featured clown sported an elegant costume, delivering the time-honored joke about "any money being better than matri-money," and naming his horse "Graphy" because when he rode him he was "Top o' Graphy." When he made the horse step out he said, "Gee o' Graphy," and when he wanted to "sell" him, he told the purchaser he "ought to buy a graphy," and so on. Tom Barry, the jester to the celebrated Eglinton Tournament, rode a donkey while carrying an umbrella, in spite of the anachronism.

Acrobatic clowns reached their pinnacle with the six Irish Hanlon Brothers, who had been trained by John Lees. They eventually took on the name Hanlon-Lees. After Lees' death in 1855, the brothers met Henri Agoust in Chicago, under whose direction they developed a series of acrobatic pantomimes, of which *Voyage en Suisse* was the most famous. Their exploits on the horizontal bars were so highly regarded that the management of Forepaugh and Sells, for whom they worked in 1899, determined that no other exhibition should be given while they performed.[33]

Beginning in the early 1850s, English clowns were in great demand, and as late as the turn of the century, no circus in Europe was considered first-class without one or more Englishmen chattering in broken French and committing acrobatic absurdities in the ring. In Franconi and Royal's Paris Circus, there was, since the ascension of Louis Napoleon, a series of Cockney clowns; Little Wheat was an especial favorite, wearing a costume embroidered in gold wheels on a black maillot, who became known as the most rapid turner of flip-flaps (or wheels) that ever appeared. Price was one of the most elegant and accomplished of comedians, who danced, sang, rode and played musical instruments while imitating

THE NEW SOCIETY FAD.—AN AMATEUR CIRCUS ENTERTAINMENT, AT HATCHESTER, WHICH INTERESTED THE "FOUR HUNDRED."—THE "BABY ELEPHANT" ACT.—FROM A SKETCH BY C. BUNNELL.—[SEE PAGE 283.]

This scene is a classic rendition of a late 19th century circus. While the trainer and the elephant bow to the crowd, the ringmaster (with his whip) and three clowns watch. The clowns are wearing the typical one-piece costume decorated with large colorful stars. The frills around neck and hands came in use by the late 1700s, while the pointed hats were popularized by Dubois. Beneath the clothing would be a rubberized "stomach" to accentuate weight, heavy men being considered jolly. The white face make-up could contain anything from egg whites and flour to white lead and benzoin. These were toxic chemicals, often causing open sores and occasionally permanent damage to the skin. (*Frank Leslie's Illustrated Newspaper*, May 18, 1889)

famous actors and actresses. His work with James Boswell in a "duel" where each shot the other became a standard. Billy Hayden, who was a jester as well as a tumbler, spoke French well enough to bandy jokes with the ringmaster, and was the darling of Paris.

The European clown had to possess a smattering of several languages from every country through which he passed and a wardrobe as complicated as any prima donna's. He never wore the same dress twice and gave great thought to his appearance, as opposed to the American "knockabout" of later years, who wore dirty, baggy suits and whose names never became familiar to the public. The costume of the clown by the 1880s rarely combined beauty and eccentricity. They wore a loose, baggy, divided skirt that began at the neck and, after cascading over a rubber stomach, terminated in two flounces at the knee or ankle. The costume, generally made of white muslin, daubed with a red moon or two, a blue donkey and a few dice in black and white, was created by two brothers whose limbs were unfortunately distorted; the loose-fitting material served to mitigate their afflictions.[34]

Delpini brought to the circus the white-face make-up, originally created with flour but later with white lead, oxide of zinc, lard and tincture of benzoin. This make-up persisted into the 1860s, and was heavily used by theatrical people, often leading to facial disfigure-ment. The bucolic red-cheeked "face" stylized by Grimaldi became vulgarized by the "auguste" into broad smudges of black over the nose and ghastly accentuations of the skull and cheek bones, caricaturing the facial features in imitation of the comic Greek mask. The two styles eventually merged: in 1842, Tom Barry's make-up "consisted of a white face with a small, delicately outlined red mouth, formalized red triangles on the cheeks, greatly exaggerated black eyebrows, and a bald wig."[35]

The earliest hat worn by clowns was the round, conical type popularized by Dubois. Billy Hayden later sported a short top hat; wigs were sometimes used, and frills appeared around the collars. By the 1870s, the "auguste" costume came into vogue, whereby the clown wore absurd clothes, much too large or much too small, a ludicrous wig and make-up. It was he who entered the ring to assist in rolling the carpets, raking the sawdust, and helping the grooms with a *bonne vitente* that was aggressively officious but always embar-rassing. He was never on time, was always in the way, and invariably disconcerted with his futility. Some skits included carrying coal to Pittsburg, and lacerating his hands when explaining the use of a razor to his friend Figero. He wanted to wash black armor white but could not find the soap, ignoring the towel and water. He never laughed or smiled, and his pompadour bristles stood up in mute astonishment as everyone refused his collab-oration.[36] This led into a two-clown act where the elegant white-faced clown played against the disreputable auguste clown, and it was always the latter who got drenched with water or whose trousers fell down.[37]

One of the most famous clowns in the latter part of the 19th century was "Chocolat," a dark-skinned Cuban attached to the Nouvean Cirque, Paris. He got his start going on one night in place of "Auguste," who was sick, and went on to be a Parisian favorite with the comic interlude "Chocolat's Wedding," which included the couple falling out of a pleasure boat into real water. In 1889, he teamed with George Footit, creating a classic clown-auguste combination.[38]

A rare female clown was Miss Williams, whose father had been a clown for 40 years. She was 25 years old and "undersized," but "with an abundance of health and energy." Her most famous trick was to dress in a cloak and bonnet and sit by a young man in the audience. During the performance she suddenly called out to the ringmaster, "Will you give me a job?" He dickered with her, and she asked what he would pay. He replied, "Ten dollars a performance." She answered, "Oh, no," and pointing to the youth, continued, "This young man here that I am engaged to will give me more than that to stop here with him." Over his great confusion, the audience roared with laughter.[39]

Circus Music

In addition to clowns, music is most closely identified with circuses. The notes of the calliope, the theme march of the animals, and the lively tunes played during a performance belong to and will always be associated with circuses. The seemingly effortless work by musicians and the astonishing coordination with acts went hand-in-hand with the overall wonder and mystery of the production. What the spectator never realized — and was never meant to — was the tremendous effort behind that awe.

In the late 1880s, the salary of a circus band member was comparable to that of a the-ater musician who worked under union rates, earning $2.50 a performance, out of which he paid his personal expenses. The circus bandleader selected and arranged music, with the added duty of matching the airs to fit ring performances. If two or three riding acts performed simultaneously, the task was relatively easy, but if acts were going on upon the ground as well as in the air, great care had to be taken not to throw off horses or artists who depended on certain musical cues. He then had to be aware of which lot took precedence, and which to make secondary, while serving both as well as possible.

In the case where a star was doing a triple trapeze act, though there were three other acts going on in other rings, the time and force of the music had to be played to suit the headliner. When he sounded his bell, the band had to play pianissimo, for that was his signal he was about to speak a word of direction and his voice had to be heard. When an astounding feat had been completed, the band broke out with a fortissimo crash, blending in the roar of the audience. No matter where the composer put diminuendos or crescendos, the bandleader was compelled to play the piece that way, whether it became unrecognizable or not, whether it suited the other performers or not, and whether people complained how badly the band played.

One point that gave a certain sameness to circus music was the compulsory emphasis of notes in a regular recurrent order, not demanded for musical expression but requisite for marking time for the horses in a menage act or some other riding. If the time were not sharply accented, the best-trained horse was liable to break stride and ruin his performance. When training a horse, one of the musicians was called upon to play the violin so as to familiarize the animal with the air to which he would be required to perform. It might take three months for a horse to match the tempo and step naturally with it.

Time was adapted to the horses to a certain degree, but still the marked accent had to be kept, creating a very strong family resemblance between the tunes — enough to make people say, "Same old tune." Elephants were trained to the same music, or so close that there were no abrupt changes, for American audiences would not tolerate the exact music all the time, no matter the preference of the animals. This was not usually the case in Europe, where the same pieces were played for years on end.

Many trapeze and specialty performers had their own music, and they were accommodated whenever possible. Generally, however, their music was arranged for string bands to be used in theaters. Circuses could not play it without rearrangement, so typically more convenient tunes were supplied. Although new music was worked in, performers preferred that which they trained with and habitually requested the band go back to their own choices.[40]

26

"A Little World in Itself"

In the year 2400, Joseph Cook says, the population of this country will be 3,200,000,000. Those of our readers who contemplate going to the circus that year will do well to purchase tickets at the down-town office to avoid the rush at the wagon.[1]

The turn of the century always seems to mark an end of the old and a beginning of the new. For the circus, that figurative transitional period could be said to have started in 1880, when Burr Robbins suffered a terrible steamboat accident. While piloting his private boat on Rock River, a mile south of Janesville, it struck a bridge, plunging him into the water. Fears for his life were entertained, but the venerable proprietor survived.[2]

That accident (and his subsequent retirement in 1887, when he sold his concern to Greiner and assumed ownership of a pleasure garden in Chicago) was a reminder that most of the surviving pioneers of the circus were getting on in age. Dan Gardner, the clown, died October 8 at age 64; in November 1881, William N. Kincade, the great leaper, was turning a double summersault over several elephants at Pulaski, Tennessee, and fell, breaking his spine and dying several days later. John H. Murray, the circus proprietor who began his career as a banjo player in a minstrel troupe in 1846, died of pneumonia in December 1881, age 53.[3] Archie Campbell, the clown, died of consumption in August 1882. The same disease took William T. Aymar in March 1883. Aymar and his elder brother John (who broke his neck in the ring on the Isle of Jersey) were early California circusmen who later performed in South America. William left Peru to return to California, where he established a livery stable and speculated in mining stock.[4]

Colonel Joseph Cushing, another early pioneer, died March 3, 1884. The attrition of proprietors continued with the death of Fayette Lodawich "Yankee" Robinson on September 4, 1884, after nearly fifty years in the business. W. C. "Fatty" Sells, one of the Sells Brothers (known as "Kale" to friends in his hometown of Decatur) died on a steamboat bound for New Orleans on November 18, 1884. Unable to reach his family, the body was buried at Paducah.[5] The depressing countdown included Frank Pastor, the last of the famous Pastors, who died June 25, 1885; while attending his funeral, Levi J. North, the beloved equestrian of a generation, caught cold and died in Brooklyn at age 71, "in possession of little or no property."[6]

C. W. Noyes died of dysentery and was buried at Goldthwaite in 1885; Andrew Haight expired from a stroke the following year. Henry M. Majilton ("Magilton"), famous for his character of "Jocko, the Brazilian Ape," originated by Henry Leech (professional name "Otto Motti"), lived out his life with paralysis of the lower extremities from a fall off the trapeze in 1861.[7] The old war soldier, Colonel Sam B. Chambers, known as "Old Silvertop," the clown and owner of Chambers' Circus, died in 1887; Will Nichols ("Nicholls"), who owned Lent's New York Circus died in 1887 at age 66 of apoplexy. Two years previous, he lost his fortune via a shipwreck off Florida and was compelled to return to riding to earn a living.[8] Spencer Stokes, who at age 17 managed Sam Stickney, the father of Robert Stickney and the man who introduced "Ella Zoyara" to the world, died at age 69 in 1888.

The seemingly unending list of notable deaths included John Robinson on August 4, 1888, who did manage to leave a large fortune. William B. "Uncle Barney" Carroll reached age 74 before dying in Westchester Village, New York. Apprenticed under George Sweet, he earned fame as a rider, leaper and acrobat before going into instructing circus performers. His wife, Mme. Carroll, was the first woman rider to jump over an object held in the air, and their daughter worked with circus leopards, marrying Ben Maginley, the actor.[9]

John Sanger, the circus manager, died in 1889; John O'Brien, another proprietor, died at Frankford, Pennsylvania, the same year, in a "somewhat embarrassed" financial condition.[10] William Hanlon, one of the famous Hanlon Brothers, fell 30 feet when a trapeze bar broke and was killed instantly on July 13, 1891. William Worrell, one of the oldest circus clowns, and father of Sophie, Irene and Jennie, the "Worrell Sisters," died at Orange, New Jersey, of a stroke. Charles J. Melville, champion circus rider, died in Pittsburg in 1893; and "Major Decker," advertised as the smallest living man, died of alcoholism at age 44 in Chicago.

The 1890s had its own share of deaths. In 1895, W. C. Coup died of pneumonia; Hyatt Frost (long manager of Van Amburgh's circus, who retired in 1884) and Thomas Coates, credited as being the first circus band leader in America and one of the original French horn players, died the same year. John S. Shorb (the first man to introduce "dime museum freaks" and cousin of Mrs. William McKinley) died in 1896. John Forepaugh died in Florida as a result of a streetcar accident in 1897; A. B. Stowe, a pioneer proprietor, died in 1898; Ephriam Sells, eldest of the Sells brothers, died of Bright's disease in 1898; while Jacob Driesbach died in 1878 and and James M. Nixon died in 1899.

Cumulatively, the loss to the circus world was staggering. But soon the circus of the 19th century was destined to change forever.

The Earth Shakes

P. T. Barnum and Adam Forepaugh spent years operating against one another, at times with serious acrimony. When they finally agreed their circus feuding was not in the best interests of business, they struck an agreement in 1886, by which they promised not to exhibit in the same territories, effectively anticipating the demise of all smaller circuses from their monopoly.[11] It did not take long. In November, W. W. Cole, despite having a good season and being $2,000,000 ahead, sold out to Barnum, the terms of the contract stipulating he cease business at the end of the year.[12] His circus was sold at auction in New Orleans, Forepaugh being a major purchaser.[13]

The following October, James A. Bailey bought the entire interest of James L. Hutchinson, W. W. Cole and James E. Cooper in the Barnum & London Circus, menagerie and

Zazel was the first person to be shot from a cannon into a suspended net when she performed the feat at the Westminster Aquarium, London. Achieving sudden fame, she and her agent/husband, George O. Starr, was brought by Barnum to America. One of her earliest feats was to jump into a net from the highest buildings in New York to illustrate the use of nets in escaping fire. During her great aerial circus dive, the "Eagle Swoop," she reached the topmost height of the Pavilion, from which she dived head foremost through the air nearly 100 feet. In the autumn of 1891, while in New Mexico with Forepaugh's circus, her apparatus was improperly fastened and she fell 40 feet. Miraculously, she survived and continued her career. (*Warren Ledger* [PA], June 11, 1895; illustration from *Oshkosh Daily Northwestern*, June 16, 1880)

hippodrome, creating a new firm called Barnum & Bailey. Bailey had formerly been a partner of Barnum's but sold out on account of ill health. The repurchase cost him 50 percent more than when he sold his shares two years previous.[14]

In 1888, the Greatest Show on Earth played the western circuit, and "4 Paw" the eastern. Under a continuation, they extended their terms through 1890: Forepaugh to have Philadelphia and Barnum to have New York, with the remainder of the country divided into Eastern and Western routes, the two shows alternating yearly.[15]

On January 22, 1890, Adam Forepaugh died at his residence in Philadelphia of influenza. He was 68 years old and left an estate estimated at over $1,000,000. He was survived by his second wife and his son, the animal trainer Adam Junior. Hardly a month later, James E. Cooper, former senior member of the firm of Cooper & Bailey, purchased the vast circus plant and title for "a princely sum," the show to be managed by Forepaugh Jr.[16]

A New York dispatch of April 7, 1891, brought other earth-shaking news: P. T. Barnum had died. According to articles of agreement with his equal partner, James A. Bailey, the show went on as usual, with Bailey quickly announcing, "the show will continue with its policy entirely unchanged. The capital of $3,500,000 will remain intact." Bailey remained as manager. News quickly spread that as Bailey had been responsible for all the "big circus ideas" for the past dozen years, no alterations were on the horizon.[17]

Next to Mrs. Barnum, the largest bequests went to Barnum's daughter, Mrs. Caroline Thompson, and his grandchildren, Helen Barnum Grinnell and Julia H. Clarke, who received $100,000 each. In consideration of a prior bequest to his daughter, Helen M. Buchtelle, she was left nothing in the will. To his favorite grandson, Clinton H. Seeley (who was widely believed to be the principal heir), Barnum left $25,000 on the condition that he legally change his name to Clinton Barnum Seeley, as Phineas left no male issue and wished to perpetuate his name. Seeley also received $30,000 and 3 percent of the net profits of the Barnum & Bailey show, up to $10,000 a year, provided he travel with and perform personal service to the show. Among other minor bequests, Barnum left $1,000 for a statue of Henry Bergh, of the Society for the Protection of Animals. The great showman was buried in Mountain Grove Cemetery, in Bridgeport.[18]

With Barnum and Forepaugh gone, mergers continued with great rapidity. In June 1891, one third of Sells Brothers circus was sold to Adam Forepaugh, Jr., and John A. Forepaugh, Forepaugh, Sr.'s nephew. The two had reportedly been dissatisfied with the sale of the Forepaugh Circus to James Cooper and were eager to have their own concern.

Adam Forepaugh's Shows advertised that "We pay one feature [artist] more salary than our country pays its president." In 1891, Forepaugh's was the "Oldest, Largest, Richest Exhibition in the world." Beginning in 1864, this marked its 28th year. Grown considerably larger than its Civil War beginnings, the exhibition was said to have $3,000,000 invested, with $5,000 daily expenses, 1,200 men and horses, 50 railroad cars and 4 railway trains. (*The Morning Review* [IL], May 3, 1891)

The plan called for Adam Jr. to assume charge of the show while John looked after the privileges.[19]

Events took another turn on January 1, 1892, when James E. Cooper died from pneumonia complicated by the grip (influenza).[20] It was not long before James A. Bailey bought control of the Forepaugh Circus, making him a very formidable competitor. His power was not lost on the smaller concerns, and in 1893, circus men, primarily from the west and southwest, formed a protective trust. The stated aim was to collectively boycott any town that fixed an exorbitant license fee, or any bill-poster or tradesman who did not give them fair prices for services rendered. Each member set his own prices and arranged his schedule. Among the larger members were the John Robinson Show, Sells Brothers, Ringling Brothers, Sell & Rentfrom, Walter L. Main, F. J. Taylor, L.W. Washburn, Baldwin & Cumming, Locke and C.E. Lee.

Individual members of the association wrote to Bailey, urging the advantages of mutual cooperation, but having already set out routes for his two concerns, Bailey declined by observing that his shows were so powerful "there is no reason why they should join with any other circuses."[21]

Things did not go well for Bailey. Devoting all his time to Barnum & Bailey (he continued to use Barnum's name, as it was the latter's wish his name should be connected with the show for 50 years after his death),[22] Bailey selected his brother-in-law, Joseph McCadden, to operate Forepaugh's show. Thomas Evans, who had been Barnum's representative, became secretary, and T. F. Callan, one of the fastest ticket-sellers in the business, was included. Shortly after the show went on the road, McFadden made several changes. He installed his nephew as cashier and changed Callan to the Barnum & Bailey show. In October 1893, Bailey reported that $100,000 had been stolen from Forepaugh's in a conspiracy involving employees in all departments. Evans and McCadden were said to be free from suspicion, but in light of the theft, Bailey declared he would not send Forepaugh's out again.[23]

In December 1894, Bailey entered into a partnership with William F. Cody ("Buffalo Bill") and his agent, Nate Salisbury (Sallisbury), with a view to organizing a "Wild West" show for 1895, to include a circus and several new features.[24] Still not content with his control of circus entertainment, Bailey consolidated the Sells Brothers and Forepaugh's shows, giving him control of three of the greatest shows on earth.[25] It would seem he had everything well under control. But trouble was brewing.

Rise of a Big Show by Push and Indomitable Courage

The names of most proprietors disappeared by the turn of the 20th century, but three survived to epitomize the American circus in the 1900s: Barnum, Bailey and the Ringling Brothers. The story of the latter began in 1882, when five brothers (Al, Otto, Charles, Alf T. and John), then known by the surname "Rungeling,"[26] were living in Wisconsin. Already accomplished musicians, having been the mainstay of the Baraboo brass band for several years, they witnessed the success of a small fly-by-night hall show with a brass band accessory. Realizing the potential for success, they organized their own hall show and performed at local towns. The venture proved successful, and the following winter they toured with a more extensive show. That summer, they added three or four wagons of their own

The Ringling Brothers started out from a small Wisconsin town with their musical instruments and a few wagons. By 1892, they were one of the largest exhibitions in operation. Their show for 1892 offered a "Real Roman Hippodrome" with 2- and 4-horse chariot racing, elephant and camel racing, and pony races with monkey drivers. They also displayed "Caesar's Triumphant Entry into Rome," and included the Mikado's Troupe of Royal Japanese and Moscow's Far Famed Cathedral Bells. (*Eldora Weekly Ledger* [IA], July 7, 1892)

construction, three horses and a dozen rented mules, calling themselves the Ringling Bros Classic and Comic Concert Company.

At this point it was not a circus, but they caught the eye of Yankee Robinson, who sponsored them. In 1884, they bought a small tent, 45' by 90', seating 600 people, brought their capacity up to nine wagons, and toured with Robinson as "Yankee Robinson's Great Show, Ringling Brothers Carnival of Novelties and DeNar's Museum of Living Wonders." Before the season ended, Yankee Robinson died, and the Ringling Brothers secured his interest in the show.

Continued success brought expansion. By 1889, they had 110 horses; in 1890, they had grown too large for a "mud show" (travel by wagon) and put the concern on their own railroad cars. In 1891, they boasted 22 cars; ten more were added the next season. (Other accounts put the railroad numbers for those years at 18 and 25.)[27]

Advertised as Ringling Brothers' United Monster Railroad Shows, the brothers boasted 200 Star Circus Performers, 250 horses and 80 Sensational Acts on 10 acres of exhilarating sights.[28] By 1893, the Ringling Brothers' "World's Greatest Shows, Now Beyond All Comparison, the Largest and Grandest Exhibition on Earth" featured a Real Roman Hippodrome, Equine Carnival, Chariot Races, the Largest Living Giraffe and the great Charles W. Fish, champion somersault rider.[29] Even if that claim were true at the time, the brothers were quickly usurped by James Bailey, first by his acquisition of Forepaugh's and later by the monster union with Sells. What began as a heated rivalry quickly developed into what contemporary newspapers styled "Circus Wars."

The first and most obvious battle was fought by bill-posters and advertising men, as they squabbled over available space to display their art. Accusations flew fast and furious as to who covered up whose billboards, each taking the high moral ground when pointing a finger at the other. In 1896, Ringling Brothers published a 15-paragraph letter to the public — not to elicit sympathy that they "didn't need," because such were "the fortunes of a circus war," but rather to give their side in the "frothy attack" by their rivals.[30] Next came their advance man Mr. Coxey's abandonment of billboards, relying on huge newspaper advertising to get the word out.[31]

Newspapers receiving the benefit of massive advertising dollars tended to take the side of their client[32]; others praised Bailey for putting together such a monster show because "patrons will get more — and the very best of everything — without a penny's additional cost."[33]

An end to the war, as far as Barnum & Bailey was concerned, happened when Bailey took the circus to England. Rumors began swirling that he was moving his exhibitions into a limited liability company, whereby he would receive $2,250,000 for the property and trademark, obtaining two-thirds in money and one-third in stock. In March 1899, the London correspondent for the *Clipper* announced the rest of the 400,000 shares would be offered to the public at £1. Vast buildings were to be erected, with Bailey as managing director.[34] Bailey's representative, Whitney Allen, qualified the deal by stating the proposed negotiations were still under consideration, as the show cleared $500,000 profit in England the previous season and there was no hurry to settle. He added:

> That show is Mr. Bailey's pride, his very life. To him the title, "The Greatest
> Show on Earth" means exactly that. Mr. Bailey took the show to England expressly
> for the purpose of proving his entire right to the distinctive name which an admiring
> American public had bestowed upon the enterprise. Now that he has done so, he will
> bring it back home.[35]

Understandably, James A. Bailey was a huge personality in England. Details of his life, given by R. F. Hamilton, were published, whereby it was stated Bailey had been born in Detroit in 1846, and was orphaned at age eleven. Although his father left a fortune of $25,000, J. A. Gordon (Bailey being an adopted name) ran away from home a year later over disagreements with his cruel guardian. Working as a cowboy and a bell-boy (using the name Jimmy Fitzgerald while working in Cincinnati),[36] he was befriended by Fred Bailey, an advance agent of a show, who offered him work, first as a bill-poster and, by age 18, as an agent. For a number of years, Bailey worked for Cooper & Whitby's Circus until being given an interest in the show, after which it was called Cooper & Bailey's.

After touring with the show in Australia, Tasmania, New Zealand, India and South America, Bailey returned home just as a printing company was laying a lien on Howes and Cushing's circus, to whom they were in debt for $160,000. Their show was offered to Bailey for a quarter of its value, and he bought it. After competing and crossing swords with Barnum, the two became partners in 1880, with Bailey becoming manager of their combined exhibitions. Success followed, and by 1897, Bailey not only owned three great circuses, but five-eighths of the wild animals in the Central Park Zoological Garden, New York, and all the animals in the Washington Garden.[37]

The End of the Century

Instead of returning to the United States, Bailey made plans to take his Greatest Show to Germany. By themselves, Forepaugh and the Sells Brothers seemed to have fewer problems with the Ringling Brothers. People continued to patronize circuses, and the rich got richer, Ringling Brothers representing a cash investment of $3,700,000, with a seasonal operating cost of $200,000.[38] Their five-long train of cars used for transporting the circus represented a floor space greater than 130 ordinary railroad cars.[39]

Whether an "old" or a "new" circus, centennial peanuts and pink lemonade continued to sell as briskly as ever, with 30,000 pounds of ice being required for one 2-day period,[40] while the addition of "frankforts" went with a rush.[41] Harkening backward, Ringling's offered a new version of the "genuine white elephant"[42]; poor old Dan Rice was sent to the work house on a 30-day sentence of loitering[43]; and the Salvation Army declared a war of its own by pasting Scriptural text and religious warnings over circus billboards.[44] Conversely, at Bonesteele, South Dakota, Archie P. Brewer, owner of a small tent show, was brought up on murder charges for killing the "missing link," after town officials decided it was more human than monkey.[45]

Circuses began offering special accommodation for "wheels" (bicycles),[46] elephants displayed terror at the smell of "automobiles,"[47] and the combined management of the "Great John Robinson and Franklin Brothers' Enormous Shows Combined" secured the most thoroughly finished and speedy "horseless carriages" for their concern.[48]

A positive note going forward was the strong influence of the American Humane Society, that resolved to see abuses arising from carelessness, ignorance or thoughtlessness to animals stopped and ultimately prevented. Toward this end, members began inspecting circuses and menageries to see that their animals were treated in a humane manner, had enough room, were fed properly and sufficiently, and were not abused.[49]

As the 1800s drew to a close, two quotations stand out, both as a summary and a look forward, the first from 1899:

> Buffalo Bill has probably been seen by more human beings than any other professional, but his name attached to a show is not worth a cent unless he appears himself. It was the same with [Edwin] Booth, who was the greatest of actors and Patti, who is the greatest of singers. A theatrical troop traveling under Booth's name or an opera company under Patti's name, would not draw any more than Buffalo Bill's company without Buffalo Bill. The name "Barnum" attached to a show is worth a million dollars.[50]

And lastly, from 1877:

> The ring is destroyed, the sawdust blown away, the hand-organ and steam piano are mute, the real lemonade has evaporated, the high-priced equestrienne, the five elephants, the only living eland, and the unicorn of holy writ have taken themselves legs and walked away, and the mourning small boy goeth about the streets looking for base ball, for verily the circus is not.[51]

At least not until next season.

Glossary

Alw Top ranking; a star performer.

Acherner Epitome.

Acrobatic slang Included such terms as "understander," "middleman" and "top-mounter."

After-piece An "extra" act performed after the main attractions.

"Angel" Someone willing to put up money.

Annex A side-show to the circus (circa late 1870s).

Arena A circus ring where acts are performed.

Barker A man with a persuasive voice who sought to entice people into the show.

Big Show The circus, usually in reference to combined shows.

Bills Circus posters or placards.

Bon Mot From the French ("good word"), meaning a clever remark.

"Bones" Slang for dice.

"Boodle" A wad of money; stake.

"Boom" To manufacture support and enthusiasm.

"Boozer" A man who drinks to excess.

Break (to break) To fail; go bankrupt.

Buffer Circus assistant; one who seated the crowd.

Burletta In the 18th and 19th centuries, a musical drama with rhymed lyrics, resembling a comic opera or a play delivered in song.

"Butcher" A catch-all term referring to those who sold peanuts, lemonade, palm leaf fans, animal and song books, and concert tickets.

"Cackle" Circus slang for "speech" or "jabbering."

Camp The circus dining tent where most circus men obtained their meals.

"Candy butchers" Men who sold confections during a circus performance.

"Catch penny concern" Common expression for a one-horse circus, circa 1870s.

"Chain Lightnings" Circus slang for a ticket seller, so-called because of the speed of his operation, usually applied to those who made a living out of giving incorrect change.

Chancery A high court of equity in England and Wales with common-law functions.

Chevy Chace A performance of dance, divided into segments.

"Cinch" Something settled beyond all doubt; from the saddle girth tightened by the Spanish method of a complicated knot that will not come undone; hence, a sure thing, or all settled beforehand.

Circus In early American usage, "circus" often meant the building rather than the performing company.

"Collar" Slang for policeman.

Corde volante A rider who performed leaps on the horse.

"Cracker" English term for clown.

Crook A class of circus followers whose methods were outside the law, such as pickpockets, gamblers and short-change men.

"Cully" Circus slang for "comrade."

Curious Its use in the 18th century referred to anything unusual or uncommon rather than the modern definition of strange or odd.

cwt. Hundredweight.

"Dead-head" Someone who attempts to get into the circus without paying; the recipient of a free circus pass.

"Depot" See "Fence."

"Ditched" Expressing ruin and collapse, from railroad men.

Drawing cards Popular attractions.

Dress/dresses Costumes.

Dude/s A common 19th century expression referring to young men dressed in a "sporty" style; fops. Also a term for a clown that plays a dude.

Dutch courage Fortified by liquor.

"Dutch metal" Fool's gold.

Exchanges Newspaper exchanges; newspapers that shared articles with one another.

"Fence" A receiver of stolen goods; originated in London.

"Fixer" A "general fixer" was the circus agent in charge of getting licenses for showing in towns and obtaining permits for street parades.

"Flipping the bones" Rolling dice.

"Fly by night" An expression meaning "to fail."

"Fly workers" Men who sold candy, peanuts and lemonade quickly, or "on the fly."

Fun makers Clowns.

Garter A ribbon, used in reference to acts of jumping or leaping over heights either by gymnasts or equestrians.

"Gilly" Slang for a dupe.

Goad A pole or stick with a hook attached, used in controlling animals, usually used in reference to elephants.

Goggles Circus slang for "eyes."

Grafter See "Crook."

Ground tumbling Acrobatics, including somersets, cartwheels and hop-frog.

"Hammer, the" "To escape the hammer"—An expression meaning to avoid bankruptcy.

"Hey, rube" A circus battle cry to arms, alerting all hands that danger was present; used particularly when mobs threatened violence.

Hippodrama A dramatic hybrid performed in a circus, with a play including live animals.

Hoodoo; to be "hoodoed" A jinx or Jonah in reference to a person, place or thing.

Hornpipe An energetic, solo folk dance set to music.

Horse boat A floating circus; a circus on a steamboat.

Horse Opera A small circus with various entertainments, so named because exhibitions of this type often played inside opera houses.

Hurdle riding An act where horse and rider leapt over barriers; also known as hunt riding, where obstacles simulated those encountered during a fox hunt.

Hustler Used by circus men to mean "a good, lively, industrious worker."

I. T. Indian Territory.

Intrinsic attraction An act claimed to be unique to one circus.

"Jasper" See "Rube."

Jewsharp (Also Jew's harp.) A small, lyre-shaped musical instrument held between the teeth and struck with the finger.

Joberwock (Also spelled "jaberwock" and "jobberwock.") Nonsense, jibberish; obscure or unidentified menagerie animal and/or the roar it emits; from Lewis Carroll's *Through the Looking Glass* (1871).

Jump The distance from one town to another.

Jumping Traveling.

"Kid top" The side show where the "freaks" were shown.

Knockabouts Tumbling clowns.

La Perche A balancing act with a pole 30 feet high balanced on the chest of one gymnast while a second gymnast is mounted on the summit performing astonishing feats.

Leapers Men who threw somersaults over horses.

Levee A reception (in circus terms, an act) given by a person of distinction (a star performer).

"Lightning jerker" Slang for a telegraph operator.

"Lines" A performer's specialty.

Lofty tumbling Acrobatics incorporating leaping, either from a horse to the ground and vice versa, or jumping through hoops and over barrels.

"Lost his grip" A man in a temporary dilemma.

Lot The show ground.

"Lusher" See "Boozer."

"Main guy" The boss of the show.

Makeup By the late 1890s, the term had come to refer to anything striking in personal adornment, referring to clothing, as opposed to a disguise or enhancement of the features.

Manege The art of horsemanship or of training horses; used to indicate an act of horsemanship.

Master A youth; used to indicate an apprentice.

Master of the Circle Ringmaster.

Mr. Merryman A term for clown.

Mud Show A circus that traveled by wagon as opposed to one that traveled by railroad.

Musique parlante Originating in France,

"speaking music" referred to comedy or drama performed without dialogue.

Necromancy Used in the 19th century to refer to ventriloquists and magicians.

Nibs (His Nibs) Circus slang for "God."

Ombres Chinoises A shadow puppet show comprised of small figures with all the natural attitudes of acting and dancing; backdrops were frequently changed, and voices for the puppets came from off stage by actors.

"Operator" Slang for one who works a dishonest board game.

Pad rider An equestrian who rode with a saddle or "pads," as opposed to one who rode bareback.

Pasteboards Tickets; also used in reference to a deck of playing cards.

"Patter" A talking clown.

Play people A common expression for entertainers seen in the 1870s.

Polander's tricks The term comprised several displays of equilibrium, including balancing on chairs, tables, etc.

Pony Circus Typically, a performance of children performing equestrian acts.

Privileges A right, purchased from a circus proprietor or manager, to operate a side show outside the main tent; this included advance ticket sales, candy sales and exhibitions.

"Puff" Outrageous and extravagant reporting (as in a newspaper).

"Ragtag and bobtail" Slang for the thieves, robbers and murderers hanging around the outer edges of a circus; riffraff.

"Razorbacks" Circus canvasmen and other laborers.

"Red letter day" Expression from the 1880s meaning "a great day."

Red Wagon Show A circus that travels overland, as opposed to one that travels by rail.

"Reuben" A clown who plays a hick.

Rider Slang Included "rough riders," "pad riders" and "bare back riders."

Riding master A position developed to keep the horse of the bareback rider at a steady pace; later developed into the ringmaster.

Roadster A horse appearing in the cavalcade but not trained for the ring.

Rompo A mystical creature; used in early menageries to refer to a hyena.

Roustabouts Circus jacks of all trades; occasionally used in reference to circus "toughs."

"Rube" Reuben — an unflattering reference to a countryman; a hick.

Sans Souci A short comedy in which public figures and manners of the day were ridiculed.

Scenic Entertaining, attractive.

Scenic rider Scenes of action on horseback where the rider plays one or more characters.

Scooped Circus slang for duped.

Semi-Equestrians Monkeys taught to ride Shetland ponies.

Sharpers Gamblers.

"Short-change men" Circus men using various methods to give improper or "short" change when selling commodities.

Show (the Show) The technical term for a circus or menagerie; used extensively in the 1880s and beyond.

Showmen The people associated with the circus or menagerie.

"Shuck" A sweat board game consisting of a green cloth marked 1 to 6 and dice.

"Sidetracked" Temporary failure and suspension, the result of outside interference (from railroad men).

Sinking fund The reserve maintained by a proprietor to cover expenses during hard times.

Slack-rope A loosely-strung rope attached to supports on either side, suspended several feet off the ground upon which performers displayed acts of agility, later replaced by the trapeze.

Soap Artist An advertising agent who executed designs promoting the circus on windows first covered with soap film.

Somerset Also spelled "sommerset" — a somersault.

"Squeal" To confess and betray companions.

"Stake-driver" Bill poster.

Stock Circus horses.

Stock tops Horse tents.

Struck its tent Packed up and left town.

Sucker A dupe, easily fooled.

Switched Diverted; originated from railroad workers.

10-cent show A show charging 10 cents for admission; usually a small exhibition company.

Tenting season The period from April until October, depending on weather, when circuses traveled.

Tight-rope Similar to what it is today — a rope attached to supports on either side and tightly stretched to provide little give; later replaced with the tight-wire.

Top The tent. This was subdivided into the "big top," "animal top," "kid top," and "candy top."

Trampoline During the late 1700s and early 1800s, this springboard was made by pinning a stretched canvas between the sides of a wooden frame.

Transparencies Optical illusions.

Troop British spelling of the word "troupe"; from the French, circa 19th century.

Turn them, to To get a person's money without giving them any equivalent.

Vaulting rider An equestrian who leapt from horse to ground and vice versa, leapt over a moving horse's head or who performed various gymnastic feats on a moving horse.

"Wheezes" A clown's funny stories.

"Wide open" In full swing, reckless and regardless of interference; from railroad men, in reference to the throttle of a locomotive being left wide open.

"Wind-jammers" Musicians with a circus.

"Without dress" Riding bareback.

"Working off the chestnuts" An expression used by clowns in reference to using stale or tried-and-true jokes.

Yellow-jack Molasses candy.

Yellow jack Yellow fever.

Chapter Notes

Preface

1. Galveston Daily News, May 16, 1885

Chapter 1

1. *Gazetteer and New Daily Advertiser* (London), June 11, 1768
2. *London Gazette,* December 23–27, 1708
3. *Daily Post* (London), June 30, 1724; July 18, 25 & 26, 1729
4. Ibid., March 17, 1729
5. *Daily Journal* (London), December 20, 1736
6. *London Evening-Post,* March 1–4, 1740
7. *Daily Advertiser* (London), January 29, 1748
8. *General Advertiser* (London), May 9, 1748
9. *Whitehall Evening-Post; Or, London Intelligencer,* October 22–25, 1748
10. *The Spectator* (London), February 9, 1712
11. *Daily Advertiser,* February 8 & December 23, 1742
12. Ibid., February 8, 1742
13. *Antigallican Monitor and Anti-Corsican Chronicle,* 1763
14. *London Evening Post,* September 5, 1765
15. *Public Advertiser* (London), April 26, 1766
16. Ibid., May 1 & August 28, 1767
17. *Gazetteer and New Daily Advertiser,* August 1, 1767
18. *Public Advertiser,* January 25, April 16 & August 4, 1770
19. Ibid., May 6, 1772
20. *London Evening-Post,* December 26–29, 1772
21. *General Evening Post* (London), January 19–21 & January 30–February 2, 1773
22. Ibid., April 10–13, 1773
23. *Morning Chronicle, and London Advertiser,* April 5, 1774
24. *Gazetteer and New Daily Advertiser,* April 6, 1768
25. Ibid., May 30 & June 11, 1768
26. Speaight, George, *A History of the Circus,* London, The Tantivy Press, 1980, p. 24
27. *Gazetteer and New Daily Advertiser,* May 3, 1770
28. Ibid., June 18 & July 9, 1770
29. Ibid., July 23, 1770
30. *Public Advertiser,* July 17, 1771
31. Ibid., August 14, 1771
32. Ibid., April 21, 1772
33. Ibid., May 27, 1772
34. Ibid., June 16, 1772
35. Ibid., June 24, 1772
36. Ibid., July 18, 1772
37. Ibid., July 27, 1772
38. Ibid., June 24, 1772
39. Ibid., August 4, 1772
40. Ibid., August 28, 1772

Chapter 2

1. *Morning Herald and Daily Advertiser* (London), November 5, 1782
2. *Morning Post, and Daily Advertiser* (London), April 10, 17 & May 22, 1775
3. *Public Advertiser,* June 6, 19 & September 4, 1775
4. Speaight, p. 31
5. *Morning Post and Daily Advertiser,* August 28, 1776
6. Speaight, p. 32–33
7. *Public Advertiser,* March 28, 1777
8. *Morning Post and Daily Advertiser,* April 9, 1777; *Public Advertiser,* May 1, 1777
9. *Morning Post and Daily Advertiser,* April 9, 1777
10. *Public Advertiser,* June 19, September 17, 1777
11. Ibid., September 24, 1777
12. Ibid., November 18, 1777
13. *Morning Chronicle, and London Advertiser,* January 21, 1782
14. Speaight, p. 47
15. *Public Advertiser,* September 24, November 18, 1778; April 3, October 9, November 24, December 5 & 20, 1780
16. Ibid., January 1, 19 & April 2, 1781
17. Ibid., July 17, 1781
18. *Morning Chronicle and London Advertiser,* October 5, 1781
19. Speaight, p. 111
20. *Morning Chronicle, and London Advertiser,* December 13, 1781
21. Ibid., January 23 & March 29; *Public Advertiser,* March 13, 1782
22. *Public Advertiser,* April 13, 1782
23. *London Evening-Post,* May 12–14, 1774
24. *Public Advertiser,* September 15, 1778; April 4, 1780
25. *Monthly Magazine* (London), September 1, 1814
26. *Morning Post, and Daily Advertiser,* June 16, 1775
27. Ibid., June 26, 1775
28. Ibid., September 7, 1775

29. *Daily Advertiser,* January 1, 1776
30. *Morning Post, and Daily Advertiser,* January 6, 1776
31. Ibid., August 19, 1776
32. Ibid., April 25, 1777
33. *Morning Herald, and Daily Advertiser,* November 5, 1782
34. *European Magazine, and London Review,* November 1, 1782
35. *Grand Magazine of Magazines* (London), No. IV, October, 1785
36. *Morning Herald, and Daily Advertiser,* October 11, 1782
37. *European Magazine, and London Review,* November 1, 1782
38. *Morning Herald, and Daily Advertiser,* November 5, 1782
39. Ibid., November 13, 1782

Chapter 3

1. *Morning Chronicle, and London Advertiser,* April 12, 1786
2. Ibid., October 9, 1782
3. *Morning Post, and Daily Advertiser,* October 18, 1782
4. *Morning Chronicle, and London Advertiser,* November 5, 1782
5. *Morning Post, and Daily Advertiser,* November 30, 1782
6. *Morning Herald, and Daily Advertiser,* December 13, 1782
7. Ibid., January 11, 1783
8. Nicholls, Sir George, *A History of the English Poor Law in Connection with the State of the Country and the Condition of the People,* London, P. S. King & Son, 1904, Chapter X, pp. 34–38
9. *London Chronicle,* January 14, 1783
10. *Public Advertiser,* April 3, 1783
11. Ibid., June 23, 1783
12. Ibid., August 16, 1783
13. *Morning Post, and Daily Advertiser,* November 27, 1783
14. *Morning Herald, and Daily Advertiser,* December 30, 1783
15. *London Chronicle,* April 10, 1784
16. Kotar, S. L. & Gessler, J. E. *A History of the Balloon,* North Carolina, McFarland Publishing, 2010, p.
17. *Morning Herald, and Daily Advertiser,* March 8, 1784; *Public Advertiser,* March 11, 1784
18. *Public Advertiser,* March 13, 1784
19. *Morning Chronicle, and London Advertiser,* April 10, 1784
20. *Morning Post, and Daily Advertiser,* April 22, 1784
21. *Morning Chronicle, and London Advertiser,* October 2, 1784
22. *Morning Herald, and Daily Advertiser,* December 1, 1784
23. *Morning Post, and Daily Advertiser,* January 10, 1785
24. *Public Advertiser,* March 2, 1785
25. Ibid., March 23, 1785
26. *Morning Post, and Daily Advertiser,* April 9, 1785
27. Ibid., June 26 & July 4, 1785

Chapter 4

1. *The World, and Fashionable Advertiser* (London), April 20, 1787
2. *Morning Post, and Daily Advertiser,* August 2, 1785

3. *Public Advertiser,* April 25, 1785
4. *Morning Post, and Daily Advertiser,* September 1, 5, 10 & October 3, 1785
5. *Public Advertiser,* October 29 & November 10, 1785
6. *Morning Chronicle, and London Advertiser,* April 12, 1786
7. *Morning Post, and Daily Advertiser,* June 13, 1786
8. Ibid., May 6, 1786
9. *Public Advertiser,* May 15, 1786
10. Ibid., July 6, 1786
11. Ibid., April 20, 1786
12. *Morning Chronicle, and London Advertiser,* July 13, 1786
13. Ibid., August 24, 1786
14. *Morning Post, and Daily Advertiser,* July 3 & 7, 1786
15. Speaight, p. 18
16. *Morning Chronicle, and London Advertiser,* April 28, 1787
17. *The World, and Fashionable Advertiser,* April 30 & May 8, 1787
18. Ibid., April 20, August 6, 17, 21, September 10 & October 2, 1787
19. Ibid., November 19, 1787
20. Ibid., August 6, 1787
21. Ibid., February 14 & April 7, 1787
22. *Daily Universal Register* (London), July 23, 1787
23. *The Times* (London), March 17, 1788
24. Ibid., May 6, 1788
25. Ibid., July 28, 1788
26. *Morning Post, and Daily Advertiser,* June 24, 1788
27. Ibid., June 24 & 25, 1788
28. Ibid., August 9, 1788
29. Ibid., October 6, 1788
30. Ibid., August 29, 1788
31. *The Times,* October 11, 1788
32. *Public Advertiser,* February 26, 1788

Chapter 5

1. *The World, and Fashionable Advertiser,* April 14, 1787
2. *Stuart's Star and Evening Advertiser* (London), March 20, 1789
3. *The World* (London), April 27, 1789
4. *Morning Post, and Daily Advertiser,* April 17 & 20, 1789
5. *The world,* June 27, 1789
6. Ibid., August 12 & 31, 1789
7. *Morning Post, and Daily Advertiser,* August 21, 1789
8. *The World,* August 22, 1789
9. *The Argus* (London), October 13, 1789
10. *The World,* December 30, 1789
11. *Morning Post, and Daily Advertiser,* October 12, 1789
12. *The World,* January 7, 1790
13. *Public Advertiser,* April 5, 1790
14. *The Oracle; Bell's New World* (London), September 26, 1789
15. *The Times,* July 7, 1790
16. Ibid., July 7, 1790
17. Ibid., July 8 & 10, 1790
18. Ibid., July 12, 1790
19. Ibid., July 15, 1790
20. Ibid., July 13, 1790
21. *Morning Post, and Daily Advertiser,* September 22, 1790

22. *Morning Post,* April 1 & 2, 1793
23. *Morning Chronicle,* May 18, 1793
24. *Morning Post,* May 25, 1793
25. *Morning Chronicle,* June 15, 1793
26. *Morning Post,* May 25, 1793
27. Ibid., June 20, 1793
28. *The Star* (London), July 18, 1793
29. *Morning Chronicle,* April 17, 1793
30. *The Times* August 26, 1794
31. Ibid., August 26, 29, September 10, 20 & October 9 & 17, 1794
32. *Morning Post, and Fashionable World,* April 10, 1795
33. *Ibid.,* April 13, 18 & May 18, 1795
34. *St. James's Chronicle; or British Evening-Post* (London), September 3 to 5 & 5 to 8, 1795
35. *Morning Post, and Daily Advertiser,* April 7, 1788
36. *Morning Post, and Fashionable World,* April 3 & 21, 1795
37. Speaight, pp. 48–49
38. *Morning Post and Fashionable World,* September 28, 1895; *Morning Chronicle,* September 10, 1795
39. *Edinburgh Advertiser,* February 10 & March 28, 1797
40. *The Observer* (London), June 10, 1798
41. *European Magazine, and London Review,* November 1, 1784; *The Courier* (London), July 26, 1814 & January 4, 1816
42. *The Times,* August 29, 1788

Chapter 6

1. *Dunlap's American Daily Advertiser* (Philadelphia), April 1, 1793
2. *Bell's Weekly Messenger* (London), June 5, 1814
3. Chindahl, George L. *A History of the Circus in America,* Idaho, Caxton Printers, Ltd., 1959, p. 2
4. Speaight, p. 111
5. Ibid., pp. 111–112; Thayer, Stuart, *Annals of the American Circus 1793–1860,* Seattle, Washington, Dauven & Thayer, 2000, p. 1
6. "The American Revolution, 1763–1783; http://memory.loc.gov/learn///features/timeline/amrev/rebelln/assoc.html
7. Scharf, John Thomas and Westcott, Thompson, *History of Philadelphia, 1609–1884,* Vol. II, Philadelphia, L. H. Everts & Co. 1884, p. 952
8. Speaight, p. 112
9. Scharf, p. 952
10. *Federal Gazette and Philadelphia Daily Advertiser,* October 23, 1792
11. Jando, Dominique, "John Bill Ricketts," Circopedia, http://www.circopedia.org/index.php/John_Bill_Ricketts
12. Speaight, p. 115
13. Thayer, p. 1
14. Chindahl, pp. 7–8
15. Downer, Alan S. (editor), *The Memoir of John Durang, American Actor, 1785–1816,* Pittsburgh, University of Pittsburgh Press, 1966, p. 46 (Sited as "Durang")
16. "Circus in America Timeline," www.circusinamerica.org/public/timelines?date1=1793&date2=1800
17. *Charleston City Gazette,* August 14, 1792
18. Rogers, George C., Jr., *Charleston in the Age of the Pinckneys,* South Carolina, University of South Carolina Press, 1989, p. 112
19. "Broad Street Theatre" www.preservationsociety.org/HalseyMap/Flash/window.asp?HTML=10

20. Thayer, p. 2
21. *Virginia Gazette* (Richmond), May 7, 1794
22. Speaight, p. 117
23. Scharf, p. 952
24. Thayer, p. 3
25. Durang, p. 43
26. Chindahl, p. 11
27. Ibid., p. 9
28. Greenwood, Isaac John, *The Circus: Its Origins and Growth Prior to 1835;* Dunlap Society Publications, No. 5, 1898
29. Spann, Edward K, *New Metropolis,* New York, Columbia University Press 1981, pp. 134–136
30. Scharf, p. 952
31. Durang, p. 44
32. Scharf, p. 952
33. Thayer, pp. 5–7
34. Vail, R. W. G., "Random Notes on the History of the Early American Circus (reprint from the "Proceedings of the American Antiquarian Society) Worcester, Mass., April, 1933
35. Broadside from Yorkheritage.org/johndurang/wp-content/uploads/2009/12RickettsHarvard
36. Scharf, p. 953
37. Ibid., p. 953
38. Durang, p. 45
39. Ibid., p. 49
40. Ibid., pp. 69–70
41. Ibid., pp. 70–93
42. *Charleston Gazette,* November 26, 1798
43. Thayer, p. 10
44. Chindahl, p. 14
45. Durang, pp. 101–102
46. Odell, George C. D., *Annals of the New York Stage* (15 volumes), New York, 1949, Vol. 1, p. 65
47. Durang, pp. 99–100
48. Thayer, p. 12
49. *Bell's Weekly Messenger,* February 2, 1800
50. Scharf, pp. 952–953
51. Durang, p. 152
52. "Vauxhall Gardens," Preservation Society of Charleston http://www.halseymap.com/Flash/map.asp

Chapter 7

1. *General Advertiser* (Philadelphia), November 3, 1794
2. Thayer, p. 15
3. Durang, p. 97
4. Thayer, p. 15
5. Ibid., p. 15
6. Ibid., p. 16
7. *New York Tribune,* April 3, 1855
8. "John Durang," hhttp://yorkheritage.org/johndurang/?p=247
9. *Kline's Carlisle Weekly Gazette,* Pennsylvania, July 6, 1810
10. Scharf, p. 954
11. Ibid., p. 954
12. Thayer, p. 17
13. *Charleston City Gazette,* June 13, 1808
14. Chindahl, p. 15
15. Scharf, p. 1811
16. *Logansport Journal* (IN), July 30, 1879
17. Odell, Vol. II, p. 487; Vol. III, p. 38
18. Holmberg, Tom, "Great Britain: Orders in Council and Licenses, 1800–1810 www.napoleon-series.org/research/government/british/c_ordercouncil
19. Thayer, p. 19

20. *Columbian Centinel,* December 26, 1807
21. Thayer, p. 20
22. Ibid., p. 21
23. Ibid., pp. 20–22
24. Durang, pp. 103–104
25. Emery, Sarah Ann, *Reminiscences of a Nonagenarian,* Montana, Kessinger Publishing 1879; reprinted 2008
26. Thayer, pp. 23–24Ibid., pp. 23–24
27. Ibid., p. 25
28. Durang, p. 104
29. Thayer, p. 25
30. Cook, Gynger, "Richmond Theatre Fire," http:// jshaputis.tripod.com/ClayArticles/Richmond_theatre_ fire.html; "The Edgar A. Poe Calendar" http://richmond thenandnow.com/Newspaper-Articles/Richmond-The-atre-Fire.html
31. "Cayetano," The Pennsylvania Magazine of History and Biography, Vol. 15, 1915, p. 427
32. Thayer, p. 27
33. Ibid., p. 28
34. Ibid., pp. 28–29
35. Ibid., p. 29
36. Scharf, pp. 957–958

Chapter 8

1. Clapp,—, "History of the Boston Stage," cited in Scharf, p. 954
2. *Alexandria Gazette,* April 19, 1814
3. Kotar, S. L., and Gessler, J. E., *The Steamboat Era,* North Carolina, McFarland & Co., Publishers, 2009, p. 23
4. Thayer, p. 34; Unless otherwise noted, references in this chapter come from Thayer, pp. 34–52.
5. Ibid., p. 34
6. Kotar/Gessler, *Steamboat Era,* p. 26
7. Davis, Andrew, *America's Longest Run: A History of the Walnut Street Theatre,* Pennsylvania, Pennsylvania State University Press, 2010, p.79
8. *The Courier, and Evening Exchange* (London), April 4, 1801
9. *The Times* (London), July 13, 1801
10. Thayer, p. 39
11. *Freemason's Magazine,* December 1, 1796
12. Banham, Martin, *The Cambridge Guide to Theatre,* Cambridge, England, Cambridge University Press, 1995, p. 488
13. *Monthly Mirror* (London), August 1, 1801
14. *The Courier, and Evening Gazette* (London), November 28, 1801
15. *The Courier,* April 26, 1810
16. *Monthly Mirror,* May 1, 1810
17. Ibid., June 1, 1810
18. Ibid., October 1, 1818
19. *The Antigallican Monitor* (London), May 5, 1811
20. *Gentleman's Magazine* (London), August, 1811
21. *Bell's Weekly Messenger,* December 29, 1811
22. *The British Press* (London), May 25; *The Monthly Magazine* (London), June 1, 1812
23. *Bell's Weekly Messenger,* September 11, 1814
24. Ibid., June 4, 1815
25. *Morning Post, and Daily Advertiser* (London), April 8, 1791
26. *St. James's Chronicle, or British Evening-Post* (London), December 20, 1791
27. *Evening Mail* (London), December 20, 1797
28. *The Albion, and Evening Advertiser* (London), June 4 & July 15; *The Star* London), June 18, 1800
29. *The Observer* (London), June 29, 1800
30. *Bell's Weekly Messenger,* September 10, 1815
31. Thayer, p. 41
32. Davis, p. 1809
33. Hughes, Glenn, *A History of the American Theatre, 1700–1950,* New York, Vail-Ballou Press, 1951, p. 114
34. Durang, Charles, "The Philadelphia Stage," *Sunday Dispatch* Philadelphia), run in serial form beginning May 7, 1854
35. Thayer, pp. 40–41
36. Scharf, p. 956
37. Thayer, pp. 43–44
38. Speaight, p. 116
39. Davis, p. 1810
40. Thayer, pp. 45–46
41. Scharf, p. 956
42. Ibid., p. 956
43. *Ohio Repository,* September 24, 1819
44. Thayer, p. 47
45. "The Cumberland Road," www.swetland.net/ cumberland.htm
46. Thayer, p. 49
47. Ibid., pp. 51–52

Chapter 9

1. Thayer, p. 62
2. Banham, p. 839
3. Wilson, James Grant, Fisk, John, Klos, Stanley L. (editors), *Appleton's Cyclopedia of American Biography,* New York, D. Appleton & Co., 1887–1889 & 1999
4. Scharf, p. 977–978
5. Thayer, p. 56
6. Scharf, pp. 977–978
7. Thayer, pp. 56–57
8. Scharf, pp. 977–978
9. Henderson, Mary C., *The City and the Theatre"* New York, Back Stage Books, 2004
10. Thayer, p. 57
11. Scharf, pp. 977–978
12. Ibid., pp. 977–978
13. *Torch Light and Public Advertiser* (MD), October 26, 1824
14. *Ohio Repository,* October 7, 1824
15. Ibid., June 24, 1825
16. *Kentucky Reporter,* November 14, 1825
17. Davis, p. 1811
18. Ibid., p, 1811
19. Thayer, p. 67
20. Salzmann, Kenneth, "Just a Stage — A Theatrical History of Albany, New York www.zinearticles.com/ ?Just-A-Stage — A-Theatrical-History-of-Albany-New-York&id=857077
21. Thayer, pp. 67–69
22. *Torch Light and Public Advertiser,* March 21, 1826
23. Scharf, pp. 977–978
24. *Torch Light and Public Advertiser,* November 22, 1825
25. *Connecticut Courant* (Hartford), May 31, April 10, 1825
26. *Republican Compiler* (PA), February 1, 1826
27. *New York Evening Post,* reprinted in *Republican Compiler,* April 26, 1826
28. Thayer, p. 82
29. Ibid., p. 84
30. *Jackson Sentinel* (IA), April 12, 1877
31. *New York Advocate,* reprinted in *Wilmington and Delaware Advertiser,* December 21, 1826
32. *New York Statesman,* reprinted in *Torch Light and Public Advertiser,* March 7, 1825

33. *Wilmington and Delaware Advertiser*, December 28, 1826

34. *Republican Compiler*, May 10, 1826

35. *West Eau Claire Argus* (WI), July 24, 1867

36. *Sandusky Clarion* (OH), October 6, 1827

Chapter 10

1. Odell, Vol. III, p. 365

2. *Delaware Gazette*, November 22, 1825

3. *Torch Light and Public Advertiser*, August 3, 1826

4. Thayer, p. 77

5. Ibid., pp. 88–89

6. Reprinted in *Delaware Advertiser and Farmer's Journal*, November 6, 1828

7. *Delaware Patriot and American Watchman*, October 6 & 10, 1828

8. Scharf, p. 978

9. Ibid., pp. 274–275

10. Thayer, p. 100

11. *Jackson Sentinel* (IA), April 12, 1877

12. Brede, Charles Frederic, "The German Drama in English on the Philadelphia Stage from 1794–1830," Americana Germanica Press, 1918, pp. 270–271

13. *Hagerstown Mail* (MD), July 24, 1829

14. *The Miltonian*, August 22, 1829

15. *Lycoming Gazette*, April 21, 1830

16. *Onondaga Standard* (NY), October 7, 1829

17. *Torch Light and Public Advertiser*, November 5, 1829

18. *Onondaga Standard*, December 30, 1829

19. Thayer, p. 103

Chapter 11

1. *Adams Sentinel* (PA), November 2, 1835

2. *Daily Intelligencer*, reprinted in *Lycoming Gazette*, November 13, 1833

3. *Adams Sentinel*, July 6, 1835

4. Ibid., September 28, 1835

5. *Bath, Steuben Co. Farmer's Advocate*, reprinted in *Republican Compiler*, August 22, 1837

6. *Adams Sentinel*, April 8, 1833

7. Ibid., August 31; *People's Press* (PA), September 11, 1835

8. *Huron Reflector* (OH), April 18, 1833

9. *Baltimore Transcript*, reprinted in *Adams Sentinel*, November 13, 1837

10. *Adams Sentinel*, December 10, 1838

11. *New Orleans Emporium*, March 23, 1832

12. *Blackwood* (1859), reprinted in *Sparta Democrat* (WI), July 6, 1859

13. Thayer, pp. 139–140

14. *Boston Atlas*, reprinted in *Adams Sentinel*, June 2, 1834

15. *Boston Traveller*, reprinted in *Torch Light* (MD), October 2, 1834

16. *Boston Transcript*, reprinted in *Adams Sentinel*, March 9, 1835

17. Thayer, p. 148

18. *Huron Reflector*, May 26, 1835

19. Matlaw, Myron, editor, *American Popular Entertainment*, Westport, Conn., Greenwood Press, 1979, p. 179

20. Rookmaaker, L. C., *The Rhinoceros in Captivity*, Amsterdam, SPB Academic Publishing, 1998, p. 107

21. *Adams Sentinel*, July 29, 1833

22. *Ohio Repository*, October 24, 1834

23. *Hagerstown Mail*, October 14, 1836

24. *Frederick Examiner*, reprinted in *Republican Compiler*, November 4, 1834

25. *Adams Sentinel*, October 20, 1834

26. *Torch Light*, November 27, 1834

27. *Logansport Journal* (IN), July 30, 1879

28. *Stamford Journal*, reprinted in *Huron Reflector*, April 28, 1835

29. Thayer, pp. 136–137

30. *Adams Sentinel*, August 18, 1834

31. Rookmaaker, p. 107

32. *Ohio Repository*, May 31, 1838

33. *National Intelligencer*, reprinted in *Hagerstown Mail*, April 10, 1835

34. *Huron Reflector*, August 2, 1836

Chapter 12

1. Barnum, Phineas T., *The Life of P. T. Barnum*," Urbana, University of Illinois Press, 2000, p. 171

2. *Star and Republican Banner*, September 21, 1835

3. *Adams Sentinel*, November 7 & 14; *Republican Compiler*, November 8, 1836

4. *Daily Herald* (Newburyport, MA), May 14, 1835

5. *Bangor Daily Whig and Courier*, September 21, 1837

6. Thayer, pp. 57 & 124

7. Barnum, pp. 161–183

8. *Bangor Daily Whig and Courier*, July 3, 1838

9. *Star and Republican Banner*, August 14, 1838

10. *Ohio Repository*, July 29, 1841

11. *Western Statesman* (MI), July 13, 1843

12. *Independent American and General Advertiser* (WI), February 22, 1845

13. Appleton's Cyclopedia, "Fanny Ellsler"

14. *Racine Advocate*, July 9, 1844

15. *Daily Sentinel and Gazette* (WI), August 18, 1848

16. *Republican Compiler*, October 22, 1849

17. "Harmonicon," JSTOR (Organization), *The Musical Times & Singing Class Circular*, Vol. 41, New York, Novello, Ewer & Co. 1831, p. 124

18. *Republican Compiler*, October 22, 1849

19. Thayer, p. 158; *Hagerstown Mail*, August 24, 1838

20. *Adams Sentinel & Republican Compiler*, August 13, 1839

21. *Weekly Chronicle*, September 23, 1838

22. Watts, Ephraim, *Life of Van Amburgh, the Brute Tamer, With Anecdotes of his Extraordinary Pupils*, New York, 1838; from *Cleve's Gazette of Variety* (London), December 8, 1838

23. Thayer, p. 138; *Weekly Chronicle*, September 23, 1838; *Springfield Republican*, November 9, 1833; *Haverhill Essex Gazette*, November 9, 1833

24. *The Age* (London) September 16 & November 18, 1838

25. *Court Gazette, and Fashionable Guide*, (London) September 23, 1838

26. Ibid., August 25; *Weekly Chronicle* (London), August 26, 1838

27. *Western Statesman*, July 16, 1840

28. *The Age*, August 26, 1838

29. *Bell's New Weekly Messenger*, November 4, 1838

30. *The Courier* (London), September 30, 1838

31. *Bell's New Weekly Messenger*, September 30, 1838

32. *The Age*, September 16, 1838

33. *The Atlas*, September 29; *Weekly Chronicle*, September 30, 1838

34. *Court Gazette*, September 26, 1838

35. *The Courier*, September 26, 1838

36. *Janesville Gazette* (WI), November 6, 1877

37. *The Age,* October 14, 1838
38. Ibid., October 28, 1838
39. *Bell's New Weekly Messenger,* November 4, 1838
40. *The Christian Advocate* (London), January 21, 1839
41. *The Age,* February 3, 1839
42. *The Charter* (London), March 3, 1839
43. *The Age,* March 24, 1839
44. *The Charter,* August 18, 1839
45. *The Age,* September 8, 1839
46. *Weekly Chronicle,* February 17, 1839
47. *The Argus,* May 5, 1839
48. *The Argus, or Broad-Sheet of the Empire* (London), February 10, 1839
49. *The Age,* October 6; *The Constitutionalist,* October 13, 1839
50. *The Charter,* October 13, 1839
51. Thayer, p. 185
52. *The Age,* October 20, 1839
53. *Western Telegraph* (OH), June 7, 1839
54. *Weekly Chronicle,* October 20, 1839
55. *The Age,* November 24, 1839
56. *The Atlas,* February 22, 1840
57. Ibid., April 18, 1840
58. *The Courier,* June 9, 1840
59. *The Argus,* June 28, 1840
60. *Weekly Chronicle,* July 5, 1840
61. *The Courier,* June 24, 1842
62. *Weekly Chronicle,* August 13, 1842
63. *The Age,* September 11, 1842
64. Ibid., December 11; *Evening Star* (London), December 12, 1842
65. *The Age,* January 8, 1843
66. *Bell's Life in London and Sporting Chronicle,* January 22, 1843
67. *Weekly Chronicle,* January 21, 1843
68. *The Atlas,* January 21, 1843
69. *The Age,* January 29, 1843
70. *Weekly Chronicle,* February 5, 1843
71. *The Age,* February 12, 1843
72. *The Atlas,* February 25, 1843
73. *The Atlas,* March 25; *The Age,* March 26 & April 2; *Lloyd's Weekly London Newspaper,* July 23, 1843
74. *Weekly Chronicle,* August 20, 1843
75. *Church Intelligencer* (London), April 19, 1843
76. *Lloyd's Weekly London Newspaper,* February 18, 1844
77. Ibid., March 17, 1844
78. *Age and Argus,* June 15, 1844
79. *Weekly Chronicle,* July 21, 1844
80. *Lloyd's Weekly London Newspaper,* September 15, 1844
81. *The Patriot* (London), March 24, 1845
82. *Bell's New Weekly Messenger,* October 5, 1845
83. *The Atlas,* October 11, 1845

Chapter 13

1. *Independent Treasury* (OH), March 23, 1842
2. Thayer, pp. 173–174
3. *Ohio Atlas and Elyria Advertiser,* December 1, 1841
4. *Republican Compiler,* August 13, 1839
5. *Southport Telegraph* (WI), September 8, 1840
6. *Adams Sentinel,* January 27, 1840
7. *Democratic Expounder and Calhoun County Patriot* (MI), July 23, 1841
8. *Wisconsin Enquirer,* December 4, 1841
9. *Bangor Daily Whig and Courier,* September 13, 1841
10. *Tioga Eagle* (PA), March 16, 1842

11. *Democratic Expounder and Calhoun County Patriot,* July 27, 1842
12. *Huron Reflector,* August 16, 1842
13. Thayer, p. 180
14. *Freeman and Messenger* (NY), April 23, 1840
15. *Adams Sentinel,* January 3, 1842
16. *Southport Telegraph,* November 9, 1841
17. *Milwaukee Sentinel,* May 10, 1843
18. *Southport Telegraph,* May 16, 1843
19. *Adams Sentinel,* June 28, 1841
20. *Hagerstown Mail,* August 21, 1840
21. Ibid., August 31, 1840
22. *Civilian and Galveston Gazette,* June 10, 1843
23. *Bangor Daily Whig and Courier,* September 2, 1843
24. Thayer, p. 198
25. *Southport Telegraph,* April 6, 1841
26. *Newport Daily News,* December 24, 1847
27. *Milwaukee Daily Sentinel,* April 16, 1845; *Star and Republican Banner,* September 4, 1846
28. *Milwaukie Democrat,* September 20, 1843
29. *Independent Treasury,* (OH), March 23, 1842
30. *Citizen and Galveston City Gazette,* September 9, 1843
31. *Adams Sentinel,* May 6; *Lorain Republican* (OH), May 8, 1844
32. *Sheboygan Mercury* (WI), January 12, 1850
33. *Bangor Whig and Daily Courier,* September 2, 1843
34. *Hagerstown Torch Light and Public Advertiser,* December 29, 1842
35. *Bangor Daily Whig and Courier,* August 11 & September 2, 1843
36. *Grand County Herald* (WI), April 6, 1844
37. *The Experiment* (OH), October 25, 1843
38. *Independent American, and General Advertiser,* August 7, 1846
39. Thayer, pp. 150, 184, 187, 192
40. *Republican Compiler,* May 22, 1843
41. *Ohio Repository,* October 12, 1843
42. *Burlington Hawk-Eye* (IA), June 27, 1844
43. The name of the elephant is referenced from the *Philadelphia Enquirer,* reprinted in the *Daily Sentinel and Gazette,* April 28, 1847; *Adams Sentinel,* March 24, 1845; *Daily Sentinel and Gazette,* April 28, 1847
44. *Burlington Hawk-Eye,* April 15, 1847
45. *Daily Sentinel and Gazette,* April 28, 1847
46. *Ohio Repository,* May 6, 1847
47. *Star and Banner,* December 31, 1847; *Weekly Wisconsin,* January 12; *Huron Reflector,* January 18; *Defiance Democrat,* January 27, 1848
48. *Marshall Statesman,* May 16, 1848
49. *Green Bay Advocate,* January 27, 1848

Chapter 14

1. Honeywell, J. "The Menagerie," *Rock River Pilot* (WI), March 22, 1848
2. Barnum, pp. 243–295
3. *Daily Sentinel and Gazette,* June 9, 1848
4. *Albany Evening Journal,* reprinted in *Weekly Wisconsin,* May 31, 1848
5. *New York Sun,* reprinted in *Star and Banner,* November 10, 1848
6. *Daily Sentinel and Gazette,* August 2, 1848
7. *Zanesville Courier,* April 3, 1849
8. Ibid., October 25, 1849
9. *Tioga Eagle,* June 13, 1849
10. *Bell's Life in London and Sporting Chronicle,* January 20, 1850; *Newport Daily News,* February 15, 1850

11. Thayer, p. 214

12. *Bangor Daily Whig and Courier,* July 20, 1847

13. Reprinted in *Newport Daily News* June 18, 1846

14. *Milwaukee Daily Courier,* June 27, 1846; *Lloyd's Weekly London Newspaper,* August 23, 1846

15. *The Nonconformist* (London), April 28, 1847; *American Freeman* (WI), May 5, 1847

16. *Liverpool Albion,* reprinted in *Lloyd's Weekly London Newspaper,* January 30, 1848

17. *Weekly Chronicle* (London), April 23, 1848

18. *Weekly Wisconsin,* December 6, 1848

19. *Reno Evening Gazette* (NV), December 16, 1884

20. *Bangor Daily Whig and Courier,* July 8, 1844

21. Thayer, p. 206

22. *Republican Compiler,* August 18, 1845

23. *Adams Sentinel,* August 25, 1845

24. Thayer, p. 206

25. *Bangor Daily Whig and Courier,* July 20, 1847

26. *Burlington Hawk-Eye,* December 23; *Weekly Wisconsin,* December 29, *Star and Banner,* December 31, 1847

27. *Bismark Twi-Weekly Tribune* (ND), July 16, 1877

28. *Fort Wayne Times,* June 7 & 14, 1849

29. *Southport American,* July 5, 1845

30. *Alton Telegraph* (IL), May 21, 1847

31. *Independent American, and General Advertiser,* August 27, 1847

32. *Watertown Chronicle* (WI), September 1, 1847

33. *Bangor Daily Whig and Courier,* August 25, 1848

34. *Star and Republican Banner,* May 22, 1846

35. *New York Daily Times,* July 11, 1855

36. *Marshall Statesman,* September 28; *Huron Reflector,* October 19, 1847

37. *Wisconsin Democrat,* July 17, 1847

38. *Beloit Journal* (WI), July 13, 1848

39. *Newport Daily News,* September 2, 1847

40. Thayer, p. 205

41. *Republican Compiler,* July 24, 1848

42. Pilato, Denise E., "Martha Coston: A Woman, A War, and a Signal to the World," International Journal of Naval History www.ijnhonline.org/volume1_number1_Apr02/article_pilato_coston_ signal.doc

43. *Hamilton Telegraph* (OH), October 4, 1849

44. *Tioga Eagle,* January 6, 1847

45. *Marshall Statesman,* September 5, 1848

46. Thayer, pp. 333–334

47. *Burlington Hawk-Eye,* May 17, 1849

48. *The Gleanor* (Jamaica), September 10, 1892; *Burlington Hawk-Eye,* July 5 & 26, 1849

49. *Warren Ledger,* July 22, 1887; *Decatur Daily Republican,* May 11, 1886; *Indiana Weekly Messenger* (PA), August 24, 1887

50. *Sentinel and Farmer* (WI), April 9, 1842

51. *Republican Compiler,* May 19, 1845

52. Ibid., January 4, 1847

53. *Star and Banner,* January 14, 1848

54. *Tioga Eagle,* January 9, 1850

55. Ibid., April 24, 1850

56. *Fort Wayne Times,* July 5, 1849

57. *Defiance Democrat,* December 22, 1849

58. *Hamilton Telegraph,* October 11, 1849

Chapter 15

1. *Wisconsin Free Democrat,* October 1, 1851

2. *Ohio Repository,* July 28, 1852

3. *Burlington Hawk-Eye,* January 17, 1850

4. *Republican Compiler,* January 28, 1850

5. Thayer, p. 470

6. *Newport Daily News,* July 8, 1850

7. *Tioga Eagle,* July 31, 1850

8. Ibid., June 5, 1851

9. Ibid., June 19, 1851

10. *Republican Compiler,* June 14, 1851

11. *Fort Wayne Sentinel,* August 17, 1850

12. Ibid., August 17, 1850

13. *Tioga Eagle,* September 25, 1850

14. *New York Daily Times,* August 6, 1852

15. *Adams Sentinel,* September 12, 1853

16. *Milwaukee Daily Sentinel,* June 14, 1855

17. *Illinois State Chronicle,* July 10, 1856

18. *Sheboygan Mercury,* January 12, 1850

19. *Zanesville Courier,* March 16 & April 4, 1850

20. *Marshall Statesman,* June 3, 1857; *Weekly Wisconsin,* April 3, 1850

21. *Marshall Statesman,* May 15, 1850

22. *Milwaukee Daily Sentinel and Gazette,* July 4, 1850

23. *Wisconsin Argus,* July 23, 1850

24. *Weekly Wisconsin,* September 4, 1850

25. *Huron Reflector,* November 26, 1850

26. *Milwaukee Daily Sentinel and Gazette,* February 24; *Weekly Wisconsin,* February 26, 1851

27. *Daily Sanduskian* (OH), May 19, 1851

28. *Star and Banner,* August 15 & November 14, 1851

29. *Weekly Wisconsin,* September 27, 1954

30. *Star and Banner,* October 1 & 15, 1852

31. *New York Herald,* reprinted in *Star and Banner,* December 16, 1853

32. *New York Daily Times,* March 22, 184

33. *Providence Journal,* June 6, 1854

34. *New Bedford Standard,* June 7, 1854

35. William Hendrickson was listed as "E. W. Henderson" in Thayer, p. 636; *Weekly Wisconsin,* April 2, 1856

36. *Sandusky Register,* reprinted in *Horicon Argus* (WI), May 14, 1856

37. *Iowa City Reporter,* July 8, 1857

38. *Cincinnati Gazette,* reprinted in *Appleton Crescent* (WI), December 12, 1857

39. *Mineral Point Tribune* (WI), July 27, 1858

40. *Athens Messenger* (OH), August 30, 1857

41. *Newport Daily News,* May 22, 1851

42. *Defiance Democrat,* July 5 & 26, 1851

43. *Weekly Argus and Democrat,* August 31, 1852

44. *New York Daily Times,* October 29, 1852

45. Ibid., December 10, 1852

46. *Marshall Statesman,* June 15, 1853

47. *New York Daily Times,* September 1, 1854

48. *Janesville Gazette,* June 26, 1851

49. Reprinted in *Daily Free Democrat* (WI), June 16, 1852

50. Ibid., July 27, 1852

51. Ibid., August 26; *Saul County Democrat* (WI), September 7, 1853

52. Thayer, p. 376

53. *Badger State* (WI), May 13, 1854

54. *Weekly Wisconsin,* December 31, 1865

55. *Ohio Repository,* July 29, 1857

56. *Janesville Morning Gazette,* July 27, 1857

57. *Reedsburg Herald* (WI), September 17, 1857

58. Barnum, p. 348

59. *Sheboygan Mercury,* November 1, 1851

60. *Daily Free Democrat* (WI), April 30; *Sheboygan Mercury,* June 14, 1851

61. *Buffalo Democracy,* reprinted in *The Independent,* June 14, 1853

62. *Syracuse Star,* reprinted in *Hornellsville Tribune*

(NY), October 16, 1852; *Weekly Wisconsin,* January 1 &
February 19, 1851

  63. *Weekly Wisconsin,* January 14, 1852

  64. *Defiance Democrat,* July 6, 1850

  65. *Daily Free Democrat,* April 19; *Milwaukee Daily
Sentinel and Gazette,* May 3, 1851

  66. *Watertown Chronicle,* June 11, 1851

  67. *Weekly Wisconsin,* July 30, 1851

  68. *Democratic Expounder,* July 22, 1852

  69. *Marshall Statesman,* July 14, 1852

  70. *Zanesville Courier,* June 12, 1852

  71. Ibid., August 20, 1852

  72. Barnum, p. 349

  73. *New York Daily Times,* August 23, 1852

  74. Barnum, p. 349

  75. *Alton Weekly Courier,* September 24, 1852

  76. *Wisconsin Tribune,* August 19, 1852

  77. *Independent American,* May 19, 1853

  78. *Kenosha Democrat,* August 5; *Weekly Wisconsin,*
August 10, 1853

  79. *Grant County Herald,* August 10, 1853

  80. *Independent American,* August 12, 1853

  81. *Janesville Gazette,* September 3, 1853

  82. *Weekly Wisconsin,* November 8; *Janesville Gazette,*
December 2, 1854

  83. *Burlington Tri-Weekly Hawk-Eye,* November 7,
1854

  84. *Newport Daily News,* June 1, 1855

  85. *Daily State Journal* (WI), September 2, 1856

  86. *Marysville Tribune* (OH), August 1, 1855

  87. *New York Daily Times,* July 18, 1855

  88. *Hagerstown Mail and Washington County Republican Advertiser,* August 20, 1830

Chapter 16

  1. *Marshall Statesman,* February 9, 1853

  2. *New York Daily Times,* May 11, 1853

  3. *Marshall Statesman,* February 9, 1853

  4. *Daily Morning Advocate,* July 1, 1854

  5. *Fort Wayne Weekly Times,* October 16, 1856

  6. *Hornellsville Tribune,* July 16, 1853

  7. *New York Evening Times,* January 2, 1855

  8. *Daily Globe* (D. C.), January 10, 1855

  9. *Weekly Hawk-Eye and Telegraph,* August 8, 1855

  10. *Independent Democrat,* May 7, 1856

  11. *Delaware State Reporter,* April 21, 1854

  12. *Dubuque Democratic Herald,* May 24, 1863

  13. *Delaware State Reporter,* September 28, 1855

  14. *Bangor Daily Whig and Courier,* August 22, 1857

  15. *Delaware State Reporter,* September 18, 1855

  16. *Hornellsville Tribune,* July 4, 1859

  17. *Lafayette Journal* (IN), May 9, 1857

  18. *Cincinnati Commercial,* reprinted in *Milwaukee
Daily American,* September 5, 1856

  19. *Weekly Wisconsin,* December 9, 1856

  20. *Hornellsville Tribune,* September 15, 1859

  21. *Detroit Tribune,* reprinted in *Milwaukee Daily
Sentinel,* May 8, 1854

  22. *Buffalo Express,* reprinted in *Horicon Argus,* August
7, 1857

  23. *Cincinnati Gazette,* reprinted in *Davenport
Gazette,* May 6, 1858

  24. *Banner of Liberty* (NY), March 2, 1859

  25. *Grant County Witness* (WI), September 15, 1859

  26. *Janesville Morning Gazette,* June 22, 1857

  27. "Calliope" http://en.wikipedia.org/wiki/Calliope
_music

  28. *Burlington Hawk-Eye,* June 14, 1877

  29. *Indiana Progress,* May 16, 1878

  30. *Janesville Morning Gazette,* June 22, 1857

  31. *Newport Daily News,* August 27, 1858

  32. *Daily Free Democrat,* August 27, 1855

  33. *Hornellsville Tribune,* July 8, 1858

  34. *Berkshire County Eagle* (MA), December 20, 1860

  35. *Dawson's Fort Wayne Daily Times,* September 27,
1860

  36. *New-York Times,* July 31, 1860

  37. *Tioga Eagle,* April 8, 1852

  38. *New-York Daily Times,* December 29, 1852

  39. *Fort Wayne Times and People's Press,* August 24,
1853

  40. *Fort Wayne Sentinel,* September 10, 1853

  41. *New-York Daily Times,* September 14, 1853

  42. *Grant County Herald,* July 3, 1854

  43. *Hornellsville Tribune,* July 19, 1855

  44. *Dubuque Daily Herald,* January 16, 1868

  45. *Maquoketa Sentinel,* November 8, 1855

  46. *Tyrone Daily Herald* (PA), June 4, 1859

  47. *Petersburg Index* (VA), December 31, 1868

  48. *Grant County Witness,* June 9, 1859

Chapter 17

  1. *Janesville Daily Gazette,* April 4, 1862

  2. Thayer, p. 410

  3. *Daily Tribune* (WI), June 21, 1860

  4. *Hornellsville Tribune,* September 20, 1860

  5. *Jefferson Banner* (WI), June 23, 1864

  6. *Racine Weekly Advocate,* May 16, 1861

  7. *Bangor Daily Whig and Courier,* June 5, 1861

  8. *Mountain Democrat* (CA), March 16, 1861

  9. *Titusville Herald,* July 22, 1879

  10. *Daily Argus and Democrat,* August 13, 1860

  11. *Manitoba Daily Free Press* (Canada), August 9,
1888; "Leotard" http://en.wikipedia.org/wiki/Jules_L%
C3%A9otard

  12. *New-York Times,* January 17, 1860

  13. *Racine Democrat,* March 28, 1860

  14. *Berkshire County Eagle,* May 3, 1860

  15. *New-York Times,* July 30, 1860

  16. *Weekly Standard* (NC), October 24, 1860

  17. reprinted in *Milwaukee Daily Sentinel,* March 14,
1860)

  18. *New-York Times,* March 29, 1861

  19. Ibid., November 30, 1861; *Berkshire County Eagle,*
December 12, 1861

  20. *Adams Sentinel,* May 5, 1863

  21. *Cedar Falls Gazette,* June 1, 1866

  22. *Mountain Democrat,* July 16, 1864

  23. *Daily Alta Californian,* October 1, 1864

  24. *New-York Times,* February 15, 1865

  25. *Daily Milwaukee News,* July 20, 1864

  26. *San Francisco Chronicle,* reprinted in *Decatur
Daily Review* (IL), June 13, 1879

  27. *Reno Evening Gazette,* December 16, 1884

  28. *Defiance Democrat,* May 8, 1869

  29. *New-York Times,* March 26, 1862

  30. *Janesville Daily Gazette,* February 7, 1865

  31. *Daily Milwaukee Press and News,* March 7, 1861

  32. *Daily State Journal* (WI), June 24, 1861

  33. *Democratic Expounder,* November 20, 1862

  34. *Marshall Statesman,* September 2, 1863

  35. *Burlington Weekly Hawk-Eye,* May 28, 1864

  36. *Daily Argus and Democrat,* June 18, 1855

  37. *Rock County Republican,* September 3, 1861

  38. *Daily Milwaukee News,* May 8, 1860

  39. *New-York Times,* July 4; *Boston Traveller,* October

4; *Newport Daily News,* October 6; *Whitewater Register,* November 9, 1860

40. *Eau Claire Free Press,* July 5, 1860
41. *Dubuque Democratic Herald,* September 10, 1863
42. *Daily Milwaukee Press and News,* April 6; *Weekly Hawk-Eye,* May 25, 1861
43. *Semi-Weekly Wisconsin,* February 6, 1869
44. *Detroit Free Press,* June 21, 1863
45. *Cedar Falls Gazette,* July 1, 1864
46. *Fitchburg Sentinel* (MA), July 18, 1868
47. *Daily Milwaukee Press and News,* October 23, 1861
48. *Venango Spectator* (PA), February 15, 1865
49. *Grant County Herald,* May 12, 1863
50. *Alton Telegraph,* March 3; *Iowa State Weekly Register,* March 8, 1865
51. Thayer, pp. 313–314
52. *Berkshire County Eagle,* May 28, 1863
53. *Burlington Weekly Hawk-Eye,* July 9, 1864
54. *Burlington Daily Hawk-Eye,* June 1, 1866
55. *Indiana Messenger,* June 16; *Indiana Democrat,* June 17, 1869
56. *New-York Times,* January 12, 1864
57. *Berkshire County Eagle,* April 16, 1863
58. *Linn County Patriot* (IA), August 18, 1864
59. *Titusville Herald,* July 12, 1865
60. *Whitewater Register,* August 14, 1863
61. Reprinted in *Linn County Patriot,* July 14, 1864
62. *McKean Miner* (PA), September 22, 1860
63. Ibid., September 15, 1860
64. *New-York Times,* March 25, 1864
65. Thayer, p. 210
66. *Dubuque Daily Herald,* August 13, 1867
67. *Galveston Daily News,* November 23 & 28, 1867; January 14, 15, 17 & 23, 1868
68. *Berkshire County Eagle,* May 28, 1863
69. *Morning Oregonian,* July 21, 1864
70. *Racine Daily Journal,* June 8, 1860
71. *Wisconsin State Journal,* December 16, 1864
72. *Dubuque Democratic Herald,* May 5, 1864
73. *Wisconsin State Journal,* April 20; *Daily Zanesville Courier,* April 21, 1865

Chapter 18

1. *Morning Oregonian,* September 25, 1863
2. *Mexican Times* (NM), January 1 & February 13, 1867
3. *New-York Times,* July 6, 1867
4. *Democratic Expounder and Calhoun County Patriot,* June 24, 1869
5. *Cincinnati Chronicle,* October 23, 1869
6. *Glenwood Opinion* (IA), April 2, 1870
7. *Delphos Herald* (OH), April 14, 1870
8. *Waukesha Freeman* (WI), May 29, 1860
9. *Wisconsin State Journal,* July 13, 1870
10. *New York Herald,* December 27, 1870
11. *Marshall Statesman,* July 31, 1861
12. *New-York Times,* April 27; *Dubuque Daily Herald,* April 29; *Cincinnati Gazette,* April 30; *Wisconsin State Journal,* May 1; *Semi-Weekly Wisconsin,* May 2 & 5, 1861
13. *Dubuque Daily Herald,* June 29, 1866
14. *Freeport Daily Journal,* June 15, 1867
15. *Elyria Independent Democrat,* June 23, 1869
16. *Titusville Morning Herald,* May 8, 1869
17. Ibid., February 7, 1864
18. *Freeport Budget* (IL), August 20, 1881
19. *Marysville Tribune,* September 16, 1868
20. *Herald and Torch Light,* December 2, 1868
21. *Ohio Democrat,* April 23, 1869
22. *Dubuque Daily Herald,* December 12, 1867
23. *Galveston Daily News,* December 8, 1867
24. *Petersburg Index,* February 4, 1868
25. *Galveston Daily News,* March 8, 1868; June 19, 1869
26. *Hudson North Star* (WI), July 31, 1861
27. *New-York Times,* January 20, 1862
28. *Beaver Dam Argus* (WI), April 20, 1863
29. *Cedar Valley Times,* December 29, 1864
30. *Zanesville Daily Courier,* November 4, 1865
31. *Galveston Tri-Weekly News,* December 18, 1865
32. *Fort Wayne Daily Gazette,* February 22, 1866
33. *Adams Sentinel,* April 10, 1866
34. *Petersburg Daily Index,* April 27, 1866
35. *Burlington Daily Hawk-Eye,* June 22, 1866
36. *Dubuque Daily Herald,* September 2, 1866
37. *The World* (NY), July 23, 1860
38. *New-York Times,* April 25, 1864
39. *Daily Milwaukee News,* September 4, 1864
40. *New York Daily News,* October 2; *New York World,* October 10; *Cincinnati Commercial,* October 12, 1866
41. *New York Daily News,* October 2, 1866
42. *Coshocton Age* (OH), February 21, 1868
43. *Eau Claire Free Press,* June 18, 1868
44. *Cambridge City Tribune,* October 6, 1870
45. *Waterloo Courier* (IA), July 23, 1868
46. *The Constitution,* October 31, 1868
47. *Newport Daily News,* June 4, 1869
48. *New York Herald,* September 29, 1870
49. *Wisconsin State Journal,* May 1, 1871
50. *McKean Miner,* March 3, 1870
51. *New York Herald,* reprinted in *Daily Wisconsin News,* December 19, 1866
52. *Titusville Morning Herald,* November 15, 1870
53. *Marysville Tribune,* September 5, 1866
54. *Daily Milwaukee News,* November 13, 1866
55. *Defiance Democrat,* July 18, 1868
56. *Fort Wayne Daily Sentinel,* June 1, 1871
57. *New York Times,* July 19, 1868
58. *Logansport Daily Pharos,* August 29, 1884
59. *Fort Wayne Daily Sentinel,* June 1, 1871
60. *New York Times,* April 25, 1897; *Cedar Rapids Evening Gazette,* September 14, 1897; *Oshkosh Daily Northwestern,* May 29, 1896; *Anita Tribune,* April 8, 1897; *Trenton Times,* October 10, 1893; *Trenton Times,* July 24, 1889; *Piqua Morning Call,* August 27, 1884
61. *Fort Wayne Daily Gazette,* February 12; *Ohio Democrat,* February 19, 1869
62. *Democratic Expounder and Calhoun County Patriot,* December 29, 1870
63. *New York Herald,* April 16, 1869
64. *Dubuque Daily Herald,* January 19, 1867
65. *Daily Milwaukee News,* January 14, 1868
66. *Daily Gazette and Bulletin* (PA), May 9, 1871
67. *Hornellsville Tribune,* August 5, 1870
68. *Daily Kennebec Journal* (ME), July 29, 1871

Chapter 19

1. *Fort Wayne Daily Gazette,* May 1, 1871
2. *Wisconsin State Journal,* July 5, 1871
3. *Weekly Wisconsin,* July 19, 1871
4. *Monticello Express* (IA), October 13, 1870
5. *Jackson Sentinel,* October 30, 1870; *Semi-Weekly Waterloo Courier* (IA), February 3, 1899
6. *Cedar Rapids Times,* October 27, 1870
7. *Monticello Express,* May 25, 1871
8. *Racine County Argus,* July 14, 1870

9. *Rock County Recorder,* July 30, 1870
10. *Indiana Democrat,* May 4, 1871
11. *Monticello Express,* May 25, 1871
12. *Titusville Morning Herald,* July 26, 1875
13. Ibid., August 29, 1877
14. *Janesville Gazette,* January 20, 1871
15. *Portsmouth Times,* January 1, 1876
16. *Bangor Daily Whig and Courier,* July 4, 1871
17. Reprinted in *Warren Ledger,* June 20, 1879
18. *Herald and Torch Light,* September 24, 1879
19. *Jackson Sentinel,* April 12, 1877
20. *Boston Daily Globe,* April 12, 1878
21. *Hickman Courier* (KY), October 28, 1873
22. *Daily Journal* (IN), July 25, 1879
23. *Evening Gazette* (NY), November 16, 1871
24. *Warren Ledger,* April 26, 1878
25. *Janesville Gazette,* July 17, 1876
26. *The World,* December 25, 1872
27. *Herald and Torch Light,* March 10, 1875
28. *Boston Daily Globe,* September 24, 1873
29. *Algona Republican* (IA), June 11, 1873
30. *Petersburg Index=Appeal,* September 10, 1878; *Daily New Brunswick Times* (NJ), June 23, 1894; *Daily Kennebec Journal* (ME), June 24, 1895; *Hutchinson News* (KS), September 2, 1898; *Lowell Daily Sun* (MA), June 12, 1895
31. *The Courier* (London), June 5, 1837
32. *The British Banner,* June 18, 1851
33. *Coshocton Democrat,* August 18, 1874
34. *Decatur Daily Republican,* June 16, 1877
35. *Coshocton Democrat,* August 18, 1874
36. *Waterloo Courier,* August 21, 1873
37. *Dubuque Herald,* July 30, 1875
38. *Newport Daily News,* June 1, 1875
39. *London Echo,* reprinted in *Janesville Gazette,* February 23, 1872
40. *Janesville Gazette,* June 21, 1879
41. *Huntingdon Journal,* July 25, 1879
42. *Herald and Torch Light,* September 3, 1879
43. *Jackson Sentinel,* June 26, 1879
44. *Daily Kennebec Journal,* March 25, 1878
45. *Newport Daily News,* May 4, 1875
46. *Herald and Torch Light,* July 22, 1874
47. *Galveston Daily News,* February 9, 1877
48. *Indiana Democrat,* June 18, 1874
49. *Warren Ledger,* October 11, 1878
50. *New York Times,* February 10, 1878
51. *The World,* May 23, 1875
52. *Marion Daily Star* (OH), April 24, 1885
53. *Allen County Democrat* (OH), June 28, 1877
54. *Sunday Morning Herald* (NY), July 1, 1883
55. *Titusville Morning Herald,* May 4, 1878
56. *The World,* August 1, 1874
57. *Logansport Weekly Journal,* July 10, 1875
58. *Galveston Daily News,* March 13, 1874
59. *The Constitution,* September 24, 1876
60. *Coshocton Democrat,* March 6, 1888; *Morning News* (MD), May 25, 1895
61. *Daily Gazette* (IA), October 21, 1873
62. *Boston Daily Globe,* November 7, 1873
63. *Manitoba Daily Free Press* (Canada), August 16, 1886
64. *Titusville Herald,* June 4, 1877
65. *Fort Wayne Daily Sentinel,* May 16, 1872
66. *Daily Gazette and Bulletin* (PA), August 14, 1873
67. *Huntingdon Journal,* September 21, 1877
68. *Newport Daily News,* May 4, 1875
69. *Dubuque Daily Herald,* June 30, 1871
70. *Titusville Morning Herald,* August 12, 1873
71. *Newport Daily News,* July 6, 1876
72. *Galveston Daily News,* January 18, 1877
73. *Star and Sentinel,* November 23, 1877
74. *Boston Daily Globe,* May 13, 1873
75. *New York Times,* February 10, 1878
76. *Petersburg Index and Appeal,* February 19, 1878
77. *Steubenville Daily Herald and News* (OH), September 10, 1874
78. *Titusville Morning Herald,* December 6, 1875
79. *Atlanta Constitution,* March 17, 1889; *Lebanon Daily News,* April 11, 1876
80. *Warren Ledger,* May 31, 1877
81. *Daily Gazette* (IA), December 14, 1873
82. *Newport Daily News,* May 4, 1875
83. *Petersburg Index and Appeal,* August 20, 1877
84. *Titusville Morning Herald,* September 8, 1879
85. *Cambridge City Tribunal,* June 9, 1877
86. *Atlanta Constitution,* March 20, 1875
87. *Janesville Gazette,* October 14, 1876
88. Ibid., October 22, 1879
89. *Ohio Democrat,* May 31, 1877
90. Ibid., May 31, 1877
91. *Janesville Gazette,* October 14, 1876

Chapter 20

1. *Freeport Daily Bulletin,* June 30, 1880
2. *Marshall Statesman,* June 9, 1881
3. *Janesville Daily Gazette,* April 27, 1885; *Lima News* (OH), March 10, 1899
4. *Janesville Gazette,* March 3, 1881
5. *New York Times,* February 20, 1881
6. *Warren Ledger,* April 8, 1881
7. *Jackson Sentinel,* My 26, 1881
8. *Freeport Budget,* June 18, 1881
9. *Warren Ledger,* August 5, 1881
10. *Waterloo Courier,* November 9, 1881
11. *Titusville Morning Herald,* April 19, 1882
12. *Chester Times* (PA), February 12, 1883
13. *Fort Wayne Daily Sentinel,* June 9, 1883
14. *Fresno Republican* (CA), July 2, 1881
15. *The Landmark* (NC), April 7, 1882
16. *Newport Daily News,* April 4, 1882
17. *Sunday Morning Herald* (NY), April 9, 1882
18. *Fort Wayne Daily Gazette,* April 7, 1882
19. *Burlington Weekly Hawk-Eye,* May 18, 1882
20. *Oshkosh Daily Northwestern,* June 14, 1882
21. *Alton Daily Telegraph,* August 10, 1882
22. *Daily Kennebec Journal,* June 16, 1880
23. *Titusville Morning Herald,* March 16, 1880
24. *Chester Daily Times,* June 14, 1880
25. *Lloyd's Weekly Newspaper* (London), April 16, 1882
26. *Trenton Times,* September 17, 1885
27. *Sterling Standard* (IL), August 1, 1895; *Olean Democrat,* September 19, 1882
28. *Newport Daily News,* June 27 & 28, 1882
29. *The World,* September 17, 1885
30. *Boston Daily Glove,* September 17, 1885
31. *Titusville Morning Herald,* September 19, 1885
32. *Logansport Daily Pharos,* July 22, 1886
33. *Monticello Express,* September 24, 1885
34. *Huntingdon Globe,* April 14, 1887
35. *Evening Herald* (NY), April 26, 1887; *Northern Vindicator* (IA), April 19, 1894
36. *Bath Independent* (ME), February 5, 1881; *Daily Journal* (IN), May 28, 1879
37. *San Antonio Daily Light,* November 29, 1887; *Newport Mercury,* November 26, 1887
38. *Indiana Democrat,* August 13, 1885

39. *Oshkosh Daily Northwestern,* September 11, 1886
40. *Helena Independent* (MT), April 20, 1884
41. *Newport Daily News,* August 15, 1857
42. *Morning Review* (IL), April 27, 1882
43. *New York Herald,* October 22, 1872
44. *Sun and Central Press* (London), November 20, 1872
45. *Newport Mercury,* August 16, 1884
46. *Northwestern Vindicator* (IA), August 7, 1885
47. *Daily Milwaukee News,* March 26, 1866
48. *Ohio Democrat,* December 31, 1869
49. *Chicago Times,* reprinted in *Cedar Rapids Times,* June 20, 1872
50. *Bismark Weekly Tribune,* December 18, 1888; *Galveston Daily News,* December 11, 1888; *Middleton Daily Times* (NY), March 17, 1893; *San Antonio Daily Express,* January 11, 1893; *Daily Argus and Democrat,* August 15, 1855
51. *Evening Gazette* (IA), September 29, 1886
52. *Adams Sentinel,* August 11, 1851
53. *Oshkosh Daily Northwestern,* September 16, 1885
54. *The Landmark,* February 15, 1884
55. *The Constitution,* July 27, 1876
56. *Indiana Democrat,* July 16, 1885; *Rock Valley Register* (IA), March 16, 1894
57. *Milwaukee Daily Sentinel and Gazette,* June 2, 1851
58. *Gettysburg Compiler,* January 25, 1887
59. *Janesville Gazette,* November 13, 1872
60. *Petersburg Index=Appeal,* April 22, 1880

Chapter 21

1. *Indiana Progress,* June 8, 1882
2. *Monticello Express,* November 27, 1884
3. *Glenwood Opinion* (IA), September 17, 1870
4. *San Antonio Light,* November 17, 1884
5. *Indiana Progress,* June 13, 1872
6. *Daily Chronicle* (MI), April 7, 1884
7. Ibid., April 7, 1884
8. *Indiana Democrat,* March 14, 1889
9. *Sunday Morning Herald,* July 1, 1883
10. *Evening Observer,* (NY), July 2, 1884
11. *Cherokee Advocate* (OK), October 7, 1876
12. *Trenton Times* (NJ), September 1, 1883
13. *Portsmouth Times,* December 18, 1880
14. *Fort Wayne Daily Gazette,* September 22, 1881
15. *Burlington Daily Hawk-Eye,* August 6, 1882
16. *Evening Observer* (NY), July 2, 1884
17. *Daily Chronicle,* April 7, 1884
18. *Bangor Daily Whig and Courier,* July 18, 1882
19. *San Antonio Light,* November 17; *Semi-Weekly Age* (OH), July 30, 1886
20. *Evening Gazette* (NY), June 14, 1879
21. *Cherokee Advocate,* October 7, 1876
22. *Sunday Morning Herald,* July 22, 1883
23. *Syracuse Standard* (NY), July 20, 1884
24. *Galveston Daily News,* December 23, 1889
25. *Oshkosh Daily Northwestern,* June 19, 1884
26. *Boston Daily Globe,* August 1, 1885
27. *Gettysburg Compiler,* June 14, 1887
28. *Dunkirk Observer-Journal* (NY), October 17, 1887
29. *Indiana Progress,* June 1, 1871
30. *Daily Chronicle* (MI), April 7, 1884
31. *Logansport Daily Pharos,* August 19, 1886
32. *Warren Ledger,* July 8, 1887
33. *New York Times,* August 6, 1882
34. *Manitoba Daily Free Press,* August 7, 1886
35. *Boston Daily Globe,* December 6, 1883
36. *Galveston Daily News,* October 26, 1884

37. *Hamilton Democrat* (OH), July 15, 1887
38. *Sioux County Herald* (IA), August 12, 1886
39. *Logansport Daily Pharos,* August 29, 1884
40. *Daily Journal* (IN), May 19, 1881
41. *Boston Daily Globe,* June 1, 1881
42. *Glenwood Weekly Opinion* (IA), October 20, 1883
43. *Syracuse Standard,* July 20, 1884
44. *Sunday Morning Herald* (NY), July 1, 1883
45. *Titusville Morning Herald,* June 15, 1872
46. *Galveston Daily News,* May 7, 1884
47. *Daily Derrick* (PA), June 19, 1874
48. *Indiana Progress,* September 7, 1882
49. *Indiana Progress,* August 5, 1874
50. *Titusville Morning Herald,* July 15, 1885
51. *McKean County Miner,* November 21, 1884; *Boston Daily Globe,* June 20, 1897
52. *Daily Republican* (IL), July 25, 1874
53. *New York Times,* January 3, 1869
54. *Fort Wayne World,* June 20, 1885
55. *Hamilton Daily Democrat,* July 15, 1887
56. *Daily Advocate* (OH), January 22, 1883

Chapter 22

1. *Olean Democrat,* June 10, 1884
2. Barnum, pp. 349–350
3. *Logansport Daily Journal,* February 16, 1883
4. *Burlington Weekly Hawk-Eye,* May 20, 1880
5. *Boston Daily Globe,* July 18, 1880
6. *Fort Wayne Gazette,* September 14, 1886
7. *Coshoeton Age* (OH), March 15, 1884
8. *Iowa State Reporter,* January 31, 1883
9. *Chester Times,* February 12, 1883
10. *Warren Ledger,* June 29, 1883
11. *Monticello Express,* August 12, 1886
12. *Logansport Daily Journal,* June 17, 1883
13. *Daily Kennebec Journal,* June 4, 1883
14. *Galveston Daily News,* June 23, 1884
15. *Elyria Republican,* April 16, 1885
16. *New York Times,* March 27, 1885
17. *Fort Wayne World,* May 14; *Oshkosh Daily Northwestern,* June 10 & 24, 1885
18. *Boston Daily Globe,* January 14; *Logansport Daily Journal,* February 16, 1883
19. *Oshkosh Daily Northwestern,* July 8, 1880
20. *Galveston Daily News,* April 7, 1884
21. *Burlington Hawk-Eye,* May 29, 1884
22. *San Antonio Light,* April 25, 1884
23. *Olean Democrat,* June 10, 1884
24. *Bangor Daily Whig and Courier,* September 9, 1884
25. *Morning Oregonian,* June 22, 1844
26. *Weekly News Supplement* (MD), November 20, 1884
27. *Belleville Telescope* (KS), April 29, 1886

Chapter 23

1. *Clay County News* (IA), April 30, 1885
2. *Jackson Sentinel,* June 17, 1875
3. *Herald and Torch Light,* March 31, 1875
4. *Indiana Progress,* May 20, 1880
5. *Fort Wayne Daily Gazette,* September 29, 1868
6. *Bath Independent* (ME), August 25, 1883; *New Brunswick Daily Times* (NJ), July 30, 1881; *Daily Kennebec Journal,* May 14, 1880
7. *Galveston Daily News,* October 7, 1874
8. *Evening Gazette* (NY), August 11, 1881
9. *Decatur Daily Republican,* January 27, 1881
10. Ibid., January 27, 1881

11. *Indiana Weekly Messenger,* July 1, 1885
12. *Defiance Democrat,* July 20, 1867
13. *Titusville Morning Herald,* April 23, 1883
14. *Sterling Gazette* (IL), June 2, 1883
15. *Lebanon Daily News,* May 28, 11873
16. *The Globe* (KS), March 26, 1880
17. *Fort Wayne Daily Gazette,* September 19, 1882
18. *Warren Weekly News* (IN), August 31, 1882
19. *Huntingdon Globe,* June 24, 1886
20. *Titusville Morning Herald,* December 13, 1879
21. *Marshfield Times* (WI), October 21, 1882
22. *Manitoba Daily Free Press,* January 20, 1885
23. *Atchison Globe,* May 18, 1885
24. *Sunday Morning Herald* (NY), June 4, 1882
25. *Galveston Daily News,* October 9, 1886
26. *Burlington Hawk-Eye,* August 10, 1878
27. *Daily Kennebec Journal* (ME), May 29, 1899; *Syracuse Standard,* July 31, 1880
28. *New Brunswick Daily Times,* April 21, 1891; *Portsmouth Times,* July 17, 1880
29. *Galveston Daily News,* June 17, 1883
30. *Trenton Times,* July 16, 1884
31. *Oakland Evening Tribune* (CA), August 7, 1874
32. *Coshocton Democrat,* April 22, 1873; *New Brunswick Daily Times,* April 26, 1882; *Ohio Democrat,* July 26, 1877; *Athens Messenger* (OH), August 2, 1883
33. *Sunday Herald* (NY), March 8, 1891
34. *Daily Free Press* (WI), June 16, 1883
35. *Oshkosh Daily Northwestern,* August 8, 1884
36. *Atlanta Constitution,* October 22, 1882; *Oshkosh Daily Northwestern,* May 23, 1898
37. *American Newspaper Reporter,* reprinted in *Indiana Progress,* August 7, 1871
38. *Newport Daily News,* May 4, 1875
39. *Janesville Gazette,* October 22, 1879
40. *Paxton Weekly Record* (IL), November 19, 1874
41. *Titusville Morning Herald,* June 16, 1883
42. *Daily Journal* (IN), July 9, 1881
43. *Rock County Recorder* (WI), July 23, 1870
44. *Indiana Daily Messenger,* April 4, 1883
45. *Boston Daily Globe,* May 20, 1881
46. *Centralia Enterprise and Tribune* (WI), February 10, 1893; *Alton Evening Telegraph* (IL), October 13, 1896; *Newark Daily Advocate,* March 30, 1885
47. Reprinted in *Newport Daily News,* June 22, 1882

Chapter 24

1. *The Constitution,* October 18, 1876
2. *Weekly Hawk-Eye,* July 6, 1861
3. *Oshkosh Daily Northwestern,* September 11, 1882
4. *The World,* May 6, 1879
5. *Ohio Democrat,* August 11, 1881
6. *New Brunswick Daily Times,* June 20, 1879
7. *Denton Journal* (MD), May 10, 11873
8. *New York Times,* June 7, 1861
9. *Milwaukee Daily Sentinel,* September 15 & 21, 1860
10. *Semi-Weekly Wisconsin,* November 9, 1867
11. *Petersburg Index=Appeal,* November 5, 1881
12. *Oshkosh Daily Northwestern,* August 20, 1885
13. *St. Joseph Herald* (MI), April 18, 1868
14. *Indiana Weekly Messenger,* September 19, 1883
15. *Elyria Republican,* July 30, 1885
16. Philadelphia Speaks, "The Kidnapping of Charlie Ross" www.philadelphiaspeaks.com
17. Fass, Paula, *Kidnapped: Child Abduction in America,* Oxford, Oxford University Press, 1997, p. 27
18. *The World,* September 8, 1874

19. *Warren Ledger,* October 14, 1875
20. *Oshkosh Daily Northwestern,* December 9, 1887
21. *Atlanta Constitution,* May 5, 1888
22. *Daily Gazette and Bulletin* (PA), January 23, 1875
23. *Dubuque Daily Herald,* June 5, 1868
24. *Semi-Weekly Wisconsin,* July 8, 1868
25. *Dubuque Daily Herald,* July 29, 1871
26. *Daily Nevada State Journal,* July 16, 1875
27. *Piqua Daily Call,* November 1, 1886
28. *Semi-Weekly Wisconsin,* May 12, 1866
29. *Denton Journal,* May 7, 1881
30. *New York Times,* July 12, 1864
31. *Monticello Express,* August 17, 1871
32. *Marshall Statesman,* August 11, 1869
33. *Bucks County Gazette,* November 22, 1877
34. *Marion Daily Star,* May 31, 1880
35. *Sioux County Herald,* July 2, 1885
36. *New York Herald,* October 4, 1870
37. *Daily Gazette and Bulletin* (PA), September 30, 1871
38. *Fort Wayne Daily Sentinel,* May 2, 1883
39. *Decatur Daily Republican,* June 28, 1882; *Salt Lake Daily Tribune,* January 17, 1886
40. *Cambridge City Tribune,* June 25, 1885
41. *Wellsboro Agitator* (PA), May 5, 1885
42. *Reno Evening Gazette,* December 16, 1884
43. *Galveston Daily News,* May 9, 1885
44. *Ohio Democrat,* June 21, 1872
45. *Sioux County Herald,* July 2, 1885
46. *Age and Argus* (London), December 2, 1843
47. *Janesville Gazette,* November 16, 1865
48. *Jackson Sentinel,* August 6, 1874
49. *Indiana Progress,* September 25, 1873
50. *Cedar Falls Gazette,* September 27, 1867
51. *Dubuque Daily Herald,* July 13, 1871
52. *Marble Rock Weekly* (IA), October 10, 1878
53. Vey, Shaunna, Cambridge Journals, "Good Intentions and Fearsome Prejudice: New York's Act to Prevent and Punish Wrongs to Children," Theatre Survey 2001, Cambridge University Press, August 2001, Vol. 42, pp. 53–68
54. *Boston Daily Globe,* December 25, 1875
55. *Fresno Republican,* September 16, 1882
56. *Newark Daily Advocate,* November 16, 1883
57. *Decatur Daily Republican,* June 25, 1884
58. *New York Times,* August 29, 1876
59. *Indiana Weekly Messenger,* November 3, 1886
60. *Sault Ste. Marie Democrat* (MI), November 3, 1887
61. *New York Times,* March 5, 1884
62. *Galveston Daily News,* July 24, 1885

Chapter 25

1. Spoken by Colonel Peter Sells, general manager of the combined Adam Forepaugh and Sells Brothers circuses; *Logansport Daily Reporter* (IN), July 18, 1899
2. "Interstate Commerce Act" http://www.ourdocuments.gov/doc.php?flash=old&doc=49
3. *Logansport Daily Pharos,* April 1, 1887
4. *The World,* April 28, 1887
5. *Bangor Daily Whig and Advertiser,* September 16, 1887
6. *Oshkosh Daily Northwestern,* August 2, 1887
7. *Jackson Sentinel,* February 2, 1888
8. *Evening Herald* (NY), June 7, 1887
9. *Janesville Gazette,* August 14, 1880
10. *Dubuque Herald,* June 16, 1880
11. *Weekly Wisconsin,* June 22, 1881

12. *Atchison Globe,* July 9, 1884
13. *Hornellsville Weekly Tribune,* March 30, 1888
14. *Waterloo Courier,* November 27, 1889
15. *Daily Independent* (WI), January 24, 1889
16. *Boston Daily Globe,* June 27, 1889
17. *Fort Wayne Sentinel,* October 1, 1890
18. *Waukesha Freeman,* June 30, 1887
19. *Bismark Tribune,* February 18, 1881
20. *Logansport Daily Pharos,* May 23; *Oshkosh Daily Northwestern,* August 9, 1882
21. *Burlington Daily Hawk-Eye,* August 6, 1882
22. *Warren Ledger,* September 17, 1886
23. *Titusville Morning Herald,* September 22, 1886
24. *Iowa State Reporter,* June 3, 1886
25. *Daily Kennebec Journal,* June 3, 1887
26. *Monticello Express,* July 21; *Decatur Daily Republican,* July 21, 1887
27. *Dakota Bell, reprinted in Cambridge City Tribune, July 21, 1887*
28. *The Republican* (WI), July 14, 1887
29. *Bradford Era,* August 27, 1892
30. *Burlington Hawk-Eye,* September 14, 1887
31. Speaight, pp. 89–91
32. Ibid., pp. 91–92
33. *Trenton Evening Times,* May 4, 1899
34. Thompson, Alfred, "The Evolution of the Clown," published in *The World,* April 26, 1891
35. Fletcher, Ifan Kyrle, "A Portrait of Thomas Barry," *Theatre Notebook,* xvii, 1963
36. Thompson
37. Speaight, pp. 95–96
38. Thompson
39. *Evening Democrat* (PA), April 6, 1895
40. *Iowa State Reporter,* August 12, 1886

Chapter 26

1. *Burlington Hawk-Eye,* October 31, 1884
2. *Oshkosh Daily Northwestern,* January 20, 1880
3. *Lowell Weekly Sun* (MA), December 31, 1881
4. *Salt Lake Daily Tribune,* March 20, 1883
5. *Decatur Daily Republican,* December 9, 1884
6. *Syracuse Daily Standard,* July 13, 1885
7. *Warren Ledger,* April 8, 1887
8. *Piqua Daily Call,* December 14, 1887
9. *Galveston Daily News,* July 21, 1889
10. *The Ledger* (PA), September 27, 1889
11. *Galveston Daily News,* May 5, 1886
12. *Logansport Daily Journal,* November 25, 1886
13. *Gettysburg Compiler,* December 7, 1886
14. *Evening Herald* (NY), October 28, 1887
15. *Lebanon Daily News* (PA), *April 10, 1889*
16. *Salem Daily News* (OH), February 24, 1890
17. *Manitoba Daily Free Press,* April 10, 1891
18. *The World,* April 11, 1891
19. *Manitoba Daily Free Press,* June 4, 1891
20. *Daily Times* (New Brunswick, NJ), January 2, 1892
21. *The World,* February 2; *Daily Express* (San Antonio), February 3, 1893
22. *Lowell Daily Sun,* September 19, 1894
23. *Lowell Daily Sun,* October 31; *Lock Haven Evening Express* (PA), November 1, 1893
24. *Boston Daily Globe,* December 23, 1894
25. *Trenton Evening Times,* November 26, 1895
26. Speaight, pp. 143–144
27. Ibid., p. 144; *Logansport Daily Pharos,* August 19, 1893
28. *Titusville Morning Herald,* September 15, 1890
29. *Logansport Daily Journal,* August 26, 1893
30. *San Antonio Daily Light,* September 30, 1896
31. Ibid., July 15, 1897
32. *Daily Review* (IL), February 28, 1897
33. *Bath Independent* (ME), August 7, 1897
34. *Naugatuck Daily News* (CT), March 3, 1899
35. *Daily Review* (IL), March 5, 1899
36. *Steubenville Herald-Star* (OH), December 5, 1899
37. *The Echo* (London), December 27, 1897
38. *Edwardsville Intelligencer* (IL), April 30, 1897
39. *Ironwood Times* (MI), July 15, 1899
40. *Daily Review* (IL), June 16, 1897
41. *Lowell Daily Sun,* June 19, 1894
42. *Daily Auronite* (SD), June 19, 1897
43. *San Antonio Daily Light,* August 20, 1898
44. *Rio Grande Republican* (NM), February 26, 1897
45. *Scandia Journal* (KS), July 21, 1899
46. *Logansport Pharos,* August 21, 1897
47. *Daily News* (MI), November 10, 1899
48. *Marysville Tribune,* July 15, 1896
49. *Daily Iowa Capital,* June 27, 1899
50. Spoken by Charles A. Davis of Forepaugh's Circus; *Gettysburg Compiler,* September 5, 1899
51. *Titusville Morning Herald,* August 29, 1877

Bibliography

Allen, Ronald R., *Fairs and Circuses in Knoxville, Tennessee in the Nineteenth Century,* Knoxville, 2008

"American Revolution, The, 1763–1783 http://memory. loc.gov/learn//features/timeline/amrev/rebell/assoc.html

Banham, Martin, *The Cambridge Guide to Theatre,* Cambridge; Cambridge University Press, 1995

Barnum. P. T., *The Art of Money Getting,* Watchmaker Publishing, 2010

Barnum, Phineas T., *The Life of P. T. Barnum,* Urbana; University of Illinois Press, 2000

Brede, Charles Frederic, *The German Drama in English on the Philadelphia Stage from 1794–1830"Philadelphia; Americana Germanica Press, 1918 "Broad Street Theatre,"* www.preserventionsociety.org/HalseyMap/Flash/windoww.asp?HTML=10

"Calliope" httn://en.wikipedia.org/wiki/Calliope_music

"Cayetano" *Pennsylvania Magazine of History and Biography,* Vol. 15, 1915

Chindahl, George L., *A History of the Circus in America,* Idaho; Caxton Printers, Ltd., 1959

"Circus in America Timeline" www.circusinamerica. org/public/timeline?date1=1793&date2=1800

Cook, Gynger, "Richmond Theatre Fire" http://jshaputis. tripod.com/ClayArticles/Richmond_theatre_fire_html

Cook, James W. (editor) *The Colossal P. T. Barnum Reader,* Urbana; University of Illinois Press, 2005

"Cumberland Road, The," www.swetland.net/cumberland. htm

Davis, Andrew, *America's Longest Run: A History of the Walnut Street Theatre,* Pennsylvania; Pennsylvania State University Press, 2010

Day, Charles H. and Slout, William L., *Joe Blackburn's A Clown's Log;* The Borgo Press, 2007

Downer, Alan S. (editor), *The Memoir of John Durang, American Actor, 1785–1816,* Pittsburgh; University of Pittsburgh Press, 1966

Durang, Charles, "The Philadelphia Stage," *Sunday Dispatch,* (Philadelphia), serial beginning May 7, 1854

"Edgar A. Poe Calendar, The" http://richmondthen andnow.com/Newspaper-Articles/RichmondTheatre-Fire.html

Fass, Paula, *Kidnapped: Child Abduction in America,* Oxford; Oxford University Press, 1997

Fletcher, Ifan Kyrle, "A Portrait of Thomas Barry," Theatre Notebook, xvii, 1963

Greenwood, Isaac John, "The Circus: Its Origin and Growth Prior to 1835," Dunlap Society Publications, No. 5, 1898

"Harmonicon" JSTOR Organization, *The Musical Times & Singing Class Circular,* Vol. 41, New York; Novello, Ewer & Co. 1831

Henderson, Mary C., *The City and the Theatre,* New York; Back Stage Books, 2004

Honeywell, J., "The Menagerie" *Rock River Pilot* (WI), March 22, 1848

Holmberg, Tom, "Great Britain: Orders in Council and Licenses, 1800–1810 www.napoleon-series.org/research/government/british/C_orderscouncil

Hughes, Glenn, *A History of the American Theatre, 1700–1950,* New York; Vail-Ballou Press, 1951

"Interstate Commerce Act" http://www.ourdocuments. gov/doc.php?flash=old&doc=49

Jando, Dominique, "John Bill Ricketts," Circopedia http://www.circopedia.org/index.php/john_Bill_Ricketts

"John Durang" Yorkheritagesociety.org/johndurang/wp-content/uploads/2009/12RickettsHarvard

"Kidnapping of Charlie Ross, The," Philadelphia Speaks www.philadelphiaspeaks.com

Kotar, S. L. and Gessler, J. E., *A History of the Balloon,* North Carolina; McFarland & Company, Publishers, 2010

Kotar, S. L. and Gessler, J. E., *The Steamboat Era,* North Carolina; McFarland & Company, Publishers, 2009

"Leotard" http://wikipedia.org/Jules_L%C3%A9otard

Matlaw, Myron (editor), *American Popular Entertainment,* Westport, CT.; Greenwood Press, 1979

Nicholls, Sir George, *A History of the English Poor Law in Connection with the State of the Country and the Condition of the People,* P. S. King & Son, 1904

Odell, George C. D., *Annals of the New York Stage,* 15 volumes, New York; Columbia University Press, 1949

Parkinson, Robert L., *Directory of American Circuses 1793–2000;* Baraboo, WI; Circus World Museum, 2002

Pilato, Denise E., "Martha Coston: A Woman, A War, and a Signal to the World," *International Journal of Naval History* www.ijnhonline.org/volume1_number1_Apr02/article_pilato_coston_signal.doc

Rogers, George C., Jr., *Charleston in the Age of Pinckneys,* South Carolina; University of South Carolina Press, 1989

Rookmaaker, L. C., *The Rhinoceros in Captivity,* Amsterdam; SPB Academic Publishing, 1998

Salzmann, Kenneth, *"Just a Stage—A Theatrical History of Albany, New York"* www.zinearticles.com/?Just-a-

stage-a-theatrical-history-of-Albany-NewYork&id
=857077

Scharf, John Thomas and Westcott, Thompson, *History of Philadelphia, 1609–1884,* Vol. II, Philadelphia; L. H. Everts & Co. 1884

Spann, Edward K., *New Metropolis,* New York; Columbia University Press, 1981

Speaight, George, *A History of the Circus,* London; The Tantivy Press, 1980

Thayer, Stuart, *Annals of the American Circus, 1793–1860,* Seattle; Dauvan & Thayer, 2000

Thompson, Alfred, "The Evolution of the Clown," *The World,* April 26, 1891

Vail, R. W. G., "Random Notes on the History of the Early American Circus," reprinted from the "Proceed-ings of the American Antiquarian Society," Worcester, MA., April, 1933

"Vauxhall Gardens," Preservation Society of Charleston http://www.halseymap.com/Flash/asp

Vey, Shaunna, "Good Intentions and Fearsome Prejudice: New York's Act to Prevent and Punish Wrongs to Children, *Cambridge Journals,* Theatre Survey 2001, Cambridge University Press, August, 2001, Vol. 42

Watts, Ephraim, *Life of Van Amburgh, the Brute Tamer, with Anecdotes of his Extraordinary Pupils,* 1838

Wilson, James Grant, Fisk, John and Klos, Stanley L. (editors) *Appleton's Cyclopedia of American Biography,* New York; D. Appleton & C0. 1887–1889 & 1999 New York

Index